PRAISE FOR *LEAP OF FAITH*

"Did the decision to invade Iraq arise from conspiracy or long-term plot, as some people suspect? No, says Michael Mazarr—the truth is actually much darker. In this novelistic plus analytic recreation of the road to war, Mazarr convincingly argues that the most costly strategic error in modern US history was the result of mistake, blunder, a toxic combination of personality traits among political and military leaders, plus intellectual and moral hubris. *Leap of Faith* puts the Iraq war in new light, and clarifies why and how such disasters might recur."

—James Fallows, national correspondent at *The Atlantic*, and
author of *Blind Into Baghdad* and other books

"*Leap of Faith* should be mandatory reading for every US general and flag officer as well as civilian senior executives; all military officers, especially those at a US senior service college; and every graduate student at an American school of security or international studies. It is a disturbing account of negligence and myopia at the highest civilian and military levels—in how they decided to launch the 2003 Iraq invasion and in the exercise of their responsibilities for those who fought at their direction. *Leap of Faith* will become a classic; it is this generation's *Dereliction of Duty* and *Essence of Decision*."

—Lieutenant General James M. Dubik, PhD, US Army, retired;
author, *Just War Reconsidered: Strategy, Ethics, and Theory*; and
former professor, Security Studies Program, Georgetown University

"Deeply researched and written with penetrating intelligence, *Leap of Faith* is a remarkable new look at the run-up to the Iraq War. While never less than clear-eyed and fair-minded, this is ultimately a powerful and bracing indictment of a group of mostly smart, well-meaning people who talked themselves, and us, into a set of woeful miscalculations. Breathtaking in its insights, devastating in its conclusions, Mazarr's book will stand as the definitive analysis of what went wrong and how."

"The Iraq War stands as one of the greatest US foreign policy blunders in history. Michael Mazarr has written the definitive account on how the decision to go to war came about. *Leap of Faith* contains valuable lessons for how future policy-makers can avoid disaster."

"Mazarr has written an excellent antidote to the simplistic and wrong Iraq narrative that 'Bush lied, people died.' He shows how US leaders tried to confront all potential threats after 9/11, and he describes the mistakes that led Iraq from the tragedy of Saddam to the tragedy of chaos. He writes wonderfully and shows very well the dilemmas facing successive generations of leaders of what is indeed 'the indispensable nation.' Of course there have been serious errors alongside the vital, existential successes of the American Century. A world without the deep and fundamentally decent involvement of America will be far more dangerous and brutal."

"Michael Mazarr's *Leap of Faith* is an incisive inquest into America's most disastrous war since Vietnam. Writing with panache and precision, Mazarr illustrates that real ideological impulses drove the will to war in 2003. It was not a Freudian war to avenge or compete with a father, or a lunge for oil, or the product of a small cabal of ideologues who have left the scene. Rather, it was made possible by a strain of missionary zeal that lives on. Because warlike idealism lives on, the Iraq adventure was not just a problem of recent history, but is a crisis of the present. Mazarr's *Leap of Faith* is a seminal, sharp, and prophetic history. We have been warned."

LEAP OF FAITH

LEAP OF FAITH

FAITH

HUBRIS, NEGLIGENCE, *and* AMERICA'S GREATEST FOREIGN POLICY TRAGEDY

———

MICHAEL J. MAZARR

PUBLICAFFAIRS

NEW YORK

PublicAffairs
Hachette Book Group
1290 Avenue of the Americas, New York, NY 10104
www.publicaffairsbooks.com
@Public_Affairs

Printed in the United States of America

First Edition: March 2019

Published by PublicAffairs, an imprint of Perseus Books, LLC, a subsidiary of Hachette Book Group, Inc. The PublicAffairs name and logo is a trademark of the Hachette Book Group.

The Hachette Speakers Bureau provides a wide range of authors for speaking events. To find out more, go to www.hachettespeakersbureau.com or call (866) 376-6591.

The publisher is not responsible for websites (or their content) that are not owned by the publisher.

Print book interior design by Amnet Systems.

Library of Congress Cataloging-in-Publication Data

Names: Mazarr, Michael J., 1965- author.
Title: Leap of faith : hubris, negligence, and America's greatest foreign
    policy tragedy / Michael J. Mazarr.
Description: First edition. | New York : PublicAffairs, 2019. | Includes
    bibliographical references and index.
Identifiers: LCCN 2018046828| ISBN 9781541768369 (hardcover) | ISBN
    9781541768345 (ebook)
Subjects: LCSH: Iraq War, 2003-2011—Causes. | War on Terrorism, 2001-2009. |
    United States—Foreign relations—2001-2009. | United States—Foreign
    relations—Iraq. | Iraq—Foreign relations—United States. | United
    States—Politics and government—2001-2009. | Iraq—Politics and
    government—2003-
Classification: LCC DS79.757 .M39 2019 | DDC 956.7044/31—dc23
LC record available at https://lccn.loc.gov/2018046828
ISBNs: 978-1-5417-6836-9 (hardcover), 978-1-5417-6834-5 (ebook)

LSC-C

10 9 8 7 6 5 4 3 2 1

Judging is our oldest faith.

FRIEDRICH NIETZSCHE[1]

CONTENTS

A NOTE ON SOURCES
AND METHODS

This book is an account of a government policy decision, drawn from open sources and over one hundred interviews and informal conversations with participants at various levels in the decision process. I have consulted published secondary sources, especially the memoirs of government officials who have had access to detailed government records of the decision process. I have looked for every declassified document available, from both the US and British governments.

The book does not, as far as I have been able to ensure, contain information that remains classified. Every government document cited here has been declassified through official US or UK procedures. In places where the book describes the activities of US intelligence agencies, I have verified the events using memoirs that have been cleared through the CIA's publications review board. In my interviews, I asked questions about the decision process and the origins of key policies but did not try to unearth secret information about intelligence findings, US military operations, or other issues. Because I was a Department of Defense employee during the time that I did some of the independent research for this book, I submitted the draft manuscript for security clearance. It has been cleared by the official DoD process.

All of my interviews were conducted on an anonymous basis; any former officials quoted by name in this work are being cited from other published materials. In quoting from those interviews, when I use the term "senior official," I am referring to people serving at the time in positions of deputy assistant secretary or higher, including equivalent positions at the NSC or in intelligence agencies. The opinions expressed in this book are solely my own.

ACKNOWLEDGMENTS

This book has its origins in late 2003, during my time teaching at the National War College. We were already beginning to get students, both military and civilian, returning from the Iraq war, many of them bearing stories of unimaginable confusion and incoherence. At the time I had a growing fascination with the character of decision-making on complex issues, and these students' stories generated an obvious question that took me the better part of a decade to investigate: How had the Bush administration, stocked with officials of tremendous insight and staggering experience, managed to stumble into a war with so little regard for what would happen afterward? This book is the result of that insistent question, and I owe many debts to individuals and institutions who have helped to make it possible.

I would like to thank all of those—though they cannot be named—who consented to be interviewed for the purposes of this research. Some had a strong sense, I am sure, that my argument was not likely to agree with their own policy leanings, but they nonetheless gave generously of their time. My former students and colleagues at the National War College provided a stimulating intellectual environment and the continuing inspiration to pursue this book on my own time. My current colleagues at the RAND Corporation offer a daily reminder of the importance and value of rigor in research, and a culture every bit as intellectually curious and professionally rewarding as that of the War College. But this is a personal work and reflects only my own views, not those of any other organization.

I am grateful to the people who consented to read specific chapters for accuracy. So as not to saddle them with implied responsibility for the resulting material, I shall not name them—but they know who they are, and I am deeply grateful for their time and counsel.

I must offer a special thanks to my editor at PublicAffairs, Clive Priddle. He is an ideal partner in the development of a writing project: gracious in his support, sage but sparing in his advice, and friendly and engaging as discussions about the book unfolded. I am truly lucky to have had the opportunity to work with him—and I owe my colleague Linda Robinson hearty thanks for making that connection.

Finally, and always, I owe the deepest gratitude to my family: my boys, Alex and Theo; and my wife, Jen. They put up with the long hours I spent locked in my tiny writing space and with the more-than-occasional crankiness of a beleaguered author on deadline. Jen offered thoughtful ideas on the title and other aspects of the argument. But more than that, my family provides, in both immediate and lasting ways, the inspiration for everything that I do.

CHAPTER 1

UNDERSTANDING A TRAGEDY

*But where is the man, where is he so keen as to cheat the snares of the gods
with a leap? Calamity lures him, smiles, seduces him, into her net, and
no escape.*

AESCHYLUS, THE PERSIANS[1]

*This is a profound truth: The interacting processes that propel the world
produce outcomes that no one intends. The fatal conceit—fatal to the
fecundity of a spontaneous order—is the belief that anyone, or any group
of savants, is clever and farsighted enough to forecast the outcomes of
complex systems.*

GEORGE F. WILL[2]

*There is, I think, in Reinhold Niebuhr's political thought a self-limitation
which is the very reflection of the subject matter of politics. It is the
awareness, to put it in different words, of the tragic character of the
political act. We plan a political strategy in order to achieve a certain
result, but the result, more often than not, has only a very remote relation
to what we intend.*

HANS MORGANTHAU[3]

Despite being the official retreat of American presidents, Camp David is a curiously bare and rustic facility.[4] Tucked into the forested northern edge of Maryland, it consists of a handful of low-slung, wood-sided lodges set among stands of soaring trees. The camp's work-ing areas have the feel of a kindly, if second-rate, family resort, at least according to publicly available photographs: rudimentary wood panel-ing, exposed brick or stone walls, and bare working tables. Former CIA official Michael Morell described one room at Camp David as "a com-fortable, homey getaway filled with leather couches, overstuffed chairs, and a big, well-used fireplace."[5]

Presidents since Franklin Roosevelt have valued Camp David as an escape from the capital's hustle and grind. One famous picture taken at the camp shows Nancy Reagan having just stepped off a horse, leaping into the arms of her husband; both are wearing cowboy hats. But some presidents and their families have not taken to the austerity of the com-pound. Harry Truman reportedly found the facility remote, and his wife, Bess, considered it dreary. George H. W. Bush enthused, on the other hand, that "the quiet mountain setting, the trees, the trails, the movies, and the varied sports activities . . . contributed to frank conversation and the chance to get to know guests on a personal basis."[6]

His son George W. also enjoyed the place. He would write in his memoirs that Camp David, though just a thirty-minute helicopter trip from Washington, "feels much more removed than that." The crisp air and natural environment, he concluded, "[foster] reflection and clear thinking."[7]

※

On September 7, 2002, President George W. Bush gathered his National Security Council (NSC) at Camp David to decide whether to seek United Nations (UN) approval for attacking Saddam Hussein.[8] It was unseasonably warm, with temperatures pushing into the mid-eighties. Official photographs depict a brilliant, sunlit day, with officials in shirt-sleeves and sportcoats.

The previous day, the NSC had heard the emerging war plan from General Tommy Franks, chief of the United States Central Command (CENTCOM). Then the cabinet principals (the secretaries of state and defense, the national security advisor, the vice president, and others) had debated the issue without the president. Dick Cheney, continuing a theme he had struck beginning shortly after 9/11, argued for rapid military action. Colin Powell pressed for another UN resolution to provide more legitimacy.[9] The session turned into a contentious affair in which these two great elephants of the administration openly butted heads. In Bob Woodward's telling, Powell "detected a kind of fever in Cheney. . . . The vice president was beyond hell-bent for action against Saddam. It was as if nothing else existed."[10]

Powell's concerns notwithstanding, the debate was no longer about *whether* to go to war. One senior official with knowledge of Powell and Deputy Secretary of State Richard Armitage's thinking confirmed that both fully supported the idea of removing Hussein. The question was *when*, and under what conditions.[11] Donald Rumsfeld would later claim—with much justification—that while Powell quibbled about the scheduling and ornamentation of war, he never disputed the need for action.[12]

The debate reopened on September 7 at a full NSC meeting chaired by President Bush. Cheney argued for a thirty- to sixty-day ultimatum to Saddam—that he must leave power and open his country to inspections—or else, Cheney urged, the "United States should remove him by force if he did not comply." Cheney believed Saddam's weapons of mass destruction (WMD) programs were accelerating so fast that the United States had no time to spare. "It is time to act," he said. "We can't delay for another year. . . . An inspection regime does not solve our problem."[13] Bush concluded the discussion by insisting that Saddam must be brought to heel. But the president did not issue any clear guidance.

※

Within seven months of that Camp David session, US tanks would be streaming across the Kuwaiti border, headed for the Iraqi capital of Baghdad. The consequences of the resulting war remain only partly known—but what we do know is devastating. The war has been a catastrophe for the Iraqi people, at least 150,000 of whom (and perhaps close to half a million, based on the most recent estimates) died in the maelstrom that emerged after March 2003.[14] The war has been a tragedy for many of the American servicemen and women and civilian officials who served in the conflict. More than 4,400 of them made the ultimate sacrifice; well over 30,000 have been wounded, many grievously.[15] Tens of thousands suffer from damaging, and in some cases crippling, psychological traumas.

The war undermined the presidency of George W. Bush, whose blueprint for a moderate domestic agenda of education, immigration, and entitlement reform gave way to the fateful choice to become a war president. It drained US finances, both directly and indirectly: estimates of the comprehensive cost of the war, including long-term care for wounded veterans, replacing used-up equipment, and continuing operations in Iraq, range from narrow calculations of $800 billion to several trillion dollars. From a geostrategic standpoint, an effort to demonstrate the power and purpose of the United States ended up producing the reverse—global resentment at an America that seemed out of control and measurably less respected than before. Potential rivals, from Russia to North Korea to China, took the war as evidence of the need to intensify efforts to balance American power and influence. Within the region, the collapse of Iraq and entanglement of American power strengthened and emboldened Iran. Sixteen years after the war, the Middle East remains embroiled in chaos; the cause of democracy has not been measurably advanced, and al Qaeda boasts an order of magnitude more adherents than it did before the invasion. More indirectly, the disaster of an unnecessary war helped, along with the subsequent financial crisis, to further undermine American faith in politics and public institutions and to set the stage for today's hyperpolarized atmosphere.

The decision to launch an ill-conceived invasion of Iraq as the centerpiece of a war on terror has therefore turned out to be a historical misjudgment of the first order. Columnist George Will commented in 2018 that it is frequently said that the decision to invade Iraq was the worst US foreign policy decision since Vietnam. Actually, it was worse than Vietnam, and the worst in American history, for two reasons. One is that so far we probably have paid no more than 20 percent of the eventual costs of that decision that enhanced Iran's ascendancy. The other reason is that America gradually waded waist deep into Vietnam without a crossing-the-Rubicon moment—a single, clear, dispositive decision. In contrast, the protracted preparation for invading Iraq was deliberative and methodical.[16]

These and other risks involved in the decision to wage war were more than evident in September 2002. But they never came up at the Camp David session—an important step on the march toward war. Indeed, there was no single meeting at which the decision to launch a global war on terror, or an invasion of Iraq, was openly, consciously, and rigorously debated.

How was this possible? How did a group of such world-wise leaders not only allow but actively cheer on such a devastating mistake? How was it that the United States, steeped in liberal values and devoted to norms of nonaggression, could fling itself into an aggressive war so easily and with apparently so little thought? Our understanding of precisely why and how that choice came to be made remains radically incomplete: more than fifteen years after the invasion, with numerous memoirs having been published and hundreds of documents declassified, we still do not know when or how, precisely, the decision took place.

That has not kept hundreds of commentators from claiming that they know the basis for it. For the administration's fiercest critics, the war represented the rash ambitions of an aggressively militaristic clique of ideologists. Some underscore George W. Bush's longtime resentment of Saddam Hussein and his desire to finish the work his father started in the first Gulf War.[17] Others focus on Bush's psychodramas[18]—his alleged desire to "prove himself." Some view the war as an attempt to gain control of Iraq's oil,[19] bolster Israel's security,[20] or promote the fortunes of corporations with ties to Bush's inner circle. Others see the war as a scheme to build a new capitalist state in the Middle East along American lines.[21] One popular theory points to the intrigues of a "cabal" of neoconservatives who dragged the nation to war in service of imperial visions.[22] Whatever the explanation, war opponents agree on one point: it was waged on the backs of half-truths, misrepresentations, and outright lies. Representative Walter Jones, a staunch Republican from North Carolina, voted for the war, but eventually "came to believe we were misled, we were lied to."[23]

Closing in on two decades after the onset of the war, we still have no consensus on its causes or the motives of those who launched it. Wikipedia boasts an entire page devoted to the "Rationale for the Iraq War," and it comes to no firm conclusions.[24] "I will go to my grave not fully understanding why" Bush chose to invade, admits Council on Foreign Relations president Richard Haass—and he was working in the administration at the time.[25] "Iraq is the *Rashomon* of wars," George Packer lamented in 2005.[26]

These are the questions I have sought to understand during almost a decade of research, including reviewing both published sources and declassified American and British documents and having over a hundred conversations with former officials and military officers. I have become convinced that what many people think they know about the war is wrong—that it resulted from conspiracies, or the plotting of villainous officials, or the dreamy liberation narratives of second-tier neoconservatives, or craven motives like corporate profits—and most of all, that it reflected a self-consciously dishonest plot to hoodwink the American people. Part of my purpose has been to strip away the layers of supposed neocon cabals, pocket-lining oil industrialists, and intelligence failures and get to the heart of this event: a tragically typical example of how America's worthy global ambitions can go terribly wrong and how senior leaders come to intuitive, moralistic judgments as one antidote to the profound uncertainty of national strategy.

The Bush administration did not invade Iraq to grab its oil or fill Halliburton's coffers with US government contracts. George Bush was not stupid, nor was he trying to prove something to his father. The scheming of lower-level Defense Department officials adorned the process with sometimes preposterous claims and ideas but did not cause the war. Even when stretching intelligence findings to the limit of what they would support, senior officials did not consider themselves to be lying to the American people. Such arguments not only fail to match the facts, they tempt us to search for wickedness or corruption in the decision process—perversions that can be cured by a simple trade-out of people or administration.

As we will see, there was plenty of foolishness to go around, including willful negligence of historic proportions. Most fundamentally, however, my research has convinced me that two factors are especially useful in understanding how such a tragedy could occur: the fuel of American missionary ambitions and the spark of an intuitive, value-driven judgment. Those twin flaws are not the unique province of any one president or any one administration. They affect the thinking of senior officials from many eras who were trying to do their level best in the face of overwhelming uncertainty. And because they are so common, these factors lie in wait, ready to emerge in future national security decisions—a pattern that may already be recurring today in US policy toward such profound challenges as Russia, Iran, and China.

Many of those in the room at Camp David on September 7 left convinced that something had been decided. National Security Advisor Condoleezza Rice later wrote that the group "decided on a course of action. Everyone in that room heard the President say, 'Either he will come clean about his weapons, or there will be war.' . . . The way ahead could not have been clearer."[27] In his own memoirs, Cheney admits that Bush "had not yet made a decision" but saw no evidence of anyone arguing "against using military force to remove Saddam Hussein from power. Nor did anyone argue that leaving Saddam in power . . . was a viable option."[28]

Some officials told journalist Peter Baker that the September 7 session was "the turning point, the juncture at which Bush resolved to go forward."[29] Just five days later, in a seeming confirmation that the die had been cast, Bush delivered a blistering speech to the United Nations.[30] "The purposes of the United States should not be doubted," Bush proclaimed before a mostly stone-faced audience. "The Security Council resolutions will be enforced . . . or action will be unavoidable."[31]

All of this would seem to suggest that the "decision" to go to war had been made in the meeting on September 7. And yet others involved in the process disagree. One participant in the Camp David session recalled that President Bush's body language seemed to suggest that he was "still debating in his mind what to do."[32] No formal order to begin military operations emerged. Bush himself has insisted that he did not decide on military action until much closer to the invasion; one very senior official privy to the president's thinking, when asked when the decision was made, instantly replied, "March [2003]"[33]—six months after the September 7 meeting.

Bush's secretary of defense didn't seem to think a final choice had been made. The day after the United Nations speech, Donald Rumsfeld dictated a memo dismissing the need for a public relations campaign to justify war. Such an effort, he said, "doesn't come into play until and unless the President makes a decision to do something in Iraq from a military standpoint," implying that Bush had not yet done so.[34] The same day, in a different memo, Rumsfeld stated categorically that "the President has not yet recommended invading Iraq. Therefore, I do not think I should go up [to Congress] and make the case for invading Iraq."[35]

Yet such quibbling makes no sense in light of the fact that the Bush administration had been busily planning for war—if not actually deciding on it—since at least December 2001. The idea had floated to the surface amid the smoke, haze, and fury of September 11 itself, in part because many in the administration had long been convinced of the need to dethrone Saddam Hussein. Even among the small library of documents so far declassified, a tidal wave of evidence can be found that many senior officials assumed war was inevitable long before September 2002.[36] Two months earlier, in July, for example, Richard Haass, then director of policy planning at the State Department, visited Condoleezza Rice. "I raised this issue about were we really sure that we wanted to put Iraq front and center at this point," Haass said later. "And she said, essentially, that that decision's been made, don't waste your breath."[37]

In important ways, then, the essential judgment to invade was in place *at least* two-thirds of a year before March 2003 and eight weeks prior to the September meeting at Camp David—long months during which the administration routinely dismissed the idea that it had already decided to go to war. Even as the NSC was "debating" the choice of war at Camp David that September, for example, and whatever Rumsfeld's hesitations, the administration was already rolling out an elaborate public relations campaign. It was a "meticulously planned strategy," as the *New York Times* put it, "to persuade the public, the Congress and the allies of the need to confront the threat from Saddam Hussein." The campaign, like the battle plan for invasion, had been in the works for months.[38]

꙰

In evaluating the decision to go to war in Iraq, we must account, first and foremost, for the beliefs, the perspectives, and ultimately the choices of the man whose highly idiosyncratic decision-making style drove the character of that judgment.

Many of those who worked for George W. Bush describe his private kindnesses. There are hundreds of examples of his spontaneous emotionalism and graciousness in the presence of Iraqis or US servicemen. I have spoken with a number of US military officers and former White House officials who described scenes such as a visit to a US Air Force base. There, after the ceremonial part of the visit was concluded, Bush held back to spend time with a family who had lost a son in Iraq. He dismissed everyone else from the room. He dropped all artifice and spoke humbly, authentically. He shared their pain and took responsibility for the decision that cost their son his life. The visit got no media coverage and received no credit beyond those who attended.

Bush did these sorts of things, I am certain, all the time. One senior official explained that when he asked the president what he most enjoyed about the job, Bush replied that he liked touching people—touching their lives with the office of the presidency.[39] Yet such episodes only highlight the tragic paradox: How was it that a man who on an individual level possessed such a caring touch could be so disconnected from decisions affecting the lives of millions?

Officials who observed George W. Bush closely typically portray him as thoughtful and astute, entirely capable of telling insights and rapid-fire questions that drove to the heart of issues. But he could also be bewilderingly disinterested and uninformed; in a number of key planning meetings about the Iraq war, for example, he asked no substantive questions. Bush could have a brilliantly untaught sense of large trends in history and yet be spectacularly blind to the risks of his own policies. He was the son of one of America's most powerful political dynasties—and yet someone who, as part owner of the Texas Rangers, eschewed luxury boxes for regular seats behind the dugout, calling peanut vendors by name, gobbling down cheap hot dogs, chatting with fans, and bonding with Hispanic players by sputtering through conversations in his high school Spanish.[40] This fan of the energy industry and skeptic of global climate treaties built a Crawford ranch house that was, his speechwriter David Frum marveled, "a showcase of enviro technology," with passive energy, extensive water conservation systems, and propane-fueled trucks.[41]

Journalist Frank Bruni writes that he asked Bush if he believed one of the goals of 9/11 was to kill him. Bush replied, in all likelihood sincerity, that he was not thinking of himself but of the families of those who had lost loved ones, and of "the children. I am a loving guy." He then proceeded to tear up.[42] He cried when he took John Kerry's concession call; he cried when his press secretary Scott McClellan left the White House.[43] After

9/11, even as Bush endorsed a global strategy of targeted assassination and sometimes celebrated the results in brutal and seemingly callous language, his was one of the first, and ultimately one of the most consistent, voices opposing the conflation of a war on terrorism with prejudice against Muslims.

"Bush defied easy description," his former White House aide David Kuo wrote upon first meeting the man who was then Texas governor. "He seemed not just charming, but weighty, seductive yet pure, likable yet mysterious." Kuo was astonished in particular by Bush's encounters with men struggling with substance abuse. Bush would "slow down. His cadence would change. He would put both of his hands on the man's shoulders and look into his eyes. Any swagger disappeared. Something softer and perhaps more genuine took its place. He listened to each story and nodded. . . . It was one of the more Christ-like things I had ever seen a powerful man do."[44] The qualities—and flaws—of this swaggering, thoughtful, disinterested, sensitive, indolent, and deeply committed man help explain how the United States came to launch an ill-conceived and ill-planned invasion that would count as perhaps America's greatest foreign policy tragedy of the modern era.

Bush's dominant goal—in fact, his overriding motive, especially after 9/11—was to fulfill what he viewed as his sacred obligation as president: to keep the American people safe. But his personality and worldview formed a very particular vision of *how* best to do that, a vision that strongly reflected America's missionary tradition and proved vulnerable to the appeal of passionate moral imperatives that overrode conceptions of risk and cost. The result was, as many commentators have noted, a form of astonishing certainty. "I know it is hard for you to believe," he told Bob Woodward in 2002 about the ballooning war on terror, "but I have not doubted what we're doing. . . . There is no doubt in my mind we're doing the right thing. Not one doubt."[45] Fueled by such visions and certainty, he would seek to smite America's enemies and to achieve an impossibly idealistic transformation of Iraq and the broader Middle

East—objectives that were destined to crash headlong into the limits of American power and the realities of a complex world.

⁂

This book tells the story of the Iraq decision in mostly straightforward chronological terms, beginning with the moment after the first Gulf War when the US relationship with Iraq began its downward slide from wary engagement into bitter hostility. Each chapter tells the story of one key phase of the process that led to March 2003. Chapter 9 then offers a brief recapitulation of the vital weeks after the first US troops crossed the Iraqi border, when the easy dreams of a quick war gave way to a recognition of the long and bitter task ahead.

In telling this story, I have taken an approach that is at times more impressionistic than linear, dividing each chapter into a number of chronological but sometimes independent vignettes that accumulate to form a mosaic of the whole road to war. I hope by this approach to mirror in narrative style the way in which the decision itself emerged: gradual, piecemeal, with arguments and memos and events piling atop one another and building toward a final judgment. The actual decision process was emergent, indirect, and intuitive, and any telling of the story must share some of these characteristics.

The resulting narrative—emerging as it does in between the initial accounts and the eventual and more complete flood of declassified documents some years hence—does not pretend to offer the final word on every meeting, every thought, every event along the road to war. There is surely much not captured here, and some claims that future historians will need to correct. But my research convinces me that the big picture can be sketched out with some confidence—that we know enough, from interviews, memoirs, and documents, to make an updated judgment, one that builds on the important early treatments to tell the story of the origins of this war in more comprehensive terms.

Yet some will rightly ask: Why *another* book on the Iraq war? Haven't there been hundreds? Aren't all the questions answered?

A new treatment is important for three main reasons. First, while much information relevant to the decision has been published, it is scattered across early journalistic accounts and later memoirs, dozens of published interviews, and hundreds of so-far declassified documents. A number of early treatments—Bob Woodward's astonishing three-volume feat of reporting, George Packer's thoughtful archaeology of the decision in the first third of *The Assassin's Gate*—told bits and pieces of the story. But we know much more than we did in 2004 or 2008 or even 2010, and no single volume has assembled all that we know in one place.

Second, a new assessment is important because what many people think they know about the origins of the war is wrong. Stubborn and erroneous mythologies persist to this day—that the war was produced by a conspiracy of neoconservatives, that it was waged for oil or Israel or Haliburton, that George Bush was a puppet in the hands of Dick Cheney. One thing this book offers, I hope, is an antidote to some of the most misleading legends about this profound event in US history.

But the most important reason for a new look at the judgment to go to war is to deepen our understanding of the pattern that brought it to life so that we might recognize the next tragedy before it occurs. The decision-making lessons so far mined from the Iraq case are at best incomplete and, in some cases, even mistaken. The conventional narrative has long relied upon theories of deception and conspiracies, the rash belligerence of a clownish president, and the sinister machinations of senior officials. The typical story told of the origins of the Iraq war, in other words, is of a sort of malicious crime perpetrated on the American people.

Just about none of this is right. It is true that the administration concealed some of its planning and preparation—but most of the march to war was right out in the open; was advertised in State of the Union addresses, United Nations resolutions, and hundreds of news reports; and, eventually, became an appeal to Congress for formal authorization. Though inattentive, sometimes incurious, and too convinced of his God-given destiny, Bush was no fool. Invalid statements about weapons of mass destruction were made and endlessly repeated not in order to bamboozle the American people, but because—based on years of seemingly iron-clad intelligence reporting—American senior officials unquestioningly *believed* them. Partly as a result, its advocates were convinced that the war had to be undertaken for a single reason: their commitment to safeguard the American people, as they interpreted that duty, demanded it.

Author Jim Rasenberger has written an engrossing history of the Kennedy administration's Bay of Pigs fiasco called *The Brilliant Disaster*. He explains that "of the many extraordinary facts about the Bay of Pigs, the most surprising may be that it was the work of mostly decent and intelligent people trying their best to perform what they considered to be the necessary emergency procedure of excising Fidel Castro." To condemn the effort "as an act of idiocy or evil perpetrated by fools and sinners is to miss the point; worse, doing so puts more distance between ourselves and those who undertook it than either we or they deserve."[46]

In a very similar way, to dismiss the Iraq war as a bizarre outlier traceable to awful individuals is to miss its most important lesson: the judgment reflects an all-too-common case of American foreign policy decision-making gone wrong, undertaken by senior officials hoping to sustain American power and safeguard the American people and yet producing outcomes that undermined both of those goals. The scholar Patrick Porter comes to a parallel conclusion in his own recent history of the British decision for war: "Mischiefs and falsehoods can facilitate war," he points out. "They were not its driving force. . . . Britain's 'deciders' are remembered as deft propagandists, but were idealists at the core."[47] The Iraq case, properly understood, can offer us—as citizens, and in some cases as journalists, experts, and senior officials—clues about what to look for so as to be on guard against future disasters.

To be sure, this decision remains a tragic misjudgment of the first order. There is responsibility to assign, culpability to be accepted; I will build the evidence for this culpability in the course of the coming

chapters, and Chapter 10 offers a framework for evaluating the degree of
negligence involved. But if my conclusions are valid, far more important
than blame is understanding—understanding of the pattern in American
foreign policy that so consistently precedes tragedies.

Some of the reasons for this mistake can be found in the factors
specific to this case, the events and personalities that fueled this particular decision. Nine-eleven's transformative effect on the risk calculus of
senior leaders, described in Chapter 4, has no parallel in modern American history since Pearl Harbor. The particular blend of personalities in
the Bush administration, a cast of characters examined in Chapter 3,
helps to explain the ultimately dangerous way in which the judgment was
made and carried out. But I will also argue that the Iraq case highlights
two more general tendencies that conspired to bring about this disaster.
Together they form a recurring pattern: the dangerous marriage of deeply
embedded national beliefs about the country's role in the world with a
passionate, urgent, even desperate imperative to act—a feeling that over-
rides concerns about risks or costs. These two factors provide the essential
context for understanding the US decision to invade Iraq.

The dominant national belief system at work was the vigorous missionary impulse that has come to characterize America's approach to
international affairs. This instinct is far from illegitimate; it stems from an
aspiration to make the world a better and more peaceful place and from
a willingness to act in decisive, and sometimes costly, ways in service of
that purpose. In more pragmatic terms, the urge to transform the world
flows from a critical insight that forced itself on American leaders in the
1940s: in an increasingly interconnected global system, it was no longer
possible to achieve security by isolating the country from the world's
travails. To keep itself secure and prosperous, the United States would
henceforth have to work to transform the world around it—an aspiration that doubled down on the essentially idealistic values inherent in
the American national identity. Left unchecked, however, this missionary
impulse can produce a theological and absolutist conception of America's
responsibility as well as a romantic conviction that America can renovate

other societies at will, a mindset that has contributed to some of the most disastrous blunders in US foreign policy.

The power of this missionary sensibility has waxed and waned over time. Not all presidents or senior foreign policy officials share it to equal degrees, and it is not responsible for every decision or debacle. And yet, as we shall see, various aspects—both hard-edged and idealistic—of this messianic conception are central to any understanding of the judgment to go to war in Iraq. For most countries the idea of invading, occupying, and forcibly modernizing a far-off and culturally alien land of twenty-five million people would be viewed as absurd. That it was not seen that way in Washington—that so much of the US national security establishment, media, and congressional leadership endorsed what much of the rest of the world saw as an adventuristic crusade—points to the influence of the aggressively idealistic concepts underlying US national security strategy. We can learn from Iraq, then, the perils that lurk within the broadly welcome instincts of American global leadership.

Second and in a closely related sense, the pattern of misjudgment behind the war stems also from the essential character of national security decisions regarding highly complex problems clouded with vast amounts of uncertainty. Rather than a rigorous focus on consequences and careful cost-benefit analysis, major national security judgments are often much more unconscious, instinctive, and emergent; and in certain circumstances, they reflect something far closer to the application of moral imperatives than reasoned analysis. The second element of the pattern I hope to illustrate is, therefore, the concept of moralistic and value-based, rather than instrumental or outcome-oriented, decision-making.

The disaster at the Bay of Pigs, Rasenberger reminds us, "was not ginned up by a nefarious band of agents in the bowels of the CIA, but rather produced by two administrations, encouraged by countless informed legislators, and approved by numerous men of high rank and intelligence, even brilliance." And nearly all of them, he explains, were "operating under conditions that made the venture almost impossible to resist. At a time when Americans were nearly hysterical about the spread of communism, they simply could not abide Castro. He had to go."[48] So it would be, four decades later, with another enemy of America who "had to go"—Saddam Hussein. It was another time of hysteria, this time about the claimed nexus between terrorists and state sponsors. The result was a similar degree of conviction, a belief bordering on faith, a feeling of obligation so strong that it bulldozed through any objections or warnings. The leaders who advocated for and eventually decided upon the invasion of Iraq did so out of an emergent sense, built up over many years and brought to a fever pitch by 9/11, that it was the *right* and *necessary* thing to do.

One of the most notable hallmarks of such imperative-driven decision-making is that planning for the resulting action is often muddled and incoherent. Once the direction is set by such value-driven considerations, the system tends to go into a passive mode, almost as if on a form of autopilot. This is one reason why the story of postwar planning will feature prominently in the coming chapters: the pattern I am describing here produces a doubly tragic outcome—the basic judgment itself is first flawed, and then the planning to accomplish the mission becomes corrupted as well.

These themes of US foreign policy mindset remain urgently relevant today. Americans have elected three presidents in a row who have promised to bring more humility and restraint to US international endeavors— and in all cases, those presidents have ended up being pulled into foreign wars and adventures of various scope and character, almost as if by a gravitational force. It is critical that Americans understand the impulses that shape this persistent adventurism, and that senior officials take seriously the degree to which their choices often sidestep a serious analysis of consequences in favor of what come to be seen as "sacred values." The sense of strategic self-righteousness so characteristic of debacles in places like Iraq is rushing through the US national security community in torrents today, propelled by the perceived authoritarian challenge from Russia and China. The even more elaborate impulse to engage in messianic, transformative campaigns is bubbling to the surface again with regard to

Iran and North Korea. As the Iraq case shows, these twin characteristics pose tremendous dangers. If the United States finds itself at war again, these two traits will be at least part of the reason for it.

David Kaiser concludes his brilliant history of decision-making about Vietnam, *American Tragedy*, by saying that the war revealed to him "my nation as it really was: not a new and unique civilization marching ever forward down the road to progress, but a great nation like every other, driven, at bottom, more by emotion than by reason, cursed at the moment by an excess of certainty, and liable to make mistakes on the same scale as its triumphs."[49] That is the nation we continue to inhabit. The risks remain—indeed, they may be greater than ever. It is critical that we reacquaint ourselves with the pattern of thinking and action that produced the Iraq disaster for one major reason: to help make sure that we as a nation do not make the same mistake again.

CHAPTER 2

THE ORIGINS OF A CONVICTION

In the history of conflicts and wars, there are few instances that match the invasion and occupation of Iraq for complexity of motive and ambiguity of purpose.

ALI ALLAWI[1]

There is a final result of Vietnam policy I would cite that holds danger for the future of American foreign policy: the rise of a new breed of American ideologues who see Vietnam as the ultimate test of their doctrine. I have in mind those men in Washington who have given a new life to the missionary impulse in American foreign relations: who believe that this nation, in this era, has received a threefold endowment that can transform the world.

JAMES THOMSON, 1968[2]

In the tragedy of Oedipus, "illusion and truth [are] the opposing forces between which man is bound, in which he is entangled, and in whose shackles, as he strives toward the highest he can hope for, he is worn down and destroyed."

KARL REINHARDT[3]

Bob Baer is perhaps best known these days for his numerous appearances on CNN and other television news channels, dissecting national security events of the day. After his retirement from government service he penned thoughtful op-eds and essays for *Time, Vanity Fair,* the *Wall Street Journal*, and other publications. Most recently he hosted the cheeky History Network show *Hunting Hitler*, each episode representing a search for tantalizing (if ultimately unpersuasive) clues that the Nazi leader did not in fact die in 1945 but was spirited out of the country. In all these venues Baer comes off as a smart and likeable figure, a straight-talking voice of pragmatic experience; trim and boyish for his sixty-plus years, curious and dogged as an investigator.

But Baer achieved his initial notoriety as a US clandestine intelligence operative, and in the mid-1990s, he was the CIA's man on the ground in northern Iraq. Baer's mission was to cobble together the elements of a successful coup against Saddam Hussein, an experience about which he would write an engrossing memoir. (That book became part of the basis for the movie *Syriana*, and the George Clooney character in the film is partly based on Baer.) In the book, Baer claims that by 1995 a senior NSC official working on Iraq, Martin Indyk, had authorized the establishment of a base of operations, whose purpose was to lay the groundwork for destabilizing Saddam.[4] But US policy had not yet got around to formally seeking Saddam's destruction, and for his part, Indyk claims that the NSC had only set up the CIA operation with explicit orders not to take action without asking for approval first. "I thought I had made myself clear" to the CIA's Middle East operations chief and to Baer, Indyk writes.[5]

As it would turn out, either he'd been less clear than he thought, or Baer decided to take more initiative than anyone expected. As one former official puts it, the "destructive ambiguity" that had emerged at the heart of US policy—the desire to have Saddam gone, but the unwillingness to take the political risks necessary to make it happen—opened the door to free-lancing by enterprising covert operators.[6] The Iraqi exile and anti-Saddam schemer Ahmad Chalabi (about whom we will hear a great deal more) brought Baer a supposed Iraqi general anxious to turn against Saddam and insisting that whole military units were ready to defect.[7] Kurdish militia in the north stood ready to help. Chalabi himself said he had thousands of Iraqi National Congress (INC) fighters ready to go, as well as commitments from Shi'ites in southern Iraq to rise up at the same moment.

Baer says he detailed all of this in several cables to CIA headquarters—and, he claims, got no response. So Baer, by his own account, in the spring of 1995 told Chalabi he may as well start the rebellion without formal US government approval. "Washington wants Saddam out," Baer told the Iraqis, on his own initiative.[8] When I asked a former senior official whether these events reflected a rogue CIA operator going off-script, he replied, "That's certainly how it felt at the time."[9] But in Baer's mind, the general direction of US policy—getting Saddam out of power—was clear, and he was operating totally in line with that goal. He had been sent there to do a job, and he was doing it.

A fascinating question is whether Ahmad Chalabi, the organizer of Iraqi components of the coup and entrepreneur for regime change, ever really expected his exile-based rabble-rousing to work. He appears to have assumed that the United States would intervene if the insurrection looked close to success. They just needed to get the ball rolling. If they went forward, Chalabi felt, Washington would confront a choice: "Whether or not to let us be slaughtered. I told them the Americans wouldn't let us be slaughtered."[10]

But the White House got wind of the emerging fight before it commenced, and from a curious source. On March 2, 1995, the United States intercepted an *Iraqi government* signals transmission showing that Saddam had uncovered a planned uprising and placed his army on alert. Indyk describes himself as "flabbergasted"; he and his team quickly informed NSC director Tony Lake.[11] "Sitting behind his desk littered with baseball paraphernalia and files, Tony Lake absorbed our report with surprising equanimity," Indyk explains, but Lake quickly agreed the thing had to be shut down. They dispatched a terse cable to Chalabi and Baer: "The action you have planned for this weekend has been totally compromised. We believe there is a high risk of failure. Any decision to proceed will be on your own."[12]

Chalabi was furious. One of the two Kurdish leaders pulled out of the plan. The other went ahead, and ten thousand Kurdish troops, supported by a few hundred INC men, threw themselves at two brigades of Iraqi infantry. But Chalabi's grand promises turned out to be—not for the last time—groundless: in the absence of Iraqi army defections or American military force, the assault promptly fizzled. In retrospect, Baer told Seymour Hersh, "There was nothing there." Chalabi, in the CIA officer's opinion, had been "bluffing."[13]

❧

Such ill-fated lunges in the direction of regime change as the abortive 1995 coup attempt offer prime examples of the roots of the judgment to go to war in Iraq, which can be found in the continuing US confrontation with Saddam and the evolution of postwar beliefs about US foreign policy that occurred in the 1990s. The story of these years is one of growing conviction that a dangerous megalomaniac had been left in power and of the burgeoning influence of officials, former officials, and adventurers who dedicated themselves to bringing down Saddam and his regime. These engines of policy transformation would accelerate in 1998 and 1999, when a group of senior officials of the Clinton administration made a forceful case for regime change—a case largely indistinguishable, in rationale and tone, from the one that would be made by the Bush administration just three years later.

These years also represent the story of Saddam's stubborn refusal to appreciate the growing hatred for his regime and the strategic dilemma that kept him from taking credit for the most profound judgment he made during this time—to mothball his weapons of mass destruction programs. It is the story of the disintegration of Iraqi society into a miasma of corruption, criminality, and decayed infrastructure. Most of all, it is the story of how Hussein's Iraq became the singular focus of America's expansive conception of its world role.

As a result, the evolution of US policy toward Iraq during the 1990s illustrates one of the primary engines behind the eventual decision to invade. Profound strategic judgments like the choice to go to war are usually grounded in what can be called evolved collective beliefs—about world politics, the identity and role of a nation, the character of an adversary. When dealing with complex, ambiguous choices brimming with uncertainty, as all major national security decisions will be, decision-makers rely on taken-for-granted certainties. The most influential of these can usually be traced to the essential principles that inform a nation's foreign policy.

In the case of Iraq, the decisive collective belief at work was a messianic and adventuristic conception of American power that had become so widely accepted by the 1990s that it was hardly even debated any more. Gradually during the twentieth century, and with accelerating speed in the late Cold War and then after its end, the American national security establishment settled on the conviction that the United States, as the global leader and hegemon, had the responsibility, the power, and ultimately the right to shape the world in ways it saw fit. These intentions embodied a powerful idealism and boldness that are among the most admirable effects of the American national identity and that have underwritten many triumphs—from the small and personal, such as the release of human rights advocates in authoritarian countries, to grand and strategic victories as significant as the defeat of communism in the Cold War. But they also impelled the United States to meddle in the politics, economies, and societies of foreign nations in literally thousands of ways. They help explain events like the 1995 coup attempt, when Americans like Bob Baer end up thousands of miles from home, working with exiles and defectors and local insurgents to overthrow a foreign government.

By 2001, one of the most urgent expressions of this impulse was the commitment to overturn the regime of Saddam Hussein. Beyond the sometimes mind-numbing details of weapons of mass destruction and human rights violations, this remarkably ambitious idea made sense—not only to the Bush administration but to the larger bipartisan US foreign policy community—in part because it fit so comfortably into the implications of America's beliefs about itself. The problem with such beliefs is that they were just that: beliefs. They had transcended the status of hypotheses to become truth. And when the time comes to act on such powerful, nearly religious beliefs, the ultimate decision has more of the character of a reflex than a choice. Judgments of that sort, grounded in creeping certainty rather than rigorous evaluation, pose one leading danger—they are all too often blind to risks and consequences.

⁂

In 1988—seven years before Baer and Chalabi launched their ill-fated coup effort—Saddam Hussein's disastrous decade-long war against Iran was drawing to an ignominious close with Iraq deeply in debt and socially devastated. Saddam had started the war in 1980 to tame a provocative Iranian revolutionary regime and establish Iraq as the regional hegemon. But after a bitter and prolonged conflict that ended in stalemate, with perhaps half a million dead and a trillion dollars expended by the two sides, Iraq was economically shattered. In order to recover, Saddam needed his fellow Sunni Arab states to forgive loans extended to Iraq during the conflict and for Iraq to resurrect its economy with oil revenues. In the process he intended to fulfill Iraq's natural place in the order of things, which to him meant regional domination.[14]

Even in the late 1980s, Saddam hoped that Iraq could pursue these goals with American sponsorship. After all, Iraq had been a sort of quasi-partner in the effort to contain the revolutionary regime in Iran. Washington had supplied arms during the Iran-Iraq war, and after a brief flirtation with Tehran during the Iran-Contra affair,[15] the United States returned to courting Baghdad. A National Security Directive of October 1989 argued that "normal relations between the United States and Iraq would serve our longer-term interests and promote stability in both the Gulf and the Middle East."[16] As a former senior US official suggested, one fundamental assumption of the pre–Gulf War US policy was that "Saddam could be managed," that a clever and judicious "combination of carrots and sticks" could manipulate him to serve US interests.[17] And so in 1989, US secretary of state James Baker met with Iraqi officials to express a desire for improved relations—just a scant few months before the two countries would be at war.[18]

These embraces were soon constrained by a growing suspicion of Saddam's intentions.[19] US interagency sessions and intelligence reports from this period catalogue an escalating series of disputes over human rights and Iraq's weapons programs.[20] One State Department report concluded that "we believe Iraq judges a nuclear weapons capability to be essential to meet its security needs and further its regional ambitions."[21] Still, the weight of thinking in the US government continued to point to a salvageable relationship.[22]

But Saddam was Saddam—belligerent, vain, autocratic, with a grandiose conception of his role in history. He directed particular fury at the neighboring monarchy of Kuwait: It refused to forgive Iraq's loans and, Saddam claimed, exceeded OPEC production quotas and thus kept oil prices artificially low, hamstringing Iraq's recovery. The dispute reached a boiling point in the summer of 1990.

Conditioned by years of viewing Saddam as a counterweight to Iran, few in the US government thought he would actually invade an Arab neighbor.[23] Nor could others believe it: three days before the invasion, the leaders of Jordan and Egypt told Washington it was likely a bluff.[24] James Baker was on a diplomatic trip in the Soviet Union; Soviet foreign minister Eduard Shevardnadze assured him that "it would be completely irrational for Saddam to do this. It's not going to happen. Don't worry about it."[25] When Saddam finally decided to attack, some evidence suggests, he did so reasonably convinced that the United States would turn a blind eye to the aggression.[26]

Such wishful thinking was typical of Saddam. Former Iraqi officials describe him as a solitary decision-maker who would retreat into private reflection somewhere in the endless expanse of his many gaudy palaces and emerge with wild-eyed proclamations based on dreams, or intuition, or religious guidance.[27] CIA interrogator John Nixon—who had multiple sessions with Saddam once he surrendered to US forces in

2003—reports that "much of what Saddam did was improvisational." There was no grand plan at work; often, "there wasn't enough discussion of the pros and cons of a particular course of action." And when "things finally went sour, there were no plans to clean up the mess."[28]

Saddam shared these traits, as it would turn out, with those who would eventually order his destruction.

⁂

Once Iraq's army had taken Kuwait, the White House, after an initial moment of hesitation, moved toward ultimatums, economic sanctions, and threats of force, starting down a road that would culminate in a conflict that has become known as the Gulf War, or "Desert Storm."[29] As war loomed, the chairman of the Joint Chiefs of Staff—General Colin Powell—watched and worried. He feared the costs of an all-out conflict and hoped sanctions would be given more time to work. In one of the first national security meetings after Saddam's invasion, Powell wanted to know just how quickly after securing Saudi Arabia they would move to liberate Kuwait. His inquiry provoked a "chill" in the room: "The question was premature," Powell would later admit. "I had overstepped."[30] Secretary of Defense Richard Cheney brusquely reminded him to keep his advice to military matters.

The Vietnam veteran Powell wondered just what sort of war they were gearing up to fight. What would they do once they had "won" the military campaign? Powell found the planning sessions "disorderly," with "people talking at random. . . . They were all looking for a military option but had no clear idea what they wanted to achieve." They needed to "put everything on the table and have an honest discussion." If others came to see him as the "skunk at the picnic," that was fine with him. Everyone could "take a deep smell."[31]

The Bush administration dallied with sanctions for a while, but given Saddam's hubris and pride, economic pressure was never going to lever him out of Kuwait. By September 1990, a US attack seemed imminent. Powell decided that he had to speak his mind.[32] On September 24, he phoned Dick Cheney, who agreed to let the chairman make the case to the president for sanctions as an alternative to war. According to his memoir, Powell outlined both options and the risks associated with each. Bush thanked him and said that the time for patience had passed.[33]

Powell's biographer, Karen DeYoung, suggests that he walked away content that he had said his piece—that he had "done what the chiefs had failed to do in Vietnam and Beirut and that all the cards were on the table." He had done, in other words, what "his conscience and duty required," even though the intervention had not swayed the direction of US policy. George H. W. Bush had been elected to make these decisions, and now "Powell had his orders."[34] All these events amounted to a remarkable preview of an almost identical dialogue that would take place thirteen years later, between Powell and a very different George Bush.

The US military campaign, when it unfolded, was a textbook use of combined arms that evicted Iraqi forces from Kuwait in a matter of days. A ceasefire was signed within a month.

Having obsessed for weeks over the plan to rescue Kuwait, the administration suddenly drifted. No one appeared to have a clear thought of what came next. The idea was to drive Iraq out of Kuwait, one official later told an interviewer, but "that was it. There was no consideration for conflict termination—Where do you want to be politically in 20 years? What are the strategic decisions for this part of the world? None of that was considered."[35]

One thing was clear: no one was in any mood to rush to Baghdad and finish off the regime, an effort that looked like a quagmire in the making.[36] The view at the time was "let's not fuck it up" by persisting in the war, an official working the issue at the time later said. Besides, senior members of the administration assumed that the ignominious defeat had dealt Saddam a political death blow.[37] His army would turn against him, they thought, and the long-suffering Shi'a majority would rise up. There was "a lot of wishful thinking going on" within an administration that wanted to believe its work was done, the official added. "Just how the psychology takes hold" of senior decision-makers at such moments, he said, is "often lost in histories."[38]

By far the best defense of the decision to leave Saddam in power came from a senior member of Bush's administration. "The idea of going into Baghdad . . . or trying to topple the regime wasn't anything I was enthusiastic about," he told a PBS interviewer five years later. "I felt there was a real danger here that you would get bogged down in a long drawn out conflict."[39] The interviewer persisted: Wasn't Saddam a serious threat who needed to be removed? "Maybe it's part of our national character," the former official answered with the wry smile that was one of his trademarks. "We like to have these problems nice and neatly wrapped up, put a ribbon around it. You deploy a force, you win the war and the problem goes away." This was a delusion, he suggested.

> It doesn't work that way in the Middle East, it never has, and isn't likely to in my lifetime. We are always going to have to be involved there and Saddam is just one more irritant, but there's a long list of irritants in that part of the world and for us to have done what would have been necessary to get rid of him— certainly a very large force for a long time into Iraq to run him to ground and then you've got to worry about what comes after. And you then have to accept the responsibility for what happens in Iraq, accept more responsibility for what happens in the region. It would have been an all-US operation, I don't think any of our allies would have been with us, maybe Britain, but nobody else. And you're going to take a lot more American casualties if you're gonna go muck around in Iraq for weeks on end trying to run Saddam Hussein to ground and capture Baghdad and so forth and I don't think it would have been worth it.[40]

This remarkable portrait of what a US invasion of Iraq would entail was drawn by none other than George W. Bush's future vice president,

Dick Cheney. The route Cheney traveled from this pragmatic and nuanced analysis to the vehement conviction that Saddam had to be immediately driven from power is one of the most important—and, frankly, puzzling—aspects of the eventual US decision to invade Iraq.

※

The fleeting perception of success in the Gulf War gradually gave way to a creeping sense of unfinished business. As Saddam routed postwar rebellions with Iraqi army units thought to have been crushed, one former official described Colin Powell as having "blasted" intelligence analysts. "You guys must be smoking dope," Powell thundered. "We killed those divisions." It soon became clear that forecasts of Saddam's fall from power wouldn't be borne out, at least not any time soon.[41]

Over time, this frustration morphed into a powerful conviction that the hopes of 1991 had to be fulfilled, and that Saddam must go. The United States had been aware of his brutality before 1991; now his cruelty began to be seen as evidence of a megalomaniacal personality capable of any aggression. Washington had known of his pursuit of weapons of mass destruction, but now that aspiration was seen as an unacceptable risk. His intermittent flirtations with terrorists were now viewed as the machinations of someone determined to undermine the stability of other Arab and global countries. This transition—from a sense that Iraq was one problem among many to a nearly obsessive certainty that Saddam Hussein represented the single most urgent threat to US interests—became the foundation stone for a formal US regime-change policy, the origin point of the later choice to invade. And it emerged gradually, without any truly formal debate or decision.

Iraq's behavior certainly added fuel to the fire. Postwar UN weapons inspections uncovered evidence of an Iraqi "crash program" to develop nuclear weapons. Saddam had spent between $5 billion and $10 billion and employed over twenty thousand people and seven thousand scientists on an effort that UN inspectors estimated had left him between twelve and thirty months short of a nuclear bomb.[42] Nearly all of this came as a total shock to US intelligence and senior officials, and it badly spooked the intelligence community. It was, as future CIA director George Tenet would put it, "a mistake no one wanted to repeat,"[43] and so the bias flipped in the opposite direction—that of being determined to not miss evidence of accumulating risk and so end up looking foolish.[44]

Still, these changing perceptions took time to work themselves into policy. The concept that Saddam *ought* to go was one thing—making it happen was quite another. Until 2001, US administrations continued to edge up to the enterprise in a half-hearted way.[45] One former senior official told me that during the early 1990s the Bush administration kept "pushing [Iraq] under the rug," and early covert efforts to go after the regime were "haphazard and helter-skelter."[46]

The United States was not the only actor in this drama with a sense of regret and frustration in the wake of the war. CIA analyst John Nixon, who helped interrogate Saddam when he was a prisoner in 2003, reports that their conversations on the Gulf War represented "the closest he ever came to admitting a mistake." Saddam "seemed to flinch" when Kuwait came up; "his face took on an anguished look, and he tried to change the subject." One time in particular when Nixon raised the subject, Saddam "put both hands on his head and said, 'Uggghhhhh, this gives me such a headache!'" He continued to imagine that there had been an opportunity for better relations with the United States, and seemed genuinely confused about where things went sour between two countries who ought to have been natural partners against Iran and Islamic extremists. "The West used to say good things about Saddam," a morose Hussein told Nixon in one conversation. "But after 1990 all that changed."[47]

⁂

The case for ending Saddam's rule by force began slowly, almost imperceptibly, gathering momentum after 1991. During the war, a handful of officials had argued for a more decisive campaign. Zalmay Khalilzad, serving in Cheney's Defense Department and later to coordinate Iraq policy in George W. Bush's NSC, told an interviewer that he had thought at the time that "we should have helped the Iraqis get rid of Saddam. There was of course a nightmare concern, clearly, that if we went to Baghdad we might get stuck. I remember sending memos to Cheney, saying, 'You can't stop! We have an opportunity to do a bigger thing.'" Khalilzad would argue for regime change in the years after 1991 because "when I left the government there was this sense that we had not done the right thing in Iraq. We had unfinished business."[48] The former defense official Ken Adelman has said that in 1995, on a trip to Vietnam, Donald Rumsfeld spoke passionately about how the United States had ended the first Gulf War badly. Bush should not have left Saddam in power, Adelman recalls Rumsfeld arguing.[49]

Nor was such thinking limited to Republicans: former vice president Al Gore authored an op-ed in 1991 disputing the idea that "Saddam Hussein is an acceptable part of the landscape." The only route to regional stability, Gore insisted, was "if Saddam ceases to hold power, and his Baathist regime is dismantled as well."[50] A whole crowd of journalists, experts, and politicians from both parties would eventually join the call for regime change, some in the 1990s and others after 9/11. The decision, when it came, would reflect the emergent view not of one administration, but of most of the US national security establishment.

But arguably the most passionate anti-Saddam activist was Paul Wolfowitz. Already a senior Defense official in 1990, he served as the top policy and strategy official in Donald Rumsfeld's Defense Department. No US analyst or official would be more insistent in the demand for action.

The son of a prominent mathematician, Wolfowitz was by many reports strongly influenced by his personal history much of his Polish extended family had been murdered in the Holocaust.[51] Bill Keller's insightful profile in the *New York Times Magazine* observes that he "grew up in a household in which Hitler and Stalin were not abstractions," that "the world's perils and America's moral responsibility were constant topics at their dinner table."[52]

Wolfowitz undertook a career characterized by periods of senior government service interspersed with academic and research positions. He acquired a reputation as cerebral, soft-spoken, and analytical. Friends and colleagues have described him as personable and kind, and at the same time as a brilliant man who lived by his ideas and whose gentle demeanor was married to a bulldozer commitment to his beliefs.[53] Wolfowitz could be stubborn and self-righteous, pushing his views to the point of annoyance.[54] Nor, despite his multiple government posts, was he known for his focus on the implementation of his ideas or his bureaucratic acumen.[55]

Yet there is no question of his passion for liberal values, which nurtured a willingness to employ US power on behalf of oppressed peoples. Wolfowitz believed ardently in human rights. One official who was deeply angered about his stance on the Iraq war nonetheless insisted that "Paul has a conscience."[56] Even most bureaucratic rivals I have spoken with retain a soft spot for Wolfowitz, whom they view as a sincere idealist with the best of intentions. One said that he was a "great humanitarian. . . . Nobody fell for the Iraqis like Paul."[57] A dominant theme in Wolfowitz's thinking, Bill Keller wrote, is "optimism about America's ability to build a better world. He has an almost missionary sense of America's role."[58]

Wolfowitz's family history also makes it easy to understand the other side of his ideological coin, the counterpart to his romanticism—a hard-edged commitment to the employment of American power. In a spring 2000 journal article, he wrote of the importance of "demonstrating that your friends will be protected and taken care of, that your enemies will be punished, and that those who refuse to support you will live to regret having done so."[59]

Such instincts made him acutely sensitive to the risks of Saddam Hussein's encroaching power, for both the region and the United States.[60] Saddam would invade his neighbors again, Wolfowitz reasoned, and next time he would do it as a nuclear weapons state.[61] One source told me he attended a small meeting in Washington during the Clinton years where Wolfowitz spoke about the need to finish the job of destroying Saddam. He was "extremely fixated about" Iraq, this source contended.[62] The Iraqi exile Kanan Makiya claims he was giving a public presentation on Iraq in the mid-1990s, when Wolfowitz was out of government, serving as dean of the Johns Hopkins School of Advanced International Studies. "I remember him seeking me out," Makiya recalled years afterward, to say that "he felt that the United States had been wrong in 1991 in the way it had handled the uprising. To have sought me out to say this thing was touching—was something special. I took an immense liking to the man because of it."[63]

Wolfowitz knew that an outright US invasion wasn't in the cards in the years after the Gulf War. So he developed a placeholder scheme: a proposal to arm insurgent Iraqis, establish protected safe havens in northern and southern Iraq where a provisional government and defecting military units could safely gather, and allow opposition forces to eat away at the regime until it crumbled.[64] A million details of such concepts were never worked out, from how a few thousand ragtag opposition forces could defeat the Middle East's most powerful army to what would happen if they somehow succeeded. Such abstraction was characteristic, many observers have argued, of Wolfowitz's thinking, which was moved more by grand ideas than by the bothersome trivia of execution.[65] In this he mirrored, to tragic effect, the president who would finally put these Iraq visions into force.

※

Whatever his later regrets, in the years immediately after 1991, it seems that Saddam Hussein was convinced he had *won* the Gulf War, the "Mother of All Battles." He had been pushed from Kuwait but remained in power. In his cocooned, self-created world, he believed he had saved his regime and fought off the Americans, forcing them to blink. To a thug like Saddam, America looked like a country unwilling "to engage in what he regarded as real war: straight up, direct slugging it out, mano-a-mano."[66] And the next time a showdown occurred, Saddam fully expected to be able to stare the Americans down once again.

※

As the post–Gulf War conviction that Saddam had to go became more entrenched, a number of people took it upon themselves to help set the agenda for US policy. One of those people was a dapper and charming former bank manager exiled from Iraq: Ahmad Chalabi.

Chalabi, who died of a heart attack in 2015, was a balding, portly man, at once cherubic and professorial, urbane, well informed, and witty. He could discuss literature, politics, and finance with equal apparent facility. He wore expensive, hand-tailored suits; spoke fluent English in an elegant and musical accent; rented beautiful homes packed with fine art in the world's capitals; and traveled the globe to ingratiate himself to the powerful and the connected. Those who encountered Chalabi tended to have one of two wildly divergent reactions. Some saw him as a cosmopolitan, Western-leaning Iraqi with a unique drive and effectiveness. Skeptics perceived a puffed-up charlatan desperate to amass influence and wealth, a man whose rapid, self-conscious stride and perpetual half-smile made him seem like someone forever playing a role.

Chalabi arrived on the scene as a tainted figure, a banking entrepreneur and executive who presided over a series of reportedly corrupt institutions.[67] He had already been involved in anti-Saddam activities, but according to journalist Richard Bonin, his response to the banking scandal that forced him out of Jordan was to cast himself as a crusader for the liberation of his people. In this crusade he knew he needed a powerful ally. He chose the United States and set out to take his cause to the American Congress and people.[68]

Thus was born a campaign that would culminate with meetings in the vice president's office, major national newspapers parroting Chalabi's claims, and fake defectors being inserted into the stream of US intelligence. The legends regarding how important he was in bringing on the war are far greater than the reality; "I don't think," one former policy-maker contends, "that the Iraqi opposition had anything to do with the war."[69] But Chalabi's machinations helped to lay the groundwork for the invasion—and for some of his wishful American friends, with the intelligence and cosmopolitanism he embodied, he became a hopeful symbol of what Iraq could become.

But he was only one man, and he was unknown to most Iraqis.

※

The idea that the United States could seriously consider adventures as militant and elaborate as overturning the Iraqi regime flowed directly from a concept of American power and purpose that had, by the early 1990s, become firmly rooted in the American national security establishment as conventional wisdom. The foundations of that conventional wisdom were drilled deep into the bedrock of America's essential sense of itself as a nation and actor on the world stage—a sense that is fundamentally messianic or missionary in character, in ways both profoundly admirable and more than occasionally self-destructive.

The essential propositions of this worldview were straightforward. The postwar world was based on ideas and institutions dictated by the United States. The stability of that world relied on American power, credibility, and principle. By the 1990s, the United States, in the minds of its leading national security practitioners and experts, had come to a pinnacle of global power and responsibility that demanded and justified a posture of global primacy.[70] This primacy, two particularly ambitious advocates of US predominance argued, offered "the only reliable defense against a breakdown of peace and international order"[71]—and that American power could and should be used in service of values as well as interests.

The idea that the United States is a special, unique actor in world affairs is grounded in America's very self-conception. Its national myths and narratives speak to a country brought forth to help produce a better world; it was a nation founded on an idea, not territory or blood—an idea with an inherent relevance, and appeal, to people everywhere, an idea that (some believe) represents a vision of God's will for humankind. Any country fired by such a self-conception will develop some form of obligation to spread its reach. In both religious and secular guises, this notion has led many American leaders and theorists to see the country as a special power brought forth to lead and change the world.

For over a century, the practical manifestations of these ideas were largely confined to efforts to set a powerful example rather than directly engage in foreign adventures. An acceptance of restraint and limits, and especially a desire to hold the United States aloof from foreign rivalries, dominated US foreign policy thinking through the First World War, and in some ways until December 7, 1941. Indeed, the notion of "exceptionalism" is sometimes misread:[72] the founding generation indeed considered the new United States exceptional, but in the sense of being unique and apart from, rather than determined to wade into, the community of nations. The historian Walter McDougall calls this the "Promised Land" version of American foreign policy, guided by the "Old Testament" of its bible of foreign affairs—an effort to "deny the world the chance to reshape America."[73]

The gradual slide into a more ambitious interpretation of America's destiny, one that went well beyond example setting, remained largely confined to the American continent and did not, for some time, embody broader intentions to play a major role in world events.[74] Yet from fairly early on, American presidents began to weave threads of territorial expansion and religious calling into the tapestry of the young nation's exceptionalism. The language used to justify these expansionist adventures implied a very different direction from the self-protective Promised Land. It pointed, as McDougall has argued, to a far more ambitious role— the "Crusader State," a concept built on giving "America the chance to reshape the world,"[75] an instinct that has sparked "the perennial impulses that have always tempted Americans to meet discriminate challenges through indiscriminate crusades."[76]

By the 1990s, these ambitious ideas had arguably become the most dominant vein of thinking in US grand strategy.[77] They became, in fact, an accepted national value, to the point that opposition to such a vision was seen as morally wrong, as breaking faith with American traditions. The missionary role had become America's calling, and responsibility, to act in service of sacred values. Arguably the apotheosis of this sensibility was expressed in the post–Cold War exuberance of American primacy by Secretary of State Madeline Albright: "If we have to use force," she informed the world, "it is because we are America; we are the indispensable nation. We stand tall and we see further than other countries into the future." The increasingly theological language surrounding these responsibilities began to produce a sense of the non-negotiability of the basic issues at stake:[78] When foreign policy becomes sacralized, demands become absolute, while enemies become vile and wicked—not merely competing powers to be balanced and contained, but evildoers demonized to the point of irreconcilability.[79]

America's missionary sensibility is responsible for many of America's greatest successes and proudest moments: the Berlin Airlift, the willingness to defend Europe against Soviet encroachment, the choice to fight for the freedom of South Korea and Kuwait—and most broadly, bearing the burden of a tremendously successful postwar international order. Striking the right balance is the trick—and among the most difficult acts of judgment that can be expected of a democracy is to recognize when shared collective beliefs, beliefs held because they have broadly benefited the country rather than harmed it, are impelling a disaster.

Yet the tendency of a missionary, values-driven sensibility is always toward excess, and observers have warned of this from almost the founding of the republic. Arguably the most profound critic of the messianic tradition in American foreign policy is Reinhold Niebuhr, who has written of the ironic—and ultimately tragic—results of an essentially positive outlook. The founding fathers, he argued, believed "that we had been called out by God to create a new political community." Partly as a result, he worried, the American brand of global idealism "is too oblivious of the ironic perils to which human virtue, wisdom and power are subject. It is too certain that there is a straight path toward the goal of human happiness; too confident of the wisdom and idealism which prompt men and nations toward that goal; and too blind to the curious compounds of good and evil in which the actions of the best men and nations abound."[80]

These idealistic impulses had become firmly embedded in US foreign policy by the 1990s. The emerging view by that time, Christopher
Preble has explained, "was not merely that the United States *could* be a
force for good, but rather that the United States was the *engine* of all that
was good."[81] The Canadian writer (and later parliamentarian) Michael
Ignatieff is representative of the liberal internationalists who became
fired by this missionary spirit—to the point, ultimately, of endorsing the
Iraq war as part of the American duty to "bear the ark of liberties of
the world."[82] During this period, moreover, the missionary sensibility
acquired a much more aggressive cast, asserting that it was America's job
to maintain military and geopolitical primacy on the world stage. By the
time of the Bush administration, the idea had become well entrenched in
hawkish foreign policy circles that the United States had been stumbling
around the world fecklessly for eight years under the Clinton administration, that threats were looming, and that America had better get about
the business of rebuilding and projecting power to sustain its primacy.
In this worldview, the right lesson to take from Vietnam is not about
the excesses of American hubris and ambition, but about the insufficient
application of American power. And in this worldview, by the 1990s,
rogue regimes like Saddam Hussein's Iraq stood at the epicenter of the
challenge to world peace and had to be the main focus of America's transformative intent.[83]

Donald Rumsfeld relates, in his memoir, his initial conversation with
President-Elect Bush on being offered the job of secretary of defense. They
talked about a variety of issues (though not, according to this accounting,
Iraq). Rumsfeld claims he ended the conversation on a somber note. "I
had observed over the past few years," he told Bush, "that there were
ways of behaving that could invite one's enemies to act aggressively, with
unintended but dangerous consequences." He went through the usual
litany—the "Blackhawk down" calamity in Somalia, the al Qaeda attack
on the USS *Cole*. "The cumulative effect, I cautioned, suggested to our
enemies that the United States was not willing to defend our interests.
'Weakness is provocation,' I said to the President-elect, who nodded in

agreement. 'But so is the perception of weakness,' I added. As I saw it, a decade of hesitation and half measures had undermined our national security."[84]

Rumsfeld, like so many other members of the Bush national security team, was determined to do something about this.[35] If a new provocation appeared, the response would be different. The aggressor, and the world, would be taught a lesson—partly in the name of self-protection but also, quite consciously, as a reflection of concepts of American rights and responsibilities that flowed directly from the messianic streak in the US national identity. In a different interview, Rumsfeld summarized the upshot of his conversation with Bush about credibility: he told the president, "We're going to have a conflict, and there's going to be a need for a decision. I am going to be telling you that I believe our country has to lean forward and not back, or else we're going to be encouraging others to do things to us."[86]

The growing conviction that the United States had to deal decisively with Saddam Hussein's regime, then, was not arbitrary and did not emerge in a vacuum. It reflected the logical extension of the fact that America was more than a great power. It had become a missionary one, fired by an uncompromising sense of purpose. The purpose was both idealistic and punitive and, in each guise, asserted America's right and responsibility to police the world. The direct, imminent threat posed to the United States by Saddam Hussein's Iraq was not something, at that moment, that would have prompted most nations to act. But the United States is not most nations, and Saddam simply stumbled into the path of its unique style of geopolitical zealotry.

⁂

These characteristics of national identity have left the United States vulnerable to the seductions of exiles from foreign lands anxious to turn America's missionary adventurism to their advantage. In the 1990s, the latest of these adventurers was Ahmad Chalabi, whose efforts to focus this American missionary zeal on Saddam's regime started even as the first Gulf War was getting underway. Around the time of the Gulf War, under investigation for financial crimes, he had fled from Jordan to London and had settled into a fine home in Mayfair. His first meetings with Iraqi exiles there left him dismayed at their ineptitude, and with America on the verge of amassing a huge army to liberate Kuwait, he reportedly felt that a golden opportunity was being lost: there was no meaningful anti-Saddam opposition to rush into the potential chaos and seize power.[87]

Chalabi thus took it upon himself to begin a courtship of American official and public opinion.[88] In Washington he met members of Congress and penned op-eds, comparing the plight of Iraqis to the Jews of the Warsaw ghetto. "Democracy is possible in Iraq," he urged in a *Wall Street Journal* editorial.[89] And crucially, he met a number of senior US officials then working in or around the first Bush administration, establishing relationships that would serve him well in 2002 and 2003.[90]

Whatever his faults, Chalabi was a master political schemer, studying US politics and cultivating relationships. "He was a genius" at such efforts, a former US official who dealt with him recalls, "one of the giants in the history of political influence."[91] His emerging exile coalition wrote to President Bush offering a program of democratic change, and the letter got Chalabi a meeting with Richard Haass on the National Security Council. Haass told Chalabi that the United States would "support an Iraqi political movement that will come out endorsing such a program." That, Chalabi claims, "was the genesis" of what would eventually become the Iraqi National Congress (INC).[92]

Some Iraqi exiles, such as Laith Kubba, hoped for a political organization appealing to the Iraqi diaspora. Chalabi and his allies wanted instead, as Kubba has put it, to "forget about the Iraqis and appeal directly to the American governments and agencies, and work with them, because they have the key to future Iraq—not the Iraqis."[93] Chalabi won the argument, and his focus turned the emerging exile community into an organization built to do two things: assemble Iraqi paramilitary forces to destabilize Saddam Hussein's regime, and create the conditions under which the United States would forcibly remove Saddam from power.

Soon enough, as George Tenet and many other US officials have confirmed, the CIA began to see in Chalabi a potential asset. Thus began a tortuous, twelve-year relationship between the enigmatic Iraqi and his American patrons.[94] Initially the agency appears to have thought of Chalabi as a savvy operator with a load of contacts who could help them coalesce the exile community into an effective force and gather intelligence. Ahmad Chalabi seems to have thought of himself as something else: the next ruler of Iraq.

&

As the consensus against Saddam hardened during the 1990s, Chalabi and other exiles stepped up their efforts to spur action. In June 1992, the still-embryonic Iraqi exile movement held a meeting in Vienna that created what became known as the Iraqi National Congress (INC). October brought a second meeting, this one in northern Iraq, in the town of Salahaddin in US-protected Kurdistan. The resulting statement left nothing to the imagination: "The INC," it said, "endeavors to become the nucleus of an actual provisional government that will extend its authority over parts of the territory of Iraq and seek to expand it to cover all the territory of Iraq and to overthrow Saddam Hussein and his regime."[95]

Chalabi and other exiles quickly moved beyond abstract theorizing to operational planning. One early concept was dubbed the "Three Cities Plan" and called for exiles to plant the seeds of a creeping insurrection in three major urban areas.[96] A critical assumption was that they were dealing with a regime that was like a block of ice frozen at a subzero temperature: at one hard blow, it would shatter into a million pieces. The army would fragment and defect into the waiting arms of the opposition. The people would rise up. All it took was the right hammer—and someone standing by, ready to take control of the resulting fragments. Chalabi nominated himself for that role. "The time for the plan is now," he would say. "Iraq is on the verge of spontaneous combustion. It only needs a trigger to set off a chain of events that will lead to the overthrow of Saddam."[97]

Had Chalabi been making this case to most officials in most governments, he would have simply been ignored. But he was making the case to the United States, a country whose national identity was essentially tied to transformative missions abroad. And more precisely, he was making his case to a group of former (and later senior) officials who saw Saddam as a profound threat and who were in the market for actions to reaffirm the extent of American power and the seriousness of American purpose.

Yet one explanation for the eventual tragedy of America's leap of faith into Iraq is that when the moment arrived for decisive action, the US government would be relying on a deeply flawed concept. A central assumption of many war advocates was that Saddam could be toppled on the cheap: his regime was a house of cards that minimal American forces, working with Iraqi exiles and defecting army units, could knock over with little more than a nudge. Then, Washington could stand aside and watch proudly as liberated Iraqis got busy fashioning a democratic future. When this idea was broached in the 1990s, its assumptions were repeatedly shot to pieces: halfway efforts couldn't knock over Saddam's military; the exiles were weak and divided; any postconflict reality was likely to tumble into chaos for which America would then be responsible; and Iraqi society, warped by decades of Saddam's brutality, would take generations to recover.

After 9/11, when American military power was brought into the equation, the first of these flaws seemed to have been addressed. But nobody took the time to do the archaeology on the others, to recall the simple fact that there is no such thing as a light-footprint approach to installing democracy. Nobody managed to remember that in thinking they could poke over a government and walk away, they were embracing a concept that had been discredited every time it was raised. By 2001, though, the Bush administration *needed* for this idea to be true in order to fulfill the sense of imperative its policy-makers felt so powerfully. And so, in their minds, the idea would become true.

⁂

Even in the early 1990s, and even with extensive UN weapons inspections underway, the growing American obsession with Iraq took inspiration from the risks of Iraqi weapons of mass destruction (WMD) programs. Saddam possessed chemical and biological weapons, the growing consensus proclaimed; he hoped for nuclear weapons, as the terrifying near-miss before the Gulf War made clear. A tyrant as bellicose and brazen as Saddam could not be allowed to continue down that path.

And yet the history of Iraq's ambitions regarding WMDs in the 1990s makes for confused and paradoxical reading. According to the Duelfer Report—the comprehensive investigation after the US invasion— Saddam viewed such weapons as essential foundations of regime survival and symbols of national pride.[98] In the wake of the first Gulf War, the Iraqis initially tried to fool the inspectors—the UN Special Commission (UNSCOM) and the UN Monitoring Verification and Inspection Commission (UNMOVIC). This turned out to be devilishly hard, in part because the UN proved more dogged than Saddam had assumed.[99] Meanwhile, the lingering cost of the Iran-Iraq war and the Kuwaiti adventure, combined with new sanctions placed on Iraq after 1991, crippled Iraq's economy, which, in the words of the Duelfer Report, created a "tense and difficult period" that "threatened regime survival."[100]

Saddam decided that he needed a way out. In the early to mid-1990s, he seems to have made a fateful pair of decisions. He ordered the regime to destroy existing WMD stockpiles and programs while preserving the intellectual capital needed to resuscitate the effort—and, amazingly, at the same time, he told his officials to keep the decision to end the weapons program secret.[101] The fact that the second decision essentially undermined the point of the first appears to have been lost on Saddam: if he was not willing to publicly admit that the programs had ended, he would not escape sanctions. He seems to have believed that US intelligence would figure out the truth, and his complex ploy would have its intended effect even though he refused to broadcast the choice to shutter the efforts. He apparently worried, senior Iraqis claimed later, that such a public undressing would advertise Iraq's vulnerability and emasculate his pride and prestige.

The order to dismantle the programs accounts for the lack of WMDs on the arrival of US forces in 2003. But Iraq's refusal to admit as much, as well as a desire to retain the know-how to restart the program at a later date, explains the muddled intelligence picture that would emerge by 2001. Still, evidence reflecting the pause in WMD work began appearing as early as the 1990s. Hussein Kamel, former head of Iraq's WMD programs, defected from the regime in 1995 and gave persuasive testimony that Iraq's weapons programs had been shut down. UN inspectors were busily locating and removing any stockpiles of chemical and biological agents they could find. In October 1997, Hans Blix, then director general of the International Atomic Energy Agency (IAEA), reported that Iraq had no nuclear program; in October 1998, new IAEA chief Mohamed ElBaradei claimed the same thing. Such developments led some to conclude that the vast majority of Saddam's WMDs had indeed been destroyed.[102]

But Iraq's cooperation with UN inspectors remained half-hearted, and Saddam ordered scientists connected with the program to be kept on hand to "preserve plans in their minds."[103] Fueled by the resulting misimpressions, US intelligence reporting from the mid-1990s, insofar as it has been officially declassified, continued to paint a disturbing portrait of Iraq's weapons aspirations.[104] The message was colored by the intelligence community's embarrassment after the Gulf War and the resulting tendency to overcompensate in the direction of seeing, rather than missing, potential threats.[105]

Saddam's postwar FBI interrogator, George Piro, gave a 2008 interview to *60 Minutes*. "He told me that most of the WMD had been destroyed by the U.N. inspectors in the '90s," Piro said of his discussions with Saddam in captivity. "And those that hadn't been destroyed by the inspectors were unilaterally destroyed by Iraq."

"So why keep the secret?" the *60 Minutes* reporter, Scott Pelley, asked Piro.

"It was very important for him to project [possession of WMDs] because that was what kept him, in his mind, in power. That capability kept the Iranians away. It kept them from reinvading Iraq."

"He believed that he couldn't survive without the perception that he had weapons of mass destruction?"

"Absolutely," Piro concluded.[106]

The upshot, of course, was precisely the opposite of what he intended. By the end of the 1990s, US intelligence—and most US senior officials—had become convinced that Saddam had resuscitated his weapons programs, that he had significant stockpiles of chemical and biological weapons, and that he was accelerating toward a nuclear capability. When the Bush administration came to make the case for war, its terrifying claims about Saddam's WMDs—admittedly more unqualified that the intelligence itself—nonetheless reflected not a calculated lie but simply what senior officials saw as the strongest possible formulation of something they absolutely believed. Every senior national security official to whom I have spoken has said the same thing: they were all certain of this point. There were doubts about degree and timing, but almost no one doubted the basic case. And thus by keeping his WMD backtracking secret, Saddam helped to guarantee the end of his regime.

※

This confused tangle of developments meant that the Clinton administration arrived in office at the beginning of 1993 faced with an Iraq policy full of contradictions—and potential land mines, strategic as well as political. The Clinton policy would waver and wobble but remain true to the line set at the end of the first Bush administration: the United States would be better off with Saddam "gone," but no one knew what precisely that meant, or how to make it happen. The default position remained containment, while allowing the CIA to persist with futile efforts to engineer Saddam's departure.[107] America's elaborate ambitions remained bottled up by the likely costs and risks of trying to do something decisive about them—and this was a risk calculus that, before 9/11, would not support bold strokes.

Nonetheless, this calculus was evolving even before 9/11, and indeed even before the Bush administration; many Clinton administration officials would eventually come around to the idea of taking more active steps to foment regime change.[108] In his memoir, CIA analyst and NSC staffer Kenneth Pollack argues that right from the outset, the administration contained a group of Iraq hawks interested in pushing hard on several coercive levers—air strikes and covert operations—to see if they could make the regime crack.[109] An early Clinton administration policy review steered clear of anything so provocative and suggested a strategy called "aggressive containment," but even that supposedly more muted approach retained a strong whiff of regime change.

But these more hawkish sentiments remained in the background; it would take years of Iraqi provocations up through 1998 to get the Clinton administration to a place of trying more energetically to engineer regime change. For the time being, the administration settled on an approach called "dual containment," which aimed to deter threats from both Iran and Iraq without tilting toward either. It was a relatively passive approach, and for good reason: the administration's crowded foreign policy agenda was headed by such issues as Bosnia, North Korea, and managing the post-Soviet transition. Iraq was a "second-tier issue," said one former senior official.[110] Most top national security officials didn't want to invest a lot in Iraq policy—especially National Security Advisor Anthony Lake. "Tony hated Iraq [policy]—it was almost a physical thing with him," a former senior official said of his views.[111]

The administration thus returned to the wishful thinking of 1991, building policy on the assumption that "the combination of sanctions and covert operations would force the collapse of Saddam's regime in five years," according to Martin Indyk, a senior NSC staffer dealing with Iraq at the time.[112] But the policy was in essence a bluff: one former senior official suggests that elements of the US government kept brainstorming ideas, but "there was zero appetite for anything [they] came up with."[113]

Meanwhile, Saddam kept provoking an administration that would have been very happy to ignore him. Early in the administration, the Clinton team received intelligence suggesting that Saddam had ordered the assassination of former president George Bush during a planned visit to Kuwait. Clinton launched a cruise missile strike on Iraq in June 1993 as retaliation.[114] In 1994, Saddam threatened a new invasion of Kuwait. During the interagency debates about US responses, Deputy Secretary of State Strobe Talbot asked what it would mean to "defeat" Iraq this time: "Is it taking out Saddam?"

According to Indyk's notes, Secretary of Defense William Perry replied simply, "That would be my judgment. We don't want to have to go back and do this yet again."[115] "The way forward," one former senior official told me, "was to get rid of Saddam Hussein," but the process ended up taking longer than anyone assumed. It would stumble through two major covert operations before reaching a crisis point in late 1998, when all the built-up frustrations of American policy finally burst into view.[116]

⁂

But that call for more decisive action was still years away. For the time being, the halfhearted US covert plotting continued. In 1995 it produced the abortive coup attempt described at the beginning of the chapter. After the failure of that hoped-for revolt, Ahmad Chalabi returned to Washington, moved into a graceful home in Georgetown, and renewed his campaign to shape US opinion. But he also accelerated work on his exile-based ideas to destabilize Saddam. His newly revised plan now envisioned well-armed paramilitary groups seizing parts of southern Iraq, declaring a provisional government, requesting support from US air power, and gradually extending their reach throughout the country. The exile force was termed the "Iraqi Liberation Army" and was planned to be about ten thousand strong.[117] The fact that a far-better trained force of Kurds of roughly the same size had just been mauled in northern Iraq while attempting a similar gambit does not appear to have dampened Chalabi's enthusiasm.

Paul Wolfowitz had become enamored of such ideas at the tail end of the first Bush administration. Part of his conversion may have come while visiting northern Iraq to see the postwar relief operation, called Operation Provide Comfort, in the Kurdish areas.[118] In these concepts, Wolfowitz had stumbled onto the model he would continue to advocate for much of the next decade: an "enclave strategy" using local and exile forces, supported with US airpower and small US ground units, to carve Saddam's regime to pieces and ultimately drive him from power with very limited US assistance.[119] But again, every time the plan was subject to close military analysis—by the Defense Department and Joint Staff, Central Command, or outside experts not on the payroll of the INC—the answer was the same: there's no way this will work without massive US military engagement. More broadly, a former senior official explained, the Chalabi plan "smelled to the Clinton people too much like 1995—and besides, his plans, like the plans of many others, were always compromised to the regime."[120]

Nor was anyone ready to endorse the sort of robust US role likely to be required in such schemes. Before 2001, no senior US official or expert advocated an American-led war as part of the process. The conservative former official and policy analyst Richard Perle described his pre-9/11 thinking: "If Ahmad [Chalabi] had said, 'You've got to send in the marines,' he wouldn't have gotten very far in my view. But the demands were modest."[121] A senior Clinton official agreed that the administration's regime change planning was based on shattering the regime's stability, not invading Iraq. "If we gave [Saddam] enough rope," the expectation went, "he'd hang himself." Continued misbehavior could generate more sanctions, harassment, and strikes that would end his rule.[122]

Yet some of the anti-Saddam activists who pushed these enclave plans seem not to have realized the self-fulfilling momentum they were setting into motion by committing US resources and credibility to the over-throw of a foreign government. Because while Chalabi's scheme was a war plan, it was also a lure. According to one account, when Chalabi met former UN weapons inspector Scott Ritter, he showed Ritter a version of his evolving insurrection plan. Ritter told Chalabi that larger American forces would be needed. Chalabi agreed, Ritter later claimed, explaining that the plan was "a ploy" to draw the United States militarily into Iraq. He couldn't actually say that, he told Ritter—to admit the requirement for large US ground forces would be "too sensitive."[123] But the US deter-mination to oust Saddam was picking up speed, and would reach a sort of fruition long before 2003—in the more determined regime change planning that started in late 1998.

※

This growing momentum was stoked by former officials and scholars out-side government, who in the mid- to late 1990s consistently issued the siren song that Saddam constituted the focus of evil in the world. Henry Kissinger rolled out an op-ed in 1998 that both warned about many of the practical complexities of plans to liberate the Iraqi people with exile armies and endorsed that option.[124] Fred Hiatt, a *Washington Post* columnist, argued in January 1998 that "Saddam Hussein has declared a holy war against America" and was busily evading UN weapons inspec-tors. Hiatt quoted the hawkish foreign policy expert Robert Kagan to the effect that the time had come to begin thinking about an invasion.[125] Another *Post* writer, Jim Hoagland, would become one of the most con-sistent supporters of Chalabi and the INC, writing as early as 1997—and then publishing numerous columns right through 2003—demanding American support for regime change.[126]

As early as 1995–1996, a small but growing cadre of officials inside the US government began to reflect similar views: though they remained fully aware of the risks of direct US action, they began to push for bolder actions to foment regime change. Iraq stood at its weakest point, these officials would eventually argue, according to sources working in government at the time. With the likely weakening of sanctions and Saddam's diligent efforts to crush nascent opposition forces, he was likely to only grow stronger. Either the United States would find ways to arrest this trajectory and shake the stability of his regime, or else it would miss its opportunity.[127] To be clear, this group was not proposing US military action; they had in mind a more disruptive version of containment, one capable of threatening regime stability and keeping Saddam on the defensive. The goal was still regime change—but by more aggressively strangling the Iraqi government, not by attacking it.

Even in this form, however, the plan struck others as too risky. More senior members of the administration foreign policy team—notably Secretary of State Warren Christopher and National Security Advisor Anthony Lake—denied that any radical departure was called for. They worried that a bolder effort posed the risk of escalating and pushing other issues off the administration's foreign policy agenda. But to the advocates of a tougher policy, Christopher and Lake looked like ostriches: they knew they couldn't keep doing the same thing and yet decided to do it anyway. One NSC official who had been arguing for a tougher line, as one participant recalled, returned from a critical meeting very upset. "The only thing we couldn't do was refuse to make a choice," he lamented, "and that's exactly what they just did."[128]

❧

Early in 1996, with broad regime change plans still on the shelf, the Clinton administration took another run at the coup option—this time under the aegis of one of the INC's rivals in the exile community, Ayad al-Allawi's Iraqi National Accord. According to a range of public accounts, the CIA recruited participants from the tribes of western Iraq. The coup was set to occur in August 1996, and according to some reports might have been supported by US airpower had it begun to work. Some believe it posed a greater threat to the regime than the INC effort the year before.

But as many skeptics of coups had warned for years, Saddam's intelligence proved too capable. It uncovered the plot, rounding up dozens of conspirators and killing many of them.[129] Separately and in an action apparently unconnected to the coup, Saddam launched raids into Kurdish areas in the north, where, among other things, his forces slaughtered some two hundred Iraqi National Congress operatives. These and related events seemed to confirm once again the infeasibility of pushing Saddam from power with anything short of radical US action. "If we want him out now," CIA operative Robert Baer concluded from the incident, "it will probably take a war."[130] This was, in fact, the primary lesson that the agency took away from its bitter experiences of the mid-1990s. And the CIA would later convey this dispiriting conclusion to the incoming Bush administration in 2000: if you want Saddam gone, you will have to do the job yourself.[131]

At least as far as the CIA was concerned, however, it wouldn't be doing that job with Ahmad Chalabi. After years of seeing his schemes amount to nothing, after new investigations that found his hugely expensive propaganda efforts to be Potemkin programs of empty offices, the agency soured on the dapper exile. In the process, it earned the enmity of the substantial parade of friends and admirers that Chalabi had, by then, amassed in Washington. The event "triggered his resentment," one former US official suggests, and caused him to switch his focus yet again: instead of gaining broad-based popular and political support for uprisings, Chalabi would now focus on recruiting backers from the highest levels of the US government.[132] He was determined to get Washington to take action, one way or another.

☙

With sanctions eroding and the US government unwilling to commit itself to formal regime change, anti-Saddam activists turned in the last years of the 1990s to urgent calls for the end of the Saddam regime. "Toppling Saddam is the only outcome that can satisfy the vital US interest in a stable and secure Gulf region," Paul Wolfowitz wrote in 1997.[133] Wolfowitz and Zalmay Khalilzad offered the details of such a program of action in a jointly authored essay later that year called "Overthrow Him."

(The article appeared in the December 1, 1997, edition of the conservative magazine the *Weekly Standard*, whose cover broadcast the message, "Saddam Must Go: A How-To Guide.") They set out steps including working with regional allies, building up the opposition, and being ready to "provide military protection" to defecting Iraqi units.[134]

Other scholars and former officials organized two open letters to President Clinton in 1998 that accelerated the public campaign for action against Saddam. At the end of January, a group called the Project for the New American Century issued a statement arguing that the United States needed a policy of "removing Saddam Hussein and his regime from power." It was signed by a host of people who would take up positions in the administration of George W. Bush: Elliott Abrams, Richard Armitage, John Bolton, Paula Dobriansky, Zalmay Khalilzad, Peter Rodman, Donald Rumsfeld, and Paul Wolfowitz. The letter was followed with op-eds and substantial media coverage, including an ABC *Nightline* segment. Several of the anti-Saddam activists secured a meeting with Clinton national security adviser Sandy Berger, where they laid out their plan for American air power backing Iraqi insurrectionists. "I listened to that," Berger said later, "and I said, 'I've seen this movie before. It's called the Bay of Pigs.'"[135]

One source I spoke with, who was eventually to serve at senior levels in the second Bush administration, described this emerging consensus as a growing sense that the patient acceptance of Saddam Hussein's regime could no longer be sustained. A determined adversary of the United States clung to power and "spent the next twelve years [after the Gulf War] breaking free of the restraints that had been placed on him."[136] The Clinton administration "just kicked the can down the road," he concluded. "We were going to have to face this problem." Another official agreed, in even more stark terms. By the late 1990s, it had become obvious that "the world's poor record in trying to pressure [Saddam] to change his policies told us that it was unrealistic to think we could solve the Saddam Hussein problem without war."[137]

But any time such plans would emerge, the dilemma at the core of US policy reasserted itself; every time the United States came face-to-face with what a truly effective regime change policy would entail, it backed off. A few months would pass, and the urgency would dissipate. Washington remained unalterably opposed to Saddam and willing to take some degree of bold action to remove him—but beyond the limited, covert actions that had already been tried, it still didn't quite know what to do about that determination.

⁂

Meanwhile, Saddam was rethinking the value of his effort to meet the inspectors' demands. Formal sanctions were not being lifted, and it began to appear to the Iraqis that the UN teams would never be completely satisfied. And so, between August and October of 1998, after almost a year of threats, ultimatums, and games, Iraq took a bold gamble: Saddam halted cooperation with UNSCOM. "Given a choice of sanctions with inspections or sanctions without inspections," the Duelfer Report explains, Iraqi leaders decided that "they would prefer without."[138]

In response the Clinton administration launched a series of military strikes called Desert Fox, about which one hears various things. Iraqi officials reportedly told postwar investigators that if they'd known how pitiful the attacks were going to be, they would have thrown out the inspectors long before. But this may have been bravado, because US intelligence reports suggested that the raids made a substantial impact.[139] Pollack writes that "Saddam panicked during the strikes";[140] General Anthony Zinni and an unnamed US military intelligence official would later tell Tom Ricks that "Desert Fox nearly knocked off Saddam Hussein's regime."[141] Fearful of losing control, Saddam reportedly ordered mass arrests, the assassination of opposition figures, and the appointment of politically loyal officers to key posts.[142]

Just after Desert Fox, another Clinton administration Iraq hawk— Vice President Al Gore—gave an interview on CNN. "If you allow someone like Saddam Hussein to get nuclear weapons, ballistic missiles, chemical weapons, biological weapons," he asked, "how many people is he going to kill with such weapons?" Gore termed the existing inspections regime a failure. The Clinton administration, he said, would in the future be ready to "use our military to degrade his ability to get weapons of mass destruction and threaten his neighbors."[143]

Years later, speaking in captivity, Saddam brushed off the significance of Desert Fox. He claimed to have seen it as a typical lashing-out by US leaders. Every American president, Saddam told his army commanders, had to prove his manhood by attacking Iraq. "So I used to joke about it, saying, 'This is our luck. Every new president has to take a whack at us!' "[144] Yet Clinton was not, of course, by that time a new president. And what Saddam seems not to have appreciated was the rise of a much more determined American commitment to drive him from power. The move toward war after 9/11, when it happened, represented the culmination of an emergent conviction with very deep roots and broad-based support.

⚜

That trend reached a high water mark of sorts in 1998. In the US Congress, the Clinton administration, the press, and the broader national security community, the idea that Saddam had to go—and quickly— achieved a new degree of urgency. The United States, many increasingly believed, would not be able to wait on events. It would have to act.

This escalation of US rhetoric and policy produced, among other things, the Iraq Liberation Act of October 1998.[145] A legislative expression of American global ambitions, it took upon the US government the right and responsibility of regime change, by providing (1) assistance to radio and television broadcasting into Iraq, (2) $97 million in military assistance to "democratic opposition organizations," and (3) humanitarian assistance to Iraqis living in liberated areas.

The act was intimately connected to the Iraqi National Congress, from its origins to its funding. "When I originally wrote this bill," House International Relations Committee staffer Stephen Rademaker told Aram Roston, "I really just had Chalabi—well, not Chalabi—the Iraqi National Congress, the INC, in mind. That was the organization, it seemed to me, that seemed entitled to this."[146] For his part, Chalabi saw specific historical parallels at work. "I followed very closely how Roosevelt, who abhorred the Nazis, at a time when isolationist sentiment was paramount in the United States, managed adroitly to persuade the American people to go to war," he would later explain. "I studied it with a great deal of respect; we learned a lot from it. The Lend Lease program committed Roosevelt to enter on Britain's side—so we had the Iraq Liberation Act, which committed the American people for liberation against Saddam."[147]

The act passed the House by a vote of 360 to 38, and the Senate by unanimous consent. President Clinton signed it reluctantly. Secretary of Defense William Cohen tempered expectations by saying that Clinton "was not calling for the overthrow of Saddam Hussein. What he was saying is that we are prepared and will work with opposition forces or groups to try to bring about in some future time a more democratic type of regime."[148] By the end of his administration, Clinton had disbursed only $20,000 of the $97 million approved in the law.

Behind the scenes, though, by late 1998, many in the Clinton administration had come to the conclusion that regime change was the only long-term option that made sense. "We'd all gotten there," one senior official who worked the issues told me.[149] In his December 1998 address to the nation explaining the strikes he was ordering against Iraq, Clinton himself was very clear about his justification and his goals, using language that was almost a carbon copy of what the Bush administration would employ three years later. Iraq was refusing inspections of its weapons sites, he argued, and this was unacceptable; they had been given many opportunities to comply, but "Iraq has abused its final chance." Clinton insisted that "so long as Saddam remains in power, he threatens the well-being of his people, the peace of his region, [and] the security of the world. The best way to end that threat once and for all is with a new Iraqi government."[150]

Kenneth Pollack explains that, during a job interview for an NSC post in early 1999, Sandy Berger confirmed that the Clinton team was tired of dealing with Saddam. "They had decided that the only solution was to topple his regime. Sandy told me flat out that he wanted me to come back to help the administration devise a realistic regime change policy." And so, Pollack concludes, "starting in early 1999, the Clinton administration began to develop options to overthrow Saddam's regime."[151]

Pollack and his boss at the NSC, Bruce Reidel, got to work on regime change planning. But the recent US experience in Kosovo had created a poor precedent; the United States had used similar concepts of air strikes to help local clients push for regime change—and until the very last minute, there was a terrifying fear that it would fail and Slobodan Milosevic might hold on, sparking a drawn-out ground war. Milosevic eventually caved, but the experience was a near-death experience for the administration,[152] and it cast a dark pall over proposals to go after Saddam. "I don't think we were anywhere near that point" even by the end, a former senior official explains.[153]

In the meantime, US officials were having growing challenges working with their alleged partners in the scheme—the Iraqi exile community. Secretary of State Madeline Albright had appointed State Department official Frank Ricciardone as a special "representative for transition in Iraq." One source says Ricciardone was getting pressure to do something, but he also made clear his suspicions of Chalabi. "Ahmad wants to bring us to war," he told colleagues at the time. "I cannot bring myself to have the United States work for Ahmad Chalabi."[154] At the same time, various exile organizations had cropped up, leaving the INC as one of a constellation of acronyms competing to speak for dissident Iraqis. Even other members of the INC viewed Chalabi with a skeptical eye. "The opposition," Ali Allawi writes, "sank back into a confused jumble of parties, each trying to cultivate its privileged status, especially with the US government or one of its agencies."[155] It was a harbinger of what the United States would find to be true of Iraqi politics as a whole.

※

A primary claim of the liberation advocates was that Iraq had become, by the late 1990s, a modern, cosmopolitan, middle-class society, ready to be freed from the yoke of a dictator who was stifling the progress of a creative and well-educated people. Remove the repressive blockage of the regime, and progress would be swift. This assumption was an essential pillar of the plans the United States would hatch in 2002 and 2003 for how to handle Iraq in the aftermath of an invasion. It represented a sort of underlying side effect of American missionary ambitions—the tendency to see in every other society an American-style democracy, struggling to break free.

At least in the case of Iraq, this convenient narrative vastly oversimplified the reality. By the late 1990s, Iraqi society had suffered through a long, slow breakdown under the impact of United Nations sanctions.[156] After the first Gulf War, broken infrastructure—especially power-generating equipment—had been pieced together with spare parts, wire, tape, and ingenuity. The sanctions regime then prevented large-scale replacements or substantial refitting. Unemployment crippled Iraq's economy, with 60 percent of the people dependent on government handouts. The situation has been described as a "plunge from a gradually advancing middle-income country to a poor and underdeveloped one."[157]

The data supporting this dismal picture was right out in the open. Thick United Nations reports catalogued the ruin of Iraq's economy.[158] In January 2003, CARE International and Johns Hopkins University published a joint report describing an electrical power grid broken down for lack of spare parts; a water treatment and supply system in shambles, with 30–40 percent of treated water leaking away through broken pipes; and the gradual loss of trained civil servants.[159] The relief group Oxfam issued a press brief titled "Iraq: On the Brink of Disaster," documenting that a million tons of untreated water were being dumped into the Tigris River every day.[160] These calamities were well known to US intelligence: the January 2003 CIA intelligence report, "Principal Challenges in Post-Saddam Iraq," which has since been declassified, catalogued them in detail.[161]

Yet when asking officials working across the US government during 2002 and 2003 what they knew of Iraq's social and economic situation, I found a kaleidoscope of answers. "Most of this is on the internet, if you really look around," one State Department official said.[162] A different source said the administration was aware (it was "common knowledge," he said) that "the sanctions had had an effect,"[163] but admitted that he never got many details. Others complained of minimal awareness. A senior Bush administration official involved in postwar planning explained that they had little sense of the grim state of the Iraqi economy and society.[164] Another senior official said, "I don't think anybody knew the degree to which it was a failed state."[165]

Part of the problem was that the advocates of invasion had been conditioned by interactions with the urbane, middle-class exile community, most of whose leaders had left Iraq in the 1970s or early to mid-1980s, before it spiraled downward.[166] Partly as a result, the war advocates' faith in their ability to erect a secular, modern democracy relied on hallucinations of a society that had, for all practical purposes, ceased to exist. Ali Allawi, an Iraqi expatriate who became a minister in the new regime, wrote later that "in official Washington, ignorance of what was going on inside Iraq before the war was monumental. None of the proponents of the war . . . had the faintest idea of the country that they were to occupy."[167] A memo prepared within the Department of Defense in March 2003 would include the following among its list of things that had to go right for the invasion to succeed: "Sufficient Iraqi infrastructure and acceptable levels of technocratic talent will exist to provide a suitable basis for all Phase IV activities."[168]

Some of those advocating stronger action knew these realities only too well, and tried to convey the seriousness of any scheme to refashion Iraq. On the verge of war, Kenneth Pollack published *The Threatening Storm*, which was taken as an endorsement of the looming conflict. But Pollack was stern in his warnings: an invasion, he wrote, "will not be quick; it will not be easy; and it will not be cheap. Indeed, to attempt only a minimal effort toward rebuilding post-Saddam Iraq would be to court disaster." Whenever the United States made a half-hearted lunge at postconflict reconstruction, he explained, "the result has been chaos, civil war, and dictatorship. . . . All the signs indicate that the same would hold true in Iraq."[169]

The upshot of such warnings—and the broader state of Iraqi society—was the need for a much more elaborate sort of operation from the one the Bush administration eventually embraced. But by 2003, taking the prospective costs and risks of ousting Saddam seriously was something that US officials, firmly in the grip of a sense of what they "must" do, no longer had any patience for. And the wishful visions of Iraqi society that fueled these convictions had become immune to correction. These certainties gained added power for another reason: each was in some way anchored in fundamental American beliefs about itself and its role in the world.

❦

The urge for action was accelerating in part because the web of sanctions and constraints cobbled together around Iraq was collapsing. This trend is essential to understanding the sense of urgency held by advocates of bold US action. Saddam, they believed, was slipping loose from the bonds imposed on him after the Gulf War. As the sanctions regime eroded, Saddam could look forward to a time when foreign investment, technology, and arms sales would return. He could look forward, the anti-Saddam activists were convinced, to a moment when he could return to the pursuit of his violent regional ambitions—this time armed with nuclear weapons. This momentum had to be arrested.

Indeed, one effect of the United Nations Oil for Food (OFF) program had been to actually strengthen Saddam's regime by allowing his cronies to skim money off the top. One ironic result of this process was to vastly inflate the sources of money fueling the corruption in the regime and broader Iraqi society, thus accelerating the growth of the sort of kleptocracy that would prove unable to function as an effective government once Saddam's regime was gone.[170] In the last years of the 1990s, Baghdad filled with businessmen from Europe and Asia who jockeyed for the seemingly inevitable moment when sanctions finally

collapsed and foreign investment rushed in.[171] By December 1999, the
UN Security Council removed all restrictions on the amount of oil Iraq
could sell under OFF.[172]

Martin Indyk, Clinton's NSC lead on these issues, concludes his
account of the administration's Iraq policy on a somber note. After eight
years of hard work, "Saddam's containment cage was disintegrating." This
line of thinking accounts for "why President Clinton and most of his senior
advisors supported President Bush's decision to use force to topple Saddam
Hussein."[173] As one source intimately involved with the war preparations
that led to Iraq told me, Saddam was *not* "in his box"—Iraq was a long-
term problem in 2000 that wasn't going away.[174] The emergent conviction
that Saddam should be removed from power was by then well established;
all it would take was the right catalyst to light the fuse of war. When it
came, the war was the product not only of the work of anti-Saddam activists, but of a whole constellation of reasons. Dominant among those was
the fact that by 2000, the United States gazed down upon the international
system as the predominant power, fired with a sense of almost adolescent
adventuristic energy and a commitment to promote its values. It would
soon be governed by a man who would reflect—for good and ill—these
characteristics of the American national spirit.

In his final years as president, Bill Clinton had granted unprecedented access to the historian Taylor Branch. When the administrations
had turned over, with Clinton now out of the White House and the
Bush administration in place, Branch had the opportunity to ask Clinton
about the new president. One thing that worried Clinton was his sense
of "Bush's strong preference to rally against a villain. . . . He wanted to
point out the bad guys and lead a charge. 'There are not many places in
the world where that kind of leadership is going to work,' said Clinton.
'Including Iraq, where I know he wants to take on Saddam Hussein.'"[175]

⁂

Few US officials, however, had a clear sense of what "taking Saddam
on" would really entail. A disquieting lesson of the Desert Fox strikes in

1998, for example, was that if Saddam's regime did suddenly collapse, no one had any idea what to do next. General Anthony Zinni, the top US military commander in the region, describes worried Arab leaders coming to him and saying, "You almost caused an implosion." If the regime disintegrated, they told the American general, the United States would have to intervene. Did he have a plan? He did not, and he began assembling what would become an elaborate framework for humanitarian assistance and provision of civil order in the event of regime collapse.

The process of developing such a framework began with a large-scale planning exercise, called "Desert Crossing." Its "After Action Report," declassified in 2004,[176] is eerily prescient. The report points out that "early establishment of a national authority to begin taking over civil functions . . . was deemed essential." The US government needed a lot more information about the situation on the ground: "Conflicting reports abound, obscuring a sound assessment of the present conditions in Iraq."

As they waded through options during the exercise, the report makes clear, US officials could not come to agreement on one essential paradox. In working to establish postcollapse governance, should the United States find a few indigenous Iraqis and quickly hand over power, or undertake "a total US/coalition occupation" under a post–World War II "Japanese model"? No consensus emerged. "Some participants argued that the United States would have such high stakes in the outcome that it must retain tight control over the progression of events," the report explained. "Others objected, asserting that the intervention may be unduly prolonged by not encouraging the growth of indigenous leadership." The rapid emergence of a local government could occur, the report concluded, "but a Bosnia scenario is more likely—which means US involvement could last for at least 10 years." The most obvious bottom line was the requirement for planning. "Past experience has too often demonstrated that ignoring interagency coordinating mechanisms and planning tools can lead to aborted, prolonged, or failed missions. US end state objectives in Iraq will not be achieved through an exclusively military intervention."

Desert Crossing took place at the end of June 1999. More than three years later, in early 2003, as war planning was heating up, General Zinni testified on Capitol Hill and saw a former military colleague then working at CENTCOM. He asked whether planners had looked into Desert Crossing. After all, it directly paralleled the postinvasion challenges they were about to assume, and so it offered critical insights and warnings.

The officer looked at him wide-eyed and responded, "Desert *what?*"[177]

CHAPTER 3

A NEW SHERIFF IN TOWN: THE BUSH ADMINISTRATION ENTERS OFFICE

Day after day we read about them, each new man more brilliant than the last. They were not just an all-star first team, but an all-star second team as well.

DAVID HALBERSTAM, THE BEST AND THE BRIGHTEST

The ABC of our profession [of history] is to avoid these large abstract terms in order to try to discover behind them the only concrete realities, which are human beings.

MARC BLOCH[1]

What is incident but the illustration of character?

HENRY JAMES[2]

On January 30, 2001, the national security team of the new administration—fresh from the inauguration just ten days before—gathered for its first National Security Council Meeting with President Bush. The personalities who would shape Bush administration national security policy sat around the table and began, in their new roles, to take each other's measure: Vice President Richard Cheney, Secretary of State Colin Powell, Secretary of Defense Donald Rumsfeld, and National Security Advisor Condoleezza Rice. Cheney and Rumsfeld were about as close as two Washington power players can be, having worked together on and off since the Nixon administration, but neither had a notable bond with Powell or Rice. Just how they aimed to go about their jobs, and what that would mean for American foreign policy, remained to be seen.

At the head of the table sat a man who remained, to many Americans, something of a mystery. George W. Bush had been around presidential politics for decades and had served two terms as the governor of one of the country's largest states. But to many Americans, he still had the reputation as something of a lightweight, and the conventional wisdom was that he had an uphill climb to establish himself as a strong and credible president.

After a brief discussion of the Israeli-Palestinian peace process, according to former treasury secretary Paul O'Neill—who shared the events of the day with journalist Ron Suskind for his book *The Price of Loyalty*—the president turned to Condoleezza Rice and reportedly asked what else was on the agenda. "How Iraq is destabilizing the region, Mr. President," Rice responded.[3]

Colin Powell talked of a new approach for targeted or "smart" sanctions—a proposal to loosen restrictions on Iraq's nonmilitary trade to win global support for the tough enforcement of sanctions on specifically defense-related items. Donald Rumsfeld replied, "Sanctions are fine. But what we really want to think about is going after Saddam." O'Neill recalls Rumsfeld saying, "Imagine what the region would look like without Saddam and with a regime that's aligned with US interests. It would change everything in the region and beyond it." But Rumsfeld, often loath to nail himself to a firm position, quickly backtracked, saying, "It's not my specific objective to get rid of Saddam Hussein. I'm after the weapons of mass destruction. Regime change isn't my prime concern."[4] The group discussed the challenges and costs of the no-fly zones in southern and northern Iraq and how they were becoming unsustainable.

The treasury secretary left the meeting shocked at the seeming urgency. "Getting Hussein was now the administration's focus," O'Neill concluded. "That much was already clear. . . . It was all about finding *a way to do it*. That was the tone of it. The President saying, 'Fine. Go find me a way to do this.'"[5]

But O'Neill, whose background was not in national security, had read too much into the substance of the discussion. One former senior official who attended these meetings heard very typical contingency planning that did not imply a rush to regime change. This official found the basic US stance largely unchanged: an administration committed to getting rid of Saddam but unsure of how to make it happen.[6] Condoleezza Rice writes that the NSC agreed that US-Iraq policy was "unsustainable," but she saw no breathless discussion of ways to "get" Saddam.[7] Even O'Neill himself recanted on some degree of his claims, clarifying later that he didn't mean to suggest the new president was already intent on war.[8]

⁂

In the dark vision of the skeptics and conspiracy theorists, the decision to invade Iraq was indeed foreordained the instant George W. Bush was elected president. A neoconservative cabal worked feverishly with a scheming vice president to goad and trap the United States into a military confrontation with Saddam Hussein. And Bush himself needed little encouragement: he embodied a filial obsession with the dictator who had ordered a hit on his father. He was determined, some believe, to go after Saddam from the moment he took office.

This view is a caricature. Despite O'Neill's initial characterization of that first NSC meeting, there is little reason to believe that the administration, or Bush himself, had reached any firm decisions before 9/11 beyond sharing the previous administration's conviction that Saddam Hussein could not be left in power. There is no question that these broad, inchoate beliefs about Saddam remained firmly in place. The new administration did arrive in office with an especially strongly held—and hard-edged—version of the messianic conception of America's world role. And some advocates of a tougher line down in the bureaucracy, as we will see, pushed contingency planning that would produce memos and arguments leaning powerfully in the direction of decisive action. But the administration as a whole reached no fundamental conclusions during this period. The story of the Bush administration's first nine months is in fact that of a largely directionless Iraq policy process, which lurched from half-baked idea to half-made choice without ever settling on a clear strategy.

This would become a defining theme of the Bush administration, both before and after 9/11: the existence of multiple, often conflicting levels of debate and seeming decision. Upon taking office, many senior Bush officials would have agreed that Saddam could not be left in power forever; a handful of them were committed from the beginning to placing US power in service of that goal. But the administration only gradually stumbled toward the judgment that the United States should go to war to get the job done. To outsiders the conflicting statements emerging from this chaotic process would look like deceit. To many insiders, it just looked like confusion.

This chapter tells the story of a transitional moment—a period when the generalized sense that "Saddam must go," grounded in shared beliefs about American power, slowly gave way to a more focused commitment to reaching that goal. Yet the evidence suggests that before 9/11, this consensus had not yet reached the status of an imperative. No one was advocating large-scale US military action to remove Saddam, and Iraq was not yet front and center on the national security agenda. The first nine months of the Bush administration represent a sort of muddled holding pattern—a time when the missionary conceptions that had come to characterize US foreign policy were only beginning to work themselves into something more pointed and obligatory on Iraq. It would take 9/11 to transform these thoughts into a moralistic conviction to act, whatever the consequences.

If there was no clear decision in the months before 9/11, one factor did emerge that would have critical ramifications for that later choice: the looming role of personality and perspective in the new administration.

Any national security judgment will flow in large measure from the mindsets and characters of those making it. "Personalities," one former senior official explained, "are more important [in the policy process] than I ever understood until I could see them at close range."[9] A number of these famous names—Cheney, Rumsfeld, Powell, Rice—occupy dominant roles in the drama. Their worldviews, reactions to 9/11, and personalities helped lead the nation to war. And those effects were ultimately filtered through the one man whose perspective made all the difference, for good and ill: George W. Bush.

＊

During the US presidential campaign in 1999 and 2000, neither Bush nor Dick Cheney had much to say about Iraq.[10] By all reports, George Bush fully intended to become a domestic policy president. His ambitions focused on tax cuts, social security reform, and education; foreign policy did not play a leading role in the campaign.

Some published reports have suggested that Bush already harbored powerful convictions about Iraq. He tended to personalize foreign policy, one account contends, and "in the pantheon of Bush [family] enemies, none was greater than Saddam Hussein."[11] In terms of practical campaign promises, planning, and discussions, however, no one who worked in the campaign believed that Iraq emerged as any sort of obsession.[12] I spoke with several members of Bush's core foreign policy advisory group, and all agreed that Iraq played a subordinate role in their discussions.[13] Richard Haass writes that in his initial session with Governor Bush, they talked about Iraq only "when I raised it, and then only for a moment."[14] Donald Rumsfeld says that, when he first met with Bush in Austin, "the subject of Iraq did not even come up."[15] Rumsfeld's own priority was transformation of the Defense Department bureaucracy; several Pentagon officials who worked with him from the first days of the administration do not recall any special interest in Iraq.[16]

Bush also displayed, at least before coming to the presidency, a conservative's natural distaste for nation building. Partly this was a reaction to the humanitarian interventions of the Clinton years, which many Republicans saw as squandering US power on secondary missions for which the military was ill suited. In a September 23, 1999, speech at the Citadel, he proclaimed himself skeptical of "open-ended deployments and unclear military missions. . . . We will not be permanent peacekeepers, dividing warring parties. This is not our strength or our calling." He added, "I'm going to be judicious as to how I use the military. It needs to be in our vital interest, the mission needs to be clear, and the exit strategy obvious."[17] The idea of extended interventions to reshape distant societies was something Bush portrayed as a Clinton-era mistake that he had no desire to repeat.

❧

When attention did turn to Iraq, Bush and his advisors expressed strong views—but conditional ones. Asked for a point paper on Iraq during the campaign, defense expert and campaign adviser Dov Zakheim responded with a forecast that "powerful military action" might be required, but only in narrow circumstances.[18] Soon-to-be national security advisor Condoleezza Rice said that "regime change is necessary," without laying out a specific timetable or means of accomplishing the goal.[19] "If I found in any way, shape or form that [Saddam Hussein] was developing weapons of mass destruction," Bush promised, "I'd take 'em out"—presumably a reference to the weapons, not to the Hussein regime itself.[20] Cheney himself said in one interview that "if in fact Saddam Hussein were taking steps to try to rebuild nuclear capacity or weapons of mass destruction, we'd have to give very serious consideration to military action to stop that activity."[21]

But these threats were hypotheticals offered in response to questions; they did not reflect determined planning on regime change. During the campaign, Condoleezza Rice wrote a *Foreign Affairs* article designed to preview a prospective Bush administration foreign policy—and took a surprisingly qualified stance on Saddam.[22] Her language merely endorsed regime change in somewhat pro forma ways but did not promise special efforts to achieve it. The article paid far more attention to other strategic challenges, Russia and China among them. When reading the 2000

Republican Party platform, in fact, one is struck by how much Iraq gets lost in the noise. While the text condemned Saddam's rule, it only committed Republicans to using "the full implementation of the Iraq Liberation Act" as a "starting point" to develop a plan "for the removal of Saddam Hussein."[23] The Democratic platform contained notably stronger language: "As President, Al Gore will not hesitate to use America's military might against Iraq when and where it is necessary."[24]

※

As the Bush administration took office, pockets of more urgent and committed anti-Saddam activism did appear. The chief spokesman for this point of view was Paul Wolfowitz, but the new administration was stocked with other enemies of Saddam, particularly in the vice president's office and the Office of the Secretary of Defense staff. Yet a rift soon emerged between these activists and a larger and more diffuse group of national security officials who did not see Iraq as such an urgent issue. "There were clearly people who joined the administration with a desire to go to war with Iraq and take Saddam Hussein out," one senior official later recalled. But "there were others who felt that, if Saddam could be kept inside a box, he was not an imminent threat." Even those who "came into the administration wishing to overthrow Saddam Hussein did not necessarily want a US invasion."[25] In his first session with Bush and top aides, British prime minister Tony Blair found a group that "did not show much interest in tackling Saddam. . . . There was no agreement, even an understanding, about getting rid of Saddam, and hardly any mention was made of the Iraqi leader in the subsequent media briefings."[26] The CIA official who became President Bush's daily briefer during this period—Michael Morell—agrees. Bush "did not come to office with any particular ax to grind with Saddam Hussein," Morell writes in his memoir. The subject came up from time to time, but for Bush, as far as Morell could determine, "there was no early or inherent obsession with Iraq."[27]

※

But if the top officials in the new administration were not obsessed with Iraq from the beginning, some reports still point to the existence of a cabal of adventurers determined to bring about a confrontation with Saddam. Much has been made, in particular, of the role of "neoconservative" thinkers within the Bush administration—combining a moderate domestic conservatism with a value-driven, aggressively interventionist, and militantly idealistic foreign policy—in driving the United States to war. In fact, the number of true neocons was always relatively small, especially among top cabinet officials. (Neither Cheney, Rumsfeld, Powell, Rice, nor Bush himself qualify for the label.) What is much more significant is how many aspects of the neocons' foreign policy assumptions reflected the prevailing conventional wisdom in the US national security community. These values included a commitment to global predominance, the belief in the United States as the indispensable and exceptional standard-bearer of liberty, the willingness to employ force for humanitarian ends, the belief that enough effort and care could allow US power to reform failing societies—views that would almost equally well describe a set of liberal interventionists who later came to populate the Obama administration. The key influence on the Bush choices after 9/11 was not neoconservative ideology but the reigning missionary sensibility, blended, as it would be, with Bush's own sense of God-given purpose.

Different officials bought into divergent strains of this missionary impulse. Some, like Dick Cheney and Donald Rumsfeld, held more sympathy for its hard-power dictates: support for US primacy, belief that security at home justified interventions far from home, willingness to impose US choices on others. Others emphasized the value-based aspects of the missionary stance, including the importance of democracy promotion.

But the distinction between the two camps can be overdrawn. There was no more powerful advocate of liberal value promotion than Paul Wolfowitz—and he was also a firm believer in an almost premodern sense of retributional *Realpolitik*. All the administration's senior officials believed passionately in American power and purpose. Where they diverged, it was more about tactics than core principles. Powell, and to a degree Rice, were classic multilateralist Republicans who saw in international institutions and alliances a source of strength rather than weakness and who harbored an instinctive appreciation for the risks of overextension.[28] Rumsfeld, Cheney, and others had become exasperated with such thinking; when America determined upon a goal, they generally believed, it made more sense to simply act, and hope at least a few others came along for the ride. Power was its own justification and created its own duties.

But these differences were often more about tactics than fundamental goals or values. Whatever the differences among these senior officials, the consistent theme was the undeniable fact of America's world calling. Indeed, it is symptomatic of the larger mindset of American foreign policy that the first paragraph in Cheney's 2015 love letter to American primacy, *Exceptional* (coauthored with his daughter Liz, a hawkish foreign policy official in her own right), would read this way: America's founders "could not have begun to imagine the true magnitude of the role we would play 'in the great drama of human affairs.' We have guaranteed freedom, security, and peace for a larger share of humanity than has any other nation in all of history. There is no other like us. There never has been. We are, as a matter of empirical fact and undeniable history, the greatest force for good the world has ever known." They describe the United States as "freedom's defender, not just for ourselves, but also for millions around the world," a mission undertaken "because it is right, because it is necessary, because our security depends on it, and because there is no other who can."[29]

Such language borders on parody. Yet it also embodies an only slightly exaggerated statement of the conventional wisdom in US foreign policy circles by 2000, an overzealous but still largely mainstream conception of the twin variants of foreign policy missionary impulses—the value-oriented and the power-oriented—that was characteristic of many in the Bush administration. George W. Bush would eventually commit himself and his administration to both of these strains: a determination to preserve American primacy and act unilaterally and brutally when necessary, and a wide-eyed faith in the world's desire for freedom under American tutelage. This complex perspective mirrored his personality—optimistic and compassionate on the one hand, and on the other harboring an appetite for retributive justice that was nearly medieval in its brutality. He could be dreamily hopeful about a democratic Iraq and merciless in his demand to have Saddam and his regime ground to dust.

"I believe the United States is *the* beacon for freedom in the world," Bush confessed to Bob Woodward just after he had made his fateful judgments about the war on terror and its application to Iraq. "And I believe we have a responsibility to promote freedom that is as solemn as the responsibility is to protecting the American people, because the two go hand-in-hand."[30] George W. Bush, like all of his senior cabinet officials and dozens of other national security personnel throughout his administration, had come to embody the central ideas of the modern American foreign policy consensus, at once messianic and aggressive, idealistic and hard-edged. After 9/11, the more extreme and ill-considered ambitions of this worldview would break free of the constraints that had kept them in check and would propel the United States into its most disastrous national security mistake.

※

Despite the lack of early, official policy action within the new administration in the direction of regime change, those committed to Saddam Hussein's overthrow inside and outside the government did not wait long before discussing how to make it happen. Their case was by now well rehearsed: Saddam was hardly "contained"; the sanctions were collapsing, opening the way to growing Iraqi military power; covert Iraqi work on WMDs was accelerating; and US support for an insurrection could topple a fragile regime.[31] Over time, the Chalabi/INC concept of American-backed uprisings had reportedly developed under the tutelage of two key advisors: retired US Special Forces general Wayne Downing and retired CIA case officer Duane "Dewey" Clarridge. Their notion involved some five thousand INC forces supported by, in essence, US mercenaries—former Special Forces troops hired to advise the imagined liberation army. "The idea from the beginning," Carridge told the *Washington Post*, "was to encourage defections of Iraqi units. You need to create a nucleus, something for people to defect to. If they could take Basra" and deprive the regime of the majority of its oil funds, "it would all be over."[32]

Secretary of Defense Donald Rumsfeld had come into office believing that "the Iraqi 'containment' policy was in tatters,"[33] but for the time being, he did not openly advocate bold action. He had other things on his mind—transforming what he saw as a moribund defense bureaucracy, first and foremost. "This is what the president sent him there to do," a former senior official explains.[34] One Rumsfeld memo from March 2001 catalogues a raft of issues discussed in a meeting with the president: missile defense, personnel appointments, and the status of the military's special operations command. Iraq isn't on the list.[35] Rumsfeld gave a major Pentagon town hall speech—designed as a clarion call for his agenda as secretary—on September 10, 2001. It was all about defense transformation.[36]

At the State Department, neither Deputy Secretary Richard Armitage nor Secretary of State Colin Powell opposed regime change. Powell "had no problem taking down Saddam Hussein," one source told me, but for the time being saw little urgency in the job. Powell's problem was with the immense difficulty of the task and the need to build a coalition, "and he felt that those were insurmountable problems" for the moment.[37] Critically, though, the *idea* of using American power to topple Saddam did not seem normatively out of bounds to anyone. The level of urgency was simply not high enough to take the risk.

On January 30, 2001, these complex views began to work themselves into formal policy at the new national security team's first NSC meeting, described at the beginning of the chapter. The concern about Saddam was palpable, but there was as yet no dramatic break from the well-established US line of regime change. A second national security meeting took place a few days later. According to Powell biographer Karen DeYoung, somewhere in the White House, the decision had already been made "to fund exile opposition groups for new anti-Saddam activity inside Iraq." From the Department of Defense (DoD) came ideas to respond more forcefully to provocations in the no-fly zones, large swaths of airspace off-limits to Iraqi planes that were still patrolled by US aircraft at significant cost and growing risk.[38] But it remained a muddled grasping for ideas rather than a laser focus on war or imminent regime change.[39]

One issue cropped up in these sessions that would later come to be among the most controversial in modern US foreign policy: the US intelligence picture of Iraqi WMD ambitions. CIA deputy director John McLaughlin offered a measured assessment of the issue at one of these early sessions—a presentation qualified enough that one official recalled its underlying theme as follows: "It's not a case we could prove in court. It's inferential."[40] But that inference was very clear: Saddam had active and dangerous programs in place designed to produce chemical, biological, and nuclear weapons. "It is hard for many people now," Rice explains, in light of later revelations, to "appreciate how compelling the overall intelligence case against Saddam appeared to be."[41] Cheney describes a "steady drumbeat" of reports on Iraqi WMDs.[42] But another lesson can be drawn from the episode: right from the very beginning, once anyone started asking questions about the quality of the intelligence, the case for Saddam's WMD progress fell apart under scrutiny. The evidence, any close examination would soon reveal, just wasn't that good.

In the thrall of assumptions and a bitter cynicism about Saddam Hussein, no senior official demanded such an examination until it was far too late. They did not, in part, because these assumptions were so firmly and deeply held. One of the commonest things I heard from senior officials in my interviews was the strength with which the WMD case was believed. *We were wrong*, most admit, *and badly so; but you have to understand: We absolutely believed this*. The status of Saddam's weapons programs was no longer an issue for discussion—it had become an article of faith. But it was nearly universally held, and it provides a strong explanation for the lack of greater push-back on the drive to war.

꙳

After those initial NSC meetings, the broader interagency process—the mechanism of official coordination below the level of the cabinet principals, running down through various layers of the national security bureaucracy—began various reviews on Iraq policy, as they did on many issues, in the following weeks and months.[43] One senior official put it in terms shared by every interviewee I spoke with: "Iraq was on the agenda, but there was no immediacy to it."[44] Another official said that these discussions "didn't mean people were talking about going to war. Nobody was talking about that at that point." Iraq, he said, actually "didn't get much attention in those first six months."[45] Another source privy to the highest-level discussions said that there was no "front burner" quality to the dialogue about Hussein's threat. "In terms of anything that someone could remotely identify as advance notice that people in this administration would be going to war—absolutely not."[46]

The administration's early lack of focus on Iraq should not be mistaken for lack of interest. As we have seen, there were a number of very senior officials anxious to push the envelope in seeking Saddam's overthrow from the first days.[47] White House speechwriter David Frum describes a February 2001 meeting with Bush in which they discussed a range of topics. He recorded a number of Bush's views and statements, including "his determination to dig Saddam Hussein out of power in Iraq."[48] For the time being, however, Iraq remained one of many issues competing for attention. And more to the point, the administration remained trapped in the same policy limbo as the Clinton team: everyone wanted Saddam gone, but nobody had a good idea of how to make it happen.

Ultimately, the initial policy review went nowhere.[49] In the coming months, the interagency process would obsess over questions far removed from regime change—the "smart sanctions" proposal, which would actually *relieve* pressure on Saddam, and how to reduce the dangers of no-fly zones—and then grind to a halt.[50] One former senior official reports that the result was an "inconclusive" process.[51] The idea of a revised sanctions regime more narrowly focused on military items did not generate much enthusiasm;[52] Rice described it as "totally unsatisfying." Bitter arguments erupted among the deputies. The whole process "was maddeningly slow" and was not producing any clear results.[53]

One of the biggest problems was that "no one knew what President Bush's view was. The bureaucracy needs to know in what direction to march." But apart from generally hostile feelings toward Saddam's regime, Bush had no strong policy direction to give at first. He remained focused on his domestic agenda and foreign policy crises that cropped up and was still finding his feet on national security issues. And in the absence of clear presidential direction, one senior official explained, "People do what they generally do in the bureaucracy: create task forces, committees, study groups, and so on." If the "elected officials are unclear" about policy, "the bureaucracy churns."[54] And it kept churning on Iraq, right up to 9/11: Without either clear direction from the president or an obvious alternative with a hope of success, the US annoyance with Saddam continued at a low boil but did not produce clear decisions.[55]

What did begin to become apparent, however, was an emerging pattern with decisive implications for the character of decision-making in the administration: the personalities and relationships at work. The early impression was that George Bush had stocked his national security posts, both cabinet level and below, with an all-star team of experienced and respected officials. This was true to a degree, but that perception obscured two ultimately more important realities: the powerful, sometimes rigid self-confidence and commitment to their beliefs of some senior officials; and the toxic feuds that blossomed among the major national security players. Both of these factors would deeply impair the quality of Bush administration judgments about Iraq.

Vice President Richard Cheney's role in the administration, and specifically the Iraq decision, has become the stuff of legend. Elaborate portraits have emerged of Cheney as a sinister and malign manipulator of the US government. Many hold him primarily responsible for the war.

Yet I know of no serious account, public or otherwise, that paints Bush as a mindless instrument of his Machiavellian vice president. None of the senior officials with whom I spoke shared any sympathy for this view.[56] What is true is that Dick Cheney would become a powerful force demanding confrontation with Saddam Hussein after 9/11; he would promote this view, inside and outside government, with statements and tactics that bordered on—and perhaps drove right past the border of—premeditated deceit. And he played this role in part because he was not the man many thought him to be, right from the beginning.

Cheney came to the vice presidency as one of the most deeply experienced government officials in recent US history. He had gone to work in the Nixon White House at the tender age of 28, and had been in and out of the legislative and executive branches ever since. He had become White House chief of staff at thirty-four, a member of Congress at thirty-seven. He served in the House for a decade before leaving to become secretary of defense in the first Bush administration.

Across these decades Cheney acquired a reputation as a pragmatic and conventional conservative. When James A. Baker III became White House chief of staff in 1980, he reached out to men who had held the job before him for advice. According to Baker's notes, Cheney advised him, "Be an honest broker. Don't use the process to impose your policy views on [the] pres[ident]."[57] In Congress he built a name as a collegial institutionalist who got on well with Democrats. He was known as "funny and witty," a regular guy,[58] distinctly unpretentious for such an influential player. According to Stephen Hayes's biography, when he became head of a major corporation, he didn't buy himself a pricey new car, didn't frequent the country club where a membership was on file for him, and didn't travel with an entourage.[59]

In the second Bush administration, however, this reputation quickly morphed into a widely held caricature of a power-hungry vice president scheming to dominate his boss. He reportedly had an agreement with Bush in advance that he would be at "every table and every meeting" that he wanted to attend. In fact, he made one unsuccessful attempt to *control* the table: he tried to run National Security Council meetings in Bush's absence, a rather astonishing grab for a role traditionally held by national security advisors.[60]

This boldness surprised some, but it was the product of a simple fact that became more and more evident as the Bush administration unfolded. Dick Cheney had always been more uncompromising, ideologically driven, and Manichean in his thinking than most realized. His graciousness and placid style concealed a thoroughgoing conservative activist. Moreover, by the time he became vice president, Cheney had acquired a truly astonishing level of impatience with the traditions and niceties of democratic governance. By 2000, Dick Cheney had become a closet radical; on what he considered to be the most important issues, he simply decided what ought to happen and made sure that it did.[61]

He had, in truth, always been more extreme in his views than his demeanor suggested. During his congressional days, members of the House who thought him a moderate were shocked when confronted with his accumulating voting record on issues like the Equal Rights Amendment and South Africa. "I had no idea he was that conservative," House Republican leader Robert Michel would say. Stephen Hayes's thoughtful biography quotes Lee Hamilton as describing Cheney as "low-key" and "respected." But "ask his colleagues to describe Dick Cheney and few of them would offer up 'conciliator' or 'mediator.' Cheney believed in legislative compromise, in working well with others, but only to a point. And once he reached that point, he would not budge—no matter how intense the pressure or who was applying it."[62]

Cheney was courteous and honest, but when he decided on the right thing to do, he was resolute, even ruthless, in his determination to make it happen. His willingness to engage in brutal power plays showed up very

early, during his role in the "Halloween Massacre" in the Ford administration, when the president pushed aside Vice President Nelson Rockefel-
ler, Henry Kissinger, and others—including Secretary of Defense James
Schlesinger, who was replaced by a young Donald Rumsfeld. "If you're a
man of principle," Cheney would later say in interviews conducted for a
documentary, "compromise is a bit of a dirty word."[53]

When Bush talked with Cheney about the vice president's job, Cheney
urged him to be sure he knew how far to the right Cheney actually was.
"Dick," Bush reportedly said, "we know that." Cheney answered, "No, I
mean *really* conservative."[64]

Two early episodes reflected Cheney's emerging *modus operandi* in
the Bush administration. One had to do with the Kyoto Accord on climate change. After watching a debate between hard-liners and proenvi-
ronment Republicans like Powell and EPA administrator Christine Todd
Whitman, Cheney stepped in and short-circuited the process by getting
Bush to sign a letter to the Senate "clarifying" the administration's opposition to the accord. The letter was drafted in Cheney's office. The vice
president was on the way out of the Oval Office with the letter, Bush's
signature still drying at the bottom, when Colin Powell arrived moments
too late to intercept him.

The same approach would emerge after 9/11 on issues related to
the treatment of detainees and domestic surveillance programs. Working with aide David Addington, Cheney helped draft legal briefs, shared
them among a narrow group of like-minded individuals, ignored and
in fact worked to exclude the rest of the interagency process, and got
President Bush to endorse the results. The secretary of state and national
security advisor first heard about some of the executive orders dealing
with detainees on the television news.[65] Bush reportedly signed one of
the policy memos without even sitting down to read it.[66] Later, when
debates over domestic surveillance were reignited, acting attorney general
James Comey and a number of other senior Justice Department officials
threatened to quit over policies they viewed as illegal. Had they done so,
it would have likely triggered a constitutional crisis. But an unrepentant

Cheney, speaking about the event years later, insisted simply that "I would have let them resign."[67]

Washington Post columnist David Ignatius, after talking with people who had known Cheney for some time, came to the conclusion that by the second Bush administration, this style reflected a maturing Cheney's worldview—a "conviction that much of the political debate in Washington is just noise and should be ignored in favor of the country's long-term interests." It was related to a "contempt for Washington" that had its origins in Cheney's reactions to Watergate and "ripened" during his time as CEO of the oil giant Haliburton, where he became accustomed to a more directive approach to leadership.[68] It did not seem to occur to him that, in the process, he was displaying a contempt for the spirit of democracy—the mess and tangle of complicated, highly inefficient give-and-take that, in 2003, he would suggest exporting to Iraq.

In office, Cheney's bureaucratic style was to operate behind the scenes, with "no fingerprints." He preferred oral rather than written instructions and deliberation—the better to evade a paper trail.[69] As one Democratic congressional aide later described Cheney's approach, "You saw the results of his work, but you rarely saw what he did. We totally misread the guy. We thought he was more philosophical than political."[70] "Am I the evil genius in the corner that nobody ever sees come out of his hole?" Cheney himself once asked, apparently only half in jest. "It's a nice way to operate, actually."[71]

As Barton Gellman has insightfully explained, some of Cheney's remarkable influence came from his habit of "going deep" or "reaching down" into the bureaucracy. Cheney played a central role in the administration's personnel process, allowing him to stash allies throughout the interagency. During policy debates, he worked with people on his own staff and throughout the government to fashion the small details of policy to get the outcomes he wanted, outcomes that sometimes left Bush without a clear sense of what had happened. At one point NSC staffers discovered that the vice president's office was receiving a blind copy of all their memos to the president—without their knowledge, and without the courtesy being reciprocated.[72]

Beyond Cheney himself, the role of his office became equally controversial. His staff attended policy meetings as regular participants in the interagency debates and came to be known as a "shadow NSC." Contrary to popular impression, his national security staff was not enormous—just a little over ten people (not dramatically different from Gore's), crammed into a relatively small space. But they had huge influence, especially when their efforts were combined with those of the Cheney acolytes and allies who had been salted throughout the government. In the interagency process, one source said, "You knew the vice president's staff was going to be a critical part of your success—or your failure. They knew how to make themselves a force to be reckoned with."[73]

While small, moreover, the staff was led by highly experienced officials, people like John Hannah, Eric Edelman, and Lewis "Scooter" Libby. People who worked around Libby, even those who did not share his politics, describe him as one of the most competent government officials they had seen, almost always calm and cordial, willing to take seriously ideas from people regardless of their level or position. Libby was proud of his credentials as a bipartisan civil servant: a source told me that one of the most prominent displays on Libby's office wall was an award he'd received years before from the Democratic official Richard Danzig.[74] Yet there is no doubt that he sought to flex his office's muscles in ways rarely if ever seen from a vice president's staff: Libby and others from Cheney's office inserted themselves into debates in ways that made the vice president's office a seeming coequal with the State and Defense Departments in the interagency process. This, in the views of many, was unprecedented.[75]

It was also problematic. The US national security policy process is not accustomed to the other *elected* official in the executive branch mixing it up in the bureaucratic push and pull below the president in such a forceful way. A Powell duking it out with a Rumsfeld—appointed heads

of departments, all subservient to the president—is one thing. Confronting a vice president is another: there is simply a difference, in the US system, in power and deference offered to the pair of people actually elected
to their jobs. One very senior official explained that the system is not set
up to deal with a vice president who is a daily player and advocate in the
way Cheney became, and it didn't properly adjust.[76]

⁂

Another perspective on Cheney emerges from a somewhat surprising
source: People who worked in Cheney's office but were not ideological
fellow travelers. These included State Department, uniformed military,
and intelligence personnel assigned to the vice president's staff on a rota-
tional basis. Their perspective is limited, of course, because they were not
privy to Cheney's real intentions. But such people mostly describe an
office determined to serve the president, and the policy process, as well
as it could.

One senior official involved in policy discussions with Cheney said
no one was more vigorous than the vice president in demanding that the
substance of debates among principals be brought to President Bush's
attention, so that he could hear the full range of opinion and decide for
himself. When an especially important issue would come up, Cheney
would say, "The man needs to hear this—and we would replay the debate
for President Bush. His goal was to have the president hear all sides."[77]

Another senior official with close knowledge of Cheney's style suggested that he was "keenly aware that [he was] trapped in a bubble of official government information" and always sought a range of views.[78] One
former staff member said of him, "On a one-on-one basis," Cheney is
"one of the calmest, nicest guys you're going to meet." This person argues
that Cheney's reputation for being dogmatic did not seem to hold true in
smaller sessions in the vice president's own offices, where he was willing
to listen to various opinions and proved open to the ideas of subordinates at various levels.[79] In high-level meetings, Cheney was typically quiet
until he posed rapier queries.[80] When he wanted to be educated on an

issue, one former staffer said, "He wanted all sides, and sometimes would draw people out to ensure that a real debate occurred in front of him."[81]

The staff's marching orders were to get Cheney the best information they could find.[82] While the office had unusual leverage—and while Cheney picked a handful of issues where he preempted the interagency discussion—broadly speaking, there was "no intent to 'control' the interagency" on a regular basis, but only to make sure that the "big questions that should have been asked get asked," one former staffer said.[83] Yet others clearly admit that the goal, when Cheney himself did hold a strong view, was to win those debates. He wanted to be supremely informed about issues in part to ensure that when the interagency process began, he'd be the smartest person in the room. That was a major reason why, another Cheney staffer told me, "on most issues we were engaged in, he ultimately prevailed."[84]

The fact of Cheney's growing impatience with bureaucratic delays and democratic processes meant that despite many positive characteristics as a decision-maker, by the time he served as vice president, Cheney had become determined to simply bull ahead when the stakes were high enough. His commitment to open and rigorous debate would not be a sufficient antidote to his increasingly relentless drive to ensure what he saw as the right and proper outcome on a number of key issues, leaving him more than willing to violate the rules of interagency gamesmanship he had advocated for a quarter century. It justified the practice of skewing the intelligence picture being described to the world, exaggerating the risks posed by Saddam to secure the votes of key members of Congress, or making other moves to shape and ensure US action against Saddam. "Cheney's most troubling quality" by 2000, Barton Gellman concludes, "was a sense of mission so acute that it drove him to seek power without limit."[85]

※

Apart from—or partly because of—the role of specific personalities, the machinery of the national security policy process in the Bush administration quickly began to show serious failings. Many officials with long experience in government spoke of a disorganized and weak NSC system, in which issues were not fully argued out, differences of opinion were often left unresolved, and implementation was left hanging. Rumsfeld was especially critical. "NSC meetings with the President did not always end with clear conclusions and instructions," he noticed within the first months.[86] His mounting frustration produced a series of bitter memos to Condoleezza Rice, demanding more coherence.[87]

As with all NSC systems, however, this one reflected the habits and desires of the president it was organized to serve. In George W. Bush's case, that meant a president perfectly content with a process that fed his "gut" rather than one that exhaustively evaluated issues. Part of Rumsfeld's frustration was the lack of the regular, consistent, and in-depth commitment to the formalized paperwork of the interagency process—"options papers" and other tools designed to evaluate competing perspectives and alternative policies. Instead, Rice ran a "drive to consensus" model in which principals were expected to push for agreement before bringing an issue to the president. Rumsfeld argued for options papers and took the issue all the way to Bush—and figured out what Rice presumably had known all along: the president wasn't interested in reading them.[88]

Rumsfeld's vexation with the NSC process appears to have been bound up with his views toward Rice herself—and was part and parcel of a ruinous fracturing of relations among senior officials. Many observers hoped for a replay of the relatively cordial interagency relations of the first Bush administration. One senior official watching the dynamics at the time, however, recalled that the residue of good feeling among the group had started fading soon after the Gulf War. Part of it was that some relationships had always been more strict and professional than cordial anyway. In other cases, officials who had served in very different levels in previous administrations—Rice as an NSC staffer, Powell as chairman of the Joint Chiefs, and Rumsfeld and Cheney as defense secretary—were now installed, and expected to operate, as peers. Some had difficulty adjusting to the new hierarchy. And these resentments, as they will do in a bureaucracy, seeped downward. As early as mid-2001, the relations among the deputy secretaries under these cabinet officials "were already strained," one official recalls.[89] Policy disputes were becoming increasingly bitter and personal. Trust was fraying, just months into the new administration.

⁂

At the helm of this discordant process was a woman destined to become one of the more controversial members of Bush's first term. She was hardly inexperienced—by 2001, she had been an NSC staff member in the first Bush administration and the provost of Stanford University— but she was still of a different generation than her three main counterparts. Condoleezza Rice had in some ways been thrust into a no-win situation, caught between a clever but often inattentive president and a national security cabinet that showed only intermittent regard for her authority.

The testimony of Rice's former NSC staffers, and many others throughout the interagency, brims with praise for her professionalism, courtesy, and insight. By and large, these former officials describe her as open to dissenting perspectives and determined to get the best possible advice to President Bush. She confronted a crisis unlike any faced by prior national security advisors and did so by all reports with determination and grace. But the full story of her role in the Iraq war decision must account for the fact that, in some larger sense, her office failed to play the role designed for it in the national security system—a failure connected to the ways in which Rice's astonishing strengths could also serve as potent weaknesses.

Rice's biographies tell of devoted parents determined that she should emerge from the segregated Birmingham of her youth to make a mark on the world. They had her tutored in violin, flute, French, Spanish, and ballet; some say she could have been a world-class pianist. As young as ten, according to Elisabeth Bumiller's revealing biography, Rice had become "president of her family," organizing discussions to plan family trips. Even at the time, one family friend noted a characteristic that would be remarked upon again and again over her career: Rice never worried about her decisions very much—she just made them. "She never pondered over things," the friend said.[90] The result of this upbringing was a well-honed rectitude, calmness under pressure, civility, and a preternatural self-assurance.[91]

Rice skipped several grades and went off to college at the age of fifteen, later arriving at Notre Dame to pursue a masters' degree in Soviet studies at nineteen. She reportedly proposed a special independent study program to relieve her of the standardized coursework required of other students. Rice, one Notre Dame faculty member remembered, worried that "there would be little benefit for her in participating in seminars with other students or listening to lectures by professors."[92] A friend, Paul Brest, dean of the Stanford law school, later spoke about her time as provost of the university. "I don't think Condi valued, in that context, hearing diverse points of view, or hearing points of view that disagreed with or challenged her own point of view."[93] She was so good at publicly defending her positions, one colleague told Marcus Mabry, that the gift became "a curse because she then falls victim to her own convictions."[94] And the result, some who knew her have suggested, was a tendency toward magical thinking. "Condi always had the capacity to see the world she wants to see," her friend and Stanford colleague Coit Blacker has said, as "opposed to the world that actually exists."[95]

⁂

Rice's relationship with George W. Bush has come in for particular scrutiny. Many reports indicate that she was absorbed into the Bush family as more than an advisor—as a close family friend and a deep admirer of a president she routinely described as having powerful charisma. "I thought he was wonderful to be around," Rice has said of Bush.[96] In private conversations, one friend told Nicholas Lemann, she would defend policy just as adamantly as in public—"except that she is more open about her adoration of the President. 'I can't find the Archimedean point outside her love of Bush.' "[97]

For his part, Bush liked her and enjoyed her company. She was an academic who loved football, didn't take herself too seriously, and could work out as hard as he did. He trusted Rice's judgment. Early on, one senior official recounted, when Bush was asked to explain key decisions, he would suddenly say, "And now Condi will explain the rationale," without having warned her beforehand.[98]

Perhaps as a result of this bond, Bush and Rice leaned toward a particular interpretation of the national security advisor's role: serving primarily as an advisor and conceptualizer, and then determining the wishes of the president and executing them—rather than playing the role of an independent check or manager of a policy process designed to confront him with messy debates. This is not to say she did not have her own views and try to persuade the president of them; later, as secretary of state, she became a critical and independent voice on a range of issues and was a major force for the moderation of administration policy in the second term, when she regularly won policy debates with Cheney and others. But early on, when she was still finding her footing as national security advisor and on issues where Bush's instinctive direction was clear, she seemed to comprehend her role primarily in terms of "whispering in the president's ear to explain the world," as one former senior official described the pattern he saw,[99] and then sensing Bush's desires and making them a reality. It was, after all, what the president seemed to prefer.

The result, though, was a perilous mismatch. In her confidence in her own judgments and seeming emphasis on advising rather than running a tightly organized implementation process, Rice ended up exacerbating the more dangerous aspects of Bush's own decision-making style. "An inattentive president needed a vigorously strong national security advisor," one former senior official, who observed the decision process at very senior levels, later said. "Instead, he got Rice."[100]

❦

Perhaps the most important clue to Donald Rumsfeld's eventual effect on the Bush administration is that, as a young man, he was a competitive wrestler. His wrestling style, explains his biographer Bradley Graham, relied on "speed and brute force." As one former teammate put it, "He'd charge across and tear a guy down to the mat as soon as he could."[101] His goal was to pin, to control, to dominate.

As secretary of defense in a time of war, Rumsfeld was arguably the key person, other than the president, in determining outcomes related to Iraq. Many of the problems with the decision process can be traced to Rumsfeld's door—his emphasis on asking a thousand meandering questions rather than forming coherent solutions; his penchant for secrecy and refusal to take a firm stand on many issues; and above all, above everything, his combativeness.

Rumsfeld, like Cheney, was one of the most experienced government officials in the country. Like Cheney, he had held a remarkable series of jobs at an early age. He was elected to Congress at thirty and became director of the White House Office of Economic Opportunity and counselor to the president at thirty-six. He had been White House chief of staff, US ambassador to NATO, and the youngest secretary of defense in US history in 1975—all by the age of forty-three.

In the course of this extraordinary run of jobs, Rumsfeld acquired a very distinct reputation as a smart, insightful, talented, powerfully ambitious, and, when necessary, hard-edged bureaucratic operator. Henry Kissinger once described him as "a special Washington phenomenon: The skilled full-time politician-bureaucrat in whom ambition, ability, and substance fuse seamlessly."[102] In a discussion with Bob Haldeman captured on the White House taping system, Nixon said of Rumsfeld, "He's a ruthless little bastard."[103]

Part of his competitiveness manifested itself in a determination to achieve; Rumsfeld saw himself as "a man with a purpose."[104] He was in a hurry to get things done. One source related that press aide Lawrence Di Rita had a Rumsfeld doll on his desk, onto which he had taped a little yellow bubble emanating from Rumsfeld's mouth. On it was written one word: "Faster."[105] At the same time, the wrestler in Rumsfeld appeared to thrive on tension and conflict. Bradley Graham has written that Rumsfeld often "seemed driven as much by the love of the fight and the challenge as he did by a deep-seated desire to improve the order of things."[106]

What became dangerous for the administration was that these patterns—belligerence, competitiveness, urgency, and ambition—colored Rumsfeld's judgment and behavior. His pugnaciousness repeatedly undermined the administration's policy process, which was not exceptionally coherent to begin with.

General Hugh Shelton, chairman of the Joint Chiefs when Rumsfeld came into office, would later write that Rumsfeld ought to have had a sign on his desk that read, "DON'T TELL ME, I ALREADY KNOW." Shelton detected "a sense of his not really wanting to ask my advice for fear that it would be viewed as his not being in charge—viewed as weakness. *If I have to ask your advice, then you obviously know more about it than I do.*"[107] Rumsfeld often appeared more interested in reserving privileges to himself than he was in ensuring that the policy-making process—even for an issue as profound as preparing for a war—took place in an open and effective manner.[108] In his own memoir, Shelton wrote simply that it was "the worst style of leadership I witnessed in thirty-eight years of service."[109]

Rumsfeld, in the view of another source, had two basic priorities: the accumulation of bureaucratic turf and power, and the creation of a *legacy*. Rumsfeld had at one point wanted to be president. By the second Bush administration, that was out of the question—but Rumsfeld was damn sure going to leave some mark on the American political landscape. The issue he chose was the transformation of a gargantuan and often hidebound Defense Department.[110] Donald Rumsfeld was not thirsting for a war with Iraq at the outset of the administration; he was thirsting for a war with the bureaucracy. And when he got a different war from the one he expected, he continued to operate as if he was in a perpetual competition with everyone around him, striving to win the bureaucratic war as much as or more than the real one.

Some of those who worked for and with Rumsfeld rightly insist on a balanced portrait that takes proper account of his better qualities. One former aide explains, for example, that his reputation as a micromanager was not entirely warranted: he is more properly understood as an "episodic micromanager." He had great antennae for issues that could become problems, this former senior official argued, and would dive deeply into them. When he had satisfied himself that he knew about the issues and what was going on, he would hand them off to a trusted subordinate and often not look back.[111] Once trust was truly established, the micromanaging would end.

Another former senior official marveled at Rumsfeld's ability to absorb detail on complex policy questions, to master them to a degree that astonished even subject matter experts. He "just dove into [an issue]" to understand it, to "figure out what he needed to know." At one point Rumsfeld told this official, "You think I'm trying to pick on your stuff. No. I'm trying to understand it. When I understand it, and you know I understand it, then I can give you guidance." This former official found that once Rumsfeld had trust in someone, he could step back and let that person run with an issue. But he admitted that Rumsfeld would only delegate "once he had taken the measure" of someone—and that process could be harsh. "He was demanding of the people who worked for him, and not everybody took to it."[112]

Rumsfeld claimed to value dissent, and sometimes he actually seemed to do so—but only if the person could first pass his confrontational tests. There are plenty of stories of someone speaking back to Rumsfeld, disagreeing with him, feeling his wrath—and then later being put in for a promotion or important job.[113] This respect had its limits, though. If the dissenter was too far off some reservation, they would be isolated. Dov Zakheim, who served as the Defense Department comptroller in this period, has written that Rumsfeld was hugely confident in his perceptions: "And when Don wasn't right he did not like to be reminded of it."[114] When Chief of Naval Operations Vern Clark auditioned with Rumsfeld for the role of chairman of the Joint Chiefs, he made clear his intention to speak his mind and push back. He didn't get the job.[115]

One senior official said that Rumsfeld's "weaknesses are the shadow of his strengths"—the obsessive focus on tiny points of detail could transform into an obsessive and rigid commitment to some belief, and Rumsfeld could become so locked into his own perceptions of events that he would not listen carefully to briefings, not consider options or alternative positions. Rumsfeld did want alternative ideas, and he was no respecter of rank—but when he got convinced of something, his mind could snap shut.[116] One person who briefed him a number of times and watched him interact with senior military people said that briefing Rumsfeld was like "volunteering to be wirebrushed in the nude." He would ask good questions, but they were all too often preceded by pointless, picky objections designed to prove Rumsfeld's attention to detail—the size of a font, the order of slides, the way in which someone was standing by a screen.[117] He was infamous for impatiently asserting the anticipated bottom line of a presentation just as the briefer was getting started—to save time, perhaps, but mainly to demonstrate his superiority, to dominate, to overawe.

※

What became clear, too, as the administration began to unfold—in a seemingly paradoxical aspect for such a decisive decision-maker—was Rumsfeld's apparent unwillingness to take responsibility for things. Over and over again in my interviews, the same reference came up: Rumsfeld was someone who had learned the fine art of employing verbal acrobatics to keep from saying something straight out. "He was famous for not committing himself to anything," one former senior official said.[118] Another official pointed to his press conferences as a clear reflection of his analytical style: "On the one hand, on the other hand, on the third hand. . . . I never heard the secretary of defense pronounce himself one way or another on anything."[119] Condoleezza Rice explains that at meetings of the national security team, Rumsfeld "would ask Socratic questions rather than take a position."[120]

This noncommittal stance was as inherent to his way of thinking as it was a bureaucratic tactic. Many who worked with Rumsfeld praised his ability to see issues in nuanced ways.[121] But the reports leave an impression of a gadfly rather than someone who would take it upon himself to define a solution that others could pick apart. He would, as one official put it, "throw out ideas and expect people to react."[122] His decision-making style flowed from these tendencies. Rumsfeld's judgment was quick and impulsive, giving him the air of decisiveness, yet he also typically refused to show his hand. He was endlessly cautious and vague, keeping his real views and intentions to himself; he was bureaucratically clever rather than strategically clear. Over and over again, senior officials returned to the same refrain: Rumsfeld was a "no fingerprints guy; he wears rubber gloves."[123] "He was very savvy about where his fingerprints were, and where they weren't."[124]

His infamous use of "snowflakes" offers a telling example of his management style. These were little memos, a line to a page long, which Rumsfeld would cascade down on the bureaucracy, as many as sixty in a single day—asking questions, making demands.[125] "What are we doing about this or that?" the memos inquire, in an almost attention-deficit sort of way. "Have we thought about this? Have you seen this resume? What would we do if X happened, or Y?" There were so many of them that their outcomes could not possibly be tracked. Many have a surreal quality: Speculating on the best seating positions in interviews (he wanted to be able to lean forward), asking that someone remind President Bush how to pronounce the words "Muslim" and "Islam." One asked, literally, "What do we want to do about the Pentagon bureaucracy?" Few generated any sort of meaningful follow-up, though they did create enormous headaches for a bureaucracy trying to deal with them.

The snowflakes were a symptom of Rumsfeld's tendency to pull things apart rather than put them together. Former Rumsfeld speechwriter Matt Latimer has written of the Rumsfeldian habit of "parsing the question" with a hundred details. "I could ask Rumsfeld, 'How did you like the speech?' And he'd reply, 'You asked how I liked the speech.

Actually, what you really want to know is if I learned anything from it. Did I learn something? Yes, I suppose I did.' Then he could go off in any direction with his answer." Latimer relayed a routine developed by CNN's Jaime McIntyre to parody this approach: "You ask if I took out the trash. Did I try to avoid taking out the trash? No. Have I done my share to help around the house? Sure. Should the trash have gone out? You bet." An essential characteristic of such Rumsfeldian dialogues, Latimer concludes, is that he "never answered the original question."[126]

For all of Rumsfeld's image as a tough administrator, it could therefore be devilishly hard to get a simple decision or straightforward guidance out of the man. And when Rumsfeld did issue orders, there was often little follow-through. Senior leaders within DoD were heard to say of Rumsfeld's dictates, "We don't have to act on that, because within a week or two he'll be onto something else."[127] At the same time, Rumsfeld's combativeness created a general reluctance to actually make decisions, in part because the anticipation of a Rumsfeld wire-brushing tended to hinder decisions. Rumsfeld's intimidation turned his department into a place abounding in rumors and fear, resentments and grievances, group-think and failure—even outright refusal—to share key information. "He never really understood the chilling effect" of his approach, one senior official concluded.[128] Rumsfeld's instincts also left him handicapped in building coalitions across the interagency. Treating so many people with contempt often left him few willing partners in the State Department, in the intelligence community, on Capitol Hill—and sometimes, even within his own department.[129]

Rumsfeld, said one source who worked closely with him, "is so bright that he blinds others. And then he ends up blinding himself."[130]

❧

As spring turned to summer 2001 and the personalities of the new administration began to hammer out their working relationships, the policy process on Iraq continued to wander.[131] British sources suggest that the idea of regime change kept coming up in meetings, but ended up as "the dog that didn't bark."[132] Paul Wolfowitz advocated once again his Iraqi insurrection plan, built around Ahmad Chalabi's INC and the recognition of a provisional government. But the idea never got much traction.[133]

And yet the direction of policy was clear—to find ways to edge toward regime change without endorsing outright military action. A May 2001 memo from British foreign secretary Robin Cook to Tony Blair captures this tightrope walking. "No-one in the administration believes they can deliver Saddam's overthrow," Cook wrote, and Washington was "keen for us not to push [regime change language] too hard while they are focusing on the sanctions package." But the memo also proposed issuing a "contract with the Iraqi people" to lay the groundwork for a "more credible and defensible approach, when regime change moves up the US agenda"—which Cook clearly expected it to do.[134] Indeed, quietly, urgency was growing: Sanctions were eroding, and Saddam, the administration grew convinced, was making progress on WMDs. The thought at the time was that "the clock is ticking," according to one senior official.[135]

As was his habit, Donald Rumsfeld was keeping his options open. A former senior Defense Department official with frequent access to Rumsfeld recalled, "He was saying that the status quo was unsupportable." On the other hand, he wasn't recommending war—he "wasn't just looking for an opportunity to attack Iraq." And on the third hand, Rumsfeld knew that Saddam was "too important and dangerous [a problem] to do nothing about."[136] What all of that added up to wasn't clear—which was, some were beginning to become convinced, just the way he wanted it.

2%

By that summer, Rumsfeld concluded that Iraq policy was adrift.[137] On July 27, he sent a three-and-a-half-page memo to Condoleezza Rice—copying Cheney and Powell—a memo that is as clear a statement of the Defense Department's settled thinking on Iraq at that time as we are likely to get. According to undersecretary of defense for policy Doug

Feith, he and Wolfowitz, now serving as deputy secretary, drafted it for Rumsfeld.[138]

In typically Rumsfeldian fashion, the memo doesn't come right out and say, *We need to do X.* It leads the reader circuitously, almost delicately, to an implied judgment through a series of subsidiary points. After admitting that discussions on Iraq had so far been "inconclusive," Rumsfeld argued that sanctions were eroding, and attacks on US aircraft in the no-fly zones signaled "a greater degree of Iraqi aggressiveness."[139] Washington could essentially give up, the memo suggests—abandon the no-fly zones and the sanctions regime, in which case it would shortly "confront a Saddam armed with nuclear weapons." It could "go to our moderate Arab friends" to see whether they might be in the mood for "a serious regime change policy." Pursuing regime change would come with risks, to be sure—but they had to be "weighed against the certainty of the danger of an increasingly bold and nuclear-armed Saddam in the near future." The *certainty*: the implicit conviction about Saddam's WMD programs shines through.

Rumsfeld tossed out a wild third idea: to "take a crack at initiating contact with Saddam Hussein" in the hope of reaching some "accommodation." The memo quickly downplayed the chances of such an offer;[140] in his own book, Doug Feith admits that the proposal was a "straw man" that Rumsfeld didn't take seriously.

The result was vintage Rumsfeld. The memo amounted to vague, complex language pointing toward a clear inference—but one that was not stated outright, and from which he could backtrack if the need arose.

⚘

The Iraq policy process wound its way to the first official policy statement, an NSC strategy paper issued in August 2001. The idea, according to one former senior official, was "to develop a plan and a strategy to pressure the regime and ultimately to change the regime," to "exploit fissures within" Saddam's government to destabilize it. This was no agenda for invasion; in fact, in its particulars, the strategy appears to have had much in common with the never-adopted proposals for bolder action that were circulating at the end of the Clinton years. In a signal of the background noise on Iraq in the administration, however, Doug Feith reveals that the strategy did openly discuss, after arming the opposition, a "third possible step" of "action against the Iraqi regime by American forces."[141] In the broadest terms, as one former official has put it, US strategy before September 11 could be described as "pressing the edges of the box in so that Saddam Hussein would finally collapse"—an approach that "masked big differences" on policy, an exercise in straddling a policy divide that would only "set the stage for many later decisions."[142]

A clear assumption continued to be that removing Saddam Hussein from power would be a fairly easy, low-cost affair. One reason advocates were not more concerned with the postwar situation was their assumption that things would cohere quickly. James Woolsey, one of those advocates, told Seymour Hersh that "Iraq has its tribal factions and regional loyalties, but it also has a very sophisticated and intellectual infrastructure of highly educated people. There's no reason they couldn't establish a federalized—or loosely federalized—democracy."[143] Iraq, they believed, was a modern, cosmopolitan society waiting to be freed from Saddam's yoke—an assumption that, as we have seen, was dangerously misguided.

Indeed, this first bite at the apple of Iraq policy in the administration represents the first of many opportunities missed to make a better ultimate judgment. As much as there was a general agreement about Saddam's evil, the costs and risks of toppling him had not been assessed in years. It would not have been that difficult to force a renewed debate, to have options papers written, to seek expert advice on postwar realities. Discussions of doing something more serious about Iraq could and should have generated a rigorous policy process to test that proposition. But such a thing never occurred.

President Bush's feelings during this period remain ambiguous. Various written reports, and some officials I interviewed,[144] recall him asking for "options" on Iraq, but without pointedly revealing intentions or suggesting anything as direct as a desire to confront Saddam Hussein.

"Don't worry about it," he reportedly told a concerned Powell about the anti-Saddam activists busily generating proposals for bolder action. "I know what they are doing and I'm in no hurry to go look for trouble."[145]

Part of the emerging strategy was to give the CIA another crack at making something happen. Many open sources have now described the fact that the agency had an Iraq Operations Group (IOG) that oversaw covert operations against the regime. In August, according to George Tenet's memoir, it received a new chief, who reviewed the state of play and concluded that "Saddam was not going to be removed via covert action alone. As much as some would wish for an 'immaculate deception'— some quick, easy, and cheap solution to regime change in Iraq—it was not going to happen."[146] This became the consistent CIA line to policy-makers, and it meant that no US action short of direct invasion was going to topple Saddam.

⁂

As these ideas accumulated and the Iraq policy debates within the administration picked up speed, one final member of the Bush war cabinet took on increasing importance. Secretary of State Colin Powell's role in the gradual march toward war remains murky and controversial to this day.

As the leader of a major government bureaucracy, Powell would be a major success. He brought to the State Department a military-trained sense of leadership and organizational culture, and he ran the department with nearly unprecedented attention to effective management.[147] Powell quickly became known for an inclusive, respectful style that valued the opinions of even more junior Foreign Service officers.[148] These qualities made Powell widely admired, even adored, by many State Department employees—but the same attention to his department would be viewed with suspicion in an administration always on the hunt for misplaced loyalties. Donald Rumsfeld sniffed that Powell saw himself as the representative of the State Department to the president, rather than the other way around.[149] Powell, to his credit, stood up for State officials and offices that came in for bitter criticism from Rumsfeld's Defense people and the vice president's staff. But in so doing, he ended up deepening the suspicions of his fidelity.

And despite his great experience, two early policy gaffes led President Bush to view him with an even more jaundiced eye. During the press conference when Powell's appointment was announced, he angered Bush by launching into what amounted to a speech, as Bush stood impatiently to one side—the assumption had been that Powell would just offer a simple thanks and then defer to the president.[150] And in one of his first brushes with policy, on US strategy toward North Korea, Powell suggested that the administration planned to more or less continue the existing Clinton approach. This statement was badly at odds with an administration determined to distinguish itself from the Clinton crowd, and he was forced to walk his comments back in public.

Powell might have been more careful, because it was widely known that his relationship with Bush had a shaky past. As early as 1998, as the jockeying for position among prospective Republican candidates heated up, reports circulated that Powell hesitated to endorse Bush's candidacy because he worried that Bush, whom he had at times called "Sonny," was "not up to the job."[151] One senior official with knowledge of cabinet interactions says that Powell "was clearly the odd guy out among the senior officials." His style—prepared, formal, serious, disciplined—didn't mesh with Bush's informality and shoot-from-the-hip tendencies. "He wasn't on the same wavelength as his president, he really wasn't," this official said.[152] The result was that Bush and Powell never developed the instinctive level of trust so important for the effectiveness of any cabinet official.[153]

Powell may have missed some of these signs because, by many reports, he also brought to the relationship a legendary optimism. Karen DeYoung has written that Powell was convinced he'd turn on his powerful charm and win over the younger Bush.[154] One former senior official who worked closely with Powell went as far as to suggest that it added up, paradoxically in a man of such great political acumen, to a certain naivete.[155] Powell was an incredibly sophisticated thinker and politically attuned senior official who was nevertheless, in the view of many who served with him in the Bush administration, trusting in the way many soldiers are—confident that behaving honorably can inspire others to do the same. Powell "regularly told me to relax," Richard Haass explains, "that with time the early excesses of the administration would wear off."[156] Powell sought to transcend bureaucratic gamesmanship. He didn't want to "fight the little things," he would say; he wanted to save his ammunition for the big fights.[157] But this led, in the view of some at State, to Powell's being rolled on a hundred small issues to the point where the "big fights" had already been decided.

Those who later looked to Powell to obstruct the road to war also seem to have misread his actual views on Iraq. While he occasionally expressed concerns and doubts and was well aware of significance of the choice to go to war, there is no evidence that he denied the value, or even the feasibility, of military action against Iraq. He seemed happy enough for US power to be employed for such a goal, as long as they knew what they were doing. More than any personality mismatch or policy view, though, the dominant factor that would shape Colin Powell's role in the emerging Iraq debate was a simple fact: he had always been, and would remain, first and foremost a soldier. His sense of honor, duty, and commitment to follow orders meant that when a second president Bush informed him of his intention to go to war against Iraq, Powell's reaction would be the same as it had been in 1990. He would offer his best judgment and lay out the risks—and when asked for his support, he would deliver it.

⚜

In the end, though, the role of a secretary of state—or secretary of defense, or national security advisor—can be central or marginal. In the American system, the executive branch policy process typically mirrors the personality and perspective of a single decision-maker in ways not always appreciated outside government. The judgment on the Iraq war that unfolded after January 2001 served as an almost perfect mirror onto George W. Bush's strengths and weaknesses as a "decider."

Trying to pin down Bush's essential character is a devilishly hard thing to do. This is a man brimming with the most interesting contradictions: at once shrewd and intellectually lazy; aloof from the details of policy, and a recurrent micromanager of speeches and statements; humane and compassionate at some moments, and frat-boy cutting and dismissive at others; a faith-driven altruist capable of titanic outbursts of fury and profanity. Having never met him, I must confess that my research—surveying a dozen or more biographies, reading the memoirs of his aides, watching endless hours of speeches and press conferences, speaking to dozens of people who encountered him in government—left me with more than a little affection for a leader who seems, at the end of the day, essentially genuine and deeply committed to the well-being of the American people and to the promotion of freedom abroad. Yet he was also so heedless of detail as to be repeatedly shocked by the implications of his own choices, someone who had convinced himself that in going with his gut, he was operating in service of some sort of historical force that absolved him of the need to examine those choices more carefully.

In small settings, Frank Bruni has written, Bush "came across as instinctively bright, quick to the punch."[158] One former official who watched him extensively in NSC sessions said simply, "He's a *smart guy*."[159] Yet Bush defined himself in part by a devil-may-care attitude, a rejection of sophistry, a willingness to go with his gut. This nonchalance had become a sort of identity; in policy discussions he insisted on acquiring the general feel of an issue rather than what he considered mind-numbing detail.[160] A year into his administration, he could not be bothered to read the classified National Intelligence Estimate on Iraq's WMDs.[161] As Bush said, "You can't learn lessons by reading. Or at least I couldn't. I learned by doing."[162] The weapons inspector David Kay briefed Bush at the White House and later confessed, "I'm not sure I've spoken to anyone at that level who seemed less inquisitive."[163]

Famous for despising long meetings, Bush was intensely impatient; frequently his legs could be seen bouncing under tables, and he often spoke in choppy sentences.[164] He justified his impatience by styling it as decisiveness: where his father was seen as cautious, "George W. was abso-lutely fearless" as a decision-maker, one Republican Party operative told two Bush biographers.[165] The problem was, in the White House, Bush never put people around him to shape his instinct, to slow him down when he was rushing to a decision. He "assumed people were going to go off to implement his big decisions *well*," a senior official told me[166]—but he never *ensured* that this took place. "The whole White House was like that," former Bush speechwriter Matt Latimer has written, "infatuated with decisiveness, dismissive of deliberation."[167]

For all his innate compassion, Bush was a fiery commander in chief, a self-defined "tough guy" committed to the value of kicking ass and taking names.[168] He tended to see the world as a series of mano-a-mano confrontations in which demonstrations of strength and willpower were essential. In a September 2002 meeting with members of Congress, Bush hit upon an odd technique to characterize Iraqi policy toward Wash-ington: He extended his middle finger to Senate Minority Leader Tom Daschle and said, "Fuck the United States. That's what it is—and that's why we're going to get him."[169]

Some of those to whom I spoke describe a man willing to take con-structive criticism, someone who insisted that he wanted to hear what his aides really thought. Yet Bush, according to numerous testimonies, could also bristle when directly challenged. And his frat-boy persona sometimes had him on the lookout for opportunities to put others in their place—for example, he conspicuously ordered Karl Rove to hang up his jacket in one meeting, locked Colin Powell out of an early cabinet session when he was a few seconds late, and referred elaborately to "Dr. Rice" in NSC meetings.[170] According to a leading biographer, part of the problem was that George W. was simply "more Walker than Bush": the Walker side of the family was known for its roughness, its lack of intellectualism, its aggressiveness, its self-confident swagger, its pugnacity.[171]

His speechwriter Scott McClellan found Bush "plenty smart," but with an analytical style "based more on instinct than deep intellectual debate. His intellectual curiosity tends to be centered on knowing what he needs in order to effectively articulate, advocate, and defend his policies"[172]—a man who decides on impulse, then back-fills with questions to justify the course he is on. "I'm not a textbook player; I'm a gut player," he told Bob Woodward in August 2002.[173] "He tended to act by impulse, without apology," writes Robert Draper in his perceptive study, "calling himself a 'doer,' 'decider,' 'provoker,' 'charger,' and 'not a very good psychoanalyst guy.' Trusting one's gut was a good thing; gazing in the same anatomical area, at one's navel, struck him as an indulgence of the weak willed."[174]

⁂

After reading the many accounts of his life and speaking to those who worked alongside him, it is difficult to avoid the conclusion that George Bush is a man who sees the world largely through the prism of his own deeply held beliefs. Robert Draper, perhaps his most insightful biographer, describes this as an "almost petulant heedlessness to the outside world."[175] The characteristic was described more charitably by a senior official who clearly admired him: Bush, he informed me, made decisions in the privacy of his own soul, with an internal, intuitive sense of rightness.[176] In fact, Bush—much like other key members of his administration, especially Condoleezza Rice—believed in *belief* itself, the ability of belief to conquer and overcome even fact and objective reality. Draper tells the story of the January 2007 White House visit of the world champion St. Louis Cardinals. Bush explained that he had met with Tony LaRussa, the team's manager, in August; and despite a big losing streak, Bush became a Cardinals believer. "I was convinced the Cardinals were going to go all the way. You know why? Because *he* was. Because *he believed it*."[177]

This love of belief and decisiveness and toughness helped to produce, even in a man authentically humble in many ways, recurrent bouts of self-righteousness. One of his more obvious traits was a certain cockiness; he was someone so self-assured that he was not given to double-checking his instincts. (He was not a "hand-wringer," in one former official's assessment.[178]) Columnist David Brooks, after seeing Bush in the flesh, wrote in 2007 that "his self-confidence is the most remarkable feature of his presidency." It flowed, he thought, from Bush's "unconquerable faith in the rightness of his Big Idea. Bush is convinced that history is moving in the direction of democracy."[179]

When combined with his inattention to detail, these characteristics could produce policy chaos. Matt Latimer describes an amazing chain of events toward the end of the administration, during the emerging financial crisis. Bush had already committed to a $700 billion bailout package when he learned that key advisors doubted it would pass the Congress. "Then why the hell did I support it if I didn't believe it would pass?" Bush snapped. This was followed by "an uncomfortable silence." What then became apparent to Latimer was that George Bush misunderstood the implications of the financial proposal he had agreed to. "When it was explained to him that his concept of the bailout proposal wasn't correct," Latimer writes, "the president was momentarily speechless. He threw his hands up in frustration. 'Why did I sign on to this proposal if I don't understand what it does?' he asked."[180]

Condoleezza Rice is canny, offering up the following essentially as a compliment, but we can perhaps read between the lines. George W. Bush is "very intuitive and insightful. . . . He is somebody who very efficiently goes to the essence of a question." But he is also, Rice concludes, someone who "least likes me to say, 'This is complex.' "[181]

❧

More important than cleverness or academic focus, George W. Bush fervently believed, was character. And character, he had come to appreciate by the time he became president, was a product of faith.

The conventional story is that around his fortieth birthday, Bush's drinking was getting bad, his oil business had been sold, he lived in the shadow of a vice president father and an intensely demanding family—and he needed to ground himself. He had a series of dialogues with the preacher Billy Graham that led to a much deeper embrace of Christianity, and in particular (by many reports) to a hardening conviction that he had been chosen by God for some yet-undetermined mission. His faith, in the view of friends and family members who have spoken to a platoon of biographers, reportedly became the answer to his various problems— the fuel for his admirable self-discipline, his ability to keep his head in moments of unimaginable stress, his answer to progressively urgent doubts about his purpose.[182] Bush would often speak about the serenity that came from being the agent of a higher power.[183]

Later, while considering a run for president, Bush had what he has admitted was a near-religious-conversion event. Seated at his second inaugural as governor, Bush listened to Austin pastor Mark Craig preach about how "people are starved for leadership. Starved for leaders who have ethical and moral courage." Various reports suggest that his mother Barbara whispered to Bush afterward, "He was talking to you!"[184] He confessed to a preacher-mentor before 2000, "I feel like God wants me to run for president. I can't explain it, but I sense my country is going to need me. . . . I know it won't be easy on me or my family, but God wants me to do it."[185]

Bush had thus become, by 2000, a born-again man awaiting a higher purpose. On 9/11, Bush would stare into the abyss of a national tragedy and see the intersection of his personal destiny and a burgeoning appreciation for his nation's global calling.[186] Former Reagan and Bush I official Bruce Bartlett has argued that these traits explain why Bush "dispenses with people who confront him with inconvenient facts. He truly believes he's on a mission from God. Absolute faith like that overwhelms a need for analysis."[187]

※

Any tragedy is necessarily the story of individual human beings—their goals, hopes, qualities, and failings. The story of the origins of World War I, Christopher Clark writes in his magisterial history *The Sleepwalkers*, is "saturated in agency." Broad causal factors such as nationalism, imperialism, and alliances helped produce the conflict. But they can only be "made to carry real explanatory weight," Clark notes, when filtered through the decision-makers and their perspectives [183]

In this chapter I have emphasized the role of individual personalities and perspectives in the emerging Bush administration. Such an emphasis may seem obvious; what are national judgments if not the judgments of leaders? And yet the vast majority of theories and approaches on international strategy these days tend to bypass individuals on the way to a stress on *impersonal* factors—human nature, the effect of a lawless international system, the role of bureaucratic politics. What gets lost in such general theories is the role of specific leaders who come to their judgments in highly personal, idiosyncratic ways.[189]

The Iraq case highlights the importance of this role of individuals for one dominant reason: events, it turns out, don't speak for themselves. Leaders and leadership groups have to *interpret* them, to bring meaning to a messy and complex reality. Because one set of leaders can interpret the same events entirely differently from another, every big judgment in foreign policy will be, as Clark put it, "saturated in agency"; and because individuals are discovering meaning in events rather than reading it—like the results of a physics experiment—as an objective truth, there is tremendous potential for biases like wishful thinking and motivated reasoning.

After an especially brutal football game during the 1950s between Princeton and Dartmouth, a group of psychologists gave surveys to students who had seen the game, asking which team had started the rough play. Strong majorities from each college blamed it on the other side, which is perhaps to be expected. But what shocked the researchers was that, even when they *showed students from both schools an actual film of the game* and asked them to inventory nasty plays as they saw them, the answers remained just as biased. Even with the evidence right in front of them, the two sides still saw it differently. "It is inaccurate and misleading," those researchers concluded, "to say that different people have different 'attitudes' concerning the same 'thing.' For the 'thing' simply is not the same for different people whether the 'thing' is a football game, a presidential candidate, Communism, or spinach."[190]

Reaching judgments in foreign policy is first and foremost an interpretive act, discovering and bringing meaning to events that could have
many readings. In order to infer such meaning, people apply all manner of shortcuts—worldviews, analogies from experience, biases, tem-
peramental reactions, associations—to make rapid, largely unconscious
judgments.[191] The resulting process is as much about imagination as
observation: decision-makers, Yaacov Vertzberger has written, construct
"a view of the world in their minds"[192] which then shapes their understanding and behavior.[193]

The powerful force of American missionary sensibilities, and the
urgent sense of obligation created by value-driven decision-making,
played major roles in impelling the United States into Iraq. But those
factors, like all general influences on America's role in the world, can
be understood only by appreciating the ways in which they shaped and
interacted with the belief systems, personalities, leadership styles, biases,
and quirks of the individuals who brought America to war. In the Iraq
case, the traits of senior leaders included an often rock-solid belief in
their own rightness, a sometimes stubborn commitment to goals, an
impatience for rigorous analysis, a determination to demonstrate American credibility, and a powerful sense of American exceptionalism. Few
of these factors are unique to any one administration. But the particular
blend of certainty and impatience characteristic of the Bush administration helps to explain everything that would happen after 9/11.

※

By September 10, 2001, US policy toward Iraq had reached a fateful
culminating point. From the late Clinton administration, US policy had
been devoted to regime change—and now it had become clear that halfway measures would not produce that result. Senior officials in the new
administration were instinctively supportive of toppling Saddam but
were in no rush. A smaller, lower-level group of true believers saw US
action against Saddam as an urgent necessity, but their arguments had so

far produced little tangible result. US Iraq policy teetered on the edge of a tipping point, awaiting a catalyst.

When that catalyst arrived, the response would be absolute and immediate in large measure because a decade of debates on Iraq had produced an implicit consensus ready to be activated. That consensus was grounded in the messianic conception of American power that had come to dominate the US national security community after the Cold War. Thanks to this worldview, once the opportunity arrived, the choice to oust Saddam would not seem extreme at all. It would seem—to American national security experts and scholars across the political spectrum—to make perfect sense. It would seem to fit precisely into America's post–Cold War conception of itself.

The judgment that Saddam had to go had, in effect, already been made, along with an accompanying decision that the United States ought to take the lead in making that happen. These impressions or visions—for that is what they were—had arisen gradually, as value judgments more than analytical conclusions. Whenever senior US officials looked closely at the risks and costs of such a step, they recoiled, but the underlying conviction was not based on consequences so much as a driving imperative: *Saddam must go.* Layered on top of that specific implicit judgment was a broader conviction, on the part of most senior officials of the Bush administration: the United States had been acting fecklessly for eight long years, and it was time for the world's hegemon to throw its weight around.

All that was needed was the catalyst.

Thousands of miles from Washington, the machinations of Osama bin Laden and a handful of fellow terrorists were on the verge of reaching fruition. No one knew it yet, least of all the leaders of al Qaeda, but their horrific actions would provide that spark. And once the idea of going to war in Iraq moved from the realm of the theoretical to the real, other characteristics of the new administration—key senior officials overconfident in their own gut feelings, a president at once decisive and incurious, a core of anti-Saddam activists who worked to quash dissent by alternately ignoring and branding as disloyal any skeptical voices, and a national security process that was messy at the best of times—conspired to prevent any rigorous assessment of the emergent decision.

The result was that the United States would not, ultimately, make anything approaching a considered judgment to invade Iraq. Instead it tumbled into war, reacting to events and driven by half-considered assumptions and powerfully held worldviews. The judgment would leap into the minds of many senior officials on and after 9/11 not out of any careful calculation of benefits, costs, and risks but rather because—given their perceptions of the world—it simply *felt right*.

That fateful process would be set into motion on one of the most fateful days of American history—the day when everything changed.

CHAPTER 4

THE TERRIBLE SHADOW OF 9/11: AN IMPERATIVE TAKES HOLD

And in the end . . . just human, always human. What the historian is trying to capture is something living, not mechanical; biology, not metal; something called mind. . . . We're not computers, not thinking machines. We're both better and worse. We're more fallible, we're more evil, and we're more sublime than any computer can be.

PETER VIERECK[1]

Those years [as the war progressed] would show, in the American system, how when a question of the use of force arose in government, the advocates of force were always better organized, seemed more numerous and seemed to have both logic and fear on their side, and that in fending them off in his own government, a President would need all the help he possibly could get, not the least of which should be a powerful Secretary of State.

DAVID HALBERSTAM, THE BEST AND THE BRIGHTEST

One of the great mysteries to me is exactly when the war in Iraq became inevitable.

GEORGE TENET[2]

The history of American foreign policy changed irrevocably at 8:46 a.m. on September 11, 2001, when United Airlines Flight 11, flown by al Qaeda hijackers, pierced the north tower of the World Trade Center in an area above the ninety-third floor. Between 9:00 a.m. and just past 10:00 a.m., United Flight 175 struck the south tower, American Flight 77 slammed into the Pentagon, and United Flight 93 crashed in a field in Pennsylvania after passengers courageously attempted to regain control. Even before Flight 93 went down, the World Trade Center's south tower had plummeted to earth; less than half an hour later, at 10:28 a.m., it was followed by the north tower.

The resulting images—and the horrific pictures of New Yorkers stumbling through rubble-strewn streets in a tragic fog of dust and smoke—would be seared into the memory of Americans. Those profound and horrible events, an epochal event in the life of a nation that unfolded over less than 120 minutes, delivered a catastrophic blow to the psyche of the United States and the senior officials of the still relatively new Bush administration. Nothing like it had happened since Pearl Harbor, and in truth, not even then: The attacks of December 7, 1941, caused civilian deaths but aimed primarily at military targets and were confined to several military bases far from the continental homeland of the United States. The catastrophe of 9/11 struck at some of the leading symbols of American power, wealth, culture, and national identity. The country had arguably never in its history received such a blow from a foreign enemy, at least not since the early nineteenth century.

In the bloody and chaotic aftermath of the attacks, those first hours of shock and horror, the administration was in a frenzy. The president was out of town and only intermittently in touch with the White House. Other attacks were expected at any minute; F-16s crisscrossed the skies above Washington, on the lookout for more suicide aircraft, and were eventually given the heart-stopping order to shoot down any civilian airliners that seemed bent on additional attacks. Secret Service agents grabbed Vice President Cheney by the belt and hustled him almost forcibly to a secure facility. The air in that bunker quickly became so stifling that people had to be pushed out; oxygen seemed to be in short supply.[3] Witnesses have testified that amid the panic and disorder, Cheney remained impressively calm—coolly keeping order, seeking information, and issuing directions.[4]

By several accounts Donald Rumsfeld also conducted himself admirably on 9/11, showing little regard for his own safety and remaining focused and calm. He rushed to where the 757 had struck the west side of the Pentagon to help with rescue efforts but was persuaded to leave. With the bitter odor of smoke still in the air, fresh from picking his way through the destruction, Rumsfeld reportedly told Bush, "This is not a criminal action. This is war."[5] On his way back from the infamous classroom in Florida—where his initial, understandably somewhat confused reaction to the news of the tragedy would generate all manner of ridiculous and unfair criticisms and speculations—Bush was warned by Condoleezza Rice, "Mr. President, you can't come back here. Washington is under attack."[6]

These moments imprinted themselves on all senior officials of the administration, and we cannot understand the nature of the decisions they would later make on issues from Iraq to interrogation policies unless we grapple with the shattering impact of that day. George Tenet describes the heated atmosphere in the White House in the hours after 9/11 as reflecting "more raw emotion in one place than I think I've ever experienced in my life."[7] One biography of Rice describes the hours of 9/11 as "the most harrowing of her life," as she sat in the bunker with Cheney and others and tried to manage the situation amid conflicting, elusive information. An event like this "changes your psychology," she would admit later.[8]

One senior official later pointed out what it is easy to forget: Bush was still fresh into office, and now he had presided over arguably the greatest catastrophe on US soil in the modern era. The resulting "overwhelming sense of responsibility" was profound. "Every single one of them felt that way," the source explained. One cannot exaggerate "the transformative effect on your sense of responsibility of being in power on 9/11." Top administration officials would still be very much in that frame of mind a year and a half later when planning the Iraq invasion—obsessed with their responsibility to protect America "in an almost irrational way."[9]

❧

Nations do not arrive at world-changing moments like 9/11 as blank slates. Their reactions are shaped by their self-conception and the ideas and narratives that guide their roles in the world. In the case of the United States, the reaction to 9/11—both the narrower response to terrorism and the broader actions now seen as necessary—would flow from the expansive, messianic notions that fueled American foreign policy, both the idealistic and the hard-power sides of that conception. Another country might have responded to such attacks by delivering a vicious retaliation against al Qaeda and stopping there. America's ambitions, at least since 1945, have been grander than that, and its reaction to 9/11 would be no different.

But the events of 9/11 added a second profound factor to the new calculus on national security: they created the basis for a morally charged commitment to acting almost regardless of consequences. The attack made America feel vulnerable and drove home the horrible price to be paid when foreign enemies gathered the means to strike the American homeland. Senior officials of the administration were emotionally devastated by the attacks and resolved never to let anything like them happen again. The way in which they weighed costs and benefits changed forever: a number of key officials inside the administration had long believed that America had been acting too timidly anyway; they had been arguing for years to throw off the shackles limiting the exercise of American power. The attacks of 9/11 gave them the most ghastly possible justification for doing just that.

In the process, the attacks intensified a long-simmering belief in the American national security community—the idea that the United States could not tolerate a world with Saddam Hussein. The events of that day transformed that belief from an amorphous sense into an urgently felt obligation. In all these ways, 9/11 triggered the second primary element of the pattern of misjudgment I am trying to illustrate: the emergence, sometimes fairly gradual and sometimes all at once, of a powerfully felt imperative to act and a resulting mindset of moral obligation rather than analytical nuance. That conviction would then merge with the messianic impulses embedded in US foreign policy to produce a reaction at once radical, idealistic, and hopelessly ambitious. The Bush administration would not merely seek to punish the handful of men directly responsible for the crimes of 9/11. They would seek—in both the proudest and most tragic spirit of America's view of itself—to transform the world.

The story of the period after 9/11 begins to reflect a number of dominant themes of the process that led to the final decision to go to war in Iraq. It is the story of a very rapid, almost automatic decision to wage a "global war on terror"—to undertake a response not limited to the perpetrators of the attack but embodying far more elaborate ambitions. It is the story of a rush to include Iraq as a dominant component of that war, followed by a period of hesitation, an unwillingness to pull that trigger immediately. It is the story, as a result, of the emergence of formal and informal decision tracks, where a slow, public formal track did not reflect the certainty and speed of an *implicit* decision to go to war characteristic of the more informal track.

The resulting process unfolded through a series of key milestones. There were the days immediately after 9/11, in which an implicit commitment, a sort of moral imperative to act, clearly formed itself in the minds of most key decision-makers. The Camp David meeting just three days after 9/11 served as the origin point of both the formal and informal decision tracks. Two weeks later, in a personal meeting, George Bush gave his secretary of defense very specific orders: get ready for war in Iraq. And by December, as this first phase of the decision process after 9/11 drew to a close, Central Command (CENTCOM) chief General Tommy Franks would be briefing the president on the initial versions of a formal war plan.

Between September 11 and December 2001, in other words, the Bush administration—while nowhere near what would be defined as the formal "decision" to go to war—had irrevocably committed itself to the downfall of Saddam Hussein, whatever that would require. The problem was that no one took the time to stand back and ask, seriously and rigorously: Just what *would* it require—and are we really willing to pay that price? They did not do so, in part, because senior leaders of the administration were no longer thinking in terms of costs and benefits. They were thinking in terms of imperatives and obligations. Under the terrible shadow of 9/11, they had a sort of instinctive revelation of the right thing to do. And they were determined to do it.

❧

George W. Bush's reaction to the attacks was instant and unambiguous. Immediately after leaving the Florida classroom, Bush turned to his aides and said simply, "We're at war."[10] He used exactly the same phrase with Vice President Cheney and then added, "And we're going to find out who did this, and we're going to kick their ass."[11]

The most fateful decision of the entire post-9/11 era—the fundamental strategic choice to launch a major global campaign against terrorists "and those who harbor them," to declare the nation engaged in a war rather than some sort of global law enforcement action—was made by Bush himself at the White House that evening, in part responding to a draft of remarks by presidential speechwriter Michael Gerson. There was no substantial discussion among the national security principals about the idea.[12] One Cheney biographer says the president and vice president quickly agreed on the notion separately from one another without any hesitation.[13]

That judgment to undertake a broader war on terror—fairly quick, habitual, and intuitive—set the stage for everything that followed. At eight thirty that evening, Bush himself publicly enunciated this concept. In his understandably morose and somewhat halting speech to the American people, President Bush promised, "We will make no distinction between the terrorists who committed these acts and those who harbored them." And "Just like that," journalist Peter Baker explains,

"Bush declared a sweeping new doctrine in American security, one that he had not discussed in advance with Cheney, Rice, Rumsfeld, or Colin Powell."[14]

⁂

A sudden conviction of the rightness of the new cause, the marrow-deep sense of operating under history's gaze, affected all the senior officials in the administration and gave them what quickly became a belligerent devotion to their chosen course of action. They tended to see their obligations, and the policies necessarily related to those duties, in elaborate and even apocalyptic terms.[15] On the evening of September 14, the cabinet principals received a weighty sheaf of briefing papers compiled from several departments and agencies. George Tenet's reaction was symptomatic: "I remember thinking as I waded through them that hundreds of trees had been killed for no good reason. The papers were irrelevant, as near as I could tell, to anything I was going to say, and by then I was so confident in the rightness of our approach that I had little use for the half measures and unformed strategies that other agencies were beginning to trot out."[16] The "rightness of our approach," Tenet said—not the likelihood of success; not the specific consequences it would produce, developed through rigorous analysis. Increasingly, the perceived *rightness* of a given policy would be the key to understanding the administration's choices.

This conviction—this *revelation*, for in many senses that is what it was, the moralistic sense of doing the right thing—would come to affect George Bush most of all. The attack had given sudden and profound meaning to his own incipient sense of being placed at a moment in history for a reason.[17] This was now George W. Bush's purpose, his calling, and he would make subsequent judgments in primarily moralistic rather than outcome-oriented terms. He said as much in NSC meetings: responding to the attacks of 9/11 and fighting what he repeatedly described as "evil" was now his "mission."[18] And he would bring to this cause every ounce of conviction, courage, energy, boldness, stubbornness, and willful self-delusion he had at his disposal. He was fired by a determination to exact retribution, to set a precedent so fearful that no one would ever contemplate attacking America in that manner again. The sense of mission was so powerful that he would throw himself headlong into its pursuit, plunging ahead with a certainty in his course that left little room for careful interrogation of its costs and risks.

⁂

Chapter 2 argued that the collective beliefs about America's role in the world offer part of the explanation for how thoughtful American leaders and officials could set the course for tragedy. But such beliefs only open the door to a judgment; they do not force the decision-makers to walk through. The United States, after all, did not invade Iraq in 1980, or 1994, or 1998. The first nine months of the Bush administration only represented a gradual transition to a more urgent requirement to act. A generalized conventional wisdom can demonstrate why a nation tends to lean in certain directions, but it cannot explain why nations act and why they don't. For that, we need a more proximate cause. And such a cause comes from the second factor I am seeking to highlight: an intuitive, emergent mechanism of judgment that is driven primarily by *imperatives*—a sense among a nation's leadership group at a specific moment that a given choice is "the right thing to do" in a sense that is more moralistic than calculatedly rational.

Most conceptions of what is called "rational" decision-making include a few essential claims about the ways in which human beings approach choices. Someone acting rationally is trying to maximize some gain and so weighs various alternatives to judge which one will give the most value in those terms.[19] Such a conception is therefore dominantly "consequentialist." It is obsessed with outcomes, because only by taking outcomes seriously can one anticipate benefits and costs. It is also what is termed "instrumental," in the sense that actions aim to produce some outcome that serves the decision-maker's interests.

But there are powerful alternative models for human judgment, models that emphasize values rather than consequences and paint a picture of decision-makers serving an imperative or norm rather than maximizing objectives. One of these is sociologist Max Weber's concept of *value rationality*. Whereas "instrumental rationality" refers to efforts to anticipate possible outcomes and calculate advantage, value rationality describes situations in which people make decisions, not based on what they think will most benefit them, but to fulfil the right thing to do—that is, to do something right for its own sake. I am arguing that, often enough on major foreign policy issues, leaders and senior officials come to be guided by precisely such value-based, rather than instrumental or outcome-oriented, thinking. Rather than what has been called a *logic of consequences* (weighing the value and cost of outcomes relative to one's goals), they employ a *logic of appropriateness*, a form of judgment in which decision-makers are concerned about doing what is right or appropriate given their role and the circumstances.[20]

The resulting mindset looks very much like a commitment to what some scholars have labeled "sacred values." These are distinct from material interests by their moralistic case; they are, "or ought to be, absolute and inviolable."[21] They cannot be compromised or traded off against other values; they are absolute rather than instrumental, and must be followed regardless of consequences. In pursuing such sacred values, decision-makers will display "harsh trait attributions to norm violators, anger and contempt, and enthusiastic support" for the enforcement of norms against those who doubt the course of action; they will "censure" and "ostracize" those who disagree.[22] Even sacred values can promote utilitarian calculations, but more often they are "derived from rules that circumscribe certain actions independently of expected outcomes or prospects of success, and that we act in accordance with them because they are the right thing to do."[23]

Examples of such thinking are legion in the history of US foreign policy. The American commitment to Vietnam was based in part on the idea that the strategic values at stake were inviolable, that fighting communism in Southeast Asia was the right thing to do. The attack on Castro's Cuba at the Bay of Pigs emerged from a similar sense of obligation;

it had to be done, because Castro had to go. More recently, the American commitment to NATO enlargement has taken on a similar moralistic flavor: it cannot be abandoned or even qualified because the countries at stake have a right to make that choice. These and other examples demonstrate how concerns that remain political and strategic can nonetheless take on the aspect of sacred values, and present themselves not as the better or more valuable choice but as the "right" one.

I do not mean to suggest that such value-driven logics govern *all* national security decisions. Indeed, they do not determine most of them: hundreds of choices—whether to buy a specific weapons system, how many troops to deploy on the territory of an ally, where to locate a proposed air base—are usually made with powerful doses of rationalistic analysis, as the decision-makers try to measure the instrumental values involved. My goal here is merely to illustrate factors that *can* play a decisive role, at particular moments, in shaping foreign policy choices and in generating tragedies. Moralistic imperatives are certainly such a factor and have been an essential ingredient in a number of prominent disasters. This can be especially true in the realm of national security, with its implied air of moral responsibility and sacred values at stake—values that impact the lives and well-being of a nation's citizens. In periods of crisis or threat, it is all too easy for national leaders to evaluate such issues in terms of values rather than consequences.

In the process, the character of these judgments diverges in another way from the sometimes nearly mathematical calculations of classic rationalism. They emerge through a sort of intuitive imagination, a creative leap to make sense out of events rather than a weighing of anticipated gains and likely risks. Such judgments take place in much the same way as Einstein described himself making breakthroughs in science: gathering facts, allowing the subconscious to work them over, and then awaiting a form of epiphany. "Imagination is more important than knowledge," Einstein said,[24] and much the same is true for national security decision-making.

Henry Kissinger has called the practice of imaginative meaning-creation "conjecture." "The choice between . . . policies did not reside in the 'facts,' but in their interpretation," he has written. Foreign policy decision-making demands the "ability to project beyond the known." And in this area, "there's really very little to guide the policy-maker except what convictions he brings to it."[25]

This is true for one dominant reason: the overwhelming complexity and uncertainty surrounding major national security choices. There are simply too many variables at work, too much nonlinearity, to judge outcomes with any degree of precision. Decision-makers lack the sort of comprehensive information assumed by rational decision-making theories and operate instead in an environment of "deep uncertainty." And so decision-makers hunt for simplified decision rules—key values or imperatives that can slice through the complexity and offer a clear basis for choice.

Confronting such complex situations, decision-makers cannot read objective truth out of a situation—they must construct meaning from their experience. And the result is that the interaction of senior decision-makers with complex issues is a fundamentally interpretive and imaginative enterprise. Facts in such a world are like images in an abstract painting, or the cloud of shapes on a Rorschach blot—ambiguous and open to multiple understandings. Observers are *creating* meaning, not simply reading or determining it.

Walter Lippman, writing in 1922, discussed the difference between reality and our mental construct of it. The "real environment is altogether too big, too complex" to grasp, he argued, and so "we have to reconstruct it on a simpler model." The result is the "insertion between man and his environment of a pseudo-environment," a "representation of the environment which is in lesser or greater degree made by man himself." Lippmann called these "fictions," and noted that they could range from hallucinations to the use of scientific frameworks.[26]

This mechanism of judgment looks and feels to the participants like rationalism. We *feel* as if we are considering objectives, as if we are goal-directed, as if we weigh various options based on how well they contribute to clearly identified interests we are trying to maximize. In fact, though, what we're doing is internalizing a mass of information and allowing our unconscious to do mostly involuntary work in bubbling forth judgments. The philosopher Alfred Schütz referred to this approach as "an anticipation of future conduct by way of phantasying."[27] Judgment is a fundamentally *imaginative* enterprise.[28] It emerges as a vision, an illusion, an invented narrative; a conviction, a belief—anything but a formally reasoned calculation.

Such an approach to arriving at judgments allows us to see the Iraq decision for what it was: a creeping (or sudden and powerful) *feeling* that a given course of action was the *right* one, based on simple rules or convictions that were more moralistic or normative than analytical. And the fact that the decision had this character allows us to better understand many seemingly confusing aspects of it: the moralistic language that surrounded the policy process, the resistance to dissent, and the refusal to take risks seriously. Judgments undertaken in such a frame of mind have more of the cast of faith than of consequentialist decision-making, more in common with revelation than calculation. When people are applying sacred values, they come to have an almost thoughtless conviction in what they are doing. It is right—it *feels* right, from the depths of their well-honed intuitive judgment—and practical arguments have little place in such a thought process.

George Ball, the famous dissenter in the US escalation decisions for Vietnam, wrote of the fact that analytical arguments simply bounced off people who believed they "must" do something. "To my dismay," he wrote of the reactions to his prescient arguments that US strategy in Vietnam was bound to fail, "I found no sympathy for these views. Both McNamara and Gilpatric seemed preoccupied with the single question, How can the United States stop South Vietnam from a Viet Cong takeover? How did I propose to avoid it? The 'falling domino' theory was a brooding omnipresence." Official statements of US commitment to South Vietnam, Ball continued, "had the sound and solemnity of a religious oath: 'We now take the decision to commit ourselves to the objective of preventing the fall of South Vietnam to Communism."[29] *The solemnity of a religious oath*—exactly the right way, I think, to understand the convictions that burst to the fore after 9/11.

⅍

It is worth, in this connection, remembering what did not happen after 9/11. Apart from a few isolated incidents and a generalized sense of suspicion, there was no large-scale violence against or efforts to round up American Muslims.[30] No formal laws were passed to prevent speech on the war or to outlaw protests. This observation may sound blasé until one reads a little American history and realizes that in times of national crisis, the body politic has often veered into astonishingly undemocratic territory.

Whatever other mistakes he made, George W. Bush must be credited for the tolerance and restraint he displayed, under tremendous pressure, in these harrowing days. He had a history of reaching out to Muslim constituencies, and in fact had been scheduled for a meeting with Muslim-American leaders on the afternoon of September 11. On September 17 he chose to visit a local mosque, at the Islamic Center of Washington, where he rejected any effort to blame Islam for the violence. "The face of terror is not the true faith of Islam," he said. "That's not what Islam is all about. Islam is peace. These terrorists don't represent peace. They represent evil and war."[31] There can be no doubt that such statements played an important role in blunting the undeniable gust of bias and anger and suspicion directed at the Muslim community in the United States after the attacks.

At the same time, Bush dealt with great compassion and humanity with the victims and families he encountered. His thoughtfulness extended to those who worked in the White House. Two days after 9/11, he learned that a staff member had a nephew missing in New York. He called the man and offered his concern and best wishes. Bush later stopped by the man's office to reiterate his concern. And then he added, "I am going to find the people who did this and bring them to justice."[32]

❧

The central and essential effect of 9/11 on the mindset of George W. Bush and his senior aides was to transform their calculus of risk. Dangers the United States had tolerated before 9/11 could no longer be accepted.[33] Actions that had seemed too perilous were now readily entertained.

Ron Suskind claims, based on sources present in fall 2001 meetings, that Vice President Cheney enunciated what Suskind has termed the "one percent doctrine"—the idea that traditional notions of balance, prudence, and pragmatism in national security strategy had to be abandoned in favor of an urgent action. "If there's a one percent chance that Pakistani scientists are helping al Qaeda" with nuclear weapons, "we have to treat it as a certainty in terms of our response," Suskind reports Cheney as having said at a principals meeting in November 2001.[34]

One person working in Cheney's office at the time rejects portraits of the vice president as a "strategic hysteric" but nonetheless agreed that 9/11 had a profound effect on his worldview: Cheney's experiences in the White House bunker on 9/11 became the point of departure for everything that followed.[35] There was never a noticeable change in the vice president's personality; he remained calm, low-profile, personable. Arguably, however—especially as the threat perceptions mounted, with the anthrax attacks and repeated exposure to the terrifying daily "threat matrix" of imminent terrorist attacks—the urgency of his absolutism hardened. Similar attacks with mass-effect weapons would be "exponentially worse," he believed, and could not be allowed. Arguments opposed to the Iraq war struck him as anachronistic, "the worldview of a time before we had seen the devastation that terrorists armed with hijacked airplanes could cause. We had to do everything possible to be sure that they never got their hands on weapons that could kill millions."[36]

For Condoleezza Rice, "waiting until a threat explodes was not an option after the experience of 9/11."[37] One senior Defense official argued that 9/11 destroyed any hope that terrorists were after "political theater" more than wanton destruction. "They aimed to destroy us, not win our sympathy for their cause. They had no restraint. All of a sudden, the problem of terrorism looked completely different."[38]

꙳

After his evening address to the nation on September 11, President Bush gathered his national security team once again.[39] Rumsfeld immediately urged that, in his own words, "we think about the problem more broadly" than just al Qaeda. "We needed to consider other nations, including Sudan, Libya, Iraq, and Iran," countries that in his view gave "safe haven" to terrorists and helped to fund and support their activities.[40] Rumsfeld defined this worldview in more detail in his memoirs. "Punishing our enemies didn't describe the range of actions we would need to take if we were to succeed in protecting the United States," he argued. "Our responsibility was to deter and dissuade others from thinking that terrorism against the United States could advance their cause."[41]

These hours after 9/11 represent an absolutely critical moment—the initial and most encompassing strategic judgment made in the shadow of 9/11, the origin point of all others; a judgment made very quickly, collectively, intuitively; a felt obligation rather than the result of any sort of analysis. On 9/11, just about every significant official came to the same conclusion: the United States would have to undertake a broad-based, global war on terrorism and its sponsors.[42] The nation would have to do far more than deal with the attackers—it needed to strike out at targets far and wide, connected and not, to teach the world important lessons. In doing so, it would not merely defeat one threat; it would transform world politics through means both hard and soft—brute force and the spread of democracy.

This is the first decisive moment after 9/11 on the road to war in Iraq—the hours and days when this judgment was arrived at, by Bush and others, without much consideration to its wider and longer-term meaning.[43] It was a clear sort of value judgment or moral imperative rather than any sort of instrumental calculation; it emerged in the absence of analysis, debate, military planning, diplomatic consultations, and even much discussion. And it was the first, necessary step toward an invasion of Iraq.

⁂

What is remarkable about these thoughts is how consistent they were, even among US officials separated by thousands of miles. Undersecretary of Defense for Policy Douglas Feith was in Moscow with a group of US officials on 9/11. He heard Bush say, "Terrorism against our nation will not stand," and so he drew his conclusions. "The President seemed to be talking war," Feith explained in his memoir. "I took the President's words as strategic guidance." Still in Moscow, he sent Rumsfeld a memo whose essential message was this: Don't go small. Go big. Find everyone connected to terrorism and crush them.[44]

A number of officials eventually shared a plane ride back from Germany; this DoD brain trust included Feith, Lt. Gen. John Abizaid, Peter Rodman, William Luti, and Dov Zakheim. After the eight-hour trip, one former senior official related, the group had "essentially blocked out" the strategy for the war on terror. "They got off the plane with the thing formed in concept."[45] Feith's memoir defines that concept. It was "a strategy for war, rather than mere law enforcement," and the target was not merely al Qaeda, but "a wide-ranging set of individuals, organizations, and states."[46] In the weeks that followed, outside pundits added detail and emphasis to these budding ideas: a small group of conservative foreign policy experts produced, for example, a manifesto called "The Delta of Terrorism," which claimed that 9/11 had inaugurated a two-generation war on extremism, that it demanded a complete overhaul of governance in the Middle East—and that a place to begin was Iraq.[47]

This strategy, and the worldview it reflected, was to a certain degree built on a mirage. The officials never brought evidence to bear about any other terrorist groups ready to strike the United States. In fact, most terrorists had little interest in harming the American homeland, and it was not clear why a potent retaliation against al Qaeda alone could not have the desired deterrent effect. There was no coherent analysis of what states were busily arming terrorists for a war against America. The image of a global network of malefactors—states and terrorist groups with hundreds of shadowy connections, merging into a snowballing threat to the United States—was, as years of subsequent research and experience would make clear, wildly off the mark.

Nor was there any analysis of the likely consequences of such a war, only a rough sketch of the outcomes the administration intended to produce. Would a global campaign that ended in open conflict with multiple states—for that was what these first notions implied—make the United States more secure? Might it tempt, rather than deter, more attacks? Would any other countries join the effort, and if none ended up doing so, would the thing still be feasible? How much would it cost? None of these questions was evaluated in any significant degree before this emergent judgment took firm root.

The planeload of US officials returned to Washington with the same accumulating convictions as Bush, Cheney, Rumsfeld, and others: the United States was facing a global war against an implacable set of adversaries. The only appropriate response was an overwhelming one, a messianic global campaign. This was the first crucial moment; without *this* judgment, the Iraq decision would not have been made. And this conclusion was arrived at in a rush, under immense emotional pressure. One official recalled that "there was not a lot of debate" about the broad outlines of the US response "because it seemed pretty clear to everybody." The basic pillars of the approach "came up pretty quickly" and "fell into place within the first week," and the "President was there before many of the rest of us." He was there, however—secure in an accumulating decision to launch a global campaign against terrorists and state supporters—largely because, based on his worldview and reaction to the moment, he *felt* it was the right thing to do.[48]

These weeks after 9/11 thus represent a second opportunity to generate a better outcome, another opportunity tragically lost: a time when the assumptions of the broader war on terror, and key constituent parts including action against Saddam Hussein, could have been tested with more rigorous analysis and debate. The purpose would not, officially, have been to deflect the administration from its course but to identify possible risks and unintended consequences. But with a president so sure of what the moment demanded, and a policy process determined both to give him what he wanted and to use the moment for its own long-harbored dreams, there was no serious pressure for such rigorous analysis.

⁂

This accumulating sense of a need to act boldly, violently, and with vengeance, to teach a bitter lesson, fit tightly into the perspectives of senior officials who saw power and respect as the cardinal principles of world politics. The route to safety in the international system, in this view, is a credible reputation for the effective use of force. The path to credibility is toughness, demonstrated through uncompromising action.

This view was perhaps held most tightly by the most important member of the national security team—President Bush himself. The other side of the coin from his thoughtful and empathetic instincts was the blunt and brutal appreciation for retributive justice, the man who as governor brooked few exceptions to death penalty sentences, the caustic frat boy who delighted in needling his senior staff. This side of Bush came to the fore at various moments after 9/11 in dozens of curt and profane promises to annihilate whoever had done this to the United States, and whoever might be thinking of helping them. The United States was at war, he believed, and as war leader he had one job more than any other: to find America's enemies and destroy them.

"It's hard to appreciate" the crushing sense of vulnerability that arose after 9/11, a former official closely involved in the post-9/11 process explained. The natural conclusion was the importance of sending an unambiguous message to potential attackers: "You shouldn't be thinking about doing anything like this ever again."[49] The degree to which such thinking had infused the American foreign policy establishment is apparent in a 2004 essay by *New York Times* columnist Thomas Friedman, who summarized an argument he had made in several op-ed pieces before the war. "The real reason for this war," he argued—one that was "never stated"—was to

> burst what I would call the "terrorism bubble," which had built up during the 1990s. This bubble was a dangerous fantasy, believed by way too many people in the Middle East. This bubble said that it was OK to plow airplanes into the World Trade Center, commit suicide in Israeli pizza parlors, praise people who do these things as "martyrs," and donate money to them through religious charities. This bubble had to be burst, and the only way to do it was to go right into the heart of the Arab world and smash something—to let everyone know that we, too, are ready to fight and die to preserve our open society. Yes, I know, it's not very diplomatic—it's not in the rule book—but everyone in the neighborhood got the message: Henceforth, you will be held accountable.[50]

In a later documentary, Doug Feith was asked about the rationale for the war. "The idea was," he said, to "take actions after 9/11 that would so shock state sponsors of terror around the world that we might be able to get them to change their policies regarding support for terrorism and also weapons of mass destruction."[51] In this conception, the scope of the response was critical: anything too small would convey the wrong impression.

This "demonstration effect" approach was a gut instinct more than a developed and defended argument. Terrorists, in fact, don't tend to be put off by the threat of harsh retaliation. Because some of their recruiting potential was based on political and sociological grievance, in fact, there was a profound risk that a violent retaliation would at best create a trade-off: some greater deterrence in exchange for substantially increased resentment of the United States, and a bigger flow of angry volunteers into al Qaeda field offices. There were tremendous risks bound up with a global military campaign, long-term dangers of a near-permanent war footing that would face the republic.

None of this was debated. They needed to strike—and quickly. "One week from now," Rumsfeld told Chairman of the Joint Chiefs Richard Myers immediately after 9/11, "the willingness to act will be half of what it is now."[52]

As the sense emerged that US strategy would be going big, some doubts did begin to emerge, especially among the uniformed military. One source with whom I spoke was serving on the Joint Staff and found the "network of evildoers" concept unpersuasive. The motives of specific terrorist groups were varied and unpredictable; the Irish Republican Army had little in common with Aum Shinriko in Japan, or Hamas. What was the point of a global "war" against such diverse threats? And why add state sponsors to the list without clear evidence of their complicity? This officer admits that he cannot remember anyone openly speaking up against the emerging doctrine. "There must be something I do not know," he thought at first. "You had to resist disbelief, in order to do your job." Some would gently raise questions—"Have we thought about *x*, *y*, or *z*?"—but at the beginning, and in many ways throughout the whole process, no one openly challenged the emerging construct.[53]

⁂

On September 12, President Bush confirmed this broad approach at an NSC meeting. George Tenet explains that Bush "stressed in stronger terms what he had said on television the evening before: he wanted not just to punish those behind the previous day's attacks but to go after terrorists and those around the globe who harbored them."[54] That morning at eleven thirty, Bush met with members of Congress. "We will answer the bloodlust of the American people that is rightly at boil," the president told them. "We are at war."[55]

⁂

The turn to Iraq was astonishingly swift. On the afternoon of 9/11, Rumsfeld was in conversation about the attacks with one of his most trusted aides, Stephen Cambone. Cambone's notes from the meeting were later released, under a Freedom of Information Act request.[56] At 2:40 p.m., Cambone jotted this down: "Hit S. H. @ same time—Not only UBL." The notes continue, "Need to move swiftly," "Go massive, sweep it all up," and "Things related and not."

These brief notes imply that Rumsfeld was, in those first chaotic hours, already thinking of the case that would need to be built against Saddam Hussein. This was the second key milsestone after 9/11: the immediate, almost automatic reflex that if they were going to go big, then Iraq had to be part of the campaign. The 9/11 Commission report suggests, based on interview material with the president himself, that Rumsfeld "wondered immediately after the attack" whether "Saddam Hussein's regime might have had a hand in it." Rumsfeld, the report concludes, "said his instinct was to hit Saddam Hussein at the same time—not only bin Laden."[57]

Lt. Gen. Michael DeLong, at the time the deputy commander of Central Command, or CENTCOM, the US regional combatant command responsible for the Middle East, has described a videoconference that first afternoon. Rumsfeld seemed impatient with the emerging thinking. "I'm not even so sure Afghanistan is the right place to start," he said. "What if Iraq is involved?" DeLong argues that Colin Powell pushed back—al Qaeda and Afghanistan were the first concerns—and President Bush closed the discussion by saying, "Let's deal with one thing at a time."[58] At the meeting, Tenet laid out information that, at least initially, pinned the blame for the attacks squarely on al Qaeda. Just after the meeting ended, though, Rumsfeld called CENTCOM back to make his own views known. "What about Iran?" he asked, according to DeLong, and when CENTCOM commander Tommy Franks seemed to brush the question off, Rumsfeld directed a search for "as much intel as we have on whoever we think was involved."[59]

One of the passengers on the plane headed back from Germany was a military officer who later shared an anecdote with George Tenet. During the discussion on board, the officer had suggested to Doug Feith that the priority clearly ought to be a campaign against al Qaeda in Afghanistan. "To his amazement," Tenet recounts, "Feith said words to the effect that the campaign should immediately lead to Baghdad."[60]

❧

Iraq leapt into the minds of senior officials in part because of widespread assumptions—largely wrong—about Saddam's ties to terrorism and presumed support for al Qaeda.[61] In the weeks after 9/11, both Rice and Cheney pointed to evidence of such a relationship. Cheney took the more uncompromising stance, unwilling even by the time he wrote his memoir in 2011 to give up the idea that Saddam may have been supporting the group. The line out of Defense, one source suggests, was the same; they could not believe that a group like al Qaeda pulled off the attack on its own. This source recalls comments in early meetings along the lines of "There's a state sponsor here, and we have to find and neutralize it."[62]

By the time of her own memoir in 2011, Condoleezza Rice had backed off of these obsessions and wrote simply that there was no compelling evidence of a connection between Iraq and 9/11. Still, "The Vice President and his staff . . . were absolutely convinced that Saddam was somehow culpable." Cheney "latched on to every report of a meeting between Iraqi agents and al Qaeda affiliates. Many of the reports were of highly questionable origin and reliability," and the evidence for a tie between Saddam and 9/11 was weak. But "the Vice President's office remained convinced that there had been." Cheney, Rice explains, asked his top aide, Scooter Libby, to brief these notions to Bush, and Libby offered a persuasive-sounding case—but Bush, "much to my relief," seemed unmoved.[63] But there is other evidence that Bush, while perhaps resisting arguments for large-scale collaboration between Iraq and al Qaeda firmly believed Saddam Hussein was somehow involved in the attack.[64]

Whatever the president's views, the effort to build the case would hardly miss a beat: some former Cheney staffers would later help form a special cell in Defense designed to gather every bit of intelligence, verified and not, supporting the argument for a global network of malefactors, who were supposedly working in evil concert to bring harm to America. And senior officials issued a flood of comments, from as early as late 2001 through the fall of 2002, raising fears of a partnership between Iraq and al Qaeda. In the days after 9/11, when asked on *Meet the Press* whether there was evidence of Iraqi complicity, Dick Cheney answered simply, "No." But a month and a half later, on the same show, he was referring darkly to "what we now have that's developed since you and I last talked," and concluded, "The evidence is pretty conclusive that the Iraqis have, indeed, harbored terrorists."[65] In November 2002, Donald Rumsfeld claimed, "There is no question but that there have been interactions between the Iraqi government, Iraqi officials and al Qaeda operatives. They have occurred over a span of some 8 or 10 years to our knowledge. There are currently al Qaeda in Iraq."[66] President Bush himself, in an October 2002 speech, insisted that "we know that Iraq and al Qaeda have had high-level contacts that go back a decade. Some al Qaeda leaders who fled Afghanistan went to Iraq."[67] Dozens of claims from this reservoir of half-baked reports later found their way, in early 2003, into early drafts of Colin Powell's infamous United Nations speech.

Whatever her later doubts, moreover, Rice participated in the effort to drive home this connection in the minds of the American public. In September 2002, she claimed that "there clearly are contacts between al Qaeda and Iraq that can be documented; there clearly is testimony that some of the contacts have been important contacts and that there's a relationship here." One CBS News story reporting her comments noted that "Condoleezza Rice's statements . . . are the strongest yet alleging contacts between al Qaeda and the Iraqi government. Previously, evidence of the two working together was tenuous, or came from unreliable sources."[68]

※

The drumbeat in the direction of Iraq thus began as the smoke was still clearing from the attacks. As one source who attended many early planning meetings after 9/11 put it, there are "not two separate go-to-war decisions here. Iraq is directly related to the war on terror decision."[69] And the implicit assumption was that they would get to Iraq soon enough: "support for what would become" the invasion of Iraq was growing rapidly, one source close to the planning process recounted.[70] "Even before we went into Afghanistan," another source indicated, the military planning discussion was moving to Iraq.[71]

Rumsfeld is a fascinating character in this emerging policy direction. As we have seen, his natural style was to question, probe, and offer alternatives and scenarios—but rarely to settle, quickly or sometimes ever, on a simple statement of intent. Despite his clear demands for attention to Saddam Hussein in those first days, for example, one former senior official with knowledge of his thinking "does not believe Rumsfeld was keen to go to war." He was merely playing with possibilities and discussing options, "doing what he should have done"—taking seriously the possibility that an avowed American enemy might have been connected to an attack. Rumsfeld as a rule "delighted in studied ambiguity"; taking a firm position involved risk. Rumsfeld, this official claims, always hoped for some outcome besides war.[72] But such an indirect, noncommittal approach, as much as it raises good questions, doesn't always ensure that they are answered effectively, or that the answers are implemented well. The secretary of defense would leave the war planning process at times rudderless as people groped around without the clear direction that Rumsfeld often proved reluctant to give.

※

In March 2003, Vice President Cheney hosted a celebratory dinner at his home. The United States had ousted Saddam Hussein; it had finally achieved the long-standing goal of regime change, and the end of Saddam's rule was something to commemorate. Guests asked the vice president when the decision for war was made. "I am pretty sure it was decided right after 9/11 to go in," Cheney replied. "But it took us all too long if you ask me."[73]

※

More evidence on the emerging focus on Iraq in the days after 9/11 comes from Richard Clarke. A longtime nonpartisan civil servant, Clarke—a gravel-voiced bulldog of a man—had been held over from the Clinton NSC to work counterterrorism issues. He also happened to be one of the few career officials in the orbit of the Bush crowd who was tough, experienced, and frankly irascible enough to speak his mind. He had been speaking it, in fact, for months: prior to 9/11, Clarke and his counterterrorism staff had been issuing a never-ending drumbeat of warnings about an imminent al Qaeda attack, vainly demanding military action against the group's Afghan hideouts.

On September 12, expecting a session on responses to al Qaeda, Clarke walked instead "into a series of discussions about Iraq." His "friends in the Pentagon," Clarke wrote later, had already started "telling me that the word was we'd be invading Iraq sometime in 2002." In the meeting, according to Clarke, Paul Wolfowitz argued that the al Qaeda attack could not have been launched without help, probably Iraqi help. Rumsfeld referred to "getting Iraq" and, seemingly mindful of the resonance needed to achieve the goal of a demonstration effect, complained that "there were no decent targets for bombing in Afghanistan and that we should consider bombing Iraq, which, he said, had better targets." Eventually the group settled on an al-Qaeda-and-Afghanistan-first approach—but it was clear to everyone that a bigger campaign was brewing that would draw in other countries.[74] And again, this was *the day after 9/11*—it took only hours for the concept of a massive global campaign, with regime change in Iraq as a central feature, to emerge as the default policy option.

For the time being, though, the most senior officials were not ready to *formally* declare that a choice had been made to use force against Saddam Hussein. Several times between September 12 and 15, Wolfowitz pressed the same argument: go after Iraq first, or at a minimum Iraq and Afghanistan at the same time. The suggestion went nowhere. "No one supported that," in the words of a senior official present for many of these early discussions.[75] The president said it was not time to make the decision about Iraq.

But in another sense, an implicit judgment *had* been made, a natural subordinate implication of the rapidly forming notion of a global war on terror. The new risk calculus could not tolerate Saddam Hussein in power. Removing him had long been the right thing to do, but now it had become an obligation as well.

⁊₹

These two conflicting decisions, against *immediate* war but at the same time clearly in favor of *eventually* decisive action against Saddam, both emerged after 9/11. Their contradictions would make the Bush administration appear more dishonest than was really the case. To the best of my awareness, few if any senior officials saw the combination as an intentional effort to mislead the world. They did not decide to invade Iraq on 9/11, *and then* decide to cover it up. They decided *not* to act against Iraq in the first phase of the war, even though a powerful argument for doing so had been lodged. But they also knew, whether consciously or not, that they would come back to Saddam.

Such divergent impulses help to explain President Bush's reactions to these first days. He cast a skeptical eye on claims of coordination between Iraq and al Qaeda, but displayed a visceral sense of Saddam's possible involvement. Clarke has described an encounter with Bush on the evening of September 12, when the president pulled Clarke and a couple of his aides into a small conference room. "Look," Clarke quotes the president as saying, "I know you have a lot to do and all . . . but I want you, as soon as you can, to go back over everything, everything. See if Saddam did this. See if he's linked in any way." Clarke replied that al Qaeda was responsible. Bush said he knew that, but he wanted "any shred" of evidence that Iraq was involved as well. After Clarke said there was no evidence of Iraqi support for al Qaeda, Bush finally shot back, "Look into Iraq, Saddam," and left.[76]

The evidence against such a connection, however, began to pile up. An interagency group quickly convened, looked at the available intelligence, and agreed that there was "no cooperation" between Iraq and al

Qaeda. This message was sent in a memo to the president. Clarke says he got a response back from Deputy National Security Advisor Steve Hadley saying, "Do it again." Clarke assumed that the White House was angry that it hadn't received the answer that it wanted; Hadley later told *60 Minutes* that he was only doing due diligence. He asked Clarke to look again "to make sure there was no new emerging evidence that Iraq was involved."[77]

Regardless of the facts, early questions about a possible Iraqi role were already shaping public opinion. By September 13, a *Time*/CNN poll discovered that 78 percent of Americans believed that Saddam Hussein was involved in the attacks.[78] Within forty-eight hours of the 9/11 attacks, the Bush administration had Iraq clearly in its sights—and public opinion was already coalescing in support of such a gambit.

⁊₹

The emotional resonance of the attacks, and the hothouse atmosphere of fear and vulnerability, would persist for months in part due to the influence of the "threat matrix," a list of all the many terrorist threats the intelligence world was tracking at any one time. In the post-9/11 demand for more and more information, the filters of intelligence analysis and reliability had been removed, and a tsunami of terrifying, speculative reports plowed into the administration. The threat matrix ran to several pages and was given to the president and senior officials every morning. "You could drive yourself crazy," George Tenet admits, "believing all or even half of what was in it."[79] Condoleezza Rice's biographer Elisabeth Bumiller writes that Rice "felt like she was constantly on edge, in a state of paranoia, but a rational paranoia, as even old threats—and Iraq would soon be one—took on new meaning. . . . In retrospect, Rice came to believe that these frantic, emotional weeks affected the psyche of Bush and his inner circle in ways that anyone outside could scarcely appreciate."[80] One White House staffer described it as an "almost suffocating amount of tension and stress."[81]

⁊₹

Within a few days, the formal bureaucratic policy-making process of the government cranked to life and began to catch up to the visceral reactions to 9/11. On September 13, the Deputies Committee of the interagency process met to discuss an emerging options paper in advance of a larger NSC meeting scheduled for Camp David on the fifteenth. Paul Wolfowitz thought the reasoning in the draft paper was too narrow. He wanted a new memo for Camp David that would convey the truly transformative campaign he had in mind. What he was worried about—what all the Defense officials would worry about—was taking "hasty action that produced only meager effects," which would end up letting the air out of any effort to achieve a demonstration effect and encouraging US enemies. Rumsfeld himself warned against action that was "hollow, ineffective, embarrassing."[82] At the same time, neither he nor anyone else commissioned formal analysis to examine these claims: Was such an effect possible? If so, what would be needed to create one? What were the risks?

Meanwhile, they had to move quickly beyond ideas to action, but the first days produced mostly frustration, at least from the Department of Defense's point of view. The same day at a meeting of the "War Cabinet," CIA Director George Tenet laid out an aggressive covert action program to go after terrorists. The CIA concept was the only idea on offer, because the Pentagon had no Afghan invasion plan ready to go—and there was a definite appetite for action. "George Bush was going a hundred miles an hour by then," Tenet writes. "And if you couldn't keep up, he wasn't interested in you."

꙰

Another recent event began weighing on people's minds on those days: the results of an exercise called "Dark Winter," about a hypothetical smallpox attack on the United States.[83] Senior officials worried about a connection to Iraq, and Saddam's biological weapons program. But the wargame did not rely on a detailed analysis of what Saddam Hussein actually *possessed*, only what he *might be able to get* in a worst-case analysis. This line of thinking—to remove potential threats as well as actual ones, to operate

on the basis of the worst case—became a consistent theme in the arguments of war proponents. Doug Feith astonishingly suggests that even if
the intelligence did not suggest that Saddam actually possessed WMDs,
the Bush administration would still have gone to war based on the future
risk of Saddam's rearming.[84]

The changed mindset about risk helps to explain comments of
Bush administration officials downplaying the importance of certainty
behind intelligence assessments of Iraq's WMD stockpiles. For purists,
the distinction was essential: If Saddam didn't have WMDs, there was no
rationale for war. Under the new risk calculus, however, even a chance
that Saddam was headed for an arsenal he could share with terrorists was
intolerable.[85] Senior officials told a team of *USA Today* reporters that a
direct connection "wasn't necessary for Bush. He saw the threat of future
terrorism by Saddam as reason enough."[86] Paul Wolfowitz said that direct
proof of an immediate WMD threat from Iraq wasn't so much the issue.
"These people have made absolutely clear what their intentions are," and
that was good enough for him.[87]

This was the central lesson of a changed risk calculus: dangers that
before could be managed and outlasted could no longer be allowed to fes-
ter. But this too was an instinctive rather than an analytical conclusion,
and it was starkly inconsistent in its application. Pakistan, for example,
had much stronger ties to extremist groups than Iraq, as well as a large
and growing nuclear arsenal—risks that the administration was willing to
live with after 9/11. Iraq had been on the to-do list of many senior officials for years, and so it leaped to the top of the risk calculus arguments.
But they were never analytically consistent.

※

Joint Chiefs Chairman General Hugh Shelton, watching these early
days and weeks unfold, became increasingly disgusted. "At some point
Rumsfeld and Wolfowitz started pushing hard to attack Iraq," he writes,
because, in his view, they saw 9/11 as "an ideal opportunity to end the
problems we were having with Saddam Hussein—just blame the 9/11

attacks on him." Shelton saw no evidence of such links and opposed the emerging drift toward war, but from his vantage point "Rumsfeld really didn't seem to care" about such evidence "because this was a golden opportunity to go after Saddam Hussein. . . . *We gotta get this guy* was all we were hearing from Rumsfeld and Wolfowitz. . . . It was almost like paranoia."[88]

⌘

In Baghdad, Saddam Hussein, who had a long history of misreading Washington's mood, badly underestimated the growing hostility.[89] For all his adventurism and belligerence, Hussein somehow continued to see Iraq and the United States as natural allies in the battle against radical Islamic ideologies represented by Iran but also many militant groups.[90] Now, surely, Washington would turn to its erstwhile regional partner for assistance.

In one interview with FBI interrogator George Piro after the war, Saddam said that he had "wanted to have a relationship with the United States but was not given the chance, as the United States was not listening to anything Iraq had to say."[91] As the WMD allegations began to pour in after 9/11, Saddam would become confused. He had given specific orders for Iraq to be disarmed—what was the problem? American intelligence surely knew this. When he asked his senior officials if Iraq still possessed WMDs, he was told, "No."[92]

Much was made at the time of the fact that Iraq was one of the few countries in the world to "praise" the 9/11 attacks. In fact, the statement was made by Saddam's son Uday, in his personal newspaper *Babil*. "What does it matter what my son says?" Saddam demanded in 2003. "Was he a member of the government? No." Nixon told Saddam that *Babil* was taken to be a semiofficial publication, and that the US government "still thought that Uday spoke for him. Saddam just rolled his eyes and laughed when he heard this."[93] In other interviews Saddam claimed that he was sure other officials, such as Tariq Aziz, had drafted and sent letters *disapproving* of the attack.[94] One summary of the postwar interrogations

of senior Iraqis concludes that "Saddam knew that Baghdad had no connection with the al-Qaida attacks and assumed that the United States
would also know this"—it simply never occurred to him that Washington would blame him for the attack.[95]

⅔

The division between the two components of thinking about Iraq—the
sense that something would have to be done combined with a hesitation to commit to war immediately—produced an important distinction
in the American policy-making apparatus, a gap between what can be
understood as formal and informal war planning tracks.[96] The formal
track—the established NSC, principals, deputies, and other interagency
meetings to discuss Iraq options and issues—would plod along, stumbling and meandering and pulling off into cul-de-sacs. Some of the interagency groups did some important and useful work in readying various
aspects of the war plan, but in terms of the judgment itself, this track
never attacked the main question. The official line was that everything
was for "planning purposes," war was a "last option," and the "final decision" was not made until perhaps January 2003, or even later.

Running beneath this formal layer, however, was a powerful second
track, one composed of a subset of officials who worked on the understanding that an informal decision had already been reached: the United
States would do whatever was necessary, including invasion, to remove
Saddam from power. A whole series of actions emerged from this second
layer—covert actions aimed at Saddam's regime, orders to begin military
planning, national security directives to the entire government to begin
war preparations—that *presupposed* a decision long before the formal
track ever got there.

This distinction is yet another factor that accounts for the seeming
deception of the Iraq war decision. The administration would publicly
deny that a decision had been made, even as many secret activities—from
military planning to troop movements to the eventual insertion of CIA
teams to lay the groundwork for invasion—operated on the assumption

that it had. To be sure, some of the top officials recognized the distinction between formal and informal tracks and knew, to some extent, that they were playing a double game.[97] Advocates were "using the 9/11 situation to promote their Iraq preferences,"[98] one former senior official said. But many refused to admit, either at that time or later, that this was the case. As the informal track surged ahead, people restricted to operating on the formal track—due to their clearance level, position, or uncertain loyalty to the emerging cause—would be left wondering: *What the hell happened?* Some of those surprised by the accelerating momentum to war were very senior indeed. One source told me that Secretary of State Colin Powell thought he had so firmly shot down the idea of invading Iraq in the days after 9/11 that he was shocked when it reappeared, this time as the assumed direction of US policy, months later.[99]

Others sniffed out the existence of the informal track right from the start. Many of these were military officers with access to the accelerating war planning underway. As early as a month or two after 9/11, some of them began to suspect the obvious: *This is happening. There's no way we're doing all of this for nothing.* Some senior civilians began to have the same understanding. One official involved at various levels "smelled in the wind" shortly after 9/11 that war with Iraq was coming. No one had told him so directly. But he thought it was likely to happen—and like people all over the government, he began acting on the *conjecture* that it would happen, even in the absence of direct instructions.[100] We see the same pattern again and again, from late 2001 right through February 2003—people across the US government deciding to simply *assume* that a war decision had been made and behave accordingly. That was how the judgment emerged, gradually, after 9/11: the accretion of a generalized assumption rather than the exercise of a pointed choice.

※

On September 14 and 15, a third major post-9/11 milestone occurred as a number of principals and deputies gathered at Camp David for the first in-depth deliberations on the reaction to 9/11. This was the first clear moment when the formal and informal decision tracks collided. While the basic outlines of the emerging strategy were already in place—a global campaign against terrorism and its state supporters—many details remained to be worked out. The president's instinct was crystal clear: it was time to kick some ass. At a break during one early meeting, President Bush was chatting with a small group. One of them—a State Department official—suggested a diplomatic overture to the Taliban in Afghanistan. Bush said nothing until the man walked away. Then he turned to the others and said, "Fuck diplomacy. We are going to war."[101]

It quickly became clear that, given the time it would take to get large-scale military options underway, most of the initial actions would be left to the intelligence community. On September 15, Tenet laid out the emerging Afghan plan in a brief titled, modestly, "Destroying International Terrorism." The next day he sent a memo to key officials throughout the CIA. Its title: "We're at War."[102]

Even here, less than a hundred hours after 9/11, a critical point of debate was whether to include Iraq in the first phase of that campaign. Doug Feith writes that the NSC discussion paper laid out three options: go after al Qaeda alone; go after al Qaeda and the Taliban; and do both—as well as taking steps "to eliminate the Iraqi threat." Even two days after 9/11, Feith says, "it was a common assumption among government officials that a global war on terrorism would, at some point, involve some kind of showdown with Iraq." The question was whether that showdown should comprise "part of the *initial* US response to 9/11."[103] Wolfowitz remained the lead advocate for that option: he famously said at the Camp David session that there was a 10–50 percent chance Saddam was involved in 9/11, though where he got these numbers was not apparent.[104] Peter Baker's account suggests that, as Wolfowitz kept pushing the idea, Bush became terse. "How many times do I have to tell you we are *not* going after Iraq right this minute?"[105]

But Wolfowitz was not speaking out of turn. One former senior official said that while Rumsfeld "allowed Wolfowitz to make the case—which is not the same as the secretary making it" himself—this was only the no-fingerprints approach at work, and Rumsfeld did make some comments endorsing action against Iraq.[106] In fact, what is astonishing is that the *official DoD position* for the Camp David meeting mirrored Wolfowitz's argument, recommending that the United States attack Afghanistan, Iraq, and al Qaeda *as a package*. Feith says it outright in his book: he and senior Defense Department official Peter Rodman wrote the memo that argued that all three ought to be "immediate priority targets for initial action" in the emerging war on terror.[107] Within four days of 9/11, the formal policy position of the Defense Department was to attack Iraq, and do so rapidly.

But while everyone seemed to understand that this decision was coming, few were ready to commit to it this early.[108] Another official present at the meeting said that when Wolfowitz raised the issue, "no one picked up that cudgel. We stuck with Afghanistan."[109] General Shelton claims in his memoirs that President Bush asked him privately about the Iraq urgency—"What am I missing here, Hugh?"—and Shelton told him there was no link to Iraq, that he should "stand firm" against calls for quick action.[110] Colin Powell had the perception that "neither Rumsfeld nor Cheney seemed to support an early move against Saddam Hussein."[111] Condoleezza Rice would later explain that when Wolfowitz brought up Iraq, she saw it as a "huge distraction."[112] Even Cheney, perhaps reading his boss's leanings, came down against Wolfowitz, saying, "If we go after Saddam Hussein, we lose our rightful place as good guy"—which was true enough and would remain true even when Cheney chose to disregard it, in 2003.

But the decision not to go after Saddam was only tentative. All agreed that the question would recur, and President Bush specifically stated his belief that Iraq was somehow involved in the 9/11 attacks. The next day, Bush told Rice, "We won't do Iraq now, we're putting Iraq off. But eventually we'll have to return to that question."[113] One senior official said that the president said "explicitly" about Iraq that "we're not doing that" at the moment. But it just as clearly remained simmering on the back burner. Bush had a "non-hidden agenda that the United States was going to have to deal with Iraq."[114] Another senior official said that the president did not *reject* Wolfowitz's argument—he only said, "Not yet."[115]

Cheney had voted no, but it is interesting how he describes the emerging consensus in his memoirs. He writes that he made the case that "Afghanistan, where the 9/11 terrorists had trained and plotted, *should be first*" [emphasis added]. "I believed it was important to deal with the threat Iraq posed, but not until we had an effective plan for taking down the Taliban and denying al Qaeda a safe haven in Afghanistan."[116]

By September 15, therefore, the decision to remove Saddam Hussein had already been made, in the minds of all the key decision-makers. It was a question of when, not if. Yet the debate was already taking on a crimped and limited character. None of the discussion had so far even hinted at the huge questions involved: What would they do when they owned Iraq? What would come next? What would the second-order effects be? Right from the outset, the debate was about when to get rid of Saddam—not whether to do so, and not, in any meaningful sense, how to do it. They were debating the timing of an imperative rather than the costs and risks of a strategic option. The decision to use whatever US power was necessary to unseat Saddam was not a carefully considered option measured against well-defined goals. It was simply the right and necessary thing to do, and the Bush administration would now set about doing it, with barely a glance backward.

※

It cannot therefore be a coincidence that when, on September 17— according to the public report of the 9/11 Commission—President Bush signed an order for war in Afghanistan, that order also called for updated military plans for going to war in Iraq.[117] Also on the seventeenth, according to the commission, Paul Wolfowitz wrote a memo to Rumsfeld reiterating the opinions he had expressed at Camp David and calling for rapid action against Iraq. Wolfowitz wrote again the next day, pointing this time to past evidence of Iraqi involvement in international terrorism.[118]

Two days later, Rumsfeld sent a message to his regional combatant commanders (the major US warfighting commands around the world), asking for revised war plans for the campaign against terrorism and making clear the scope of what he had in mind. His message instructed them on the themes he wanted to see: "Targets worldwide, such as UBL Al Qaida cells in regions outside Afghanistan and even outside the Middle East. . . . It will be important to indicate that our field of action is much wider than Afghanistan." He wanted to show a "capability or a boldness that will give pause to terrorists and/or those who harbor terrorists." "The legitimacy of our actions" in this process would not depend on the degree of international support they could gather, Rumsfeld wrote in a different September 19 memo. "More nearly the opposite is true: the legitimacy of other countries' opinions should be judged by their attitude toward this systematic, uncivilized assault on a free way of life."[119]

This call for worldwide demonstration effects would reach sometimes absurd lengths. On September 20, Doug Feith, as he later confirmed in a public op-ed, suggested that the United States ought to hit terrorists outside the Middle East, not even connected to al Qaeda.[120] One source described a meeting at which Feith pushed attacks on supposed terrorist cells in Latin America. "Well, they all read the newspapers," he said in explaining his rationale. "If we knock one back, the others will take notice." The source explained ruefully, "I wish I could adequately describe the eye-rolling in the room at that point."[121]

By September 20, advocates of action against Iraq were speaking openly enough about their intentions that they made the *New York Times*. The report said that Wolfowitz and Scooter Libby favored attacks against Iraq "with the aim of toppling President Saddam Hussein."[122] Libby prized his anonymity, seeing it as an element of professionalism, and was reportedly horrified to see his name in the newspaper. But he did admit later that he advocated for an early Iraq option alongside Wolfowitz.[123]

Within less than a week of 9/11, there was seemingly irresistible momentum for preparing the United States for war with Iraq.

⁂

On September 18 and 19, the Defense Policy Board, a group of nongovernmental defense policy experts who gather to debate issues and conduct studies to provide input to the DoD, met to discuss Iraq. The top leadership of the department was present to hear from, among other people, Ahmad Chalabi. A *Vanity Fair* report says Chalabi insisted that "although there was as yet no evidence linking Iraq to 9/11, failed states such as Saddam's were a breeding ground for terrorists, and Iraq . . . possessed W.M.D. During the later part of the second day, Wolfowitz and Rumsfeld listened carefully to the debate. 'Rumsfeld was getting confirmation of his own instincts. . .' Richard Perle says. 'He seemed neither surprised nor discomfited by the idea of taking action against Iraq.'"[124]

By early October, Chalabi was being courted by allies inside the administration. Richard Bonin's account claims that John Hannah, a senior aide to Vice President Cheney, met with Chalabi at a coffee shop near the White House and told him that senior officials inside the administration were "looking for people who know about Iraq's weapons of mass destruction." He asked Chalabi, "Can you introduce us to any?" The reason for the request was transparent, Chalabi immediately saw. "It was to push forward the policy," he said later. "Hannah said, 'The administration needs information about weapons of mass destruction so we can move forward with this agenda.'"[125]

These interactions with Chalabi reflected the beginning of a wide-ranging search for alternative sources of intelligence on Iraq, both its weapons programs and its connections to terrorism. Like the process as a whole, there would be formal and informal channels. And the informal ones would soon be teeming with supposed evidence of Saddam's connection to terrorism and ambitions for WMDs.

A number of senior officials, including Wolfowitz and Vice President Cheney, pushed these efforts. They did not trust the US intelligence community to deliver the full story and repeatedly injected half-baked reports and unverified intelligence into the process. Meanwhile Chalabi was accelerating long-standing efforts to collect—or, some would say, manufacture—evidence that it was imperative to topple Saddam. He began proffering defectors to US intelligence and media outlets, bearing amazing stories: of terrorist training sites, ties to al Qaeda, biological weapons programs. The US media proved arguably the most gullible customer of all, scarfing up Chalabi's people and broadcasting their claims with little qualification or double-checking.[126]

Soon, Chalabi's INC was getting in on the act, throwing alleged defectors at the CIA. Every couple of weeks the vice president's office would call the CIA, one source recounted, and say, "There's a defector, and you need to talk to him." The CIA would dispatch a team and invariably find the source unreliable—or worse. One supposed eyewitness to Iraqi nuclear work had "a third-grade understanding of nuclear physics," according to a specialist in the debriefing team. In another case the INC delivered a source who had already been dismissed as a fabricator by US, British, and Austrian intelligence. "You guys pay me a salary to make these judgments," a CIA official replied to the White House—and suggested that it *just might be* that if three different intelligence services had concluded the source was unreliable, then chances were, he *was* unreliable.[127]

Meanwhile, shortly after 9/11, Doug Feith and other senior officials assembled a tiny group of people to begin to look into global connections between terrorists and their presumed state sponsors. This effort has been explained in detail elsewhere,[128] but the upshot was a massive briefing on sinister global networks of terrorist intent and capability. Much of it was based on raw intelligence that was cherry-picked and unevaluated, and the initial reactions from the intelligence community were not positive (though accounts differ on just how confrontational those meetings were). The goal of this effort was not so much to locate the truth of the matter as it was to affirm the image of a giant, global, networked conspiracy of terrorist movements that demanded a coordinated US response. This vision was indirectly tied, in that sense, to planning efforts in the Joint Staff to develop a "war plan" for the battle against this shady network. Going after al Qaeda would not be enough, these briefings implied. The campaign had to be much wider and more ambitious.

The message from more formal channels continued to be very different. Bush received a number of reports stating the intelligence community's opinion in fairly unequivocal terms: they possessed no evidence that Iraq was involved in 9/11 and had little reason to suspect deep contacts between Iraq and al Qaeda.[129] Yet Feith's informal intelligence operation—linked with sympathetic officials elsewhere in Defense and in the vice president's office—fed the preexisting conceptions of key senior leaders with portraits of a looming global alliance of evildoers. And the narrative stuck. Shortly after he received a formal intelligence briefing that meaningful ties between Iraq and al Qaeda did not exist, Bush publicly claimed, "You can't distinguish between al Qaeda and Saddam when you talk about the war on terror." Rumsfeld added a day later: "We have what we consider to be credible evidence that al Qaeda leaders have sought contacts with Iraq who could help them acquire . . . weapons of mass destruction capabilities."[130]

But if Iraq's ties to terrorism found little support in formal US intelligence analysis, the story on Saddam's WMDs was very different. The message was fairly consistent from the start: Saddam's programs were large and growing. Administration officials would exaggerate and embellish the picture they were getting in some of their public statements, but broadly speaking, everyone assumed that Iraq's WMD programs were moving ahead. This was the overwhelming impression from years of evidence that had accumulated on the issue.

There were contrary signals, if anyone had been interested in picking them up. Richard Bonin describes an interview with Amer al-Saadi, the chief of the Iraqi chemical and biological weapons program. There would have been no reason to trust the man; Iraqi officials like him had been lying for years. And so when he said, during an interview for an October

2001 *60 Minutes* broadcast, "There's nothing left, absolutely nothing left" of Iraq's WMD program, no one took the claim seriously. The following April, Bonin was back in Iraq, and several senior Iraqi officials asked him to return to Washington with a message: "Saddam was now willing to do whatever it took to avoid war," including "offering inspectors unfettered access, including surprise visits, to any of Iraq's suspected WMD sites." Bonin dutifully reported the offer to senior people at the White House and the CIA. "Both came back to me with essentially the same reaction," he writes. "The time for trusting the Saddam regime had long passed."[131]

⁊ᴇ

On September 20, President Bush met with British prime minister Tony Blair. When the subject turned to Iraq, the president repeated his line from Camp David: Iraq would not be the immediate focus.[132] Yet an equally strong emphasis of the president's conversation was that they *would* be dealing decisively with Saddam, and relatively soon. It wasn't off the table so much as pushed to one side.[133]

Great Britain's ambassador in Washington, Sir Christopher Meyer, would reflect years later on the emerging dialogue on Iraq. One critical question, he realized, is whether—as early as this September 20 meeting—Bush and Blair had decided "come hell or high water to go to war" and then afterward concealed this decision. Meyer, with access to senior British as well as American policy-makers, does not believe this was the case. "Sitting in Washington" during these months, he contends, "talking to contacts, the road to war looked to me at that time anything but straight or the destination preordained."[134]

The road may not have been straight, but the destination was indeed becoming pretty well determined. The following day, Rumsfeld jotted an idea in one of his infamous snowflakes. "At the right moment," he suggested, "we may want to give Saddam Hussein a way out for his family to live in comfort."[135]

⁊ᴇ

There was, therefore, no formal decision for war against Iraq in these early days. But in the intense and emotionally charged atmosphere of that period, just two weeks after 9/11, a critical meeting left little doubt about just where the unofficial track of policy was headed.

On September 26, Rumsfeld says in his memoir, Bush met with the secretary of defense alone, in the Oval Office. "The President leaned back in the black leather chair behind his desk," Rumsfeld writes. "He asked that I take a look at the shape of our military plans on Iraq."[136] When he returned to the Pentagon from that fateful meeting, according to several accounts, Rumsfeld jotted a note for the record. He relayed that the president had asked about Rumsfeld's son, who was fighting drug addiction. "I broke down and cried," Rumsfeld confessed. "An amazing day—He is a fine human being—I am so grateful he is President. I am proud to be working for him." Before that very personal and compassionate moment, Bush had summarized the instructions from the NSC meeting. "I want you to develop a plan to invade Ir[aq]," Bush told Rumsfeld. "Do it outside normal channels." And presumably hinting at a desire to avoid an endless nation-building exercise and exhausting occupation: "Do it creatively so we don't have to take so much cover."[137]

※

Four days later, on September 30, Rumsfeld sent a memo to President Bush—copying Cheney, Powell, Tenet, and Rice—that laid out a number of core elements of his emerging view.[138] In two blunt pages, it conveys the emerging consensus of many aspects of the "war on terror," but also betrays many assumptions that had not been examined or tested.

One basic message came through loud and clear: the goal of their combined activities was *not* merely to get al Qaeda. Instead, they ought to "capitalize on our strong suit, which is not finding a few hundred terrorists in the caves of Afghanistan." The goal must be much more ambitious and transformative: "If the war does not significantly change the world's political map, the US will not achieve its aim. There is value in being clear on the order of magnitude of the necessary change."

Warming to his theme, Rumsfeld proposed specific goals: force regime change in Afghanistan "and another key State (or two) that supports terrorism (to strengthen political and military efforts to change policies elsewhere)." Drive Syria out of Lebanon. Dismantle WMD capabilities in several states whose names have been redacted, but surely must have included Iraq. In order to heed Bush's injunction to keep the costs down, Rumsfeld took up the Wolfowitz strategy of supporting rebels to overthrow regimes rather than ordering a US invasion—at least as an opening gambit. The "US strategic theme," Rumsfeld wrote, "should be aiding local peoples to rid themselves of terrorists and to free themselves of regimes that support terrorism. US Special Operations Forces and intelligence personnel should make allies of Afghanis [sic], Iraqis, Lebanese, Sudanese and others who would use US equipment, training, financial, military and humanitarian support to root out and attack the common enemies."

Once again, vast assumptions lurked between the lines of such proposals. The biggest assumption was that terrorism flowed from hostile states, and that American toughness was needed to cow them back into line. If, instead, terrorism derived from state weakness and fragility as well as thousands of individual choices by susceptible recruits, then such a stance would certainly make little difference, and might even be counterproductive.[139] Could a global campaign achieve its goals without addressing the support for extremist groups believed to emanate from Pakistan and Saudi Arabia? None of this was subjected to any analysis.

Another key assumption in Rumsfeld's memo was the intention—an implicit preference that would guide US policy through Afghanistan and into Iraq—to go light, to use local friends to achieve the desired objectives rather than a heavy-handed, long-term US presence. But no one had a sense of whether this would work, or whether it would achieve the outcomes the administration wanted. With regard to Iraq, at least, most officials I spoke with made clear that whenever the exile-based or "enclave" strategies were raised, they were just as quickly shot down.

There would be "one meeting and then you wouldn't hear about it" again, one official explained.[140] One very senior official does not recall seeing a direct proposal for the plan and is not aware that it was briefed to the Joint Staff. The idea, he says, never had an active life among military planners.[141] But if the exiles could not do the job, and yet Saddam still had to be forced from power, that only left one meaningful alternative: invasion.

꙰

In the Pentagon on the Joint Staff, in the J-5 Strategic Plans and Policy division, a special task force had been set up—the "Strategic Planning Cell"—to develop a war plan for the Global War on Terror. The Joint Staff assembled a group of twenty to thirty officers headed by an army brigadier general—General Jeffrey Schloesser—to write the plan.[142] They worked at a breakneck pace, twelve or more hours a day, six or seven days a week, for two solid months, October to November 2001. According to Eric Schmitt and Thom Shanker, another senior Joint Staff officer, General John Abizaid met with Schloesser after just a week to convey the urgency. "'Have we killed any al Qaeda yet?' Abizaid demanded, staring at Schloesser," Schmitt and Shanker write.[143]

The planners were told to do blue-sky thinking unencumbered by constraints. "We have a unique space in time to shake the Etch-a-Sketch clean," one officer in the group later explained the message they received. "To get a lot of stuff done off of our [national security] to-do list." If planners "came back with something that applied the normal rules," another officer said, "it was kicked back" with the question "Don't you know the world has changed?" The mentality was summed up by one source: "Pretend there are no rules now. We've been given a moment in time when we can do anything we want."

From the very beginning, there was a "strong perception," another source said, that "this was much more than just al Qaeda versus the United States." It "had to be a global response, a much more comprehensive approach." Some doubted the feasibility or value of such an encompassing response. They argued that the attack and its author were very specific and that the response should be equally so. "Once we killed UBL, we'd be finished," according to this view.[144] But the guidance was clear—the United States intended to be far more ambitious than that. And so the planners pressed forward.

⁂

As they did so, however, an uncomfortable question cropped up: as far as the Joint Staff planning cell's research was concerned, Iraq's role as a state sponsor of terrorism did not warrant its inclusion as a first-stage target of the conflict. Schloesser had a blunt conversation with the chairman of the Joint Chiefs, General Myers, about why they were adding Iraq to the plan when it had no connection to 9/11. "I think this is really unwise," he said. "We're going to drain our resources and goodwill." The world was on America's side. Invading Iraq would "piddle that away."

Myers was blunt. "Get with the team," Eric Schmitt and Thom Shanker report that he told Schloesser. His message, according to that account and sources in the planning cell, was clear: their team had to get on board, to get their head into the game on Iraq and work it into the broader war.

Another person working in the cell at the time told me Schloesser came back from this this discussion in a foul mood. His reaction, in a nutshell, was, *What the fuck is this bullshit?* But he was a professional military officer, and he had been given a direct order.[145]

⁂

At about this same time, the *New York Times* reporter Bill Keller happened to be traveling with Secretary of State Powell. Powell sounded distinctly uninterested in going after Iraq. "Iraq will be sitting there after this campaign is well along," he said. "Iraq isn't going anywhere. It's a fairly weakened state. It's doing some things we don't like. We'll continue to contain it. But there really was no need at this point, unless there was really quite a smoking gun, to put Iraq at the top of the list." Later, in

October 2001, Keller "asked if [Powell] had seen anything to change his mind about targeting Iraq. He said he had not."[146]

Later, Powell would claim that he supported the idea of taking out Saddam, that his disagreements were more a matter of timing and technique. In a September 2005 interview with Barbara Walters, Powell said, "I'm always a reluctant warrior. . . . But when the president decided that it was not tolerable for this regime to remain in violation of all these U.N. resolutions, I'm right there with him with the use of force."[147]

※

Many of these same themes—a need to go after Saddam but an equally powerful requirement to do it carefully, if such a thing were possible— began to be echoed back to Washington from Tony Blair's government in London. An example is a note that Blair sent to Bush October 11—"CONFIDENTIAL AND PERSONAL FOR THE PRESIDENT"—offering his thoughts on the emerging war on terror.[148]

"I have no doubt we need to deal with Saddam," Blair wrote. "But if we hit Iraq now, we would lose the Arab world, Russia, probably half the EU[,] and my fear is the impact of all that on Pakistan." Yet he made clear he was arguing for a postponement, not taking Iraq off the list. "We can devise a strategy for Saddam deliverable at a later date." Part of the reason for this indirection was to avoid scrutiny. "We just don't need it debated too freely in public," Blair concluded, "until we know exactly what we want to do."

※

The anthrax attacks in the fall of 2001, which struck the US Congress and other targets, had an important and sometimes neglected role in solidifying the Bush administration's emerging thinking about the war. Along with other fearsome signs—such as an October report that senior officials had been exposed to botulinum toxin and would soon die[149]— this evidence of the risks of mass destruction weapons only made taking out Saddam seem more urgent.[150]

Some apparent attacks struck very close to home for senior officials. As reported by *Newsweek* in 2006, a strange letter arrived at the vice president's residence and triggered an alarm for anthrax. Cheney and his family went on an antibiotic regime and seemed, for a time, to have assumed they had been exposed. It turned out to be a false alarm.[151] In another case his daughter Liz got a call that her home had been infected with anthrax, and she had to have her nanny evacuate her children. It proved to be another false alarm, but the risk was clear: a state-terrorism nexus that supplied such weapons to those ready to attack the United States could not be tolerated.[152]

⁂

By early 2002, the outcome of the campaign in Afghanistan would create a convenient and newly minted analogy for advocates of action in Iraq. The Afghan mission took place in a physically and culturally demanding country, the place where "empires go to die." Many worried before the campaign that US forces would end up battling shadowy Taliban armies for years and taking huge casualties, as the Soviets and British had done in prior Afghan adventures.

And then, in a flash, it was all over, and advocates of action against Saddam received a gift-wrapped analogy to employ in making the case that their proposed operation could be accomplished at low cost.[153] Afghanistan was "supposed to be so hard," one source recalled. But instead it was "cheap and lean and it worked so easily" that it created an entirely different mindset—a model that could be replicated. The United States had done just what Wolfowitz and others had always suggested: used air power and small ground forces to empower local allies to win the war, all the while pushing back aggressively against ideas of long-term reconstruction projects and delegating the burden of postwar security mostly to allies.[154] (Wolfowitz himself pushed these concepts in internal debates on Afghanistan: Don't go in heavy, he suggested. Empower the militias. Don't liberate Afghanistan ourselves, but play "a supporting role, *helping Afghans liberate themselves* from the Taliban."[155]) In so doing, the

Afghan campaign suggested that the United States could kick over a hostile government and then promptly leave, sidestepping the sort of long-term nation building that was anathema to Rumsfeld, Bush, and others. "The US forces will not stay," Bush said at one NSC meeting, according to Bob Woodward. "We don't do police work."[156]

Coalition forces ended up taking down the government of a country of twenty-nine million people (several million more than Iraq's population) with some nine thousand US forces. They managed to find and install a friendly leader, Hamid Karzai. The effort gathered international support. It all seemed to work—and, according to the former senior official, "We thought that these concepts . . . might have some applicability in Iraq."[157] In Britain, too, some came to believe that Tony Blair's change in attitude toward Iraq in early 2002 was grounded in the experience of Afghanistan.[158]

Perhaps one of the most pernicious lessons of the Afghan experience was that the issue of governance could be jury-rigged after the fact, once the fighting was over. The administration set about the task once the Taliban had effectively been swept away and found Hamid Karzai, a candidate broadly acceptable to all the concerned parties. They convened an international conference in Germany to establish an international consensus on a way forward in building a new Afghan government, and they recruited international support for peacekeeping and economic assistance. It all seemed—for a brief, shining moment—so neat and clean. This experience may well have undermined any sense of urgency, as they turned their attention to Iraq, to address the governance issues well in advance.

Of course, in the longer term, this light-footprint vision in Afghanistan turned out to be fatally flawed, and the initial euphoria surrounding a seemingly quick and easy victory turned out to be wishful thinking. The Afghan government was too weak to keep order. Chaos returned, the Taliban strengthened, and the United States found itself gradually ratcheting up its presence to keep the country in one piece. When Bob Woodward interviewed Bush as early as August 2002, the analogy should have been collapsing—because, as Woodward writes, "The theoretical pronouncements Bush had made about not nation building have been discarded almost wholesale in the face of the need to keep Afghanistan together. He was at times acting like the Afghan budget director and bill collector."[159] That role metastasized over time, and the United States still has large military contingents in Afghanistan today, sixteen years after 9/11; in 2018 alone, the US budget for its Afghan mission was $45 billion—almost $20 billion more than the entire Department of Energy budget, two-thirds as much as the US federal government spent on the Department of Education, and equal to the entire budget of the Department of Homeland Security. At the time, though, the seeming confirmation of the light-footprint model provided potent fuel for wishful thinking that the United States could fulfill its perceived obligation to act without significant cost. In this way it empowered the disregard of costs, risks, and consequences that would be a centerpiece of the imperative-driven thinking on the choice to go to war in Iraq.

⁊⧸

One of the many ironies of the process was that the United States actually hesitated in the face of opportunities—costly though they may have been—to get Osama bin Laden during the concluding phases of the Afghan campaign. When bin Laden and his al Qaeda group holed up in a remote and complex system of caves in the Afghan-Pakistan borderlands known as Tora Bora, the administration did not drive home an uncompromising, all-out attack. It drew back and turned much of the battle over to its anti-Taliban Afghan allies, for reasons that remain perplexing to this day. When Bush heard the news of this failure, writes CIA official Michael Morell, "he was madder than I have ever seen him." Bush exploded: "How the hell could you lose him?"[160]

In his memoirs Rumsfeld offers various excuses. Local tribes didn't like outsiders. It would have taken too many troops. The intelligence on Tora Bora was uncertain. As is so often the case, he deflects responsibility:

"I believed a decision of this nature, which hinged on numerous operational details, was best made by the military commander in charge." It does appear that Franks offered some bracing advice about the constraints in applying US military power in those remote areas. Rumsfeld claims that he *offered* more troops, if anyone had just asked. He sent a memo to George Tenet, wondering whether they "might be missing an opportunity at Tora Bora."[161]

A group attacks the US homeland in one of the most heinous attacks of modern times. A president promises unremitting vengeance. And when it looks as if they have the architect of the attack cornered, they back off? They defer to the military commander? The secretary of defense *sends a memo?* While being prepared to launch a worldwide military campaign, alter long-standing US legal and traditional practices of human rights, and authorize wire-tapping of US citizens—all because of the intense risk posed by terrorists—this same administration then blanches at the precipice of early success?

Some have found these choices so astonishing that they must imply a conspiracy—to keep the basis for war alive, for example, and justify further aggression. If such a motive was explicitly in the minds of any senior officials, I have not seen evidence of it. But such ideas were, in more muted, strategically conceived, and (to their way of thinking) defensible terms, an important part of the thought process at the time. Rumsfeld himself has offered the explanation that an "emphasis on bin Laden concerned me. Our country's primary purpose was to try to prevent terrorists from attacking us again. There was far more to the threat posed by Islamist extremism than one man."[162] They were not as focused, Rumsfeld implies, on punishing those who conducted the attack than with sending much more general and profound messages. They were after a demonstration effect. Extinguishing al Qaeda in the first weeks after 9/11, Rumsfeld's comments seem to suggest, would have been an incomplete fulfillment of the obligation to drive home the consequences of trifling with the United States.

A senior administration official later told Peter Baker that "the only reason we went into Iraq . . . is we were looking for somebody's ass to kick. Afghanistan was too easy."[163]

⁓

On November 15, top Blair aide Jonathan Powell penned a memo to his prime minister titled "The War: What Comes Next?"[164] It was filled with a foreboding of rapid American action against Saddam. "There is a real danger that we will part company with the Americans on what comes next," Powell wrote. Right-wing Republicans "will want to carry on by bombing Iraq and Somalia. Bush's natural tendency would be to support them unless presented with an alternative." London needed a complete Iraq policy overhaul, Powell recommended. Its objective now had to be regime change, not just more inspectors—because, he suggested, a measured, nonbelligerent approach would no longer "cut any ice with the Americans."

⁓

A senior official agreed that, at first, he saw Rumsfeld's first orders to rehabilitate Iraq war plans as dusting off an aging planning document rather than getting ready to launch an imminent war. Rumsfeld, as far as this source recalls, did not push hard in the fall of 2001 for briefings or information on Iraq—he was concerned with the overall war on terror and Afghanistan.[165] But the military planning machine was clearly grinding into action, partly on Rumsfeld's orders. "The only thing they were thinking about was Iraq," one officer working in an air force strategy office said.[166] The implicit message was this: "We're gonna go in and finish what we didn't finish in '91."

Bob Woodward reports that Bush pulled Rumsfeld aside after a National Security Council meeting on November 21 and asked about the status of Iraq war plans. He told him to begin considering "what it would take to protect America by removing Saddam Hussein if we have to." He told Rumsfeld to do it quietly, without involving too many people.[167]

According to the chairman of the Joint Chiefs of Staff, General Richard Myers, Rumsfeld contacted him that same day to say "the president wants to know what kind of operations plan we have for Iraq." Six days later, Myers was on a plane to CENTCOM headquarters in Tampa, Florida, to discuss a revamped war plan with Rumsfeld and CENTCOM chief General Tommy Franks. Rumsfeld ordered him to "dust off your plan and get back to me next week." But as Myers makes clear later, Rumsfeld also "insisted on the strictest possible security for our planning," so that for the next six months, only a tiny group of military officers would be included.[168]

Rumsfeld's talking points for this discussion have been declassified—having originally been classified "Top Secret Close Hold"—and they depict an administration already leaning far forward in the saddle.[169] They refer to taking "slices of action" aimed at "building momentum for regime change"—slices as elaborate as efforts to "seize or destroy missile sites," "seize or destroy Republican Guard," and "deploy ground forces in western desert or south of Baghdad." Rumsfeld's handwritten notes on the talking points add a question of sequencing: "What order to create likelihood of collapse?" The talking points offer several rationales for escalating attacks on Saddam, including "Dispute over WMD inspections"; they make clear that the United States should not reduce its regional footprint (Rumsfeld's notes say, "Enhance current footprint") and must "be ready to strike from a standing start."

Very clearly, then, within two months of 9/11, the Defense Department was engaged in vigorous planning for actions that would collapse the Iraqi government. Notably, there is little mention here of the aftermath, and some of the approaches discussed were fairly minimal—military actions to create the conditions for Saddam's downfall, rather than an invade-and-occupy design. The talking points appear to reflect Rumsfeld's mindset throughout the planning: the United States was preparing to shove Saddam aside, not run Iraq. But as less elaborate, more indirect options began to emerge as infeasible, the focus of planning quickly moved to a classic, large-scale US military operation. But whether the light-footprint assumptions of the more indirect, Afghan-like options could be sustained once US tanks were parked in Baghdad—or whether, at that point, there would simply be no way to avoid the massive responsibility of a long-term occupation—was never broached.

One officer doing high-level planning work at CENTCOM[170] remembers very clearly that before Christmas of 2001, the focus had shifted to Iraq. It was a "foregone conclusion. . . . The dominant narrative was Iraq, I can say that definitively." No one was ready yet to say that it was happening; it was a lot of winks and nods. The officer and others asked their chain of command: What's this about? They "must have asked a hundred times," he recalls. And the answer kept coming back: We are telling you to rethink the war plan. Just do it.

⁂

Another set of British policy documents from the end of November and the beginning of December refers to strong pressure coming from Washington to make the choice—and perhaps act—as quickly as possible. "To meet US impatience," one memo bluntly concludes about possible new demands for WMD inspections, "a 12–18 month time-frame should be imposed."[171]

The British memos also began to emphasize a theme that would become commonplace over the coming year: an effort to use what just about everyone realized was a fruitless nod toward diplomacy to help *justify* military action, rather than providing a meaningful *alternative* to it. The coalition would demand that Saddam allow inspectors back in; "If this does not happen [we] will take action on Iraq." But it was "important not to be specific about what the action will consist of and not to set a deadline. . . . If asked, say regime change would be desirable, but not our formal objective for the moment." In other words, dissemble: insist that a "formal" judgment to invade had not been made—while continuing rapidly ahead with planning based on a clear and widely understood informal judgment to do exactly that. And ignore, essentially, the question of whether such an act would be justifiable under international law.

This covert strategy emerged clearly in another British memo of December 4—"The War Against Terrorism—the Second Phase." The original was marked "Top Secret/Personal/Eyes Only." There were only six copies, individually numbered.[172] One can see why: the memo essentially laid out a mechanism for tricking Western publics into war.

"Any link to 11 September and AQ is at best tenuous," the memo admitted, and publics were not ready to go after Saddam. "So we need a strategy for regime change that builds over time." Phase one would be "softening up"—focusing on Saddam's flouting of UN resolutions, saying "regime change is 'desirable' (though not yet setting it as a military objective)," supporting opposition groups, and demanding new inspections. The United States and Britain would do this "without specifying that we will take military action if the demand is not met," while signaling that "nothing is ruled out. But our time frame is deliberately vague."

"This is presentationally difficult," the memo confessed. They were making threats they didn't want to carry out for some time, until they had given Saddam the space to hang himself. The plan then suggested efforts to pressure Syria to reduce oil supplies to Iraq, boost support to oppositionists, "mount covert operations"—and "when the rebellion finally occurs we back it militarily," with air power and other support (the Afghan analogy once again). It was a strategy to sidle up to war "without so alarming people about the immediacy of action that we frighten the horses, lose Russia and/or half the EU and nervous Arab states and find ourselves facing a choice between massive intervention and nothing." Another British policy memo revealed the broader mindset at work: "Behind this Iraq agenda," it explained, lay a desire for a "climatic change in the psychology of regimes in the region."[173]

※

On December 4, 2001, Tommy Franks and an aide briefed the evolving war plan to Donald Rumsfeld and General Myers. Franks assumed that the goal was regime change, and Rumsfeld did not correct him. The existing concept had been to employ a massive force of some five hundred thousand troops, a number that Franks was already hacking away at—he had it down to four hundred thousand and was continuing to cut, he told Rumsfeld. Rumsfeld urged him to become more radical—to create an even slimmer, leaner option. Rumsfeld urged that Franks work the planning process faster than normal with a very small, leak-proof group of planners. "The President wants to see the concept soon, General," Rumsfeld pressed on December 19, according to Franks's own memoir.[174]

General Michael DeLong's version stresses the same sense of urgency. "We want this ready to go if need be," Rumsfeld told his CENTCOM commanders. DeLong writes that "President Bush and Rumsfeld were insistent on being able to kick off any conflict with Iraq on short notice."[175] In the final days of the month, Franks again presented the latest version of the plan to the president. Bush told them that he remained committed to diplomacy—but that he was equally committed to keeping WMDs out of the hands of regimes like Saddam's.[176]

A fascinating clue to the president's evolving thinking comes in Bob Woodward's book *Plan of Attack*. Bush said he watched Franks's "body language" very carefully, presumably to get an assessment of the general's confidence in assembling the war plan. "Is this good enough to win?" he asked the general, and Bush recalls Franks replying that it was, although it could get better. Bush told Woodward "we weren't ready to execute then," but that he left the meeting "with two things on his mind: 'Saddam's a threat. This is an option.'"[177]

Note his phrase to Woodward—they were not yet "ready to execute," rather than saying he had not yet made a decision. And the military briefing had created the impression in the president's mind of a feasible option assembled by a general who had just won a surprisingly easy conflict in Afghanistan and a Secretary of Defense who was among the most intellectually curious, demanding, assumption-challenging members of the cabinet. As one source told me: Remember, just after Afghanistan, DoD was riding high and appeared to have demonstrated a cheap and easy way to fight wars.[178] The danger, of course, was that such a line of thinking closed out the numerous other factors—from world opinion to postwar planning—that would play such a decisive role in determining the success or failure of the Iraq mission writ large.

Already the problem of how to manage the postwar was beginning to inch its way to the top of lists of potential risks. In a military plan, "Phase IV" refers to the posthostilities period of stabilization and return to civilian rule. For Phase IV in the emerging Iraq plan, under "duration," the CENTCOM briefing charts at this point simply said, "Unknown." But from the beginning, the clear assumption in everyone's mind was that the American stay in Iraq would be short. They wanted to hand off power quickly to an Iraqi provisional government and a US civilian overseer, and then get out.[179] This was a natural extension of the line of thinking established in October, reemphasized by the Afghan campaign: a light touch, relying on Iraqis to do much of the work. They proposed, in other words, to fight a war on the cheap.

> ❧

By December 2001, the Iraq decision was unfolding in bits and pieces, across the government, without clear coordination. In some ways the ultimate decision had already been made—the imperative was fully in place. In a formal sense, though, it would not be made for a year and a half. In a hallmark of the emerging decision process, the case for war was never made formally or explicitly. One former senior official involved in the planning told me that the decision process "zigged and zagged" its way to Iraq without a clear strategic mindset.[180] One later report quoted a senior State Department official as saying, "It simply snuck up on us."[181] There was no single meeting, no formal options paper, no significant debate about the consequences.[182]

Meanwhile, people not invited into the narrower, informal decision track remained blissfully ignorant of the speed and scope of these implicit judgments. Unanimously, they described themselves as surprised by the speed with which a decision to "confront Saddam" was reached—absent any discussion in the interagency process, even at the principals' level. One source would explain that between the fall of 2001 and the spring of 2002, the president had come to the position of regime change, by whatever means turned out to be necessary. But it was not so much a decision as an attitude, arrived at instinctively, by emergent feelings rather than deliberate assessment.[183] Another senior official close to the planning process denies a "final decision" was really made until 2003. Yet he recognizes that the abstract process of mental commitment is hard to pin down. In terms of the transition from "a problem to deal with" to the actual mental commitment to go to war: "The answer is that it's an unknowable."[184]

The formal planning process would now stretch on for over a year. It would never be very rigorous because it was, in a sense, beside the point—thus laying the basis for a closely related danger, that of policy implementation on autopilot. "By mid-2002," Richard Haass had become convinced, "the president and his inner circle had crossed the political and psychological Rubicon."[185] Over at State, Haass directed a thoughtful, perspicacious—and largely futile—stream of advice and warnings at Colin Powell, some of the initial examples of what would become a blizzard of cautions that would emerge through January and February of 2003. In one memo he argued in favor of continued containment, an attitude rapidly going out of fashion in the administration. The costs of a full-on invasion, he kept reminding his boss, would be enormous. "Should Saddam be removed and Iraq occupied by American forces," Haass wrote, "the country's future will become primarily our responsibility."[186] But such warnings would have little effect on a decision that had been, effectively, already made or on a planning process that was rushing forward largely on autopilot.

CHAPTER 5

JUSTIFYING INVASION: JANUARY TO JUNE 2002

Being a policy-maker "unwilling to incorporate any information contrary to your firmly-held idea immediately puts you in fantasyland, because you only see what you want to see."

FORMER SENIOR US NATIONAL SECURITY OFFICIAL[1]

T.S. Eliot announced no fresh discovery when he wrote that "Humankind cannot stand too much reality." Myths are an age-old form of escape, and they rarely fade completely; people will continue to believe what they want to believe.

GEORGE W. BALL[2]

In an engrossing essay titled "The Rubicon Theory of War," political scientists Dominic D. P. Johnson and Dominic Tierney explain that people wagering on horses become more confident in their wager after they have placed their bet. "The simple act of committing to a decision alter[s] their assessment of the probability of success,"[3] they write. The confidence-boosting effect of making a commitment is well documented: Once people have made a decision, two other scholars explain, they become "narrow-minded partisans of their plans of action."[4] People tend to process information in different ways, it turns out, depending on

what phase of a decision they believe themselves to be in. An important
threshold is the moment after a decision has actually been made, when
the decision-maker has created a goal that "the individual feels committed to achieve."[5]

For Johnson and Tierney, one implication for national security affairs
is the importance of the moment in a rivalry or crisis when decision-
makers—consciously or subconsciously—come to view war as inevitable.
From this instant, the time that leaders think of themselves as past the
point of choice, they are less likely to be deliberative and more likely to be
shopping for information that confirms a judgment already made. They
tend to become dangerously overconfident. And the especially perilous
thing is that this transition can occur long before a "decision" is formally
reached; once leaders begin to assume, implicitly and intuitively, that war
is inevitable, they have *in effect* crossed the Rubicon of judgment, even
though consciously they would deny they had made a choice for war. The
conscious part of their mind—the part that calculates their responsibilities as senior leaders and weighs costs, benefits, and consequences—does
not fully appreciate the significance of the moment.

This mechanism of threshold crossing has much in common with
the value-driven feeling of rightness that played such a significant role in
the Iraq case. When decision-makers apply values rather than weighing
consequences, the rightness of a course can leap into their minds very
quickly. Once it has done so, they are already across the threshold of
commitment—and already, from the first moments, resistant to contrary
perspectives. They are operating on conviction, on faith. They have not
so much reached a calculated and tentative decision as they have fallen
under the sway of a kind of revelation.

Many senior Bush administration officials had crossed this Rubicon
by January 2002—in many ways, within a week of 9/11. They were not,
for the most part, consciously deceitful when, in their public statements,
they said that they had not "decided" on war. This was in one sense true.
But consciously or subconsciously, most knew it was coming. And this
made all the difference in terms of how they would process information

in the coming year—including warnings that their presumed course of action was either unnecessary or infeasible. Without fully appreciating it, they had become narrow-minded partisans, defending their favored course of action against the tests of contrary facts.

This sort of single-minded thinking on the part of war advocates occurred within government but also outside of it. It is reflected, for example, in a January 2002 *Weekly Standard* essay by Robert Kagan and William Kristol. Saddam had to go, they argued—*immediately*. His threat burgeoned "with every day that passes." It was, for them, the defining choice of the emerging world order, which would be either a world "conducive to our liberal democratic principles" or one in which "brutal, well-armed tyrants" run amok. "No one questions" the threat posed by Saddam's weapons of mass destruction, Kristol and Kagan argued: "Iraq possesses the necessary components and technical knowledge to build nuclear bombs in the near future." Saddam was clearly in league with al Qaeda. "So," they concluded simply, "there is no debate about the facts"[6]—except, of course, that many of their "facts" were not facts at all.

⁂

As the administration headed into 2002, the overt decision track on Iraq remained ponderous and uncertain. Nothing had been decided, the public line claimed; all options remained open, and the assumption was that the administration still hoped to avert war. But a second line of thought—which dominated the perspective of a handful of senior officials and lurked, subconsciously, behind the hesitations of the rest—fully recognized that the decision had, in effect, already been made. Saddam would go, whatever it took.

Indeed, amid a growing flood of war planning orders, some military officers began to get the impression that their secretary of defense wanted to be ready to go to war very quickly—in that summer of 2002. It "took a lot of convincing" to get him to believe that the military just didn't have sufficient supplies in its inventory to be ready in that time frame, one source suggested. "I remember some of the relief that went through the building" when word went around that Rumsfeld had given in.[7]

Those not privy to the underlying track are to this day mystified that the process was accelerating right beneath their noses. "I still have a question in my own mind of how this happened," one senior official explained.[8] In January 2002, according to Karen DeYoung's account, Colin Powell thought he had plenty of time to stave off war. "The whole idea seemed far in the distant and unlikely future."[9] But it was hardly that—something that would become clear in a critical series of developments beginning with the famous State of the Union address in January 2002.

This unfolding decision process displayed hallmarks of the two elements of the pattern of misjudgment I am developing here: the influence of missionary conceptions of American foreign policy, which would be evident in both public statements and internal documents, and the catalytic effect of a moralistic imperative to act. By early 2002, the combined effect of these factors had begun to produce what would become a leading and disastrous side effect—the hectic forward momentum of policy on a sort of autopilot. As can so often happen when people are acting in a sort of reflex to serve a perceived obligation or imperative, the requisite attention was never paid to implementation. The critical thing was to act, to fulfill the need. Consequences were secondary.

This chapter continues the story of the emerging decision process by describing a series of key events and themes that unfolded in the first half of 2002. Many of the basic hallmarks of the decision had already been established: a continuing division between formal and informal planning tracks, an intensifying search for ways to justify and pave the way toward decisive action, and deepening efforts to shape a formal war plan. The decision process in these months would be characterized by a number of key moments: the January 2002 State of the Union address, a remarkably unambiguous statement of the administration's new direction; the beginning of a formal interagency process for war planning; and a series of trips and meetings in March and April that cemented the course of action.

Through it all, Saddam watched and wondered in Baghdad, alternately brushing off the growing danger and ordering his regime to take steps to head it off. But as the Americans would remind anyone who asked, the time for Saddam to avoid war had passed.

※

Within a day of 9/11, according to Michael Isikoff and David Corn, members of the Iraq Operations Group (IOG) at the CIA were beginning to revisit their plans for threatening Saddam's regime. There is no evidence that, at the time, this reflected anything more than intelligence operatives taking some initiative. This planning accelerated during "an intense forty-five day period beginning in late 2001," they report, when the team put together a long list of ideas from "recruiting disgruntled military officers" to financial sanctions to direct sabotage.[10] They were rethinking long-discarded ideas about how to drive Saddam from power short of war, but no one was persuaded that these tactics in themselves would do the job.

After 9/11 there wasn't an immediate explosion of interest or commands regarding the IOG's planning. Most of the CIA was obsessed with postattack counterterrorism and the unfolding Afghan campaign. For about three months, the IOG was put on hold, still working but without the resources they would need to conduct the ambitious operations they had sketched out. During this period, George Tenet has written, "Iraq was not uppermost in my mind." The CIA was rushing to expand its counterterrorism center and conduct a war in Afghanistan. "If someone had told me to quit paying so much attention to terrorism in the months following 9/11 and to start boning up on Iraq instead." Tenet writes, "I would have stared at them in disbelief."[11]

Nonetheless, planning and discussions continued, spurred by a quick return to the perennial question: What, if anything, could the CIA do to unseat Saddam Hussein? On January 3, 2002, members of the CIA's Iraqi Operations Group came to brief Cheney on this planning at his request. The IOG director told him that, in the face of Saddam's brutally effective intelligence services, the CIA "could not, by itself, oust Saddam." Saddam had killed, run off, or intimidated too many potential assets. For them to throw their support behind an effort to foment regime change, Cheney was told, "we would need to convince the Iraqis that this time we meant it."[12] One source familiar with the session recalled Cheney ruefully commenting about unfinished business from his last stint in government—business that he now firmly intended to conclude.[13]

Some in the administration continued toying with the exile-based "enclave" ideas of previous months, but it was increasingly clear that such schemes did not offer a real option. Condoleezza Rice has described a flurry of principals meetings that began in January 2002 to reconsider Iraq policy, going through the usual set of issues—sanctions, no-fly zones, support for exiles, and Wolfowitz's enclave notions (which "gained little credence," she writes). These were secretive affairs that, according to Rice, reviewed a range of issues but determined little and left most of the decisions for the lower-level interagency discussions that occurred later. But one conclusion did emerge from those discussions: As Rice explains, "We were really down to two options if we wanted to change course: increasing international pressure to make him give up his WMD or overthrowing him by force."[14] The preference of those advocating for Saddam's removal was clear. By January, Cheney aide Scooter Libby was pushing the State Department to generate an international conference of exiles, in part to lay the foundation for an interim government and post-Saddam rule.[15]

One source described a CIA briefing for senior administration officials on these emerging plans to destabilize Iraq in early 2002. "Let's give them something that will scare them," they had been told. A CIA officer jotted down a bunch of the ideas they had been toying with, including some of their wilder ideas. At the meeting, he briefed it all, and no one seemed to have a problem with any of it. On leaving, the CIA officer remarked to his colleagues, "Now I'm scared. They scared me. They're willing to do anything."[16]

❧

A critical step in the road to war, and one of the first unambiguous public signals of how serious things had become, was the January 2002 State of the Union address—destined to become the infamous "axis of evil" speech. The focus on Iraq was now unmistakable. Presidential speechwriter Michael Gerson reportedly told his aide David Frum, "Make the best case for war in Iraq, but leave exit ramps."[17] Frum apparently wanted to use "axis of hatred," but Gerson preferred "axis of evil" because of its "theological resonance," as journalist Jeffrey Goldberg explained.[18]

Indeed, the first drafts of the foreign policy section dealt almost entirely with Iraq, amounting to a clear nomination of the next target in the global campaign against terrorism. The singular focus concerned Condoleezza Rice, who worried that people would see it as a de facto declaration of war—because, of course, that is essentially what it was. And so the speechwriters tossed in two other countries and grouped the three together, without discussing the long-run strategic consequences of calling out these regimes as a package. Rice, as one biographer puts it, had "backed into the phrase without thinking it through."[19]

The lines in the speech dealing with Iraq ended up being astonishingly blunt anyway. In one of the most resonant phrases, Bush said, "We'll be deliberate, yet time is not on our side. I will not wait on events while dangers gather. . . . The United States of America will not permit the world's most dangerous regimes to threaten us with the world's most destructive weapons." This is one of the earliest examples—a full fourteen months before the war began—of the president and the administration making crystal clear the direction they planned to head. Yet somehow the distinction between a commitment to oust Saddam and a decision for war continued to leave room for passivity and wishful thinking, both inside the administration and outside. No one—in the executive branch, in Congress, for the most part in the media—saw any need yet to demand a deep and rigorous interrogation of what it would actually mean to undertake regime change in Iraq. And by the time the commitment morphed into a decision, it was too late.

Some, though, took clear note of the State of the Union's implications. In the wake of its fiery threats, columnist Charles Krauthammer wrote that if there had been any debate within the administration about Iraq, "that debate is now over. The speech was just short of a declaration of war." It was not a statement characteristic of a "president husbanding political capital," Krauthammer concluded—or, we might say, in the throes of a careful assessment of risks and costs. "This is a president on a mission."[20]

※

In Baghdad, Saddam and his cronies listened to the State of the Union address with some alarm. According to interviews conducted with Iraqi officials after the war, for the first time since 9/11, they were now seriously concerned about the extent of US intentions. Some officials suggested that the time had come to "step forward and have a talk with the Americans"—in part to make clear that Iraq had no relationship with al Qaeda. Saddam rejected the idea. He had become convinced that the United States was deaf to his approaches. What was the point?[21]

※

On February 7, 2002, Tommy Franks presented a modified war plan to the president. He argued that the best time to initiate military action would be between November or December of 2002 and the end of February 2003. According to Bob Woodward's account, Franks thought the briefing went well, and that "he had some time before war." Colin Powell drew the conclusion that "no one seemed trigger-happy."[22]

The degree of US war preparations was increasingly clear, though, even outside the government. Warren Strobel and John Walcott published a report on the McClatchy News Service on February 13, based on interviews with administration officials. Bush "has concluded that Saddam and his nuclear, chemical and biological weapons programs are such a threat to US security that the Iraqi dictator must be removed," they wrote. The report quoted an unnamed US official saying that "this is not an argument about whether to get rid of Saddam Hussein. That debate is over. This is . . . [about] how you do it."[23]

In her memoir, Condoleezza Rice explains that she and Chief of Staff Andy Card were with Bush at Camp David in February, and "Iraq was on his mind." They talked openly about the threat of force to change Saddam's behavior.[24] Both seemed perfectly willing to accept the natural implication: in a process of coercive diplomacy, if the threat of force does not work, then war is the only remaining option. Except, of course, that coercive diplomacy would never really be given a chance: Senior administration officials had come to the conviction that no limits on Saddam's ambitions could be trusted. Inspections had failed. It was never clear, from the beginning, what the threat of force was expected to achieve, apart from creating the firm impression that alternatives to war had been given a reasonable hearing. Because of the prevailing beliefs about Saddam's character, they never were.

Despite the detail that by this time had gone into such planning, three months later, in May, speaking in Europe, President Bush would blithely wave off claims that he was on the verge of attacking Iraq. "I have no war plans on my desk," he would say—a statement that, while perhaps literally true at that precise moment, was profoundly misleading. And in late May, Tommy Franks would go as far as to claim, when asked what an Iraq war plan would look like: "I don't have an answer because my boss has not yet asked me to put together a plan to do that."[25]

Franks was not the only one forced into outright dissembling by the twin-track process of war planning. Before long, the issue arose of how to pay for something that had been neither officially decided nor publicly announced. These resource demands put Pentagon comptroller Dov Zakheim "in a quandary," he would later write. The administration was vigorously denying its intention to go to war. How was he supposed to legally release funds to prepare for an unauthorized conflict—especially given that they would have to begin building some of the logistical basis for the war and when, by law, he needed the approval of the military construction subcommittees in Congress to pay for any infrastructure projects?

In his memoir, Zakheim is quite direct. Going to Congress would "open a Pandora's box of debate over Iraq when the administration was not yet ready for one. . . . I was in no mood to take those kinds of chances." He and his staff hit upon mechanisms to covertly fund the emerging war—hiding money under the aegis of the ongoing operations against residual Taliban forces, for example. If anyone asked, Zakheim thought, he'd say he was paying to build infrastructure and sending supplies to the Gulf region to support operations in Afghanistan.[26]

⁂

George Tenet describes how, as early as February 2002, the CIA began the "painstaking" process of rebuilding its Northern Iraq Liaison Element (NILE) groups of agents embedded with Kurdish forces in northern Iraq. It would take several months to get the teams up and running. "We wanted them," he says of their Iraqi recruits, "to take aggressive actions to challenge the legitimacy of the regime wherever they could, sabotage railheads, disrupt communications nodes, attack local Ba'ath Party headquarters, and communicate their actions with the military to maximize their effectiveness."[27]

By early 2002, the "rumint and gossip" at the CIA was that the agency was gearing up to prepare for the war.[28] The whole purpose of this activity, one source said—the "whole purpose of assembling a team from the very first conversation"—was to "prepare the battlefield for the invasion." Tenet confirms this, indicating that the CIA's role was to lay the groundwork for and then directly support military operations.[29] They were told, the source explains, that "You need to hurry, you need to go now. . . . We need people in there as fast as possible. War is coming soon. . . . The decision has been made, we're going to invade, we need guys on the ground."

Indeed, the available public sources make clear that by February of 2002, the emerging elements of a plan to unseat Saddam were beginning to unspool in a serious way. The CIA presumably started establishing its NILE teams that month for a reason. Both Isikoff and Corn and Rowan Scarborough point to a presidential order on February 16; the former describe it as a presidential finding authorizing covert actions against Iraq, while the latter claims it was a broader presidential directive "for going to war with Iraq."[30] In one volume of his post-9/11 trilogy, Bob Woodward refers to it as an intelligence order and summarizes its main components—typical covert actions designed to destabilize a hostile regime.[31] Former CIA operative Charles Faddis writes that he had been "told by the White House in January 2002 that war in Iraq was imminent." Faddis recruited his team in February and had them "ready to go to war in Iraq by early March of 2002, on schedule."[32] The Iraq Operations Group, as noted above, had been "put on hold" for the first months after 9/11, while still getting strong indications that they would be called back into action soon enough. There was "nothing as dramatic as where they all [NSC members] say, 'We're going to overthrow Saddam Hussein.'" Over time, though, "word got to us: 'We're gonna do this.'"[33] And that word apparently began coming in the first months of 2002. Public reports began to seep out that took for granted this line of thinking. A January 28 *Newsweek* story reported "that a 'general consensus' has emerged among Bush and his top advisors for a 'regime change' in Iraq. But Saddam will not be attacked 'tomorrow or unilaterally.'"[34]

This accelerating work naturally raises the question of whether a meeting occurred during this period when the president and national security principals sat around a table, looked each other in the eye, and declared—formally, definitively—that they were agreed on going to war. No evidence has yet emerged supporting such a formalized decision for invasion this early. Numerous participants describe later discussions with the president that made clear the final judgment was still to be made, suggesting that at least some degree of finality was left hanging after February 2002. But one determination *had* clearly been made by the beginning of 2002—Saddam had to go, and quickly. If the public accounts of it are accurate, the February order, whatever its precise categorization, reflected a formal US government commitment to achieve that goal.

Between orders to intensify war planning and expanded covert activities, the Bush administration was taking vigorous steps in that direction while deferring the actual choice to go to war and continually denying that such a choice had been made. But the distinction was obviously meaningless: the intelligence community had *already told* the administration that if they wanted to get rid of Saddam, covert action would not do it, and nobody in the administration took seriously the occasional suggestions that Saddam could be bribed out of power. A decision to unseat Saddam therefore *was* a decision to go to war and could easily have been understood as such in these first weeks of 2002. But the administration stubbornly clung to the idea that while it had decided to remove Saddam from power, it had not yet decided on invasion to accomplish that goal. The problem with this approach was that by assuming a likely need to go to war but never, until the very last minute, accepting it openly enough to warrant serious debate about its costs and risks, they left dozens of assumptions and questionable claims unexamined, and vast amounts of essential planning were left undone until it was too late.

※

Christopher Meyer, the British ambassador in Washington, sent a lengthy cable to London at about this time. "The Administration appears to be gearing up for a decision on removing Saddam," he wrote, while admitting that they were "not quite there yet. The 'how' is still difficult. The debate looks likely to come to a head this month." Dick Cheney was set to travel throughout the Middle East in March, Meyer wrote, and "it would be wise to assume that by then, the US will have a reasonably clear vision, for which they will want our endorsement."[35]

Meyer made clear the growing tension between the two tracks, open and subterranean, in the decision process. "The line that no decision has been taken . . . may still formally be correct," he wrote, but "there are few parts of the Administration that see any alternative to US action—the real questions now are what, when, and (from our point of view) how much international legitimacy the US will seek to build." An emerging diplomatic track had a very clear purpose: to grease the skids for war. US inspection demands would lead to an ultimatum designed to "set the bar so high that Iraq will never comply in practice."[36]

꙰

Washington Post columnist Jim Hoagland, who obviously was on the receiving end of lots of material from Defense and the vice president's office, emerged as a semi-official voice reflecting the views of many war advocates in the administration. By February 2002, he was beating the Iraq war drum. "Iraq is America's most important unfinished business abroad," he wrote in his *Washington Post* column of February 17.[37] Already then—and he could not have written this without some inside word—he was telling his readers not to pay too close attention to debates over use of force, discussions of smart sanctions, and weapons inspections. "Much of this," he concluded, "is dust in the eyes." The real decision had been made.

Hoagland would betray himself as a staunch supporter of Ahmad Chalabi and the INC. Already at this point he was referring to the "three to six months needed to train and equip Iraqi dissidents to play a significant role in toppling Saddam Hussein." And Hoagland reflected another major assumption of war planners: "Fears that Iraq will fall apart" when Saddam was deposed "are both exaggerated and irrelevant." The moral case for removing him from power was absolute, Hoagland implied. Fears about what might come next are "almost always an excuse for doing nothing." Hoagland's columns are indicative of a fact that was disquieting for the American media: the drumbeat for war was increasingly heard from major newspapers and magazines, and little critical analysis was focused on the implicit decision that, when pressed, so many in and around Washington knew had been taken. This must count as another tragic lost opportunity—the fact that, apart from a handful of examples, the US media spent so little time trying to answer the question of what war would actually mean.

⁂

Meanwhile, in Baghdad, Saddam Hussein had decided that the evidence of an emerging threat was sufficient to do something—but not the sort of bold concessions that would have been necessary to derail the movement toward war. In February he ordered his aides to agree to UN weapons inspections, but only after bargaining for at least partially lifted sanctions. He therefore laid the groundwork for the signals Iraq would consistently send in the inspections process: limited, partial, and grudging cooperation.[38] This failure to appreciate the seriousness of the moment emerged when the International Atomic Energy Agency's chief inspector, the professorial Swede Hans Blix—a former foreign minister and experienced diplomat, possessor of both a doctorate and a law degree—sat down with Iraqi officials to get the new inspections organization, UNMOVIC, into Iraq. The Iraqis seemed to be more concerned with presenting themselves as victims. "I did not have an impression of a lack of sincerity," Blix would write later, but "rather of a people living in another world of thinking,"[39] a world that could not yet take seriously the fact that the Bush administration had effectively decided to unseat them.

⁂

As the unspoken decision for war gained steam, it became increasingly apparent that its justifications were complex, shifting, and sometimes contradictory. Different senior officials held very different reasons for needing Saddam gone. The tensions would not be resolved by the time of the invasion, creating massive disconnects in the war and postwar planning.

One former official who had a window into the thinking of senior administration leaders stresses that "different actors were converging on Iraq for different reasons." Some really believed the emerging democratization narrative—freeing Iraq would spark a cascade of liberty in the Middle East. Many saw Saddam as a persistent threat that needed to be removed. Wolfowitz saw it as an exercise in liberating an oppressed people, whereas others—Cheney and Rumsfeld in particular—seemed much more motivated by punishment and the removal of a threat. Some even saw an endless series of regime-change operations stretching out to the strategic horizon, to run the table on the rogue enemies of American power. One place where everyone's thinking continued to converge was in the area of risk calculus. President Bush and Vice President Cheney "really bought into the one percent doctrine," a former senior official said—the idea that the United States could no longer allow Saddam's regime to persist primarily due to the potential nexus between lunatic regimes with WMDs and terrorist groups.[40]

Yet the goal of democracy promotion remained dearly held by many senior officials who advocated for the war. One such official later recounted:

> I don't think that the President decided to overthrow the Saddam Hussein regime so that the US could promote democracy in Iraq. I think he decided to do it because of the national security danger that that regime embodied. Having decided to take military action, however, the President understood that a successful effort to build democratic institutions in Iraq could beneficially transform the Middle East, contributing to our goal of countering ideological support for terrorism. Even those of us who were most interested in the beneficial effects of democracy understood, however, that it would be difficult to build democratic institutions in Iraq. But if the payoff, if our efforts are successful, could be large. . . . We knew before 9/11 that the United States could benefit from substantial political reform in the Middle East. After 9/11 the importance of such reform grew, as people throughout the US government realized.[41]

One key actor seems to have been fully committed to the democratization rationale: George W. Bush. His former speechwriter Scott

McClellan writes that one of Bush's "core beliefs is that all people have a God-given right to live in freedom. There was nothing I would ever see him talk more passionately about than this view." McClellan, watching Bush on an almost daily basis during this time, became convinced that Bush's primary motive in launching the war "was an ambitious and idealistic post-9/11 vision of transforming the Middle East through the spread of freedom."[42] The implications of this view would become apparent once US forces were in Baghdad: if the requirement for promoting democracy was to stay and make a long commitment, then George Bush would be all in. But the real causal links involved in such a process—how exactly invading Iraq was supposed to manufacture a democracy; what the regional effect would be; and how, even if protest movements arose, that would manage to produce stable democracies in such an inhospitable region—were never discussed, let alone debated.

The rationales for the war were thus a messy tangle of concepts: among them the ideals of demonstrating power, seeking out WMDs, and promoting liberty. Different ideas were held in different measure by different actors and were never spelled out clearly, prioritized, weighed against one another, or weighed against the likely risks. But because the decision had been *obliquely* made—because they had crossed that Rubicon of commitment without a true debate or analytic choice—they subconsciously arrived at a place where they saw little need to double back and unearth those fundamental questions. And increasingly, anyone who expressed doubts would be pushed aside with that most common dismissive quip directed at dissenters: *you just don't get it.*

※

And yet when asked, top administration officials continued to downplay how far this implicit judgment had progressed. At a February 2002 press conference, Secretary of Defense Rumsfeld was asked if he supported regime change in Iraq. He proceeded to give a master class in obfuscation.[43] "Well," he said, "I think Congress passed legislation relating to regime change." He then launched into a variety of circuitous

ambiguities. "I don't know many people," he began, "who have developed
a great deal of admiration for that regime and the way it treats its people
and the way it treats its neighbor[s], and the fact that it's engaging in the
development of weapons of mass destruction. The timing, and whether
or not anything is done with respect to any country is something that is
for the president and the country to make those judgments. And it's not
for me to express views on that. So I don't." Again Rumsfeld was asked,
"Would it be accurate to say that" the Pentagon was actively planning for
an Iraq war? "This building has always been attentive, for at least more
than a decade now, 10, 12 years, to Iraq," he replied.

The answer did not technically constitute a lie—but to any
uninformed American listening, it was the functional equivalent of a
falsehood, because it left the impression of an outright denial. *No*, it's just
that we have always been considering Iraq; *no*, there's nothing unusual
going on. But of course there *was* something unusual going on, dramatically so, and there had been from the first hours after 9/11—when Rumsfeld himself dictated lines that would lead the United States to begin
plotting against Saddam.

At the same press conference, Rumsfeld was asked about Iraqi weapons of mass destruction and terrorism, and about reports that there
was no "direct evidence" of a link between Iraq and al Qaeda. And he
responded with one of the most famous Rumsfeldisms of all time—
gesturing with an index finger as if lecturing a class: "Reports that say
that something hasn't happened are always interesting to me," he pronounced, "because as we know, there are known knowns; there are things
we know we know. We also know there are known unknowns; that is to
say we know there are some things we do not know. But there are also
unknown unknowns—the ones we don't know we don't know. And if
one looks throughout the history of our country and other free countries,
it is the latter category that tend to be the difficult ones." There was some
muffled laughter in the briefing room. But the reporter wouldn't let it go.
"Excuse me," he continued. "But is this"—that is, Iraq's connections to
terrorism—"an unknown unknown?"

"I'm not—" Rumsfeld began.

"Because you said several unknowns, and I'm just wondering if this is an unknown unknown."

"I'm not going to say which it is," Rumsfeld said, shuffling his briefing papers on the podium, a wry grin on his face.

"Mr. Secretary, if you believe something—" the reporter continued, desperately trying to get an actual answer.

Rumsfeld pivoted to another question.

A few minutes later, another reporter accused him of trying to "cleverly bury" the issue, and asked again: Did Rumsfeld have actual evidence that Iraq was supporting terrorists?

Rumsfeld, clearly perturbed, shot back, "Yeah, I am aware of a lot of evidence involving Iraq on a lot of subjects. And it is not for me to make public judgments about my assessment or others' assessment of that evidence."

⁊⁊

As winter turned to spring in 2002, the initial set of cabinet meetings that had begun in January—and already appear to have coalesced around a tentative decision to unseat Saddam, somehow and on some schedule—grew into a more comprehensive interagency process. It would occur at several levels: some among the cabinet deputies and some at lower interagency levels, occasionally among principals. Doug Feith describes the deputies' meetings, noting that they included him, Deputy National Security Advisor Stephen Hadley, Deputy Secretary of State Richard Armitage, Under Secretary of State Marc Grossman, Deputy CIA Director John McLaughlin, General Peter Pace from the Joint Staff (or General George Casey), Scooter Libby from Cheney's office, and a senior NSC staffer—General Wayne Downing, Zalmay Khalilzad, or Frank Miller.[44]

It soon became clear that the point of this process was not to *decide* whether the nation would go to war—or even to debate that proposition and flow analyses up to the principal-level decision-makers. That overall decision had been seeping out of the ether, emerging in some mysterious way. The point of the interagency process was instead to busily get about the task of planning a war that had not been formally decided upon. Here we run into another lost opportunity for a better choice, a more rigorous process: in theory, the president or national security advisor could have demanded that this planning process begin with the question of whether the United States *should* take Saddam out, before it moved on to the issue of *how* to do that. There would have been discomfort and impatience—many senior officials would have described it as a waste of time—but it could surely have been done, and it might have unearthed some of the dilemmas and risks that ended up being ignored.

As one participant in these sessions later recounted, "It was really weird. It was never explicit: *We're going to invade Iraq and take down the regime, so let's meet*. It was much more abstract." The meetings had a hypo-thetical feeling—*if* war were to break out and the United States needed to do *x* or *y*, how would it do that?[45] Many of the meetings amounted to organized brainstorming sessions—"that was one of the weird things about it," said one of the participants.[46] CIA Director George Tenet wrote later,

> In talking now to those who did attend, I'm told that the sessions . . . seemed odd. A presidential decision on going to war was always alluded to by the NSC in hypothetical terms, as though it were still up in the air and the conferees were merely discussing contingencies. Sometimes there would be lengthy debates over such arcane details as how quickly after the war began could we replace Iraq's currency and whose picture should be on the dinar. . . . In none of the meetings can anyone remember a discussion of the central questions. Was it wise to go to war? Was it the right thing to do?

"What never happened, as far as I can tell," Tenet adds, "was a serious discussion of the implications of a US invasion. What impact would a large American occupying force have in an Arab country in the heart of the Middle East? What kind of political strategy would be necessary to cause the Iraqi society to coalesce in a post-Saddam world?" The process reflected a disastrous "lack of curiosity in asking these kinds of questions, and the lack of a disciplined process to get the answers before committing the country to war."[47]

One participant in these sessions explained that "there was never a time" when the principals "sat around the NSC table and everyone was asked for their views" about invading Iraq. Was it a good idea? What would the risks be? "It never happened."[48] There simply wasn't "the same crispness of approval with this administration" that had existed in earlier ones, an experienced official remarked.[49]

Another participant lamented, "What surprised me was how *little* was decided at the deputies meetings, and even the principals meetings" during this time. There would be two to three meetings a week; massive preparation would take place for them (developing briefing slides, writing memos), and staffs would wait to hear what had been decided and for the implementation orders. And then: silence. Meanwhile, a crucial mechanism for interagency effectiveness—the network of lower-level "action officers" on issues who get to know one another, talk, trade issue papers, and keep one another informed—"broke down," in part because of interagency rivalry and in part because Defense seemed to be vacuuming up all authority. "As I learned later," one former senior official said, "the decisions were being made outside these meetings"[50]—by the president, the vice president, the secretary of defense, a handful of people outside the context of a traditional decision process. More than one senior official, especially at State, said more or less the same thing as a senior State Department official: they first learned about the seriousness of the intention to take down Saddam "from the newspapers, actually."[51]

Only later, in August 2002 with the formation of what was called the Executive Steering Group (ESG) under Frank Miller at the NSC, would some sort of more disciplined, formalized war planning get underway. Even then, however, it remained focused on a specific handful of war planning issues, despite Miller's exhaustive efforts. To make matters worse, the ESG was more of a working-level group, and other series of meetings around the government ended up having intermittent contact with the ESG, except to the extent that individual people happened to attend both sessions.[52] One official I spoke with said simply it was "not clear *who was in charge* in this period."[53]

A senior official who attended many interagency meetings recalled that the planning process ended up being "a very disjointed affair" in terms of the messages being sent out. He did, however, have the sense that Bush was "all in favor" of the direction from the beginning. Bush, Cheney, Rumsfeld—once 9/11 had occurred, they were all "certain from day one" about toppling Saddam. As far as this source could tell, attending deputies and principals meetings, it was obvious by January that "These guys are serious. At that point I was one hundred percent certain. We had been told, we're going to overthrow Saddam Hussein."[54]

※

One foundational issue that quickly emerged was the question of governance—who would run Iraq when the United States took the place over. Effective governance is critical to security in any post-conflict situation; without a competent administrative entity ensuring basic physical safety, no other postwar objectives can be met. But this crucial issue would become the central gathering point for all the dilemmas poisoning the US mission, dilemmas that flowed directly from the broadest of all origin points: an unwillingness to take seriously the costs and risks of a missionary approach to foreign policy. There were, in effect, two basic choices for how to handle the issue. When US forces seized Baghdad, Washington could either find some Iraqis to quickly take over or embark on a years-long occupation. Each of those options embodied tremendous risks for the United States, risks that the planning process did not take seriously.

From the beginning, Defense officials became advocates of a rapid handoff to Iraqi control. Some used the term "provisional government" to refer to this rapid process—generating a temporary governing structure of Iraqis and equipping it with some staff and resources to take over. Others seem to have been thinking in even more streamlined terms, believing that an effort to assemble such a provisional government would take too long.[55] State Department officials would gradually propose a concept that would become known as the "Transitional Civil Authority" that presumed the necessity of a longer stay and more extended US responsibility.[56] But the options remained poorly defined, and the formal pros and cons were never laid out in a comprehensive decision brief.

Conspicuously absent from this emerging process was the firm hand of an organizing office in the interagency that should have grabbed hold and coordinated—the National Security Council—as thinking about a potential Iraq operation spun essentially out of control and was never brought back into line. As Condoleezza Rice's thoughtful biographer, Elisabeth Bumiller, puts it, Rice helped facilitate each action "as a logical consequence of what had already been decided. In not challenging the moves toward war, she saw herself as carrying out Bush's wishes."[57] She set in motion two major NSC planning processes that achieved something. But never did she attempt to impose any large-scale strategic vision, or any operational planning discipline, on the process until it was far too late.

To be fair to Rice, her job was fatally complicated by the bitter internal politics of the administration—and the fact that two of the key players, Rumsfeld and Cheney, gave every impression of simply not respecting her and refusing to recognize her authority. Cheney offers several dismissive references to Rice in his memoirs, none more so that when he has her "tearfully admitting" mistaken judgments about public apologies for intelligence mistakes.[58] For his part, Rumsfeld "resented" Rice's role as the broker and referee of policy, she wrote later. At one point when Rice asked him why they couldn't work well together, Rumsfeld replied bluntly, "You're obviously bright and committed, but it just doesn't work." Why it didn't work, he did not say. Meanwhile Cheney's office, she contends, "seemed very much of one ultra-hawkish mind" and was "determined to act as a power center of its own," undermining the authority of the formal NSC staff.[59]

⁂

Rigorous examination of the consequences of war was obstructed by various factors. One of the most powerful was the truly astonishing degree of wishful thinking, including on the part of some very senior officials, that was practiced around the question of how an invasion could be pulled off at little cost or risk. The release of hundreds of British documents from this period offers a fascinating window into the emerging mindset of both British and US senior leaders. In brief, that mentality, as of early March 2002, could be described as a determination to take Saddam down without causing a political disaster.

One options paper from March 8 drafted by the Overseas and Defence Secretariat of the Cabinet Office outlined three options to accomplish regime change: "covert support to opposition groups to mount an uprising/coup," "air support for opposition groups to mount an uprising/coup," and "a full-scale ground campaign." The memo went on to suggest that "these are not mutually exclusive. Options 1 and/or 2 would be natural precursors to Option 3. The greater investment of Western forces, the greater our control over Iraq's future, but the greater the cost and the longer we woul[d] need to stay. The only certain means to remove Saddam and his elite is to invade and impose a new government, but this could involve nation building over many years." The paper saw little hope for covert action alone. (The authors referred to Ahmad Chalabi as "a Shia and convicted fraudster, popular on Capitol Hill.") Comparisons with Afghanistan "are misleading," the paper contended: "Saddam's military and security apparatus is considerably more potent and cohesive. We are not aware of any Karzai figure able to command respect inside and outside Iraq." The authors concluded, "In sum, despite the considerable difficulties, the use of overriding force in a group campaign is the only option that we can be confident will remove Saddam and bring Iraq back into the international community."

Yet if London and Washington were to take on this mission, one major stumbling block was the annoyingly inconvenient fact of international law, which tended to look askance at unprovoked territorial aggression. One of the most profound statements in all the documents so far declassified by London or Washington is a March 21 memo from John Grainger, the British government's legal counsellor. He had been asked to render a verdict on the legality of an Iraq invasion, and he did not mince words. "No group of states has the right to intervene . . . for any reason whatever, in the internal or external affairs of any other state. Armed intervention and all forms of interference" were thus clearly "violations of international law," the memo said. As a result, "Any action by HMG [Her Majesty's Government] to assist any group, internal or external, to overthrow the regime in Iraq by violent means would be contrary to international law."[60]

How, then, to justify a preemptive war?

"A legal justification for invasion would be needed," a separate March 8 British memo had admitted, anticipating the legal advisor's opinion. "Subject to Law Officers advice, none currently exists. This makes moving quickly to invade legally very difficult." Difficult indeed—but not, as it turned out, impossible. What they needed was a "staged approach" to build pressure on Saddam and generate international support while "developing military plans."[61] In the process, the United States and Britain would build themselves a legal justification—and the most iron-clad basis, this memo and others began to reason, would be Iraqi noncompliance with UN mandates on WMDs. Because, the paper admitted in contradiction of claims coming out of Washington, "there is no recent evidence of Iraq complicity with international terrorism," there was therefore "no justification for action against Iraq" based on 9/11 under the self-defense principles enshrined in the United Nations Charter. Instead, the authors of the memo proposed exhuming UN resolutions from the dim history of the Gulf War: "Offensive military action against Iraq can only be justified if Iraq is held to be in breach of the Gulf War ceasefire resolution, 687. 687 imposed obligations on

Iraq with regard to the elimination of WMD and monitoring these obligations. But 687 never terminated the authority to use force mandated in UNSCR 678 (1990). Thus a violation of 687 can revive the authorization to use force in 678." This was a byzantine legal ruse, dredging up decade-old authorizations as if the Gulf War had only been placed on pause. And it had a major flaw: only the UN Security Council could trigger a reauthorization of force under Resolution 678. For this to happen, "they would need to be convinced that Iraq was in breach of its obligations regarding WMD, and ballistic missiles. Such proof would need to be incontrovertible and of large-scale activity." At this point the memo laid out yet another inconvenient fact about the state of knowledge about Iraqi WMDs, a fact that stood in dumbfounding contradiction of just about everything that would come out of the British and American governments for the next year: "Current intelligence is insufficiently robust to meet this criterion."

Still the authors did not give up. There was a way around even this obstacle: if the United States and Great Britain made a fresh demand for large-scale inspections to enforce the existing resolutions, and if "Iraq refused to readmit UN inspectors after a clear ultimatum by the UN Security Council," or if the inspectors "were re-admitted to Iraq and found sufficient evidence of WMD activity or were again expelled trying to do so," then the legal road to invasion would have been cleared. These Iraqi actions could provide the magical connection to UN Resolution 687, the undead war justification from a decade before.

This, then, would quickly become the leading understanding for the UN diplomatic and inspections process that would get underway within a few months. In many officials' minds, the intent was never really to make war unnecessary by disarming Iraq, but instead to provide a basis for war under international law by demonstrating Iraqi noncompliance. Most top US officials have unfailingly claimed that—in Cheney's words, as one example—they ardently sought a "diplomatic resolution," and only "if we couldn't achieve one, we would be compelled" to go to war.[62] Yet virtually none of them appears to have had the slightest belief that such a resolution would be possible. If that was true, the only possible role for a diplomatic effort was to make war possible rather than avoid it.

⁂

In anticipation of Tony Blair's planned Crawford ranch visit in April, Blair's foreign policy advisor David Manning traveled to Washington and reported back on the state of thinking about Iraq. Condoleezza Rice's "enthusiasm for regime change," he wrote in a March 14, 2002, memo, is "undimmed. But there were some signs, since we last spoke, of greater awareness of the practical difficulties and political risks." President Bush had yet to figure out most of the "big questions," such as "how to persuade international opinion that military action against Iraq is necessary and justified" and "what happens the morning after?" Manning worried that "there is a real risk that the Administration underestimates the difficulties. They may agree that failure isn't an option, but this does not mean that they will avoid it."[63]

⁂

In the middle of March, Vice President Cheney traveled through the Middle East to sound out Arab leaders on the possibility of removing Saddam from power.[64] He stopped first in London to exchange blunt words with Tony Blair, who made clear once again his own determination to be rid of the Iraqi regime. Cheney promised that if Bush "decided to go to war, we would finish the job. We would remove Saddam Hussein, eliminate the threat he posed, and establish a representative government." He stopped in Jordan and Egypt to convey a similar message and to discuss the things the United States would need from these countries if it went to war in Iraq.[65] "The president has decided that we have to deal with Saddam," Cheney told the leaders he met. We're going to act, and you'll be required to decide how to respond. The administration had not yet decided what that meant—but it surely meant something decisive.[66]

Although publicly the regional answer was hesitant—we don't want war; instability will result—privately, senior officials of countries across the Middle East made clear that they would not consider it a great trag-edy if Saddam were removed from the scene.[67] But the United States had to be serious about it; no one wanted any more half measures. They had seen enough of that.

⁂

As the administration's engagement with Capitol Hill ramped up, two journalists have reported that Condoleezza Rice hosted three senators at the White House in March. They talked of the plans for Iraq: Could we do it through the UN? Could we assemble a coalition?

President Bush dropped in and said hello. The group mentioned they were discussing what to do about Iraq. "He waved his hand dismissively," the account suggests. And he said simply, "Fuck Saddam. We're taking him out."[68]

⁂

On Sunday, March 17, Paul Wolfowitz lunched with British ambassa-dor Sir Christopher Meyer. London "backed regime change," Meyer told him, "but the plan had to be clever and failure was not an option." One way, Meyer suggested in line with the emerging concept, would be to "wrongfoot Saddam on the inspectors and the UN SCRs [Security Coun-cil Resolutions]. . . . If all this could be accomplished skillfully, we were fairly confident that a number of countries would come on board."[69]

In a later newspaper column, Meyer was blunter about the idea. "What was needed," he said he urged on Wolfowitz, "was a clever plan that convinced people there was a legal basis for toppling Saddam." And one way to do this would be to "demand the readmission of UN weapons inspectors into Iraq. If [Saddam] refused, this would not only put him in the wrong but also turn the searchlight onto the Security Council reso-lutions of which he remained in breach." Wolfowitz "listened carefully," Meyer recalled, "but he was noncommittal."[70]

What Wolfowitz did strongly concur with, according to Meyer, was a focus on Saddam Hussein's atrocities as the rationale for war. Meyer mentioned that London "was giving serious thought to publishing a paper that would make the case against Saddam" in specifically human rights terms. On this, according to Meyer's memo to London,

> Wolfowitz said that he fully agreed. He took a slightly different position from others in the Administration, who were focussed on Saddam's capacity to develop weapons of mass destruction. The WMD danger was of course crucial to the public case against Saddam, particularly the potential linkage to terrorism. But Wolfowitz thought it indispensable to spell out in detail Saddam's barbarism.[71]

The convergence between the decision on regime change and the decision on war shines brightly in the final paragraph of Meyer's memo. Wolfowitz, he wrote, scorned the idea of a military coup to topple Saddam. The Iraqi generals all "had blood on their hands," Wolfowitz reportedly said. "The important thing was to try to have Saddam replaced by something like a functioning democracy."[72]

⁂

At about this same time, the *New Yorker* writer Nicholas Lemann had a number of interesting conversations with senior administration figures. The discussions led Lemann to the conclusion that "the chain of events leading inexorably to a full-scale American invasion [of Iraq], if it hasn't already begun, evidently will begin soon."[73]

Both sides of US missionary impulses—the hopeful and the hawkish—were on full display in these exchanges. Lemann met with Condoleezza Rice, who spoke in terms every bit as messianic as her boss, proclaiming that the terror attacks of 9/11 constituted "one of those great earthquakes that clarify and sharpen." She raised comparisons with 1945 and 1947, implying a new moment of American responsibility to remake the world: world politics were in flux, and it was the United States' job to mold their new shape.

Lemann also talked to Scooter Libby, Cheney's senior foreign policy aide. Libby told him that the rise of terrorism could be traced to
American weakness—a lack of responses to the Somalia debacle, to terror
attacks in the 1990s. "If you look at that long list and you ask, 'Did we
respond in a way which discouraged people from supporting terrorist
activities . . . ? Did we help to shape the environment in a way which
discouraged further aggressions against US interests?'" Even in the spring
of 2002, Libby was very clear. "The issue is not inspections," he said. It
was the series of broken Iraqi promises, the inability to trust the Hussein
regime—the same rhetoric President Bush would later use to justify war.
Lemann asked Libby if he had any hope that the Iraqi regime would
"change its behavior in a way that you will be satisfied by. . . . He ran his
hand over his face and then gave me a direct gaze and spoke slowly and
deliberately. 'There is no basis in Iraq's past behavior to have confidence
in good-faith efforts on their part to change their behavior.'" He was all
but saying there was nothing Iraq could do.

※

On March 25, British foreign minister Jack Straw wrote to Tony Blair
about an upcoming Crawford meeting with Bush. The problem, he
suggested, was that, while Blair might be committed to war, the reasons for it weren't being communicated. Other countries "know that
Saddam and the Iraqi regime are bad," Straw continued. "Making that
case is easy. But we have a long way to go to convince them as to: (a)
the scale of the threat from Iraq and why this has got worse recently;
(b) what distinguishes the Iraqi threat from that of eg Iran and North
Korea so as to justify military action; (c) the justification for any military
action in terms of international law; and (d) whether the consequence
of military action really would be a compliant, law abiding replacement
government."[74]

Before *convincing* people of those facts, though, US and British
officials had to actually settle, for themselves and posterity, that they
were indeed true. And this simply never occurred. Having crossed the

Rubicon, in thrall to imperatives that made their proposed course right and true, they were looking ahead to the glorious results—liberation, democracy, a blow against the confidence of their enemies—which their faith in a course of action made mandatory. Whether these aims were also realistic, or even possible, was an entirely different question.

※

By many reports, the April 2002 Bush-Blair Crawford summit did not produce a formal agreement on war. One Blair aide told a British journalist that "The idea that Bush and Blair were prepared to invade Iraq during Crawford is complete bullshit."[75] Of course, Bush was *more* than prepared to do so, and fairly soon, if the supposed diplomatic alternatives failed. Blair's conditions for support centered around those alternatives, and he began a consistent (and at best partly successful) effort to pin the Americans to the UN route. Christopher Meyer would write much later that Cabinet Office notes of the meeting "recorded that Blair told Bush that Britain would support military action 'provided that certain conditions were met,'" conditions like a real effort to secure UN approval and taking a renewed run at the Arab-Israeli peace process, one of Blair's hobby horses. But Meyer began to notice that when pressed, Blair would emphasize the *promise of support* side of the equation more than the *required conditions* side. At one point Blair said that when "America is fighting for those values, then, however tough, we fight with her—no grandstanding, no offering implausible and impractical advice from the touchline." This gallant proclamation caused Meyer to wonder, "When is a condition not a condition? . . . Preconditions do not mix easily, if at all, with a commitment like that."[76]

When Blair returned to London, he reported to his cabinet, and the supposed conditions seemed to be melting before their eyes. Robin Cook reports Blair's summary of the meeting in the form of a crudely simple oath: "I do believe in this country's relations with the US." When other cabinet members urged the importance of a serious and extended period of UN diplomacy, Blair would not commit himself. "Rather more alarmingly," Cook wrote, Blair said that "the time to debate the legal base for our action should be when we take that action."[77]

For his part, Bush's public statements were also becoming increasingly unconditional. As early as April 2002, in an interview with the British ITV television network, Bush said, "I made up my mind that Saddam needs to go. . . . The policy of my government is that he goes." When asked how he planned to attain this goal, Bush replied, "Wait and see."[78]

æ

The question of the postwar—what the United States planned to *do* with this country of twenty-five million people once it gained possession of the place, who would govern it, and through what mechanisms—remained vague through the spring of 2002. To help address the question, that spring the State Department undertook an ultimately abortive effort that would become known as the "Future of Iraq Project."[79] The project's briefing books came to more than two thousand pages of detailed thinking about a post-Saddam Iraq.[80] The core of the effort involved bringing together American officials with Iraqi exiles to develop principles for a postwar Iraq, and by implication to bring those exiles into the running of that government.[81] Very quickly, though, the Future of Iraq Project laid bare simmering disputes about the role of exiles in postwar Iraq. A stern hand on the wheel of the process would have forced a compromise resolution once it was obvious that the issue was a serious problem. But the central problem with the war planning, and indeed the larger implicit judgment, was that there was no hand on the wheel at all.

In the end, the Future of Iraq Project—both its engagement of exiles and its analytical components—would have to be described as a failure. It did not involve high-level involvement at State. It was, Karen DeYoung has written, "physically and psychologically far removed from Powell," who "paid little attention" to it.[82] It largely ignored the expertise of those with the most experience in postwar political-military planning.[83] Its reports were not anything resembling "plans"; they were extended analyses, ruminations, thought pieces, and interesting background material—all far too bulky to be useful to anyone engaged in the rushed and urgent task of planning a war.

One source described the effort as bringing together very smart, hard-working people to generate "silly, useless ideas" that were "at best postreconstruction" in nature. There was "no coherence" to the reports or proposals; they were "all over the place."[84] NSC officials later invited the State Department officer leading the project to brief the Executive Steering Group; the brief, one participant explained, "told us nothing. There was nothing there."[85] Some reports pointed to the Future of Iraq work as reflecting significant foresight and a meaningful strategy for the postwar, but in fact, "State didn't have the answer. We didn't know how hard it was going to be. The Future of Iraq [Project] wasn't a plan. It was the beginning of a plan."[86]

※

In the late spring, George Bush conducted a diplomatic tour of Europe. Condoleezza Rice explains that Bush discussed Iraq with many European leaders. "There was general support for raising the profile of the Iraq problem," she writes, "and we returned to Washington confident that it was time to do so."[87]

In Baghdad, meanwhile, Saddam was trying to lie low. He would agree to inspections in due time, he appears to have figured, and deprive the United States of an excuse to provoke a war. And he seems to have thought, by this strategy, that he would avoid one.[88]

Part of the problem, it turns out, may have been that Saddam, in power for a quarter of a century, had lost the taste for daily affairs of state. By 2003, according to what he told his American interrogators after being captured, he focused on "things other than the humdrum business of government"—including, among other projects, writing a novel. (Repeatedly, while in captivity in later years, he railed against the Americans' refusal to provide him with paper and pens. "I am a writer!" he would thunder at his captors.) He had "delegated much of the running of the government to his top aides." In the process he had become "clueless about what was happening inside Iraq," had stopped receiving regular intelligence briefings, was "inattentive to what his government was doing," and had "no real plan to prepare for the defense of Iraq." He was completely detached from the military situation; shown a map of the battlefield, he proved unable to say anything meaningful about the movement of forces during the conflict. Saddam, as it turned out, was just winging it, and hoping things would turn out for the best.[89]

In the oddest of parallels, this pattern—of improvising on the road to war under the influence of the felt "rightness" of a cause and a direction—turned out to be equally, and disastrously, true in both Washington and Baghdad.

⁂

As the planning continued, it gradually became clear that the Defense Department intended to control postwar political outcomes in Iraq. But an unplanned outcome of this grab for control was to send an ultimately disastrous signal: because the civilians in Defense had oversight of the postwar governance problem, the military planners at CENTCOM could safely ignore it. The uniformed military had natural antibodies to conducting postwar stabilization anyway; the idea that Defense civilians wanted the job was all the excuse they needed. "I think we just dodged a big bullet," Tommy Franks reportedly said coming out of one meeting with Rumsfeld and Feith, when it appeared that Feith would be responsible for postconflict security and reconstruction.[90] Yet in typical Rumsfeld management style, all of this was left more abstract than specific. Responsibilities were mostly left unassigned, and few things were formally decided.

As the process crawled forward, the rest of government continued to discover the extent of planning indirectly and, as often as not, come to the self-generated conclusion that they had better get busy thinking about the postwar.[91] One official figured things were getting serious when he saw CENTCOM's charts on temperature changes in Baghdad.[92] Even now, months after the implicit decision to act had been taken, State people were shocked when the seriousness of war planning was revealed. "We thought the president was in a different spot," one senior State official explained. "We had no idea he had decided to do it when he did. . . . We thought he was more deliberate."[93]

As they came to these conclusions, apart from the relatively small number of people directly involved in the military planning group, other knots of officials within various departments and agencies began thinking about what it would take to pacify and administer a country of twenty-five million people. They did this at first (and for months on end) without any clear guidance, coordination, or even awareness of what was actually going on. Those government officials who saw the white smoke and guessed correctly about the direction of policy—notably at the CIA and the US Agency for International Development (USAID)—were better prepared when the decision was formally announced than those who continued to hope or believe that all options were still on the table.

Just how far advanced thinking was by spring 2002 is apparent from a declassified memo titled "Scenarios for the 'End Game,'" which is dated April 23. It does not list an author, but it was classified by the Near East South Asia office of OSD Policy.[94] The three-page memo made a clear assumption that the direction of US policy would unseat Saddam Hussein, by force if necessary.

The memo then went on to list a number of fantasies. When the regime fell, "we will need to start a 'Bonn process' immediately"—as if the UN-led conference of Afghan leaders that had been held in Germany in December 2001 could be re-created for Iraq. The United States "should train opposition groups to run the POW camps"—which would amount to placing ambitious and totally untrained exiles who had been out of the country for decades in charge of angry, resentful former regime elements in captivity. "Opposition group members must be ready either to take command of defecting military units, or to work with their commanders," and also to "review the military officers currently in command of units in Iraq . . . and decide which ones might be acceptable and which ones would have to be replaced immediately."

The idea that arriving exiles, fresh from the coffee shops of Europe and trained for careers as engineers or professors or lawyers or barbers or mechanics, could slide into command of battle-hardened Iraqi military formations in the name of an invading and occupying army is nothing short of insane. But such delusions were an essential support system if the emerging US concept had any hope of working. For the memo concluded, with astonishing simplicity, "The earlier a provisional government can be established, the easier it should be to turn over tasks to it, thus allowing the US military to leave."

This emphasis on a rapid handover would become a common refrain among advocates for regime change, who loathed the idea of an "occupation" and had no interest in getting sucked into an interminable process of nation building. During the Afghan campaign, Rumsfeld had written Bush, "We ought not to make a career out of transforming Afghanistan."[95] He would say much the same things in the Iraq debate, and was one of the great skeptics of the democracy agenda as a primary mission.[96] In September 2002 testimony, he said bluntly that "going the next step and beginning to talk about democracy or things like that is a step I can't go."[97]

But leaving Iraq a functioning democracy was the clearly expressed goal of many other policy memos, and would soon become the oft-repeated public commitment of the US government. It was the abiding dream of such humanitarians as Paul Wolfowitz—and, of course, the deeply held commitment of President Bush himself. All of which raised this question: If the United States would not stay behind during the post-invasion chaos to stabilize the country and build democratic institutions, who, exactly, was going to do the job?

※

Some in the administration remained determined to justify action against Saddam by establishing his ties to al Qaeda, and more directly, to the 9/11 attacks themselves. But the US intelligence community was steadfast in its insistence, from the first day, that Iraq had nothing to do with it. That this was not going to sit well with the war advocates became apparent in June 2002, when the CIA circulated two papers on Iraq's nonconnections to terrorism.

Cheney aide Scooter Libby called the lead agency analyst, Jami Miscik, in a fury. The argument in the paper was wrong, he barked. CIA official Michael Morell reports that Libby screamed, "Withdraw the paper!" loudly enough that everyone in the room on Miscik's end of the call could hear it. She refused. Libby called her boss, John McLaughlin, to vent his fury; Miscik said "she would resign before withdrawing the paper." To their credit, McLaughlin and Tenet backed her. Libby's meddling, Morell writes, "was the most blatant attempt to politicize intelligence that I saw in thirty-three years in the business."[98]

When Miscik later briefed Bush, the president himself let her know, as Morell puts it, that "he had her back." He wanted his intelligence people to "call 'em like you see 'em." But they had only begun fighting the war against pressure to gin up the case against Saddam, pressure that would culminate in the days before Colin Powell's February 2003 United Nations speech. Senior officials intent on confronting Saddam would not hesitate to intimidate and suppress unwelcome intelligence and perspectives.

ə⃟

Meanwhile, the diplomatic and inspections path gathered momentum but could not generate any decisive results or findings. Between May and July of 2002, IAEA inspections chief Hans Blix held a series of meetings with Iraqi negotiators, who continued to demand concessions for cooperation and otherwise showed no signs of representing a regime under threat. Even by July 2002, Iraqi officials clung to the idea that they were in a strong bargaining position. "They were still balking and focused exclusively on their effort to limit the scope of inspections," Blix would later write. "The Iraqi stance was puzzling. Talk of armed action was growing louder. . . . Was Saddam Hussein not well informed or was the Iraqi conduct simply a piece of hard bargaining in the bazaar?"[99]

We now know that Saddam remained in the grip of misconceptions that had poisoned his thinking for years. The US threat was, to him, just another in a long line of standoffs, mutual bluster, and eventual negotiation that hardly threatened his regime.[100] He knew that Iraq did not have a close relationship with al Qaeda, that his regime had not been involved in 9/11—and so, naturally, the Americans *could not possibly mean* what they said about Iraq as the center of a global axis of evil. He knew, as well, that the American charges on WMDs had to be hot air; he had ordered the weapons to be jettisoned after the inspection and sanction crises of the 1990s. He told his postwar interrogator, "We destroyed them. We told you, with documents. That's it." By means of proof, he also said his behavior during the US invasion made clear his lack of capability. "By God, if I had such weapons, I would have used them in the fight against the United States."[101]

On June 1, 2002, President Bush gave a hard-nosed speech at the West Point graduation ceremony. "The gravest danger to freedom lies at the perilous crossroads of radicalism and technology," President Bush said. "Containment is not possible when unbalanced dictators with weapons of mass destruction can deliver those weapons on missiles or secretly provide them to terrorist allies. . . . [If we] wait for threats to fully materialize, we will have waited too long."

In Baghdad, Saddam Hussein decided that Bush must have been talking about North Korea.[102]

CHAPTER 6

MUDDLING TOWARD WAR: JUNE TO AUGUST 2002

The problems of a great country are exactly the kinds of problems most resistant to bold strokes.

BUSH SPEECHWRITER DAVID FRUM[1]

I just presumed that what I considered to be the most competent national-security team since Truman was indeed going to be competent. They turned out to be among the most incompetent teams in the post-war era. Not only did each of them, individually, have enormous flaws, but together they were deadly, dysfunctional.

KENNETH ADELMAN[2]

None of these judgments had any reality outside the subjective thoughts of the officials who asserted them.

DOUGLAS FEITH[3]

In August 2002, a new spate of warnings about the potential costs and risks of an Iraq adventure appeared in the press. On July 28, Tom Ricks had reported in the *Washington Post* that "many senior US military officers contend that President Saddam Hussein poses no immediate threat and that the United States should continue its policy of containment rather than invade Iraq to force a change of leadership in Baghdad."[4]

Former national security advisor Brent Scowcroft warned on CBS's *Face the Nation* in the first days of August that going after Saddam "could turn the whole region into a cauldron and, thus, destroy the war on terrorism."[5] Speaking in Hanover, German chancellor Gerhard Schröder declared that his government would not support a war.

According to Bob Woodward's reporting, Colin Powell was affected by some of these cautions. Powell "basically agreed" with Scowcroft's worry, Woodward explains. "He realized that he had not laid out his own analysis to the president directly and forcefully" and decided that he "owed Bush his understanding and his views on all the possible consequences of war."[6] Powell asked Condoleezza Rice if she could help arrange a private meeting at which he could air his concerns. She did so, and the three gathered in the first week of August.

This was the backdrop to one of the most potentially important milestones on the road to war—the moment when the American secretary of state, a man of tremendous insight and profound military and diplomatic experience, took the opportunity to speak directly and personally to his president about the dangers of launching a far-off war. It was the only time, as far as my research has uncovered, when a cabinet member took such pains to highlight the risks of conflict. And although the war was still eight months away, the rapid emergence of an implicit moral conviction about regime change meant that this offered perhaps the last real opportunity to generate any meaningful hesitation.

Indeed, it may already have been too late. Just how difficult it would be for Powell to gain any traction against the momentum toward war was clear from statements of congressional leaders who appeared on the weekly talk shows on the same Sunday that Scowcroft aired his doubts.[7] The Democratic senator Joseph Lieberman, a well-known national security hawk, argued that "every day Saddam remains in power with chemical weapons, biological weapons and the development of nuclear weapons is a day of danger for the United States of America." Even the Democratic minority leader in the Senate, Tom Daschle, said that "we all support strongly a regime change [in Iraq]." His only concern was that "we've got to get our ducks in order."

If Powell was going to make a powerful case to avoid war, then, he had an uphill climb. But as it turned out, he was not going to make such a case at all.

࿊

From June through August 2002, the planning process for the war ramped up inside government. Yet during all this time, it remained something short of a formal *decision*, in the classic sense of governmental policy. The unfolding discussion inside the administration reflected intentions and hopes, the planning documents made increasingly clear, but no final judgment had been made official. And one lesson of the Iraq case is that it turns out to be painfully difficult to plan for a war that no one will admit is going to happen.

The early summer of 2002 should have been a period of intensifying preparation for the implications of invasion. Instead, critical issues—from the role of exiles in postinvasion Iraq to the ownership of post-war planning to the basic governance model for that moment—were left unresolved. Senior officials with the understanding and power to have thrown themselves across the tracks of the accelerating rush to war, notably Colin Powell, took halfway steps in that direction but quickly concluded that the decision was, in effect, made. And the upshot of all of these developments was that looming disasters were left in the path of the emerging American commitment to transform Iraq, the Middle East, and the world.

This chapter surveys a number of developments on the path to war during these months. One of the most important was the debate about the role of Iraqi exiles in any postwar situation. By mid-2002, they had become essential to many assumed American strategies for handling the postwar in ways that had been neither subject to any real analysis nor even cleared with the president. But as it turned out, George W. Bush was uninterested in picking the "right" Iraqis to run the country after the United States got there—a decision that, while it reflected a genuine commitment to democracy, would throw a devastating wrench into the plans of many war advocates.

As the decision became increasingly formed during these months, one central dilemma began to peek forth from all the memos, meetings, and discussions: how the United States proposed to both liberate and control Iraq. Spurred by both the hawkish and dovish sides of its missionary sensibility, the United States had acquired a sense of moral obligation to drive Saddam from power and transplant a democracy in place of his regime. To do this, though, would require something far more elaborate than the light-footprint, brief-stay approach long favored by liberationists. It would require, most likely, a coercive and lengthy occupation to make sure that the US invasion did not simply open the way for another maniacal dictator—or Islamic extremists—to seize power, replacing one tyranny with another. But such an occupation necessarily implied risks and costs that few would have been consciously willing to embrace, and that would shock the American people when they came to pass.

This was the most painful dilemma that confronted American ambitions in Iraq—how to set a people free and determine their course at the same time. It would never be resolved. In some important ways, in fact, the United States is still looking for a way out of this dilemma, sixteen years later.

⁂

As a potential war drew closer, US Army general George Casey at the Joint Staff—first as the director of the J-5 strategy division and then as the Joint Staff director—decided on his own initiative to form a planning group, the J-5 Post-War Planning Group, which would become the Iraq Political-Military Cell, or IPMC.[8] A senior participant in the group told me that Casey was concerned that nothing was being done at the NSC or in the interagency to assess the requirements for an operation that seemed increasingly likely.[9] It was a working-level group staffed mostly with officers on loan from the Joint Staff, though there were representatives from

State, CIA, the vice president's office, and other departments. The group met weekly, eventually tied into the NSC process, and occasionally more senior officials sat in.[10] It aimed to identify essential strategic tasks that would have to be performed in the event of war.

Despite Casey's initiative and the best efforts of everyone concerned, the IPMC eventually conformed to the pattern of just about all the many postwar planning efforts that bloomed and then died off during 2002 and early 2003: it came to little. One participant said that "a lot of the preparatory work we did was wasted."[11] I asked if this officer had noticed any dissent—anyone raising serious questions, debating the very feasibility of the operation. He "never sensed serious discussion that it couldn't be accomplished." Why wasn't there more pushback, I continued? Why didn't someone start asking the bigger questions? Largely, the officer said, because they all figured the decision had already been made. Regime change was "given to us as an end state." Their job was to assess its requirements, not question its feasibility. And here, too, a pattern would be set that would replicate itself throughout the decision process after June 2002: almost nobody asked hard questions about the biggest issues in going to war, because they saw no point.

Some senior officials who might otherwise have raised more doubts fell victim to another symptom of imperative-driven thinking: they did not appreciate the degree of momentum for war. In July, State Policy Planning head Richard Haass met with Condi Rice at the NSC to express concerns about a possible war—only to be told not to waste his breath, that it was a done deal. He dashed back to the State Department, straight into Colin Powell's office. "It seems as if we're going to war," he told the secretary. Powell "was typically relaxed," Haass wrote later, "skeptical that things had gone that far, thinking either Condi was exaggerating or I had misread 'my girlfriend,' as he teasingly tended to refer to her in my presence."[12] Of course it was Powell who was misreading and who had been doing so for months.

One thing many people involved in the Joint Staff planning process did notice, as planning for the postwar crawled toward actual choices, was that, in the words of one officer, "a lot of faith was being placed in the exiles." And the man who had spent the 1990s angling to produce decisive American action against Saddam—Ahmad Chalabi—remained at the center of that group, by his own design as much as anything else. There was a long tradition of buccaneers using America's messianic conceptions of its role in the world to serve their purposes. Chalabi was well aware of this history and thirsted to become the latest example. He would not achieve his personal goals, but the role of the exiles more broadly emerged as a critical support pillar for the assumptions of many war advocates.

War advocates were taken in by Chalabi in part because they were being told what they wanted to hear. Iraq was ready for democracy, he insisted. Expatriates would flood back into the country and run its major ministries, carrying democratic habits and Western technocratic approaches with them. As the decision hardened in the summer, such testimony allowed anti-Saddam advocates to fortify their conviction that war would be easy: administration leaders "believed what they were being told," a US official says. Chalabi's fellow exile leader Kanan Makiya, the official said, "now admits he was wrong, but [all the US officials] wanted to believe it, and were told [these things] by people they trusted."[13] Over time, some anti-Saddam activists had come to see in Chalabi the personification of their hopes for a cosmopolitan Iraq—and, having vested him with their dreams, reacted with fury against anyone who dared challenge his credibility.

The story of the exiles, and of Chalabi in particular, has become enshrouded in myth and legend. Even today, many participants in the drama differ starkly about his role. We know that during the 1990s, successive US governments funded Chalabi and his Iraqi National Congress (INC) as part of a largely half-hearted effort to destabilize Saddam. At first the CIA ran the Chalabi account, but gradually soured on him. The agency decided that Chalabi's so-called intelligence was garbage. He made a lot of claims about getting "couriers" from inside Iraq that people in the agency came to see as bullshit. The CIA had "created" Chalabi, another source told me, but over time "we realized that this was a bad thing."[14]

So the agency sought to off-load his account, and for a time he was transferred to the State Department, which funded INC programs to accomplish such tasks as beaming anti-Saddam propaganda into Iraq. But a September 2001 report by the State Department Inspector General found substantial problems with the INC grants, including over half a million dollars of cash payments without adequate records.[15] The report exacerbated tensions between State and Chalabi sympathizers, especially at the Office of the Secretary of Defense (OSD) and in the vice president's office. In January 2002, prompted by a *New York Times* piece claiming that State was abandoning the INC, Rumsfeld reportedly brought the matter up at a lunch with Powell. According to a snowflake he dictated to Wolfowitz later that afternoon, Rumsfeld asked "why State is halting support for the Iraqi exile group. He said they are not, but are continuing at $500,000 per month so they can keep functioning." Powell did mention "an audit problem" and the uncomfortable fact that the INC was proving "unwilling to tell [State] how they are spending the money." Rumsfeld instructed Wolfowitz to get senior officials across government focused on the issue: "You ought to get the Deputies back on this subject, I would think."[16]

Meanwhile, State heard rumors that Chalabi was using the funds to develop a secret intelligence network on the ground in Iraq—a task beyond what US government economic support funds are legally allowed to accomplish. But neither State nor any formal US intelligence agency was getting any of the intelligence from the contacts Chalabi was bragging about; if he was gathering it, it was ending up somewhere else. One source told me that a State official traveled to London to confront Chalabi. *Either you give us the results of this supposed network*, he was told, *or we are going to cut your funds.* Chalabi, furious, eyes bulging, told the official that such a step would "cut the heart out" of the INC. He fumed that the State Department was not committed to the liberation of

Iraq—perhaps, Chalabi spat, because it was filled with "Saddamists."[17] Chalabi's fans would become bitterly convinced that, in broadcasting these doubts, State and the CIA had undermined a transformative opportunity to install a friendly leader of Iraq.[18] The writer George Packer says that much later, as postwar Iraq descended into chaos, Vice President Cheney "approached his longtime colleague Colin Powell, stuck a finger in his chest, and said, 'If you hadn't opposed the INC and Chalabi, we wouldn't be in this mess.' "[19]

Defense decided there was only one thing to do—adopt the INC themselves. One source told me Powell finally said, "Don asked one too many times, so I gave it to him. I told him, 'You want it, you got it,' "[20] and Chalabi became the responsibility of the Defense Intelligence Agency (DIA).[21] The DIA connection would continue until May 2004, a year after the invasion; Defense officials said Chalabi was by then part of the governing council, and it would be inappropriate to have a foreign official on an intelligence payroll. Other reports claimed that the full scope of the INC's intelligence fabrications was coming to light, and DIA wanted to cut ties before Chalabi and his crew became an embarrassing liability.[22]

⁂

What remains hotly disputed is to what degree backers of the war truly intended to put Chalabi in power. People involved in the debates at the highest levels offer starkly differing accounts.

The defense analyst Richard Perle, closely connected to many Defense officials and a passionate anti-Saddam activist, admitted to Richard Bonin that in order to fashion a postinvasion government, "We had to work with somebody, and I thought [Chalabi] was the right person." Bonin also reports that Harold Rhode, an Islamic studies specialist who would work in OSD Policy under Feith, talked in almost religious terms: "Once I met Ahmad, I intuitively understood that there was hope. Hope for what? A better future for the Middle East." He spoke of Chalabi as the "Charles de Gaulle of Iraq."[23]

Such comments are symptomatic of an undeniable fact: right up to the war (and afterward), Chalabi retained a significant core of supporters. Many in the Washington conservative policy community were "supporting the INC wholeheartedly" during this time, one official told me.[24] State Department consultant David Phillips, who helped to arrange many early meetings with Iraqi exiles, quotes a Defense official who he claims said, "Ahmad Chalabi is like Prophet Mohammed. At first people doubted him, but they came to realize the wisdom of his ways."[25] Some former senior officials with whom I spoke were told quite specifically, "We are going to make Ahmad Chalabi the next King of Iraq." But they heard this from the same middle-level zealots who were going around saying a lot of histrionic things. Most senior officials to whom I spoke claim they never heard such people as Vice President Cheney or Defense Secretary Rumsfeld endorse Chalabi in such unqualified terms.[26]

One source closely involved in war planning says it was very evident to him that, for some of the war hawks, it was all about Chalabi. The INC leader's enthusiasts imagined a magical transition in which Chalabi would move into one of Saddam's residences with his palace guard and the Iraqis would call out, "The king is dead; long live the king." Yet even this source admitted that "with some exceptions, the more senior you go, the more recognition there was" that such a model was a fantasy.[27] One very senior official explained, "Rumsfeld said many times: 'Chalabi is the best politician they have got.' But Rumsfeld never bought into Chalabi one way or the other. And I don't think Wolfowitz was necessarily as close to him as some believe."[28] A source with close knowledge of the issue said support for Chalabi centered on Wolfowitz, Defense and NSC official William Luti, Feith, and some in the vice president's office such as John Hannah. As for Rumsfeld, "I never found him to be an INC guy."[29] Yet another source who participated in multiple meetings with Wolfowitz came away with the impression that Chalabi was favored, but not in any wholesale way. Wolfowitz saw him as "one of the guys we can work with" but never simply said, "We have to make Chalabi the leader."[30]

Yet counterbalanced against these recollections must be placed contrary reports—many in the media, but some from interviews with senior officials—suggesting that leaders like Cheney and Wolfowitz were strongly committed to Chalabi. One senior official said quite directly, "Oh, yeah, he was their guy. He was going to bring democracy, change the Middle East," and reestablish relations with Israel. "Don't let them tell you now," this former official told me passionately, jabbing a finger for emphasis, that the advocates weren't buying into Chalabi—they absolutely were. I asked whether these officials made clear that Chalabi would run Iraq after the invasion, and he replied simply, "Yup." When I mentioned that other senior leaders had denied giving Chalabi any special treatment, he waved off the suggestion. Who was the United States primarily backing, with funds and direct support? What was the only organization for which the United States was training a private army?[31]

With regard to Wolfowitz, few in government saw evidence of a nuanced view. Most viewed him as an unhesitant champion of Chalabi and the INC. One published source suggests that Wolfowitz lobbied the CIA to stop belittling Chalabi, that he was really not the "scoundrel" that some claimed. At other times Wolfowitz darkly hinted that those who opposed the INC leader were "undermining the president."[32] Chalabi met with Wolfowitz and others directly in private meetings in 2002, another former official said.[33]

A senior official who participated closely in the interagency debates on the INC said the idea that Defense people never preferred Chalabi is "at best half true. . . . I sat in on many meetings where I observed up close the personal relationships between Chalabi and DoD officials." Those officials did not *say* they wanted to put him in charge; it did not appear that they had to.[34] US policy was obviously based on a major role for exiles, and Chalabi was the chief exile. Former Pentagon comptroller Dov Zakheim relates in his memoir that when one Defense official offered the simple suggestion that they could decide who to work with once they got to Iraq, the comment earned him a trip to Doug Feith's woodshed. "You don't get it," Feith told the official. "Chalabi's our guy."

Jay Garner would later claim that Feith suggested that he simply declare Chalabi president; Frank Miller of the NSC has testified that Wolfowitz and Feith made the case directly to President Bush for putting Chalabi in charge.[35]

Yet a critical and undeniable fact is this: the ultimate decision-maker in the US government, George Bush, had significant doubts about Chalabi. When given an opportunity to weigh in, Bush made it clear: US policy would not pick any leader for post-Saddam Iraq.

By all reports, Bush saw through Chalabi from the start. On many occasions before and after the invasion when Chalabi's influence seemed apparent—such as when he somehow appeared, sitting behind Laura Bush, at a State of the Union speech—Bush was noticeably upset. Later, when evidence emerged that Chalabi had revealed crucial US intelligence to Iran, Bush ordered him completely cut off—and was furious when the Defense Department dragged its feet on the order.[36] In at least two different meetings with Defense officials, Bush was unequivocal: he would not "put [his] finger on the scale"[37] relative to various Iraqi leaders. One source recalled that Bush "slammed" either Wolfowitz or Feith when they kept making the case for Chalabi.[38] Another source said he heard Bush say outright, "This guy is not going to be president [of Iraq] as long as I am president."[39]

But if Chalabi and his INC would not take over in Iraq after the Americans got there, it was not clear who would.

⁂

Indeed, the dispute about Chalabi partly obscures a larger and much more important issue: the role of exiles—or, as many OSD policy memos refer to them, "oppositionists"—in US planning for what would happen in Iraq once US forces had kicked Saddam's regime aside. Defense plans relied on expatriate Iraqis to come into the country and begin playing a major governance role immediately.[40] But nobody had reason to believe they could do such a job—none of them had the political or managerial experience, or contemporary contacts in Iraq, to take on such a monumental task. Imagining such a role for small knots of cultured exiles, most of whom had mostly been gone from their native country for years or even decades, was pure fantasy.

Yet that precise idea crops up again and again in DoD planning documents. A May 9, 2002, memo to Rumsfeld from Defense official Peter Rodman is emblematic of the pattern: Rodman suggested the need to "make sure the wrong people don't fill the vacuum" in Iraq, and proposed marshaling "the Iraqi Opposition to assist with regime change." Rodman argued that it was critical to "ensure that the post-Saddam vacuum is filled quickly by the right people."[41] This basic notion—making sure the "right people" rose to the top after an invasion—would remain central to thinking in Defense and the vice president's office right up to, and after, the beginning of the war.

Handwritten notes on the Rodman memo indicate that Rumsfeld liked it and requested an extended version to send around to the principals under Rumsfeld's own signature. This longer memo appeared on July 1. "Organizing the Iraqi opposition to assist with regime change is needed for two reasons—to ensure legitimacy . . . and to make sure the wrong people don't fill the vacuum created by the end of the Saddam regime," it began. There were "undesirable opposition elements" inside Iraq that needed to be shunted aside after an invasion. By creating a strong force of exiles aligned with US goals and ready to rush into Iraq, Washington could "avoid a chaotic post-Saddam free-for-all." The key line in the memo was the following: "An attempt to run Iraqi affairs by ourselves *without* a pre-cooked umbrella group of Iraqi Opposition leaders could backfire seriously."[42]

Many war advocates continue to insist that they did not pick specific favorites, and perhaps that is true in the strictest of terms. But they did not have to. They were creating the conditions under which the postwar US administration would have no choice; the policy would direct them to prepare the ground for a set of exiles, and Ahmad Chalabi was the most "pre-cooked" of all. More fundamentally, this memo hints at the crippling dilemma at the heart of the American project—a lesser version of the dilemma affecting the broader missionary conception of foreign policy. The United States, the memo made clear, wanted both to set Iraq free and to determine its future. It wanted to be liberator and hegemon at the same time.

But the president would soon reject the idea of the Chalabi-as-king model, and the idea of installing exiles never entered into the formal NSC planning for the postwar. And so a continuing pattern of this policy on autopilot persisted: different players in the drama marched forward with diametrically opposed conceptions of how it would unfold—dilemmas that were never even well understood, let alone resolved.

⅔

Ambitious exiles like Chalabi and their backers in the US government are representative of a concept that helps to explain the emerging place of Iraq in US foreign policy: the role of what have been called "policy entre- preneurs." In foreign policy as in other issue areas, at any one time dozens of ideas are swirling for attention. Some get picked up and implemented, others do not; some hang around for years before their time arrives. These outcomes can be partly explained by the activities of organized advo- cates for specific policies—people who devote their time and prestige to achieving a prized outcome on an issue of passionate interest to them.[43]

The political scientist John Kingdon has described the role of what he calls "policy communities." These are groups of people—officials, former officials, think tank analysts, scholars, journalists, and members of Con- gress and their staffs—who share similar ideas, outlooks, and perspectives.[44] They develop shared belief systems, theories, and agendas. Certain espe- cially energetic and dedicated members of these communities, the policy entrepreneurs, are prepared to commit significant time and personal capital campaigning for their favored policies.[45] They are highly motivated advo- cates lying in wait in and around government, on the lookout for policy windows so they might focus events to justify their pet projects.

Such activists are not motivated as much by a desire to solve spe- cific problems as they are in realizing their long-incubated concept: they develop the ideas, and then they wait "for problems to come along to which they can attach their solutions."[46] This is just what the anti-Saddam activists did, spending years laying the groundwork of ideas and foreign policy consensus—which made them ready, after 9/11, to transform an attack by an obscure extremist group into a campaign for regime change. Advocates of confronting Iraq were "using the 9/11 situation to promote their Iraq preferences," one former senior official explained.[47] Immediately after September 11, "Paul Wolfowitz was interested" in going after Iraq, said another, and so "Paul took his shot, because that's how you do it." Wolfowitz's advocacy "wasn't surprising to me at all. It represented intelligent people of excellent bureaucratic skills using an opportunity to press their agenda."[48]

One dangerous side-effect of policy communities, though, is to reinforce tendencies to motivated reasoning. By creating self-selecting forums for dialogue and by circulating confirming evidence, the communities serve to reinforce the view of their participants. A mutual confirmation bias is at work, in which members of these policy communities continually reaffirm the core tenets of their thinking, raising those tenets to the level of accepted faith.

Another danger of policy entrepreneurship is that, when an option is worked out in advance and slipped into policy during a crisis, it will escape rigorous debate—because advocates are convinced they have already thought the problem through. In the Iraq case, as we have seen, before 9/11 anti-Saddam activists had not been imagining a US invasion—they planned to use exiles and defecting Iraqi army units and Kurdish forces to topple Saddam with limited US help, and then to rely on those liberationists to run the country afterward. That postwar was never well defined, but that didn't much matter when the United States would not be responsible for it. Perhaps because they had been incubating a policy option that allowed a limited responsibility for the postwar, anti-Saddam activists could not break out of the mental map that told them that phase would take care of itself. In the process, policy entrepreneurs set themselves up to be overtaken by imperative-driven thinking: the very nature

of policy entrepreneurship is to settle on a form of imperative, an outcome that is the "right thing to do," and await a catalyst or opportunity
to push it into place.

The Iraq case thus reinforces a recurring lesson: when a crisis gives
policy entrepreneurs the chance to push a coveted idea through a policy window, it will often be ill-considered and poorly conceived. As the
scholar Nelson Polsby explains, a crisis can help advocates with ready-
made solutions to get them enacted, "but it cannot make the policy
actually work afterward." Policy advocates thus "have to be reasonably
confident of the efficacy of the alternatives they propose—or they may
get what they 'want' and find it was not worth getting."[49]

⁂

What the war advocates believed to be imperative, of course, was decisive
action against Iraq, and it quickly became clear that they were willing
to sidestep inconvenient obstacles like international law to get it. On
July 23, 2002, the British cabinet met with Prime Minister Tony Blair
to discuss the emerging Iraqi war plan and US policy. Present at the
meeting were such principals as the defense secretary, Geoffrey Hoon;
the foreign secretary, Jack Straw; the head of MI6, Sir Richard Dearlove (code-named "C"); Tony Blair's chief of staff, Jonathan Powell; and
several others.[50] The report of this famous session, which has become
known as the "Downing Street Memo," is actually an official set of meeting notes. The most widely quoted passage is this:

> C reported on his recent talks in Washington. There was a per-
> ceptible shift in attitude. Military action was now seen as inevit-
> able. Bush wanted to remove Saddam, through military action,
> justified by the conjunction of terrorism and WMD. But the
> intelligence and facts were being fixed around the policy. The
> NSC had no patience with the UN route, and no enthusiasm for
> publishing material on the Iraqi regime's record. There was little
> discussion in Washington of the aftermath after military action.

It "seemed clear" to Foreign Secretary Straw, according to the notes, that "Bush had made up his mind to take military action, even if the timing was not yet decided." Straw worried, however, that "the case was thin"; Saddam "was not threatening his neighbours, and his WMD capability was less than that of Libya, North Korea or Iran." His recommendation was that "we should work up a plan for an ultimatum to Saddam to allow back in the UN weapons inspectors. This would also help with the legal justification for the use of force."

This line of thinking—war was legally suspect, and Washington and London needed to engineer some sort of Iraqi noncompliance to justify action—was, as we have seen, well established by the spring of 2002. A March 14 memo from David Manning to Blair lays it out quite clearly: the challenge was that the "issue of the weapons inspectors must be handled in a way that would persuade European and wider opinion that the US was conscious of the international framework, and the insistence of many countries on the need for a legal base. Renewed refus[als] by Saddam to accept unfettered inspections would be a powerful argument."[51] A "Note by Officials" produced by the London Cabinet Office on July 21 states quite explicitly that it would be "necessary to create the conditions in which we could legally support military action." Yet this would be a complex task, in part because of what was likely to happen once the demand for inspectors was on the table.

> In practice, facing pressure of military action, Saddam is likely to admit weapons inspectors as a means of forestalling it. But once admitted, he would not allow them to operate freely. UNMOVIC (the successor to UNSCOM) will take at least six months after entering Iraq to establish the monitoring and verification system. . . . Hence, even if UN inspectors gained access today, by January 2003 they would at best only just be completing setting up. . . . It is just possible that an ultimatum could be cast in terms which Saddam would reject . . . and which would not be regarded as unreasonable by the international

community. However, failing that (or an Iraqi attack) we would be most unlikely to achieve a legal base for military action by January 2003.[52]

Which is to say: If we are intent on generating a process to manufacture a legal justification for the war, we had best get cracking.

A declassified US Defense Department memorandum from the same time period reflects a similar turn of mind, outlining ways to use inspections as a catalyst for war. The United States had a public strategy of regime change, the memo began. Once that policy moved into its end-game, however, "Saddam is likely to believe that he cannot physically survive," and "he may not be interested in exile." Therefore, "he may figure he has little to lose by using WMD." The implication was clear: "We should aim to delay Saddam's recognition of the *imminence* of his downfall for as long as possible" and "convince him that he has more time to maneuver than he actually does. When the end comes, it must come quicker than he imagines." At that point, Washington would say the time for inspections had passed, and would deliver an ultimatum demanding (1) disarmament, (2) handing over of "all al Qaida suspects in Iraq," and (3) unrestricted inspections accompanied by US troops—all to be agreed to within a number of days.[53] Saddam would refuse, and the United States would have a legal basis for war.[54]

The appreciation that the inspections process was a huge gambit rather than a serious effort to disarm Saddam without war was widely held within the administration. One official I interviewed, not in the neocon camp, nonetheless was clear-eyed enough to see the inspections for what they were. The idea that this process would make war unnecessary was "my hope, not my belief," he said calmly. "I viewed it entirely as a preparation for war, to build international support for war if it happened."[55]

❧

As the planning process for that war ramped up during the summer, where exactly Colin Powell was on all this remained something of a mystery. At a minimum, Powell did not become a vocal advocate for alternatives other than invasion. He must have "questioned the need to take down Saddam Hussein," one State official suggested. "I'm certain that he did,"[56] though he never said as much publicly. I have heard the same impression from people at State, Defense, the NSC: "Powell's heart wasn't in it." Officials in Defense and the vice president's office were convinced Powell opposed them. But he would not speak up—forcefully, definitively—among the principals. Several subordinate State Department officials describe Powell as essentially backing away, as appearing to give up. In his view, most likely, he was following the lead of a president he was duty-bound to serve.

He may also have been caught somewhat unaware. For the longest time, according to testimony from close associates as well as public statements, Powell seems to have discounted the likelihood of war. And then, suddenly, he began getting signals that it was more than likely—the decision had been made.

Some in State began to assume that the cynics at Defense and the vice president's office were right—that Powell and Deputy Secretary Richard Armitage really wanted the whole thing to run off the rails. They wanted the neocons to fall on their face, and so they responded to Rumsfeld's stiff-arms in the interagency by essentially saying: *Fine, asshole—you want it, you got it.* One USAID source recounted that they got to brief Powell for *ten minutes* on their postwar planning for reconstruction. This would inevitably be a major part of State's role, and they were working long hours to be ready. Ten minutes? It didn't make sense. Powell didn't throw his weight behind the Future of Iraq Project and did not pick up the multiple warnings that came his way and wave them in the face of the president.

One nonideological Defense official explained that "State had lots of people who were engaging in what I would call guerrilla warfare against the president's policies—trying to slow-roll everything in the hope that the war wouldn't happen."[57] That is very likely untrue, at least in terms of active subversion, but the lack of enthusiasm was palpable.

Another State official recalled, "A lot of us trying to work the issue did not feel a clear sense of direction from the top of our building." Powell, the official said, "*seemed* opposed" to the drift toward war, "but I didn't see evidence of work to take the military option off the table." It all "seemed very passive-aggressive to me." A senior official who worked with the cabinet members said that Powell "did not ever come out and advocate" for a contrary view. He was clearly unenthusiastic, they could tell that, but he didn't offer alternatives. "He never said, 'Don't do this.'" Powell "needed an idea," this official continued, "and State didn't have any. State had no useful ideas for the president about what to do about any of this," distinct from the line being pushed by Defense. "There was no positive agenda, just nit-picking. . . . The president was an activist. He gravitated toward those who gave him something to do, for better or worse."[58]

Powell offers an interesting theory of responsibility and loyalty in his memoirs. To cope with the sometimes crushing bureaucracy of the army, he wrote, you cannot simply refuse orders. Instead, you "give the King his shilling" to "get him off your back, and then go about doing what you consider important." Powell had little regard for officers with a demonstrated "stubbornness about coughing up that shilling. They fought what they found foolish or irrelevant, and consequently did not survive to do what they considered vital."[59] Paying the shilling earned you the right to take positive action on issues important to you. These and similar anecdotes tell a dominant story about Powell: he was first and foremost a soldier, and following orders was for him an honorable reflex action.

This may go to the heart of the man who participated in the policy process in the run-up to the Iraq war. His temperament simply didn't allow for any sympathy for policy tantrums or refusing to go along. Moreover, he had his goals—leading the State Department, conducting diplomacy with an able and moderate hand—and if he had to "pay a shilling" on the Iraq adventure, so be it. He would survive to do what he considered vital. And so, when the president said get ready for war, he got ready. When the president asked, *Are you with me?*, his answer was going to be *Yes, Mister President*, because it simply could not be anything else. Powell's "willingness to support his president runs exceedingly deep—and it goes back to the day he became a US soldier," one senior US official told me. Had someone asked, this official said, "How could you possibly support this decision?", the answer most in tune with Powell's value system would have been very simple: "How could I *not?*"[60]

🎄

Powell did take one opportunity to speak up—just as he had in the Gulf War, and with the same effect—at the dinner with the president on August 5, 2002, the outcome of his request, mentioned at the beginning of the chapter, for an opportunity to make a direct appeal.[61] President Bush, Condoleezza Rice, and Powell met together, had dinner and continued to talk in Bush's White House residence office. It was, as far as is known, the only time President Bush received any sort of serious catalogue of the risks and consequences of going to war. And it ended up being highly constrained, a calm discussion of things that "could" go wrong.[62] Karen DeYoung summarizes the case he made as reviewing "all the potential consequences that Bush would have to consider before making a decision to invite Iraq." Powell told DeYoung he said that once they went into Iraq, it would be a "crystal glass . . . it's going to shatter. There will be no government. There will be civil disorder."[63]

Yet Powell did not urge Bush to rethink the war, nor did he make the case for waiting, containing Saddam, or some other course that he felt had already been ruled out. He simply said, *Try to build a stronger coalition*. President Bush listened and took the suggestion seriously, and eventually, despite his frustrations with the idea of UN diplomacy—and overruling severe objections from Vice President Cheney and others—he agreed to an additional round of United Nations consensus-building led by Powell.[64]

At the time, Rice pronounced the August 5 meeting "terrific" and told Powell, "We need to do more of those."[65] Years later, though, writing in her memoirs, she had come to a different view of Powell's various interactions with Bush. She writes that she was surprised that he did not speak more bluntly and openly about his concerns. Referring to interactions broader than merely the fateful August meeting, Rice points to various times she had heard out Powell's frustrations and organized meetings with the president in which she expected him to hit Bush hard with his views. When they met, though, "he didn't, and the President sometimes had difficulty gauging the extent of Colin's dissatisfaction." Rice writes, "I did sometimes wonder what held Colin back; perhaps the 'soldier' felt constrained."[66]

⁂

The days and weeks after 9/11 are the first key moment in the march to war, when the idea of linking Iraq to a global war on terrorism first took root. January and February of 2002 represent a second decisive period, when war planning and covert operations begin to heat up and some of the first formal directives appear to have emerged. August 2002, then, is a third critical threshold, when the implicit decision began to take on more concrete form at the highest levels of government. That this increasingly determined course did not, even at this stage, generate a formal consideration of *whether* to go to war—or even a truly rigorous assessment of risks—reflects value-driven decision-making in action. But it also represents yet another missed opportunity to take a step back and subject the rapidly coalescing decision to something like critical analysis.

The very day after Powell's dinner with the president, on August 6, Condoleezza Rice distributed a paper called "Liberation Strategy for Iraq." Feith quotes from the paper's introduction. "When we move to bring about a change of regime in Iraq," it began—*when*, not *if*—the United States should not assume the role of overbearing invader. The eviction of Saddam Hussein should "be perceived as a liberation of the Iraqi people by the US as opposed to a hostile, exploitive occupation." And yet to have "the most confidence in achieving US objectives," US forces would have to remain "in significant numbers for many years to assist in a US-led administration of the country."[67] These goals reflected Bush's powerful view that a primary purpose of any war should be the liberation of the long-suffering Iraqi people, which could start a domino effect of freedom throughout the Middle East.

This message didn't go over well with those committed to a much shorter stay—a quick in-and-out plan of toppling a regime. It was a remarkable admission, if taken seriously, one that would be contradicted by most of the administration's public statements over the coming year about the likely duration and cost of the war. At a Principals Committee meeting three days later, Rumsfeld came out clearly against such extended meddling in Iraq's affairs, or any devotion to promoting democracy. After the meeting, Feith says he spoke to Rumsfeld and suggested perhaps he shouldn't sound so negative on the subject of democratization. I get your point, Rumsfeld told him, but "democracy is complex; it is a lot more than just organizing an election." They spoke, Feith says, about Edmund Burke, whose thinking "supported Rumsfeld's view that US officials should refrain from suggesting that we would push Iraq to copy American political models."[68] Rumsfeld has argued that the democracy idea never occupied much time in NSC discussions of Iraq.[69]

The Secretary of Defense, in other words, was on a completely different page from his president about the goals of a looming war. And if the United States did end up "owning" Iraq for years, as Powell worried it would and as the strategy document seemed to agree—and if Rumsfeld's hard-nosed assumptions about the vexing challenges of democracy turned out to be right—nobody would have the slightest clue what to do about it.

※

Alongside planning for the war, the administration began—in even more organized and diligent ways—to sell it. In August 2002, a new organization called the White House Iraq Group was formed to make the public case. According to a raft of reports that have now emerged, the group met in the Situation Room each week. It included Karl Rove, Karen

Hughes, Mary Matalin, Rice, Hadley, and Libby.[70] Bush speechwriter
Scott McClellan has described it as a process to develop a "strategy for
carefully orchestrating the coming campaign to aggressively sell the war."
At the time it seemed to him fairly unexceptional—not intentionally
manipulative, just Public Relations 101.[71]

The group was working from a reasonably strong base. An August
2002 opinion poll found 69 percent of Americans believing that military
action to remove Saddam was justified; 79 percent believed Iraq posed
a threat to the United States.[72] But the support seemed to be contin-
gent on a low-cost, light-footprint operation. Another poll, a CNN/*USA
Today* survey conducted by Gallup in August, found public support for
a ground invasion of Iraq declining steadily—down to just 53 percent,
compared to 74 percent in November 2001 and 63 percent as recently
as July 2002. And only 41 percent expressed support for any action that
might have to last longer than a year.[73] The window of opportunity, in
other words, was already closing.

In the first days of August, senior US officials from Defense and State met
for discussions with key exiles, including Ahmad Chalabi and Abdul-
Aziz Hakim of the pro-Iranian Shi'a group SCIRI.[74] The official press
statement after this meeting read that the United States shared with the
exiles a "vision of a better future for the Iraqi people after the departure of
Saddam Hussein and his regime."[75] Ali Allawi writes that the exiles took
away the message to "organize a broad conference . . . in preparation for
the possibility of military action to overthrow the regime."[76]

On August 14, according to reports from a number of official memoirs and declassified documents, a national security principals session
chaired by Rice took another critical step in the direction of war:[77] they
approved a national security presidential directive on goals and objectives
of US strategy toward Iraq.[78] The direction of policy was hardening—
even though, in technical and formal terms, nothing had been actually
decided.

Despite the growing conclusiveness of this planning, or perhaps because of it, Colin Powell stepped up his call for a more active effort to generate a United Nations process that would lend legitimacy to the war the United States now planned to fight. At an August 16 NSC session, with Bush on video from his ranch at Crawford, Powell made the case for a UN route that in his mind would include weapons inspections as well as resolutions with ultimatums for Saddam. Even Cheney agreed. They talked about a plan in which Bush would go to the UN in September and make a case against Saddam.[79]

Meanwhile, planning for the civilian components of a war accelerated, though it remained largely uncoordinated and ad hoc. An NSC-based coordination group called the Executive Steering Group (ESG), headed by Senior Director for Defense Planning Frank Miller, had been formed in July, and it began meeting on August 12.[80] The ESG's focus was on the political-military minutiae of a war: getting access to bases, providing for stockpiles of food and medicine to be ready in case of a humanitarian disaster, building coalitions, worrying about WMD use and supplies. It was very much about "the military getting to Phase III"—the main warfighting phase, one participant recalled.[81]

One participant said the problem was unintentionally magnified by the massive scale of their task and the press of time. Frank Miller—a dedicated, highly experienced, blunt, and tough-minded civil servant—"ran very tightly focused meetings." He had to—he had little time for broad objections or discussions of theoretical issues. But the result, some participants said, was an environment with precious few opportunities to raise problems, assumptions, or flaws.[82] "No one asked," another participant said, "Are you *ready* to go to war? Are you ready to build a government?"[83]

※

This was the central, essential issue that leaps out of all accounts of these late-summer planning meetings. Above and beyond some of the more prosaic issues involved in postwar planning, the key fact that began to emerge in these weeks was that the administration had no coherent concept for what to do with Iraq, as a functioning society, once it took possession of the country. In all of the declassified memos and cabinet member memoirs that have been released about the planning process, there is almost no hint of a truly rigorous analysis of what it would take to get Iraq up and running after Saddam Hussein's regime fell. One officer recalled, "We lost a year of planning" because of the refusal to take the postwar seriously. There were "only cursory glances" of what would happen after they got to Baghdad. They ended up with "nat's-ass detail about [target] sites"—but if you asked them about the status of police in Baghdad, "you got this big hush—not a damn thing was known."[84]

In terms of military planning, the issue was how to handle governance in Phase IV, the postwar phase of any war plan. This same officer pointed to the essential dilemma. From a military planning standpoint, the process was looking at every possible disaster. In terms of Phase III— the major combat operations of a war—"the questions we were getting asked were all worst-case": What would happen if Saddam set the oil fields ablaze? How would they respond to a chemical attack? These issues were partly the province of the ESG, and indeed some good preventive planning was done on them. But when they turned to the postwar and issues like governance and reconstruction, suddenly all the assumptions were *best*-case: they would be welcomed with open arms, the Iraqi government would continue running, and police would maintain order. And the catch-22 of the thing was that the worst-case assumptions about the combat phase kept them from having any time to interrogate the best-case assumptions about the postwar. As a result, postwar conceptualizations became all "hand-waves and generalizations."

Not only were questions not being asked, but in more than a few cases, senior leaders in the military hierarchy actively shut down efforts to expand the postwar analysis. According to one planner, some senior leaders would respond to nettlesome questions by huffing, "You're not getting my message. You need to focus on the close fight. It's about the fight." This officer felt "strong pressure" not to have anyone in his shop working postconflict issues. At one point a small group questioned the assumption that it would take a multiweek campaign to get to Baghdad, and raised concerns about what would later be known as "catastrophic success," moving so quickly they outstripped the planning timeline for the postwar. In exchange for their prescience, this group "had their lips ripped off" for suggesting the big fight might not be as bad as some assumed.[85]

⁂

Partly as a result of such constraints, the United States would rush into Iraq seven months later without a clear idea of how it intended to govern the country. Some of the ideas on this score that began to circulate in the spring and summer of 2002 were half-baked and frankly nonsensical.

As we have seen, the default approach to postwar governance could be described as "decapitation": trade out the very top layer of the regime (in significant measure with favored exiles—the "right people"), and the rest of the Iraqi bureaucracy and the country as a whole would churn forward without missing a beat. Occupation was never part of the plan, nor—despite the comments to the contrary in some NSC strategies— was a long-standing US military presence. One senior official claimed that Feith and Wolfowitz so abhorred the idea of an occupation that they banned the term from appearing in documents.[86]

"We'll stay there about a month," one source described the basic idea, then "hand it off to the Iraqis, and come home."[87] The concept, one official recalled, was that you would "cut off the head" of the Iraqi regime and then witness a "rapid and inevitable march toward Jeffersonian democracy."[88] (The image was perhaps unintentionally revealing; not many things can make an energetic march with their head cut off.) Barbara Bodine, a highly experienced State Department Mideast expert who became involved in the postwar governance of Iraq, incredulously explained the idea to documentarian Charles Ferguson: "We would go in, and there would be a fully functioning Iraqi bureaucracy. They would all be in their offices, at their desk, pen and paper at the ready. And we would come in and, essentially, you know, take them off the pause button."[89]

One senior official suggested that the war advocates fell into this concept as a way of avoiding costs. His hunch, he said, was that they had persuaded themselves of it because they so desperately wanted to do something about Iraq, and taking seriously the true costs of unseating Saddam would undermine their whole case.[90] This was yet another product of faith-driven decisions guided by sacred values: when the imperative pushes leaders to ignore consequences but the reality of those consequences keeps pressing itself on them, decision-makers have to generate a scheme that resolves the resulting cognitive dissonance, one that allows them to believe that they really *are* dealing with those consequences. In the case of Iraq, that scheme was simple: the United States simply wouldn't be involved in the messy aftermath. A Department of Defense memo from August 23, 2002, includes a section called "Vision for Iraq's future," which concluded simply, "We will stay around for as long as necessary, but not a moment longer. . . . We are already working with Iraqi opposition groups to plan for the post-Saddam regime."[91]

All of this, of course, ran flatly in the face of every nation-building exercise of the 1990s, from Panama to Haiti to the Balkans, where the NATO-led Implementation Force (IFOR) had initially employed some sixty thousand troops to keep order and where IFOR's successor, the Stabilization Force, still had some twelve thousand troops as of 2002. But those were tainted, Clintonite efforts. It also ran up against the findings of just about any meaningful study of Iraqi society, which made clear that corruption ran marrow-deep and that no technocratic elite remained from which to fashion a thriving society. But the advocates had a gleaming counterexample to flash at any doubters, a powerful reservoir of fuel for their own wishful thinking about the burden the United States would face in the aftermath: Afghanistan. Washington had installed a government and got out, apart from small residual forces. It had worked, they thought at the time, beautifully. Some military officers and Defense civilians alike "seemed so intoxicated by their success in Afghanistan" with new models of light-footprint warfare, one source explained, that "nobody was interested in contingency planning in case these assumptions didn't materialize."[92] These perceptions, of course, were cropping up before the hard work in Afghanistan had really begun—before the nation building was underway, without which the regime change could not be cemented into place; before the deadening awareness that the Taliban could not actually be defeated; before anyone would anticipate that the United States would still be there in 2018, spending *$45 billion* in a single year on its unrelenting Afghan project. But no one was looking that far ahead.

The decapitation concept was also part and parcel of the larger illusion of Iraq as an advanced, technocratic, middle-class society just waiting to be set free from Saddam's tyranny. "We were predisposed" to believe certain things about Iraqi society, one DoD official explained. It was a "misreading of what the climate was." Yet even when I spoke with him years after the invasion, he would not surrender an essential faith in the vision of a "democratic beachhead" in the Middle East. "If there was a place it could work, it would be Iraq."[93]

In fact, there was plenty of evidence that if there was one place it would *not* work, it was Iraq—not after decades of kleptocratic dictatorship and years of grinding sanctions. If true, a logical implication was that there was no quick and easy, light-footprint solution to be had, at least if the United States didn't want to leave a murderous carnage in its wake. James Fallows wrote in the *Atlantic* as early as November 2002 that "The in-and-out model has obviously become unrealistic." Any US operation would place "tens of thousands of soldiers, with their ponderous logistics trail . . . in the middle of a foreign country when the fighting ended. . . . Having taken dramatic action, we would no doubt be seen . . . as responsible for the consequences." Most of the experts Fallows consulted for his piece told him the same thing. "Military action is a barbed hook: once it goes in, there is no quick release."[94]

Yet advocates of invasion clung to this mythical idea—dropping into Iraq, putting hand-picked exiles in charge, and leaving. In later years some would grumble that the president had mysteriously, and disastrously, abandoned this sensible approach at the last minute, allowing Paul Bremer to embroil the United States in a grinding occupation.

Others would pin blame on schemes to smear Ahmad Chalabi. There had been an idea of "helping the Iraqis liberate themselves," Richard Perle has said, "which was a completely different approach than we settled on. We'll never know how it would have come out if we did it the way we wanted to do it."[95]

Yet such questions remain as wishful a sort of thinking today as they were at the time, because there were always massive disconnects buried within the light-footprint concepts. One source closely involved in planning suggested that Paul Wolfowitz had the strong sense from early on that much of the Iraqi army would have to be disbanded, because of its complicity in the former regime's crimes and other issues. How this squared with a simple trade-out strategy isn't clear; in a military dictatorship, once the army disappeared from the equation, the rest of the government couldn't be far behind.[96] And the faith in a quick exit contradicted, even at the time, numerous quotes in the open press in which officials recognized the need for a multiyear occupation.[97] In one example, Vice President Cheney said on *Meet the Press* that "we clearly would have to stay for a long time, in terms of making sure we stood up a new government," and he warned that the resulting process could be "very costly."[98]

Similar appreciation for the scope of the task at hand, if the United States was really serious in its intentions, was also bubbling up outside the government. James Fallows interviewed retired army general William Nash, who spoke of the need, in postconflict stabilization operations, for military units to "find the village elders. . . . Right away you need food, water, and shelter—these people have to survive. Because you started the war, you have accepted a moral responsibility for them. And you may well have totally obliterated the social and political structure that had been providing the services." Fallows warned of a spree of revenge killings, and quoted Phebe Marr, one of the few true Iraq experts in the United States: "If firm leadership is not in place in Baghdad the day after Saddam is removed, retribution, score settling, and bloodletting, especially in urban areas, could take place." General Nash spoke from his experience in post–Gulf War Iraq in 1991, overseeing groups of refugees and Iraqi soldiers, watching disputes and riots break out. "And when that happens," he said, "you have no idea of what kind of vendetta you've just fallen into the middle of. . . . I take that experience from 1991 and square it fifty times for a larger country. That would be postwar Iraq."[99]

But somehow, Bush administration officials remained eerily sanguine about all of this. Wolfowitz was particularly cheerful. He was quoted in a September 22 *New York Times Magazine* story by Bill Keller. Wolfowitz said he was aware of the risks of an invasion and took them seriously. But he mentioned mostly military operational things, like Scud missiles and oil supply disruptions. "I think getting in is the dangerous part," Wolfowitz said. Keller concluded that Wolfowitz "worries considerably less about the day after."[100]

⁂

The planning process for "the day after" therefore remained jumbled and kaleidoscopic, with overlapping, uncoordinated efforts underway in a dozen places around the US government.[101] The labels used in the debate could seem rather semantic: "Transitional Civil Authority" versus "provisional government" or "Interim Iraqi Authority." But what they implied for the duration, cost, and risk of the mission was absolutely central to the whole enterprise. Was the United States invading Iraq to shove Saddam aside, hand the keys to the kingdom to some group of reasonable-seeming Iraqis, and leave (as in the "provisional government"–based schemes)? Or was it going to dig in, undertake an extended occupation, and run the place itself for years, molding Iraqi governance and society into something fundamentally different with its own hands (the implications of State's Transitional Civil Authority)? The question was rarely raised in explicit terms and had not been resolved even as US tanks crossed into Iraq the following March.

The issues at stake in this debate cropped up in an August 17, 2002, memo from senior Defense official Peter Rodman—the person who had been writing about exiles and occupation back in May—to Rumsfeld.

He explained that State had proposed a Transitional Civil Authority to run Iraq after the war. State's idea, he argued, was based on the assumptions that "(1) the Iraqi opposition is too divided to fill the vacuum on its own, and (2) the US will want to control what happens with Iraqi WMD, oil, etc."[102] Rodman admitted that Iraqi exiles would have "much further to go before they would be capable of a provisional government," but he urged that the United States make the effort to get them ready. He rejected World War II–style occupation analogies ("We will have nowhere near the total control in Iraq that we had in Germany and Japan") and preferred a French analogy: not the defeat and occupation of an enemy nation, but the liberation of an ally with the help of Free French forces. In Iraq, he argued, "there are bad guys all over," from radical Shi'a to communists, "Wahhabis, al Qaeda," who would "strive to fill the political vacuum," and he claimed that an "occupation government will only delay the process of unifying the moderate forces."

This didn't sound like the incipient middle-class democracy that was depicted in other planning documents. If the country was so full of powerful and dangerous political entities, it was unclear how Rodman or anyone else expected a nascent group of externals to pop in and coalesce into a governing body without a US occupying authority back-stopping them. Still, Rodman urged accelerated efforts to unify the opposition "into a coherent political force" with a common program and establish a "Provisional Government in the near term."[103]

This essential debate—with State coalescing around a transitional authority to govern for an extended period, and Defense arguing for a quick handoff—embodied several ironies. Some in Defense were convinced that State, shot through with narrow-minded "Arabists" who refused to believe Middle Eastern countries were capable of true democracy, would never buy into the mission of democratizing Iraq. But the ideas State proposed were actually *more in line with* laying the groundwork for a functioning democracy than a quick trade-out model was. Indeed, if those passionately committed to the democratization of Iraq wanted to locate the foremost opponent of their agenda, they didn't have to look far—he was working on the E ring of the Pentagon, in the secretary's office, and his name was Donald Rumsfeld.[104]

One White House official explained that there was an idea of an "early transition to a sovereign Iraqi transitional government. But our experience with an interim government gave us no assurance" that such a thing would work. It seemed a "short road to chaos," partly because it "risked transferring authority to expatriates, people who had not been in the country."[105] But it remained the default proposal of war advocates—in part because Feith and others at Defense saw a longer-term transitional authority idea as a plot to keep Ahmad Chalabi and his associates from having any influence in a postwar Iraq.[106]

This was the essential contradiction of the US governance challenge, cropping up yet again: a fragmented Iraq demanded strong leadership to be reassembled, but firm control by outsiders, especially foreign military forces, was anathema to proudly nationalistic Iraqis, and was not what most US planners had in mind. There was really no way to bridge this paradox, a fact very much in evidence at the various conferences of exiles brought together under the Future of Iraq Project at State. The Iraqi expatriates at those sessions wanted a logical impossibility: an extensive US commitment to stabilizing and rebuilding Iraq—without an occupation. The "US should make [a] commitment to Iraq like Japan and Germany," said one US government summary of the discussions at an exile conference. Yet its very next bullet pointed to the problem: "Military government idea did not go down well."[107] Everyone thirsted after the *outcome* of the German and Japanese experiences, but nobody, especially at Defense, was interested in paying the price.

But if the United States wasn't going to keep order, it wasn't clear who would. One person closely involved in these debates saw the problem clearly. "My big concern," he said, "was that key Iraqi infrastructure officials would disappear after the war, and there would be no one left to run the place."[108]

※

As the planning continued for military operations in the main combat phase, Rumsfeld began a process of overwhelming micromanagement that drove senior military officers to distraction.[109] He demanded to approve every unit put into the war plan, every Request for Forces (RFF).[110] It became, in the words of one military source, a "constant planning cycle" that never ended. A truly final war plan could never emerge, because the pressure just kept coming to shave down the numbers. "You will go extremely light and extremely fast" were the instructions, and the word to the planners was that this was coming direct from Rumsfeld.[111]

One obvious goal was to serve Rumsfeld's transformation agenda and to conduct the operation in as streamlined a manner as possible. And so the perpetual demand was to cut—cut force levels, cut units from the plan, build "off ramps" so that planned deployments could be abandoned if they did not prove absolutely necessary. Rumsfeld was "ensuring that the size of that force was as small as he wanted it to be," one officer said, summarizing the broad view of many at the Pentagon.[112] One very senior leader who worked with Rumsfeld said he never dictated a specific number; it wasn't how he worked. Instead he would probe, ask questions, guide briefers to revise their estimates.[113] He would question proposed force deployments down to the level of the "fire team"—four- to five-person units and military working dogs, sometimes asking why specific *individuals* were being requested. Always, the questions were the same: Why do you need this person? Why do you need ten people instead of five, or a brigade instead of a battalion, or a battalion instead of a company? "Simple decisions could become so cumbersome," one participant in the process explained. "What should have taken hours would take weeks."[114]

Any request for units with an even number of troops immediately set off warning bells with Rumsfeld. How could a generic number like that—one hundred or one thousand—be the result of specific analysis? At one point the air force submitted a requirement for a unit of personnel to support an "air bridge"—a support unit to flow forces to the theater. Their best-guess number was that they'd need five thousand people for the task. When briefed to Rumsfeld, his reaction was, metaphorically if not literally: *Bullshit—there's no way a rigorous process could have generated a number like that. You probably just made it up. Do it again.*

This demand was relayed from the briefers down to the Air Staff office, and a senior officer cut through the Gordian knot. "Send it back," he told the staff, "and use the number 4,987."

A junior officer asked, "If Rumsfeld demands to know where we got that number, what do we tell him?"

"Tell him I used the BHAM," the senior officer replied.

The younger officer asked what the acronym meant.

"It stands for the 'Big Hairy-Ass Model,'" the general replied.

Presumably, they would not have told Rumsfeld as much—but I was told that the acronym "BHAM" actually appeared on a piece of official paper that went back up through the chain of command. The new estimate passed muster, and the air bridge request was approved.[115]

Rumsfeld's maniacal micromanaging of the planning process had a number of disastrous results. One was to distract and infuriate planners who already had too little time to think about the postwar. More directly, the result of Rumsfeld's obsession with a light footprint was to leave the United States deeply unprepared for the aftermath. He would excuse this lack of preparation by claiming that "you go to war with the army you have"—but as Richard Haass trenchantly points out, the United States actually went to war in Iraq "with much less than the army it had. The Iraq war was a war of choice twice over: that it was fought and how it was fought."[116] And both turned out to be tragic misjudgments.

❧

Senator Trent Lott attended meetings with Bush during the spring and summer of 2002. "I knew," Lott would later write, "that the president wanted to go in like lightning, remove Saddam and his family from power, and replace the brutal dictatorship with democracy. Bush wasn't interested in half measures." Bush's approaches to the Congress weren't subtle; what he wanted, it was very clear to Lott, was the authority to "wage war on Iraq."[117]

Lott, however, saw meek and confusing public signals. He knew that if the American people were going to be whipped into a war frenzy, more would be needed than this. And so, "On a Sunday in mid-August, I called [Dick] Cheney. . . . 'Dick, I think you may have a big problem here with public perceptions of a possible Iraq War,' I told him. 'The case hasn't been made as to why we should do it, and, furthermore, the administration seems to be speaking through surrogates.'"

Cheney was reassuring. "Don't worry," he told Lott. "We're about to fix all that. Hold on."[118]

In his own memoir Cheney admits that, by August, he had begun to worry that Bush, under the influence of Powell and Blair, was going soft and becoming obsessed with the inspection route. One source I spoke with talked of a particular meeting when he heard Cheney say very clearly about the UN route, "We're not going to get tied down in that process."[119] Diplomacy wouldn't work, Cheney believed, and was becoming a distraction from the main effort of getting ready to oust Saddam.

Cheney decided to broadcast the truth as he saw it in an infamous August 26 speech at the Veterans of Foreign Wars meeting, which essentially said inspections were a hopeless stupidity.[120] Someone working in Cheney's office at the time recalled that the speech was written in a very close-held manner; only a handful of people even knew it was being prepared. Staff members would be asked to develop evidence for parts of it, but the whole text was not circulated within the interagency. And it is easy to see why: Cheney's speech essentially said that any hope in UN inspections—the route to which President Bush had now publically committed himself as about the last practical alternative to war—was pointless.

Powell was taken by surprise by the speech; he'd had no warning.[121] CIA Director George Tenet was troubled by the bluntness of Cheney's claims. Cheney asserted that, "Simply stated, there is no doubt that Saddam now has weapons of mass destruction"; and, later, "Many of us are convinced that [Saddam] will acquire nuclear weapons very soon."

Tenet writes that the speech "caught me and my top people off guard." It had not been cleared, as speeches purporting to be based on intelligence routinely are, with the intelligence community—and it "went well beyond what our analysis could support." (The community thought Iraq could get nukes by the end of the decade, not "very soon.") Tenet's interpretation was that the speech was "an attempt by the vice president to regain the momentum toward action against Iraq"—toward war.[122]

Even Bush was startled by the speech, and asked Condoleezza Rice to call Cheney and remind him, "I haven't made a decision." Cheney coyly asked for language to walk back his position; Rice provided it to Scooter Libby, and Cheney included it in his next speech.[123] But the blunt claims and passionate urgency of the VFW speech left an indelible imprint on the public debate. It reflected Dick Cheney's increasingly apparent way of operating: when he decided on what he believed was the right thing for the country to do, he simply set about making it happen, in whatever ways he knew how.

⁂

One declassified document—an unobtrusive Joint Staff briefing called simply an Operation Iraqi Freedom "History Brief"—contains many well-known dates and decisions. And then the briefing makes a reference in passing to a potentially decisive moment in the decision process: "29 Aug 02 / President approves overthrow of Saddam Hussein regime."[124]

This document—"Iraq: Goals, Objectives, Strategy"—was distributed by National Security Advisor Rice on August 29. A version of it crops up as a modified, unclassified attachment to an October 29 memo that was released as part of the documentation for Doug Feith's book.[125] The Special Inspector for Iraq Reconstruction quotes the original memo liberally, noting that it called for using "all instruments of national power" to effect regime change. The United States would "work with the Iraqi opposition to demonstrate that we are liberating, not invading Iraq, and give the opposition a role in building a pluralistic and democratic Iraq, including the preparation of a new constitution." It appeared to commit the United States to a much more elaborate postwar role than Rumsfeld had in mind, because it said that US strategy ought to "demonstrate that the United States is prepared to play a sustained role in the reconstruction of post-Saddam Iraq" in a way that "preserves but reforms the current Iraqi bureaucracy and reforms Iraqi military and security institutions."[126] At the same time, as if providing nods and winks to all sides in the continuing debate about how to govern Iraq once the United States owned it, the memo also called for the establishment of an interim Iraqi administration and a transition to Iraqi rule "as quickly as practicable."

This collection of evidence suggests that a decision of some sort—to commit "all instruments of national power" to unseat Saddam Hussein—was *formally* made no later than the end of August 2002. One could quibble, and surely senior officials would do so, that such a decision did not commit the United States to war; it remained possible that other "instruments of national power" (such as economic sanctions or covert action) could pry Saddam out of his chair. But by this time, nobody really expected any of those other tools to work.

The very same day, administration spokesmen admitted to CNN that the president intended to work with Congress for a resolution authorizing force against Iraq. "But this should not be taken," one White House official said, "as the administration making a decision."[127]

Rice stresses that neither she nor Bush wanted to go to war, and that they looked for alternatives. She claims that Egypt passed word that Saddam and his sons might leave power for a billion dollars—and Bush agreed to pay, if they'd go. It proved a false hope.[128] She explains that retired air force general Chuck Boyd offered the concept of "armed inspectors" as an extension of the UN process which might, Boyd thought, so humiliate Saddam that another Iraqi general might move against him. Rice said she and Bush were both intrigued with the idea, but that it was shot down in an NSC meeting. "The fact is," Rice concludes, "we invaded Iraq because we believed we had run out of other options" to achieve the outcome they knew was required. They had, she wrote, "come to the conclusion that it was time to deal with Saddam."[129]

This is true enough, in one sense. They had arrived at a powerful "feeling of rightness," a moralistic conviction, about a given course of action. But even as the downhill momentum for war picked up speed, senior officials insisted on remaining maddeningly opaque about their intentions. At about the same time, according to one person with whom I spoke, senior State Department official Marc Grossman called a member of the vice president's national security staff and asked him to meet, quietly and personally. They had coffee at the Hirschorn Museum in Washington, not far from the White House. Grossman asked, "Just tell me—has the president decided to go to war?"

"The president has decided," the official responded, "that the problem of Saddam Hussein has to be resolved, one way or another. Whether that means war, I can't say."[130]

But with the Iraq decision implicitly made, the pressure on perceived dissenters continued to grow. One source summarized a theme I heard from many outside of the White House, Defense, and the vice president's office. Some things, he said, people were simply not allowed to question: the viability of the decapitation or trade-out strategy, faith in Ahmad Chalabi, and the likelihood that Iraq would welcome US troops. Meanwhile, no one really debated, or even much discussed, the likely sources of order after Saddam was gone. It was never imagined that the most potent force holding the country together was exactly what Saddam Hussein said it was—the threat of retaliation from his security forces—and that, once it disappeared, order would collapse. Anyone raising such fears was simply brushed aside.[131]

The problem—for analysis, for debate, for choice—was that the case for war had been essentially sealed in cognitive amber the moment the planes struck the towers on 9/11. It was not an analytical case; it was an instinctive one, and it was no longer open for debate. And in the "interagency" debate, such as it was, theoretical issues such as *why* the United States was going to war were never resolved, because they were never raised. They didn't have to be. Everyone "knew" at a gut level—or knew in their own way, because not all perspectives entirely agreed—and didn't need an extended academic discussion to rationalize it for them. They knew it because they felt it was right; and the fuel of that belief, that faith, was their absolute commitment to protecting the American people, and their conviction that the only way to do this was to overturn a hostile government thousands of miles from home in part to spread democracy and reshape perceptions of American power throughout the world. Heroic to the point of folly, this vision nonetheless made sense, at some instinctive level, in part because it comported so well with the messianic tradition in American foreign policy.

The resulting choice could not be pinned to a specific place or time. It arose. It grew; it spread. "It was an accretion, a tipping point," Richard Haass told George Packer. "A decision was not made—a decision happened, and you can't say when or how."[132] We *can*, in fact, trace its course and understand its evolution—the period from September 2001 to March 2003 represented a decision process that can be laid out and dissected. But Haass's point is fundamental to the *character* of that judgment: emergent, intuitive, reflecting unconscious imperatives more than explicit, objective calculation. And the result, because of this character as much as anything else, would be tragedy.

CHAPTER 7

A JUGGERNAUT FOR WAR: SEPTEMBER TO DECEMBER 2002

Without strong public support [in a war] the administration and
allied political leaders would likely not be given the necessary time.
The administration said several years ago that US troops would be out
of Bosnia in 6 to 12 months. They are still there, all these years later.
We need to be honest. Arguments of convenience put forth to pacify the
public ultimately damage credibility.

DONALD RUMSFELD, 1999[1]

I felt as though an accelerating current were propelling us faster and faster
toward a gigantic waterfall. Yet no one was questioning the navigation,
only how to rev up the engines to make the ship run faster. "How?" was the
obsessive question. . . . Men with minds trained to be critical within the four
walls of their own discipline—to accept no proposition without adequate
proof—shed their critical habits and abjured the hard question "why." Once
they caught hold of the levers of power in Washington, they all too frequently
subordinated objectivity to the exhilaration of working those levers and
watching things happen. The lessons of history, to my surprise, were disdained.

GEORGE W. BALL, ON THE AMERICAN ESCALATION IN VIETNAM[2]

They misjudged the world. And, most of all, they misjudged themselves.

JOHN MCCAIN, ON THE "BEST AND BRIGHTEST"[3]

For some time, as planning for the war accelerated, Paul Wolfowitz had been beavering away at the concept of generating Iraqi units of some kind—a sort of analogy to the Free French Army that accompanied Allied forces into Europe in World War II—to ride into Iraq at the head of an invading column.[4] No one else much liked it; State and CIA saw it as a cover for helping Chalabi's Iraqi National Congress (INC) build a private army, and the military planners on the Joint Staff repeatedly shot down the idea as pointless. Nonetheless, it kept percolating and at some point morphed from a proposal for full-scale military units into a more modest concept for training and deploying a group of guides and translators for US forces.[5]

George Tenet has written in his memoir that "months in advance of the start of the war," a US Army colonel showed up at the CIA's Iraqi Operations Group with news that they would be assembling a "fighting force of Iraqi exiles."[6] The goal, the colonel said, was a force of fifteen thousand. Experienced CIA officers told the colonel, Tenet recounts, that "this was a fantasy, that he would be lucky if he could get a thousand men. No, we were assured, a force of twelve to fifteen thousand was entirely doable if the United States focused on it, and for that the colonel offered no less an authority than Ahmed Chalabi." Many of the diaspora Iraqis didn't have passports; even if they did join a nascent liberation force, they wouldn't be able to get to any training sites. CIA officials told the planners that the diaspora Iraqis were "coffee-shop heroes"; they had comfortable middle-class lives and would be entirely uninterested in going off to war. Nonetheless, they soon heard that someone connected with the enterprise was passing out flyers in mosques and coffeehouses in Europe, recruiting for a war that had not been declared.

On August 12, Defense official Doug Feith sent Donald Rumsfeld an action order for signature; it was addressed to the chairman of the Joint Chiefs and demanded a "plan to recruit, train, and equip Iraqi armed opposition elements to enable them to participate in operations aimed at replacing the Saddam Hussein regime. The operations should enable the opposition to be militarily useful and a constructive force in post-Saddam

Iraq."[7] General Franks and CENTCOM brushed off the idea of babysitting nominally trained civilians. "Doug, I don't have time for this fucking bullshit," Franks reportedly told Feith after one fall 2002 briefing.[8] Still the program went forward, coordinated out of Frank Miller's NSC planning group and the Defense Department, and exile groups reportedly "submitted" some six thousand candidate names (though how many were legitimate is hard to know). The US government managed to vet about six hundred of them. It dispatched five hundred invitations, and ninety-five people showed up in response.[9] I have heard various numbers of those who completed training—one account says seventy-three; two sources to whom I spoke said seventy-seven. An official Joint Staff history concludes simply: "31 Mar 03. Free Iraqi Force (FIF) training suspended; 76 graduates."

In the third week of September 2002, US Army general David Barno received a series of frantic calls suggesting that elements within the military and DoD hoped to establish a group of Iraqi exiles to participate with US forces in the invasion of Iraq and directing Barno to begin planning for such an initiative.[10] At first there were references to a Free French–style mechanized brigade, but that quickly gave way to humbler suggestions of small groups who had language skills, cultural knowledge, and local contacts that would be useful to US forces. The unit assembled to run the operation was dubbed Task Force Warrior and consisted of troops from thirty-one different units, totaling more than one thousand US personnel.[11]

Meanwhile, the State Department had been tasked with finding a covert training site able to handle "thousands" of volunteers. They eventually settled on Hungary.[12] Kellogg Brown & Root built a large facility there. The INC would do the recruiting—which "became the flaw in the entire concept," one source suggested, because when that single pipeline didn't produce enough recruits, Washington had nowhere else to turn.[13]

As various elements of what would become the US training force began to assemble, the promises flowed in from the advocates at Defense. "You're going to be getting thousands" of Iraqis to train, US personnel were assured. The trainers focused on their more modest goal of preparing Iraqis to serve in advisory roles—a choice that did not sit well with some of the Iraqis, who had arrived with grand notions of steering their American-issued tanks into Baghdad at the head of an invading army like a scene from a World War II movie. Training in Hungary did not begin until February 1, 2003, just over a month before the war.[14]

The Iraqis were enthusiastic, and most of them seemed committed and dedicated.[15] But their numbers remained tiny, and task force leaders thought, "Whoa—this is one hell of a lot lower than the predictions. . . . This is not good."[16] Up in Washington, at one NSC meeting when the Free Iraqi Forces' problems cropped up, Frank Miller kicked everyone out of the meeting except the CIA and Defense representatives. "What the hell is going on?" he demanded. "This isn't getting anywhere. Why not?" No one had any answers.[17]

Most of the Iraqis came from the United States, many from Michigan. A handful came from Europe and elsewhere, however, which led to the sort of result one could only imagine in a Joseph Heller novel: the task force had to hire interpreters, at significant cost, to translate for Iraqis recruited to serve as guides and translators for US forces.[18] Later on, rumors circulated that Ahmad Chalabi was about to show up with several hundred volunteers directly from Iran. This caused some alarm, because no one was sure of their reliability or what sort of training they might have. In any event, he never appeared.[19]

As the war loomed, the handful of exiles was gathered up and sent off to join the forces preparing for war, and then no one in Task Force Warrior quite knew what to do.[20] There was some discussion of moving the whole task force to Iraq, perhaps to serve as the embryo of an organization to train Iraqi military forces. But it never happened, and instead the large US force simply sat there on the now-empty facility, waiting for additional trainees to show up before the war ended. US officers set up sightseeing trips around Hungary to keep the troops entertained—an odd sort of "mission creep," as one officer said. Once the major offensive phase of the war ended in April 2003, Task Force Warrior was sent home and disestablished.

In terms of facilities built and US military salaries paid to over one thousand troops for a year, journalist Aram Roston suggests that the price tag of the abortive Free Iraqi Forces scheme may have been as high as $200 million[21]—something like $2.5 million dollars apiece to train seventy-odd men. CENTCOM deputy commander General DeLong says that some of the Free Iraqi personnel melted away once in Baghdad.[22] Some reportedly served well and bravely with US forces, but the ultimate value of the effort was negligible. The Task Force Warrior mission was built on faulty assumptions and had not been thought through before it was shoved at dedicated troops who saluted and moved out to do it— which is, of course, the story of the entire Iraq adventure, in microcosm.

꙰

The last few months of 2002 proved to be a peculiar time in the history of the Iraq war decision. The most fundamental judgment, to remove Saddam, had long been made. It had risen to the surface in the weeks after 9/11, become firmly entrenched by February 2002, and by August had mutated into a more formalized commitment to regime change.

Yet the truly final choice, the moment when President Bush told a range of senior officials that war was inevitable, did not occur until the first days of 2003. In between was a strange no-man's-land of warnings missed and opportunities for more effective preparation forgone. All along, the decision and planning process remained a fragmented mess. It stayed that way in large measure because of the essential character of this judgment, as I have tried to argue: when a group of officials, and a broader government, are plowing forward to make good on what is perceived as a moral obligation—when they are operating on the basis of a revelation rather than a calculation—doubts and arguments come to be seen as something worse than a distraction. They become, in an almost pure sense of the term, blasphemy.

This, then, is the primary story of the Iraq war decision in the last few months of 2002. Little active discussion was going on at the highest levels about *whether* to go to war, because that decision—presuming

Saddam Hussein did not simply pack his bags and move into exile—had effectively been made. The closer the war loomed, the more seriously people were forced to consider what it might mean and how the United States would deal with the aftermath. Yet that discussion was constricted and warped by the refusal to plunge into postwar planning until the last minute, the general air of loyalty-enforcing groupthink, and the wishful thinking that was so characteristic of a number of key war advocates. During these months, Congress approved a war resolution, and the administration made its intentions ever more clear. But no one, it seemed, was willing to step back and ask—seriously and rigorously—the most profound question: *Are we really ready to do this?*

⁂

During this period it is striking how little outside advice Bush sought, how few tough questions were asked of knowledgeable observers. He admitted to Bob Woodward that he simply never asked Powell whether the secretary of state thought attacking Iraq was the right thing to do. Rumsfeld himself, when asked by Woodward if he had recommended a war, said this: "It's an interesting question. There's no question in anyone's mind but I agreed with the president's approach and his decision. Whether there was ever a formal moment when he asked me, Do I think he should go to war, I can't recall it."[23]

"The Iraq decision was never systematically vetted," one senior official explained. "To the best of my knowledge there never was a formal decision meeting. There never was a place where people formally argued it out. . . . The purpose of bureaucracy, of the policy process, is in part to save administrations from themselves—to slow things down, not as an end in itself, but to make sure that policies are properly vetted."[24] Another source told me, "I was never privy to any discussion of should we go to war, why should we go to war, what are the strategic risks of going to war." The inevitable answer to such queries was, "The decision has already been made. Don't ask questions." Because of this environment, this source concludes, "smart people weren't asking the right questions."[25] After one meeting, a senior representative from one of the participating agencies, on the way back to his headquarters, exclaimed, "What the fuck? I don't understand. Can't we do any better than this?"[26]

People did not share their real thoughts in part because of an accumulating lack of trust. They used National Security Council meetings as much to sniff out the positions of other senior leaders as to make any coherent decisions.[27] A close observer described the whole tenor of the dialogue as follows: "Either you 'get it' or you don't get it." There was "lots of groupthink going on," he said. "There was no rigor in the debate," no "serious argument, no back and forth." The military planned brilliantly for the initial operation. But "when it came to the policy side, it was buffoonery. It was fucked up."[28]

Those who did have doubts made their own calculations. Richard Haass, at the time heading the State Policy Planning office, pauses at several points in his memoir to explain why—though surprised and at times worried by the drift of events—he did not speak up more forcefully: simply put, he writes, oppositional voices get sidelined. In policy arguments, "it is usually of little or no value to place yourself totally outside the debate and raise concerns that are judged to be irrelevant." For State officials to have spoken up more violently, he was convinced, would have felt good but also would have diminished their ability to influence "planning for the war and its aftermath." And so he placed his focus on where the action was: that if they went to war, "we do it right."[29]

This is, obviously, an indictment of the government organization that is supposed to organize the policy process—the NSC. One senior official who watched Condoleezza Rice operate admired her deeply and acknowledged that she had to deal with "two gray elephants who hated each other" in Powell and Rumsfeld. But the source also admitted that Rice oversaw a process that often failed to resolve issues—and not just issues surrounding Iraq.[30] Another former official traces the real problem a level higher: "The national security advisor is the president's creature," he explained. Bush and Rice appear to have settled upon an approach that placed her in the role of advisor, not an iron hand on the interagency process. And however

close they may have been, Bush did not clearly back her. In NSC meetings, he would sometimes refer to her exaggeratedly as "Dr. Rice," and in
some cases when she and others went to Bush for help with Rumsfeld,
Bush simply sloughed it off. "You and Don work it out," he would say.[31]
Rice herself tells a poignant story of trying to get Bush to raise the issue of
postwar security—only to have him march into the room and begin the
meeting by saying dismissively, "This is something Condi has wanted to
talk about"—a single comment that "completely destroyed any chance of
getting an answer," Rice explains.[32]

The effectiveness of a national security advisor is a function of many
things. Two of the most important are a clearly defined role based on
the president's appreciation for the sort of advisor he or she wants, and
unambiguous presidential backing for the advisor's authority. Whatever
one says about the way Rice herself approached the job, in the end, the
simple fact is that George Bush provided Condoleezza Rice with neither
of these things.

As the war planning accelerated into the fall, the question of whether
to establish a formal postwar planning office reared its head. As early
as June 27, 2002, at a deputies' lunch, someone had proposed an "Iraq
coordinator" to begin thinking about such issues, but it was deferred. On
October 18 Rumsfeld told Feith to form such an office—then reversed
himself, "without explanation," according to Feith. Deputy national
security advisor Steve Hadley would later tell Feith that Bush was worried that "setting up a postwar planning office at that moment would
undercut his diplomacy,"[33] the efforts to generate support for coercive
actions through the United Nations. If other countries assumed that the
United States was already determined to attack, they would likely stop
cooperating with that process.

Rumsfeld writes as much in his own memoir, saying he worried about
"the wisdom of even conducting large-scale planning" given the effects
it would have on diplomatic efforts.[34] A senior Defense official recalled

that the word came down: "People who were opposed to the president would have used that as proof positive" that Bush was unserious about diplomacy and was merely preparing for war.

I pressed him: "Everyone knew war was at least an option," I said. "Would planning for the aftermath really have been so different from deploying forces to the region?"

He shook his head and quietly answered, "You just didn't go there."[35]

Another senior official said that the real barrier was the lack of a formal decision for war, which, he suggested, did seem to make open planning for the postwar inappropriate.[36]

As legitimately as they may have been held at the time, in retrospect these fears appear absurd. On the one hand, the administration was massing a vast army in Kuwait and giving every indication of being ready to go to war. On the other, it was wringing its hands over creating a tiny postwar planning office in the Pentagon because it might destroy US credibility.[37] It made no sense. In fact, the administration had been working closely with Iraqi exiles to think about postwar Iraq since mid-2002—and doing so *in the open*, in public conferences that were reported in the press.[38] It held numerous meetings and commissioned studies on postwar Iraqi realities, which were leaked. "This was such bullshit," one official said bitterly about the excuse not to start postwar planning. "I was stunned at this charade." Washington openly supported the INC and exile planning; "we didn't seem too shy about that one. And they had the Future of Iraq Project" fully out in public, with "people all over the country and the world talking about this." They had speakers going around to the Iraqi exile community and to Arab states, telling them, "You guys gotta get serious, Saddam's days are numbered. This notion that they were worried about tipping their hand—ridiculous."[39] Whatever the reasons, the implications, as we will see in Chapter 9, were disaster.

❧

Early in September, Bush instructed the principals to begin drafting a congressional resolution authorizing war with Iraq. The next day he shared his skepticism of UN weapons inspections with Powell and Rice but agreed to keep giving the UN route a try while he prepared for more decisive action.

On September 3, the White House Iraq Group, conceived in August, held its first meeting to plot the public marketing of the war. Just five days later, the Sunday talk shows featured a phalanx of senior White House officials trumpeting the threat from Saddam's regime—including Rice, who used the infamous phrase "We don't want the smoking gun to be a mushroom cloud." About the phrase, Rice said later, "I liked it. What it meant was, we've almost always been surprised by nuclear explosions—India, the Soviet Union, China. . . . And usually when we know somebody's got a nuclear weapon, there's already been an underground mushroom cloud. So that's what that meant."[40]

Yet this was deceptive, because none of the intelligence available to the administration suggested that Iraq was close to acquiring nuclear weapons. The way she was beginning to speak—and would, along with other senior administration officials, continue to speak, right up until March 2003—would, intentionally or not, mislead the American people about the imminence of the Iraqi threat.[41] It was one thing for the administration, in its own internal calculation of risks, to conflate the issues of what Iraq had and what it might someday have. It was quite another to intentionally blur that line for public consumption, to sell a war based on a very particular calculation of dangers. Because the senior officials were firmly convinced that the threat was real and immediate, I do not believe that this rises to the level of conning the American people into war. But it did represent a degree of exaggeration and threat-mongering that helped to foreclose a more elaborate public debate—a debate that was badly lacking in the run-up to the war.

꙳

At about the same time, Iraqi exiles were meeting in London under the auspices of the Future of Iraq Project.[42] The US officials at the meeting came predominantly from the vice president's office, the Joint Staff, and

Defense.[43] The war advocates hoped they were setting up the embryo of a government in exile, and the dialogues among the Iraqis themselves seemed surprisingly productive.[44] One US official later recalled that the London conference made people "optimistic" that this group or parts of it, working with people inside Iraq, could become the nucleus of a post-war regime. No one knew who the "internals" might be, leaders inside Iraq who were experienced, expert, untainted by deep association with the Saddam regime, and willing to throw in with an invading Western power. And yet, the official says, "We were convinced they were there."[45]

⁂

On September 7, the NSC session at Camp David described in Chapter 1 took place. It became another example of a decision made and not made at the same time. The discussion of possible risks and consequences remained perfunctory. According to George Tenet's memoirs, the briefing book for the session laid out the case for liberating Iraq, how Iraq would be governed after the US forces arrived, lessons learned from the World War II occupations of Germany and Japan—in other words, supportive information to back an already strong momentum toward war. Only at Tab P in the briefing book did the participants discover a CIA analysis called "The Perfect Storm: Planning for Negative Consequences of Invading Iraq." This analysis had been published on August 13 and said "worst-case scenarios" upon invasion could include "anarchy and the territorial breakup of Iraq," instability in surrounding Arab nations, "a surge of global terrorism against US interests fueled by deepening Islamic antipathy toward the United States," and disruptions of oil supplies.[46]

But arguments made at Tab P seldom sway national security choices, and Tenet admits that while the agency had real reservations, it did not forcefully articulate them. "Had we felt strongly that these were likely outcomes, we should have shouted our conclusions," he wrote in his memoirs. "There was, in fact, no screaming, no table-pounding. Instead, we said these were *worst case*. . . . We had no way of knowing then how the situation on the ground in Iraq would evolve. Nor were we privy to some of the future actions of the United States that would help make many of these worst-case scenarios almost inevitable."[47]

﹡

At about this time, CENTCOM chief General Tommy Franks briefed Bush about the emerging war plan. According to Michael Gordon and Bernard Trainor, Bush asked if the plan would work—if they would "win."

Franks replied, "Absolutely."

"Can we get rid of Saddam?" Bush asked.

"Yes, sir," Franks answered.[48]

There is a plan, Bush was being told. *It will work. My general is telling me it will work.*

﹡

During this period a handful of observers and participants did try to tell the war advocates that they were rushing ahead without adequate thought. In an early September meeting at the White House, House Majority Leader Dick Armey—a Republican but no fan of the careless employment of military power—confronted Cheney. "You're going to get mired down there" in Iraq, one report suggests that Armey told the vice president.

"We have great information," Cheney replied. "They're going to welcome us. . . . They're sitting there ready to form a new government. The people will be so happy with their freedoms that we'll probably back ourselves out of there within a month or two."[49]

﹡

On September 12, 2002, President Bush went to the United Nations and delivered a speech that made his intentions crystal clear: "Our greatest fear is that terrorists will find a shortcut to their mad ambitions when an outlaw regime supplies them with the technologies to kill on a massive scale. In one place—in one regime—we find all these dangers, in their most lethal and aggressive forms, exactly the kind of aggressive threat the United Nations was born to confront." This, of course, was Iraq. He offered a stark ultimatum: "If Iraq's regime defies us again, the world must move deliberately, decisively to hold Iraq to account. We will work with the U.N. Security Council for the necessary resolutions. But the purposes of the United States should not be doubted. The Security Council resolutions will be enforced . . . or action will be unavoidable. And a regime that has lost its legitimacy will also lose its power."[50]

It was, in effect, a declaration of war—but an indirect one, which allowed the US government to continue sidestepping a formal justification under international law. One US official intimately involved in planning had been thinking up until that time that "no decision had been taken"—but the speech struck him as "pretty definitive."[51] Yet some news accounts actually depicted it as a step *back* from conflict, in the sense that it offered conditions Iraq might actually meet. In London, Robin Cook wrote in his diary that Tony Blair "has not entirely lost hope that the UN process might provide a diplomatic solution." Blair really wanted to avoid war, Cook still believed, and the domestic price he would pay for one. "Bush, by contrast, would be aghast if the UN process produced a successful result in terms of getting Iraq to comply with its obligations, as by definition that would leave Saddam still in place." Cook saw this; Blair, as far as Cook could tell, did not, which left Cook—and others like him—"trotting alongside the juggernaut for war, privately asking rational questions about whether this is the direction in which we all want to go."[52]

He did not trot all the way, however. Almost unique among US and British officials, Cook would ultimately resign before the war began— choosing principle over continued service in a government whose policies he could no longer support.

⁂

At a September 14 deputies meeting, after some fairly unqualified statements from Doug Feith about Iraqi weapons of mass destruction, Robert

Walpole, the national intelligence officer for strategic programs, said the United States would be hard-pressed to use the intelligence about these programs as the justification for war. To some his comments seemed to come out of left field, contradicting as they did everything the war advocates *knew* in their bones about Saddam Hussein's Iraq. According to George Tenet, Walpole went on to explain that North Korea was a far greater WMD threat—and "when that gets out, you guys will have a devil of a time explaining" why the United States went to war. Others at the meeting suggested that, on the terrorism issue, Iran was a bigger menace than Iraq. Doug Feith reportedly called their comments "persnickety,"[53] and the meeting moved on to the next topic.

࿔

Within Feith's OSD policy shop, as war planning grew more intensive, the staffing level of the relevant office (Near East and South Asia, or NESA for short) began to become an issue. It was responsible for just about all the countries drawn into the war on terror in addition to Iraq. By the summer of 2002, William Luti, the NESA head, had fewer than ten people working the Iraq account—and with a war approaching, he needed more. Feith got permission from Wolfowitz to add a dozen or more people to the office, and as a result Luti decided to restructure NESA into various directorates. The Northern Gulf Directorate—the Iraq account—became the Office of Special Plans (OSP), directed by Abram Shulsky. They gave it an ambiguous name to avoid media attention.[54]

What became the Iraq war planning office worked with Iraqi exiles, prodded and aided the effort to build the Free Iraqi Forces to support an invasion, and developed the texts of resolutions for the United Nations process.[55] While its members had many ties to Chalabi's Iraqi National Congress, contrary to some reporting at the time the OSP did not "run" the INC intelligence collection program; it was run out of the DIA's Defense HUMINT Service.[56] OSP staffers did, however, reportedly prepare talking points based on selectively culled intelligence, and many reports suggest that staff members of the office worked closely with war advocates outside the government to publicize their claims.

In the process, the Office of Special Plans became one of the most infamous cells of work to prepare for and promote the war. But it was just a handful of people, operating at a relatively low level. Though the evidence and arguments the group generated helped reinforce established preconceptions, nothing it produced determined the thinking of the president, the vice president, or anyone else. The United States was hurtling toward war in Iraq for far bigger reasons than the machinations of a few true believers in the Pentagon.

※

Even as the US planning and decision process rolled forward, the role of the United Nations, as well as its weapons inspection organizations and teams, was about to become much more significant. On September 16, Iraqi foreign minister Naji Sabri provided UN Secretary General Kofi Annan and Arab League Secretary General Amr Moussa with a letter indicating that Iraq would readmit inspectors without conditions.[57] The director of the International Atomic Energy Agency (IAEA), Hans Blix, outlined his plans to the Security Council on September 19; it would take about two months to get the inspections rolling, he predicted.[58]

The reaction in some offices at Defense was one of horror. This was the beginning of precisely what they had feared: an endless round of fraudulent Iraqi concessions that led nowhere. The White House quickly rejected the offer. They were gearing up to unseat Saddam, not enable his continued rule through a sham inspections process.

On September 18, Rumsfeld testified before the House Armed Services Committee.[59] He laid out the case against Iraq: the risk of WMDs given to terrorists, the genocide, the record of regional aggression. Some had worried, Rumsfeld said, "whether an attack on Iraq would disrupt and distract from the US global war on terror. The answer is that Iraq is part of the global war on terror." Yet he also claimed, "No one with any sense rushes into war. It is something that everyone thinks through very,

very carefully. And that is why the President has not made a judgment as to precisely what he believes needs to be done. He has laid out the problem and he is looking for ways that it can be dealt with." Later he was even more unequivocal: "The President has obviously not made a decision." One artifact of the dual-track decision process underway in the administration was that such a statement could be both technically true and profoundly misleading at the same time.

Meantime Rumsfeld left the impression that the whole endeavor would simply not be that big of a deal. "It is not knowable what a war or a conflict like that would cost," Rumsfeld told the Congress. "You don't know if it is going to last two days or two weeks or two months." One thing Rumsfeld was sure of: "It certainly isn't going to last two years." The price tag, he assured the Congress, "would be modest, to be sure." Part of the reason for his faith was the limits to US ambitions. "We are not looking to occupy any country. Our goal is to be helpful and then go about our business." That was Rumsfeld's goal—but whether it was possible to achieve, in light of all the other US objectives in Iraq and in particular the president's strongly expressed desire to promote freedom, was something that seems never to have occupied the attention of even a single cabinet meeting.

✺

A week later in London, Tony Blair presided over what Robin Cook found to be a "grim meeting" comprised largely of "a succession of loyalty oaths for Tony's line." Most expressions of doubt among the cabinet had faded away in the face of Blair's obvious determination to press toward war. Only Cook and Clare Short continued to resist military action. The following day, the UK government would present its own intelligence case for war—a report, later known as the "dodgy dossier," filled with dubious evidence that would collapse under later scrutiny.

"When I came to read the dossier," Robin Cook wrote in his memoir, "I was surprised that there was so little new material in it. There was no new evidence that I could find in it of a dramatic increase in threat requiring urgent invasion." He found specifically false claims—an alleged chemical weapons plant in Falluja, for example, which had already been visited by not only a UN inspection team but also a German television crew that past July. Both found it to be a ruined hulk, with no activity underway whatsoever. When Cook confronted other officials about the need to correct these public misrepresentations, he was waved off.[60]

⁂

On September 28, the United States shared the draft of a war resolution with fellow Security Council members France, Russia, and China. The terms of the draft did precisely what had been sketched out in those springtime memoranda written in Washington and London: create a basis for war by throwing conditions at Saddam he could not and would not meet. The resolution gave Iraq only seven days to provide a full and comprehensive declaration of all of its weapons programs, and twenty-three days after that to open all of its WMD sites. It proposed the establishment of military bases within Iraq, presumably staffed by US troops, from which weapons inspectors would operate, and no-fly and no-drive zones around suspect sites. These were demands no self-respecting sovereign state could possibly accept. And in the event of noncompliance, the draft resolution authorized UN member states "to use all necessary means to restore international peace and security."[61] Russian and French officials immediately recognized the resolution as a ruse, designed to be rejected and to create the conditions for war.[62]

⁂

Meanwhile, the thinking underway within the Bush administration about what the United States would do with this country of twenty-five million people continued to meander through various ill-defined concepts. An October 2, 2002, document out of Defense's NESA office called "A Political Roadmap to a New Iraqi Government" showed the emerging trend of thinking about postwar governance, and highlighted again the growing divergence between the accumulating ambitions of this most

messianic of transformational projects and Rumsfeld's assumptions that
the United States would be able to simply "be helpful and go about its
business." Some components of the plan laid out in the eight-page memo
reflected the preference for exile-based quick handovers, but others were
all over the map. "Prior to Liberation," it suggested, "the Iraqi opposition should take the initiative to organize a political conference" that
would "publish a Bill of Rights," promote an independent judiciary, and
"guarantee free exercise of faith and a separation of mosque and state."[63]
Even before the invasion, right from the get-go, US policy was aiming
to dictate political outcomes in the name of granting freedom. "Stability
and a representative government will be best ensured by a constitutional
bicameral federal system," the memo went on to argue, choosing a form
of government before Iraqis of any sort had a chance to weigh in. It went
as far as to propose that the new Iraqi constitution should abolish the
death penalty—but only for "political crimes." The memo suggested that
US forces would "announce intention to hand power over to Iraqis"—
but would not, in fact, do so: a US "military administration" would run
Iraq. It would, for example, "manage all Iraqi government television and
radio stations"—and do so "in consultation with the Iraqi opposition."[64]
This didn't sound much like the scenario Rumsfeld had sketched out for
the Congress, but no one was riding herd on the competing ideas.

One set of ideas circulating around the Defense Department was
gradually distilled into a concept known as the "Interim Iraqi Authority."
One former senior official stressed the importance of each of the three
pieces of the title: it was *Iraqi*, he insisted, not American; *interim*, not
permanent; and merely an *authority* rather than a government.[65] The
title gave an impression of a coherent plan when in fact it was hopelessly
vague; ill defined; and in fact not even conveyed to the people who would
be implementing policy on the ground, many of whom had never heard
of it by the time the invasion took place. Its central assumption was that
a permanent government could well up, organically, from Iraqi society—
that very same society that had been warped into a brutal Hobbesian war
of all against all by Saddam's cruelty.

Among the exiles, the spirit of cooperation, which had been taken by some as a harbinger of a smooth postwar transition was disintegrating. On October 4, 2002, the Future of Iraq Project's Democratic Principles Working Group met at Wilton Park, England, to review progress. The meeting quickly turned into an INC power grab. A key INC staffer, Salem Chalabi—Ahmad's nephew—arrived with a thick report titled "Transition to Democracy in Iraq," authored by fellow exile Kanan Makiya, that purported to answer all the questions the group had supposedly gathered to discuss. The plan envisioned a dominant role for Iraqi exiles in forming a rapidly generated transitional government.[66] Makiya himself seemed upset that anyone would take issue with the plan, especially when no others had alternatives to present. "It's the architect in me," Makiya later told George Packer. "Architects are such megalomaniacs."[67]

They were not, seemingly, the only ones. On October 7, inside the Pentagon, Defense officials were drafting the "SecDef Directive to the Military Governor of Iraq," a template for orders Rumsfeld could use to guide his commander's actions after invasion. "You must initially assume command of the Iraqi government," it said unequivocally. "Your responsibility is to maintain security in Iraq so that infrastructure can be rebuilt and daily administration resume. . . . You must police cities, towns, and the countryside to discourage and prevent blood revenge and vigilante justice." OSD staff also wrote up the "Structure, Organization, and Staffing of the US Military administration" on October 7; among other things, it directed that "the military governor will appoint US specialists to assume responsibility in each ministry in order to replace Ba'ath party officials."[68]

Who would do all of this was unclear. The emerging US military plans called for a rapid withdrawal, and General Franks was telling everyone inside government who would listen that he had no intention of getting embroiled in postinvasion security requirements or political disputes. Some mythical figure would materialize, these memos seemed to imply, to accomplish the tasks that no one was prepared to offer the manpower or resources to fulfill. And these instructions comported not at all with Rumsfeld's promises, just weeks before, to the Congress and the American people that the Bush administration was "not looking to occupy any country."

Meanwhile, the double messaging about the imminence of war continued. A White House official told British ambassador Christopher Meyer that the US military buildup had not yet reached a point of no return. "The president had not yet signed off on going to war," the official claimed. "Nothing was yet irrevocable."[69] Yet Rumsfeld was by this time sending around snowflakes like the one he dispatched to Franks on September 30: "If the UK isn't going to work in the north and the Turks may not, and the Kurds may not be enough, we are going to need some US forces. Let's discuss."[70] And on September 26, Bush spoke with eighteen members of the House of Representatives. "If we use force, it will be fierce and swift and fast," he said. "I have been looking each general in the eye and asking them whether or not they see any problems for a regime change. They do not."[71]

⁂

An important part of the history of the congressional resolution that explicitly authorized the use of force was the capitulation of many Democrats, something that can only be understood in the context of the conventional wisdom by then-governing US foreign policy and the degree of agreement on the threat posed by Saddam Hussein's Iraq. Three senators, one Democrat and two Republican—Joseph Biden, Richard Lugar, and Chuck Hagel—tried to draft a less comprehensive resolution that would have authorized Bush only to go after WMD sites. The White House sent over clear instructions to Senator Trent Lott: kill it, and "make certain it didn't pollute the strong language they required."[72]

There is little evidence that many members of Congress exhausted themselves in any sort of independent evaluation of the likely consequences of war. Congressional aides, for example, told the National Intelligence Officer dealing with the issue that just six senators and a "handful" of House members read any more than the five-page executive summary of the National Intelligence Estimate on weapons of mass destruction.[73] The discussion and debate over the resolutions, then, represent another missed opportunity for more elaborate investigation of the case for war and its likely risks.

On October 10–11, 2002, Congress approved the use-of-force resolution. The House version passed on October 10 by a vote of 296 to 133; the following day, the Senate version passed 77 to 23. In the Senate, Democrats like Joe Biden, Maria Cantwell, Max Cleland, Hillary Clinton, Tom Daschle, Christopher Dodd, John Edwards, Dianne Feinstein, Tom Harkin, John Kerry, Blanche Lambert Lincoln, Harry Reid, and Chuck Schumer—all experienced and tough senators who should have been able to stand up to the president if they had thought the looming war unwise—all voted for it. Twenty-three courageous Democrats cast a skeptical eye, including Jeff Bingaman, Kent Conrad, Ted Kennedy, Carl Levin, Barbara Mikulski, Jack Reed, and Debbie Stabenow.

Their lonely dissent was swamped by the war cries of fellow Democrats. "We have no choice but to eliminate the threat," Joe Biden claimed on *Meet the Press*. Hillary Clinton was equally hawkish: Saddam Hussein, she argued, parroting the White House talking points, had "given aid, comfort, and sanctuary to terrorists, including al Qaeda members." Whatever his various deceits, Donald Rumsfeld was dead on the mark when he later complained that Democratic leaders had voted for war—and then, when the vote became politically inconvenient, "they acted as if they had never said any such thing."[74]

※

A few weeks before, in September, a second interagency planning team, paralleling the Executive Steering Group, had cranked to life, headed by Robin Cleveland of the Office of Management and Budget and the NSC's Elliott Abrams.[75] Termed the Iraq Relief and Reconstruction Working Group, it had been created by Frank Miller as a sort of subgroup of the ESG to focus specifically on postwar humanitarian challenges.[76] The group had about ten members from various departments and agencies when it got underway, and eventually grew to about thirty.[77] It met for several months—at least once a week, often twice—through January 2003. "We were going to invade Iraq," one participant described the basis for the group's charter, "and take over and displace the government"; their job was to look at the postconflict period, specifically "on the human side."[78]

The new group undertook a broad-based social assessment of what would be required to get Iraq back up and running as a functioning society—but hanging in the background was always the presumption that this was short-term planning. Nobody had the idea that they were going to stay ten years and rebuild the country. "Nothing happened in Iraq that we didn't talk about," one participant recalled, with one exception: the shape of postconflict governance. They were told to leave it alone. A couple of State people who asked why this was were told, "Don't go there. Drop it."[79]

The group openly discussed just how ambitious the reconstruction efforts ought to be. One participant said Cleveland instructed the group that Iraq would be returned to prewar levels only; its oil wealth would pay for its longer-term development. The source recalled building a series of indicators—three-, six-, and twelve-month metrics of progress, "and then we're out of there" by that point.[80] Other sources do not necessarily recall such a precise, one-year timeline but do agree with the general sense it conveyed: short-term responses to get the country back on its feet were "our responsibility." Beyond that, "at a certain point, we have to let the Iraqis take over." When I asked if, during all this planning, anyone had ever told this group how long the United States anticipated remaining in Iraq, one official said simply, "No." Did the group assume, I then asked, that long-term development was not going to be a US responsibility? "In a word," the former official said, "yes."[81]

One participant told me that troublesome questions were distinctly unwelcome. "When you raise your hand and express objections," the official said, "you get shot to pieces." Statistics and projected numbers were being pulled out of thin air. "If you wanted to stay in the game and keep your agency in play, you had to make up shit."[82] Another former official had a searing recollection of a particular session[83] during which Abrams asked the temporary USAID representative—Ambassador Frank Almaguer, who had been brought in from the cusp of retirement by USAID Administrator Andrew Natsios to help coordinate postwar planning—what the agency planned to do in the aftermath.

"We have a lot of postwar experience," Almaguer said. "We'll be working human needs, health, and related issues."

This official said that Abrams replied, "There won't be a need for any of that."

Almaguer countered that postwar contexts almost always produce human dislocation, including internal refugees who may need humanitarian assistance, such as water and sanitation. These immediate responses then lay the foundation for longer-term development. "None of that is going to happen," Abrams told Almaguer flatly, in the memory of this participant. What they did want was for schools to reopen within weeks of Saddam's unseating. And they wanted them equipped with new textbooks, stripped of Ba'athist propaganda. They wanted USAID to develop, write, edit, and print millions of new textbooks—in Arabic—in a matter of a few weeks.

Almaguer was flabbergasted. Even if it were possible, he said, it would cost a huge amount of money. Where was USAID supposed to get it? USAID had the capacity to respond to humanitarian disasters, such as temporary shelters, water, and sanitation, but longer-term development issues like school materials demanded more lead time for planning and the commitment of resources. And USAID had very limited Arabic-speaking staff in the education sector who could be mobilized for such a massive textbook rewrite.

Almaguer returned from the meeting and shared the story with USAID administrator Natsios, who said the idea was "full of shit." He told Almaguer to go back and say USAID would need some random amount up front—$50 million—to do the book revision, printing, and distribution job—and that they couldn't guarantee it would get done in the necessary time in any case. This idea was quickly shot down, and nothing came of the proposal.

The episode illustrated again the central dilemma in the US approach. If America wanted to leave Iraq as a protodemocracy, it couldn't very well depart the country with Iraqi schoolchildren still learning from Ba'athist propaganda. But if it was determined to change the society down to the level of textbooks, it was in for a far longer and more expensive mission than anyone was buying into. "I don't know what's going on," a senior USAID official said at the time, in the recollection of one source. "But it sounds like insanity."

Others are somewhat more positive about the achievements of these planning groups, and the Abrams-Cleveland process in particular. Whatever his notions about individual issues, Abrams—like his counterpart Frank Miller—was an able and experienced civil servant, and several participants said that the group efficiently ran through many major issues.[84] They took steps to mitigate various risks, such as humanitarian crises. But their good intentions and hard work could not overcome the massive dilemmas involved in a project that aimed at once for US control and complete liberation, nor could they compensate for a striking inattention to postwar issues at the top of the policy-making pyramid.

❧

At the US Agency for International Development, the lead organization in the US government responsible for rebuilding underdeveloped nations—and in theory the logical place to centralize planning for reconstruction of a postwar Iraq—nobody had been brought into war planning in any extensive way at senior levels.[85] Many interviewees describe an outright hostility toward USAID at Defense. It was not universal, and it did not prevent USAID from ultimately having a substantial role. But it amounted to subterranean bureaucratic warfare that ate away at efficiency and subverted the potential of the agency in the US government best positioned to support the ambitions of the postwar US goals in Iraq.

By the fall of 2002, a handful of USAID officials were just starting to think through what might be needed of them if the United States invaded Iraq. They had no formal guidance but were reading about the looming potential for war in the newspapers.[86] It "never crossed our minds that [US]AID wouldn't be in charge of the development aspects of it," one official said later.[87] So in October they set up a working group and put Ambassador Wendy Chamberlin—recently returned from Pakistan—in charge. She developed what became known as the "horse blanket," a giant sheet of paper laid out across a table or desk in her office, with columns or rows for various categories of aid issues, lists of possible initiatives, and estimates of potential costs. USAID was trying to design postwar plans without working from an official policy, or even being able to admit to many people outside their group what they were doing. Chamberlin wanted to write requests for proposals to be ready to get contractors spun up when she needed them—but she couldn't write the requests without a formal government position on the war.

USAID officials gradually became aware that the NSC relief and reconstruction group was largely interested in short-term humanitarian issues. Iraqi oil was going to pay for longer-term reconstruction and social renewal, US plans seemed to be assuming. People with serious experience in such situations found this attitude to be naive; postconflict societies don't jump back to their feet in an instant, and short-term relief always gets nested in longer-term programs. And so they kept planning, and got ready. They developed detailed programs in three-, six-, and nine-month increments. They looked at categories—electricity, opening three thousand schools by the beginning of the new school year, rural preventive medicine, basic democracy programs. The price tag for all of this ballooned to $90 billion, a number that would have gagged Defense officials who were busily assuring the public that Iraqi oil revenues would pay for everything.[88] Missionary zeal, as it turned out, was an expensive proposition.

President Bush signed the war resolution on October 16. As he did so, he insisted that "I hope the use of force will not become necessary."[89]

Two days later, Donald Rumsfeld finally asked Doug Feith to establish a postwar planning organization—and then withdrew the order once again. Feith says Stephen Hadley told him that they somehow still could not be seen to be planning for the war—the very same war that they had just publicly asked Congress for permission to wage.[90]

At about this same time—the beginning of October—columnist William Raspberry penned a stinging attack on the concept of invading Iraq, asking many hard questions. Rumsfeld apparently read the column and told his staff to give him some answers.[91]

How long would public support last, Raspberry had wondered? "In Vietnam, support for the war remained high even as we started taking casualties in large numbers," the Defense Department staff memo cheerfully informed the secretary. "Majority public support lasted into 1968, by which time about 30,000 American servicemen and women had died." In answer to the query "How will you govern a defeated Iraq?" the memo offered two brief bullet points (one referring to exile planning) and then concluded its entire analysis of the issue by asking a question of its own: "Why do we assume that the Iraqi people are unable to provide themselves with a decent government?" (One answer might have been: Because of *everything* the US government knew about the fractured state of Iraqi society.) But the most astonishing claim came in answer to the question of how many Americans would die to unseat Saddam Hussein. The memo concluded simply, "None." American combat deaths would be incurred for the purpose of "defending our country and defending its vital interests," the memo proclaimed. This was, by implication, a wholly different thing.

※

Despite the USAID and State efforts to begin strategizing about postwar economic and social requirements—or perhaps, in reaction to them—by this time Donald Rumsfeld was pressing for the Defense Department to control postinvasion reconstruction. He did so, in the view of one former official privy to his thinking, not because he thought the Defense Department should actually do the job entirely alone—he knew other agencies would be involved—but because of his devotion to the concept of "unity of command," and his sense that *some* department needed to have overall responsibility.[92] According to Bob Woodward's account, another motive was to avoid the sort of embarrassment that occurred in the early days of the Afghan operation, when the CIA was the only agency prepared to offer immediate strategies and solutions. The next time a major operation cropped up in this war, Rumsfeld reportedly decided, Defense would be running the show.[93]

And so about this time a crucial aspect of the postwar was decided: The Department of Defense would be in charge. Rice and Powell agreed without dispute. A civilian administrator would be appointed for governance and reconstruction issues, but that person would report to Rumsfeld. "It was not at all controversial," Rice said later about the decision. "I mean, how else were you going to do it?"[94] Some senior officials saw little risk, because as one source familiar with the thinking of people at State put it, they "never dreamed that State would be eliminated" from the planning process.[95] Defense might be in charge—but surely, it would welcome and ensure the participation of everyone who had something to contribute. To do otherwise would risk the success of the postwar mission.

Within the US government, debates over the UN resolution continued. Colin Powell worked with his British counterparts—Foreign Secretary Jack Straw and Blair foreign policy advisor David Manning—to get their governments to submit a modified, less exacting resolution that could gain Security Council approval. On October 23, US ambassador to the United Nations John Negroponte gave the five permanent members of the Security Council a new draft while making clear rising US impatience.[96] In large measure because of the pressure from Blair, Bush would not abandon the effort to gain international legitimacy.

On October 30, the IAEA's Hans Blix, as he continued to report on the results of inspections, made a remarkable visit to the White House. Blix sensed that the administration wanted to hug the inspectors close to show that it was embracing multilateral diplomacy. The IAEA officials met with Cheney, who, Blix writes, "did most of the talking and gave the impression of a solid, self-confident—even overconfident—chief executive." Inspections "cannot go on forever," he intoned, and "the US was 'ready to discredit inspections in favor of disarmament.' A pretty straight way," Blix continued, of making clear that the United States was determined to disarm Saddam on its own. Blix shortly thereafter sat with Iraq's UN ambassador. Iraq was trying to prove that they had no weapons of mass destruction, but faced a dilemma. "What if," the Iraqi diplomat asked Blix, "there was nothing to report?"[97]

※

During this period, Donald Rumsfeld composed a memo listing thirty-five or forty things that could go wrong during an invasion. According to one source, its concerns generated some work afterward—Pentagon officers were tasked with generating contingency plans against some of the items on the list, such as the "Fortress Baghdad" scenario.[98] In his memoir Rumsfeld says he read the list to a principals meeting and later sent it to Bush.[99]

After years of speculation about its contents, the memo was finally released in a set of documents declassified in connection with Rumsfeld's book.[100] It turned out to be a fairly random catalogue of dangers, ranging from a lack of UN mandate to disruption of oil supplies to other rogue states using US distraction in Iraq to launch attacks elsewhere. Several are rather interesting, in hindsight:

- Number 13: "US could fail to find WMD on the ground in Iraq and be unpersuasive to the world."
- Number 19: "Rather than having the post-Saddam effort require 2–4 years, it could take 8–10 years, thereby absorbing US leadership, military and financial resources."

- Number 20: "US alienation from countries in the EU and the UN could grow to levels sufficient to make our historic post World War II relationships irretrievable, with the charge of US unilateralism becoming so embedded in the world's mind that it leads to a diminution of US influence in the world."

Equally notable, though, is what is absent. Looting is nowhere mentioned, nor is a generalized collapse of civil order. Number 27 mentions the risk that "Iraq could experience ethnic strife among Sunni, Shia and Kurds," but the idea of a full-blown civil war, or near-civil war, does not appear.[101] Nor, apart from some very limited attention within Defense, was there a significant effort to follow up in any serious way on the memo's warnings—no interagency process, no Defense working group, no comprehensive risk mitigation effort. Even Condoleezza Rice, watching from the NSC, "suspected that the Defense Department's motive was really to issue a documented warning just in case the whole endeavor failed." She confirms that "there were no implementation plans to address the conclusions."[102] When I asked a senior member of the Iraq Political-Military Cell (IPMC), the Joint Staff group that comprised one of the lead interagency groups tasked with preparing for the war, about the memo, his response was simple. He had never heard of the thing.[103]

It appears, however, that Rumsfeld never saw himself as accountable for such risks anyway. As he put it in his memoirs, his Defense team had "prepared for these contingencies in our area of responsibility." But no one made sure, he continued—the worldly sigh heaving off the page—that there was "a systematic review of my list to the NSC."[104] Apparently the responsibility of the secretary of defense extended to issuing warnings, not doing anything about them.

※

Within the military commands responsible for the war, some degree of "Phase IV" planning was beginning to take place—mostly disconnected from parallel efforts like the Executive Steering Group and the relief and reconstruction team. The officer who would come to run one piece of that effort, Colonel Kevin Benson, had arrived at CENTCOM in July 2002. He found a staff obsessed with the "major combat" (Phase III) part of the war, lacking the time or direction to plan for the postwar, and decided to establish a small group to begin thinking through the Phase IV challenge. This work got underway in mid-2002 and continued through the end of the year, but remained very rudimentary.

On December 14, the tiny postwar planning unit briefed the Joint Staff on their embryonic analysis. "We were assuming that there would be no government that moves in," one officer involved said afterward, "so we were anticipating chaos."[105] The brief made enough of an impression to prompt the Joint Staff director, Lieutenant General George Casey, to establish a larger dedicated organization for Phase IV planning beyond the limited Joint Staff planning cells already in place. This more self-contained effort would come to be called Combined Joint Task Force IV (CJTF-IV). But CENTCOM's war planners kept at the task as well, and it was unclear how the two groups were meant to relate to one another. By January, the Office for Reconstruction and Humanitarian Assistance (ORHA) would also be established, yet *another* layer on the cake—layers not fully integrated with one another, or with the NSC-led organizations covering some similar ground. Meanwhile, the State Department's Future of Iraq Project continued to limp along, and USAID was doing its own independent planning.

General Casey put General Steven Hawkins in charge of CJTF-IV, and Hawkins went to see CENTCOM—only to be given the brush-off. They were crashing at breakneck speed to get ready for Phase III; nobody had any time or resources to worry about the aftermath. Hawkins had to move into a nearby warehouse and scrounge supplies for his task force. They began looking into all aspects of Iraq—history, current situation, postwar issues—once again starting from scratch and duplicating the efforts of a half-dozen other groups.[106]

CENTCOM commander Tommy Franks's discussion of Phase IV planning in his memoir is revealing, in a disheartening sort of way. Like Rumsfeld's memo on the larger geopolitical risks, it has the flavor of an observer who is not really responsible for what he is describing. "Throughout our planning of 1003V," Franks writes, using the numerical designation for the war plan, they "discussed" Phase IV. They assumed they would have Iraqi military units to work "side-by-side with Coalition forces to restore order" after the invasion. He expressed a genuine wish that some wonderful Iraqi would emerge to be crowned as leader but admitted he didn't much like Ahmad Chalabi. He read newspaper stories and watched television accounts of a possible occupation of Iraq, casting him as the MacArthur of the tale, and he "weighed the obvious pluses and minuses of such an occupation." In the end, the man commanding all US forces about to launch into Iraq lays out his bottom line: "I could see no elegant solution to this very complex problem."[107]

A major source of Franks's apparent indifference no doubt stemmed from his conviction that he had off-loaded the postwar mission. When asked in meetings, one source recalls, Franks "would say Phase IV is Doug Feith's responsibility."[108] Planners began to recognize the problem of shortage of numbers. One of them later told the Iraq Special Investigator's office that "the thing we kept going back to was we've only got so many people." But the war plan called for numerous tasks—border security, hunting WMDs, protecting oil pipelines, humanitarian relief, basic public order.[109] It was becoming increasingly obvious that Rumsfeld's insistence on a small footprint was dooming the postwar, but the insight never had much impact.[110]

General Richard Myers, serving as chairman of the Joint Chiefs at the time, writes in his memoir that he tried to push Franks to realize a significant chunk of Phase IV was still his job. "I had trouble that fall getting Franks to focus on" it, he writes. "Despite several phone calls and personal messages to Franks, CENTCOM's planning for Phase IV never improved."[111] A major reason why was the stubborn assumption of a relatively short sojourn for American forces in Iraq. Military forces were going to be the catalyst to bring the dictator down, not the support system to raise a new nation up.[112] A leading assumption of their thinking, Colonel Benson makes clear, was that "we would be able to recall the Iraqi army and the Iraqi governmental bureaucracy . . . and the removal of Ba'ath party members would be limited to senior-level bureaucrats and officers."[113] Yet even *with* these starkly optimistic assumptions, their analysis of the requirements of administering Iraq generated an estimate of three hundred thousand troops—roughly double the size of the force that Franks and Rumsfeld hoped to get away with.[114]

Faith in a plan that would leave US forces only briefly in Iraq was the load-bearing pillar of the wishful thinking that helped propel the United States into the war so unprepared. One official with knowledge of Pentagon thinking said that "We weren't talking about a lot of troops staying, and they weren't going to stay for a long time. . . . Everything that I saw" pointed in the direction of a plan to "get rid of Saddam, and get out of there." Rumsfeld, this official thinks, may have been influenced by a Panama analogy: In that operation, the United States had raced in to unseat the dictator Manuel Noriega and then raced out again.[115] One official from another department with close connections to the military planners said the idea that "we'd be in and out" very quickly was such a strong presumption that it was virtually "burned into our brains."[116]

But just who, someone should have pressed Rumsfeld, *will keep order to allow your forces to leave? A reconstituted Iraqi military? What about what your own deputy, Paul Wolfowitz, reportedly said in multiple meetings: that the Iraqi army was tainted by its war crimes and would have to be rebuilt from the ground up?* A senior official involved in the process said that the "in-and-out" concept was "not thrashed out" in the government—and the assumptions about a key leadership role for Ahmad Chalabi and his Iraqi National Congress were "not shared by the president."[117]

⁂

"So here's the irony," one former senior official explained. Donald Rumsfeld came into office after "watching the whole Bosnia thing unfold" and was determined not to make a similar mistake. Meanwhile, he had been questioning why US forces remained stuck in deployments that to his mind weren't justified—in Europe, Greenland, and Korea. So the "animating idea of postwar Iraq was not to stay long. The last thing he would have wanted is an occupation." He was, famously, given to tough questioning of loose assertions, and had, it was widely thought, one of the most incisive minds in government. How, then, did he preside over such a poor process that led to exactly what he wanted to avoid?

This official shook his head ruefully and sighed. 'I haven't been able to explain it since it happened." The best reason he could come up with was that "he thought the postwar thing was being handled," and he was "focused on winning the war."[118]

Several sources with knowledge of Rumsfeld's thinking suggest that he was not simple-minded enough to believe that US forces could be *expected* to be out within a couple of months.[119] Rumsfeld did not speak, or perhaps even think, in such absolutes. But again: if not, why give so little attention to what would happen once they were there?

I asked another former senior official intimately involved in war planning: How could you plan to be there for so short a time, and still imagine you would stabilize the country? His face screwed up into a dismissive sneer, and he said, "We did not sit around predicting—pretending we knew—how long our forces would be in Iraq doing what. People don't understand the difference between planning and predicting. The idea that we are crystal ball readers is stupid."[120] Which is of course beside the point—the issue wasn't predicting; it was *deciding* on a firm, coherent concept for what the United States intended to do. But such a concept never really congealed out of the oozing muck that was the interagency debate about postwar governance.

Those who pointed out these shortcomings were subdued or bypassed. Another senior official closely involved in the planning said he saw briefings that proposed to cut US force levels down under sixty thousand by September 2003. He says he thought the assumption was crazy, and objected to it. His objection was dismissed, and so he concluded that, because the truth would only emerge with events anyway, the only thing to do was register his views and move on.[121] There is, of course, the other possible reason why such objections had no meaningful effect: the possibility that Rumsfeld fully appreciated the risks of chaos but fully expected that the United States would be able to off-load them onto the Iraqis themselves.

▪

Part of the distraction was that many of those involved in advocating *this* war were also involved in advocating *other* ones.

The war on terror, from the beginning, was going to be a series of operations to wipe the slate clean of hostile regimes and groups, with Iraq merely the opening gambit. One source explained that on a flight of war planners headed to Italy, a senior Defense Department staffer was walking up and down the aisles saying, "This isn't the battle for Baghdad. This is the first battle for Tehran."[122] A former Bush administration Pentagon official related a phrase he said he heard a number of times around the halls of the building in those days: "Recocking the pistol."[123] It meant firing off one operation and rapidly reloading the expeditionary capability of the US military to fire off another—presumably, at places like Syria, at Hezbollah, and at Iran. George Tenet writes of having to repeatedly shoot down amateur covert operations planning by Defense Department officials from Feith's office working with anti-Iranian activists outside government—an effort to make contact with Iranians willing to join a regime change operation aimed at Tehran.[124]

This was the most militantly aggressive version of the US missionary sensibility. It appears to have been held, as an imminent hope, by only a few officials in the Bush administration. But for those concerned to run the table past Baghdad, to get bogged down in Iraq would be a nightmare because it would reduce their freedom of action in dealing with subsequent targets.[125] It's "no wonder [Rumsfeld] was only giving Franks 100,000" or so troops for the Iraq mission, said another Pentagon planner, relaying the rumors and speculation that were rife at the time. "Because six weeks into this we were going to Syria."

※

By the fall of 2002, if the postinvasion interviews with senior Iraqi officials are to be believed, Saddam glowered and mulled his options in Baghdad. His primary obsession remained internal security—coups, uprisings, Iranian meddling with the Shi'ites in the south. He continued to imagine that an American invasion was impossible. He placed his faith in the French and Russians, who he believed would forestall any American effort to gain UN approval for war.[126]

And if war did come, Saddam thought, he could bloody US forces until they left. The Americans didn't have the stomach for real casualties, he was convinced. (He was a fan of the film *Black Hawk Down*.) He figured they would use air power alone, which he could ride out, as he had in 1991.[127] He convinced himself, repeatedly on the road to March 2003, that his worst fears could not possibly be true.

※

In the first week of November, the United States presented a third Security Council resolution, one that loosened some of the earlier demands and threatened Iraq with the vague prospect of "serious consequences" for misbehavior. France and others quickly agreed to it, and it became Resolution 1441, passed fifteen to zero by the Security Council.

Each side in the debate at the UN willfully interpreted the wording of the resolution to serve their own purposes. Other members of the Council thought they had restrained the Bush administration by forcing changes in the language. Looked at in the harsh light of retrospect, this was clearly wishful thinking.

The accompanying UN press announcement made burningly obvious these differences in interpretation. "The representative of France," it said, "welcomed the two-stage approach required by the resolution, saying that the concept of 'automaticity' for the use of force had been eliminated."

Meanwhile, "the United Kingdom's representative said the resolution made crystal clear that Iraq was being given a final opportunity. The Iraqi regime now faced an unequivocal choice: between complete disarmament and the serious consequences indicated in the resolution."[128]

⁂

The other element of the UN role in the unfolding drama—the weapons inspection teams—was also picking up speed. On November 18, a group of twenty-six specialists arrived in Baghdad, led by Hans Blix. Iraq soon notified the Security Council that it was having difficulty assembling its full declaration of WMD programs, in part because the precise requirements were so vague, but the process ground forward. The first formal inspection took place on November 27; within a week, twenty inspections had occurred. The specialists actually found some material—a few mustard gas shells at a known storage facility.[129] But at the same time, Blix began to appreciate that it was all a distraction; press reports quoted US officials saying they would prefer if Hussein simply refused the inspections. They wanted to get on with the main event.

Five days before in Washington, a November 13 Rumsfeld memo for the president called "Next Steps in Iraq"[130] had already made clear that Blix's fears were wholly justified. The inspections process, Rumsfeld wrote, "has important implications for US military planning." Saddam had been given a choice. "The task is to test—sooner rather than later—which choice he has made." When would they know? "It could be early, if he makes some early blunder." It could take a month, if he furnished a "blatantly false" declaration to the UN Security Council. "Or it could be many months away, after the inspectors have begun their work." Either way, Rumsfeld said military preparations needed to continue to be "ready to move relatively quickly should Saddam do something that leads you to decide to act." Comprehensive military preparations would "have us ready by February," Rumsfeld argued, but they would be ready to act even sooner if needed—jumping into the northern areas of Iraq, grabbing Basra in the south, or generally acting to "create a shock effect which, with a great deal of good fortune, could hasten the crumbling of the regime." He was leaning as far forward in the saddle as he could muster while still maintaining the fiction that the choice for war was yet to be made.

⁂

Meanwhile, the efforts to assemble the embryo of a new government in Iraq, to which the United States could rapidly transfer authority in the event of an invasion, continued. On December 14–17, the United States organized a new conference of Iraqi exiles in London.[131] Zalmay Khalilzad was now leading the US delegation as special envoy. He said that Washington planned to integrate the exiles "in our plans as we prepare for liberation," but hinted that Iraqis had to develop their own approaches to postwar Iraq. Not all the Iraqis reacted well. One told reporters, "We want the Americans to help us overthrow Saddam. They seem to want to do it themselves."[132] Khalilzad had to take charge to make things happen, but on the bigger question he remained convinced that a US-led occupation "might create a scapegoat and a common enemy for Iraqis."[133]

The exile meeting quickly degenerated into a microcosm of the subsequent US experience in Iraq. The groups squabbled about Shi'ite versus Sunni versus Kurdish representation on the committees, while US negotiators tried desperately to stitch together shifting, brittle alliances. Ahmad Chalabi and key INC allies fumed that they were not being allowed to orchestrate events to the degree they had expected.[134] US officials, including reportedly Khalilzad himself, worried openly about Iranian meddling, a perception hardly eased by the fact that Chalabi had arrived in London straight from Tehran, where he had been engaged in cozy tête-à-têtes with senior Iranian officials.[135] Even Doug Feith had to admit that the delegates "differed sharply among themselves on many issues."[136] If this was a preview of postwar governance, it did not bode well.

These accumulating signals of impending disaster finally led Steve Herbits, a senior aide to Donald Rumsfeld, to find time with the secretary of defense on December 5. Rumsfeld should take a look at the postwar, Herbits implored, as related by Bob Woodward: "It is so screwed up. We will not be able to win the peace." Rumsfeld, nonplussed, called a meeting with Doug Feith and ordered him to "get this on track."[137] But that was apparently as far as the follow-up went. At this point, there was simply no appetite to start rethinking fundamentals.

⁂

Late November and early December brought the fire drill of the full Iraqi weapons of mass destruction declaration—an official statement to the world of their complete nuclear, chemical, and biological infrastructure. As Hans Blix recognized even at the time, the whole affair was frankly ridiculous—expecting "a country with a sizeable petrochemical industry" to provide "within thirty days a full description of all its peaceful chemical programs," among hundreds of other requirements. The Iraqis had complained from the beginning that they didn't have enough time—but this, of course, was the whole point.[138]

Still, the Iraqis went through with the charade, handing twelve thousand pages of documents over to an UNMOVIC staffer on December 7, who flew immediately to New York. One set of the papers was helicoptered to Washington, while UNMOVIC staff made other copies.

By December 19, Blix was ready to give his report to the Security Council. In the first of many such instances, he emphasized one side of a complex story—that Iraq was not complying with what was being demanded of it. While he understood how difficult it would be for any government to produce such information on such a short timeline, "the declaration had certainly not been used as the hoped-for occasion for a fresh start, coming up with long-hidden truths. It looked rather like a repetition of old, unverified data." US Ambassador to the UN John Negroponte lost no time in drawing the long-sought-after implication. Iraq, he said, was in "material breach"[139] of United Nations resolutions.

The day before the UN sessions, at a December 18 NSC meeting, President Bush and his senior national security team had debated what to do about Hans Blix's expected findings. They discussed the semantics of whether Iraq had indeed violated its UN obligations, and what that would mean. According to Doug Feith's account, Bush said, "It's clear that Saddam is not cooperating."

"That's right," Colin Powell replied.

"The president took this as a grave judgment," Feith wrote, "and his face showed it. 'That's a significant statement. . . . It means it's the beginning of the end for the guy.'"

Later, Bush would ask Powell, "Is war inevitable after you say 'material breach'?" Powell said no. Bush disagreed: "I think war is inevitable."[140]

In March, when he finally ordered the onset of war, Bush would write to his father that he had "decided a few months ago to use force, if need be, to liberate Iraq and rid the country of WMD."[141] When exactly that decisive moment was, he did not say; he probably could not have pointed to a single moment.

⁂

Even at this late date, many obvious questions were not being asked. Some of them were about the postwar. Others were about the status of Iraq's WMD programs, and the quality of US intelligence about them. Whenever it was pressed, the US intelligence community actually seemed to admit fairly quickly that the status of its knowledge was less than definitive, especially about Iraq's nuclear capabilities. But it was seldom pressed; and on one infamous occasion when it was, the senior intelligence advisor to the president offered a simple answer that camouflaged a far more complex reality.

This was the famous "slam dunk" meeting, which took place on December 21. CIA Deputy Director John McLaughlin was briefing on Iraq's WMD programs. The presentation was nuanced and qualified—which apparently shocked some in the small audience, who found it hardly as definitive as they had expected. The implicit commitment to go to war had long been made; senior officials were by this point looking for evidence to make a case, and what they were being presented didn't sound that compelling. As McLaughlin offered his facts "in a dry, academic fashion, none of us was very impressed," Dick Cheney explains.[142]

When McLaughlin finished, there was a pause. According to Bob Woodward, Bush, seemingly nonplussed, interjected, "Nice try. I don't think this is quite—it's not something that Joe Public would understand or would gain a lot of confidence from."

This is a critical moment; one wonders if it appeared so to anyone in the room. The president of the United States had been making the case for war based on assumptions about the degree of certainty in US intelligence. Presented with a comprehensive summary of that intelligence, he has just realized that those assumptions were built on sand.

He wasn't the only one who had this reaction. Condoleezza Rice, and not for the first time, was unconvinced. Bush's chief of staff Andrew Card was so worried by the tentativeness of McLaughlin's presentation that it caused him to wonder whether there might not be any "there there" on the intelligence.

Bush turned to CIA director Tenet. "I've been told all this intelligence about having WMD," he said testily. "And this is the best we've got?" And then Tenet—not once but twice—answered the president with the now-infamous phrase: "It's a slam dunk case."[143]

Of course, by December of 2002, none of this probably made any difference; the die had been cast. Repeatedly, however, when confronted with the actual details of the best evidence of Saddam's WMD ambitions, senior officials were not persuaded. President Bush did not come face to face with this dissonance until it was too late. We will never know what would have happened if the realization had been forced upon him earlier.

Tenet's memoirs offer an astonishing account of a White House session several days after December 21, designed to improve on the McLaughlin brief. Robert Walpole, the National Intelligence Officer for strategic programs, was going through elements of a proposed National Intelligence Estimate, saying things like "we assess" and "we judge." At some point Condoleezza Rice stopped him.

"Wait a minute. Bob, if you are saying these are *assertions,* we need to know this now," she said. "We can't send troops to war based on assertions."

Walpole then dug into a few distinctions, explaining, for example, that the intelligence community had "high confidence" that Iraq possessed chemical weapons. Rice reportedly asked what "high" meant—90 percent? That was about right, Walpole replied. To which Rice replied, "That's a heck of a lot lower than we're getting from reading the PDB."[144]

There are paradoxes here—because despite the skeptical reactions to some of these overview briefings on WMDs, senior officials are also fairly uniform in insisting that they were being exposed to truckloads of facts and reports that left no doubt about the status of Iraq's programs. As one very senior source put it, "For many of us this was the most specific and extensive information we'd ever seen" on any similar kind of issue.[145] They were provided with photographs of supposed sites, recordings of Iraqi officials talking to one another, evidence of their behavior in advance of UN inspections; it all seemed entirely consistent with the conventional wisdom about Saddam's ambitions. One of the "greatest of all the mysteries" about the Iraq war, this official suggested, is how there could have been essentially nothing there when they arrived, when they were confronted with a seeming avalanche of prewar information suggesting the opposite.

Part of the answer, of course, is that much of the stuff being thrown at senior officials was raw intelligence—suggestive, circumstantial hints, many of them unverified reports, that did not necessarily prove anything. In fact, doubts about the intelligence did exist. They were reported, at the time: the *Christian Science Monitor's* Jonathan Landay was one of the few to question the conventional wisdom. He noted, "Senior US officials with access to top-secret intelligence on Iraq say they have detected no alarming increase in the threat" posed by Saddam Hussein.[146] One senior DoD official told me later that he was watching all the WMD intel go by, thinking, *This stuff just isn't definitive. Where's the smoking gun?* "There was always this assumption," he said, "that there is some open-and-shut case buried over at the CIA that we don't know about."[147]

Clear statements of the limits of US knowledge were readily available, for anyone who was interested. One of the most powerful is a Joint Staff briefing from the J-2, the intelligence division of the staff, and which has since been declassified. Produced in September 2002, it is titled "Iraq: Status of WMD Programs."[148] In the cover memo, Major General Glen Shaffer, the director of the J-2, stated quite clearly, "We've struggled to estimate the unknowns. . . . We range from 0% to about 75% knowledge on various aspects of their program." The second bullet in the actual brief is quite blunt: "Our assessments rely heavily on analytic assumptions and judgment rather than hard evidence." The third bullet admitted, "The evidentiary base is particularly sparse for Iraqi nuclear programs."

At the bottom of the first slide, in a box, *in italics*, was this warning: "*We don't know with any precision how much we don't know.*" The slide on nuclear programs was specific: "We do not know the status of enrichment capabilities"; at the bottom, again in italics and boxed, was this statement: "*Our knowledge of the Iraqi nuclear weapons program is based largely—perhaps 90%—on analysis of imprecise intelligence.*"

The slides dealing with Iraqi biological and chemical programs contained more detailed information but still pointed to huge gaps in US knowledge. "We cannot confirm the identity of any Iraqi facilities that produce, test, fill, or store biological weapons," the next slide explained. On chemical weapons, the brief concluded that Iraq had the "knowledge" to build them, but said, "We do not know if all the processes required to produce a weapon are in place," and "We cannot confirm the identity of any Iraqi sites that produce final chemical agent." It admitted that most of what they knew had to do with "infrastructure and doctrine." In terms of actual chemical weapons stockpiles and facilities, "knowledge is 60–70 percent incomplete."

The cover memo was addressed to the chairman and other top military leaders. The copy declassified in 2011, however, is prominently stamped, "**SECDEF has seen.**"

Others in the Pentagon had come to similar conclusions. Sometime in 2002, the air force—worried that it would be called upon to destroy Iraq's WMD sites—set about developing a targeting list. As people involved in the process have suggested to me, they had intricate, off-the-shelf targeting plans for things like Iraq's Integrated Air Defense System (IADS), but nothing for WMDs. So the air force pulled together a "Tiger Team" of staffers which began talking to the intelligence community and tried to round up a list of WMD sites. "And we could never find anything," one staffer involved in the process said.[149] They'd discover some evidence for dual-use items or facilities, like crop dusters that *in theory* could be used to spread chemical weapons. But in terms of actual production or storage of WMDs—nothing. It became a running joke with their superiors: the team would say they hadn't found any worthwhile targets; their bosses would reply, "You're just not looking hard enough."

In Iraq, though the air force team couldn't have known it, UN inspectors were equally frustrated. "If our goal is to catch [the Iraqis] with their pants down," one inspector told the *Los Angeles Times*, "we are definitely losing. We haven't found an iota of concealed material yet." UN officials said that cooperation was relatively good, despite some low-level harassment and signs that the Iraqis seemed to know where the inspectors were heading. But "I must say," one inspector said, "that if we were to publish a report now, we would have zilch to put in it."[150]

And yet, like most of the inspectors, the air force team never fundamentally questioned the assumption that Saddam did have WMDs. "He's got this stuff, we just don't know where it is," they figured. "We were convinced that he was just really good at hiding it." Some members of the air force leadership, as in other places in the DoD hierarchy, retained visceral memories of the UNSCOM inspection process in the 1990s. Their life experiences told them that Saddam *had* to be hiding WMDs. It reached the level of a "religious belief" with some, and there was "no convincing them otherwise."[151]

One officer who worked with WMD evidence before the war talked of junior analysts coming back and saying, "Sir, I'm just not seeing it."

But the much greater pressure was in the other direction: "The narrative shaped the lead question," he said, "and it shapes how you think and analyze." And the narrative was that Iraq had WMDs—a conviction, a certainty, shared by most senior officials across government. "Everybody wanted to be the guy who found confirmation" of that fact—and suddenly, "everything you see is a potential confirmation."[152]

Eventually, the Tiger Team was disbanded, and the members moved on to other things. Years later, one of them talked with a former boss about what he considered a personal failure; he'd never considered the alternative scenario, that Saddam really didn't have WMDs. His one-time boss waved it off. "You would never have gotten anywhere with it" anyway, he said. Everyone *knew* that Saddam had WMDs, and no amount of apparent evidence—or the lack of it—was going to convince them otherwise.

That conviction, moreover, was about to be blared from the rooftops, without qualification. At the beginning of January, the CIA issued its public white paper on Iraq's WMD programs.[153] The first paragraph read this way: "Iraq has continued its weapons of mass destruction (WMD) programs in defiance of UN resolutions and restrictions. Baghdad has chemical and biological weapons as well as missiles with ranges in excess of UN restrictions; if left unchecked, it probably will have a nuclear weapon during this decade."

⁂

Postwar interviews with Iraqi officials revealed that the accelerating rhetoric of the Bush administration had finally, by the fall of 2002, convinced Saddam Hussein and his regime that Washington was serious. Bush's September UN speech "unsettled" the Iraqi leadership, according to the Duelfer Report; even three weeks later, Saddam appeared "very stiff" when talking about it. He was clearly still "feeling the pressure," according to other officials. But Saddam was somehow still confident; he said, "What can they discover [in the inspections process] when we have nothing?" And so, in December 2002, he told his government to "cooperate completely" with the UN inspectors.[154]

Such actions stood to make little difference at this point, of course. In Washington, Saddam's lack of compliance was a forgone assumption. One anonymous memo, likely from Defense's policy shop (Doug Feith's office) from this period—December 18—lays out ideas for dealing with the forthcoming Iraqi weapons declaration, which everyone expected to be a collection of lies.[155] "Claiming that the Iraqi declaration is false is a momentous step," it began. In doing so, "we are in effect saying that inspections cannot serve their purpose." Although unstated, this was clearly the background assumption of the document. "We should be ready to use strong language—such as accusing Iraq of a 'material breach' of UN Security Council resolution 1441 as soon as we are ready to take decisive action, *but not sooner*," the document continued. Preparing the argument would "take weeks," during which time they would "Get our own case concerning the falsity of the declaration in order (and it isn't yet)." Meantime they would continue with the most important preparation for their intended course: "Continue flowing forces to the region."

⁂

It was just before Christmas that George Bush did something unusual: He asked a senior national security official, directly and unambiguously, whether war was a good idea. He may have been getting anxious; by this time, annoyed with the failure to gain consensus at the UN, he had remarked to Rumsfeld, "This is a quagmire of my own making."[156]

"Do you think we should do this?" he asked, as he and Condoleezza Rice stood alone in the Oval Office.

"Yes," she replied.[157]

In a way the question was unnecessary. Both already knew it was something they had to do, and no one in the administration was making powerful contrary arguments. They had been informally committed to removing Saddam since the days after 9/11 and had formally committed to doing so since at least August 2002 and in some fashion since the previous February. Their powerful sense of rightness about the need to unseat Saddam—and quickly—had only gained strength, and become a form of moral convinction. The result was a form of psychological clo-sure throughout the executive branch. "Once the president decides," a senior official told me, "the only thing anyone cares about is making what he wants happen."[158]

⚹

By the last months of 2002, in the NSC planning group on postwar relief and reconstruction, Robin Cleveland and especially Wendy Cham-berlin had begun to get concerned about the lack of security provided by the plans. None of the elaborate humanitarian and reconstruction programs would have any effect if the security situation collapsed. The two of them tried to go to CENTCOM to ask questions—and CENT-COM, through interagency channels, blocked the trip. They were busy planning a war. Chamberlin sent a lower-level staffer, whose discussions had little effect.

Chamberlin kept raising the issue with everyone she could think of. She laid out her concerns in a formal memo, which was drafted as being from USAID administrator Natsios to Colin Powell. Natsios approved and signed it, and then delivered it to Powell, telling him, "I think you should share this with the White House." It was the last the USAID people ever heard of it. More typically, Chamberlin got a more straight-forward reaction, along these lines: *Don't worry about it. We don't need more security. People will fall in line—the local police will take over. The big fight will be in Baghdad. The rest of the country will be quiet. There won't be a need for any big presence.* Which sounded, people at USAID later recalled, like code for "We don't have enough troops anyway, so what are we going to do about it?"

The problem, a USAID source said, was that Chamberlin was "argu-ing the right point from the wrong platform": Who was going to take seriously a military security argument from a USAID person? (Of course, she was precisely the right person, because she and others like her knew what risks postconflict situations would offer.) And Chamberlin and other USAID staffers got virtually no time with Powell, so they could not bring their concerns to him. Finally, someone came to her and said, "Will you please shut up about the security thing? You're making people uncomfortable. You're being too vocal."[159]

These episodes were beginning to reflect what would be a dominant trend of the final three months before the invasion, a theme of warnings ignored. An obvious question is why—why a group of tremendously smart and experienced senior officials who legitimately wanted the best for their country could have refused to take seriously the risks, and in fact go beyond that to actively suppress discussion of them. I asked a senior official in a position to be aware of the consequences of the invasion, in fact himself an advocate of it, about his expectations as he watched the march to war unfold. Didn't he worry that they had not done enough?

"Once you remove a regime in a country like Iraq," he admitted, "you're going to have very little control over what happens next."

"Okay," I replied, "but what did you truly *expect?*"

"There were too many uncertainties to have a coherent plan," he added. "No amount of prior planning would have prepared us for the magnitude [of the effects] we would get when the lid came off."[160]

"What was so hard," another former official recalled, "was to be in the middle of it and see it going so wrong—and having no one listen" to the warnings. This official "never saw a deliberative process" in the issue of going to war or planning for the aftermath, and assumed that the major decisions were all taken by a tiny handful of people—President Bush, Vice President Cheney, Don Rumsfeld, Condi Rice. "I didn't know, as a middle-ranking person, how to impact it." The person wrote memos about what appeared to be going wrong, sent them up the chain, and got no response. "Beyond literally *screaming*" at people, those who harbored doubts and wanted to express them didn't know what else to do.[161]

I asked another person privy to segments of the planning and interagency process: When you saw looming disaster, why didn't you or others raise a huge stink? "There was a cloud that hung over the decision-making process," he explained. "Regardless of what reality was, the ground truth you felt in your bones was that the decision had been made, primarily driven by Cheney and his group, approved by the president. You could go to Condi—nobody was going to go to Rumsfeld—but you did not go to Cheney. You'd just get shot in the face." Even going to Rice wouldn't help, because you'd be told, "that's been decided." Cheney was the "unseen but felt 800-pound-gorilla in the room. That was the ambiance in the decision process."[162]

Military officers were particularly muzzled by the dynamic between Rumsfeld and the uniformed military. There was a "horrible, horrible culture" between the two in the Rumsfeld Pentagon, one officer told me. The civilian attitude was that "you guys are just minions to execute our mission. Don't call into question what we are doing."[163]

Still, given what was at stake, senior military leaders could, and should, have done more. The source described what he believed to be a "cataclysmic failure of leadership on the part of the Joint Chiefs" not to become more involved on the issue. He described how when Hugh Shelton became chairman, he had distributed copies of H. R. McMaster's book *Dereliction of Duty*—the tragic tale of the US military leadership's failure to question Vietnam strategy and escalation decisions—to all the chiefs, as a quiet message: "Not on my watch" will such things happen. But it's not clear that this gesture had the intended effect. "Not one person in NSC meetings at which I was present stated or hinted that they were opposed to, or even hesitant about, the President's decision" to go to war as it unfolded, Donald Rumsfeld claims in his memoirs.[164] I have found no evidence to contradict him.

Beyond that, however, and even more fundamentally, the Iraq war decision was grounded in sacred values, in deeply felt imperatives—the United States *must* not allow regimes with ties to terrorists to have weapons of mass destruction; the United States *must* remove Saddam from power. And so the proposition that the United States must fight such a war was resistant, even immune, to serious confrontation with consequences. Warnings become the siren song of the wicked and the deluded. Like any dissolute temptation, they must not only be ignored—they must be actively resisted. And so they would be, right up until US forces vaulted into the unknown. As 2002 drew to a close, three months remained before they would do so—three months from the final and fateful crossing, the tragic plunge into the abyss. But the time to rethink the course, to step back and ask hard questions, had long passed.

CHAPTER 8

"ALL IS TBD"—ON
THE VERGE OF WAR:
JANUARY TO MARCH 2003

I think if I had been delphic, and had seen where we are today, and people had said, "Should we go into Iraq?," I think now I probably would have said, "No, let's consider other strategies for dealing with the thing that concerns us most, which is Saddam supplying weapons of mass destruction to terrorists." . . . Could we have managed that threat by means other than a direct military intervention? Well, maybe we could have.

RICHARD PERLE, IN 2006[1]

The only sober moment we've had in the past four decades was 9/11, and we spoiled that by invading a place where the attack didn't come from, full of people who didn't cause it, for reasons we pulled out of our butt.

P. J. O'ROURKE[2]

The American war decision in Vietnam was "absurdly constricted," yet even that narrow issue was never settled, nor any clearcut decision made. The momentum of events carried us constantly forward, and, so long as no one challenged the fundamental assumptions on which our involvement rested, events, not design, would determine the future.

GEORGE W. BALL[3]

The decision to go to war had essentially been made by January 2003, when the formal and informal tracks of the decision process merged. President Bush had made clear to several top officials that he had come to his judgment—the United States would undertake regime change in Iraq. But the decision to do something and the choice of *how* to do it are two different propositions, and while the war plan itself was coming together, the practical details of the postwar continued to elude close analysis. More and more people noticed the gap and pointed, in some cases urgently, to the massive hole where a clear concept for the postwar ought to be. But their concerns made little impression on leaders who were already fully committed to what they saw as a form of moral imperative.

Partly as a result, the period of January–March 2003 was one of warnings ignored. The overwhelming question by January was obvious: *We are headed into Iraq—but what happens when we get there?* And on that issue, signs of impending danger flooded in between January and March, from inside the outside government: *You are buying into a calamity*, they would say, *and you are not prepared to deal with it.* Yet awareness of this fact would not sink in. The available evidence suggests only one interpretation: senior members of the Bush administration had by that time so committed themselves to a course of action that warnings about costs and risks had become essentially irrelevant. This pattern revealed itself at a number of especially significant moments in those last three precipitous months: when a powerful memo cataloguing postwar risks was thrown into the Defense planning process, to little effect; when the Defense Department grabbed authority for the postwar; and at an astonishing planning conference which revealed—just a month before the invasion—that disaster was looming.

※

Even as the commitment to war hardened, evidence was accumulating that Iraq's WMD programs were less significant than the US administration assumed, but few were paying attention. By mid-January 2003, UN inspection teams had made 237 visits to suspect sites and found nothing. CENTCOM was having the same experience. It repeatedly asked the CIA for intelligence to do target planning on WMD sites. When the CIA finally opened up, one CENTCOM source says, the intelligence "was crap," much of it dating to 1991. Pictures showed buildings without any sense of what was inside.[4]

Saddam continued to drag his feet and dissemble, which played into US hands. In the Baghdad talks in January, the Iraqis offered few new concessions, leaving the IAEA's Hans Blix wondering just what they could possibly be thinking.[5] Blix's statements in these weeks were maddeningly opaque. "One must not jump to the conclusion that they exist," he said of Iraqi WMD. "However, that possibility is also not excluded."[6] Blix's comments were beginning to sound a lot like Don Rumsfeld.

Just after New Year's Day 2003, Bush met privately with Rice and said the inspections were not working. "We're going to have to go to war," he told her.[7] By January 8, he was admitting to Republican congressional leaders that war was likely. On January 13, he informed Colin Powell. In stark contrast, the day before Bush met with Rice to say war was inevitable, Hans Blix had written in his diary: "I do not think that the US has made up its mind to go to war even though they are taking all the steps in that direction. It serves to scare the Iraqis."[8]

❧

Even at this time, the interagency process still grappled with basic questions about what form postwar governance would take. When those involved in the process expressed concerns about the state of such planning, "no one wanted to hear it," another senior US official recalled.[9]

The indecision was reflected in a January 17, 2003, memo—less than sixty days before the war—from Defense, which said straight out, "No decisions have been reached on the post-Saddam governance of Iraq." It went on to list options "under consideration" that embodied a three-phase process consisting of an immediate posthostilities "military administration" followed by a "transitional authority" to lay the groundwork for elections, and finally "transition to broad-based Iraqi government."[10] This matches reasonably closely the process that eventually unfolded on the ground—but such an extended vision of the plan to generate a new Iraqi government shares little in common with the assumptions being made by the military and many at the Defense Department that the United States would be getting into and out of Iraq very quickly.

The issue of US influence cropped up in a "Draft Agreement between USG [US Government] and 'Iraqi Interim Authority' (IIA)," issued on March 3.[11] In the proposed agreement, meant to serve as the blueprint for the formal arrangement that would exist after the war, Washington would recognize the IIA as the "legitimate governmental authority of Iraq." But the transfer of authority only went so far, because the proposed agreement then demanded that the supposedly independent IIA take a host of actions, including "treat all Iraqis equally, regardless of religion or ethnicity," "return all individuals and property illegally held in Iraq," shut down the Ba'ath party, "disband military and security agencies that are tainted with the crimes of the Ba'ath regime," and vet all "military, security and law enforcement personnel to remove all who are tainted with the crimes of the Ba'ath regime." This was an awful lot to decide on behalf of the supposedly sovereign government of a newly liberated country.

But these were only DoD proposals; the US government had not yet settled on a clear governance model. It all hung in the air, with nothing resolved.[12]

❧

Meanwhile, the administration's public campaign to build support for war was having an effect. A mid-December ABC News/*Washington Post* poll found that 81 percent of Americans perceived Iraq as a "threat to the United States"; 64 percent of these saw it as a "substantial" threat, and 44 percent viewed it as an "immediate" danger. Almost 60 percent wanted to see more evidence before Bush took action[13]—and they would

soon get it from a number of war-selling initiatives, most famously Colin
Powell's UN speech.

The same poll revealed the striking effect of months of exaggerations.
Over 40 percent of Americans "said that Iraq already possessed nuclear
weapons." A Pew Research Center/Council on Foreign Relations survey
made public on February 20 "found that 57% of those polled believed
Saddam Hussein helped terrorists involved with the 9/11 attacks." In an
early March *New York Times*/CBS News poll, 45 percent agreed with the
statement " 'Saddam Hussein was personally involved in the Sept. 11 terrorist attacks,' and a March 14–15 CNN/*USA Today*/Gallup poll found
this apparently mistaken notion holding firm at 51%."[14]

Once internalized, such views became hard to shake. How else can
we account for the fact that, even by September 2003, six months into
the war and after dozens of major news stories corrected the impression,
69 percent of Americans *continued* to believe that Saddam Hussein was
involved in the 9/11 attacks? Andrew Kohut of the Pew Research Center
told the *Washington Post* that the best explanation he could come up
with was self-delusion. It was almost as if people desperately needed to
believe this, he said, in order to justify their support of a president and
a war they were too afraid to jettison.[15] In this they were little different from the senior officials whose looming war they felt duty-bound to
support.

⁂

On January 10, President Bush and Vice President Cheney hosted three
Iraqi dissidents in the Oval Office and asked them about the postwar transition. "People will greet you with flowers and sweets," one of them said.
When the president asked how he knew, the man said he was in touch
with people inside Iraq. Later, Bush told the exiles that when Saddam was
thrown out, "now there [will be] a void. What's your vision?" No one had
a clear answer. Bush continued, "How do we deal with the impression the
US is bringing a leader in, imposing our will?" Again, no coherent answer
was forthcoming.[16]

Jim Hoagland would later report that Iraqis at the meeting "were surprised at how little [Bush] seemed to know about the embryonic plans for a democratic, federal Iraq or about the organized opposition to Saddam Hussein."[17] In the midst of the discussion of postwar planning, according to George Packer, Bush said to Rice, "A humanitarian army is going to follow our army into Iraq, right?" She said yes.[18] Cheney insisted that the United States would have a "light hand in the postwar phase," but some of the Iraqis urged a powerful US role of at least two or three years. The risks of getting the balance wrong were stated by one Iraqi participant, who predicted that the United States would have about two months to show serious progress toward effective governance. Otherwise, "you could see Mogadishu in Baghdad."[19]

It turned out that, at about the same moment, a few officials and military officers in Doug Feith's Defense policy shop were starting to worry about just that scenario.

₹₺

One of my interviews was with a former senior Bush administration official, who voiced a common planning assumption of the invasion. They went in, he said, under the view that "there would be institutions." You could take off the top layer, and the governmental ministries and agencies and other social institutions would keep right on running underneath. That assumption, he admitted quite forthrightly, was wrong. "The institutions just evaporated. That, we had not expected. *No one expected that.*"[20]

Some did, though, and issued pointed warnings in the months before the invasion. And probably the most elaborate and detailed warning came about by accident, because a Defense official happened to be sitting in on a meeting for his boss.

This was a report produced by the office of the Deputy Assistant Secretary of Defense for Resources and Plans, Chris Lamb. Lamb was a Foreign Service officer who transferred to the Department of Defense in 1990. When Lamb's boss was transferred to run another office, Lamb began attending Under Secretary Douglas Feith's staff meetings. And so it was on a day in late 2002—probably December, according to the recollections of participants—that Lamb was present when Feith questioned whether his team had done all the necessary preparatory work for war in Iraq. The UN resolutions process was underway, Feith announced, and the march toward action in Iraq had been delayed. "We may as well use the time profitably," sources remember him saying.[21] Feith asked the room, "Can anyone think of any issues we haven't covered?"

Chris Lamb tentatively raised his hand. During the first Bush administration, his office worked on a study about lessons from the failure to plan the aftermath of the US invasion to topple President Manuel Noriega in Panama.[22] He mentioned it to Feith and his assembled subordinates, saying, "We typically forget about the postconflict period, and especially the need for security in the immediate aftermath of an invasion. Large-scale civil disorder has caught us by surprise in the past."

Feith agreed and told Lamb to look into it. So Lamb went back to his office, found a marine colonel, Steve Busby, and asked him to take the lead in drafting a paper.[23] Lamb initially told Busby to produce something in three or four days, but eventually it would grow to three weeks.[24]

Colonel Busby tried to get access to the war plan under construction, but he was turned down. *Too secret*, he was told. With Lamb's assistance, Busby eventually got a forty-five-minute look at PowerPoint slides dealing with Phase IV—about twenty slides, the "sum total" of what the planners had on paper about the postwar by that moment in the process. Busby spoke to contacts at CENTCOM and explained what he was doing. Their reaction, as they were neck-deep in war and postwar planning, was not favorable. "Why the hell are *you* doing that?" was the basic gist. Busby asked if they could share any information; the answer was a curt no. Still, as Busby and others explored the issue, they became "ever more convinced that there was a problem."[25]

Colonel Busby talked to OSD intelligence experts and gathered up research reports and intelligence documents on Iraq. He read about the US experience in Panama. He met with people in the Office of Special

Plans, who, according to sources in the office, he found "not forthcoming with information . . . not forthcoming with anything, really." He went to the Internet and downloaded anything he could find that bore on post-conflict security and Iraq. He ended up with a pile of documents three or four feet tall stacked in his office. And he proceeded to draft a memo that was as prescient as anything written about what the United States could expect in postwar Iraq, a clear-eyed prediction that the US plans and force levels were not adequate to provide the postconflict security that experience suggested was absolutely essential to success.

The office took the first draft of the memo to Feith. He pronounced it "pedestrian" and demanded a rewrite. They produced one. They submitted the second version and waited. As time went on, they began to pester their bosses. They recommended that the issue be brought to Rumsfeld's attention and that Feith highlight it during his regular meeting with the vice chairman of the Joint Chiefs, marine general Peter Pace.

Feith's book released a declassified version of the memo itself, presumably the second draft, dated February 9, 2003—just over one month before the war would begin. The study forecast a collapse of civil order in Iraq upon the entry of US forces, partly due to a massive disconnect between civilian and military planners. "The post-war planning office expects that CENTCOM will provide forces for maintaining order from the beginning," the report explained. "CENTCOM believes these forces have other priorities." The memo warned that key assumptions being made to rule out the possibility of chaos were also made "in Operation JUST CAUSE in Panama and proved wrong; massive civil disorder began almost immediately."[26] The bottom line was unambiguous. "The potential for civil disorder to undermine military successes is a 'win the war but lose the peace' scenario."[27] In his two-page executive summary, Busby put the same conclusion in even starker terms: "Disorder of this magnitude could become 'Win the War' but 'Lose the peace' events."

The memo argued that the issue should be raised at the highest levels of government—principals- and deputies-level meetings. But it also sketched out, in fourteen detailed pages of "background planning considerations," the skeleton of a program for maintaining order in Iraq through a whole range of actions—information operations, using what elements of the Iraqi police forces could be salvaged, deploying rapid reaction US forces to "flash points" when disorder emerged, and much more. It defined the problem, but also pointed to a solution.

⁊₭

A permanent replacement for Lamb's boss had come in, Ryan Henry, and Lamb no longer attended meetings with Feith. He wasn't getting an answer on the memo, and he asked Henry, "Do I continue pursuing this, or do I drop it?"

A source in OSD told me that Henry took the issue to Feith, who was "totally on board" with the idea of expanded police presence in liberated areas. Henry's office then brought the concept to CENTCOM, where it was promptly shot down. A combination of insufficient force levels to both wage the war and police Iraq—and, sources suggested to me, a continuing lack of respect at CENTCOM for Doug Feith—generated a simple answer. "Don't you guys get it?" CENTCOM replied, in effect. "This war plan is all about getting to Baghdad. We can't get there if we're dropping troops off on the way."[28]

So eventually, Lamb got his answer. "You can stand down."

I asked an OSD official involved in the process why they didn't begin causing trouble at that point, demanding that the issue be addressed. The problem, he explained, was that it was obvious CENTCOM just wasn't going to give. "You're pushing a rope. You can go beat your head against a door that won't open, or you can deal with problems that you can solve."[29]

One person who worked in Lamb's office thought blaming CENT-COM was disingenuous, noting that the Defense leadership at that time was notorious for "how they micro-managed everything. It was excruciating." Besides which, CENTCOM had a point—it *was* running a thousand miles an hour trying to be ready for Phase III and doing so under a constant assault of questions, demands, and revisions imposed by a peripatetic secretary of defense. Upon reflection, the source believes other factors explain the failure of OSD to follow up on the staff's postwar planning memos: "I had the impression that everyone thought that this was going to be a very quick evolution—quick in and out." The problem was, to make that assumption you had to make another one: that the United States could "put a thousand years of history behind us."[30]

Whether or not postwar security could be achieved was not some marginal issue, however—it was widely known to be essential to anything the United States hoped to accomplish in the aftermath of an invasion. Just before the events surrounding this warning memo had unfolded, someone in OSD had prepared a two-page bullet memo titled "Post-War Tasks."[31] It was a list of all the things the United States would need to do when it got hold of Iraq. It was a daunting and frankly delusional list, including items such as the following: "Organize for decentralization of government services and paying salaries at municipal level"; "Develop provincial dialogue process—create environment to identify local talent and capacity." At the top of the list was the following bullet: "Create transitional security force equipped to handle post-conflict security needs."

※

Other warnings had already been flooding in before Colonel Busby's perspicacious memo. At some moment in the fall of 2002—I have heard estimates of September through mid-December—the Near East Affairs bureau of State generated "The Perfect Storm," a worst-case assessment of the chaos that could ensue when the tight lid on a fractious multi-ethnic state was pried off. (To make matters confusing, the title duplicated the CIA memo on similar issues.) It raised the prospects of looting, the collapse of government authority, ruined infrastructure, tribal leadership turning against the United States, Kurdistan breaking away and Turkey going to war as a result, Iran getting engaged in the conflict, ethnic battles for power, and much more.[32] But it did not go beyond State, it is not clear Powell himself ever read it, and its character as a "worst-case assessment" ruined its predictive and policy value.

At about the same time, the intelligence community began to generate a number of analyses that should have served as powerful red flags.
But it did so in a haphazard, often self-generated fashion. Because the
depressing truth is that no one—from the president on down—ever
asked the intelligence agencies for a formal assessment of what would
happen when Saddam's regime fell. "Many at the Agency were concerned
that bringing down Saddam would open a Pandora's box," senior CIA
official Michael Morell explains in his memoir. He thought, as a result,
that the agency had a "responsibility prewar to produce a detailed analysis of the likely postwar scenarios." But he then admits that such a paper
"was never written. . . . No analyst initiated such a paper and no one in
the chain of command, from a first-line supervisor at CIA all the way to
the president, requested it."[33] He does not explain why.

Despite the lack of guidance, individual offices and analysts did take
their own initiative to produce briefings and reports. A DIA brief given
in January 2003, for example, was "aggressive" in its warnings about the
postwar, as were State Intelligence and Research (INR) office and Joint
Staff assessments.[34] Up at the Army War College in Carlisle, Pennsylvania, a senior army general tasked the Strategic Studies Institute to consider Phase IV risks. In late January it came out with a report warning
that "instability may emerge in the aftermath of the dictator's removal.
In particular, tensions among Iraqi religious, ethnic, and tribal communities are expected to complicate both the occupation and efforts to build
a viable postwar government."[35]

The National Intelligence Council (NIC) issued two reports the same
month: "Principal Challenges in Post-Saddam Iraq" and "Regional Consequences of Regime Change in Iraq." Sometimes wrongly attributed to
the CIA, these were in fact products of the NIC, the broadest and (in
theory) highest-intelligence-production office in the government.[36] No
one in the executive branch had asked for them, and so without a formal request, National Intelligence Officer for the Middle East and South
Asia Paul Pillar took it upon himself to initiate the two estimates in late
2002. The NIC staff put in some three months of "rigorous review and

coordination" on the reports. In the end they "received the unanimous concurrence of all the intelligence agencies."[37]

The primary report, declassified in large part in 2007, told policy-makers that the biggest challenge in post-Saddam Iraq would be "the introduction of a stable and representative political system. . . . The building of an Iraqi democracy would be a long, difficult, and probably turbulent process." The challenge was especially problematic because the hardest nuts to crack in this regard were "most deeply rooted in Iraq's history and culture and least susceptible to outside intervention and management." "Any new authority in Iraq," it went on, "would face a country with societal fractures and significant potential for violent conflict among domestic groups if not prevented by an occupying force." The report warned that "Iraq's history of foreign occupation . . . has left Iraqis with a deep dislike of occupiers. An indefinite foreign military occupation . . . would be widely unacceptable." The overall message of the reports, Pillar wrote in a later essay, "was summed up by one of my colleagues on the NIC. . . . As he said, no one who accepted and reflected upon the assessments' conclusions could possibly think the war was a good idea."[38]

But that is too pat. The assessments themselves, which have been released in only slightly redacted form, are hedged and qualified; they include possibilities of some good outcomes as well as bad ones. And more fundamentally, as intelligence professionals are the first to admit, the judgments may have been wrong. "Reflecting on" the assessments may merely have produced the skeptical reaction—as it did in the minds of a number of war proponents—that the intelligence analysts were reflecting long-standing biases against the possibility of democracy in the Middle East.

A 2007 Senate investigation reviewed many of the intelligence reports that emerged in the months before the war. None of them, it concluded, offered anything like specific guidance to policy-makers trying to decide, *Will this really work?* As one example, in August 2002, the CIA asked, "Can Iraq Ever Become a Democracy?" Its answer: *Well, yes, maybe . . . sort of.* The country lacked the prerequisites to do so, the report argued. On the other hand, Iraq had "several advantages"—exiled elites and oil wealth—that might be helpful. On the third hand, "None of these factors should be seen as minimizing the obstacles to democratization in Iraq after Saddam."[39] And so it went, report after report that offered few concrete judgments to hang any hats on.

"These were all just projections," one former intelligence official said later, when asked why they didn't deliver blunter and more unconditional warnings. "We could have been wrong, and the rosy-glass-wearing neocons could have been right. . . . Nobody's got a crystal ball. It would have been hubris to start shouting, 'This is going to happen.'" Another intelligence professional said, "We did our best to anticipate things. Nobody predicted the institutional vacuum to the degree that it did emerge."[40] A former official deeply involved in war planning is quite direct: "We never saw" serious intelligence estimates that the plan was bound to fail, he said. If intelligence officials really believed that, he argued, they could have found senior officials to pull aside and warn, or they could have generated more unqualified statements of likely postinvasion chaos. They simply did not.[41]

The response, when the two estimates were published in January, was a deafening silence. The single reaction one NIC member received was from a senior policy-maker who replied, "You guys just don't see the possibilities. You're too negative." One senior official who received the reports, when asked whether they made him think twice about the advisability of the war, told me, "The intelligence reports weren't an epiphany. They never give you that. That's not what intelligence does, and I think sometimes people come to believe that intelligence can do more than it actually can. . . . There are lots of opinions running around [in a decision-making process]. Some have more credibility than others. Intelligence is one of those, but only one; and when dealing with intelligence, you always have to ask, 'How do they know that?'"[42]

For those in OSD and the Pentagon, besides, Don Rumsfeld had already been ahead of the curve—back in October, he had issued *his* memo outlining all the things that could go wrong. They knew about all that; they had internalized the risks, domesticated them. The new reports told them nothing.[43]

⅍

On January 13, President Bush finally became direct with Colin Powell. "I really think I'm going to have to take this guy out," he said. Powell told a biographer that he replied by asking the president if he knew what he was getting into. Bush answered, "Yes, I do." Bush asked if Powell would support him, and Powell said yes. One senior official who worked with cabinet officials points to this moment as perhaps the time when one could say that a hard-and-fast decision had been made. By asking Powell for his support, Bush had made clear that he had "probably decided that there was no way to resolve this short of war." And yet Powell, the inveterate optimist, plunged ahead with his diplomacy. He said in an interview later that he still thought perhaps he could divine a difference between "reaching a conclusion and [making] a decision to be implemented." Bush thought there was no alternative to war, Powell thought—but he had not yet ordered war.[44] One source who knows him well is certain Powell thought he could derail the path to war right up until the end.[45]

⅍

Two days later, on January 15, NSC official Elliott Abrams gave a briefing on postwar planning to the president in the White House. Abrams spoke about supplies of food, water, funds, and other logistical preparations in case of refugee flows, temporary starvation, or other short-term humanitarian crises. The focus was on meeting very immediate, quick-reaction needs of people displaced by war. There was nothing in the briefing about providing security for the whole of Iraq, rebuilding the country from the ground up, or refashioning a functioning government from scratch— that was simply not the remit of this group.[46]

What the president did not know was that in a few days, the brief he had just received would become irrelevant: Abrams's group would be out of business. Control for postwar Iraq was about to shift to the Defense

Department, and when it did, much of the careful planning that had just been laid out to him would be cast aside. The new Defense organization to manage the postwar would begin essentially from scratch. More than one person involved in the NSC effort believes that the net effect of the January briefing was a sort of bait and switch: showing the president a picture of a cheerful future that depended on the functioning of a very specific mechanism—a tight planning process led by the NSC—and then throwing that mechanism away.

Five days after that briefing, Bush and Cheney met with the assembled Joint Chiefs of Staff. Bush asked if anyone had concerns about their ability to execute the conflict. Only Chief of Staff of the Army Eric Shinseki spoke up, raising a number of fairly technical issues about force flow and Turkey's role—code, one would presume, for a general sense that the light-footprint approach carried big risks. But it was hardly a full-throated warning, and Bush simply offered thanks.[47] No one else raised any objections.[48]

⁂

On that same day, January 20, the NSC issued a national security presidential directive in Bush's name. Titled NSPD-24, it was the eventual outcome of Don Rumsfeld's bid for control, formally vesting Defense with the administration of postwar Iraq.[49] One result would be the formation, finally, of an official mechanism for orchestrating the postwar: the Office of Reconstruction and Humanitarian Assistance (ORHA), led by retired general Jay Garner.

At one level, the origins of NSPD-24 are fairly straightforward. According to one participant, Doug Feith came to see Steve Hadley and Frank Miller sometime in mid-December 2002 with a Joint Staff official in tow. Feith shared with them a draft directive and asked them to coordinate it. It was circulated for comment, in this official's recollection, and State only objected to a single provision—a statement that after the invasion, the US ambassador in Iraq would be subordinate to whatever civilian viceroy was temporarily running the country.[50] The NSC was aware of it, and the general existence or content of the document should not have come as a surprise to cabinet-level officials.

When it finally emerged, however, NSPD-24 caused consternation throughout the lower ranks of an interagency process that was largely unaware of this higher-level coordination and that still had no clue that Defense was going to run the show.[51] One of those who had been participating in the Abrams-Cleveland interagency process recalled Feith explaining the order: *We—DoD—will do all postwar humanitarian and immediate reconstruction tasks*, he said.

"I don't remember any debate," the former official said. "I don't remember any discussion. There were no papers written with the pros and cons of this kind of DoD takeover." It was just: "Done!"[52] Another planner involved in the early phases of ORHA said, "My first thought when I saw it [NSPD-24] was, I can't believe Secretary Powell has agreed to this."[53] I asked one participant why no one questioned the new order; he said simply, "You have the president's *signature* on this thing!"[54] What few realized that the time was that, in ways no one intended, NSPD-24 would further undermine any hope for a coherent postwar plan.

Jay Garner was introduced at one of the meetings. He didn't have much to say, in part because he had as yet no idea what was going on. He had only been contacted with an offer to run ORHA on January 9; after a few days of hesitation, Doug Feith called him on January 13—the same day Bush was telling Powell he had decided to go to war—and persuaded him to accept the job.[55] The self-inflicted wound of waiting until the very last minute to begin postwar planning now left the administration rushing to cobble together the crude semblance of a postwar office in a matter of days.

※

It did not go smoothly. The bureaucratic wrangling that would characterize ORHA's whole existence—partly a product of the persistently venomous interagency relationships—began almost immediately. According to one source, the senior USAID official Wendy Chamberlin was present at one of the meetings with Jay Garner. She told him about the USAID planning process and mentioned that she was well along in the development of a nearly $3 billion reconstruction program. She had plans, and she had people. They now, according to this document, belonged to Garner. "Tell me," she said, "when you have the office space, because you now own them."

"That's great," Garner replied. A dedicated, thoughtful, collegial military officer, avuncular and deeply respected in parts of Iraq for his work coordinating the post–Gulf War relief operations largely in Kurdish areas, he was anxious for all the help he could get and deeply respectful of USAID from his prior leadership of humanitarian operations. "Let's have lunch," Garner said to Chamberlin, and even suggested that she might come out as his deputy.

In this source's recollection, at this point Doug Feith, also at the meeting and listening in to the discussion, jumped up and nearly shouted, "No! No! That won't work."[56] It was one of the first signs that when the Defense Department said they'd taken the authority, they meant it—and would exercise an iron grip on just who would be allowed to play in their sandbox. Rumsfeld pestered Garner endlessly about who would be on his team, insisting that they be "DoD people."[57] At least one senior official saw the Defense bid for control as a transparent effort to help their favorite exiles.[58] The result was to begin a process of freezing out other agencies of the government, some of whom had done extensive postwar planning.

Though Defense officials had been participating in the Executive Steering Group and other NSC-led processes in meaningful ways up to January, several sources agree that from the point that NSPD-24 was announced up to the early phases of the war, the nature of Defense support for non-DoD processes rapidly diminished. Defense officials increasingly spurned the ESG's work; Defense staff wouldn't show up for its sessions, or they would arrive late and leave early. They often refused to share information and would sit silently through the meetings, playing dumb. One participant put it this way: "OSD came when it wanted,

and fucked around."[59] Another participant related that DoD representatives would say, "I don't feel the need to say anything in this setting";
this person's opinion was that DoD "didn't do a goddamned thing." On
issues from translators to generators to various sorts of equipment that
was needed, it was left to Frank Miller and the ESG to fight the interagency battles.[60] Miller, like many others, was told, "You don't need
to worry about the nuts and bolts of basic reconstruction. It's now an
OSD operation." Thereafter, "it was 'you guys stay out, we don't need
your help.'"[61]

When I asked a senior Defense official about these charges, he simply
shrugged. The Pentagon had a "not invented here" approach to planning,
he said. They did not see Miller as "part of the team." Although this official was not personally aware of specific efforts to spurn the ESG, such
actions would have been "consistent with my understanding" of how the
DoD viewed Miller and his efforts.[62] I asked someone who was serving in
a senior State job at the time why people didn't confront the Defense representatives. He gave a knowing smile and, referring to bitter interagency
feuding, replied, "It was *so* prevalent. . . . That's just the way they did it
all day, every day."[63]

Even in cabinet meetings, Rumsfeld often would not distribute
his briefings in advance, and he refused to allow people to keep information from them—because, he claimed, he wanted to avoid leaks. If
people began taking notes, he would sometimes tell them to stop.[64] In
one such session, according to someone present, Rice said she wanted to
keep her copy of the slides. Rumsfeld refused and reached for them. The
two were actually pulling the slides back and forth until Rice appealed
to Bush, who was sitting at the head of the table: "Mr. President, I need
to keep these." Bush merely shrugged and left the room. Rice eventually
surrendered her copy, but sent a staff member to the Pentagon to find
another.[65] Such evasiveness left Rice no option but to send her staff on
snooping missions, gathering information on the sly by sneaking into the
Pentagon. Her biographer, Elisabeth Bumiller, suggests that Rice "belit-
tled her predicament, chalking it up to Rumsfeld's personality. 'Don is a

bit of a curmudgeon, all right? And he can be irascible and short and I'd known Don for years, and that's just Don.'"[66]

Such behavior, though, was part and parcel of an interagency process that had become, as one participant later recalled, an "idiosyncratic mess." By this time, agencies and departments were constantly backstabbing each other. And it was, in large measure, the tragic product of mistrust and divisions among the key senior officials—Rumsfeld, Cheney, Powell, and Rice. "When you're a nation on the cusp of going to war and you have cabinet officials who are not clicking," this former official said, "it has ripple effects."[67]

All instruments of national power needed to be brought to bear to ensure success—and fairly quickly, it was obvious that NSPD-24 was having exactly the opposite result, quickly turning into an exclusionary, hostile Defense approach that shut out State, USAID, and CIA. "DoD could not throw us out," one USAID official said—but they did everything short of that, taking a "hostile" and "ideological" attitude toward the one agency most capable of bringing rapid economic and institutional relief to postconflict Iraq. This was the "initial mistake," an ORHA official explained, "that led to all others," because NSPD-24 "put planning in the hands of a department that is allowed to isolate others from planning. The NSC should have been running this thing."[68]

The problem was exacerbated by Donald Rumsfeld's belief that only national security principals could make significant decisions. This meant that any serious issue had to be kicked up to the Principals Committee meetings—and that his senior aides, given no authority to do otherwise, essentially boycotted the critical Deputies Committee sessions, which are usually an essential mechanism for getting work done. Doug Feith, one source explained, would sit in Deputies Committee meetings and say, "I can't commit to anything"; then, after the principals had made a decision, he would say, "I can't talk about that." There were times "when I thought Rich Armitage was going to reach across the table and wring his neck," the source recalled. "DoD committed the cardinal bureaucratic sin of seizing the bureaucratic turf and doing nothing with it."[69] Condoleezza

Rice is remarkably direct about this bureaucratic warfare in her memoirs. President Bush told Rice to watch over planning for postwar administration, but to use a "light touch" because Defense had the lead on postwar planning. "But he didn't mean," Rice writes, "that it should do so in the high-handed, dismissive way that emerged. Almost immediately [Doug Feith] . . . made clear that the Pentagon neither needed nor welcomed the opinions of others. He treated Frank [Miller]'s Executive Steering Group as a nuisance and the NSC Deputies Committee with only slightly more respect."[70]

This is true enough, but what is equally true is that Rice, more than any other cabinet officer save Powell, had the most intimate knowledge of these burgeoning maladies of the emerging planning. She could—and probably should—have done more, pushed harder, insisted on better coordination. Yet, as we have seen, she was caught in multiple dilemmas, especially by January: Bush was not taking the postwar risks seriously, Defense owned the process and was elbowing the other departments to one side, and Powell was sticking to his lane. One senior official involved in the process later claimed, "The NSC process failed,"[71] but it is perhaps more accurate to say that the *president's* leadership of that process failed— and then Defense's leadership of the war planning failed as well.

Rice can rightly be faulted for not doing more. But it must be recognized that in order to do so, in large measure because of the predicament Bush left her in, she would have had to have taken a nearly self-immolating degree of risk with every ounce of political capital she owned. This she would not, it seemed, be willing to do—yet another example of the pattern, so common in this tragedy, of painful judgments that are not so much venal or stupid as profoundly human.

⁂

Meanwhile, the diplomatic process at the United Nations, the last hope of those who prayed for an alternative to war—and the great worry of those determined that it should happen—ran over a French-speaking land mine.

Since November, when the initial UN resolution had passed, France had been signaling its distance from the United States. It was not at all convinced of the urgency of going after Saddam, and much more worried about the consequences of a calamitous war in the Middle East. On January 20, French foreign minister Dominique de Villepin made comments at a foreign ministers' meeting and then a press conference in which he essentially abandoned support for a second resolution. "There is no reason to go to war while we can still improve the path of cooperation," he said. "We don't believe the world is ready."[72] US officials had been engaged in behind-the-scenes negotiations with the French, and claim they received no hint that the public denunciation was coming. Colin Powell was reportedly furious, believing de Villepin had stabbed them in the back.[73]

Some US officials, still hoping that coercive diplomacy could have caused Saddam to give in if he really thought the world community was united against him, saw the French move as destroying the last chance for a peaceful resolution of the crisis.[74] This is of course exaggerated— many in Washington were headed toward war long before the dispute with Paris. And in any event, it was not France's responsibility to play an assigned role in a finely tuned diplomatic dance to walk America up to the edge of conflict in the probably futile hope that it would convince Saddam to surrender or walk away from power. A week and a half later, Bush would endorse one last effort to secure a second resolution—but the die was by this time really cast.[75]

On January 27, Hans Blix and Mohamed ElBaradei reported to the UN Security Council on the IAEA's latest round of weapons inspections. ElBaradei, for his part, was quite direct: "We have to date found no evidence that Iraq has revived its nuclear weapon program since the elimination of the program in the 1990s."[76] Yet Blix continued to make statements seeming to support the American line. "Iraq appears," he said, "not to have come to a genuine acceptance—not even today—of the disarmament which was demanded of it and which it needs to carry out to win the confidence of the world and to live in peace." He felt unwilling to ask for more time for inspections, he would later write, because he just wasn't convinced the Iraqis would ever come around.[77]

When Blix's report was predictably taken up as ammunition to prove the US case, the diplomat insisted that had not been his goal. "My intention had been only to render an accurate report," he claims in his memoirs.[78] He said he favored peaceful disarmament, but once again reiterated that, unlike ElBaradei, he was not asking for more time "because I haven't seen a change of attitude on the part of Iraq."[79]

࿔

President Bush's January 29 State of the Union address offered a very specific ultimatum to Iraq. "Today, the gravest danger in the war on terror, the gravest danger facing America and the world, is outlaw regimes that seek and possess nuclear, chemical, and biological weapons," Bush thundered. "Trusting in the sanity and restraint of Saddam Hussein is not a strategy, and it is not an option. . . . Let there be no misunderstanding: If Saddam Hussein does not fully disarm, for the safety of our people and for the peace of the world, we will lead a coalition to disarm him. . . . And if war is forced upon us, we will fight with the full force and might of the United States military—and we will prevail."

Britain's ambassador Christopher Meyer saw these statements as the final death knell of any chance of avoiding invasion. If Bush had previously intended to leave himself "any space to step back from war, he closed it down early" in this speech, which Meyer found to be, "even by Bush's standards . . . unusually messianic in tone. The destruction of Saddam was a crusade against evil to be undertaken by God's chosen nation."[80]

࿔

Even as Bush spoke, random ideas were still firing around the US government about the precise shape of what would happen when the United States crashed into Iraq. The imperative to act was front and center; the potential outcomes of US action were left swimming in vagueness.

The very day of Bush's State of the Union address, a memo written by an anonymous office in the Pentagon laid out an agenda that looks, in retrospect, frankly Herculean. It proposed that the United States would resolve the "legal basis (Iraq Constitution, substantive criminal law, law of criminal procedure, organic police law, etc.) for law enforcement reform, development and operations" in Iraq. But that was hardly all: "Police leadership would need to be vetted." The US governing authority would require a "legal basis for establishment and leadership of Iraq Corps of Public Service" and a "code of professional conduct for public officials and employees." On and on this astonishing memo goes, casually laying out the signposts for an agenda to remake Iraq as a legal and constitutional entity from the ground up.[81]

A month and a half later, on March 19, Bush would give a speech as the war began. "We have no ambition in Iraq," he would claim, "except to remove a threat and restore control of that country to its own people."

⁊⃛

As the effort to sell the war shifted into high gear, the line between what was known to be true about the threat posed by Saddam Hussein, what was suspected—and what the intelligence agencies had in fact quite directly told senior officials was *not* true—became increasingly blurred.

On February 5, Condoleezza Rice appeared on *Larry King Live* and spoke about alleged ties between Saddam Hussein and al Qaeda. "There is no question in my mind about the al Qaeda connection," she announced in her trademark decisive and precise tones. "It is a connection that has unfolded, that we're learning more about as we are able to take the testimony of detainees, people who were high up in the al Qaeda organization." Saddam, she claimed, "became impressed with what al Qaeda did after it bombed our embassies in 1998 in Kenya and Tanzania, [and] began to give them assistance in chemical and biological weapons, something that they were having trouble achieving on their own." Rice went on to refer to the "potential marriage of weapons of mass destruction with terrorism" and the fact that Saddam

Hussein, who had such weapons, could "easily transfer" them "to one of his terrorist associations."[82] On February 6 Bush repeated the charge. "Saddam Hussein has longstanding, direct and continuing ties to terrorist networks," he claimed. "Senior members of Iraqi intelligence and al Qaeda have met at least eight times since the early 1990s. Iraq has sent bomb-making and document forgery experts to work with al Qaeda. Iraq has also provided al Qaeda with chemical and biological weapons training."[83]

We now know that the US intelligence community had looked in vain for serious ties between Iraq and al Qaeda, and had reported the lack of evidence to Rice, Bush, and the rest of the administration's senior officials. The intelligence agencies had been doing so, in fact, since immediately after 9/11. The tiny office established in Defense that produced its overheated spider charts of global terrorist conspiracies didn't persuade anyone of their validity. British intelligence had come to the same conclusions. As early as November 2001, a UK Joint Intelligence Committee Assessment stated simply, "There have been contacts between UBL and Iraqi officials in the past, but these did not lead to practical co-operation. Saddam has refused to permit any Al Qaida presence in Iraq. He is ideologically poles apart from the Sunni extremist networks linked to UBL and fears their impact on the population."[84]

A story like that, however, would not inflame public opinion and justify a war. And so, administration officials worked busily to create an impression of a connection that did not, as far as their intelligence services believed, actually exist. Despite the clear statements of the intelligence community, senior CIA official Michael Morell has written, "There were senior administration officials, most significantly the vice president, who continued to imply publicly that there was a current connection between Iraq and al Qa'ida. This was inconsistent with the analysis, but the implications continued—all to the detriment of the American people's understanding of the truth."[85]

※

The effort to make the case for war reached a grim apogee on February 5, when Colin Powell gave his infamous presentation to the United Nations—promising an airtight case on WMDs, reading horrifying testimony from defectors, shaking a vial of poison, declaring Iraq in breach of its UN obligations. The purpose of the speech was clear to everyone: it was meant to serve as a final clarion call to, and legal justification for, military action.

Powell had been well aware of the war advocates' efforts to exaggerate the intelligence, and as the speech approached, he decided to go out to the CIA personally to work through the evidence. He arrived with several staff members to discover proposed draft material, dozens of pages presumably generated at the White House and filled with claims and supposed evidence the intelligence people had never seen. Powell's staff plunged in—with the help of George Tenet and the CIA—to separate fact from fiction and rumor. Powell insisted that there be multiple sources for every assertion.[86]

CIA official Michael Morell dug into the source of the draft—and found out that much of it had been lifted from memos and background papers written in Cheney's office. Not only that, but Cheney's people then "parachuted into CIA headquarters to lobby for their point of view." Endless debates commenced in which intelligence community analysts had to fend off piles of uncorroborated reports. One official recalled that the Defense and Cheney staffers "had this huge stack of papers." Someone would ask, "Where did this [piece of intelligence] come from?" The advocates would "look through his stack and come up with a page and say, 'DIA report 2934 such-and-such.' We'd look it up on the CIA computers and see that it was completely out of context."[87] Some of the offending passages still made the case that Saddam was somehow connected to al Qaeda, and so to 9/11. Those sections were stripped out, but only after a bitter fight.[88]

Morell had not been deeply involved in the WMD account within CIA. When he watched the analysts pore over the specific evidence with Powell, he reflected the universal reaction of intelligence-savvy officials confronted with the actual facts: *This is all we've got?* As Powell and his aides questioned every claim in the speech, Morell writes, "many seemed to fall apart before my eyes. And the material falling apart was not the White House additions. My team had already removed these. No, what was collapsing was some of the facts used in the National Intelligence Estimate (NIE) to support the judgments there." He did not speak up about his doubts, in part because he simply decided, as had many before him, that *surely, this couldn't be everything.* Surely, there had to be knock-out evidence to support the bold claims the cabinet members had been making to the American people and the world.[89] Surely, it was a slam dunk case—everyone *knew* it.

Of course, it wasn't. And when the speech was delivered, chock-full of bad intelligence and hyperboles, many informed observers, watching in Washington and around the world, were horrified. US intelligence officials, observing the secretary of state power through his assertions, were aghast that the speech included claims known to be false and references to human sources that had long been discredited. Allied officials and intelligence analysts asked themselves, *Doesn't he know those sources are wrong?*

"What blissfully did not occur to me" during the presentation, Hans Blix would later write, was that while Powell had supported inspections, now "the administration was using him and drawing on his credibility to show the world what it 'needed to see.'"[90]

The reaction of war supporters, on the other hand, is perhaps best reflected in a comment from columnist Jim Hoagland. "To continue to say that the Bush administration has not made its case," he wrote in the next morning's *Washington Post*, "you must now believe that Colin Powell lied in the most serious statement he will ever make, or was taken in by manufactured evidence. I don't believe that. Today, neither should you."[91]

After the speech, Powell, ever the good soldier, ever the optimist, returned to Washington and ordered a special plaque designed for everyone in the State Department who had worked on the speech with him, a token of the hard effort that had gone into the document by dedicated professionals. His senior aide Larry Wilkerson, increasingly cynical about the drive to war and disgusted at what they had done, refused his copy.[92]

⁂

Hoagland was not the only cheerleader for the war in the mainstream media. More than one senior official has remarked afterward how much pressure they felt to act from *outside* the administration—not merely from Defense or the vice president's office, but from major daily newspapers and commentators. The fact is that the American media became caught up in the same emotion-fueled imperatives as the administration, and simply did not do its job as a corrective check on power while the United States rushed to war.[93]

"After Secretary of State Colin L. Powell's presentation to the United Nations Security Council yesterday," the *Washington Post* announced in an editorial on February 6 titled "Irrefutable," it is "hard to imagine how anyone could doubt that Iraq possesses weapons of mass destruction." The *Post* continued in language that could have been taken directly from administration talking points: "Whether Iraq is disarmed through the authority of the United Nations or whether the United States effectively assumes responsibility depends on how the Security Council responds. . . . Twelve years of experience have demonstrated that it is impossible to strip an unwilling totalitarian government of its weapons" through the inspections route.[94] And this was just one of many *Post* editorials making the case for war.

The *New York Times* hardly accumulated a better record, publishing dozens of front-page articles reporting on evidence of Iraq's weapons programs that more or less made the administration's case for it. Many conservative opinion writers endorsed the war—Charles Krauthammer, George Will, William Kristol, Stephen Hayes, Robert Kagan, and many others—but so did a number of liberals and moderates, including Thomas Friedman, Richard Cohen, George Packer, Christopher Hitchens, and Peter Beinart. Newspapers across the country amplified Colin Powell's February presentation and other administration claims into an airtight case for Iraqi WMDs.[95] Even the *New Yorker*'s editor, David Remnick, endorsed the project, arguing that

> the United States has been wrong, politically and morally, about Iraq more than once in the past; Washington has supported Saddam against Iran and overlooked some of his bloodiest adventures. The price of being wrong yet again could be incalculable. History will not easily excuse us if, by deciding not to decide, we defer a reckoning with an aggressive totalitarian leader who intends not only to develop weapons of mass destruction but also to use them. . . . A return to a hollow pursuit of containment will be the most dangerous option of all.[96]

George F. Will eventually became a bitter skeptic of the American project in Iraq—but in early 2003, his attitude brimmed with disdain for anyone opposed to the idea that America should unseat Saddam. Colin Powell went to the UN, he wrote, to "tutor slow learners" about Iraq's possession of WMDs; fatuous skeptics included the "Vichyite French government." Will spent more time mocking the French ("How many soldiers does it take to defend Paris? No one knows because it has not been tried for so long") than he did seriously investigating Powell's claims.[97] Elsewhere Will wrote of the "futility of the inspection process"[98] with breathless enthusiasm to get the fighting started, scolded people "who still deny the need for force," and offered his vision of "a satisfactory outcome: Saddam Hussein removed, the United Nations reduced."[99] As a good conservative, Will should have been asking some hard questions about what would happen to Iraq at that moment—how, exactly, conservative principles would allow for the rapid transformation of a society. Rather than mocking those skeptical of war, he could have realized that they, rather than the war promoters, were reflecting truly conservative principles.

The failures of the rush to war were not merely failures of one administration; they seldom are. They were failures of American democracy, including the institution that is supposed to cast a skeptical eye on such ill-thought-through adventures: the media.

※

On February 11, Doug Feith and his counterpart, Under Secretary of State for Political Affairs Marc Grossman, testified before the Senate Foreign Relations Committee. The decision for war still had not been made, they said. If war did come, America planned to transfer authority very quickly to Iraqis.

The unsettled nature of the planning ought to have been apparent from the way Grossman described the basis for their testimony. Their appearance before the committee, he said, would "in some ways be like a consultation. Many of the policies Under Secretary Feith and I will describe are still under discussion in the Administration."[100] Feith, too, was vague on details of how political power would be handed over. He offered a lot of possibilities—"an Iraqi consultative council *could* [emphasis mine] be formed to advise the US/coalition authorities. . . . Town and district elections *could* be held soon after liberation to involve Iraqis in governing at the local level."[101] But nothing was set in stone—less than one month before American forces would go crashing into Iraq.

Inside the administration, some were starting to get jittery. This included the anonymous Defense Department author of a memo written five days before Feith and Grossman's testimony. Titled "Justice Sector Major Decision Issues," it echoed many of the concerns of Colonel Steve Busby's analysis. "Absent four thousand (4,000) or so US/international civilian police or three thousand (3,000) international constabulary forces," it warned with repeatedly underlined emphasis, "US military must provide police service" in the postconflict environment. But this was a problem, because "all anecdotal evidence indicates that JTF4 force structure is not adequate to meet this requirement." The next paragraph asked, "Is USG comfortable with constructing and deploying a sizable CivPol-like US civilian police force throughout Iraq" and doing so without the benefit of UN mandates? "Such a force does not now exist," the memo made clear. The "cost to recruit, train, deploy and operate it [would] approximate $700M for first year! Are funds of that magnitude available?" Likely not, it admitted, because at the same time it warned that "there are no funds presently available/earmarked with which to commence preparations for civilian law enforcement and justice sector management, monitoring and/or reformation."[102]

Similar concerns animated several senior State Department officials who sent a pointed memo to Paula Dobriansky, undersecretary for global affairs, the very next day. Dobriansky, the memo makes clear, had recently been to visit CENTCOM, had responsibility for some issues related to Iraq, and apparently seemed a good person to warn. And so on February 7, 2003, Lorne Craner, Arthur Dewey, and Paul Simons wrote her a note saying that their "experience in other post-conflict situations" and their observation of planning for Iraq had made them increasingly convinced that there could be "serious planning gaps for post-conflict public security and humanitarian assistance between the end of the war and the beginning of reconstruction."[103]

I spoke with someone familiar with the memo's origins. It partly stemmed, he explained, from concerns of State bureaus likely to have people on the ground in postwar Iraq, bureaus which had come to realize that there "wouldn't be a security environment permissive enough to do what they needed to do."[104] They got little if any reaction. The reply kept coming back: *The military just doesn't have enough people.* It appeared to one official that postwar public order "wasn't a high priority for anybody."[105]

I pressed back in this interview: "You knew this was a problem. You knew there was a risk of chaos after the invasion. Why didn't you go around raising holy hell?"

The former senior official gave me a rueful look. "This was the most difficult issue I ever worked on," he said. State people were being demonized all over, being thrown off the Garner team. "People became very reluctant to say very much, or express concerns that might call into question their loyalty to the overall enterprise." On postwar order issues,

"I had a reluctance to raise these issues because I feared we would be removed from the team. . . . It was an intimidating environment. We saw others being removed from the team." To remain engaged in the debates, he said, "You had to be careful about how you raised issues."

"Come on," I said. "You wanted the mission to succeed. Your message was simple: there's a risk of postinvasion chaos. Couldn't you have hit that harder?"

He shook his head and quietly explained the depth of suspicion and mistrust that had emerged by February 2003. "If you pushed that message too hard, you would inevitably be perceived as challenging the cakewalk philosophy that undergirded the whole enterprise and be viewed as not with the program." Everyone knew that Secretary Powell had already made the same arguments and had been ignored. If *he* hadn't made any headway at the top, why refight the battles in the middle of the bureaucracy? Finally, this official admitted what, frankly, was on many sometime-skeptics' minds just before March 2003: *You know, this might all just work out.* "At the end of the day," he said, "we didn't know what would play out. We didn't know it wouldn't play out the way some of the cocky guys [advocates of war] felt."

Maybe, he and others imagined, it would be a cakewalk after all.

⁊❦

On February 14, Blix and ElBaradei presented yet another inspections report to the UN Security Council.[106] Blix said they had found no evidence of WMDs, no smoking guns; yet he also admitted that Iraqi compliance left much to be desired. (One senior British official told a journalist, "The problem with Blix was that he was a typical diplomat. He did not want to upset anyone—not even the Iraqis."[107]) ElBaradei was more direct: while a few technical questions remained, he said, Iraq did not appear to have an ongoing nuclear program.

ElBaradei said the last nuclear weapons–related issues could be resolved by about April 15 with Iraqi cooperation. Blix, though, ever cautious, wasn't sure if the chemical and biological issues could be finalized by then. And so he asked Powell: What about giving it until April 15 to make another round of progress? The American brushed it off. "He said it was too late."[108]

Others were hoping it wasn't—or were at least determined to let the world know of their deep worries about the slide into war. The same day as the latest IAEA inspections report, French foreign minister Dominique de Villepin gave an eloquent speech before the Security Council, building on his comments of a month before and hammering a last nail into the coffin of any hope for French support of a second resolution. The world had not yet exhausted the UN inspections route, he insisted. "Real progress is emerging." The French government firmly believed, he said, that "the use of force is not justified at this time. There is an alternative to war: Disarming Iraq via inspections."[109] For most in Washington, of course, that had simply never been a viable option.

⁂

Also on February 14, across town from the UN where the IAEA inspectors were delivering their report, Donald Rumsfeld gave an astonishing speech called "Beyond Nation Building"[110]—astonishing for the secretary of defense of a country about to invade and take possession of a nation of twenty-five million people. Rumsfeld spoke about ongoing operations in Afghanistan. "From the outset of the war," he said, "our guiding principle has been that Afghanistan belongs to the Afghans. The United States does not aspire to own it or run it. . . . The objective is not to engage in what some call nation building. Rather it's to try to help the Afghans so that they can build their own nation. This is an important distinction."

It was indeed, but anyone familiar with the Afghan situation even then could have told Rumsfeld there were already stirrings of the instability that would drag the United States back in. They could have reminded him about the commitments and goals Washington had broadcast, including a functioning Afghan government to prevent a return of the Taliban or al Qaeda. They could have pointed to the Bonn Accords, an elaborate agenda for Western-style democracy in a country that had never known anything of the sort. But Rumsfeld continued to pour scorn on the idea of more elaborate commitments. "In some nation building exercises," he added,

> well-intentioned foreigners arrive on the scene, look at the problems and say let's fix it. This is well motivated to be sure, but it can really be a disservice in some instances because when foreigners come in with international solutions to local problems, if not very careful they can create a dependency. . . . A long-term foreign presence in a country can be unnatural. This has happened in several places with large foreign presence. The economies remained unreformed and distorted to some extent. Educated young people can make more money as drivers for foreign workers than as doctors and civil servants.

Rumsfeld insisted in the speech that "the President has not made any decision with respect to the use of force in Iraq"—weeks after Bush had told Rice, Powell, and others that he had come to precisely that conclusion. But if the decision were to be made, Rumsfeld calmly assured the audience, the US position would be that "Iraq belongs to the Iraqis and we do not aspire to own it or run it. . . . The goal would not be to impose an American style template on Iraq, but rather to create conditions where Iraqis can form a government in their own unique way just as the Afghans did."

Rumsfeld had, as we've seen, been saying similar things inside the government since the middle of the Afghan campaign.[111] But given the history of every American intervention of recent vintage, given that postwar chaos would serve as a breeding ground for precisely the sort of terrorism the administration was ardently trying to stamp out, given the multiple warnings his department had received about the postwar, and given the incredibly ambitions agenda for transforming Iraq reflected in dozens of official Defense memos and briefings, it is mind-boggling that

Rumsfeld could not have seen the obvious contradiction. There was simply no way they could do what they were planning to do, as defined in both internal and public statements, while adhering to his rule of staying aloof from "other countries' political disputes." But somehow, in the fevered grip of an urgent imperative to act, with their wishful thinking fueled in part by the habits and assumptions of a missionary conception of America's role, some of the most experienced national security officials ever to work in the US government managed to overlook signs of an impending disaster.

More evidence of these dilemmas would emerge at an elaborate postwar planning meeting just three weeks before the war began. By that time, however, the ball was rolling too fast downhill to do anything about it.

∂₹

This was a meeting on February 21 and 22, when planners and military officers from around the US government—including representatives from General Garner's newly formed Organization for Reconstruction and Humanitarian Assistance (ORHA)—gathered at the National Defense University in Washington for a planning conference, commonly referred to as a "rock drill," to see where they stood.

Many of the briefings were delivered by ORHA's new staff members. Some of these reports have been declassified, and they tell a dispiriting tale.[112] Under the category of "fundamental assumptions," the charts listed several claims that could—and should—have been easily punctured. "Sufficient infrastructure exists—buildings, roads, transportation, comm[unication]s," one slide insisted—when information was readily available that the country's infrastructure was a mess. They assumed that "Free Iraqis/expats can identify reliable Iraqis with relevant experience who can be entrusted with positions of responsibility," when those working with the exiles knew very well that none of them had been to the country for years and had no contacts with anyone.[113]

One briefing laid out the main elements of Iraqi institutions critical to postwar stability, such as security forces. And then, *seven slides later in the same brief,* ORHA's justice and law enforcement team could be found admitting that "Saddam's political appointees will likely remain in the ranks of the police, judiciary and prison administration"; and in part because "Existing police/security forces lack any legitimacy with Iraqi people," the "extent of public voluntary compliance with law will be low." Another slide said, "Existing Iraqi institutions responsible for public security and judicial processes likely will be in disarray."[114] This was precisely the opposite assumption about the Iraqi police being made by the planners at the NSC.

A presentation from ORHA's postconflict planning group used some of the same phrases and then put the conclusion even more starkly. "**Post conflict conditions**," the final bullet on a key slide argued—in boldface, no less—"**will overwhelm Iraqi capabilities to maintain public order**." It drew the obvious conclusion. "In the absence of a credible, indigenous police force, the burden of both executive-level law enforcement and oversight of Iraqi police will fall on the US Military occupation forces (MPs and infantry)."[115] This would have come as a surprise to military planners (and frankly, even at this late date, President Bush himself), who had no interest in making the US Army the new police force of Iraq.

ORHA's right hand was making glaringly clear the risk of public disorder, which would threaten Iraqi governing institutions and public infrastructure—all the capacities on which ORHA's left hand was depending for the success of its mission. This briefing embodied the same calamitous dissonances infecting the entire American project in Iraq: what needed to be true for the sanguine assumptions of postwar security could not be true given the accurate but dismal assumptions about what Saddam's spiteful rule had done to Iraqi society.

The briefings also announced stunning disparities between ORHA's looming tasks and its actual capabilities. ORHA would own the "responsibility for vetting Iraqis (to determine their suitability for employment)," the slides say—hundreds of thousands of Iraqi employees of dozens of ministries and agencies; indeed, over a hundred thousand police alone. What organization could parachute into an alien land and vet hundreds of thousands of people for reliability? But that was hardly all: ORHA would also develop and issue a new national currency and create an "organizational/budgetary mechanism to pay civil servants," presumably from scratch. "Civil Administration (CIVAD) must immediately provide stability, predictability and continuity in essential government services."

All of this was utterly at odds with the goal of avoiding "other countries' political disputes," as Donald Rumsfeld seemed to want. But the result of his light-footprint assumptions was a grievous lack of resources. If at that meeting you had turned to the briefing slide about "Civil Administration, Current Manning," for example, you would have found that ORHA had *thirteen people* on its staff to handle governance issues one month before the war began. "Awaiting detailees from State, Commerce," the slide announced, rather pathetically. "Need more intell community support for vetting." The next slide added that "critical shortfalls" existed in such areas as "culture and religious affairs, Immigration and consular affairs, Trade, commerce and industry." Another slide talked of the need to begin contracting "for appropriate personnel/vendors to accomplish" the mission of supporting the emergence of Iraqi governance—except that government contracts can't be published, won, approved, funded, and put into the field in a month. But, anyway, the same slide admitted that "there are no funds available to start hiring processes," so the timing problem hardly mattered anyway. One especially poignant slide on "critical mission support," such as computers, technicians, and translators, concluded simply: "All TBD."

If you had then advanced two slides down to "Funding," you would have discovered that the civil administration component of ORHA thought it required between $425 million and $1.1 billion to accomplish its various tasks—a figure that represents only a fraction of what the US occupation authorities would ultimately spend, and an amount that, even at that early date, was obviously insufficient for such herculean tasks. (The briefing posited a miniscule total of $40 million for law, justice, *and* border security functions.) And yet the slide went on to indicate, after listing these estimated requirements: "Currently available or committed: $0M. Shortfall: $425M to $1.1B."

⁊

The litany of unpreparedness continued, one "rock drill" briefing after another. ORHA's energy team laid out an impressive agenda to get Iraq's energy sector back on its feet, which sounded great—until you got to the slide on "Energy Team Organization" and realized that ORHA owned a grand total of *three people* working the issue. Under "Critical Shortfalls," the slide listed a need for more than twenty additional staff plus "funding required for DoD contractors." Of estimated requirements of between $2 billion and $16 billion to rebuild the energy sector, the team had identified $146 million in available funds.

The slides on plans for indigenous Iraqi media nearly hummed with another of the essential dilemmas of the whole project—the tension between liberation and control. The "vision" was to "reconstitute indigenous Iraqi media as a model for free media in the Arab world." Money was requested to fund new Iraqi radio and television networks. But the following slide made clear other motives: US objectives included efforts to "inform the Iraqi public about USG/coalition intent and operations," "provide Iraqis hope for their future," and "begin broadcasting and printing approved USG information to the Iraqi public very soon after cessation of hostilities." Or, as another bullet summed up the whole purpose of the investment, "Help justify USG actions." In effect, ORHA was proposing to trade one captured state media for another.

But the biggest hole in the proposed postwar effort continued to be the gap between the requirements of stability and the troops available to ensure it—precisely the problem that had been identified by Steve Busby's memo, the warnings at State, and many other analyses. ORHA's justice and law enforcement group argued in its presentation that the United States "must establish interim public security whatever the cost." A slide called "Show Stoppers" said simply, "Early reestablishment of public order under rule of law is critical to success but is achievable only if funds and staff are made available **now**." Yet the discussions revealed that the US military was planning to move fast, bypass resisting cities, get to Baghdad, and end the war. In the words of one participant, "It became clear that they had no troops to leave behind for stability operations." USAID and others asked about the security of the aid workers necessary for the long list of humanitarian objectives. One military officer replied, "You expect to lose things in war, don't you?"[116] In another conversation, a senior CENTCOM officer suggested that the aid agencies "hire warlords," not recognizing that in Iraq, unlike Afghanistan, there were no warlords to hire.[117] "That was when our jaws dropped," one participant from outside Defense said. "We were on our own."[118]

※

As the "rock drill" progressed through one unanswered question after another, the tenor, in the view of many participants to whom I spoke, turned demoralizing. A meeting that had begun with the excitement of "We're here to plan victory" gradually became "Oh, shit, here's yet *another* issue we don't know how to handle." One participant recalled angrily, "You could just tell, as the various elements" made their pitch, that "we were totally out to lunch. They're missing an awful lot of information that had been accumulated over the last six months."[119] A former staffer from Cheney's office spoke to people who had been present: "As far as they were concerned," he said, "there was almost no one in the room who knew what they were doing."[120]

One senior official explained that some of his people returned from the NDU meeting saying the operation was a looming disaster.[121] Another official met staffers returning from the meeting saying it "looked like total chaos."[122]

"We were horrified," one of the participants bitterly remembered. "This had catastrophe written all over it."[123] Garner was well intentioned and trying to do his best, and one source later claimed he was well aware of the problems and very explicit about his own judgment: they were not ready.[124]

The concluding meeting notes from the rock drill, quoted later in the Iraqi Special Investigator's Report, offer a bracing message. "It seems likely that we will begin military action before we know whether sufficient Phase IV funds will be available," the report admitted. Partly as a result, there would likely be "economic-related violence. . . . Civil unrest will be the rule, not the exception." And hanging over the whole enterprise were two powerful, interrelated issues. "What sort of future Government of Iraq do we have in mind, and how do we plan to get there?"[125] Leaving such questions unanswered posed massive dangers, the report concluded. "We risk letting much of the country descend into civil unrest [and] chaos, whose magnitude may defeat our national strategy of a stable new Iraq."[126]

Four days after that session, in a major speech in Washington, President Bush reassured the world about American planning for the coming war. "If we must use force," he promised, "the United States and our coalition stand ready to help the citizens of a liberated Iraq. . . . America has made and kept this kind of commitment before—in the peace that followed a world war. After defeating enemies . . . we established an atmosphere of safety, in which responsible, reform-minded local leaders could build lasting institutions of freedom."[127]

The very day the rock drill concluded, Paul Wolfowitz was in Michigan, energizing Iraqi-Americans for the conflict. "The United States and the international community will ensure the rapid flow of humanitarian relief and the rapid start of economic reconstruction efforts," he assured them. Planning for this was well underway, he assured the exiles.[128] The Iraqi-American moderator of the meeting thanked Wolfowitz for his "wonderful, comforting, reassuring remarks."

❧

One official perfectly placed to both recognize these emerging risks and convey them to the president was not the one who tried, if halfheartedly, to do it—Colin Powell—but one who did not, Dick Cheney. He had been engaged in a war with Iraq once before and had expressed skepticism about occupation. He presumably knew how to recognize bullshit planning when he saw it. He had the president's ear—and his trust. Cheney was both renowned and feared for mastering issues to an intimidating level of detail.

An official deeply familiar with Cheney raised the obvious question in one of my interviews: How could someone as rapier-sharp as Dick Cheney not see the evidence of a looming disaster? Why, "if it was so obvious to us" what could go wrong at the time, "wasn't it so obvious to someone as experienced as the vice president?"[129] The official answered his own question: "Cheney had one major Achilles' heel: the nature of his relationship to Don Rumsfeld." Rumsfeld had hired Cheney in their early days and mentored him through a series of senior government positions. This official believed that Cheney "never outgrew that relationship in some sense; he still felt a sense of loyalty." In most cases, Cheney was clearly capable of separating the personal from the political—but "I don't think Cheney was capable of making those judgments with Rumsfeld," the source suggests. Another official who was working in Cheney's office at the time believes that this implicit trust had been reinforced by how well the campaign in Afghanistan had gone, which bolstered his faith in Rumsfeld's war planning.[130] At Rumsfeld's retirement ceremony years later, Cheney would give heartfelt remarks in which he said simply, "I have no better friend, and ask for none." He then called Rumsfeld "the finest secretary of defense this nation has ever had."[131]

When Don Rumsfeld said about Iraq, "Don't worry, I've got it"; when postwar Iraq was formally assigned to DoD responsibility; when Rumsfeld's prestige and accountability were on the line—to have raised concerns, thrown wrenches in the works, and/or gone directly to the president would have constituted disloyalty to the very man who had *made* Dick Cheney who he was. And it appears Cheney, a man for whom loyalty is one of the chief virtues, was not about to do that.

Instead, according to Bush's own memoir, the vice president issued no warnings, and instead bluntly pressed his boss to shit or get off the pot. At a private lunch in February, Cheney growled, "Are you going to take care of this guy or not?"[132]

⁊

In the weeks before the invasion, George Bush met with the preacher Pat Robertson.[133] Bush was "the most self-assured man I ever met in my life," Robertson would later tell a journalist. "He was just sitting there, like, I'm on top of the world, and I warned him about this war. I had deep misgivings about this war, deep misgivings. And I was trying to say, Mr. President, you better prepare the American people for casualties. [But Bush responded,] Oh, no, we're not going to have any casualties. Well, I said, it's going to be. . . . The Lord told me it was going to be, A, a disaster and B, messy." It is not clear how exactly Robertson had accessed this divine guidance on war outcomes, but the president brushed it off. When asked why Bush dismissed his warnings, Robertson replied, "I just think he was so sure that this man was a tyrant, he was evil and he needed to be taken out. I mean, he just felt it." Bush was seized with the rightness of a course of action, and there was no way he was going to fail in what he now perceived as his duty.

⁊

The idea from the beginning was that ORHA would be temporary, designed to oversee an American transitional effort of limited duration. The tiny organization—at about 150 people, it was smaller, at the beginning of the war, than a single US Army infantry company—was never really designed to "run" Iraq. It was supposed to fit between the military headquarters and a quickly emergent Iraqi transitional authority. Rumsfeld wanted "to parachute Jay in, make some recommendations, clean the thing up, and get out," one former senior official said.[134] They'd "peel off the top layer of bad guys and put in technocrats," as one former ORHA staffer put it.[135]

As a result, "Garner was never made 'the man'" in a way that would have allowed him to exercise more decisive influence, one source confided.[136] The Joint Staff denied an initial ORHA request for ninety military personnel—too many people, they said, they couldn't afford it. State stood aloof: one source claimed that Garner didn't even find out until the late-February planning session at the National Defense University that there had been such a thing as the Future of Iraq Project.[137] Yet at the same time, in a signal of the continuing confusion in the scope of the mission, NSPD-24 gave ORHA eleven colossal missions ranging from reestablishing the government to turning on the lights in Iraq to finding WMDs.[138]

Late in January a retired USAID official named Larry Crandall had stopped by at the ORHA offices to check on the status of thinking about postwar development. What he found was confusion:

> I went into Jay Garner's office—this was before he actually left for Kuwait—and on one wall of a large meeting room in Garner's suite of offices was a whole maybe 20 or 25 eight-by-11 pieces of paper pasted to the wall with sort of Economics 101 representations of what you would have to do to address each and every concern, economic concern, around the country. I looked around and looked at my colleague and said, "Hmmmm," and started asking questions of some of the staff who were responsible for those pieces of paper on the wall. Then we began to think these people really don't get it.[139]

Some officials justified the halfhearted nature of the effort by claiming that there had been lots of planning already; ORHA's job was merely to "pull it together" and make it happen.[140] But there had been no coherent effort to do that; ORHA was too small and had too little time even to comprehend all the preparatory work that was underway, let alone coordinate it. "It was a clusterfuck at the Pentagon," one official assigned to ORHA in those early days recalled. "Chaos, badly organized. Everyone was frustrated."[141]

Very quickly, the organization ran headlong into an issue that would bedevil Garner and his staff through their whole time in Iraq—the role of the exiles. As we have seen, the exile community had been involved in postwar planning for months, in some cases with exaggerated assurances from midlevel US officials about their future authority. As a result, many simply didn't take ORHA seriously. One ORHA staffer who worked with the exiles said some assumed they were going to run Iraq. Did they say this outright? I asked. "Sure," he said. "Some explicitly said, 'I should be in charge.'"[142] But there was no consensus on these issues across government, and without knowing it, Garner had dropped into a vicious bureaucratic war: Defense people thought State and the CIA hated the exiles; State people thought Defense was trying to install Chalabi as king of Iraq.

Within ORHA, some senior people initially remained confident. Don Eberly, who signed up early on, wrote later that "optimism ran so high that no one seemed too concerned about what would follow" in the postwar phase. They were buying into the "decapitation" model: with the Ba'athists gone, Iraqi civil society could rise up and flourish. "Any doubts were expressed quietly in side conversations." He is quite open about their frame of mind. "Like my ORHA colleagues," he explains, "I was prepared to act on faith."[143]

Despite the optimism, ORHA's deficiencies in personnel and resources were obvious to everyone involved. The group had very few Arabists or true experts; agencies and departments were slow to respond to requests for personnel to fill out ORHA billets, and the ones they did get arrived randomly, in dribs and drabs, barely having time to learn each other's names before the war kicked off.[144] Garner brought resource requests to the NSC, to Condoleezza Rice, money needed to undertake critical postwar activities in areas such as law enforcement, media, and refugee support. "Never did get any of those," Garner said later. At one point he sent a list of essential reconstruction tasks to Rumsfeld, who asked for a cost estimate. Garner suggested a billion dollars. "My friend," Garner said Rumsfeld told him, "if you think we're going to spend a billion dollars of our money over there, you are sadly mistaken."[145]

As ORHA staff rushed to figure out what was going on and make their own plans and judgments, as far as anyone at the NSC could tell, much of the prior planning went up in smoke. ORHA ignored most of the work done in the Abrams-Cleveland process, one source fumed, "And when [Paul] Bremer showed up he ignored all of it. . . . Lots of useful stuff [was done] there, that went nowhere as far as I could tell." This participant recalls General Garner walking into a meeting of Abrams's group, presumably in late December or January; nobody had a clue who he was. "Who the hell are you?" Abrams asked him.

"I'm in charge now," Garner answered.[146]

The NSC team was then asked to turn their files over to ORHA. "This," one senior member of the NSC effort suggested, "is the equivalent of burning them. Because nothing ever comes of it. All of our efforts are for naught. They disappear into chaos—the one-word summary of ORHA." General Garner, this official worried, was extrapolating from his earlier experience running post–Gulf War relief operations in Kurdistan, where everyone had loved the Americans. By this point, watching ORHA from the outside, the official began to get the distinct impression that "this was all hopeless," that "this Garner thing was a mess."[147]

And yet, as with so many other key people in key places, he did not relay these thoughts to others. Something intervened—some psychological process, some mental block—between the hard and fast knowledge that ORHA was a debacle waiting to happen and the awareness that the larger US plan to liberate Iraq was a brewing tragedy. The official has no recollection of "thinking or saying that this invasion will be a mess." He did not write a memo. He did not raise hell with his superiors. "Which is a little bit odd, as we have this conversation," he admitted, years after the war started, rattling off all the reasons he had at the time to expect a disaster. "Because why not? Why didn't we say more? That's a good question. I don't know the answer."

As a product of its limited role and strength, ORHA was not designed to be competitive with or parallel to CENTCOM—it was supposed to *report to* the regional combatant command and be its implementing arm for the post-conflict phase.[148] The *command* was the accountable entity, one senior US military officer recalled. "CENTCOM was clearly given the responsibility for the postwar. We told them. There is no doubt in my mind."[149] As we have seen, the Chairman of the Joint Chiefs, General Myers, sent Franks a number of messages to this effect during the fall. A senior official with close responsibility for these issues confirmed seeing one of these orders telling CENTCOM they were fully responsible for the postwar.[150] But CENTCOM didn't act like they'd been given the mission; just about every time it came up, General Franks took pains to make clear he saw it as a Defense Department job.

In his memoirs Franks relates that Rumsfeld told him about ORHA. He then quickly writes, "Washington would be responsible for providing the policy . . . to win the hearts and minds of the Iraqi people." Some senior official in Washington would do it—not CENTCOM, not the people on the ground in Iraq. "Washington," he says a few pages later, to drive the point home, "needed to get ready for the occupation and reconstruction—because combat operations just might be over sooner than anyone could imagine."[151] Just before ORHA left for the Middle East, another source explained that Tommy Franks said of postwar planning, "I don't want to be involved in managing bus schedules."[152]

But senior Defense people were not giving much thought to the postwar in large measure because they were—as they had always been—planning for a quick exit.[153] When he asked, at one point, about creating a plan for Iraq's postwar political order, Garner was told not to worry about it—the United States, he was assured, was going to transfer authority to the Iraqis so fast that he wouldn't need one.[154]

❧

Army chief of staff Eric Shinseki was preparing for congressional testimony on February 25. To estimate potential troop requirements for occupying Iraq, the army staff had drawn together projections from several sources. They all came out in the multiple six-figure range, three hundred thousand and above, for occupation requirements.[155]

These numbers were brought to the attention of General Shinseki before his testimony. He knew he was likely to get a question about the numbers issue, which was being hotly debated in the press. One source suggested that a staff advisory group urged Shinseki not to answer that question directly, because of the implications for him and for the army: it was going to piss Rumsfeld off. "And I'll never forget what Shinseki said," the Pentagon official recalled. "The statute says I am supposed to give my best military advice. It doesn't say the secretary of defense has to like it."[156] Rumsfeld didn't, in part because he believed he'd given Shinseki ample opportunity to speak up on the issue before. The secretary of defense felt blindsided by Shinseki's warnings on the Hill.[157]

Two days after Shinseki testified, Paul Wolfowitz went before the House Budget Committee and made his own case.[158] Without referring to Shinseki by name, he called the estimate "quite outlandish" and said straight out that "the notion that it will take several hundred thousand US troops to provide stability in post-Saddam Iraq" was "wildly off the mark." Speaking quietly and with great confidence in his professorial manner, Wolfowitz insisted that the liberation of northern Iraq after the Gulf War had disproved the need for a major occupation force. They would, he claimed, have large numbers of Free Iraqi Forces ready to keep order.

"There's been none of the record in Iraq of ethnic militias fighting one another," he cheerfully announced, "that produced so much bloodshed and permanent scars in Bosnia, along with a continuing requirement for large peacekeeping forces to separate those militias." And finally he continued to insist that, while "we can't be sure that the Iraqi people will welcome us as liberators," in point of fact, he really *was* sure of that: "Based on what Iraqi-Americans told me in Detroit a week ago . . . I am reasonably certain that they will greet us as liberators, and that will help us to keep requirements down." Wolfowitz concluded that he found it "hard to conceive that it would take more forces to provide stability in post-Saddam Iraq than it would take to conduct the war itself and to secure the surrender of Saddam's security forces and his army."

It should hardly have been difficult for Wolfowitz to imagine the need for significant postwar policing, in part because we know he was familiar with an article from just three years before that described precisely such risks—risks that stem from trying to create democracy out of thin air in societies that are not ready for it. The article said, in part:

> Both because of what the United States is, and because of what is possible, we cannot engage either in promoting democracy or in nation-building simply by an exercise of will. We must proceed by interaction and indirection, not imposition. In this respect, the post-World War II examples of Germany and Japan offer misleading guides for the present. What proved feasible following total victory and prolonged occupation—in societies that were economically advanced but, at the same time, had profoundly lost faith in their own institutions—does not offer a model that applies to other circumstances.[159]

We know that Wolfowitz was familiar with those lines for a very simple reason: He wrote them.

⁂

On March 6, in a televised evening press conference, Bush continued to claim that that he had not made the decision to use force. "I believe Saddam Hussein is a threat to the American people," he said. "I take the threat seriously, and I'll deal with the threat. I hope it can be done peacefully."[160] This was nearly a month after he had told Colin Powell he had decided to go to war, and two months since he'd indicated the same thing to Condoleezza Rice.

The following day, Hans Blix offered a new report on Iraqi inspections compliance to the Security Council, during which he once again refused to be conclusive.[161] "At this juncture we are able to perform professional, no-notice inspections all over Iraq," he said. And "the question is now asked whether Iraq has cooperated, 'immediately, unconditionally and actively,' with UNMOVIC, as is required under Paragraph 9 of Resolution 1441." Yes, Mr. Blix—that was indeed the question on which the decision for war or peace now hung.

"The answers," he continued in his maddeningly elliptical way, "can be seen from the factor descriptions that I have provided. However, if more direct answers are desired, I would say the following: The Iraqi side has tried on occasion to attach conditions, as it did regarding helicopters and U-2 planes. It has not, however, so far persisted in this or other conditions for the exercise of any of our inspection rights. If it did, we would report it."

Divining the meaning of such Delphic utterances was almost impossible. In his memoirs, Blix explains that he told an American friend he thought it would have been "presumptuous of me" to make a clear judgment. To which his friend replied, "Hans, they wanted you to be presumptuous!"[162]

⁂

The first formal Principals Committee meetings on the full Interim Iraqi Authority (IIA) proposal, which remained at that point "a concept (not yet a detailed plan)," were held on March 1 and 7—respectively, three and two weeks before the war began.[163] Doug Feith made the case to "recognize the IIA as the *legitimate governmental authority of Iraq*" as soon as possible after the war. The proposal appeared to allow the United States the right of appointing IIA members, and held a majority of IIA seats for exiles—because they would be "better positioned to understand concepts of democracy" that had badly atrophied within Iraq. This was an odd claim for an administration counting on the fact that the country they were about to liberate was an incipient democracy waiting to break free of its constraints, but no one apparently challenged the contradiction. State disagreed only on several minor counts, for example, in preferring that the United Nations be allowed to select IIA members.[164]

The architects of these governance concepts were trying to have and eat several cakes at the same time—go fast, be comprehensive, retain absolute American control, liberate the Iraqis, and determine who runs Iraq while allowing the Iraqis to determine the same thing. One senior official conveyed to me his skeptical reaction to the IIA concept on first being briefed. "It didn't adequately take into account," he said, "the fact that we [would have] just blown the shit out of the place." Once US forces swept aside the regime, there would be "no civil society, no leadership." The invasion would release "fifty years of pent-up demand"; were they ready to handle it? He worried that assumptions necessary to a quick reboot—such as the idea that Iraqi oil would start to flow quickly and smoothly to finance a domestic rehabilitation—were not adequately tested. The whole concept just "wasn't sufficiently political" but reflected a technocratic solution to a social problem.[165] This official tried to raise some of these concerns at the time. And for his trouble, he was told, more or less, to mind his own business.

At one of these meetings, according to published and interview sources, President Bush asked Tommy Franks directly: Was he ready to ensure security in the postwar? Michael Gordon and Bernard Trainor have reported that Franks claimed he would be installing "lord mayors" in all the significant towns of Iraq.[166] According to Franks, "It was all taken care of," as George Tenet recalled the promise.[167] In fact, Franks had prepared no such plan, had provided for no real postwar security concept, and was telling everyone who would listen that the postwar was someone else's problem and that US forces would be leaving as quickly as they arrived. The result of the conversation was to slam the door shut on any further debates about the immediate postwar: the president had asked his commanding general very directly if he had the ball, and the general had said yes. There was, now, really nothing anyone else could do.

᠀

In his March 8 radio address, Bush said, "We are doing everything we can to avoid war in Iraq. But if Saddam Hussein does not disarm peacefully, he will be disarmed by force."[168] Two days later, French president Jacques Chirac built on his foreign minister's skeptical stance of a month before, making clear his own distinct lack of interest in supporting a second war-endorsing resolution at the United Nations. Chirac said France would veto a new resolution "because she considers this evening that there are no grounds for waging war in order to achieve the goal we have set ourselves, i.e. to disarm Iraq." British tabloids had a field day. The *Sun* exclaimed that, "Like a cheap tart who puts price before principle, money before honour, Jacques Chirac struts the streets of shame. . . . We will never forgive the French."[169]

※

On March 10 and 12, the NSC and Defense provided Bush with two sets of briefings.[170] At one point Garner briefed on ORHA's postwar plan—a presentation that lasted less than an hour. This first briefing, on humanitarian and postconflict development issues, consisted of roughly a dozen very general PowerPoint slides.[171]

On the issue of de-Ba'athification, while rejecting the idea that "those who ran Saddam's Iraq" could have any role in the future, the briefings argued that only about twenty-five thousand Iraqis were "active and full members" of the Ba'ath party—only a small proportion of the Iraqi bureaucracy's two million employees. The slides called for vetting procedures to figure out who fit this category. They discussed the potential for a truth and reconciliation process in Iraq, and the parallels in places like South Africa. The concept was for a minimal form of de-Ba'athification that weeded out the smallest number of senior party leaders.

Yet this treatment of the issue—a dozen slides with about fifty total bullets' worth of information—raised far more questions that it answered. Imagine cleaving off the top twenty-five thousand officials in the US government—would it still function properly? In a totalitarian state, lower-level officials are accustomed to avoiding responsibility rather than exercising it. Could the second- and third-tier Iraqis step up? Who would do the promised vetting, with what information, and over what period of time? Were there *any* examples on record of a successful "trade out" strategy being employed for regime change in large nations, one that absolved the invader of any real need for occupation?

These critical briefings offered three lonely slides on "post-conflict policing and justice," which reflected one of the more problematic assumptions of the trade-out strategy: that Iraqi police were generally effective and well trained and could continue keeping order after the invasion.[172] The truth of what was actually believed, and officially reported, on this issue remains elusive. Many Defense and NSC officials I spoke with are convinced that the CIA assured them that the police would keep functioning—but agency officials flatly rejected the notion that they would ever have offered such a judgment. Some recall saying quite explicitly that the Iraqi police were not trained to keep the peace— they were trained to inform, and to enforce Saddam's orders.[173] (This was reportedly also the verdict of the CENTCOM intelligence office, which was presumably not made available to the NSC.[174]) These confusions were never resolved, and many senior officials took away from these discussions a remarkable conviction that they could rely on Saddam Hussein's police force to maintain order in a newly liberated Iraq.

The second briefing discussed how to handle Iraq's Ministry of Foreign Affairs; it suggested that US forces would "seize" the ministry building, throw out the top leaders, vet the rest, and "appoint technical advisors to begin reorganization plans." The slides then ran through a gamut of complex issues: who, with the government toppled, would conduct foreign affairs; how would they ensure border security; what would happen to embassies and ambassadors abroad; and how would they handle a possible flood of expatriates clamoring to return to Iraq. A bullet on one slide said, "May need to destroy stocks of Iraqi passports; create new." These issues alone reflected a hornet's nest of Gordian knots that would take years to untangle.

And then the second brief turned to an issue critical to the postwar— the status of the Iraqi army. As with de-Ba'athification, the goal was to use as light a touch as possible; the briefings made clear that by keeping the regular army intact, US forces would have an essential partner in providing security in the chaotic aftermath.[175] But the slides did call for the dismantlement of all of Iraq's security services and paramilitary units as well as the Republican Guard and Special Republican Guard—hundreds of thousands of the most dedicated and highly trained of the regime's security services. The idea that the initial plan was to keep the "Iraqi army" intact has always been somewhat misleading. From the beginning, the US intent was to demobilize vast swaths of the Iraqi military, which would always have put tens or hundreds of thousands of resentful military men on the streets. The briefing proposed reconstituting one piece of that military—the regular army—and corralling it for temporary duty as a "national reconstruction force," though whether any self-respecting army would allow itself to be used as contract labor by an invading occupier seems a heroic assumption.[176]

Officials involved in the process indicate that the briefings produced clear implementation memos. By the time they were issued, however, they had been watered down, and the directions to key departments were imprecise. And in any event, all of these decisions would prove fleeting. When the time came, Paul Bremer would make decisions about de-Ba'athification and the future of the Iraqi army that violated most of them. One of the slides on the Iraqi army concludes quite pointedly: "Cannot immediately demobilize 250K-300K people and put on the street." In the event, that is precisely what Bremer did—and when that moment arrived, President Bush appeared not to understand the significance of the difference. But again, given the US intention to disband the most loyal elements of Iraq's military—the Republican Guard, Special Republican Guard, and security services—US plans were *always* going to throw well over one hundred thousand angry, highly trained soldiers into the streets.

Another irony of these sessions is that one of their critical conclusions undercut a major assumption—at least in the minds of some advocates—of the trade-out strategies: that Iraqi exiles could play a major role in filling gaps in leadership after the invasion. In these final planning meetings,

President Bush refused to endorse specific exile groups, saying, "I will not put my thumb on the scale" in determining the outcome of postinvasion politics. Bush's instinct here was canny—unwilling to short-circuit the democratic process, suspicious of Chalabi himself. Yet he missed, along with everyone else, the core dilemma that this reluctance produced: if they were not going to install specific people, if instead they were going to preside over the extended birth of Iraqi democracy, then this was going to become a drawn-out affair, which was exactly what the plans were designed to avoid.

I asked one senior Defense official whether, by the time the war started, there was a clear concept for governing Iraq when US forces got there. He said simply and emphatically, "No." The reason was that "nobody would make a decision. We had some plans" at DoD, he said, but State had objections and "would never sign off," and as a result, it was "never clear how Iraq would be governed." There were "a lot of ideas floating around that we would have liked to have seen become plans," but they were not hard-and-fast operational expectations, because the interagency process at the principals level had not fully bought into them. "As far as having a plan together, it was Keystone Cops," he concluded.[177]

On March 16, Dick Cheney appeared on *Meet the Press*. When asked by host Tim Russert, "What do you think is the most important rationale for going to war with Iraq?" Cheney replied, "Well, I think I've just given it, Tim, in terms of the combination of his development and use of chemical weapons, his development of biological weapons, his pursuit of nuclear weapons."

Russert pressed him: "And even though the International Atomic Energy Agency said he does not have a nuclear program, we disagree?"

Cheney said, "I disagree, yes. . . . We believe he has, in fact, reconstituted nuclear weapons. I think Mr. ElBaradei frankly is wrong."[178]

These words constituted another powerful misrepresentation of the state of intelligence: to suggest that Saddam had "reconstituted nuclear weapons" was vastly beyond anything they had information to support.

On the question of the potential for hostile reaction to a US invasion—the possibility of "a long, costly, and bloody battle with significant American casualties"—Cheney, who had once spoken of the terrible risks of a US occupation of Iraq after the first Gulf War, now changed his tune. "Well, I don't think it's likely to unfold that way, Tim, because I really do believe that we will be greeted as liberators," he said. "I've talked with a lot of Iraqis in the last several months myself, had them to the White House. . . . The read we get on the people of Iraq is there is no question but what they want to get rid of Saddam Hussein and they will welcome as liberators the United States when we come to do that." When asked about General Shinseki's estimate of three hundred thousand or more troops required to keep the peace, Cheney smirked and grumbled. "I disagree. We need, obviously, a large force and we've deployed a large force. . . . But to suggest that we need several hundred thousand troops there after military operations cease, after the conflict ends, I don't think is accurate. I think that's an overstatement."

⁂

In the final days before the war, Saddam's thinking cartwheeled through various contradictory beliefs. At one point he worried that an invasion was imminent and settled on a new strategy—at least according to what he told his FBI interrogator, George Piro, after the war. "What he asked of his military leaders and senior government officials," Piro says Saddam told him, "was to give him two weeks. And at that point it would go into what he called the secret war . . . Going from a conventional to an unconventional war."[179] One senior US official told me that during the period of combat operations, he traveled to Kuwait and was furnished by senior Kuwaiti military officials with a captured order signed by Saddam Hussein. In the event that Baghdad fell, he had instructed his forces to loot, burn, and demolish the ministry buildings, to ensure that nothing of value would be left behind for the Americans.[180]

❧

A senior foreign policy maven, writing a few years before, had reviewed the troubled history of Clinton-era nation-building efforts. Recent experiences—in the Balkans, in Haiti—made clear the utter irresponsibility of trying to remake a society by force. "Leadership has a responsibility not to raise false expectations," he argued, "which encourages others to change their behavior and . . . to put their lives at risk. If expectations are raised falsely, then we share responsibility for the deaths, and both we and they would have been better off had we not intervened in the first place." If the United States "seriously question whether or not we are capable of doing something successfully," this experienced senior official insisted, "then it is, without question, best not to try."[181]

That was Donald Rumsfeld, writing in 1999. But things were of course different now, after 9/11, in the new world of risk. The imperative to act pressed on the administration—and the broader American national security community, Congress, and the media—with irresistible force. The United States was about to do precisely as Rumsfeld had feared and warned in 1999, and the result would be tragedy. Just how tragic the outcome would be, few could have imagined in those last days and hours before the United States undertook its war of choice.

CHAPTER 9

THE AFTERMATH

We as a nation fucked up so bad on the day after piece. . . . We took a hard thing and made it impossible. . . . I ask myself, what was this all for? It was such a waste. We could have done something right, and we did everything wrong. . . . We took the manual of what not to do, and followed it to the letter.

FORMER SENIOR US GOVERNMENT OFFICIAL[1]

Many people who supported the war no longer do.
Yes.
They feel that they were suckered.
Yes, probably. . . .
Do you feel any discomfort with that?
No. We are in Baghdad now.

AHMAD CHALABI[2]

In a tragedy, men assume they are acting freely but in fact fate is in the saddle, and "their actual decisions are determined by forces beyond their control and almost beyond their knowledge."

C. M. BOWRA[3]

In August 2003, I traveled to Iraq for the first time.

DOUGLAS FEITH[4]

Beginning on March 20, 2003, thousands of US military personnel swarmed across Iraq's border with Kuwait, rushing toward Baghdad. The Americans found, at first, a mostly friendly populace. Bedraggled lines of Iraqi troops crawled or walked up to the roadsides to surrender, sometimes sullen and sometimes openly curious. Crowds of civilians cheered passing US units, waving and jumping and smiling. Flocks of skinny children gave thumbs-up signs as they sprinted next to crawling, whining tanks. In fact, speaking to many Iraqis, it becomes clear that the war advocates would prove right on at least one point: the vast majority of the country was relieved, in some cases overjoyed, to have been rescued from Saddam's tyranny. But two things quickly became obvious. Someone was going to have to govern the country—and Iraq's new liberators had no meaningful plan, or any seeming intention, to do so.

The Iraq war, it soon became apparent after March 2003, had been unleashed on the backs of a herd of faulty assumptions. There were, famously, no WMDs. No one has found evidence of a serious collaborative effort between Saddam Hussein and al Qaeda, or any other terrorist group posing an imminent threat to the United States.[5] The Iraqi political system was catastrophically unripe for the institutions, habits, or procedures of a stable democracy. But the war represents an authentic tragedy most of all because its authors, as I hope the preceding narrative has made clear, were not evil or pernicious human beings. Nearly all were intelligent, well-intentioned, highly experienced senior officials urging courses of action they genuinely believed to be vital.

Yet in the end their good intentions were ruined by their very human, and in some cases truly poignant, flaws—including a conviction that they were operating out of some sort of historical obligation, a moral imperative, that foreclosed critical thinking and quashed doubts. Most fundamentally for our understanding of strategic judgment, their choice reflected an intuitive sense of the rightness of a course of action—a leap of faith—that led the United States into Iraq. Before we turn to a final evaluation of the character of that judgment, to understand its full tragedy we must first some to grips with the manner in which specific misjudgments played themselves out on the ground.

In the face of ballooning violence and disorder, American officials and military officers improvised as they made judgments on the fly and tried their best to comprehend a nation that was a mystery to all of them. Some of these judgments turned out to be sensible, others badly misguided—but the real cause of the postwar chaos was not the choices made in its midst, even those as seemingly decisive as the decision to disband the Iraqi army. The larger truth is that these American officials had been fatally handicapped by the largest misjudgment of all: the idea that the United States could crash into Iraq, cobble together a government, and get out, without major cost to itself or injury to the Iraqi people. This was the ultimate hallucination of the US decision to invade; it was a product of a decision poorly made and poorly executed, and it fatally handicapped the often courageous and insightful American military and civilian leaders who tried to make the best of an unfolding disaster.

※

Lieutenant Colonel Chris Hughes, commander of a battalion of the 101st Airborne Division, was emblematic of many US officers who went to Iraq to fight a war and ended up as a civil administrator of a country he did not comprehend. He inherited an area of thirteen thousand square kilometers in the area of Mosul and Hillah, in northern Iraq, overseeing four sizeable cities and scores of dusty towns and villages.[6] Hughes swiftly recognized that his job was political and social rather than military, and set about discovering ethnic boundaries, meeting tribal leaders, mapping local power structures, and pleading with Iraqis to govern themselves.

But local self-sufficiency was slow to emerge. Soon after he'd arrived, Hughes started "getting laundry lists" of things to fix, he later told an oral history project—water, sanitation, power. He asked, "Have you ever had this before?"

Iraqis would answer, "Oh, no, but you're Americans. You can make things happen right now."[7]

Still, Hughes felt welcomed, and he and his men worked hard to deliver what they could. "I will say from the very beginning [the Iraqis] were very comfortable with us. . . . It's frustrating because it went really well. Some of us saw some things go tremendously well."[8]

Vice President Richard Cheney, watching the early returns from Washington, was thrilled. "We were greeted as liberators," he boasts in his memoirs, "when we freed the Iraqi people from Saddam's grip."[9] Yet liberating an oppressed people from a tyrant turned out to be a devilishly complex business.

᪸

Some time ago, a prominent Western country set about to liberate another nation—smaller, brutally injured by a vicious occupier, but with an ancient and brilliant history—from the danger of chaos and takeover by a totalitarian movement. In the first days, arriving troops "were greeted with enthusiasm."[10] They promised the rapid installation of a democracy and started working with the hand-picked leader of a provisional government.

Yet within days, power struggles and social tensions rent the fabric of the nation. Militias turned on one another. Riots erupted. Labor strikes paralyzed the economy. Score-settling emerged—beatings and confiscations and brutal killings, the welling-up of decades of grievance. Faced with an increasingly restive population, the Western forces had to use force to impose order—curfews, arrests, retaining walls, interrogations, an incessant hunt for criminals and insurgents. These harsh measures were married to "clumsy diplomacy" that caused the intervening power "to be seen . . . as would-be imperialist oppressors of a liberated people."[11]

An incipient civil war now exploded into greater violence and terror. The Western power's embassy "resembled a besieged outpost" and was regularly taken under fire; staff there had no electricity and subsisted on army rations. When high-ranking visitors arrived, they were rushed through the bullet-ravaged streets in armored cars. Eventually the

Western military commander appealed for a whole division of extra men, a request that shocked his government, which had anticipated a painless restoration of order followed by a smooth and speedy exit. Eventually the intervening power would dispatch over ninety thousand troops to pacify the nation it had arrived, with the best of intentions and a powerful dose of naivete, to liberate.

The intervening power struggled to form a legitimate regime that could impose order and facilitate a withdrawal. The ambassador of the Western interventionists remarked acidly that "at its best" the country was a fiasco of "muddle, incompetence, evasion, corruption, political persecution and lack of planning and control."[12] The resulting civil war lasted over three years and has been described as a period of "continuous horror"[13] for the people. It left behind a devastated and divided nation that suffered, by some estimates, over 150,000 dead, with many more wounded and uncounted numbers harassed, tortured, and traumatized.

The experience to which I refer is the 1945–1947 British intervention in Greece, and on closer examination it obviously carries haunting lessons for any would-be liberator. US Assistant Secretary of State Dean Acheson visited the country in December 1944 and produced a memo for Roosevelt aide Harry Hopkins. Liberated populations, Acheson observed, "are the most combustible material in the world. They are fighting people. They are violent and restless."[14]

The advocates of the Iraq war often used European liberation narratives to justify their assumptions of what postwar Iraq would look like. But the analogies they held in their minds were nostalgic, abridged versions of the bitterly complex realities that tormented much of Europe after 1944. Perhaps the best account of postwar chaos is Keith Lowe's *Savage Continent*, which begins with a bracing portrait. "Imagine a world without institutions," he wrote. "There are no governments any more, on either a national scale or even a local one. . . . Law and order are virtually non-existent, because there is no police force and no judiciary. . . . Goods belong only to those who are strong enough to hold on to them, and those who are willing to guard them with their lives. Men with weapons roam the streets, taking what they want and threatening anyone who gets in their way."[15]

Lowe is describing, again, ruinous patterns that emerged in the heart of *Europe*, a continent with extensive experience in democracy and the rule of law. Lowe is especially powerful on the subject of vengeance. In the Balkans alone, seventy thousand alleged Nazi collaborators lost their lives. In Greece, thousands were hauled off to "reeducation camps" in the mountains to be tortured and indoctrinated. "We could see the physical destruction," Lowe quotes a shocked Dean Acheson, musing on the effects of the war on liberated countries. But "the effect of vast economic disruption and political, social and psychological destruction . . . completely escaped us."[16]

⁊

It should therefore have come as little surprise that the initial welcome in Iraq was destined to congeal into something far more ferocious and grim. Iraqis with ties to the old regime were violently opposed to the American presence from the first days. In other cases, as expectations were dashed, optimism gave way to confusion, resentment, and finally antagonism. The fundamental dilemma at the heart of the whole enterprise—that is, was America coming to install a new set of Iraqis in charge, or to take charge itself?—had been left hanging, in part because either choice offered crippling risk. Refusing to run the country would lead to chaos; running it would produce anger and rebellion. "The reality," a senior US official admitted later, "is that we never resolved the issue."[17]

Perhaps the most fundamental discovery of those early days was not the absence of WMDs. It was that the well-educated, technologically sophisticated, middle-class nation imagined by the architects of the invasion turned out to be a mirage. And partly as a result, the idea of a Western power coming to rule Iraqis in the name of liberation embodied a fatal contradiction in terms, destined to explode into violence.

⁊

Most US troops arrived in Iraq unsure of their roles in an environment that was, at first, weirdly calm. A Pentagon planner in touch with American units and officials on the ground in the first days and weeks after the invasion described a pattern of "stumbling in the dark." US officers and officials "were making stuff up as they go,"[18] because they had not been equipped to do anything else. One Third Infantry Division officer to whom I spoke remembered getting the division's "Phase IV" instructions, which governed the postconflict stage of operations. The message has since been declassified: "This phase is event-driven and will change based on current conditions of the Iraqi military or political change in the regime," it reads. "This phase ends on receipt of change of mission instructions."

Well, shit, that's great, the officer thought—*a "big hand wave."*[19]

As US marines came in from the south, there were flowers and sweets and thanks from the Shi'a population that had been mauled by Saddam over the years. But many marines, inveterate readers of the corps's *Small Wars Manual* and practitioners of low-intensity warfare, had an innate sense of disquieting calm before a storm.[20] Some took solace from the claim that, according to the war plan, they would leave about as quickly as they arrived—redeployed to the States within weeks. But as the effects of long-suppressed resentments bubbled to the surface of the liberated society, it became clear that they would be needed for much longer than that. "We asked a lot of questions; we didn't get a lot of answers," one officer recalled. "The teams we were told were coming never came. . . . That was the worst thing" about the campaign, this marine lamented. "There was never any [concept for the] ending. . . . You've got to understand, the fundamental mindset was, we thought it was *over*. You started to hear, State's coming in. Bremer. You started to hear these names. We assumed there was a plan there."[21]

"There was a moment—there was absolutely a moment," full of promise and potential, one army officer explained.[22] But just what kind of a moment it was, few understood. "Questions we should have been asking for a year were only now being asked. You got to Baghdad; then what?" There were success stories, to be sure, as US troops and US Agency for International Development (USAID) staff and some contractors and many thousands of Iraqis coped as best they could. Thus a pattern was set of heroic, creative tactical adaptation in the face of strategic incoherence. But unless and until that incoherence was resolved, the tactical successes would be for naught, lost in a countervailing wave of grievance and violence.

※

Whether by design or happenstance, the looting changed everything. Not expected, not planned for, it began in the days after the regime collapsed and quickly escalated. Buildings were stripped down to bare concrete, doors and windows torn out, plumbing borne away, metal edges pulled from concrete steps to be melted down for scrap. Wiring was yanked out of hacked-apart walls; HVAC systems were heaved onto trucks and carted off. In those early days before a heavily guarded "Green Zone"—days when newly arrived Americans could change into civilian clothes, walk onto the streets and hail a taxi—Iraqis flowed into American-controlled areas and made off with generators, water pumps, desks, and chairs.[23] When one group of US soldiers visited a printing plant to make up some leaflets, one source remembered with a sort of awe, they found that looters had brought in cranes and hauled off the printing presses. The things weighed five tons apiece.[24]

"We weren't ready for the looting," a senior defense official said.[25] Apart from the physical destruction of Iraqi ministries that had been counted on to continue running the country, the psychological shock and the insult to the credibility of the US presence were immense. Average Iraqis retreated behind their walls to wait it out, to find a fence to sit on; and the Americans would never, in some critical sense, win most of them back.[26]

In northern Iraq, one source explained, US forces arrived at weapons depots to find most of the arms carted off. "The Kurds were coming out with vast, vast quantities of this stuff," whole convoys of trucks loaded so full they could barely move. It wasn't clear how things would turn out, this US official remembers thinking. "What was clear was that we were not in control of the situation."[27]

⁂

The United States had gone to Iraq, in substantial measure—in dominant measure, according to the public and official case—to strip Saddam's regime of WMDs. Given the prominence of the mission, it might have been reasonable to expect airtight planning for the WMD search in the aftermath. Instead, the effort was rushed, confused, and ad hoc. Units were hastily assembled and repurposed to the task.[28] Troops in the field kept getting urgent, disjointed messages from the White House: *Check this site. Trucks are rolling here, go take a look. We've got WMD over there.* None of the clues turned up anything.

One of the first senior Iraqis to be captured was the man who'd served as one of Baghdad's main interlocutors in the prewar weapons inspection process, Dr. Amir Al Sa'adi. As he surrendered, he told German television reporters: "There are no weapons of mass destruction and time will bear me out."[29]

In the Pentagon, senior officials under Donald Rumsfeld waited for US forces to encounter the WMDs—and then waited more. "A numbness set in," one told me, as time passed and no weapons showed up. Intelligence assessments had claimed that there would be WMD hidden under mosques. "We were really surprised when the mosques ended up just being mosques."[30]

⁂

Those who suffered the most intense effects of US misperceptions and planning gaps were the Iraqis themselves. One Iraqi to whom I spoke was living in Baghdad on the eve of the war, working at a government ministry. Eventually he had emigrated to the United States.[31] "The Iraqi people knew war was coming" months beforehand, he explained to me over tea and sweets in his compact, tidy Virginia apartment. He said this matter-of-factly but with great emphasis, and some disgust. "But the leader, Saddam, didn't know. He thought the same thing would happen as in 1991—America wouldn't come. Finally in March, he started to prepare everything very suddenly."

Another Iraqi émigré, a powerfully built former army officer, explained that in the last days before the war, government officials were running around handing out weapons to anyone who could carry them. "Saddam was trying to make civilian people become military. Arm all the people." The regime was suggesting that it would be like the first Gulf War of 1990–1991, with America drawing back—but "our experience told us, this time they want to change the regime."[32] I asked him, as a military man, how he reacted. "I am confused at this moment," he replied. "Do I welcome the Americans? No. I am a soldier. If someone attacked America, what would you do? But did I want to continue with a dictator? Did I want to change to something when we didn't know what would come next? After 2003, what we got was a mess. Chaos."

Complicating matters was the fact that, before the invasion, Iraqis had an outsized view of what Americans could accomplish. A former Iraqi government official lamented that "people expected *like this*"— snapping his fingers—"Iraq would be like America or Dubai. There won't be any more power cuts again."[33]

"If we can change the regime," another Iraqi said the thinking went, "we'll be like Germany." His father had assured him that "America, if they are serious, they will make Iraq like Japan. Because the Americans—they are the most intelligent people."[34] A former Iraqi engineer admitted that he and his friends were "desperate for change. I hated the regime. . . . The Iraqi people welcomed the Americans with flowers—in the early days." America was a great country, and Iraqis expected great things. After one conflict, Saddam had restored electricity to Baghdad in forty-three days. "We thought the Americans would do it within two hours."[35]

Another source used a medical analogy to describe how America had ravaged Iraq. "I give you an example," he said. "Someone is sick. He has a cancer in his body. They take him to the hospital. . . . Then when they open his stomach, and they cut the cancer, the doctor, he says—that's it! And he leaves the stomach open. And the man, he becomes infected. I completely agree, Saddam was a dictator. But this is the result: America made a surgery but left the wound open."

≫

Despite the accumulating evidence of pandemonium, a giddy sense of historical achievement pervaded the Bush administration in those early weeks. Dick Cheney hosted a celebratory dinner at his home and invited his aide Scooter Libby, Deputy Secretary of Defense Paul Wolfowitz, and others—but not Rice, or Powell. "We were euphoric," former senior official Kenneth Adelman recalled. "The mood and feeling were just wonderful. I just thought it was a magical moment." Rice describes an air of "hubris" among war advocates and says Cheney confronted her with a challenge: "The Pentagon just liberated Iraq. What has the State Department done?"[36]

Meanwhile, CIA officers were arriving back at the agency's Langley headquarters to find that it was becoming impossible to get anyone to focus on the burgeoning violence in Iraq.[37] Another agency source spoke of a general "euphoria," partly based on natural pride that they had done something well. As to what happened next, "that's not our problem—we don't have a day-after piece."[38]

The sense of "mission accomplished" extended even to Baghdad and senior military commanders. Less than a month after the invasion, on April 16, 2003, General Tommy Franks dispatched a cable to Donald Rumsfeld.[39] "Personal for SecDef," it was headed. Franks declared that the time had come to initiate Phase IV of the operation—stability operations, the postwar. "The arrival of additional international combat and police/paramilitary forces will allow us to accelerate the withdrawal of our troops," the CENTCOM commander claimed—though just who these forces were, he did not say. Franks would also soon submit his retirement papers, a rather shocking act for a general in the middle of a war—"certainly not what you would have expected," in the words of a former senior Bush administration official.[40]

The whole tone, the guiding theme of the US military effort in Iraq, was to finish the job and get out. Most US units had plans to be gone by the fall. Nobody wanted to get sucked into the politics of the postwar. The first line of Franks's cable had read, "Mr. Secretary, we have achieved decisive military victory in Iraq."

⁂

Yet that victory was already in great peril, despite the tireless and often heroic efforts of Americans on the ground, in large measure because the planning effort for the postwar had never settled on a concept for what would come next.[41] "There was no clear plan for establishing a provisional government," one participant said. "It was all on the fly, seat-of-the-pants. . . . [The US government] hadn't put a lot of thought into how they were going to do governance. . . . I don't think anybody understood that the center of gravity was going to be governance."[42]

In fact, some had understood just that, and as we have seen, a fair amount of effort had gone into planning for it. But key choices had never been made. Some former officials have claimed that Defense's proposal of an Interim Iraqi Authority (IIA) reflected a fully coherent plan for postwar governance. This is at best an exaggeration; the dialogues behind the IIA had produced a shifting kaleidoscope of ideas, half-baked notions, and barely understood proposals for how Iraq would be governed. The result was chaos, as ill-prepared officials scrambled to understand the country they were about to inherit. According to someone working the issues at the time, one senior ORHA leader busied himself with the task of assembling a design for Iraqi ministries by downloading their organizational structure from the internet.[43]

Don Eberly, a senior advisor in ORHA, was shocked to arrive just weeks before the invasion to find no clear plan for postwar governance. "Was this simply a case of one hand not knowing what the other was doing," he wondered, "or was it possible that this type of planning had simply not been done?" Whatever the case, "An operational plan for post-war civil administration simply did not exist."[44] In his memoirs, NSC official Zalmay Khalilzad admits that despite months of discussion and debate, "the concept for when and how to transfer power to the Iraqis remained unresolved."[45]

A senior official intimately involved in the postwar political process confirmed that the governance plans were anything but formal. He was "not party to any discussions on the transfer of power," he says. "Nor was I aware that there was any serious or sustained dialogue on that. I certainly had the impression that there wasn't." Once in Iraq, the initial efforts to develop governance structures on the ground would become "totally ad hoc." He and his colleagues were "making it up as we went along. . . . There was no plan going in."

"And so," I asked, "as far as you could tell, the plan was that you were simply going to show up in Iraq and figure it out as you went along?"

"That's certainly how it seemed to me," he said.[46]

Seven months before, in August 2002, a CENTCOM brief had articulated the leading assumptions necessary for the success of the enterprise. One had to do with postwar governance. The State Department, the planning document read, would "promote creation of broad-based, credible provisional government—prior to D-day."[47]

❧

As Washington scrambled to respond, State Department Arabist Ryan Crocker and senior White House official Zalmay Khalilzad were dispatched to begin a process of bottom-up conferences in several Iraqi cities to create the foundation for just such a provisional government.[48] They and their staffs made diligent and often heroic efforts to cobble something together in the face of ballooning disorder. But a former staffer involved in the process admitted that "we were winging it off of a broad concept. The problem is, this takes time. In the Arab world, nothing happens that fast."[49]

One senior official believed in retrospect that the Americans had underestimated the degree to which Saddam's regime had affected the mindset of the Iraqi people, their willingness to take responsibility. "We were counting too much on the Iraqis to say, 'Thanks very much, we'll take over.' . . . Most people thought an Iraqi leadership would arise. I never bought into the idea that we would be 'liberators'—but I did think they would appreciate their freedom and take responsibility for their country."[50]

Yet it didn't take much research, one US military officer serving in Iraq in those early days found, to discover that the country had become a collection of "miniature kleptocracies knitted together under Saddam Hussein," with no true degree of effective governance or rule of law, and that any expectation of Iraqis taking rapid, effective responsibility for their own governance was bound to be disappointed.[51] The entering assumption was that "the Iraqis are going to step up" and create a functioning democracy—but "we were fucking idiots to believe" that story, the officer said later. "Because the evidence was to the contrary." The officer summarized the postwar governance plan as he experienced it: "You're free, now make shit happen. And shit didn't happen."

Anxious efforts to implement the Defense Department's concept of an Interim Iraqi Authority continued after the beginning of hostilities. A week into the invasion, on March 30, Defense's policy shop produced a large packet of materials (since declassified) to support a principals meeting the next day.[52] A free Iraq should be many things, one memo argued, including "Friendly to the US." The document admitted that democratization would require "breaking with Iraq's history of domination by the Sunni Arab majority—a potentially painful political process." How this was to occur, and the possible risks and costs of such a transition, were left to the imagination. "The new Iraq," it concluded, would require, among other things, "Representative institutions (power sharing among the ethnic and sectarian groups). Rule of law and individual liberty. Private property and private enterprise." But of course any plan to achieve such outcomes—in terms of time, resources, scope of coalition mandate, and so much else—called for precisely the sort of extended presence and intrusive nation building that was anathema to many US officials, and indeed *to the IIA concept itself.*

These documents leave no doubt that the IIA aimed to pick winners from among the Iraqis contending to rule post-Saddam Iraq. Saddam's system had scarred his people, one memo concluded, and it would "take time before many become familiar with democratic ideas and before democratic-minded leaders can emerge." It was in the US interest "to give those who share the President's ideas a head start in the post-Saddam political process." Yet a mission conceived to liberate Iraqis to run their own affairs could not also be grounded in the assumption that the society was too traumatized to take advantage of that opportunity; an effort to allow a people to govern themselves could not simultaneously predetermine political outcomes. As we have seen, too, President Bush had on at least two occasions definitively—even angrily—rejected the idea of pre-cooking the leaders of an exile transitional government.

The authors of this particular memo acknowledged these paradoxes and made their preference clear. "There is tension between our interests in steering the process toward a moderate and free Iraq, and our interest in winning immediate broad support in and out of Iraq for our policy," the memo conceded. But an "excessively 'hands off' approach may produce an anti-democratic result," raising the specter of Algeria, in which hasty elections brought "Islamist extremists" to power. "As we have to start somewhere," the IIA summary and action plan added, "we should start with Iraqis with whom we are familiar and who have already endorsed principles that the USG supports."

At a principals meeting on the morning of Monday, March 31, Donald Rumsfeld reintroduced the IIA concept. "Getting an Iraqi face" on the government would be critical, his talking points assert.[53] His script explicitly called for choosing US-friendly leaders, saying that "Leadership of the Free Iraqis could form a core group of an Organizing Committee." On the declassified draft talking points, that phrase is underlined and emphasized—as is the following one, directed to President Bush:

"This is the best way to support moderate Iraqis who support your vision for Iraq."

But the principals meeting produced inconclusive results, and the next day Rumsfeld dispatched a blunt memo to Bush.[54] It was crucial "to convince the Iraqi people" that America was "intent on changing the regime" and that the "new regime is going to be a free Iraqi government, not a US military government," he wrote. "We have developed a mechanism to do this"—the IIA. "We have got to get moving on this. We can't afford to have a protracted interagency debate. This is now a matter of operational importance—it is not too much to say that time can cost lives."

Indeed it could, but a coherent process was slow in coming. As late as April 28, five weeks into the war, an OSD briefing book included a memo that concluded, "US government interagency process have yet to decide upon a final structure for the IIA, and have not announced an approach or timetable for implementing the concept."[55]

❦

Ahmad Chalabi suddenly materialized in the Iraqi desert on April 6, airlifted by the US military with several hundred men he claimed belonged to his infamous "Free Iraqi Forces" but who had nothing to do with the few dozen men trained by the US military. Chalabi stepped proudly off an American transport aircraft like a conquering hero. To this day it is difficult to find anyone who can explain exactly how he arranged this ride. Back in Washington, Condoleezza Rice "was visibly startled by press reports" of Chalabi's arrival, and Colin Powell "learned about it by reading the newspapers."[56]

The same day Chalabi peacocked into Iraq, Vice Chairman of the Joint Chiefs Peter Pace was asked about foreign jihadists. He replied, "Militarily it's not significant at all. If they join the fight, they will die. . . . I've heard reports of—in the hundreds [of fighters]—but it is not militarily significant." In the same interview, the host, Tim Russert, asked Paul Wolfowitz about the rumored Free Iraqi Forces. Were there indeed,

Russert asked, "five or six hundred" of them? Wolfowitz cagily answered, "The number initially trained was smaller, but the number keeps growing daily."[57]

❧

To govern, or assist in the governing of, a country of twenty-five million souls, ORHA had a budget of $37 million and a staff of 167.[58] When finally allowed to load up and move to Baghdad, staff members arrived to discover that there were whole Iraqi ministries they hadn't known about.[59] One of the Americans discovered that the ministry she would be responsible for—social welfare and labor—included the prison system. She'd had no idea.[60] "I just remember running into her in Kuwait City and going, 'Oh, my god,'" USAID staffer Denise Dauphinais explained to an oral history project. "That's what she kept saying, too: 'Oh, my god.'" Dauphinais had "asked repeatedly for things like an organizational chart of the Iraqi government and local government structures. Nobody seemed to be able to get any of that." Meanwhile, on arriving in Baghdad, ORHA had no facilities and no phones. But that mattered less at first because it had no idea of who it wanted to call, or what their phone numbers would be—it had no Baghdad telephone directories.[61]

At the end of March, someone in Washington sent out a list of proposed ministers for the interim government. Lawrence Summers, the famed economist—and then-current president of Harvard University, if anyone cared—appeared on the list as finance minister. Jack Welch of General Electric would be minister of electricity. Former US secretary of education Bill Bennett would run the schools.[62] In the event, none of these people were involved in the occupation.

The planning assumption continued to be that the US presence would quickly wind down. General Garner, one ORHA staffer recalls, kept repeating that he "would only be there for a short time."[63] Another remembers a Garner speech to the group a week before they left. "We're going in to help the Iraqis," he said, "for about ninety days. Then we're out of here."[64] A senior US civilian administrator remembered that "everybody was planning to do this for a few months and then go home." General Garner, he said, made it plain he had a civilian job to get back to.[65]

Back in Washington, even the Defense Department was having a hard time keeping track of events on the ground. Outsiders have "no idea how bad communication was in those first weeks," one Defense official explained. "We weren't getting much," and in fact Defense members often kept track of events in the same way the public did: by watching television.[66] One senior official said they resorted to getting updates from "a British guy on the scene" who was sending situation reports to Tony Blair, who would forward them to President Bush.[67]

Reports did begin trickling in about the condition of Iraqi infrastructure. US Army Corps of Engineers units scoured the country for power plants and related civil infrastructure. What they found was badly decayed and jury-rigged. The whole thing was such a mess, in fact, that one source recalled that the issue wasn't finding *an* Iraqi engineer to repair a given power station or water treatment plant—they needed to find *the* guy who'd worked on it in order to comprehend the byzantine mishmash of spare parts, half measures, and duct tape that kept the thing sputtering along.[68] US planners had done their postwar reconstruction planning based on "very little on-the-ground knowledge," one US official admitted; it turned out to be "pretty staggering what we were up against"— decades of "sheer and utter neglect."[69] Estimates started circulating of $35 billion in necessary infrastructure reconstruction investments.[70]

Iraqis looked on, alternately bemused, concerned, and infuriated. Iraqi exile and soon-to-be official Ali Allawi decided that Garner was "out of his depth in both Iraqi politics and the battle for supremacy over Iraq policy" within the US government.[71] Garner was "one of the smartest guys I've worked with," in the view of a former senior State official on the ground in those first weeks, "a sly old fox"[72]—but he had been given a mission that would make anyone look bad. New batches of people were arriving with the idea that they were responsible for some issue, and in some cases, they had little desire to be managed. One ORHA member remembers Garner remarking ruefully, "I don't know how Rumsfeld expects me to do this. Every time I turn around another former ambassador shows up. I can't tell these people what to do." Garner maintained a rotating list of the "top ten issues" to raise with Rumsfeld. At one point, things seemed so overwhelming that, this source recalled, Garner remarked, "I can't figure out any more what ten things to talk about."[73]

At the same time, John Abizaid, one of the few US generals with personal experience in the Arab world, told General Garner that he had been watching Iraqi media very closely. "I'm telling you," he concluded. "We're going to have a guerrilla war on our hands."[74]

❧

By April 9, with ORHA finally ready to relocate to Baghdad, the air was still full of ambiguous discussions of a "rolling transfer of power" to an Iraqi authority.[75] But none of the details had been worked out. Senior ORHA staffer Don Eberly was trying to work with Iraqi exiles brought in to help the US transitional administration, and he was not encouraged. "They were a fragmented group, torn apart by competing agendas, delicate egos, and ambition," Eberly wrote later. Some of the exiles told Eberly that Paul Wolfowitz had assured them they would be "running Iraq" when they got there—very likely an exaggeration, but one that created dangerous illusions.[76]

On April 12 General Garner put out a proposal for "big tent" meetings to begin organizing Iraqis for self-governance. Along with Crocker and Khalilzad,[77] he set up a series of regional conferences designed to coalesce an interim leadership—a first one on Nasiriyah, in April; a second in Kurdistan in the north; and a third in Baghdad. There was to be a fourth, also in Baghdad, this one a national conference to draw the regional pieces together.

Khalilzad—an elegant, thoughtful Afghan-born national security specialist who had been in and out of government for more than a decade and who would become the highest-ranking Muslim-American in the Bush administration—began talking about a rapid handover to a collection of local and diaspora Iraqis. At one point, in the memory of another participant, he used the phrase "in a couple of weeks"—and the source wondered what in the world he could be referring to, as if there was any group of Iraqis that could be ready to run the country in weeks, or even months. But Khalilzad's priority seemed clear. "Zal knew that they must get internals and indigenous Iraqis into the process," one observer insisted. "He wanted to avoid being an occupying power, and wanted to transfer authority as quickly as possible."[78]

This was an entirely sensible judgment—but an Iraqi sense of ownership, so essential to the US goal of a rapid handover, turned out to be elusive.[79] Exile writer and activist Kanan Makiya wrote to Douglas Feith during these weeks, warning that the IIA concept was falling apart. It was "overly complicated, theoretical," too "drawn out. . . . anarchy is in essence breaking out." Iraqis wanted "a tangible, palpable and simple sense that some Iraqi/Iraqis are in charge. This is non-existent at the moment. The feeling that I am referring to is primal, very basic and goes to the heart of what politics is all about." By April 22, Feith admits in his memoir, he knew that the effort was "not going well."[80]

❧

At about this time CENTCOM commander Tommy Franks arrived in Baghdad for the first time. He met with military aides and told them to begin planning the American withdrawal from Iraq. They should be "prepared to take as much risk departing as they had in their push to Baghdad," he directed. On the same day Franks arrived, senior US officers participated in a video conference with President Bush and Donald Rumsfeld—both of whom "reinforced Franks' directive for a quick redeployment."[81]

International peacekeepers were coming, Franks assured the troops. A new Iraqi government would be in place within two to three months. He wanted as many as fifty thousand troops withdrawn per month; by September, he wanted no more than a US division numbering thirty thousand personnel remaining in Iraq. (Troop numbers *would* continue to fall, in fact, down to just over one hundred thousand by February 2004, even as violence mushroomed.) President Bush called and congratulated everyone. According to a *New York Times* report, they then "posed for photos and puffed on victory cigars."[82]

In Baghdad, a news report from about the same time described the reality of post-liberation Iraq as opposed to the emerging fantasy that was fueling these rapid-withdrawal plans. "Fearful of going out after dark," it explained, "waiting up to 10 hours to fill their cars with gas, spreading rumors in the absence of reliable media, watching landmark buildings set on fire and wondering who is in charge, the residents of this capital are growing increasingly impatient with the deepening disorder that is plaguing their lives more than a month after US troops took over the city."[83]

⁂

At the April 28 governance conference in Baghdad, Ali Allawi discovered burgeoning speculation about the imminent declaration of a provisional government.[84] Exile Kenan Makiya later wrote, "The sense of the mood of that meeting was, 'we want a government and we want it now.'" The Americans running the session were "on the verge of losing control, because they didn't have answers." Makiya added, "[An American] gets up there . . . and somebody says, 'You mean you don't have a plan for the government?' He says, 'No, we are here to meet to discuss that. This is your government, not our government. We don't want to impose this government on you.' It all sounds so ridiculous. . . . It sounds so stupid."

And yet the paradox was obvious: when the Americans *did* try to exercise control, the Iraqis recoiled at that too. Makiya himself displayed the tension in his next comment: "What people wanted was authority, a sense of exertion of responsibility—that is, democracy."[85]

A remarkable April 21 *Washington Post* story quoted senior US government officials dismissing growing talk of a long-term presence. "These officials are leaning toward a quick exit," the article explained, with rebuilding turned over to "an Iraqi interim authority, which could control key aspects of Iraqi governance within months." The sources were clearly Defense Department and White House advocates of the IIA. "I don't think it has to be expensive," one of them told the *Post* of the US stay, "and I don't think it has to be lengthy. Americans do everything very quickly."[86]

Khalilzad wasn't so sure. Touring a decrepit but eerily quiet Baghdad, the American envoy appears to have been struck by the magnitude of the job—and as he writes in his memoirs, he came to the conclusion that the United States was not up to it. "I became even more convinced that we needed an Iraqi government to take over as soon as possible. We needed an Iraqi in charge—a Karzai—someone to whom the Iraqis could go with their problems." And, he writes, "The principals apparently agreed, deciding that the United States would begin the process of forming an interim authority by the end of May."[87] That critical choice about the character of the US role in Iraq—to find an Iraqi leader or leadership group and transfer provisional authority very rapidly—would last almost precisely one week.

On May 5, Garner published the names of a nine-member Iraqi leadership group and said that an Iraqi provisional government could be recognized by the middle of the month. Yet that same afternoon, according to Allawi, Khalilzad and Crocker admitted "unease about vague signals" coming from Washington about the risks of such a quick move.[88] Nonetheless, Chalabi would claim to *Frontline* that he met privately with Khalilzad and Garner, who told him of a plan to establish the provisional government as quickly as possible. Khalilzad was about to head back to Washington; he promised to be back in ten days to begin working the details of the transition plan. As events transpired, however, he wasn't able to keep the promise. "He went," Chalabi said, "and never came back."[89]

※

In those first days of May, a prominent Washington foreign policy expert, a former US senior official and ambassador, was listening with alarm to a radio report of emerging US policy in Iraq. As he drove to work at a new Pentagon job, the official would later explain, "The lead story on the

6:00 A.M. news had been that Jay Garner had announced his intention to appoint an Iraqi government by May 15. I almost drove off the George Washington Parkway. I knew it would take careful work to disabuse both the Iraqi and American proponents of this reckless fantasy—what some in the administration were calling 'early transfer' of power—animated in part by their aversion to 'nation building.' "[90]

This sort of deep skepticism about a quick turnover flew squarely in the face of whatever limited concept for governance was in place at the time of the invasion. A long-term supervision of Iraq would turn fundamental US intentions for postwar Iraq on their head and would make monumental demands on US national resources.

However valid or dangerous, these new doubts would soon define US policy. Because the man struggling to keep his car on the road was one L. Paul Bremer, and he was about to barge into Iraq and change everything.

※

Eventually the speed of the handover process, and the first signs that it might be breaking down, caused even some of the IIA supporters to hesitate. News reports in the second week of May were rife with signs of an administration alarmed that their Iraq gambit was falling to pieces. "Unless we do something in the near future," one administration official told the *New York Times*, "it is likely to blow up in our face."[91] The decision Khalilzad had momentarily sensed—of an administration ready to place its bet on a rapid handover—was coming unglued.

The evidence of burgeoning chaos was everywhere. By mid-May the Baghdad police force was still unaccounted for. Looting had left almost every police station a ruined, emptied hulk. Armed gangs roamed the streets, carjacking Iraqis and grabbing aid from foreign NGOs. Gunfire punctuated the nights. American soldiers struggled to keep order as they were pulled more and more deeply into the most obscure local disputes. "It's kinda fucked," one trooper told *Newsweek*, "to take a bunch of infantry who're trained to kill" and ask them to "mediate who ran over somebody's dog."[92]

Three years before the invasion, during the 2000 presidential campaign, Condoleezza Rice had penned an article for *Foreign Affairs*. Among other things, Rice heaped scorn on the nation-building policies of the Clinton administration. "The president must remember," she lectured, "that the military is a special instrument. It is lethal, and it is meant to be. It is not a civilian police force. It is not a political referee. And it is most certainly not designed to build a civilian society."[93] Now she was helping to preside over the beginning of a romantic effort to transform a society that would dwarf everything from the 1990s put together.

In Washington, even Rumsfeld, the bitter skeptic of nation-building crusades, was growing worried enough to consider delaying the handover process. He began to waver on a quick exit, expressing a desire to have US forces in place to look for WMDs and ensure that al Qaeda could not take root. He thought Garner and Khalilzad seemed to be handing authority to a confused, unprepared bunch of Iraqis who had no idea what they were doing.[94] But these impulses remained inchoate. A senior White House official confirmed that Khalilzad's transfer efforts remained fully in line with the White House approach, at least the one in place at the beginning of May. "I'm not sure Zal was out ahead of the rest of us," he said.[95] As the fatal inconsistencies of American policy began to play themselves out, US officials and officers on the leading edge of the operation surfed a tsunami, trying to improvise their way to some sort of coherent outcome.

Meanwhile, and at first unbeknownst to those officials, US policies were changing rapidly. In the first days of May, Crocker and Khalilzad returned to the White House to give a status report. Both assumed they'd quickly head back to continue overseeing the handover. As he has described in his memoir, Khalilzad continued to press the concept of a bottom-up provisional government alongside regional and national conferences, to thrust as much governance authority into the hands of Iraqis as quickly as possible.[96] A cryptic response came back: Condoleezza Rice "wasn't sure that's the way we were going to go."

❧

Some time earlier, more than a week at least, in a process that Khalilzad and others in Baghdad were unaware of, Wolfowitz and senior Cheney aide Scooter Libby had been in touch with a former US Foreign Service officer and ambassador named Paul Bremer. Would he be interested, they had asked, in running Iraq?[97]

The postwar plan had always assumed that Garner would only be on the job for a short time, to be replaced by some sort of civilian overseer, and that ORHA would give way to a more permanent representative office. But the character of that position—whether ambassador or occupier—had never been clearly defined, and the person who'd hold the job had never been selected. Only now, *after* the invasion, with US policy collapsing around them, was the administration trying to recruit someone for this superhuman task.

When first contacted, Bremer replied that he had a job, with the finance firm Marsh & McLennan, and so he "couldn't serve for long."

"Not to worry," Libby told him. What they had in mind "wouldn't be a full-time job. Perhaps 90 days." Bremer was brought down to Washington for an in-person audition with Paul Wolfowitz, who asked Bremer point-blank: "Do you believe in democracy with the Arabs?" Bremer did.

Wolfowitz continued, "Would you be willing to have your name considered in running the occupation of Iraq?" Bremer said he had to speak with his wife, and then he agreed.[98]

By May 2, the first public reports emerged suggesting that President Bush intended to appoint Bremer.[99] Garner and ORHA had barely established themselves in Baghdad, and now they were about to be superseded—by someone whose instincts ran very much against the assumptions of an early handover.

As he began to get his bearings, working out of a hastily arranged Pentagon office, Bremer was visited by the postwar stabilization expert James Dobbins of the RAND Corporation. Dobbins delivered a copy of a bracing study that concluded pacifying Iraq would require half a million troops. "The analysis was stunning," Bremer concluded. He had a short summary quickly prepared and dispatched to Rumsfeld. "I think you should consider this," Bremer wrote. He never got an answer.[100]

On May 6, the White House officially announced Bremer as new US civilian administrator. In the following days he met Bush for a fateful lunch in which the two discussed the scope of Bremer's authority.[101] Bremer told the president he believed in the principle of "unity of command," and he insisted that he couldn't have others in Iraq "saying they too represented the president." He was especially vexed by Zalmay Khalilzad's meetings with Iraqis.[102] Bremer also brought up the RAND report and his concerns about troop levels.

In his memoirs, Bush confirms that Bremer talked of a study "and thought we needed more troops in Iraq." Bush says he discussed "the question of troop levels with Don Rumsfeld and the military leadership. They assured me we had enough." Bush, as was his habit, "accepted Don and the military's judgment."[103]

Khalilzad still assumed he was headed back to Iraq to generate a provisional Iraqi government.[104] One source claimed that Khalilzad's little group had its bags packed and literally had cars waiting to take them to Andrews Air Force Base for their flights before they were called back.[105] "We had cleared both announcements," Khalilzad would later tell *New York Times* columnist Roger Cohen, "with Bremer to run things and me to convene the loya jirga, both as presidential envoys. We were just playing with a few final words. Then the game plan suddenly changed: we would run the country ourselves."[106]

Colin Powell called to ask, " 'What happened?' And [Khalilzad] said, 'You're Secretary of State and you're asking *me* what happened!' " Powell would describe himself as equally staggered. "The plan was for Zal to go back. He was the one guy who knew this place better than anyone. I thought this was part of the deal with Bremer. But with no discussion, no debate, things changed. I was stunned."[107]

The whole US approach to postwar governance, long predicated on the idea of a rapid handover, was about to be capsized. As one senior official closely involved in these discussions would later remark with a rueful shake of his head, "I don't think anyone ever intended that." Bremer later claimed that he was assured by people in Washington that "some time" after March 10, when the NSC approved the IIA in concept, Bush essentially reversed his position and "decided the idea of a short occupation and a quick handover wasn't going to work. But the problem was, I don't think it was ever documented. No one ever put a piece of paper in front of him and said, 'Here's the new guidance,' and so there was a lot of confusion."[108]

One very high-ranking Defense Department official confessed that he initially assumed Bremer had been brought on board to implement the IIA. When Bremer got out to Iraq and abandoned those plans, this official assumed that conditions on the ground must have forced the switch. Only when this senior official read Bremer's memoir years later did he realize that the new US proconsul had intended to scrap the rapid turnover plan *from the time he took the job*. This official was dumbfounded.[109]

Everything in the US approach to Iraq had been predicated on a short deployment and a quick exit. No one had made plans for an extended stay. What would they do now?

૨૬

Meanwhile, the national security policy process, not efficient in the best of times, became even more confused. Bremer claims that he began quickly to notify Rumsfeld of his plans for a longer handover period; Rumsfeld says he didn't get the message, and assumed the guts of the IIA were still in force all through the summer of 2003.[110] The dam held until September 8, when Bremer wrote a *Washington Post* op-ed disparaging rapid turnover and admitting that a full conversion to Iraqi sovereignty could take years. Defense officials were mortified, but it was too late to turn back.

Long before then, however, more or less as soon as Bremer was appointed, signs of a changed approach had been leaking out. As early as May 8, reflecting the new thinking, the United States and Britain sought a United Nations resolution giving them the status of occupying powers. Ali Allawi writes, "The Iraqis were completely flabbergasted by this reversal. Within the space of a few days, the entire process that was to lead to a provisional Iraqi government had been abruptly stopped, and then upended." The switch, he believes, "effectively undermined the credibility of the parties with which the USA had been engaged, with varying degrees of enthusiasm, for the better part of a decade."[111] Senior Iraqis "were stunned," Khalilzad explains. "We had given our word" that power would be rapidly transferred. "Breaking this promise would call into question our motives for intervening in Iraq."[112]

On that very day, however, senior officials gathered in Washington to hear a report on "Next Steps Toward an Iraqi Interim Authority"—that is, steps toward *precisely the approach that the new head of the US mission was busily discarding.* Declassified documents from the meeting depict a proposal for "a nationwide conference of roughly 250–300 delegates." The memos argued that if a conference were to occur, "the USG [US government] should convene the meeting and control the invitation list."[113] But Rumsfeld wasn't at the meeting, and Powell used it, according to Feith, as an opportunity to attack the concept. Rice didn't clarify matters, and confusion reigned. What the hell were they actually trying to do in Iraq?

On May 11, the administration announced that Garner would be coming home within a week.[114] On May 16, the United States formally postponed the effort to assemble a transitional Iraqi authority. Also on the sixteenth, Bremer issued a prominent directive: a ban on government service by the top thirty thousand or more Ba'ath Party members. His order for de-Ba'athification, according to the bulk of the contemporary reporting,[115] seems to have been relatively uncontroversial. One doesn't get a sense, reading accounts of the time, of the overriding consensus that has since emerged: that the order reached dangerously far down into the ranks of average Ba'ath party members, excluding from effective roles the only people who knew how to run the country. Garner and a CIA officer did strongly object, citing the risks, but were brushed off.

On May 23, Bremer issued a second order, disbanding the Iraqi army.[116] This action drove a stake into one of the most foundational assumptions of US postwar efforts. Planning documents are filled with references to a rapidly reconstituted Iraqi army as a critical tool in the governance of postwar Iraq. Bremer and others involved in this decision have justified it with the claim that the Iraqi army essentially disbanded itself—it had fled, scattered to the winds. I have spoken to a number of sources that disagree vehemently; they had been collecting lists of names and units, they said, and while it would have taken effort, they were laying a basis to call back much of the army. Iraqi commanders were showing up, pleading for the resources to reassemble their units.

To be fair, this choice was more complex and difficult than is generally understood. The Iraqi army was dispersed, and some felt creating a new institution would be not much harder than reassembling the former body. It was a Sunni-dominated institution, moreover, and others involved in postwar planning believed that to rely on it would have produced an immediate Shi'ite uprising. The idea, moreover, was to put combat units back together so as to employ them as public works laborers in the employ of a Western invader, and it is not clear if Iraqi troops and officers would have stood for this, even if it had been attempted.

The choice was therefore a hard one, and the decision Bremer made is more defensible than critics sometimes admit. But there is absolutely no question that the prewar planning had clearly stipulated that the regular army would be kept together, to avoid further chaos and to provide a critical signal of Iraqi ownership of the new situation. It is not clear how much of this Bremer was aware of as he discussed the issue with Rumsfeld during the first weeks of May. On the twentieth, he sent a letter to Bush outlining his intention to disband the army, but only in passing and without emphasizing the significance of the step or the ways in which it conflicted with prior plans. "You have my full support and confidence," came an eerily pro-forma reply.[117] On the twenty-second, Bremer presented his plan via video link at an NSC meeting, and again Bush approved it, though it came as a surprise to many others in the room.[118]

Unlike the de-Baathification order, the decree disbanding the army provoked immediate and widespread alarm. All the military planning assumptions were predicated on the idea of a coherent Iraqi army serving as a major partner in security and reconstruction—and now it had been eviscerated by a signature. "In retrospect," George W. Bush confides in his memoirs, "I should have insisted on more debate on Jerry's [Bremer's nickname] orders."[119] When interviewed for an earlier book on his presidency, Bush was more direct. Asked when he first heard about the policy change, he told Robert Draper, "Yeah, I can't remember, I'm sure I said, 'This is the policy, what happened?' "[120]

Zalmay Khalilzad's memoir reveals a man anguished by the disintegration of the policy process around postwar governance. The NSC principals lost focus on Iraqi policy once Bremer was in place, he surmises. The president thought he had given the job of running Iraq to Defense— but Rumsfeld "disengaged from day-to-day oversight of policy" because, he told Khalilzad, "the White House had taken over that role." Bremer, after all, was not Rumsfeld's guy. "None of the principals, in my recent conversations with them, could recall a meeting in which they decided whether to disband the Iraqi army." Khalilzad's verdict is spare but clear. "I cannot help but conclude that the principals failed in their responsibilities for oversight."[121]

⁂

A rather important constituency not brought up to speed on these new plans was the US military, which at first clung doggedly to its intention to leave Iraq as fast as possible. Tommy Franks hoped to begin ushering forces out of Iraq at a rapid clip, and this was the assumption inherited by his successors. All through the summer of 2003, US Army general Ricardo Sanchez said later, "the services were operating under the guidance and expectation that a rapid withdrawal was to be expected." Only in July were the brakes put on.[122]

"The administration," a New York Times story explained on May 3, "does not want substantial numbers of American forces to be tied down in Iraq. It is eager to avoid the specter of American occupation, and it is hoping to shift much of the peacekeeping burden of stabilizing Iraq to other governments." Meanwhile, President Bush was giving speeches promising to bring order to all of Iraq. Getting the troops out quickly would depend on restoring electrical and water supplies, rebuilding Iraq's infrastructure, and forming a new government. "But the administration is calculating that these are temporary problems and that political trends will improve and will allow the disengagement of most American troops."[123]

꙳

As ORHA gave way to Bremer's Coalition Provisional Authority (CPA), the ranks of the American mission in Baghdad came to be filled more and more with political types, many of them astonishingly young. The key qualifications in many cases were Republican Party loyalty and connections to top Bush administration policy-makers.[124] Beyond the politics was the sheer disorganization of the staffing process. One official told me people would randomly show up—from the White House, from DoD: *Here I am, come to transform Iraq! Where do I bunk?* As late as June 2004, when new ambassador John Negroponte arrived in Baghdad, the staff had to admit that they had no firm idea of how many people were there, or who they were.[125] "Bodies were being thrown at Baghdad without any sense of what they would do," people who were "completely and utterly clueless" and out of their depth, one senior State Department official told me.[126] In one billet related to the administration of police training, they got a young woman, just a couple of years out of college, who'd been working in Republican state politics but who had no background in or familiarity with police issues.[127]

USAID staffer Denise Dauphinais explained that CPA had no way of getting real input from Iraqis, which led to an ironic result: "We went in to defeat what was essentially an old-fashioned, Soviet-style, centralized-planning regime—with a great deal of brutality tossed in. We replaced it with a warmer, kinder, gentler, fuzzier, Soviet-style centralized-planning regime, which maybe didn't have a lot to do with what Iraqis needed, wanted, or could have dealt with."[128] The irony hung like a suffocating haze over the project: an avowedly conservative administration had worked itself around to embracing an experiment in social reform and central planning that would have made America's 1960s progressives blush, in a country none of them remotely understood.

⁂

As late as September 2003, with violence surging and chaos metastasizing, Donald Rumsfeld visited Iraq and drafted a triumphalist memo for President Bush.[129] He pronounced Iraq "different . . . from many of the press reports. Conditions have improved since my visit in April," he claimed. The coalition had performed six thousand civil affairs projects. The morale of US troops was high. "Iraq is a country with good potential," he argued; the "ingredients for success are there." Rumsfeld wrote that the security context "is improving, and better than reported."

This was one of Rumsfeld's "fatal mistakes," a senior Bush administration official would explain: the stubborn aversion to seeing reality for what it was.[130] The same day he was writing his cheery note to the president, the US Army announced that it would have to involuntarily extend the tours of Reserve and National Guard troops in Iraq to a full year, to meet force requirements in the face of burgeoning violence.

One US officer had a chance to discuss the growing dangers with one of the best-known of the senior Iraqi prisoners—Tariq Aziz, the former foreign minister and deputy prime minister under Saddam. Aziz was famous for his fluent, musical English; his shock of white hair; and his oversized black glasses. He retained some of the swagger of his former life; at one point he ordered his captors to bring him tea. When asked about the growing resistance, Aziz told the Americans they had forfeited their chance. "The first few days were quiet, weren't they?" he asked (one can imagine the grim, knowing smirk). "People were waiting for you to tell them what to do. They wanted to be told what to do." But America hadn't come to tell Iraqis what to do. It had come to let them figure it out for themselves.

⁂

And then there was Paul Bremer, an American viceroy of a new style, point man for the messianic application of American foreign policy in an alien land. Bremer was many things: former career foreign service officer and ambassador to the Netherlands; regal, cosmopolitan, and elegant—a tall, handsome, dark-haired diplomat right out of central casting; and also a hard-nosed manager who demanded results, someone prone to bouts of screaming, fist-pounding, and belittling. But Bremer was also courageous, committed, and determined, a man who would brush off numerous assassination threats and visit the most dangerous areas of Iraq. As to his qualifications, Charles H. Ferguson puts it this way: "His only experience with any Muslim society was an assignment in Afghanistan in the 1960s. He had never served in the military, had never worked in the Middle East, had never worked on Persian Gulf issues, spoke no Arabic, had never worked in any postwar occupation or reconstruction effort, had no experience with the oil industry, and had never managed any large budget or organization."[131] Other than that, he was the ideal man for the job. And then, too, as a hallmark of the war planning process, one can do little better than this devastating fact: by the time he ensconced himself in a Pentagon office to begin serious research and thinking for his new mission, Paul Bremer had roughly a week before he departed to run a nation to which he had never traveled before in his life.[132]

As it turned out, according to the testimony of many who worked in the CPA in those days, Bremer's style was often autocratic and peremptory. Decisiveness was the goal, though decisions often lagged in the overall confusion. To his defenders, his authoritative approach "held the country together" in those first months.[133] But in the process he often appeared to brush off the State Department; the United Nations; his own Defense Department sponsors; and even the US military commander, General Ricardo Sanchez, with whom he had a rapport that could best be described as frosty.

Bremer's relationship with the organization best equipped to play a central role in reconstructing Iraq—the US Agency for International Development (USAID)—was especially toxic. Many USAID officials became convinced that Bremer loathed their agency. He "antagonized and tortured" USAID staffers, one former official reported, accusing them of disloyalty and disobedience. "He threatened to take away [USAID's] money every day," the official recalls. He displayed intense frustration with USAID's sometimes arcane contracting regulations—which were, annoying as they might be, grounded in law. At one point all the abuse and impossible demands got so bad that a group of USAID staffers at CPA gathered together and sent a message to Andrew Natsios, the head of their agency: "This is bullshit," they said. "We're out of here." They were prevailed upon to stay.[134]

Despite everything, Bremer had determination and charisma too. He obviously wanted to help Iraq make the transition to a better future, and he put his life on the line to do it. One former CPA employee told me that a group of them would meet for meals or drinks for years afterward. They gathered to reminisce and chat and catch up. But what really brought them together was a chance to see Paul Bremer. He inspired fierce loyalty among a select group of mostly young staffers who worked in Iraq in those tense days. Bremer would scream at you one day and praise you the next, some said, but it made them stronger. There was an esprit d'corps among his close staff members, who felt that he trusted and would be loyal to them. Of Bremer, this former CPA official said simply, "We all loved him."

⁂

Washington Post reporter Jim Hoagland accompanied Paul Wolfowitz into postwar Iraq in July 2003. The scene has a surreal quality: here is Wolfowitz, the pensive, kindhearted scholar, hoping to "offer firsthand testimony about things I have only read in books until now," speaking of his passionate optimism that the Iraqis "are remarkable people who can achieve a change in their lives that will also mean much for the whole region."[135] Some months before, in fact, in late February, Wolfowitz had visited a group of Iraqi exiles. "Let me assure you once again," he had told them, "that the United States will be committed to liberating the people of Iraq, not becoming an occupation force." Wolfowitz was quite explicit: "The answers to these questions are not for America nor for the international community to dictate. Iraqis need to answer them for themselves."[136] And he quoted a passage from the Quran, sura 13, verse 11: "Surely God has not changed the condition of a people until they change their own condition."

According to a version of the Quran that I possess, at least one translation of the verse offers a far more perilous warning. "Lo! God changes not the condition of a folk until they (first) change that which is in their hearts," it reads. "And if God wills misfortune for a folk there is none that can repel it, nor have they a defender beside Him."

Even as the violence mushroomed, even as the prospect of WMDs melted into air, many of the war advocates clung to the idea that invading Iraq had been the right thing to do. Many cling to it even today. Eliminating even the *risk* that Saddam would have built a nuclear program, they say, was worth it. Look at North Korea today, on a trajectory for a hundred or more nuclear devices, a geopolitical nightmare of the first order. Iraq may not be a democracy yet, but give it time. Violence has all but ceased. In some months of 2017, deaths from social unrest had fallen to just over one hundred per month, the lowest in several years. There have been no more mass-casualty attacks on the United States, an outcome that the war advocates must surely associate with the demonstration effect they sought. All of this will look very different in fifty or a hundred years, they assert, when the long-term goals of the project are borne out.

Some of it, war advocates will surely claim, is already beginning to look different. Taking advantage of a decline in violence and the at-least-temporary forbearance of the religious edicts of Shi'ite militias, as of mid-2018 Baghdad had become somewhat more open and liberated. A small explosion of culture and entertainment was underway, with singers and poets and authors able to express themselves in ways not seen for decades. "Fifteen years after the US-led invasion of Iraq," a recent

Washington Post story explained, "Baghdad is undergoing a renaissance of sorts. . . . There's a widespread consensus that at no time in the past 40 years, since Saddam Hussein acquired absolute power and led Iraq into a series of ruinous wars, has Baghdad been as free and as fun as it is now."[137]

These claims bear some truth. One cannot deal legitimately with the goals and arguments of an experienced, well-intentioned crowd of senior officials without taking their perspective seriously. If Saddam had a nuclear program to rival Kim Jong-un's today, it would indeed be a serious danger. Embers of hope do glimmer in Iraq's political process, and in the hints of social liberation we can detect in today's Iraq. Iraqis are freer than they have been in decades, and whatever the brutalities of the country's current politics, they cannot rival the bloated torture chamber that was Saddam's regime.

But the idea that America's misadventure in Iraq should best be viewed as a profoundly sensible judgment waiting to emerge from short-term cynicism cannot withstand scrutiny, for several overwhelming reasons.

There were, first of all, clear alternatives at the time to achieving most of America's goals in Iraq, alternatives that did not require going to war. Intrusive inspections combined with close international attention could have kept the lid on a WMD program that, as we have seen, had already been mothballed in any case. Deterrence—of Iraqi aggression and use of WMDs—could have worked, as it has in many other places. Even at the time, it was widely known that Saddam had little to do with al Qaeda; gutting the terrorist group's capabilities could have been achieved with a regional and global law enforcement and covert action assault of the kind that has more or less been underway since 2002, a campaign that would have been far more diligent and persistent without the distraction of Iraq.

Second, there is simply no evidence—and there never was—for the diaphanous precedent-setting justifications for war. No meaningful study would have proved in 2002 that toppling Saddam's regime would convince others to cease planned attacks against America. The portrait of a global spiderweb of terrorists and state supporters was always wildly exaggerated, as was any potential "demonstration effect." Nor was there reason to believe in a hopeful, liberationist precedent—the claim that toppling Saddam would set off a wave of democratic reforms in a region not yet ready for them. In fact, any truly meaningful risk analysis would have highlighted the danger that emerged. The Iraq war's primary lesson to the world was actually that America had lurched into a quagmire of its own making and then proceeded to exhaust itself, financially and politically, in the resulting conflict—which left Iran much strengthened in the region, America's word and reputation deeply wounded, and other US rivals badly spooked. Instead of constraining hostile trends like the North Korean nuclear threat, American adventurism in Iraq and Libya accelerated them.

Consider, for example, the true results of the regional demonstration effect some hoped for. Advocates argued that a transition to democracy in Iraq would set an example for the Arab world. Inspired by this, people would throw off their oppressors and rise up. This is more or less what happened (for reasons, experts are fairly unanimous in explaining, that mostly had nothing to do with Iraq) in the Arab Spring. And what were its outcomes? Variously, depending on the nation and context: chaos, violence, civil war, and return to military rule; an accelerating regional rivalry for power; the requirement for US and allied military interventions to prevent bloodbaths, interventions that spawned yet more violence, with tragic results—at least in Libya—for American diplomats and security officers and a toxic conspiracy theory in American politics; and the firm decision by American rivals, at a minimum in Russia and North Korea, that all of this demonstrated an America out of control, a nation whose power had to be checked more forcefully. Even if the hopeful signals today in Iraq take deeper root, they will not be able to serve as any sort of balm for the global reaction the invasion helped unleash.

Third, a clear test of the "time will bear us out" argument is to imagine that the advocates made their current-day argument in 2002, and guess at the popular, congressional, and global reaction. That is: "Iraq does not have WMDs, and may be years from a nuclear weapon. The formal operational ties to al Qaeda are negligible. While Iraqis thirst for freedom, the short-term prospects for anything resembling a democracy are minimal. Moreover, if we do this, we will spend a decade, thousands of American lives, and hundreds of billions of dollars—and pour much of the goodwill of the post-9/11 era—into a project that ultimately leaves Iraq fragile, fragmented, and deeply embedded with Iranian influence. But Saddam will be gone; there will be no short-term risk of his acquiring WMDs; and after a decade and a half of brutal violence, parts of Iraq will begin to emerge into normalcy and a hopeful future." Had this been the argument in 2002, who would have possibly endorsed the mission?

Fourth, the breast-pounding defense of the invasion on the grounds that we *thought* Saddam had WMDs, and no state sympathetic to terrorists could be allowed to have them, is built on significant degrees of hypocrisy. As experts knew well at the time, far more support for extremist groups was flowing from places like Saudi Arabia and Pakistan than from Iraq. While the degree of "official" support for extremism in Riyadh and Islamabad is often exaggerated, some elements in their power structures viewed—and continue to view—the sponsorship of extremist groups as an entirely legitimate tool of statecraft, in ways that Saddam simply never did on the same scale. Pakistan had a sizeable, and growing, nuclear arsenal in place when Iraq had only aspirations. Meanwhile, North Korea's nuclear stockpile grows by the month, to a size at which it could theoretically be comfortable selling fissile material. As some comments by war advocates in the 1990s made clear, Iraq was a target because it was doable, not because it was the epicenter of the terrorists-with-WMD peril. As a result, invading Iraq did not mitigate that danger; indeed, by hardening the resentment of the United States in some Muslim lands and serving to boost North Korean nuclear ambitions, in some ways it made the problem worse.

Fifth, the evidence, almost twenty years into the larger war on terror to which the invasion of Iraq was supposed to contribute, is clear: global Islamic extremism in general, and al Qaeda in particular, are vastly stronger than they were on 9/11. Former FBI counterterrorist agent Ali Soufan noted in October 2018 that in the decade after 9/11, "al-Qaeda's membership grew by an order of magnitude—from 400 to around 4,000." It gained offshoots and adherent organizations in a dozen countries and regions, including Somalia, Yemen, Syria, north Africa, and Iraq itself. The movement's ideology remains strong—in part because of the convenient targets the United States has provided for that narrative, including the invasion of Iraq.[138] That same month, US chairman of the Joint Chiefs General Joseph Dunford admitted that "little progress has been made in addressing the underlying conditions that lead to violent extremism,"[139] a rather dispiriting (though bracingly honest) conclusion to reach seventeen years into a campaign to address precisely such conditions.

Defenders of the war on terror point to the absence of other large-scale attacks on the United States as evidence of that war's success. This is an important fact, and we can credit the global assault on al Qaeda with keeping the group off balance and reducing its capacity for such operations. But the war on terror—and its component, the war in Iraq—were explicitly designed to do something more. They were designed to end global Islamic extremist terrorism, in part by setting loose a train of democratic reforms that would destroy the basis of that movement and its supporting states. In regard to this objective, the campaign has manifestly failed. Global extremism is far stronger than on 9/11, and if it ever turns its malign intentions back to the United States in a large and persistent way, the results would be catastrophic.

Sixth and finally, the calamity of this judgment comes not only from its strategic incoherence, but also from the way in which it was pursued and implemented, from process as much as outcome. A decision to invade a foreign land—even if one hopes the stay will be brief—is a profound choice. But the planning for what happened after the United States arrived was, as we have seen, unaccountably ham-handed and shoddy. One cannot possibly defend the Iraq war judgment, in the larger sense, as sensible and effective *given the way it was made*. This extends not only to the lack of postwar planning but to the discussion of risks and costs. In the next chapter, I outline several criteria for what I term a "doctrine of policy negligence." These criteria apply largely to the way in which a judgment is reached rather than its outcomes—and by these standards, the Iraq judgment was clearly negligent.

Some cling tightly, still, to the imagined dreams of glorious liberation, which was cruelly denied by avoidable mistakes foisted on the operation by skeptics and cynics. What if, they insistently ask, the implementation had been better? What if the postwar planning had been extensive and effective? What if some of the advocates' dream of a quick handoff to Iraqis had been accomplished?

But these questions search after a mythical outcome: there was no way to escape the dilemmas waiting like land mines in Iraq. "Better" post-war planning would not have prevented a general collapse of order, given the typical patterns of postliberation societies. There *were* no Iraqis ready to assume power apart from exiles with no political base in the country and no experience governing anything. The issue wasn't just planning but also resources: there never could have been enough US troops to strictly govern a country of twenty-five million people, and there was no way the Bush administration would have devoted the tens of billions it would have required to rush adequate supplies, specialists, and capabilities into Iraq to begin to effect the sort of rapid transformation that might have staved off chaos.

Ultimately, the argument comes back to the strategic incoherence of the whole enterprise. Why try to "do better" when the conceptual argument for a thing makes so little sense in the first place?

᯼

In December 2003, after months of searching, American forces finally discovered Saddam Hussein, cowering in his infamous hole in the ground. A series of CIA and FBI interrogators then had precious months in which to question him before he was turned over to the Iraqi government and ultimately hanged. When he first met the initial CIA team, writes John

Nixon, Saddam "paused to make eye contact with each of us, moved toward us and smiled warmly. He shook our hands and said hello like a Boston pol working the room." He continued to view himself as a brilliant leader. "Why don't you ask me about politics?" he demanded of one of his CIA interlocutors. "You could learn a lot from me."[140] And one of his most consistent taunts was both simple and haunting: the Americans, he assured his captors, had no idea what they had gotten themselves into.

"Wahhabism is going to spread," Saddam claimed at one point about the especially austere and sometimes violent version of Islam. "And the reason why is that people will view Wahhabism as an ideal and a struggle." Iraq, he continued, "will be a battlefield for anyone who wants to carry arms against America. And now there is an actual battlefield for a face-to-face confrontation." Saddam held little hope for the American project. "You are going to fail," he said from his interrogation room. "You are going to fail in Iraq because you do not know the language, the history, and you do not understand the Arab mind."

"Next summer, when it is hot," he continued, chuckling, "they might revolt against you. . . . You might put that in parentheses for President Bush!" As events transpired, it did not even take that long—by January an insurgency was already flaring, and US military officers approached Saddam with the somewhat insolent request that he beg the insurgents to stop fighting. He waved the request aside. "The occupier who comes across the Tigris to our country and asks the occupied to stop fighting— that is not logical. We will say, 'If you want to stop the bloodshed, you should leave.' You will lose nothing by leaving, but we will lose everything if we stop fighting."

Lt. Col. Hughes—the dedicated and thoughtful US military officer quoted at the beginning of the chapter, who led a unit into early occupation duty—figured something out on his return to the United States. "When I entered the city of Najaf and we stood at an intersection," he said, "and had an incident when I was over there, it didn't mean jack squat to me. . . . When I came back here, I learned that when I stood at that intersection, I was the thirty-first commander of a foreign army in the history of Mesopotamia to seize that road intersection. In hindsight, we're just another group of people coming in there to oppress them."

So his interviewer asked, "What is the solution? Just get out?"

The previous thirty eventually left, Hughes replied. "It just took some of them a long time to figure that out."[141]

CHAPTER 10

LESSONS

The first, the supreme, the most far-reaching act of judgment that the statesman and commander have to make is to establish . . . the kind of war on which they are embarking; neither mistaking it for, nor trying to turn it into, something that is alien to its nature.

CARL VON CLAUSEWITZ[1]

If my son succeeds, he will be the marvel of all men; but if he fails—he is not accountable to anyone. If he lives, and returns home, he will rule the country as before. The country is his.

ATOSSA, MOTHER OF XERXES, IN THE PERSIANS[2]

We had a really good idea. We had really, really good people. And yet we still screwed it up.

SENIOR BUSH ADMINISTRATION OFFICIAL[3]

Some time ago, the head of a great nation led his country into a poorly conceived adventure against a hated enemy. He did so, some historians have suggested, recklessly and without adequate information or planning. His father had been the nation's leader before him, and the son sought to emulate his success—to go one better, in fact, by finishing a job left undone, to wipe away the one nemesis who still mocked his father's legacy.

The unfortunate son was the Persian king Xerxes, who came to power in the fifth century BC. Xerxes is caricatured as the effete, body-pierced weirdo who directs the Persian hordes to the slaughter of the fearless Spartans in the film *300*. In real life, a surely more conventional Xerxes led the world's greatest assembly of military might into Greece and managed to sack Athens before his fleet was destroyed at Salamis and he withdrew with part of his army to Persia. The force he left behind fought inconclusive battles with the Greeks; the two sides remained at war for over a decade, but Persia never again threatened the Greek mainland—and the costs of the expedition seem to have contributed to the decline of the Persian empire.

In his play *The Persians*, the Greek dramatist Aeschylus conjures imagined differences between father and son, Darius and Xerxes. Darius was the wise, prudent, thoughtful king; Xerxes was instead "impetuous," a "stubborn fool" guided by a "powerful Spirit" that tended to "relieve him of his wits" with a "disastrous result."[4]

Much of this is surely dramatic license. The real Xerxes was likely no fool, and had the best of intentions—as he saw them—for Persia. Yet as depicted by Aeschylus, he was also subject to tragic flaws, some of which may have been present in the real man: arrogance, boldness to the point of irresponsibility, an urge to dominate the quarrelsome Greeks, and a burning desire to outdo his father in war.

Tragic flaws, as distinct from malevolent or senseless ones, have played a similar role in bringing about more recent conflicts. Christopher Clark has examined the road to World War I in his magnificent book *The Sleepwalkers*. He dismisses villainous theories of the war's origins, "in which a coterie of powerful individuals, like velvet-jacketed Bond villains, controls events from behind the scene in accordance with a malevolent plan." Instead, what would become the most horrific conflict in human history was produced by mostly gifted, pragmatic statesmen with the interests of their nations fully in mind. "The outbreak of the war," Clark concludes, "was a tragedy, not a crime."[5] So it is with countless US foreign policy calamities—the Bay of Pigs, Vietnam, Libya, and of course Iraq. The actions of the United States government in deciding to go to war in Iraq reflected an all-too-common descent into wishful thinking and hubris—and the only question now is whether this experience becomes a path to collective self-knowledge. This lesson suggests, among other things, that it will not be enough to locate a new gang of the "best and brightest" and install them at the tiller of American foreign policy. To the extent that they remain embedded in that policy's messianic tradition and their judgments are still subject to the urgent imperatives of categorical values, crises and temptations will emerge that render them once again mostly blind to the consequences of their actions.

Iraq was a mistake and a tragedy, I have argued, rather than an intentionally cruel act or a mendacious conspiracy. But it *was* still a mistake, and it represents a deeply flawed judgment—arguably the single most flawed judgment in the record of modern US foreign policy. So who is to blame: Amid all the errors of belief and judgment outlined in the preceding chapters, is there any room to assign culpability? And does placing blame do any good?

＊

The problem of blame is a difficult issue to resolve in complex judgments. Because there is no obviously right answer in such kaleidoscopic problems, it may be challenging to assign culpability for errors. If the mistake was entirely understandable, made using the best information people had available to them and undertaken in service of productive goals, then on what basis can we say in retrospect that the choice was "wrong"?[6] If decision-makers cannot possibly know how their judgment will turn out, then how can they be held accountable for outcomes that are so dependent on the whims of chance? I have spent a career studying such events, speaking to the senior officials who shaped them, and seeing a very small dose of the process up close, and I'm confident that declaring such strategic calamities as Vietnam and Iraq to be the products of intentionally criminal or deceitful behavior, while emotionally satisfying, rarely matches the facts. Senior officials operate in the service of sometimes crimped ideologies, personality quirks, imprisoning experiences, and other limits to reasoning. They can be bull-headed and obtuse, immune to corrective information. But all of that only makes them human, not evil.

Yet if we cannot assign blame, then senior officials will escape just about any accountability for the results of their actions—and this, I believe, is the reality in foreign policy today. Because we know the leaders and their senior advisors are basically guessing, we are loath to punish them afterward if the guesses were wrong, as long as the resulting policies adhere to some basic legal and procedural standards (and sometimes, not even then). When was a secretary of state or national security advisor last held personally liable for the choices he or she recommended, or conspired to produce? How often do the coauthors of disaster retire back to well-compensated positions in academia or the corporate world, their misjudgments having no long-term effect on their reputation? There is, at least in democracies, always a form of collective accountability; parties and governments can be turned out by the voters. But is it ever reasonable to pursue *individual* accountability for the roles senior officials play in midwifing disaster?

I have argued that it is wrong to search for villains in stories that are primarily about people struggling to do their best. But going to the opposite extreme—abandoning the assignment of any responsibility and hanging medals around the necks of those whose errors helped pave the way to tragedy—is just as wrong-headed. Leaders and senior officials make much of the agonizing duties on their shoulders, and of the differences between their positions of responsibility as "policy-makers" and the more crank-turning blandness of lower-level bureaucrats (or, worse, the ivory-tower shelter of academics). Given these duties and this power, they are surely responsible for something.

More than that, there is a difference between a truly honest, well-informed mistake—in which the decision-maker has acquired and taken seriously every piece of information possible to reasonably assess and has promoted rigorous thinking and open debate—and a mistake that even at the time reflects powerful degrees of ignorance, refusal to accept contrary information, stubbornness, and Machiavellian tactics. The difference lies between making a mistake after doing everything possible to avoid one, and making it out of some dereliction of responsibilities, even if well intended.

⁊ₑ

One of the senior officials I interviewed for this work was describing the uncooperative—indeed, actively subversive—behavior of Donald Rumsfeld's Pentagon during the later war planning process. It was, this former official said bitterly, nothing less than "criminally negligent." At the time I took it for a metaphorical claim, a sort of allusive reference. But the more I have thought about it, the more I believe that the concept of criminal negligence offers perhaps the best avenue to a conceptual framework for assessing accountability in national security contexts. I would propose what might be called a *doctrine of policy negligence* to apply to future cases.

Negligence in a criminal setting refers to a failure—through action or inaction—to meet an established obligation to some person or group. It does not encompass true accidents; for example, auto makers are not held liable if someone has a heart attack at the wheel and drives his or her car into a tree. But if the auto maker *knew* that the steering system had a flaw and did nothing to correct it, and accidents result, they can be held to be criminally negligent in a court of law. The responsibility involved derives from what is termed a "duty of care" that arises in certain relationships—sellers and buyers, managers and employees. When someone has such a duty of care, they acquire a "reasonable person" responsibility for exercising that duty. Failing to do so makes them negligent.[7]

Legal negligence generally has four components. In order to be liable, (1) a person must *owe a duty of care* to the victim; (2) he or she must *breach that duty* by acting, or failing to act, in ways that violate it, as would be judged by a "reasonable person"; (3) those actions (or lack of action) must be *causally responsible* for the injury; (4) and the plaintiff *must be harmed*. "Stated simply," one legal source suggests, "the defendant likely will be found negligent if the average person, knowing what the defendant knew at the time, would have known that someone might have been injured as a result of his or her actions—and would have acted differently than the defendant did in that situation."[8] Critically, what matters for culpability is what the potentially liable person *should have known* at the moment he or she took the action. If there was no reasonable way to appreciate that an act or decision was likely to cause harm when the judgment was made, there cannot, by definition, be negligence.

Judgments involving senior national security officials deciding on questions of war and peace seem to meet at least three of these conditions. By their position, by their power, and by the oaths they take, such officials have an obvious duty of care to their citizens and to the military personnel and civil servants they supervise and, in some cases, order into combat. In many cases their decisions for war do become the primary causes of injuries suffered by Americans or others. (This is not always true, as in the cases of the unintended effects of policy, but a decision to go to war is clearly a proximate cause of the *effects* of that war.) And in war, people do suffer injuries. The only question, then, is whether a decision such as the one to go to war in Iraq can meet the final criterion of the four: Would an average person judge that the decision-makers had breached their duty of care? I would argue that in the Iraq case, as in Vietnam and many other demonstrable mistakes, the answer is clearly yes.

An obvious barrier is the problem of uncertainty. Many officials might contend that they can never be held liable for negligence because there is no way to determine whether they are making the right choice at the time. Suppose the United States did *not* go to war in 2003; suppose also that Saddam eventually got nuclear weapons and used them against Kuwait or Israel or American troops. Would we then hold US officials negligent for having *not* invaded? Opting to drink and drive is an obviously negligent choice at that moment. Preferring negotiations over war in Korea, or sanctions over intervention in Syria, will never be demonstrably negligent relative to alternative options at the time they are made. This is the primary difficulty with applying these standards to national security choices: If we cannot know which course will lead to a better outcome, how can any choice on such issues ever be described as negligent?

The Iraq case suggests that such a standard is indeed possible—not by reference to the outcome of the decision, but the process. Precisely because these choices are so complex, negligence typically arises not from the substance of the choice that is made (though that could be true for a handful of issues where moral, legal, or ethical considerations loom especially large, such as torture and mass bombing of civilians). More commonly, it can be found in the *quality* of the decision: senior decision-makers fail in their duty of care when they make their judgments in a fashion that reasonable observers would assess as not meeting the standards of rigor appropriate to the stakes. Four criteria can identify when that is the case.

- The first asks whether decision-makers have *carefully interrogated the rationale* for a proposed action. Decision-makers acting responsibly have to give deep and careful thought to their reasons for acting, asking whether those reasons are persuasive and whether their proposed course will really solve the problem. If not, they cannot demonstrate that the proposed actions are likely to produce the desired ends; if they do not have a coherent theory of success, they are swinging wildly at events.
- The second criterion emphasizes the importance of *thorough processing of information relevant to the choice*. Irresponsible judgments take place without acquiring all the information that is available at the time, and in a manner that refuses to see facts clearly or that allows the beliefs and expectations of decision-makers to cloud the objective assessment of evidence.
- Third, responsible decision-makers must *deeply and seriously consider potential risks and take meaningful steps to mitigate them*. Irresponsible judgments occur without assessing and working to mitigate risk of failure from issues that can easily be anticipated. When decision-makers ignore or disparage warnings of what can go wrong, they are not fulfilling their duty of care.

- Finally, a responsible decision process must *approach the debate about the choice, both internal to government and in the wider democratic society, in as open and honest a manner as possible, one designed to generate the freest possible debate*. When judgments occur in a way that, intentionally or not, suppresses information contrary to their established views and/or misleads the elite or general public about the basis for the judgment and its potential consequences, they become irresponsible.

When senior officials violate these rules, they ought to be held liable for what might rightly be termed "policy negligence." Quite apart from any accusations of "Monday morning quarterbacking," these are standards that can be evaluated while a decision process is underway.

⁂

How, then, does the judgment to go to war in Iraq (as a subset of the larger decision to launch a global war on terror) stack up? The manner in which this judgment was reached, in my view, as well as the specific actions of certain individuals, fails every one of the four proposed criteria for fulfilling the duty of care that senior officials possess. And the failures are especially painful because this was a war of choice—a luxury rather than a necessity, a situation where all options still remained open.

It is worth addressing one possible objection—that we should apply these criteria, at least in the US government on national security issues, to only one person. In the American system of government, the president alone makes the final call in the executive branch. There is no majority vote, no rule by committee. An essential truth about the American system, one former official emphasized in our discussion of culpability, "is that it is the *president* who decides—especially in foreign policy."[9] An argument could be made that neither Donald Rumsfeld nor Dick Cheney nor Condoleezza Rice can be held responsible for the demonstrably bad judgment on Iraq; it was ultimately George W. Bush's choice. By this standard, some might suggest, he and only he should be held accountable.

But this is too simple. Presidents, like other national leaders, do not have the time to master the complexities of every decision. They often lack significant experience in foreign affairs or military operations. They count on their senior advisors to *present* choices in ways that enhance their opportunity to make a well-informed guess and minimize the chances that they will engage in negligent behavior. "I'll go back to a very basic tenet of staff work in government," the national security official William Bundy explained after the Bay of Pigs: "You're responsible for the impression created in the head of the [person] you are advising."[10] Many senior officials of the Bush administration helped to produce impressions in the mind of President Bush that contributed to disaster. To that extent, senior advisors, and not only the primary decision-maker, bear some share of blame for the outcome, and we can and should assess the actions, statements, and beliefs of those who directly advise the president for evidence of culpability.

Previous chapters in this book consist, among other things, of a comprehensive catalogue of evidence on all of the criteria listed above. The rationale for going to war was not deeply interrogated—indeed, it was never even debated in an NSC meeting. The president and his senior officials did not make certain to acquire all the information available at the time; repeatedly, they ignored or bypassed the testimony of experts on issues as critical as the nature of Iraqi society, the demands of nation-building enterprises, and likely regional effects. Efforts to mitigate the risks of failure were half-hearted at best and confined largely to problems of major combat operations and the immediate aftermath. Finally, all senior officials disregarded very direct warnings without examining them in detail, and several actively suppressed contrary views while, in some cases, issuing misleading statements of their own.

There were also, previous chapters argued, clear opportunities to do better, opportunities missed because those involved were not mindful of something like the four principles outlined here. Before 9/11, for example, initial proposals for more decisive action against Saddam (though still far short of direct US military action) should have called for an in-depth examination of precisely how this would work and what the costs and risks might be. After 9/11, when the idea of going after Iraq first floated to the surface, someone could have demanded a formal debate about whether it was a good idea before it became an assumed course. As the decision took hold, the intertwined issues of postwar security and governance—and the multiple dilemmas attached to the question of how Iraq would be run after the invasion—could and should have been made the focus of extensive analysis and debate.

These facts allow us to conclude that the Bush administration was guilty of policy negligence. Manifold failures produced a situation in which they ultimately breached their duty of care—for the United States, its civilian officials, its military personnel, and the people of Iraq.

The pressures on President Bush's shoulders after 9/11 must have been crushing, an insistent compulsion to protect the American people from further attack. To his credit, Bush, unlike some others, has never flinched from shouldering the responsibility for his choices—either as president or afterward. That he was forced into the role of wartime president by the actions of others rather than seeking it out nominates him, in my own estimation (somewhat like Lyndon Johnson before him), as an essentially tragic figure. It would have taken a remarkable leader to compartmentalize his or her feelings after the horror of 9/11 and force a more considered analysis of the long-term response. But the fact remains that Bush allowed the two most momentous policy proposals that welled up from advocates in the US government—to initiate a "global war on terror" and to invade Iraq—to be decided without any serious critical analysis. Once the direction was set, other characteristics of Bush's leadership style—the tendency to scoff at deep analysis, incuriousness, a refusal to confront bureaucratic malice, the driving certainty that came from a sense of being on a God-given mission—conspired to undermine all the criteria for responsible decision-making outlined above.

Others then magnified—or failed to counteract—these problems in ways that leave them implicated in the charge of policy negligence. The handful of obsessive war advocates (most notably the vice president) energized the rush to judgment and took many opportunities to shoot down contrary views, acting only, or almost entirely, as advocates of a specific outcome, and not in any meaningful way as the guardians of a sound decision process. Donald Rumsfeld endorsed the proposed war through his usual approach of indirection, did not ensure an adequate consideration of the postwar, demanded that his department be given responsibility for that challenge yet did far too little to ensure it would be fulfilled effectively, and cowed dissent with an aggressively confrontational leadership style. Condoleezza Rice was placed in a grim situation—hindered by senior officials who often defied her influence, serving a president with little stomach for policy debates and even less instinct for safeguarding her position—but did not, ultimately, take the bold actions that would have been necessary to overcome these barriers and force a more considered policy.

Nor did the military leadership. Tommy Franks assured President Bush that "they had a plan" that would work, and that he had the postwar security situation all sewn up. Given repeated opportunities to speak up, the Joint Chiefs and other senior officers did not, in any serious way, do so.[11] Those few military officers who did state forceful concerns inside the policy process, such as Lt. Gen. Greg Newbold (Ret.), were either ignored or told to get with the program.[12]

A quirk of the current command structure in the US military helped to produce this result. In today's "combatant commander"–dominated environment, the regional command chiefs (such as the CENTCOM commander), working for the secretary of defense—and not the Joint Chiefs of Staff, the chairman of that group, or the wider Joint Staff that supports them—have the lead in generating and executing war plans. An immense deference has emerged to this arrangement of authorities, to the point that the Joint Chiefs, even the chairman, have become loath to interfere in that command relationship. And the combatant commanders sometimes actively resist oversight: Tommy Franks's dismissive reference to "Title Ten motherfuckers" (Title 10 being the statute that governs the Joint Chiefs), while more profane than most, captures the views that some regional commanders have of the Washington military hierarchy.[13] The Iraq case is yet another reminder that the statutory role of the chairman and service chiefs as military advisors to the president and the National Security Council—and secondarily, their role in offering military advice, after notifying the secretary of defense, to the Congress—is now among the most underdeveloped checks in the process of deciding on and planning for war.

This concept of policy negligence and its associated criteria are meant to apply to the executive branch—the senior officials of national security who debate and discuss and contribute the key advice to a judgment. But a lesser yet still significant degree of blame must be shared by some of the legislators in office at the time. The US Congress is constitutionally charged with the solemn duty of declaring war, something the nation has been incapable of doing for half a century in a full and complete manner, despite all the wars the United States has fought. Yet most of the members who voted for the stand-in declaration of the Iraq war resolution—in some cases endorsing that resolution in language that mirrored the administration's talking points—did strikingly little due diligence about the degree of preparedness, the nature of the war plan, or conceptions for the postwar. It would not have taken very much digging by serious, enterprising congressional staff to have turned up evidence of a brewing fiasco. That senior members of Congress did so little to inhibit the rush to war must count as one of the signal failures of legislative oversight in the modern era.

The failure was equally troubling on the part of another critical social institution that is supposed to provide a check on governmental power in a democracy: the media. Apart from a few lonely reports and essays, the American national media turned remarkably little critical attention to the rising commitment to invade and occupy a far-off land. Many newspapers, magazines, and columnists in fact ended up editorializing in favor of the war, without bothering to do much investigation of either the general requirements of such an operation or the condition of the Bush administration's planning for it. Like so many inside government and like society at large, the media appears to have been caught up in the same cascading momentum, the same sense of imperative, the same view that there wasn't much point debating the issue because the decision had really been made. The result was that like so many others in this tragic drama, the media as an institution bears some proportion of the overall charge of negligence.

Indeed, a related lesson of the Iraq case is that presidents cannot typically manufacture national security tragedies out of whole cloth. Patrick Porter dismisses the idea that Britain's commitment to the Iraq blunder was Tony Blair's personal failure. "Why were people so easily 'charmed,'" he asks, "including Blair's most committed and bitter opponents outside and inside his own party, who were not in the habit of being seduced?" Blair could cajole and persuade, Porter rightly argues, but "did not, and could not, foist the venture on his other compatriots in the dead of night. He could not have undertaken it had the ground been infertile. . . . Even Blair, armed with a well-honed propaganda machine, could only lead Britain to war because many were already receptive to the doctrines in which it rested." Porter concludes: "This was Britain's war too, not just Blair's."[14]

So it was, as we have seen, in the United States: Bush and his administration could lead the country to war only because many of the evolved collective beliefs in the American national psyche made the ground fertile enough to weaken any opposition. Yet this hardly excuses the degree of policy negligence involved—if anything, it magnifies the importance of approaching such decisions with the greatest procedural care. Because what the Iraq case makes clear is that by the time a president and his or her cabinet are ready to bring the nation to war, the checks and balances built into the American system of government will in most cases already have been fatally weakened. The justifications for the war are likely to be too broadly held for the Congress or even the media to put up much of a fight. Diligent, responsible conduct of the executive decision, then, will often be the only barrier to disaster.

The final question, then, is what to do when negligence occurs. Although I have drawn on legal concepts in developing this notion, I do not believe it would be helpful to prosecute, or undertake civil proceedings against, those who engage in policy negligence. Typically, unless the crimes are extreme, holding senior officials legally responsible for their actions will be politically infeasible and socially destabilizing. It would be a start, instead, to establish a more informal norm assuring that decisions will be scrutinized for the criteria outlined above (or something like them) and that officials will be subject to an organized and rigorous assessment—by the media, by scholars, and by former colleagues—to reach a verdict on whether they satisfied their duties of care in the way in which they made their most profound judgments.

This already occurs today, of course, in a broad-based, haphazard, and often partisan manner. Perhaps one way to institutionalize the process and create a more singular evaluation would be to establish a standing national commission, composed of independent thinkers—scholars, former officials, retired military officers—without allegiance to any administration and willing to offer tough and honest opinions. Such a body could receive briefings during an administration on the evolving course of policy debates on the biggest national security issues, especially those involving peace and war. Its members could offer ongoing feedback to the president on what they are finding and then conduct a summary investigation once the administration has ended to reach a final, formal, and public verdict on the quality of the decisions and the potential existence of policy negligence on the part of the outgoing group. A harsh judgment from such a body would impose a price on those who had performed poorly, at least in terms of reputation.

But perhaps the bigger advantage of such a commission would be to create an outside channel of direct, blunt advice to the president—people coming to his or her office more willing to speak openly than many senior and midlevel officials—and thus help head off disasters before they become the basis for a charge of policy negligence. Had such an organization and such a process existed in 2002, President Bush would presumably have received numerous warnings that the Iraq war decision process had been incomplete and that the accompanying planning process was disastrously fragmented. We cannot know if this would have made a decisive difference—but given the stakes of failure in the largest national security judgments, it seems unworthy not even to try.

⋇

We are still left, though, with the problem of explanation—the question of *why*. At least within an administration preparing to go to war, why did profoundly experienced, politically savvy, and in some cases brilliant senior officials not do better? Why did more people not speak up against the emerging decision when it bore such obvious unattended risks?

George Bush's CIA director, George Tenet, implies in his own writings that he disagreed with the decision to go to war. Yet Douglas Feith writes, "I sat with [Tenet] in many of the meetings, and no one prevented him from talking. It is noteworthy that Mr. Tenet met with the president for an intelligence briefing six days every week for years. Why didn't he speak up if he thought that the president was dangerously wrong or inadequately informed?"[15] Rumsfeld has leveled the same charge at Colin Powell, arguing that he debated the timing and packaging of the war but not its essence. President Bush apparently asked senior military leaders in more than one session whether any of them saw reasons not to go to war; none, by all reports, spoke up.

The Iraq case provides helpful—if ultimately disheartening—insight into the reasons why warnings can fail in the midst of a policy headed for disaster. Some of these reasons are well-known hallmarks of motivated reasoning: senior decision-makers, like people in general, typically arrive at their convictions first and then look for evidence to support them. The case for action was grounded in heartfelt beliefs—that Iraq was ready for democracy, that the post-9/11 world demanded a bold and brutal exercise of power to reestablish American credibility—that overrode warnings. The environment of senior government decision-making emphasizes the need to protect one's reputation and hoard political capital, which tends to discourage blunt and open dialogue. And finally, because of the profound uncertainty surrounding such choices, anything less than an unambiguous, shouted-from-the-rooftops alarm will have little effect.

The Iraq case illustrates other barriers to effective warning, and to the operation of the checks and balances within a democratic government that are designed in part to head off such misjudgments. One is a version of the "crying wolf" problem: once one or more senior officials have raised a danger and been rebuffed, the message is sent—to them and others—that the "case has been made" about possible risks and there is little point in further quibbling. In the Iraq example, there are at least a half-dozen potent examples of this phenomenon: Colin Powell's intervention with the president in August 2002, Condoleezza Rice's attempts to get Bush to take postwar security seriously that fall and into January and February 2003, Rumsfeld aide Steve Herbits's direct warning to his boss, the Steve Busby memo and others like it, and Richard Haass's urgent notes to Colin Powell. Many officials told me that in one way or another, these and other futile efforts to highlight dangers convinced them that there was no point to pushing the issue. If warnings are raised, often hesitantly and with insufficient bluntness, evidence, and clarity, and those warnings fail, that halfway attempt can inoculate the process against more serious interrogation of the risks involved.

Yet another way in which warnings failed was that they often flowed upwards to people and offices without the power or, at the moment they got the messages, inclination to do much about them. As various State officials worried to Powell about postwar security, he seems to have thought both that he had already spoken his piece and that those issues were in Don Rumsfeld's lane. Warnings to CENTCOM arrived at a military command working at a feverish pace to ready themselves for major combat operations. Catalogues of risks directed at Rumsfeld were never going to achieve much; he apparently convinced himself that the United States would not be staying long in Iraq and therefore would be absolved of any major perils attendant on a messy postwar period. The seemingly baroque issue of lanes of responsibility turns out to be significant in this regard. After January 2003, with the issuance of NSPD-24, Defense had taken the ball on the postwar; to go directly to Rumsfeld with warnings of impending disaster would have been pointless, while to go around him would have been viewed as a violation of the chain of command.

Warnings must therefore be targeted rather than fired at random. Some former senior officials who might have been more willing to cause trouble were mostly left in the dark about the growing fears at the time. "I would love to have heard those warnings," one claimed ruefully upon reading several of the memos written during the run-up to war. "Whoever they were, they never told anyone who could have done anything about it. . . . If they harbored serious doubts, they could have and should have taken me aside and said, I am really worried. None of them did that."[16] In fact, many thought that they had spoken up in some way. But the Iraq case tells us that, in the byzantine world of national security decision-making, getting the right warnings to the right people at the right moment turns out to be an exercise in navigating a very daunting maze.

Of course, senior leaders can create a culture that is either supportive or dismissive of such efforts. And one obvious reason why the warnings failed in this case is that Rumsfeld, Cheney, and indeed—despite his own belief that he welcomed contrary views—George Bush himself cannot escape accountability for having created a policy environment in which dissent was viewed as pointless and, in the minds of some to whom I have spoken, viewed as a career-endangering act.[17] The almost universal response I received when asking senior officials why they didn't speak out more forcefully was a rueful shake of the head and a quiet statement to this effect: *nobody was going to take it seriously, so why try?* The existence of such a perception throughout government is a leading clue toward solving the riddle of policy negligence behind the Iraq war decision: such self-censorship can exist on a generalized scale only when senior officials have undermined the criteria for meeting a government's duty of care to its people, its soldiers and civil servants, and those in other countries affected by its actions.

A review of the roles of the most senior officials does not, of course, exhaust the question of responsibility. Others such as Paul Wolfowitz,

Douglas Feith, and Scooter Libby pushed for a war with urgent conviction, but without taking care to be sure their assumptions were correct.
Others throughout the bureaucracy with concerns and doubts could have
spoken up more vigorously (or at all). But a critical lesson of this case is
that the overall context for a decision can exercise a critical influence over
the degree to which it will be carefully interrogated—whether the highest
officials will care much about consequences. And the pressure-packed
environment in the Bush administration after 9/11, combined with the
overwhelming (and sometimes quite openly stated) belief that the president had already made his choice, undermined rather than promoted
these goals of careful and responsible judgment. In this they were joined
by the two broader, more timeless factors I have emphasized in earlier
chapters: the missionary sensibility in US foreign policy, and the perceived moral imperatives of a value-driven decision process.

꙰

Vital national security decisions seldom accrue out of thin air, nor do
they represent entirely discrete calculations of costs and benefits. In most
cases, there are ideas at work—ideas motivating the main actors, ideas
at large in the strategic culture of nations, ideas that shape the environment in which choices are made. These ideas inspire, they constrain, they
help fashion the frames and lenses through which decision-makers view
events. And when they are fundamental or foundational enough, they
loom over a judgment process, skewing every thought and debate and,
very often, ruling out objections and concerns in ways that contribute to
disaster.[18] In fact, the most influential ideas can sometimes be the least
apparent: they have become so fundamental and taken for granted that
the main actors in a decision process simply cannot imagine thinking any
differently.

In the Iraq case, the substratum of ideas and beliefs that justified
and propelled the judgment to go to war arose from widely held conventional wisdoms about America's role in the world. Those beliefs reflected
a uniquely messianic notion, grounded in the founding myths and

essential identity of the country, that was turbocharged in the 1990s by the United States' predominant global position and eventually reflected in the views of a number of especially influential groups in the American foreign policy community. Only in light of this broad set of ideas can we understand the case for placing American military might in service of global norms and precedents, or the argument for invading and transforming a culturally alien country of twenty-five million people thousands of miles from America's shores.

This essential notion did not, as Walter McDougall and others have made clear, always have an adventuristic cast. At first, the United States seemed determined to play this role through force of example rather than force of arms. But the underlying ideology creates a foundational expectation that America is duty-bound to point the way to a safer, freer world. How the nation fulfills this responsibility has changed over time, but this basic message can be found embedded in the speeches of presidents and leaders of American foreign policy, and then in US national security documents, over the life of the nation. America is, by its founding identity and national disposition, a missionary nation.

Over time, it became clear that even an idealistic sensibility embodied two sometimes complementary and sometimes conflicting elements: a romantic, value-promoting interpretation of this vision, one that inspired foreign aid and humanitarian missions and sponsorship of human rights; and a hard-edged component—the belief that American military primacy was an essential support system for the obligations of American power, and the claim of a right to undertake coercive actions, including war, to achieve its goals.

The hallmarks of this missionary sensibility, in both its value-promoting and power-seeking guises, are plastered all over the impulses and beliefs that helped produce the decision to invade Iraq. It can be seen, for example, in the idealistic demonstration effect sought by those who hoped that freeing Iraq would set a regional precedent and transform the nature of politics in the Middle East. It emerged in the faith-driven, very consciously messianic intentions of George Bush. It found

expression in the often wild-eyed aspirations of the war-planning documents, which assumed that the United States had the right to sketch out
future political, economic, and social realities in a distant country. In
sum, the United States' decision to invade Iraq was a product, in part, of
its specific conception of itself and its rights and responsibilities on the
world stage.

Administrations that operate in service of this spirit—and all have,
to one degree or another, since about 1943 or 1944—are not composed
of imperialists and warmongers, but instead of well-meaning men and
women who believe that the power and influence of their nation should
be placed in service of something beyond its own selfish interests. The
senior officials of the Bush administration were no different: No different, in the wellsprings of their worldview, than the members of the Truman administration who helped reconstruct a shattered Europe and sent
US forces to counter communist aggression in Korea. No different from
the leaders of the first Bush administration who dispatched US troops
to reverse Iraqi aggression in Kuwait and bring aid and comfort to the
suffering people of Somalia. No different from the Clinton administration foreign policy team that employed US power to end wars and ethnic
cleansing in the Balkans and to enlarge the NATO alliance right up to
Russia's doorstep.

The missionary instinct is not inherently malign or injurious to US
interests. The trick is in distinguishing feasible, pragmatic expressions of
this impulse from its excesses; once a nation has taken up the mantle of
global police officer, it becomes difficult to look away from any crime.
Testing proposed adventures with rigorous analysis and debate will
help—a testing process that involves working diligently to meet the criteria for avoiding policy negligence outlined above. Failure to meet those
criteria, in Iraq as in other cases, is an invitation to catastrophe. The first
factor to look for in emerging tragedies, then, is the American missionary
spirit run riot, heedless of consequences.

But a generalized missionary sensibility is often insufficient to produce the worst tragedies. For that we need a second factor: a moralistic, often event-driven *imperative to act*. The absence of a powerfully felt imperative kept the United States from invading Iraq before 9/11; after that event, the distorted risk calculus and fear of imminent further attacks produced exactly such a value-driven imperative. At such times, judgments are driven by what the decision-maker thinks is the right thing to do rather than what will produce the best outcomes. These imperatives tend to emerge gradually, under the influence of largely unconscious factors. They are not decided upon as much as grown into, not chosen as much as gradually felt, not calculated as much as believed.

Implicitly or explicitly, this tendency has driven many US foreign policy decisions—and those of other major powers as well—over the last seventy years, from the urgently felt need of the British and French to reaffirm their Middle Eastern hegemony in Suez to the Soviet Union's perceived requirement to plunge into Afghanistan. And one of this tendency's primary results is to produce a policy on something like autopilot; when a government is in thrall to a moralistic sense of rightness, it drives forward largely heedless to contrary evidence or argument. Once that sort of conviction has taken hold, doubts become seen as infidelity. Consequences become largely irrelevant; the nation is acting on a form of sacred value. And the resulting policy becomes, in the purest sense of the term, a leap of faith.

Part of the reason decision-makers embrace such imperative-driven thinking is out of a need to deal with the crushing ambiguity of complex jugments. Dozens or hundreds of variables are at work on any national security issue, swirling and interacting in ways that make a classic rationalistic approach of measuring the value of different outcomes unsuited to the task. Decision-makers dealing with such issues are in the market for simplifying rules, principles that cut through the fog of uncertainty and provide clear guidance. Value-driven imperatives—especially tied to the essential beliefs of a nation's foreign policy—help deal with such complexity by simplifying what are otherwise impossibly complex judgments. In their purest form, imperatives specify what *must* be done. They pull the decision-maker out of the baffling, swirling kaleidoscope of events and perceptions and factors and offer a pristine way forward by pointing to the *right thing to do*.

These moralistic imperatives do not, typically, emerge out of thin air. They generally require some sort of catalyst—usually the action, or anticipated action, of a rival or adversary. The United States acquired a moralistic conviction to act in Vietnam in response to perceived communist aggression. The Soviet Union became certain that it had to act in Afghanistan, out of an ultimately incorrect view that the United States was trying to take over the government there. And 9/11 activated a sense of urgency that drove US policy into a value-driven cast of mind that proved—as such value-based thinking tends to be—immune to a serious confrontation with consequences.

What makes such convictions especially destructive of good judgment is that as much as the resulting conclusions will *feel* like reasoning to the decision-makers, they typically arise in largely unconscious, intuitive, emergent ways. This, too, tends to seal them off from critical analysis. Psychologist Robert Burton argues that judgment on complex issues reflects "neither a conscious choice nor even a thought process. Certainty and similar states of 'knowing what we know' arise out of involuntary brain mechanisms that, like love or anger, function independently of reason."[19] This process is gradual, emergent, incremental: Decision-makers absorb information and form impressions, and a judgment *arises* over time—it is not "reached" in one decision moment. It is less of a conscious decision or judgment, in fact, and more of a revelation.

Jonathan Haidt's "social intuitionist" model similarly suggests that "moral judgment is caused by quick moral intuitions and is followed (when needed) by slow, ex post facto moral reasoning."[20] It is, as he argues, "a kind of cognition, but it is not a kind of reasoning." One just "knows" the answer without rational reflection on costs and benefits. And this is precisely the problem with value-driven decision-making in national security: the leaders and officials involved "just know" that something is the right thing to do. They have arrived at a place where analysis and questioning are not only unnecessary—but, all too often, they are perceived as very nearly immoral. Doubters and critics are not, typically, confronted with detailed arguments and data as much as with the accusation that represents a leading hallmark of many value-driven judgments: *you just don't get it.*

The judgment to invade Iraq gives every indication of embodying this sort of value-driven imperative, this kind of revelation, rather than a truly objective calculation of likely costs and benefits. The themes of a value-driven imperative crop up again and again in the decision-making process leading to March 2003.

They crop up, for example, in Dick Cheney's uncompromising conception of the national interest (his "one percent doctrine"), and the obligation for senior officials to protect the American people—an end that justified just about any means. They emerge in President Bush's repeated reference to his certainty that the administration was doing the "right thing" and in his references to the sacred values at stake in responding to the attacks of 9/11. This general theme, that the security of the nation had become a sacred trust that could not be traded off against anything as prosaic as domestic or international law or international public opinion, became universally held within the administration. It was the essential imperative and conviction of the post-9/11 period and explains the mindset of urgency and unconcern for costs and consequences. Value-driven decision-making also emerged in the American duty to protect and spread democracy abroad, something felt powerfully by President Bush and a handful of other senior officials in the administration, and it, too, took on a suddenly moralistic cast.

The power of these and related values helps to explain the rude treatment which greeted anyone in the interagency process who expressed doubts about the proposed course of action, either the general war on terror or the attack on Iraq. They were not merely viewed as offering policy arguments; they were seen as morally tainted.

John Agresto is a former college president and university professor who signed on to go to Iraq and work with ORHA and then CPA to help reform Iraq's higher-education system. He argues that those who went were not part of any cabal or conspiracy; they simply wanted to do good, to promote American national interests, or serve some other goal. The problem was not evil intent. It was, as he wrote years later, "fooling ourselves—fooling ourselves with optimism, with hope, with 'happy talk' as we called it in Baghdad, and with a blindness to the character of our enemies, blindness to the character of the Iraqis we liberated, and blindness to America's own limitations as a liberating power." When people are determined to pursue a mission, "we only see what we want to see, not what's visible," Agresto writes. "Hope may well be a virtue—but in foreign policy, it is more often a sin, a temptation to willful blindness."[21]

Robert Burton's focus in his fascinating book on decision-making is actually on the concept of "certainty," and it is an important and productive theme. Evolving toward a feeling of rightness involves an unconscious process of absorbing information and producing a conviction, and the result of the process can more accurately be described as belief or faith than as reason. "It is impossible to overlook the shared qualities of the *feeling of knowing*, a *sense of faith*, and feelings of *purpose* and *meaning*," Burton writes. "All serve both motivation and reward at the most basic level of thought."[22] Indeed they do, but it is often when leaders reflect such motivated thinking and are caught up in the iron grip of a deeply felt imperative that disaster can ensue.

The challenge is especially acute in high-level political leadership because these positions demand two very different sets of qualities. In order to lead effectively and decisively, senior leaders need certainty and confidence. And in order to avoid errors of judgment, they must retain a deeply felt humility in the face of events and a natural curiosity and hesitation about leaping to conclusions. Striking this balance turns out to be one of the most difficult aspects of leadership on national security issues; specific presidents and senior officials tend to reflect one or the other side of this dichotomy but seldom both. The two factors that helped to fuel the Iraq war—the American missionary sensibility and the urgently felt imperative—had their malign effects in part by skewing this balance, putting all the emphasis on certainty and action rather than care and deliberation. One obvious lesson of the Iraq case, then, is to watch carefully for the hallmarks of such a balance—of leadership, of national mindset and mood—going badly out of whack.

⁊⛵

It is the marriage of these two factors—the driving engine of the messianic sensibility in US foreign policy and the emergence of a specific moralistic urge to act in service of sacred values—that so often produces disasters. The missionary sensibility alone will not, in many cases, overcome the tendency to muddle along, which is the default setting of government policy-making. An urge or imperative, on the other hand, is often just an inchoate feeling without broader philosophies to shape and direct it. It is when the two emerge together that a tragedy or farce ensues: in the toxic combination of messianic anticommunism and anti-Castro desperation that produced the Bay of Pigs; in the same anticommunist obsession and the urgent fear of falling dominoes that propelled the United States into Vietnam; in the Brezhnev Doctrine of holding allies and proxies tightly in the communist orbit, combined with urgent fears that the United States was conspiring with local turncoats, that drove Moscow into its ill-fated adventure in Afghanistan.

I have argued that one of the most important reasons to reconsider the experience of the decision to go to war in Iraq is to draw lessons that can help inform national decisions today. Part of the reason why this is so timely and important is that we see, once again, worrisome hints of this same pattern emerging on major issues of national security.

We see these hallmarks, for example, in the growing moralism and belligerence of US policy toward Russia, a trend that is intensifying an increasingly perilous standoff with the world's other extensively nuclear-armed nation. Our missionary sensibility demands that the United States assert its rights to influence events in Russia's immediate neighborhood, even if the issues involved are secondary to the United States. At the same time, the addiction to primacy in our approach to the world stands as a powerful roadblock to giving Russia a meaningful voice in regional affairs. Russia certainly hears the messianic tone and objectives of US foreign policy, especially in the wake of events like the color revolutions in Europe and the US regime change operations in Iraq and Libya, and fears that it will soon be in the crosshairs of American ambitions. And now, under the influence of recent aggressive actions by Moscow, from poisonings of regime opponents abroad to meddling in democratic processes, many in Washington have descended into an imperative-driven degree of moralism in regard to the necessary US response.

None of this is to excuse Russia's very real violations of norms, any more than the case against war in 2002 constituted an endorsement of Saddam's brutality. This is a connection we must break: anyone who opposes the adventuristic assertion of power is now accused of harboring a decadent approval of the target state's behavior. Just because an autocratic regime is misbehaving, however, does not mandate—or even justify—a belligerent US response. To believe that is to vastly overstate the lesson of the 1930s, which has given the missionary sensibility in US foreign policy a distinctly militant cast. Some read that lesson in the most elaborate way: potential aggressors must be confronted and fought at every possible inch, or they will gain irresistible momentum. But this has rarely been true throughout history and need not be so today. Very few aggressors are Nazi Germany. Most are, like the majority of great powers throughout history, often pragmatic and capable of being deterred or even worked with on shared interests.

Some of the same worrisome signs are apparent in US policy toward Iran. America's missionary sensibility propels us to oppose the regime in Tehran on essentialist terms, and causes us to see it as an irredeemably theocratic, militaristic, revisionist power rather than the troublesome but largely pragmatic regime it has now become. Its nuclear ambitions have provided the spark for a renewed sense of sacred imperative: the whiff of regime change again surrounds US policy.

Perhaps most perilously, the same pattern is beginning to shape the US approach to China. The American missionary spirit creates an inherent tension in this relationship to begin with, both because it commits—on the basis of principle, not judgment—American power to the containment of Chinese regional ambitions, and because Chinese leaders perceive that the United States ultimately desires regime change, at least of a sort. The sense is growing in Washington that the United States simply may not be able to share the world stage with this ever-more-powerful autocracy, dedicated as it seems to be to developing horrifying technologies of repression, obtaining a veto power on all activities in Asia, and dominating key elements of the global economy. These are absolutely areas for concern, and to be fair to the rising group of China hawks in the United States, it is not clear whether China's domestic and international behavior will remain moderate enough to avoid a severe break. But the American brand of messianic self-conception imbues this trajectory with a particular danger: the implicit objective is not merely to fashion a wary but stable relationship with a tough competitor, but rather to bottle up China's demand for equal status and to transform Chinese governance and society along American lines. This Beijing cannot abide.

This sense of urgency and imperative to confront China seems to be growing by the day. In some cases this is warranted; neither the United States nor the other value-sharing democracies can sit idly by while China steals intellectual property; forces foreign companies to turn over prized secrets for the right to operate there; engages in repeated cyberintrusions of Western governments and businesses; and buys up foreign companies to obtain their technology, patents, and human capital. But competitions can take many forms—calm, unemotional, persistent, and restrained; or moralistic, ardent, paranoid, and overdramatized. The patterns illustrated by the Iraq decision, if applied to specific choices in the emerging rivalry with China—and if they generate a policy on autopilot of an urgent, suspicious cast—could push the United States toward judgments far more perilous than the Iraq war.

⚜

What, then, can we do about these risks? How can the United States—officials of future administrations, members of Congress, the American people—avoid another misjudgment on the scale of Iraq? Doing so demands, first of all, awareness: an official class, legislative branch, national media, and voting populace that all possess a more self-conscious appreciation for the risks of the messianic turn of mind. That way of thinking remains alive and well throughout the US national security community, ready to stand behind US policy, especially in moments of crisis, and shove it into new calamities.

The trick is to avoid throwing the benefits of American global activism overboard even as we draw limits on its ambitions. America's postwar effort to build the architecture of a global order has had important benefits for the United States and the world. It also provides the United States arguably the most significant competitive advantage ever enjoyed by a great power: it has allowed us to rally the efforts of dozens of value-sharing democracies and, often, to speak in their name as a defender of such principles as nonaggression. The American advocacy of human rights and democratic values has helped to embed those hopeful principles in world politics and provided an inspiration to activists the world over.

But the time for a course correction has clearly arrived. When we encounter new proposed missions, Americans must be willing to cast a more skeptical eye—to empower those participants in the debate who believe in American power but who have no interest in seeing it squandered on reckless adventures. We must be willing to admit that when other countries take hostile actions, they are sometimes reacting to what the United States is doing to *them*, not (always) acting out of premeditated malice. We must be ready to take other countries' interests seriously, rather than writing them off as an inconvenient and ultimately illegitimate speed bump in the way of American value promotion.

The Iraq experience provides the American people with a very specific roster of questions to ask a president before approving any new global adventure. As might be expected, they reflect the concerns expressed in the criteria for policy negligence outlined above. Does the threat truly justify massive military action? What are the precise risks, and have they been mitigated? Who, inside or outside government, has expressed doubts, and have they been heeded? Are you certain that some of your senior officials are not quashing internal dissent or broadcasting exaggerated justifications? Are you prepared for the aftermath of your gambit, and if so, how?

This will take effort, because, as I have argued, the urge to load up the troop ships seldom emerges out of thin air. It comes in the aftermath of a crisis or an attack. It has been whipped into a preset frenzy by months or years of demonizing another country or leader. And when it arrives, the "feeling of rightness" that presses itself upon a nation—not merely upon senior officials—produces a passionate urge to abandon critical analysis, throw caution to the wind, and *just act*.

The next time—even after a national tragedy on the scale of 9/11— the American people need to make clear that their first demand, before retribution, before lashing out, is for their leaders to *think*.

※

One of the sources I consulted in the course of my research was a highly experienced civil servant, a senior official in the Bush administration who had worked up close with Rumsfeld and Rice and Wolfowitz and Feith and Libby, and who spoke of his frustration with the "policy types" who pushed an ill-informed concept without a clear sense of how they were going to make it happen. The problem was, he pointed out, that such missionary thinking was endemic to our system: US administrations, whether Democratic or Republican, were typically populated with senior national security officials whose ideology was infused with the collective myths of the nation and fired by the commitment to personal visions— visions sometimes disconnected from reality. Iraq was far from the first example of this type of excessive, imperative-driven expression of our deeply admirable, but nonetheless volatile, national instincts. And, he worried, it would not be the last.

As he showed me out of his office, I thanked him for his time. He paused, remembering the theme on which we had finished and its implications.

"You know, it will happen again," he said. "We'll do it again."

NOTES

1. Friedrich Nietzsche, *On Truth and Untruth*, trans. and ed. Taylor Carman (New York: HarperPerennial, 2010), 131.

CHAPTER 1: UNDERSTANDING A TRAGEDY
1. Aeschylus, *Persians*, in *Aeschylus: Complete Plays*, vol. 2, trans. Carl H. Mueller (Hanover, NH: Smith and Kraus, 2002), 126.
2. George F. Will, "Let America Plunge Toward Our Fast-Unfolding Future," *Washington Post*, June 21, 2017.
3. Hans J. Morgenthau, "The Influence of Reinhold Niebuhr in American Political Life and Thought," in Harold R. Landon, ed., *Reinhold Niebuhr: A Prophetic Voice in Our Time* (Greenwich, CT: Seabury Press, 1962), 106.
4. More than you would ever want to know: http://aboutcampdavid.blogspot.com/.
5. Michael Morell, *The Great War of Our Time* (New York: 12 Books, 2015), 61.
6. George H. W. Bush and Brent Scowcroft, *A World Transformed* (New York: Knopf, 1998), 74–75.
7. George W. Bush, *Decision Points* (New York: Crown, 2010) 185.
8. Bush, *Decision Points*, 238.
9. Interviewee 24; the debate is described in Karen DeYoung, *Soldier: The Life of Colin Powell* (New York: Alfred A. Knopf, 2006), 409.
10. Bob Woodward, *Plan of Attack* (New York: Simon and Schuster, 2004), 175.
11. Interviewee 7.
12. Donald Rumsfeld, *Known and Unknown* (New York: Sentinel, 2011), 437–438.
13. Bush, *Decision Points*, 239.
14. Marina Koren, "New Estimates Suggest US War Led to Nearly Half a Million Iraqi Deaths," *National Journal*, October 15, 2013. See also Philip Bump, "15 Years After the Iraq War Began, The Death Toll Is Still Murky," *Washington Post*, March 20, 2018; and http://www.iraqbodycount.org/.
15. The official US Department of Defense casualty figures can be found at https://dod .defense.gov/News/Casualty-Status/.
16. George W. Will, "The Second-Most Dangerous American," *Washington Post*, March 23, 2018.

17. Russ Baker, "Real Reason for Iraq Invasion, Finally?" *Huffington Post*, February 7, 2011, http://www.huffingtonpost.com/russ-baker/real-reason-for-iraq-inva_b _819426.html.

18. See, for example, Justin Frank, *Bush on the Couch: Inside the Mind of the President* (New York: HarperCollins, 2004), 12. Frank contends that Barbara Bush's rather distant maternal style and other characteristics of the Bush family cultivated in the young George Bush an inability to adequately internalize mature conceptions of complex, nuanced realities; of a mixed and balanced portrait of himself; and of a vision of the world composed of grays rather than blacks and whites. The result, Frank claims, was "the cultivation of a fantasy world dominated by the struggle between good and evil" and the experiencing of enemies as "evil and one-dimensional, rather than integrated in his mind as a whole people. Because he experiences them in this way, he feels free to harm them without pity or loss."

19. Alan Greenspan wrote in his memoir that "the Iraq War is largely about oil." Graham Petersen, "Alan Greenspan Claims Iraq War Really Was for Oil," *The Times (UK)*, September 16, 2007. Greenspan later backtracked somewhat; see Bob Woodward, "Greenspan: Ouster of Hussein Crucial for Oil Security," *Washington Post*, September 17, 2007. A leading proponent of this viewpoint has been Michael Klare; see Klare, "Blood for Oil, in Iraq and Elsewhere," in Jane K. Cramer and A. Trevor Thrall, *Why Did the United States Invade Iraq?* (London: Routledge, 2012), 129–144. See also John S. Duffield, "Oil and the Decision to Invade Iraq," in Cramer and Thrall, *Why Did the United States*, 145.

20. The most mainstream version of this argument—and the connection between pro-Israel views and neoconservative activists—is made in John Mearsheimer and Stephen Walt, *The Israel Lobby and US Foreign Policy* (New York: Farrar, Straus and Giroux, 2007). A different take can be found in George Packer, *The Assassin's Gate: America in Iraq* (New York: Farrar, Straus and Giroux, 2005), 30. For an effective critique of the Iraq war argument, see Jerome Slater, "Explaining the Iraq War: The Israel Lobby Theory," in Cramer and Thrall, *Why Did the United States*, 101–113.

21. See, for example, Naomi Klein, "Baghdad Year Zero," *Harpers*, September 2004, http://harpers.org/archive/2004/09/0080197.

22. See Michael Lind, "Neoconservatism and American Hegemony," in Cramer and Thrall, *Why Did the United States*, 114–128; and Lawrence Wilkerson, "The White House Cabal," *Los Angeles Times*, October 25, 2005.

23. James Dao, "Antiwar Republican Is No Longer Party's Pariah," *New York Times*, June 6, 2011.

24. http://en.wikipedia.org/wiki/Rationale_for_the_Iraq_War.

25. Richard Haass, *War of Necessity, War of Choice: A Memoir of Two Iraq Wars* (New York: Simon and Schuster, 2009), 234.

26. Packer, *Assassin's Gate*, 46.

27. Condoleezza Rice, *No Higher Honor: A Memoir of My Years in Washington* (New York: Crown, 2011), 180–181. Bush offers precisely the same quote in *Decision Points*, 239.

28. Dick Cheney, *In My Time: A Personal and Political Memoir* (New York: Simon and Schuster, 2011), 390–391.

29. Peter Baker, *Days of Fire: Bush and Cheney in the White House* (New York: Doubleday, 2013), 216.

30. "The history, the logic, and the facts," Bush said in the speech, "lead to one conclusion: Saddam Hussein's regime is a grave and gathering danger. . . . To assume this regime's good faith is to bet the lives of millions and the peace of the world in a reckless gamble. And this is a risk we must not take." He demanded not only a full accounting of WMDs, but also an end to support for terror, to repression, and to the oil-for-food corruption, as well as the return of remaining Gulf War prisoners; see White House, *Selected Speeches of George W. Bush, 2001–2008*, 145.

31. On the afternoon of September 7, British prime minister Tony Blair had arrived at Camp David to join the conversation. When he and Bush spoke to the press that afternoon, Blair wasted no time jumping to the bottom line. "The threat from Saddam Hussein and weapons of mass destruction—chemical, biological, potentially nuclear weapons capability—that threat is real," he told the gathered reporters. "And the policy of inaction is not a policy we can responsibly subscribe to." When it was his turn to speak, Bush agreed. "Well, as you know, our government in 1998—action that my administration has embraced—decided that this regime was not going to honor its commitments to get rid of weapons of mass destruction. The Clinton administration supported regime change Many members of the current United States Senate supported regime change. My administration still supports regime change." The CNN commentator who came on immediately afterward described the process as one designed to seek "support when it comes to military action and ousting Saddam Hussein"; "Bush, Blair Address Reporters," CNN Transcript, September 7, 2002, at http://www.cnn.com/TRANSCRIPTS/0209/07/bn.01.html.

32. Interviewee 24.

33. Interviewee 39.

34. Donald Rumsfeld, Memorandum, "Testimony on Iraq," September 13, 2002, 2:39 p.m., declassified January 9, 2009, and available on the Rumsfeld Papers website, http://papers.rumsfeld.com/.

35. Donald Rumsfeld, Memorandum, "Hill Expectations," September 13, 2002, 12:36 p.m., declassified January 9, 2009, available at Rumsfeld Papers website.

36. As early as July of 2002, Rumsfeld had written other NSC members about organizing the Iraqi exile community "to assist with regime change," in part "to make sure the wrong people don't fill the vacuum created by the end of the Saddam regime." Regime change, the memo continued, "should not be simply the result of an American 'invasion.'" Donald Rumsfeld, Memorandum, "Supporting the Iraqi Opposition," July 1, 2002, declassified October 12, 2010, available on Rumsfeld Papers website.

37. Quoted in Nicholas Lemann, "How It Came to War," *New Yorker*, March 31, 2003, 4. The account is described in Haass, *War of Necessity*, 4–6.

38. Elisabeth Bumiller, "Bush Aides Set Strategy to Sell Policy on Iraq," *New York Times*, September 7, 2002.

39. Interviewee 39.

40. Peter Schweizer and Rochelle Schweizer, *The Bushes: Portrait of a Dynasty* (New York: Doubleday, 2004), 389.

41. David Frum, *The Right Man: The Surprise Presidency of George W. Bush* (New York: Random House, 2003), 67.

42. Frank Bruni, *Ambling Into History: The Unlikely Odyssey of George W. Bush* (New York: HarperCollins, 2002), 9.

43. Scott McClellan, *What Happened: Inside the Bush White House and Washington's Culture of Deception* (New York: PublicAffairs, 2008), 235, 301–303.

44. David Kuo, *Tempting Faith: An Inside Story of Political Seduction* (New York: Free Press, 2006), 113, 117.

45. Bob Woodward, *Bush at War* (New York: Simon and Schuster, 2002), 256.

46. Jim Rasenberger, *The Brilliant Disaster: JFK, Castro, and America's Doomed Invasion of Cuba's Bay of Pigs* (New York: Scribner, 2011), 390.

47. Patrick Porter, *Blunder: Britain's War in Iraq* (Oxford: Oxford University Press, 2018), 1.

48. Rasenberger, *Brilliant Disaster*, xv.

49. David Kaiser, *American Tragedy: Kennedy, Johnson, and the Origins of the Vietnam War* (Cambridge, MA: Harvard University Press, 2002), 495–496.

CHAPTER 2: THE ORIGINS OF A CONVICTION

1. Ali A. Allawi, *The Occupation of Iraq: Winning the War, Losing the Peace* (New Haven, CT: Yale University Press, 2007), 1.

2. James C. Thomson Jr., "How Could Vietnam Happen?—An Autopsy," *The Atlantic*, April 1968.

3. Karl Reinhardt, "Illusion and Truth in *Oedipus Tyrannus*," in Harold Bloom, ed., *Sophocles' Oedipus Rex* (New York: Chelsea House Publishers, 1988), 102.

4. Baer's volume was cleared by the CIA's prepublication review board. Unfortunately, the CIA censor removed a key word or phrase at just this point in Baer's memoir. As he writes, the CIA's goal was "to [DELETED] the Iraqi dissidents overthrow Saddam"; Robert Baer, *See No Evil: The True Story of a Ground Soldier in the CIA's War on Terrorism* (New York: Crown, 2002), 174.

5. Martin Indyk, *Innocent Abroad: An Intimate Account of American Peace Diplomacy in the Middle East* (New York: Simon and Schuster, 2009), 160.

6. Interviewee 66.

7. This event is also described in Kenneth M. Pollack, *The Threatening Storm: The Case for Invading Iraq* (New York: Random House, 2002), 72–73.

8. Richard Bonin, *Arrows of the Night: Ahmad Chalabi's Long Journey to Triumph in Iraq* (New York: Doubleday, 2011), 98; Baer, *See No Evil*, 180–187.

9. Interviewee 66.

10. Bonin, *Arrows of the Night*, 101.

11. Indyk, *Innocent Abroad*, 160.

12. Bonin, *Arrows of the Night*, 101–103; Baer, *See No Evil*, p. 173; Aram Roston, *The Man Who Pushed America to War: The Extraordinary Life, Adventures, and Obsesions of Ahmad Chalabi* (New York: Nation Books, 2008), 111.

13. Hersh, "The Iraq Hawks."

14. Charles A. Duelfer and Stephen Benedict Dyson, "Chronic Misperception and International Conflict: The U.S.-Iraq Experience," *International Security* 36, no. 1 (Summer 2011): 84–85.

15. Saddam was "deeply disturbed by what he saw as American double-dealing," former CIA officer John Nixon explains. He and his top aides "struggled for weeks to comprehend it." It didn't make sense: Ronald Reagan had struck against Libya in 1986 but was now cozying up to Iran, which "plays a greater role in terrorism," as Saddam told his interrogators. John Nixon, *Debriefing the President: The Interrogation of Saddam Hussein* (New York: Blue Rider Press, 2016), 78–80.

16. James A. Baker, *The Politics of Diplomacy: Revolution, War and Peace, 1989–1992* (New York: G. P. Putnam's, 1995), 262–263. See also Pollack, *The Threatening Storm*, 28; and Richard Haass, *War of Necessity, War of Choice: A Memoir of Two Iraq Wars* (New York: Simon and Schuster, 2009), 43–47.

17. Interviewee 68. The overall policy, as summarized by a US Joint Staff paper of the period, suggested the "use of economic, political and military incentives to increase US influence, enhance US access and moderate Iraqi behavior." Declassified cable from Commander, US Central Command to Joint Staff, "Proposed US-Iraq Military Initiatives," November 29, 1989.

18. The preparatory memo for the meeting listed among its "key points" that "our interests argue for a strengthened relationship with Iraq"; US Department of State, Memorandum to Secretary Baker from James H. Kelly, "Meeting with Iraqi Foreign Minister Tariq Aziz," October 4, 1989, declassified February 11, 1993. There was "no evidence" of Iraqi chemical weapons use since 1983, the memo stated, though it did admit that Iraq "is developing a BW [biological weapons] capability." In October, Baker saw Iraqi Foreign Minister Tariq Aziz and assured him that "the United States valued its relationship with Iraq and wanted to see it strengthened and broadened." In January 1990, the Bush administration extended Iraq $200 million in new credits for grain purchases, and Baker told Aziz that this "reflects the importance we attach to our relationship with Iraq"; Baker, *The Politics of Diplomacy*, 264–267. The Iraqi regime continued to worry that the United States sought their removal from power, and complained about supposed efforts to Baker, who replied with a private message to Aziz through the US Embassy in Baghdad. "The United States," it said, "seeks a broadened and deepened relationship with Iraq on the basis of mutual respect. That is the policy of the president." He promised Aziz that "the United States is not involved in any effort to weaken or destabilize Iraq." Such efforts, Baker continued, would be "completely contrary to the president's policy, which is to work to strengthen the relationship between the United States and Iraq whenever possible." US Department of State, "Message from Secretary Baker to Tariq Aziz," October 21, 1989, declassified May 31, 1994.

19. An April 1990 State Department cable from the US Embassy in Baghdad suggested that recent Iraqi actions had "caused a sharp deterioration in US-Iraqi relations." Since the previous fall, there had been a "series of disappointments which have raised real concerns about Iraqi intentions." Iraq had been criticizing the US role in the Gulf; it had an "abysmal human rights record"; an Iraqi diplomat had been expelled from the United Nations; and Baghdad had tried to avoid continuing sanctions by smuggling arms; US Embassy Baghdad, Cable to US Embassies in Paris and Moscow, "Background on Relations with Iraq," April 29, 1990, declassified January 29, 1993.

20. See, for example, US Department of State, Information Memorandum, "DC Meeting on Iraq," April 1990, declassified February 3, 1993; State Department Cable from Secretary of State to US Embassy Baghdad, February 27, 1990, "Assistant Secretary Kelly's Conversation with Iraqi Ambassador," declassified May 4, 1994; and US Department of Commerce, "Interagency Meeting on Iraq," June 11, 1990, declassified September 28, 1992.

21. US Department of State Office of Intelligence and Research, Memorandum to the Secretary, "Iraqi Nuclear Program," March 30, 1990, declassified December 7, 1993. An April 16, 1990, Deputies Committee session requested an options paper, which outlined a range of actions that could respond to recent Iraqi provocations, from simple economic sanctions to "a virtually total economic embargo and political break with Iraq"; US Department of State, Memorandum for Brent Scowcroft, "Options Paper on Iraq," May 16, 1990, declassified on May 28, 1992.

22. As late as the end of May, a point paper in advance of a Deputies Committee meeting extolled the "actual and potential" economic opportunities in closer US-Iraqi ties, and contended that "Iraq does not want to damage its relationship with the US and has so signaled in a variety of ways"; US Joint Staff J-5, "Position Paper," May 25, 1990, declassified on March 7, 1994.

23. In a cable on July 22, a week before the invasion, the US Embassy in Baghdad concluded that "Arab diplomats here are somewhat 'optimistic' . . . that Iraqi political, media and military posing is solely for the purpose of ensuring higher oil prices and some cash infusion from Arab sources, and is likely to diminish after July 25," assuming the OPEC meeting on that day went well; US Embassy Baghdad, "Kuwait: Iraq Keeps Up the Pressure," July 22, 1990, declassified October 18, 1991. As Richard Haass explains in his memoir, the history of US policy may have inclined the administration away from thinking Saddam would actually invade. Other Arab countries worried that harsh threats might actually goad Saddam into action rather than deterring him. The direct messages they sent were couched in language designed to preserve the potential for good relations, which may have watered down their deterrent effect; Haass, *War of Necessity*, 56–59.

24. Baker, *The Politics of Diplomacy*, 274; on this period see also Haass, *War of Necessity*, 48–59.

25. William Taubman, *Gorbachev: His Life and Times* (New York: Simon and Schuster, 2017), 566.

26. *Comprehensive Report of the Special Advisor to the DCI on Iraq's WMD*, vol. 1 of 3, September 30, 2004, 42; hereafter cited as the Duelfer Report.

27. "Saddam's supreme, even mystical, confidence in his own abilities and wisdom allowed him to ignore or discount the practical considerations raised by others," one analysis, based in part on testimony of Iraqi generals, has concluded; Kevin M. Woods, with Michael R. Pease, Mark E. Stout, Williamson Murray, and James G. Lacey, *Iraqi Perspectives Project: A View of Operation Iraqi Freedom from Saddam's Senior Leadership* (Norfolk, VA: Joint Center for Operational Analysis, US Joint Forces Command, March 2006), 12.

28. Nixon, *Debriefing the President*, 134.

29. On August 20, George H. W. Bush issued National Security Directive 45, on "US Policy in Response to the Iraqi Invasion of Kuwait," which spelled out the series of actions including military force authorized to reverse Iraqi aggression. NSD was declassified on November 22, 1996.

30. Colin Powell, *My American Journey* (New York: Ballantine Books, 1995), 451.

31. Karen DeYoung, *Soldier: The Life of Colin Powell* (New York: Alfred A. Knopf, 2006), 194–195.

32. Powell, *My American Journey*, 457.

33. Powell, *My American Journey*, 466–467.

34. DeYoung, *Soldier*, 198, 201.

35. As the army's official history puts it, the "cease-fire occurred more quickly than anyone expected," and the "postwar process that had existed only in concept was now imminent"; quoted in William Flavin, "Planning for Conflict Termination and Post-Conflict Success," *Parameters* (Autumn 2003): 99, 109.

36. "The truth is there was no interest in going to Baghdad," Richard Haass explains. "I do not recall any dissent on this point"; Haass, *War of Necessity*, 131.

37. There is little mention of this expectation in George Bush and Brent Scowcroft, *A World Transformed* (New York: Alfred A. Knopf, 1998), 484–492. James A. Baker, *The Politics of Diplomacy* (New York: G. P. Putnam's Sons, 1995), 442, says quite explicitly that regional allies expected a coup against Saddam within a year, and that while deposing Saddam was never a formal goal of the Gulf War "we never really expected him to survive a defeat of such magnitude."

38. Interviewee 66.

39. Quoted in "Oral History Interview: Dick Cheney," PBS *Frontline*, "Bush's War," 1996, available at http://www.pbs.org/wgbh/pages/frontline/gulf/oral/cheney/2.html.

40. Dick Cheney, *In My Time: A Personal and Political Memoir* (New York: Simon and Schuster, 2011), 226.

41. Interviewee 66.

42. Jay C. Davis and David A. Kay, "Iraq's Secret Nuclear Weapons Program," *Physics Today*, July 1992, 21–27.

43. George Tenet, *At the Center of the Storm: My Years at the CIA* (New York: HarperCollins, 2007), 330.

44. Policy-makers learned their own lessons from the experience: US intelligence tended to underplay, rather than exaggerate, emerging threats. Even some nuclear inspectors made this case forcefully. A leading example was David Kay, the most prominent member of the 1991 inspections team, who argued that "the only way out of this is the replacement of Saddam"; see "Interview: David Kay," *Frontline,* "Spying on Saddam," 1999, available at http://www.pbs.org/wgbh/pages/frontline/shows /unscom/.

45. "It must be said," Richard Haass admits of Bush administration policy after the war, "that US policy during this period was ragged." The administration had exhausted itself planning and preparing for a successful war—and as is so often the case, simply hadn't had the mental energy to think through what would happen afterward; Haass, *War of Necessity*, 136. His mention of postwar discussions of regime change is on pp. 148–149.

46. Interviewee 66.

47. Nixon, *Debriefing the President,* 141–142.

48. John Lee Anderson, "American Viceroy: Zalmay Khalilzad's Mission," *New Yorker,* December 19, 2005, 62–63. Khalilzad himself describes this turn of views in his memoir, *The Envoy* (New York: St. Martin's Press, 2016), 69–71.

49. Bob Woodward, *State of Denial: Bush at War, Part III* (New York: Simon and Schuster, 2006), 77.

50. Al Gore, "Defeating Hussein, Once and For All," *New York Times,* September 26, 1991.

51. Thomas Ricks, *Fiasco: The American Military Adventure in Iraq* (New York: Penguin Press, 2006), 16.

52. Bill Keller, "The Sunshine Warrior," *New York Times Magazine,* September 22, 2002, 54.

53. One account of his post-Pentagon tenure at the World Bank spoke of a leader known for "adopting a single-minded position on certain matters, refusing to entertain alternative views, marginalizing dissenters"; Steven R. Weisman, " 'Second Chance' at Career Goes Sour for Wolfowitz," *New York Times,* May 18, 2007, http://www .nytimes.com/2007/05/18/washington/18worldbank.html?pagewanted=all&_r=0.

54. See Weisman, " 'Second Chance' at Career Goes Sour for Wolfowitz." See also Todd S. Purdum, *A Time of Our Choosing: America's War in Iraq* (New York: Times Books, 2003), 14.

55. Interviewee 27. Some tell stories of his absentmindedness; when president of the World Bank and visiting a local market, he had to borrow ninety dollars to buy some token goods because he had not brought any money. John Cassidy, "The Next Crusade: Paul Wolfowitz at the World Bank," *New Yorker,* April 9, 2007, 36.

56. Interviewee 11.

57. Interviewee 42.

58. Keller, "The Sunshine Warrior," 50–51. One longtime friend told an interviewer that "Paul is a bit of a softie. . . . He really believes in helping people who are economically deprived or who have nasty or corrupt governments." The writer

Christopher Hitchens described Wolfowitz as a "bleeding heart. His instincts are those of a liberal democrat, apart from on national security"; Cassidy, "The Next Crusade," 36, 39, 41.

59. Paul Wolfowitz, "Remembering the Future," *The National Interest*, Spring 2000, 35–41. A good discussion of this aspect of Wolfowitz's worldview is Andrew J. Bacevich, "A Letter to Paul Wolfowitz," *Harper's Magazine*, March 2013.

60. For an excellent history of Wolfowitz's statements and evolving thinking on Iraq, see James Mann, *Rise of the Vulcans: The History of Bush's War Cabinet* (New York: Viking, 2004), 234–238.

61. Bonin, *Arrows of the Night*, 59.

62. Interviewee 27. The former Bush administration official Dov Zakheim agreed in his memoir that Wolfowitz had become "haunted" by the choice to let Saddam stay in power; Dov S. Zakheim, *A Vulcan's Tale: How the Bush Administration Mismanaged the Reconstruction of Afghanistan* (Washington, DC: Brookings Institution Press, 2011), 30.

63. See "Interview: Kanan Makiya," http://www.pbs.org/wgbh/pages/frontline/shows /truth/interviews/makiya.html.

64. DeYoung, *Soldier*, 212; Paul Wolfowitz, "Rising Up," *New Republic*, December 7, 1998, 12. Zalmay Khalilzad explains that Wolfowitz pressed unsuccessfully for such a plan at the end of the Gulf War—having the American aircraft already patrolling the postwar skies begin launching raids in support of the Iraqis who had risen up against Saddam. The two argued the case so insistently that Powell called Wolfowitz and told him to get his "civilians in the Pentagon" to stop advocating military plans; Zalmay Khalilzad, *The Envoy: From Kabul to the White House, My Journey through a Turbulent World* (New York: St. Martin's Press, 2016), 72–73.

65. See, for example, Haass, *War of Necessity*, 235–236.

66. Woods et al., *Iraqi Perspectives Project*, 15–16.

67. Roston, *The Man Who Pushed America to War*, 43–63. Andersen auditors found that a later financial institution founded in Jordan had inflated its claims of available capital by a factor of ten; Bonin, *Arrows of the Night*, 31–44.

68. Bonin, *Arrows of the Night*, 51.

69. Interviewee 66.

70. Barry Posen has argued that the post–Cold War debate has not been about whether to seek primacy, but what sort of primacy to seek; see, for example, Barry Posen, "Command of the Commons: The Military Foundation of US Hegemony," *International Security* 28, no. 1 (Summer 2003): 6. See also Posen, "Stability and Change in US Grand Strategy," *Orbis* (Fall 2007): 563. A classic argument about the role of liberal ideals in shaping American political culture is Louis Hartz, *The Liberal Tradition in America* (San Diego: Harcourt, Brace, Jovanovich, 1955). For more modern arguments about the missionary sensibility, see Christopher Layne, *The Peace of Illusions* (Ithaca, NY: Cornell University Press, 2006); Fred Kaplan, *Daydream Believers: How a Few Grand Ideas Wrecked American Power* (New York: John Wiley and Sons 2008); and Barry Posen, *Restraint: A New Foundation for US Grand Strategy* (Ithaca, NY: Cornell University Press, 2015).

71. William Kristol and Robert Kagan, "Toward a Neo-Reaganite Foreign Policy," *Foreign Affairs* 75, no. 4 (July–August 1996): 23. Patrick Porter shows than even presidents who come into office overtly skeptical of this instinct eventually get converted by it; Patrick Porter, "Why America's Grand Strategy Has Not Changed: Power, Habit, and the US Foreign Policy Establishment," *International Security* 42, no. 4 (Spring 2018).

72. For a discussion of the historiography here, see Michael Adas, "From Settler Colony to Global Hegemon: Integrating the Exceptionalist Narrative of the American Experience into World History," *The American Historical Review* 106, no. 5 (December 2001).

73. Walter A. McDougall, "Back to Bedrock: The Eight Traditions of American Statecraft," *Foreign Affairs* 76, no. 2 (March–April 1997), 135. For the full version of his argument, see *Promised Land, Crusader State: The American Encounter with the World Since 1776* (New York: Houghton Mifflin, 1997).

74. One measure of the nation's habitual aloofness was that just two months before Pearl Harbor, only 17 percent of Americans wanted their country to get involved in the war; Walter A. McDougall, *The Tragedy of US Foreign Policy: How America's Civil Religion Betrayed the National Interest* (New Haven, CT: Yale University Press, 2016), 209. For a broader view of the constraints on crusaderism before World War II, see pp. 30–31.

75. McDougall, "Back to Bedrock," 135.

76. McDougall, *The Tragedy of US Foreign Policy*, 2, 6.

77. For more recent arguments about the missionary sensibility, see Christopher A. Preble, *The Power Problem: How American Military Dominance Makes Us Less Safe, Less Prosperous, and Less Free* (Ithaca, NY: Cornell University Press, 2009); Robert W. Merry, *Sands of Empire: Missionary Zeal, American Foreign Policy, and the Hazards of Global Ambition* (New York: Simon and Schuster, 2005); Andrew J. Bacevich, *The New American Militarism: How Americans Are Seduced by War* (New York: Oxford University Press, 2013). Perhaps the single classic work is Reinhold Niebuhr, *The Irony of American History* (Chicago: University of Chicago Press, reprint ed., 2008).

78. James Chace, "Imperial America and the Common Interest," *World Policy Journal* 19, no. 1 (Spring 2002): 7.

79. John Judis, "The Chosen Nation: The Influence of Religion on US Foreign Policy," Brookings Policy Brief No. 37 (March 2005), available at http://carnegieendowment.org/files/PB37.judis.FINAL.pdf.

80. Niebuhr, *The Irony of American History*, 24, 69–70, 133.

81. Preble, *The Power Problem*, 4.

82. Michael Ignatieff, "The American Empire: The Burden," *New York Times*, January 5, 2003.

83. For a powerful statement of this worldview, see William Kristol and Robert Kagan, "Introduction: National Interest and Global Responsibility," in Kristol and Kagan, eds., *Present Dangers: Crisis and Opportunity in American Foreign and Defense*

Policy (San Francisco: Encounter Books, 2000), 10, 21. Elsewhere, Kagan and Kristol called for a "benevolent global hegemony": "In a world in which peace and American security depend on American power and the will to use it," they argued, "American hegemony is the only reliable defense against a breakdown of peace and international order." William Kristol and Robert Kagan, "Toward a Neo-Reaganite Foreign Policy," *Foreign Affairs*, July–August 1996.

84. Donald Rumsfeld, *Known and Unknown* (New York: Sentinel, 2011), 282–283.

85. In December 2001, Rumsfeld himself translated some of these ideas into a paper on deterrence to guide thinking in the still-embryonic war on terror. It began with a list of American failures in the 1990s—the 1993 attack on the World Trade Center, the April 1993 assassination attempt against former president Bush that "went unpunished," Somalia, "softness" on North Korea, the USS *Cole* bombing, and so on. "In short," the memo argued, "for some eight years, the US deterrent was weakened as a result of a series of actions that persuaded the world that the US was 'leaning back,' not 'leaning forward.'" Such actions "contributed to a weakened deterrent in that they told the world that the US, if tweaked, would flinch, thereby persuading hostile nations and actors that they can harm the US without risk to themselves." Donald Rumsfeld, "How US Deterrence Has Been Weakened," December 11, 2001; attached to Rumsfeld, "Paper on Deterrence," memo to Paul Wolfowitz, January 4, 2002, released through DoD FOIA process, available at DoD FOIA website, Rumsfeld folder.

86. Evan Thomas, Tamara Lipper, and Roy Gutman, "Chemistry in the War Cabinet," *Newsweek*, January 28, 2002, 26.

87. Indeed, a US State Department options memo from May of 1990 had concluded that "The political opposition to Saddam and the Ba'ath Party, such as it is, is down-at-the-heels, mostly in exile, and (apart from some Kurds) lacks a following in Iraq." The paper mentioned a possibility of supporting such groups but concluded that "There is little to recommend this option"; US Department of State, Memorandum for Brent Scowcroft, "Options Paper on Iraq," May 16, 1990, declassified on May 28, 1992.

88. Bonin, *Arrows of the Night*, 52–60.

89. Roston, *The Man Who Pushed America to War*, 69–71.

90. Khalilzad, *The Envoy*, 73–75, describes his initial meetings with Chalabi, and his intense frustration at the barriers thrown up by the US government to meetings with Iraqi exiles.

91. Interviewee 70.

92. "Interview: Ahmad Chalabi," *Frontline* documentary, "Truth. War and Consequences," available at http://www.pbs.org/wgbh/pages/frontline/shows/truth/interviews/chalabi.html, accessed February 6, 2007. Haass later confirmed the essence of the report in an interview. See "Interview: Richard Haass," http://www.pbs.org/wgbh/pages/frontline/shows/truth/interviews/haass.html.

93. See "Interview: Laith Kubba," http://www.pbs.org/wgbh/pages/frontline/shows/truth/interviews/kubba.html.

94. Tenet, *At the Center of the Storm*, 397, states that "Following the first Gulf War, [Chalabi] was instrumental in creating, with CIA assistance, the Iraqi National Congress."
95. Roston, *The Man Who Pushed America to War*, 89–92.
96. Roston, *The Man Who Pushed America to War*, 106–107.
97. Seymour M. Hersh, "The Iraq Hawks: Can Their Plan Work?" *New Yorker*, December 24 and 31, 2001, quoted from www.newyorker.com/printable/?fact/011224fa _FACT, 1. Former CIA case officer Robert Baer reports being briefed on the End Game plan in August 1994, by which time, according to Baer, it had been "well shopped around Washington." Robert Baer, *See No Evil: The True Story of a Ground Soldier in the CIA's War on Terrorism* (New York: Crown, 2002), 188.
98. The Duelfer Report, 24–26, 29.
99. Industrious inspectors like David Kay led IAEA groups on high-speed chases to run down Iraqi trucks carrying nuclear components. Other inspection leaders, such as Bob Gallucci, faced down Iraqi guns and refused to yield. Some of this background can be found in Hans Blix, *Disarming Iraq* (New York: Pantheon Books, 2004), 24–28.
100. The Duelfer Report, 42.
101. "Ultimately," the Duelfer report explains, "his top priority (after survival) was to get out of the UN constraints. That priority underlies the actions of the Regime during the past 13 years. This may seem obvious but is easily forgotten"; the Duelfer Report, 8.
102. The IAEA brought together a group of high-level nuclear experts in 1992 to review the evidence gathered after the war. This group found "important bottlenecks" in the Iraqi program that would have extended the time required to get a bomb to "at least twice as long as" the twelve to eighteen months commonly claimed; Paul Lewis, "U.N. Experts Now Say Baghdad Was Far from Making an A-Bomb Before Gulf War," *New York Times*, May 20, 1992; available at http://www.nytimes .com/1992/05/20/world/un-experts-now-say-baghdad-was-far-from-making -an-a-bomb-before-gulf-war.html. On the Kamel episode, see the transcript of the UNSCOM interview with Kamel, available at http://www.casi.org.uk/info /unscom950822.pdf, accessed February 7, 2006. On this episode see also Blix, *Disarming Iraq*, 29–30; John Barry, "The Defector's Secrets," *Newsweek*, March 3, 2003, available at http://www.commondreams.org/headlines03/0226-01.htm, accessed February 7, 2006. The Blix report is available at http://www.iraqwatch .org/un/IAEA/s-1997-779.htm, accessed February 7, 2006. See also Scott Ritter, "The Case for Iraq's Qualitative Disarmament," *Arms Control Today*, June 2000.
103. The Duelfer Report, 9.
104. See, for example, CIA Nonproliferation Center, "The Chemical and Biological Weapons Threat," unclassified report, March 1996.
105. Kamel's defection, despite his claims of a terminated program, produced disturbing evidence of past Iraqi activity—from weaponized biological weapons to a crash nuclear program in 1990—that reinforced the skeptics in their view that Saddam had been fooling them all along.

106. CBS News, "Interrogator Shares Saddam's Confessions," January 27, 2003, transcript; available at http://www.cbsnews.com/stories/2008/01/24/60minutes/main 3749494.shtml.

107. Bonin, *Arrows of the Night*, 86–87.

108. Martin Indyk, a senior White House official, relates that he traveled with Tony Lake and Sandy Berger to see candidate Clinton during the campaign. Speaking of Iraq and Iran, containment wasn't enough, Clinton told the three future officials: "We had to find a way to change their behavior or change the regimes." Indyk, *Innocent Abroad*, 31.

109. Pollack, *The Threatening Storm*, 66.

110. Interviewee 68.

111. Interviewee 66.

112. Indyk, *Innocent Abroad*, 36–39.

113. Interviewee 66.

114. Pollack, *The Threatening Storm*, 67. In this action Clinton overruled some aides who had suggested a far stronger and wider-ranging blow against Saddam's elements of regime authority, but still representing an endorsement of a hard-line strategy of confronting Saddam for perceived aggression.

115. Indyk, *Innocent Abroad*, 153–155. Pollack describes a January 1995 debate within the administration; it is not clear if he is talking about the same meeting: Pollack, *The Threatening Storm*, 71–72.

116. Interviewee 68.

117. Michael R. Gordon and Bernard E. Trainor, *Cobra II: The Inside Story of the Invasion and Occupation of Iraq* (New York: Pantheon Books, 2006), 12; Roston, *The Man Who Pushed America to War*, 126–132. Michael Isikoff and David Corn characterize Downing as an out-and-out anti-Saddam hawk; Michael Isikoff and David Corn, *Hubris: The Inside Story of Spin, Scandal, and the Selling of the Iraq War* (New York: Crown, 2006), 81.

118. Ricks, *Fiasco*, 9–10.

119. Interviewee 8; Bonin, *Arrows of the Night*, 121–123. Most of the officials I spoke with were familiar with a variant of such plans involving the southern city of Basra; another source described a Chalabi proposal to start in the north using Kurdish peshmerga and "INC forces" and work from the north down, defeating Iraqi regular military units as they went.

120. Interviewee 8.

121. Bonin, *Arrows of the Night*, 144.

122. Interviewee 68.

123. Jane Mayer, "The Manipulator," *New Yorker*, June 7, 2004.

124. Henry Kissinger, "Bring Saddam Down," *Washington Post*, November 29, 1998.

125. Fred Hiatt, ". . . And a Crisis in Iraq," *Washington Post*, January 25, 1998.

126. See for example Jim Hoagland, "How CIA's Secret War on Saddam Collapsed," *Washington Post*, June 26, 1997.

127. Interviewee 66. See also Pollack, *The Threatening Storm*, 57. In his book Pollack summarizes the case made by the advocates of a tougher stance: the United States

"could adopt a policy of aggressive regime change in the hope of capitalizing on Saddam's current weakness, or else its position would inevitably weaken and it would find itself fighting a long rearguard action in defense of containment"; Pollack, *The Threatening Storm*, 78.

128. Interviewee 66.

129. Indyk, *Innocent Abroad*, 166. Tenet writes of this period that it was a time of "painful experience" for the CIA. "Our attempts to identify a Sunni military leader with the capability and following to take on Saddam's elite units proved difficult. Saddam regularly shuffled or even killed senior officers just for the sport of it, and this greatly increased the challenge of getting access to the right networks without being compromised." Many CIA-recruited Iraqis had been killed, found out or perhaps just randomly taken down by Saddam's security services, Tenet reports; Tenet, *At the Center of the Storm*, 385.

130. Baer, *See No Evil*, 213.

131. Indyk, *Innocent Abroad*, 163.

132. Interviewee 70.

133. Paul Wolfowitz, "Rising Up," *The New Republic*, December 7, 1998, 12–14. He laid out once again the strategy he had favored at the end of the Gulf War: arming the Iraqi opposition to Saddam and using "American forces to create a protected area in which opposition forces can organize and to which units from Saddam's army can defect." See also Paul Wolfowitz, "Rebuilding the Anti-Saddam Coalition," *Wall Street Journal*, November 18, 1997.

134. Zalmay M. Khalilzad and Paul Wolfowitz, "Overthrow Him," *Weekly Standard*, December 1, 1997. Khalilzad authored pointed essays making the case that Saddam was an urgent danger, and the United States needed a coherent strategy to unseat him. Zalmay Khalilzad, "The US Failure in Iraq," *Wall Street Journal*, September 10, 1996; Khalilzad, "It's Not Too Late to Topple Saddam," *Wall Street Journal*, February 25, 1998; Khalilzad, "A Turning Point for Iraq Policy," *Wall Street Journal*, November 13, 1998; and Khalilzad, "Air Strikes Aren't Enough in Iraq," *Wall Street Journal*, March 5, 1999. His bottom line was that the existing US approach had "run its course." Either the United States had to live with a Saddam who had a growing WMD program and regional ambitions—or make a "sustained and serious effort to help the Iraqi people get rid of their oppressive government and to allow Iraq to take its proper place in the region and the world"; Khalilzad, "A Turning Point for Iraq Policy."

135. Berger speaking at an HBO History Makers series at the Council on Foreign Relations, quoted in Bonin, *Arrows of the Night*, 149.

136. Interviewee 22.

137. Interviewee 9.

138. The Duelfer Report, 11, 55–57.

139. Indyk, *Innocent Abroad*, 193–201.

140. Pollack, *The Threatening Storm*, 93.

141. Ricks, *Fiasco*, 19–20.

142. Woods et al., *Iraqi Perspectives Project*, 26; Pollack, *The Threatening Storm*, 93.
143. Quoted in Frank P. Harvey, *Explaining the Iraq War: Counterfactual Theory, Logic and Evidence* (New York: Cambridge University Press, 2012), 50; see more broadly on Gore's role in the administration, pp. 47–52.
144. Nixon, *Debriefing the President*, 141.
145. The Iraq Liberation Act, PL 105–338, October 31, 1998.
146. Roston, *The Man Who Pushed America to War*, 155–156.
147. Mayer, "The Manipulator."
148. Not all the signals were so negative: in one meeting with Iraqi opposition leaders, National Security Advisor Sandy Berger reportedly outlined a goal to unseat Saddam by the end of Clinton's second term. But this was a select audience, and most public statements remained highly guarded; Vernon Loeb, "Saddam's Iraqi Foes Heartened by Clinton," *Washington Post*, November 16, 1998, A17. See also David Isenberg, "Imperial Overreach: Washington's Dubious Strategy to Overthrow Saddam Hussein," CATO Institute Policy Analysis, November 17, 1999, 2–3.
149. Interviewee 66. An example of the evolving thinking has come to light in the form of recently declassified talking points and transcripts from late 1998 for conversations between President Clinton and Crown Prince Abdullah of Saudi Arabia. Although the audience and context have to be taken into account—Washington would want Riyadh to think it was tough on Saddam—nonetheless, the documents are revealing. The November proposed talking points for President Clinton include the statement "I believe it is now imperative that we begin to take the decisive action necessary to change the Baghdad regime. It will take time to get rid of Saddam but we should start in earnest now." They referred to efforts that represented "the necessary first step in a long-term plan to get rid of Saddam." The memo summarizing the actual call has Clinton notifying Abdullah of upcoming military strikes and arguing that the strikes would "further our long-term goal of changing the leadership in Baghdad." The White House, "Telephone Call with Crown Prince Abdullah," memo and talking points, November 3, 1998, declassified 2009; the White House, "Memorandum of Telephone Conversation," December 15, 1998, declassified 2009. It is not clear if the talking points were for this call, but it appears to be the case.
150. "Transcript: President Clinton Explains Iraq Strike," *CNN*, December 16, 1998.
151. Pollack, *The Threatening Storm*, 95.
152. Pollack, *The Threatening Storm*, 99.
153. Interviewee 68.
154. Interviewee 70.
155. Allawi, *The Occupation of Iraq*, 78.
156. As journalist Todd Purdum puts it, "the country's economy was a shell of its former self and the fabric of society was in tatters"; Purdum, *A Time of Our Choosing*, 24.
157. Special Inspector General for Iraqi Reconstruction, *Hard Lessons: The Iraq Reconstruction Experience* (Washington, DC: US Government Printing Office, 2009), 5–6, available at http://www.sigir.mil/files/HardLessons/Hard_Lessons_Report.pdf.

158. Rajiv Chandrasekaran, *Imperial Life in the Emerald City: Inside Iraq's Green Zone* (New York: Alfred A. Knopf, 2006), 151. An article in the British medical journal *The Lancet* chronicled how a decade of war and sanctions "have left the country's economy and infrastructure in ruins"; "Health of the Iraqi People Hangs in the Balance," *Lancet*, February 22, 2003, 623–625.

159. CARE International in Iraq and the Johns Hopkins University Center for International Emergency, Refugee and Disaster Studies, "Humanitarian Assistance Capacity in Iraq: Part I," January 2003, available at http://www.who.int/disasters/repo/9353.pdf.

160. Oxfam, "Iraq: On the Brink of Disaster," January 23, 2003, available at http://www.reliefweb.int/rw/rwb.nsf/AllDocsByUNID/b0b4dab0d4ec89e1c1256 ccc0053668c. Despite the issue date on the website, references internal to the document make it clear that it was written in late 2002.

161. National Intelligence Council, "Principal Challenges in Post-Saddam Iraq," January 2003, declassified and released in Senate Select Committee on Intelligence, *Report of the Select Committee on Intelligence on Prewar Intelligence Assessments About Postwar Iraq*, 110th Congress, 1st Session, available at http://intelligence.senate.gov/prewar.pdf, 54, 62, 77, 79.

162. Interviewee 40.

163. Interviewee 39.

164. Interviewee 28.

165. Interviewee 36. When ORHA deployed into Iraq later that year, according to one of its senior officials, Don Eberly, "I was struck again and again by how little we knew about Iraqi ministries and the realities of the country's basic infrastructure"; Don Eberly, *Liberate and Leave: Fatal Flaws in the Early Strategy for Postwar Iraq* (Minneapolis, MN: Zenith Press, 2009), 51.

166. Chandrasekaran, *Imperial Life in the Emerald City*, 114, 149–150, 111.

167. Allawi, *The Occupation of Iraq*, 7. Allawi refers to the work of a famous Iraqi social scientist, Ali al-Wardi, who had argued that the modernist aspects of Iraqi society were a facade. Tribal values still governed the lives of many Iraqis, he believed. The "sense of a conflict-strewn society," Allawi writes, "permeates the work of al-Wardi: tribe versus tribe; tribe versus government; intra-urban violence between neighborhoods; tribe versus town; town versus town; town versus government." This was changing, but not with any speed. "Transformation of society was a painfully slow process, subject to frequent setbacks and reversals, with old patterns of behavior often returning to the ascendancy"; Allawi, *The Occupation of Iraq*, 14–15.

168. No author, "Memo to Deputy Director," January 29, 2003, declassified through DoD FOIA process, available at DoD FOIA site.

169. Pollack, *The Threatening Storm*, 409.

170. Interviewee 13.

171. The Duelfer Report, 11. See also Egypt: Trade with Iraq Reportedly Growing," *BBC Monitoring Middle East*, November 10, 2001, 1; "Iraq's Vice President,

Syria's Economy Minister Discuss Free Trade Zone," *BBC Monitoring Middle East*, November 3, 2001, 1.

172. Allawi, *The Occupation of Iraq*, 70.

173. Indyk, *Innocent Abroad*. See also Pollack, *The Threatening Storm*, 103.

174. Interviewee 8.

175. Taylor Branch, *The Clinton Tapes: Wrestling History with the President* (New York: Simon and Schuster, 2009), 657.

176. United States Central Command, "Desert Crossing Seminar: After Action Report," June 28–30, 1999, declassified July 2, 1994.

177. Thomas E. Ricks, *Fiasco* (New York, Penguin, 2006), 87.

CHAPTER 3: A NEW SHERIFF IN TOWN

1. Quoted in George Packer, *The Assassin's Gate: America in Iraq* (New York: Farrar, Straus and Giroux, 2005), 102.

2. James quoted in Robie Macauley and George Lanning, *Technique in Fiction*, 2nd ed. (New York: St. Martins Press, 1987), 91.

3. Ron Suskind, *The Price of Loyalty: George W. Bush, the White House, and the Education of Paul O'Neill* (New York: Simon and Schuster, 2004), 73–74.

4. Suskind, *The Price of Loyalty*, 85. At the meeting, CIA director George Tenet showed some intelligence photographs, spoke about the limits of US assets inside Iraq, and said his agency had made little progress in covert means to unseat Saddam; Karen DeYoung, *Soldier: The Life of Colin Powell* (New York: Alfred A. Knopf, 2006), 314–316.

5. Suskind, *The Price of Loyalty*, 75, 86. See also Bryan Burrough et al., "The Path to War," *Vanity Fair*, May 2004, 234.

6. Interviewee 4. In January 2004, reacting to the release of O Neill's book, President Bush refuted his former Treasury secretary's characterization of events. The distinction Bush tried to make was between regime change and invasion: "Like the previous administration," he told a news conference, "we were for regime change." He admitted that his administration was working from its first days to investigate ways to make this happen. But those ways, Bush insisted, did not include contemplating a US invasion—only more covert means, a continuation of no-fly zones, and other ways to pressure Saddam Hussein; Richard W. Stevenson, "Bush Disputes Ex-Official's Claim that War with Iraq Was Early Administration Goal," *New York Times*, January 13, 2004.

7. Condoleezza Rice, *No Higher Honor: A Memoir of My Years in Washington* (New York: Crown, 2011), 31. They spent a lot of time before 9/11 "trying to figure out something else on Iraq," she would later say. "I went to more meetings about strengthening sanctions than I did about anything else"; Elisabeth Bumiller, *Condoleezza Rice: An American Life* (New York: Random House, 2007), 137–141. For a response at the time, see Stevenson, "Bush Disputes Ex-Official's Claim."

8. Quoted in Daniel Drezner, "Thoughts on Paul O'Neill," *Foreign Policy*, January 12, 2004.

9. Interviewee 27.

10. As journalist James Mann has suggested, the Bush campaign did not give "any par-
    ticular emphasis to the issue of Iraq. If George W. Bush thought that Saddam Hus-
    sein's brutal mistreatment of the Iraqi people . . . was so outrageous as to require
    outside military intervention, he managed to get through an eighteen-month race
    for the presidency without saying so"; James Mann, *Rise of the Vulcans: The History
    of Bush's War Cabinet* (New York: Viking, 2004), 258.

11. Peter Schweizer and Rochelle Schweizer, *The Bushes: Portrait of a Dynasty* (New York:
    Doubleday, 2004), 533.

12. Clinton administration follies in Bosnia were a much more common topic of con-
    versation, one source argued; Interviewee 1. Those who claim that George W. Bush
    arrived in office with a preset agenda on Iraq point to stories such as the one told
    by Texas author and friend of the Bush family Mickey Herskowitz. He was working
    on an autobiography with Bush—but then later, as the campaign heated up, his
    draft work would be judged unacceptable, and he was dropped from the project.
    Herskowitz claims that, in one of their conversations, Bush said, "One of the keys to
    being seen as a great leader is to be seen as a commander-in-chief. My father had all
    this political capital built up when he drove the Iraqis out of [Kuwait] and he wasted
    it. If I have a chance to invade Iraq, if I had that much capital, I'm not going to waste
    it. I'm going to get everything passed I want to get passed and I'm going to have a
    successful presidency"; Kim Cobb, "Writer Says Bush Talked About War in 1999,"
    Houston Chronicle, November 1, 2004. The same quote, or a version of it, seems to
    reappear in Robert Draper, *Dead Certain: The Presidency of George W. Bush* (New
    York: The Free Press, 2007), 173. This is a controversial quote. Herskowitz offered
    it to freelance journalist and blogger Russ Baker, who posted it on a partisan site
    called the Guerrilla News Network. Herskowitz later claimed that it was taken out
    of context: Bush was not promising to invade Iraq; he was contrasting his leadership
    style from his father's, claiming that he would perhaps be more bold and decisive.
    Herskowitz also pointed out that Bush had said, in many other public forums, that
    he would deal decisively with Saddam Hussein if the need arose. Seen in this light,
    the quote does not suggest any preset agenda.

13. Interviewee 39. Iraq, the prominent Vulcan and future DoD appointee Dov
    Zakheim would later contend, served as only one of many prominent foreign policy
    issues under discussion; Dov S. Zakheim, *A Vulcan's Tale: How the Bush Adminis-
    tration Mismanaged the Reconstruction of Afghanistan* (Washington, DC: Brookings
    Institution Press, 2011), 14.

14. Richard Haass, *War of Necessity, War of Choice: A Memoir of Two Iraq Wars* (New
    York: Simon and Schuster, 2009), 169.

15. Donald Rumsfeld, *Known and Unknown* (New York: Sentinel, 2011), 418.

16. See, for example, Zakheim, *A Vulcan's Tale*, 53.

17. Quoted in Draper, *Dead Certain*, 128. In an October 2000 presidential debate he
    would say on the same topic: when the US sends in troops, "the mission must
    be clear. Soldiers must understand why we're going. The force must be strong
    enough so that the mission can be accomplished. And the exit strategy needs to

be well-defined"; quoted in Lou Cannon and Carl M. Cannon, *Reagan's Disciple: George W. Bush's Troubled Quest for a Presidential Legacy* (New York: PublicAffairs, 2008), 170, 172.

18. Zakheim, *A Vulcan's Tale*, 32.

19. Gerald F. Seib, "Campaign Query: Who Will Act to Oust Saddam?" *Wall Street Journal*, June 28, 2000, A24. Robert Zoellick, then a general foreign policy advisor, was repeatedly quoted on the need for tougher steps, including cementing opposition groups' control over certain parts of Iraq. "We have started to do that in the north" of Iraq, he said publicly in May 2000. "I believe we could do that in the south. I believe that in part this involves [American] air power. It might involve more." John Lancaster, "In Saddam's Future, A Harder US Line," *Washington Post*, June 3, 2000, A1. Another senior advisor to Bush told a reporter, 'In the intervening decade, the behavior of Saddam has not improved and many people have come to the view that perhaps eviction is in order"; Steven Mufson, "A World View of His Own: On Foreign Policy, Bush Parts Ways with Father," *Washington Post*, August 11, 2000, A1.

20. Lancaster, "In Saddam's Future." For an article discussing the importance of the "missing consonants"—whether Bush meant "them" or "him"—see Frank Bruni, "Bush Has Tough Words and Rough Enunciation for Iraqi Chief," *New York Times*, December 4, 1999, A12. Bush is quoted explicitly as explaining that he meant "them"—the weapons—and did not mean to suggest that he would go after the regime. And yet during one of the debates in question, after saying "take 'em out," Bush continued to say, "I'm surprised he's still there." Clearly, the removal from power of Saddam Hussein was on his mind.

21. Nicholas Lehmann, "The Iraq Factor," *New Yorker*, January 22, 2001. See also Stephen F. Hayes, *Cheney: The Untold Story of America's Most Powerful and Controversial Vice President* (New York: HarperCollins, 2007), 318. Cheney made other, similar threats. During the October 2000 vice presidential debate, Cheney was asked, "If Iraq's President Saddam Hussein were found to be developing weapons of mass destruction, Governor Bush has said he would 'Take him out.' Would you agree with such a deadly policy?" Cheney responded: "We might have no other choice. We'll have to see if that happens. . . . I certainly hope he's not regenerating that kind of [WMD] capability. But if he were, if in fact Saddam Hussein were taking steps to try to rebuild nuclear capability or weapons of mass destruction, you'd have to give very serious consideration to military action to stop that activity. I don't think you can afford to have a man like Saddam Hussein with nuclear weapons, say, in the Middle East"; "Excerpts from the Debate between the Vice Presidential Candidates," *New York Times*, October 6, 2000, A28.

22. "Saddam Hussein's regime is isolated," she wrote, "his conventional military power has been severely weakened, his people live in poverty and terror, and he has no useful place in international politics. He is therefore determined to develop WMD. Nothing will change until Saddam is gone, so the United States must mobilize whatever resources it can, including support from his opposition, to remove him." Condoleezza Rice, "Promoting the National Interest," *Foreign Affairs*, March–April

2000. One former government official told Seymour Hersh that Rice was signaling in the piece that Iraq would not, in fact, be a priority. The key issues would be Russia, China, NATO expansion, India, and Africa; Hersh, "The Iraq Hawks," printable web version, 2.

23. A copy of the platform can be found at http://www.presidency.ucsb.edu/ws/index.php?pid=25849#axzz1n92eRBBp.

24. The Democratic platform is available at http://www.presidency.ucsb.edu/ws/index.php?pid=29612#axzz1n92eRBBp. In fact, several sources have argued that Gore advisors had sketched out a plan to seek regime change more actively, by ripening the Iraqi opposition into a stronger, unified group that could attract international and especially regional support; see Seib, "Campaign Query," and Lancaster, "In Saddam's Future."

25. Interviewee 4; also Interviewee 39. In her memoirs, Condoleezza Rice explains that Iraq was indeed a "preoccupation of the national security team" from the outset of the administration—but the focus, she contends, was not on regime change. Instead, they were trying to tighten sanctions, which were fraying; Rice, *No Higher Honor: A Memoir of My Years in Washington* (New York: Crown, 2011), 29. On January 29, 2001, President Bush met at the White House with Imam Sayed Hassan al-Qazwini, head of one of the United States' largest Islamic mosques, the Islamic Center of America in Detroit. The two men knew each other—they had spoken several times during and after the election about the problem of Iraq. Imam Qazwini told the *New York Times* that at this meeting Bush supported efforts to unseat Hussein, although "No method was discussed at all. It was a general desire to regime change." See Richard W. Stevenson, "Bush Disputes Ex-Official's Claim That Iraq War Was Early Goal," *New York Times*, January 13, 2004. In January 2001, even before George W. Bush was inaugurated as president, Vice President-Elect Cheney asked outgoing secretary of defense William Cohen to brief President-Elect Bush. He did not, however, want the "routine, canned, round-the-world tour"; instead, according to Bob Woodward's account, he "wanted a serious 'discussion about Iraq and different options.' . . . Topic A should be Iraq." But while Cheney apparently saw Iraq as a serious issue, he was not, at that point, advocating any specific near-term US policy options. Bob Woodward, *Plan of Attack* (New York: Simon and Schuster, 2004), 9; Hayes, *Cheney*, 318–319.

26. Con Coughlin, *American Ally: Tony Blair and the War on Terror* (New York: HarperCollins, 2006), 122. One UK official told Coughlin that, "pre 9/11 Washington's main fixation was missile defense and China. Nothing else seemed to matter."

27. Michael Morell, *The Great War of Our Time* (New York: 12 Books, 2015), 78–79.

28. On Powell's views, see Bill Keller, "The World According to Powell," *New York Times Magazine*, November 25, 2001.

29. Dick Cheney and Liz Cheney, *Exceptional: Why the World Needs a Powerful America* (New York: Threshold Editions, 2015), 1, 257.

30. Woodward, *Plan of Attack*, 88. In his second inaugural address, Bush would arguably go even further, arguing that "America's vital interests and our deepest beliefs are now one." Quoted in Christopher A. Preble, *The Power Problem: How American*

Military Dominance Makes Us Less Safe, Less Prosperous, and Less Free (Ithaca, NY: Cornell University Press, 2008), 122.

31. Richard Bonin, *Arrows of the Night: Ahmad Chalabi's Long Journey to Triumph in Iraq* (New York: Doubleday, 2011), 1–4, 172, 176.

32. Lang, "Drinking the Kool-Aid," 44. For further information on Downing, see Richard Leiby, "The Secret Warrior: Gen. Wayne Downing, From West Point to White House," *Washington Post*, November 20, 2001, C1. Other background on this issue was drawn from Interviewee 8 and Bonin, *Arrows of the Night*, 178–181.

33. Rumsfeld, *Known and Unknown*, 418.

34. Interviewee 69.

35. Donald Rumsfeld, "3/28/01 Meeting with the President," March 30, 2001, available at www.rumsfeld.com.

36. Interviewee 1, Interviewee 11; see also Bob Woodward, *State of Denial: Bush at War, Part III* (New York: Simon and Schuster, 2006), 25.

37. Interviewee 11, Interviewee 9. This view is strongly reflected in Haass, *War of Necessity*, 167. Powell received a memo from Edward Walker, the head of his Near East office at State. The memo began, "You asked about the origin of our regime change policy in Iraq." Walker explained the 1990s history—the Iraq Liberation Act and the very strong statements from President Clinton about the threat posed by Saddam and the need for his removal. Department of State, Information Memorandum from NEA—Edward S. Walker Jr., to the Secretary, January 23, 2001, declassified January 19, 2005. But the memo did not advocate a more elaborate course of action, and from the beginning Colin Powell appears to have viewed Saddam as a problem to be managed, not an imminent threat.

38. DeYoung, *Soldier*, 317. Rumsfeld discusses the problem of no-fly zones in Rumsfeld, *Known and Unknown*, 419.

39. George Tenet again characterized it as merely a typical beginning-of-administration policy review. George Tenet, *At the Center of the Storm: My Years at the CIA* (New York: HarperCollins, 2007), 303. See also Bumiller, *Condoleezza Rice*, 141.

40. Interviewee 24.

41. Rice, *No Higher Honor*, 168, 198.

42. Dick Cheney, *In My Time: A Personal and Political Memoir* (New York: Simon and Schuster, 2011), 367.

43. Rumsfeld, *Known and Unknown*, 305.

44. Interviewee 7; similar sentiments were expressed by Interviewees 3, 11, and 13.

45. Interviewee 64. "It's undeniable that there were some [in the new administration] who thought we should have finished it in '91," recalled another senior official. "And in the period from 1999 to 2001 Saddam was becoming increasingly obstreperous." But nothing decisive emerged. "I didn't have the sense that there was a drumbeat campaign" to oust Saddam before 9/11, this official says: Interviewee 69.

46. Interviewee 19. Someone who worked in the vice president's office described a "crisis of the day" focus before 9/11, a focus on a variety of national security issues among key Cheney aides like Scooter Libby and John Hannah, but no sense of a driving, singular agenda on an issue like Iraq; Interviewee 17. For similar views see Sir

William Paley, chief of UK Foreign Office Middle East department in 2001, quoted in UK Iraq Inquiry testimony, November 24, 2009, morning session, 25; available at http://www.iraqinquiry.org.uk/media/40656/20091124am-final.pdf.

47. I did receive one powerfully discordant view on the priority granted to Iraq early in the administration. This source told me that even before 9/11, "It was very clear that the one issue that was dominating the NSC agenda was Iraq." When I suggested that Iraq was not a top-tier issue, this source said, "No. I disagree vehemently with that. . . . I saw one or two Russia issues for every five or six Iraq issues." The source especially recalled his first meeting with the senior Pentagon official William Luti, before 9/11. "This is a done deal," Luti was saying. "We are taking Saddam out. Two squadrons of F-18s could topple the guy"; Interviewee 54.

48. David Frum, *The Right Man: The Surprise Presidency of George W. Bush* (New York: Random House, 2003), 26.

49. Richard Haass "spent hours at the CIA" discussing available options, none of which seemed feasible. That spring he sent Powell a memo that concluded that "the only sure way to oust the regime and put something better in its place is through prolonged military occupation and nation-building." That, he implied, was a bridge way too far—and he argued that sanctions and containment were working and ought to be reinforced; Haass, *War of Necessity*, 181.

50. One report suggests that the "process swiftly became bogged down in bitter interagency disagreements." Those involved in the process told several *Vanity Fair* reporters that "at first the president seemed in no hurry to deal with Saddam. 'Faced with a dilemma, he has this favorite phrase he uses all the time: Protect my flexibility,'" one "administration insider" contended. And thus the overall administration Iraq policy "remained stuck" in "gridlock" until September 11, this report suggests; Burrough et al., "The Path to War," 234. Seymour Hersh, in "The Iraq Hawks," *New Yorker*, December 24, 2001, web version, pp. 4–5, discusses the role of deputy secretary of state Richard Armitage in slowing the drift toward anti-Saddam options. Hans Blix describes how he visited Washington in April 2001 and heard little talk of impending conflict; Hans Blix, *Disarming Iraq* (New York: Pantheon Books, 2004), 55–56.

51. Interviewee 64.

52. For a description of the process, see Haass, *War of Necessity*, 174–180. At Defense, the idea was greeted with outright disdain. In one November 2002 snowflake, Rumsfeld observed that the existing Oil for Food program was already "just a sieve" and concluded simply, "Smart sanctions do not work." Donald Rumsfeld, "Oil-for-Food," memo to Doug Feith, November 18, 2002, released through DoD FOIA process, available at DoD FOIA website, Rumsfeld folder.

53. Rice, *No Higher Honor*, 31.

54. Interviewee 4.

55. Interviewee 12.

56. Barton Gellman's detailed portrait suggests that Bush was entirely on board with an activist vice president, and ultimately reserved the right to decide; see Barton Gellman, *Angler: The Cheney Vice Presidency* (New York: Penguin Press, 2008), 35, 52.

57. Barton Gellman and Jo Becker, "'A Different Understanding with the President,'" *Washington Post*, June 14, 2007, A12.

58. Lou Dubose and Jake Bernstein, *Vice: Dick Cheney and the Hijacking of the American Presidency* (New York: Random House, 2006), 49.

59. Hayes, *Cheney*, 179, 272.

60. Bumiller, *Condoleezza Rice*, 137.

61. Gellman, *Angler*, 9, 49.

62. Hayes, *Cheney*, 183.

63. Quoted in the Showtime documentary "The World According to Dick Cheney." See http://www.sho.com/titles/3370771/the-world-according-to-dick-cheney.

64. Peter Baker, *Days of Fire: Bush and Cheney in the White House* (New York: Doubleday, 2013), 27, 34–35. A persuasive analysis in *The New Republic* by Spencer Ackerman and Franklin Foer contends that the vice president's foreign policy radicalism was not, as some accounts have suggested, a result of a reaction to 9/11. They describe Cheney's unsuccessful battle in the first Bush administration to shift US Soviet policy away from Mikhail Gorbachev and toward an effort to collapse the Soviet Union and promote democracy. Their sources described a willingness, even then, on Cheney's part to "circumvent the typical bureaucratic channels to gain advantage over his rivals." Spencer Ackerman and Franklin Foer, "The Radical: What Dick Cheney Really Believes," *New Republic*, December 1 and 8, 2003, 17–18.

65. Superb examples of the Cheney style are offered in Gellman and Becker, "'A Different Understanding,'" A12–A13; for the torture memo case, see Gellman and Becker, "The Unseen Path to Cruelty," *Washington Post*, June 25, 2007, A7.

66. Bumiller, *Condoleezza Rice*, 170–171. The pattern would continue. By late 2005, President Bush was ready to support a congressional compromise on detainee treatment. Cheney's staff got ahold of the draft presidential statement and literally changed the language to a bland assertion of unfettered presidential power. Essentially the whole rest of the national security establishment—the CIA, Justice Department, and Defense and State Departments—came out against the resulting proposal. "None of that mattered," Gellman and Becker explained. "With Cheney's weight behind it," the new, hard-line draft was sent "to Bush for his signature." Gellman and Becker, "The Unseen Path to Cruelty," A8.

67. Quoted in "The World According to Dick Cheney."

68. David Ignatius, "Cheney's Enigmatic Influence," *Washington Post*, January 19, 2007, A19.

69. Dubose and Bernstein, *Vice*, 19–20.

70. Dubose and Bernstein, *Vice*, 69.

71. Quoted in Hayes, *Cheney*, 3.

72. Gellman, *Angler*, 52–55, 189.

73. Interviewee 17.

74. Interviewee 41.

75. My interviews with former officials confirmed the impression left on one former Bush administration staffer, quoted by Spencer Ackerman and Franklin Foer in *The*

New Republic: the vice president's office was often "driving the policy, leading the debate, leading the arguments, instead of just hanging back and recognizing that the vice president is not supposed to be driving the policy." Ackerman and Foer, "The Radical," 20. The same argument is made by Daniel Benjamin, "President Cheney," *Slate*, November 7, 2005, http://www.slate.com/id/2129686/nav/tap1, accessed February 1, 2006. See also Haass, *War of Necessity*, 183.

76. Interviewee 4.

77. Interviewee 39. Admittedly, it may be that this impression became more pronounced in the second term, when issues were going against Cheney more often than they had in the first.

78. Interviewee 64.

79. Interviewee 17.

80. Interviewee 36. Ironically, this source told me, Cheney saw as one of his main roles grabbing the reins on "an issue where people seemed to be racing off" without careful enough thought.

81. Interviewee 41.

82. Interviewees 36, 64.

83. Interviewee 36. One person with knowledge of the office's workings said Cheney "wanted to be extremely well informed" but was strict about the staff not speaking in his name—in fact *not* trying to exercise some secret veto power on his behalf; Interviewee 64.

84. Interviewee 41.

85. Gellman, *Angler*, 389.

86. Rumsfeld, *Known and Unknown*, 319, 326–327.

87. According to Bradley Graham, Rumsfeld himself came to resent what he saw as the inefficient management of the NSC process under Rice. Bradley Graham, *By His Own Rules: The Ambitions, Successes, and Ultimate Failures of Donald Rumsfeld* (New York: PublicAffairs, 2009), 345–346.

88. Graham, *By His Own Rules*, 348.

89. Interviewee 69.

90. Bumiller, *Condoleezza Rice*, 19.

91. "Rice not only believes in herself," Nicholas Lemann wrote in 2002; "she believes in belief, as an all-conquering force. Doubt, ambiguity, and caution are just not part of the picture—if Rice ever experienced them, she has either put them somewhere out of view or completely willed them away"; Lemann, "Without a Doubt," 168. See also Marcus Mabry, *Twice as Good: Condoleezza Rice and Her Path to Power* (New York: Modern Times, 2007), 36.

92. Bumiller, *Condoleezza Rice*, 66.

93. Bumiller, *Condoleezza Rice*, 113.

94. Mabry, *Twice as Good*, 213.

95. Glenn Kessler, *The Confidante: Condoleezza Rice and the Creation of the Bush Legacy* (New York: St. Martin's Press, 2007), 19.

96. Mabry, *Twice as Good*, 151–154, 209. One White House official told Elisabeth Bumiller that there was "an extraordinary emotional bond" between the two; Bumiller, *Condoleezza Rice*, xvii, 127.

97. Lemann, "Without a Doubt," 167.

98. Interviewee 39.

99. Interviewee 5.

100. Interviewee 39.

101. Graham, *By His Own Rules*, 23.

102. Quoted in Katie Bacon, "Rumsfeld's Roots," *The Atlantic*, November 1, 2003.

103. "Nixon and Bob Haldeman on Donald Rumsfeld," March 9, 1971, Miller Center presidential recordings, University of Virginia, available at http://millercenter.org /presidentialclassroom/exhibits/nixon-and-bob-haldeman-on-donald-rumsfeld.

104. Graham, *By His Own Rules*, 27, 56.

105. Interviewee 13.

106. Graham, *By His Own Rules*, 61. Condoleezza Rice, a frequent victim of Rumsfeld's urge to win, would later write that he "rarely saw shades of gray on an issue, while Colin [Powell] almost always saw nuances." She refers to Rumsfeld's mindset as a "black-and-white view of the world." Rice, *No Higher Honor*, 20.

107. Hugh Shelton, *Without Hesitation: The Odyssey of an American Warrior* (New York: St. Martin's Press, 2010), 403, 408.

108. Graham, *By His Own Rules*, 392, 410–411, 673, 678. See, for example, Rumsfeld's famous evasions in press conferences—"we didn't need to anticipate this," "we shouldn't have prepared for that"—rather than simple acceptance of accountability. When the Iraq war plan began getting criticism, he was quick to point out that "I keep getting credit for it in the press, but the truth is. . . . It was not my plan. It was General Franks's plan." Later, when Franks decided, in a highly suspect move, to put General Ricardo Sanchez's understaffed V Corps headquarters in charge of operations in Iraq, Rumsfeld wrote internal memos claiming he had no knowledge of the decision.

109. Shelton, *Without Hesitation*, 401, 413.

110. Interviewee 11.

111. Interviewee 42.

112. Interviewee 69.

113. See for example Zakheim, *A Vulcan's Tale*, 60–61.

114. Zakheim, *A Vulcan's Tale*, 50.

115. Woodward, *State of Denial*, 67–68, 70.

116. Interviewee 30.

117. Interviewee 58.

118. Interviewee 27.

119. Interviewee 7.

120. Rice, *No Higher Honor*, 16, 19, 87.

121. Interviewee 12.

122. Interviewee 1.

123. Interviewee 13.

124. Interviewee 42.

125. A massive collection of these has been declassified and is available at https://nsarchive .gwu.edu/briefing-book/foia/2018-01-24/rumsfeld-snowflakes-come-cold.

126. Matt Latimer, *Speech*less: Tales of a White House Survivor* (New York: Crown, 2009), 130.

127. Interviewee 30.
128. Interviewee 36.
129. Interviewee 42. The same confrontational mindset helped to create what one Defense official referred to the "henchmen" phenomenon. Some especially aggressive aides took his supposed desires and extended upon them; they tried to please by doing more than the boss thought he ever wanted, including in confronting and at times subverting the activities of other departments. One senior official put it to me this way, about several top Defense officials: "Their mission in life was to find out what Rumsfeld wanted and do it in spades." Interviewee 13.
130. Interviewee 13.
131. Douglas J. Feith, *War and Decision: Inside the Pentagon at the Dawn of the War on Terrorism* (New York: Harper, 2008), 199–204.
132. Sir Peter Ricketts, director general political in the Foreign Office, quoted in UK Iraq Inquiry testimony, November 24, 2009, morning session, 26, 101–102; Simon Webb, policy director, Ministry of Defence, 41; available at http://www.iraqinquiry.org.uk/media/40656/20091124am-final.pdf.
133. DeYoung, *Soldier*, 345.
134. Memorandum from Robin Cook to Tony Blair, "Iraq: US/UK Policy Review," May 4, 2001, declassified by the UK Iraq Inquiry, available at http://www.iraqinquiry.org.uk/.
135. Interviewees 9 and 13.
136. Interviewee 9. The concern about the no-fly zones was especially intense in the military. General Jim Jones—at the time serving as commandant of the Marine Corps, later to be NSC advisor under Barack Obama—wrote a scathing memo to the chairman of the Joint Chiefs on August 31 highlighting precisely these dangers. The current approach of limited responses "is a high risk strategy without clear objectives or a desirable end state." Eventually they would lose an aircraft. They had backed into a "tit-for-tat approach that is at odds with our status as a great power. . . . It has become a campaign without purpose." The memo was Jones's statement of his "non-concurring" with established policy. J. L. Jones, "Memorandum for Chairman, Joint Chiefs of Staff, 'US Military Responses in Iraq,'" August 31, 2001, declassified September 8, 2008, released with documents released to Donald Rumsfeld through MDR, available at DoD FOIA website.
137. Rumsfeld, *Known and Unknown*, 419.
138. Feith, *War and Decision*, 210–212.
139. US Department of Defense, Memorandum, Donald Rumsfeld to Condoleezza Rice, July 27, 2001, declassified May 10, 2007. Available at http://www.gwu.edu/~nsarchiv/NSAEBB/NSAEBB326/doc06.pdf.
140. In his memoirs Rumsfeld is more charitable to the idea, wondering if "the right combination of blandishments and pressures might lead or compel Saddam Hussein toward an improved arrangement with America. While a long shot, it was not out of the question." Rumsfeld, *Known and Unknown*, 420–421.
141. Feith, *War and Decision*, 206.
142. Interviewees 3, 4, 12, and 22.

143. Hersh, "The Iraq Hawks," web printable version. 6.

144. For example, Interviewee 7.

145. Woodward, *Plan of Attack*, 22.

146. Tenet, *At the Center of the Storm*, 304.

147. DeYoung, *Soldier*, 307–309.

148. One senior State official said that Powell was "always open to all points of view" and enjoyed debating the elements of policy. "He would challenge you," but clearly in service of better ideas. When a decision had been reached, he marched forward and expected others to do the same; Interviewee 52.

149. Rumsfeld, *Known and Unknown*, 322.

150. DeYoung, *Soldier*, tells the Clinton Haiti story, 249–250, and the Bush story, 297–298.

151. Peter Schweizer and Rochelle Schweizer, *The Bushes: Portrait of a Dynasty* (New York: Anchor Books, 2005), 467. Powell wouldn't commit to Bush during the primaries and went as far as to admire John McCain's Vietnam service while casting a skeptical eye at Bush's National Guard war avoidance; DeYoung, *Soldier*, 286, 288–289.

152. Interviewee 64.

153. Haass, *War of Necessity*, 185.

154. DeYoung, *Soldier*, 301–302.

155. Interviewee 11.

156. Haass, *War of Necessity*, 185–186.

157. Interviewee 27.

158. Frank Bruni, *Ambling Into History: The Unlikely Odyssey of George W. Bush* (New York: HarperCollins, 2002), 35, 55, 270. After a 2007 interview with Bush, columnist David Brooks wrote that he was a "smart and compelling presence in person"; David Brooks, "Heroes and History," *New York Times*, July 17, 2007; Baker, *Days of Fire*, 114.

159. Interviewee 71; also Interviewee 39.

160. Draper, *Dead Certain*, 165, 131. Bush's speechwriter Matt Latimer has described an episode in which a speech draft referred to the *conservative movement*. "What is this movement you keep talking about in the speech?" Bush asked impatiently. Latimer tried to explain—the modern conservative movement, William F. Buckley and so forth. "The president either had no concept of what I was talking about, didn't want any part of it, or both." Bush said, "Let me tell you something. I whupped Gary Bauer's ass in 2000. So take out this movement stuff. There is no movement"; Latimer, *Speech*less*, 250.

161. Michael Isikoff and David Corn, *Hubris: The Inside Story of Spin, Scandal, and the Selling of the Iraq War* (New York: Crown, 2006), 137, 296. Same issue raised in Ron Suskind, *The One Percent Doctrine: Deep Inside America's Pursuit of Its Enemies Since 9/11* (New York: Simon and Schuster, 2006), 72–73.

162. Draper, *Dead Certain*, 36.

163. Isikoff and Corn, *Hubris*, 310.

164. Woodward, *State of Denial*, 366.

165. Schweizer and Schweizer, *The Bushes*, 337.

166. Interviewee 36.

167. Latimer, *Speech*less*, 184.

168. Compared to his father, Condoleezza Rice wrote with apt conciseness, Bush was "quicker to anger and less given to shades of gray." Rice, *No Higher Honor*, 24.

169. Isikoff and Corn, *Hubris*, 117.

170. Draper, *Dead Certain*, 23, 102, 221–222, 248–249, 255, 360–361.

171. Schweizer and Schweizer, *The Bushes*, 134–135.

172. Scott McClellan, *What Happened: Inside the Bush White House and Washington's Culture of Deception* (New York: PublicAffairs, 2008), 145.

173. Woodward, *State of Denial*, 11.

174. Draper, *Dead Certain*, 7, 54.

175. Draper, *Dead Certain*, 416.

176. Interviewee 39.

177. Draper, *Dead Certain*, 409.

178. Interviewee 39.

179. Brooks, "Heroes and History," A21. See also Woodward, *State of Denial*, 325.

180. Latimer, *Speech*less*, 257–261.

181. Nicholas Lemann, "Without a Doubt: Has Condoleezza Rice Changed George W. Bush, or Has He Changed Her?" *New Yorker*, October 14 and 21, 2002, 177.

182. Schweizer and Schweizer, *The Bushes*, 332–335.

183. Draper, *Dead Certain*, 190. See also Frum, *The Right Man*, 30.

184. Schweizer and Schweizer, *The Bushes*, 438.

185. Cited in Stephen Mansfield, *The Faith of George W. Bush* (New York: Penguin Group, 2004), 109.

186. Peter Baker contended that the result suggested to Bush that "he had been saved to accomplish great things," which led to a "messianic" streak of idealism that ran through all of his major policies; Baker, *Days of Fire*, 17. See also Jeffrey Goldberg, "The Believer: George W. Bush's Loyal Speechwriter," *New Yorker*, February 13 and 20, 2006, 64; and David Kuo, *Tempting Faith: An Inside Story of Political Seduction* (New York: Free Press, 2006), 111, 113.

187. Quoted in Ron Suskind, "Without a Doubt," *New York Times Magazine*, October 17, 2004, 46.

188. Christopher Clark, *The Sleepwalkers: How Europe Went to War in 1914* (New York: HarperCollins, 2012), xxix.

189. Most textbooks of international relations, for example, scan a wide range of theories—structural, human nature, environmental—without giving any serious attention to the role of individual perspectives in state behavior. One example is James E. Dougherty and Robert L. Pfaltzgraff Jr., *Contending Theories of International Relations*, 4th ed. (New York: Longman, 1997).

190. See Scott Plous, *The Psychology of Judgment and Decision Making* (New York: McGraw-Hill, 1993), 18–20.

191. Studies of leaders' belief systems, the scholars Stephen Walker and Mark Schafer conclude, demonstrate that "a leader's belief system may reflect an idiosyncratic constellation of influences from more than one cultural tradition, which makes leaders indispensable psychological agents rather than interchangeable

creatures of systemic constraints or cultural forces in the explanation of foreign policy decisions." Walker and Schafer, "Theodore Roosevelt and Woodrow Wilson as Cultural Icons of US Foreign Policy," *Political Psychology* 28, no. 6 (2007): 749.

192. Yaacov Y. I. Vertzberger, *The World in Their Minds: Information Processing, Cognition, and Perception in Foreign Policy Decision Making* (Stanford, CA: Stanford University Press, 1990), 1.

193. As a result, it does little good to figure out how a generic set of decision-makers would view a situation; what is important, one scholar has argued, is to capture the world "of the decision makers as *they* view it. The manner in which *they* define situations becomes another way of saying how the state oriented to action and why." Richard C. Snyder, H. W. Bruck, and Burton Sapin, *Foreign Policy Decision-Making Revisited* (New York: Palgrave Macmillan, 2002), 59. In this approach, the individual represents the *point of integration* for the many factors influencing judgment, the decisive engines of meaning-making that produces a judgment; see, for example, Valerie M. Hudson, "Foreign Policy Analysis: Actor-Specific Theory and the Ground of International Relations," *Foreign Policy Analysis* 1 (2005): 1, 3, 5. Elsewhere she argues that "the point of intersection is the human decision maker"; Hudson, "Foreign Policy Decision Making," in Snyder, Bruck, and Sapin, *Foreign Policy Decision-Making*, 3–4.

Chapter 4: The Terrible Shadow of 9/11

1. Peter Viereck, "Clio is no Cleo: The Messiness of History," *Society*, March/April 2004, 14.

2. George Tenet, *At the Center of the Storm: My Years at the CIA* (New York: HarperCollins, 2007), 301.

3. Stephen F. Hayes, *Cheney: The Untold Story of America's Most Powerful and Controversial Vice President* (New York: HarperCollins, 2007), 333, 335, 343.

4. Barton Gellman, *Angler: The Cheney Vice Presidency* (New York: Penguin Press, 2008), 116–118.

5. Rowan Scarborough, *Rumsfeld's War: The Untold Story of America's Anti-Terrorist Commander* (Washington, DC: Regnery Publishing, 2004), 1.

6. Robert Draper, *Dead Certain: The Presidency of George W. Bush* (New York: The Free Press, 2007), 139.

7. Tenet, *At the Center of the Storm*, 170.

8. Elisabeth Bumiller, *Condoleezza Rice: An American Life* (New York: Random House, 2007), xx.

9. Interviewee 36.

10. Peter Schweizer and Rochelle Schweizer, *The Bushes: Portrait of a Dynasty* (New York: Doubleday, 2004), 513.

11. Ari Fleischer, *Taking Heat: The President, The Press, and My Years in the White House* (New York: William Morrow, 2005), 42. Cheney's own reactions were, if possible, even more unqualified: he referred to the attack as 'the most devastating blow to our homeland in its history"; Dick Cheney. *In My Time: A Personal and Political Memoir* (New York: Simon and Schuster, 2011), 330.

12. Bob Woodward, *Bush at War* (New York: Simon and Schuster, 2002), p. 30; Bumiller, *Condoleezza Rice*, xvii.

13. Hayes, *Cheney*, 345.

14. Peter Baker, *Days of Fire: Bush and Cheney in the White House* (New York: Doubleday, 2013), 131.

15. Speechwriter David Frum has described the "blood-red fury that swept the country" after 9/11, a sentiment that infused the administration as well; David Frum, *The Right Man: The Surprise Presidency of George W. Bush* (New York: Random House, 2003), 136.

16. Tenet, *At the Center of the Storm*, 176.

17. Frank Bruni, *Ambling Into History: The Unlikely Odyssey of George W. Bush* (New York: HarperCollins, 2002), 247.

18. See for example Woodward, *Bush at War*, 102.

19. Gerd Gigerenzer and Reinhard Selten, "Rethinking Rationality," in Gigerenzer and Selten, eds., *Bounded Rationality: The Adaptive Toolbox* (Cambridge, MA: MIT Press, 2002), 3.

20. James G. March, *A Primer on Decision Making* (New York: The Free Press, 194), 2–3, 100–102; James G. March and Johan P. Olson, "The Institutional Dynamics of International Political Orders," *International Organization* 52, no. 4 (Autumn 1998): 949; and James G. March and Johan P. Olson, "The Logic of Appropriateness," *ARENA Working Papers*, 04/09, 3, at https://www.researchgate.net/profile/Johan_Olsen3/publication/5014575_The_Logic_of_Appropriateness/links/55d2f0c808aec1b0429f03e4.pdf.

21. Scott Atran, Robert Axelrod, and Richard Davis, "Sacred Barriers to Conflict Resolution," *Science* 317 (August 24, 2007): 1039.

22. Philip E. Tetlock, "Social Functionalist Frameworks for Judgment and Choice: Intuitive Politicians, Theologians, and Prosecutors," *Psychological Review* 109, no. 3 (2002): 458–460.

23. Gregory S. Berns et al., "The Price of Your Soul: Neural Evidence for the Non-Utilitarian Representation of Sacred Values," *Philosophical Transactions of the Royal Society* 367 (2012): 754.

24. Michele and Robert Root-Bernstein, "Einstein on Creative Thinking," *Psychology Today*, March 31, 2010.

25. Kissinger quoted in Niall Ferguson, "The Meaning of Kissinger: A Realist Reconsidered," *Foreign Affairs* 94, no. 5 (September–October 2015): 138.

26. Walter Lippmann, *Public Opinion* (New York: Free Press, 1997), 10–11.

27. *Dewey's Human Nature and Conduct*, quoted in Alfred Schütz, "Choosing Among Projects of Action," *Philosophy and Phenomenological Research* 12, no. 2 (December 1951), 162.

28. See Fernando J. Cardim de Carvalho, "Keynes on Probability, Uncertainty, and Decision Making," *Journal of Post-Keynesian Economics* 11, no. 1 (Fall 1988): 74–75.

29. George W. Ball, *The Past Has Another Pattern: Memoirs* (New York: W. W. Norton, 1982), 366, 369.

30. David Frum catalogues the internal debate on this issue extensively in *The Right Man*, 152–154.

31. Samuel G. Freedman, "Six Days After 9/11, Another Anniversary Worth Honoring," *New York Times*, September 7, 2012, available at http://www.nytimes.com/2012/09/08/us/on-religion-six-days-after-9-11-another-anniversary-worth-honoring.html?_r=0.

32. Baker, *Days of Fire*, 137.

33. One senior official who was present for many of the post-9/11 discussions put it this way: "The tolerance for risk after 9/11 dropped precipitously" in regard to state sponsors of terrorism; Interviewee 64.

34. Ron Suskind, *The One Percent Doctrine: Deep Inside America's Pursuit of Its Enemies Since 9/11* (New York: Simon and Schuster, 2006), 62.

35. Interviewee 17.

36. Cheney, *In My Time*, 330–331, 388. Richard Bonin, on the basis of interviews with people inside and outside Cheney's office, believes that the bioweapons angle was crucial—that America's vulnerabilities on this score, combined with his belief that Saddam possessed the weapons and was willing to use them, led to an urgent commitment to overthrow the Iraqi leader; Richard Bonin, *Arrows of the Night: Ahmad Chalabi's Long Journey to Triumph in Iraq* (New York: Doubleday, 2011), 194; Baker, *Days of Fire*, 150–151.

37. Condoleezza Rice, *No Higher Honor: A Memoir of My Years in Washington* (New York: Crown, 2011), 79, 103–104, 198.

38. Interviewee 9.

39. Hayes, *Cheney*, 2–3.

40. Bradley Graham, *By His Own Rules: The Ambitions, Successes, and Ultimate Failures of Donald Rumsfeld* (New York: PublicAffairs, 2009), 284–285, 288. General Shelton's memoir concurs, saying Rumsfeld made the case to "go after all the countries who provide any kind of support" to terrorism: "Afghanistan, Sudan, Libya, Iran and Iraq." He quotes Rumsfeld: "We must think broadly." Hugh Shelton, *Without Hesitation: The Odyssey of an American Warrior* (New York: St. Martin's Press, 2010), 437.

41. Donald Rumsfeld, *Known and Unknown* (New York: Sentinel, 2011), 342.

42. There was at least one prominent exception: State Policy Planning Director Richard Haass, who wrote Colin Powell a measured note after the attacks, casting doubt on the wisdom of a "war" on terror and conceiving of terrorism "as akin to disease, an all but inevitable facet of modern life that one must constantly struggle against with a range of measures"; Richard Haass, *War of Necessity, War of Choice: A Memoir of Two Iraq Wars* (New York: Simon and Schuster, 2009), 188–189.

43. Frum, *The Right Man*, 141–142.

44. Douglas J. Feith, *War and Decision: Inside the Pentagon at the Dawn of the War on Terrorism* (New York: Harper, 2008), 3–4.

45. Interviewee 69.

46. Feith, *War and Decision*, 5–11.

47. Bob Woodward, *State of Denial* (New York: Simon and Schuster, 2006), 84–85.

48. Interviewee 39.

49. Interviewee 69.

50. Thomas Friedman, "Liberal Hawks Reconsider the Iraq War," *Slate*, January 12, 2004, available at http://www.slate.com/id/2093620/entry/2093763/.

51. Quoted in MSNBC documentary, "Hubris," broadcast February 19, 2013; see http://tv.msnbc.com/2013/02/19/watch-hubris-documentary/. On Dick Cheney's understanding of the demonstration effect, see Gellman, *Angler*, 231–233.

52. Rumsfeld, *Known and Unknown*, 343.

53. Interviewee 6.

54. Tenet, *At the Center of the Storm*, 175. "The president said that this was a war, and that it was the Pentagon's responsibility," Feith said. "He wanted it fought in the right spirit. People came away saying it was clear he wasn't talking about half measures"; Burrough et al., "The Path to War," *Vanity Fair*, May 2004, 236.

55. Baker, *Days of Fire*, 134.

56. Notes from Steven Cambone from meeting with Defense Secretary Donald Rumsfeld, September 11, 2001, as released via Freedom of Information Act Request, February 2006. See http://www.tomflocco.com/Docs/Dsn/DodStaffNotes.htm. The same material had already been referenced in Bob Woodward, *Plan of Attack* (New York: Simon and Schuster, 2004), 25.

57. Final Report of the National Commission on Terrorist Attacks Upon the United States, *The 9/11 Commission Report*, Authorized Edition (New York: W. W. Norton and Co., 2004), 334–335.

58. Lt. Gen. Michael DeLong, *A General Speaks Out: The Truth About the Wars in Afghanistan and Iraq* (St. Paul, MN: Zenith Publishing, 2007), 19–20.

59. DeLong, *A General Speaks Out*, 20.

60. Tenet, *At the Center of the Storm*, 306, xix. Feith has denied a number of different accounts that claimed he urged such attention on Iraq in these early days. In a sense it is beside the point; by September 14, at Camp David, the official Defense position was urging such a focus.

61. Interviewee 9.

62. Interviewee 6. Cheney continued to make the case for these connections in his memoir; see Cheney, *In My Time*, 396, 414–419. As Rice explains, "That an unconstrained Saddam might aid a terrorist in an attack on the United States did not seem far-fetched," especially given his established "pattern of recklessness"; Rice, *No Higher Honor*, 170.

63. Rice, *No Higher Honor*, 170–171.

64. See for example Woodward, *Bush at War*, 167.

65. The White House, "The Vice President Appears on NBC's Meet the Press," transcript, December 9, 2001, https://georgewbush-whitehouse.archives.gov/vicepresident/news-speeches/speeches/text/vp20011209.html.

66. Thom Shanker, "Rumsfeld Sees Lack of Proof for Qaeda-Hussein Link," *New York Times*, October 5, 2004, at https://www.nytimes.com/2004/10/05/politics/rumsfeld-sees-lack-of-proof-for-qaedahussein-link.html.

67. This quote appears in a helpful list of many administration statements connecting Iraq to al Qaeda: "The World: What the Bush Administration Said," *New York Times*, June 20, 2004, https://www.nytimes.com/2004/06/20/weekinreview/the-world-what-the-bush-administration-said.html.

68. Quoted in Sue Chan, "Bush Administration Links Iraq, al Qaeda,' CBS News, September 26, 2002, https://www.cbsnews.com/news/bush-administration-links -iraq-al-qaeda/.
69. Interviewee 6.
70. Interviewee 55.
71. Interviewee 56.
72. Interviewee 69.
73. Baker, *Days of Fire*, 266.
74. Clarke, *Against All Enemies*, 30–31. DeLong describes Rumsfeld's frustration with a lack of targets in *A General Speaks Out*, 34; Woodward has Rumsfeld pointing to Iraq as a target on the twelfth—see *Bush at War*, 49.
75. Interviewee 64.
76. Clarke, *Against All Enemies*, 32. Several reports claim to refer to other government staffers who witnessed this exchange. One of them—Philip James, "Running Scared," *Guardian*, March 26, 2004, available at http://www.guardian.co.uk /uselections2004/comment/story/0,14259,1178658,00.html, accessed February 7, 2006—was written by a Democratic party operative, and so his citing of an anonymous eyewitness may have political motivations. On first broadcasting its interview with Clarke, though, CBS News found two sources, one an eyewitness to the actual meeting, who confirmed Clarke's account; see http://www.cbsnews.com /stories/2004/03/19/60minutes/main607356.shtml, accessed February 7, 2006. Still, when Clarke's book came out, the White House said they had no record of the meeting. Michael Morell, the president's CIA briefer and around him far more than Clarke in those early days, describes Bush as repeatedly demanding to know who was responsible, but not with a fixation on Iraq. But the questions would have been perfectly consistent with a general sense that Iraq hung in the background of 9/11, directly or indirectly. See Michael Morell, *The Great War of Our Time* (New York: 12 Books, 2015), 52–55.
77. Bonin, *Arrows of the Night*, 196–197.
78. Dana Milbank and Claudia Deane, "Hussein Link to 9/11 Lingers in Many Minds," *Washington Post*, September 6, 2003, A1.
79. Tenet, *At the Center of the Storm*, 231–233. See also Morell, *The Great War of Our Time*, 66–67.
80. Bumiller, *Condoleezza Rice*, 167–169.
81. Baker, *Days of Fire*, 157.
82. Douglas J. Feith, *War and Decision: Inside the Pentagon at the Dawn of the War on Terrorism* (New York: Harper, 2008), 49–50.
83. Feith, *War and Decision*, 216–217; Rumsfeld, *Known and Unknown*, 356.
84. The "rationale for war," Feith says straight out, "did not actually stand or fall on the accuracy of CIA and UNSCOM assessments of Iraq's WMD stockpiles. The danger was that Saddam might someday soon provide terrorists with WMD"— based on his potential to do so, not merely his current stockpiles; Feith, *War and Decision*, 225.

85. "September 11th highlighted the special dangers that come from the connection of weapons of mass destruction to state sponsors of terrorism," Feith told a 2003 gathering of reporters. "That's a different issue from the analysis of whether one believes that the Iraqis possessed" WMDs ready to use at the time; Douglas Feith and William Luti, "DoD Briefing on Policy and Intelligence Matters," Department of Defense News Transcript, June 4, 2003, available at www.defenselink.mil /transcripts/2003/tr20030604-0248.html, accessed February 21, 2006.

86. John Diamond, Judy Keen, Dave Moniz, Susan Page, and Barbara Slavin, "Iraq Course Set from Tight White House Circle," *USA Today*, September 11, 2002, available at http://www.usatoday.com/news/world/2002-09-10-iraq-war_x.htm.

87. Bill Keller, "The Sunshine Warrior," *New York Times Magazine*, September 22, 2002, 50, 53.

88. Hugh Shelton, *Without Hesitation: The Odyssey of an American Warrior* (New York: St. Martin's Press, 2010), 441–442. See also Woodward, *Bush at War*, 61.

89. *Comprehensive Report of the Special Advisor to the DCI on Iraq's WMD*, vol. 1 of 3, September 30, 2004, 12; hereafter cited as the Duelfer Report.

90. Charles A. Duelfer and Stephen Benedict Dyson, "Chronic Misperception and International Conflict," *International Security* 36, no. 1 (Summer 2011): 83–84. He "denied any connection to al-Qaeda," the CIA analyst John Nixon, one of his interrogators, explains, "insisting he was a determined foe of the group." Because 9/11 was clearly the work of Islamic extremists, Saddam "thought the United States would need his secular government to help fight the scourge of Wahhabist militancy"; John Nixon, *Debriefing the President: The Interrogation of Saddam Hussein* (New York: Blue Rider Press, 2016), 108, 111–112.

91. Joyce Battle, ed., "Saddam Hussein Talks to the FBI," National Security Archive Electronic Briefing Book No. 279; casual conversation, June 11, 2004, available at http://www.gwu.edu/~nsarchiv/NSAEBB/NSAEBB279/24.pdf.

92. Battle, "Saddam Hussein Talks to the FBI," casual conversation, May 13, 2004, available at http://www.gwu.edu/~nsarchiv/NSAEBB/NSAEBB279/23.pdf.

93. Nixon, *Debriefing the President*, 108, 111–112.

94. Battle, "Saddam Hussein Talks to the FBI," casual conversation, June 28, 2004, available at http://www.gwu.edu/~nsarchiv/NSAEBB/NSAEBB279/26.pdf.

95. Duelfer and Dyson, "Chronic Misperception and International Conflict," 86.

96. This interpretation comes from a wide variety of evidence, but was explicitly laid out by Interviewee 11.

97. See for example the quotes in Glenn Kessler, "US Decision on Iraq Has Puzzling Past," *Washington Post*, January 12, 2003.

98. Interviewee 3.

99. Interviewee 3.

100. Interviewee 8.

101. Michael Morell, *The Great War of Our Time* (New York: 12 Books, 2015), 63.

102. Tenet, *At the Center of the Storm*, 177–179.

103. Feith, *War and Decision*, 48–49. A DoD briefing paper for the meeting, which was provided in the meeting's briefing book, did suggest "three priority targets

for initial action," according to the 9/11 Commission: "Al Qaeda, the Taliban, and Iraq," with a special emphasis on al Qaeda and Iraq. *The 9/11 Commission Report*, 335.

104. Woodward, *Bush at War*, 83–84.

105. Baker, *Days of Fire*, 144.

106. Interviewee 69; Woodward, *Bush at War*, 84.

107. Feith, *War and Decision*, 51. Confirmed by Interviewee 9; Bumiller, *Condoleezza Rice*, 165.

108. One senior participant in these discussions would later recall, "Clearly, there were those who were saying, 'Do Iraq now.' They made the argument because of what they saw as the connection between WMD and terrorism—at least that's how I understood their argument. But we had all we could do with Afghanistan, and . . . there were not a whole lot of people saying we should do Iraq first. Generally it wasn't that blatant." Interviewee 12.

109. Interviewee 7. Another who was not there but who got an immediate read-out from some who had been present said that it seemed that, at Camp David, "good decisions had been made"—the administration was sticking with Afghanistan and bin Laden; Interviewee 11.

110. Shelton, *Without Hesitation*, 444.

111. Karen DeYoung, *Soldier: The Life of Colin Powell* (New York: Alfred A. Knopf, 2006), 352.

112. Rice, *No Higher Honor*, 86–87. Rumsfeld was mum, Rice would later suggest. "Don may have said something like, 'The question of Iraq presents itself, Paul wants to say something,' but Don didn't offer an opinion about Iraq," Rice said later. "And I think the president was a little taken aback because Paul's not a principal and so I think he just wanted it off the table because it was a distraction"; Bumiller, *Condoleezza Rice*, 165–166.

113. Woodward, *Bush at War*, 91, 99; Baker, *Days of Fire*, 145; Rumsfeld, *Known and Unknown*, 359; Woodward, *Plan of Attack*, 25–26; Bill Keller, "The World According to Colin Powell," *New York Times Magazine*, November 24, 2001, 4; Hayes, *Cheney*, 352. Shelton has a different recollection, that Rumsfeld and Cheney were open about their support for rapid action against Iraq; *Without Hesitation*, 444. He describes the meeting as "turning ugly," which is stronger language than most other participants use, including participants I interviewed. Tenet writes that Bush "listened to Paul's views but, fairly quickly, it seemed to me, dismissed them. So did I. Rumsfeld did not seem nearly as consumed with the Iraqi connection as was his deputy, and he did not join in this portion of the debate in any meaningful way." Tenet recalls a vote being taken among the principals "on whether to include Iraq in our immediate response plans," and the result being "four to zero against it, with Don Rumsfeld abstaining"; Tenet, *At the Center of the Storm*, 306.

114. Interviewee 39.

115. Interviewee 9. For his part, Wolfowitz drew a clear conclusion from the Camp David sessions: "There was a long discussion during the day about what place if any Iraq should have in a counterterrorist strategy. On the surface of the debate

it at least appeared to be about not whether but when. . . . To the extent it was a debate about tactics and timing, the President clearly came down on the side of Afghanistan first. To the extent it was a debate about strategy and what the larger goal was, it is at least clear with 20/20 hindsight that the President came down on the side of the larger goal"; Deputy Secretary Paul Wolfowitz, interview with *Vanity Fair* magazine, May 9, 2003, DoD transcript of interview available at http://www.dod.gov/transcripts/2003/tr20030509-depsecdef0223.html, accessed February 7, 2006.

116. Cheney, *In My Time*, 334.
117. *The 9/11 Commission Report*, 335–336; and Glenn Kessler, "US Decision on Iraq Has Puzzling Past," *Washington Post*, January 12, 2003. Based upon its interviews, the Commission suggests that the motivation remained merely precautionary—to have war plans ready in the event that Saddam Hussein tried to use the disarray provoked by 9/11 to move against US or allied interests. This interpretation seems to vastly underestimate the subconscious commitment to unseating Saddam that had arisen in the minds of most senior administration officials.
118. *The 9/11 Commission Report*, 335–336.
119. Feith, *War and Decision*, 50, 55–56. See also Douglas J. Feith, "A War Plan That Cast a Wide Net," *The Washington Post*, August 7, 2004, A21.
120. In a later op-ed, Feith explained his rationale for such a suggestion: The enemy in this war "was not a single distinct organization," he wrote, but "was understood to comprise all those who contributed to the terrorist threat to the United States, of which Sept. 11 was just the most serious instance to date. The enemy was thought of as a network of individuals, groups and states that committed or supported such acts of terrorism." As a result, he thought it sensible to consider "military options that might: Shock the enemy network. . . . Show seriousness of US military purpose. . . . [and] show that the war would not be limited geographically to Afghanistan." Feith, "A War Plan That Cast a Wide Net." See also Mark Hosenball and Michael Isikoff, "Secret Proposals," *Newsweek*, August 9, 2004.
121. Interviewee 6.
122. Patrick E. Tyler and Elaine Sciolino, "Bush Advisers Split on Scope of Retaliation," *New York Times*, September 20, 2001.
123. Woodward, *Plan of Attack*, 50. Pressure to think seriously about Iraqi scenarios was reportedly coming from another angle as well: CENTCOM Commander Tommy Franks; see *The 9/11 Commission Report*, 336.
124. Burrough et al., "Path to War," 236.
125. Bonin, *Arrows of the Night*, 193–194.
126. Bonin, *Arrows of the Night*, 197–200.
127. Interviewee 54.
128. See, for example, Dana Priest, "Pentagon Shadow Loses Some Mystique," *Washington Post*, March 13, 2004, A11; Douglas Feith and William Luti, "DoD Briefing on Policy and Intelligence Matters," Department of Defense News Transcript, June 4, 2003, available at www.defenselink.mil/transcripts/2003/tr20030604-0248.html, accessed February 21, 2006; Inspector General, US Department of Defense,

Review of the Pre-Iraqi War Activities of the Office of the Under Secretary of Defense for Policy, February 9, 2007, declassified version available at www.dougfeith.com, 2; James Risen, "How Pair's Finding on Terror Led to Clash on Shaping Intelligence," *New York Times*, April 28, 2004; Feith, *War and Decision*, 117–118; Select Committee on Intelligence, US Senate, *Report on the US Intelligence Community's Prewar Intelligence Assessments on Iraq*, 108th Congress, July 7, 2004, 307; and Republican Policy Committee, United States Senate, "Disaggregating the Pentagon Offices: The Department of Defense, the Office of Special Plans and Iraq Pre-War Intelligence," February 7, 2006, 5; available at http://rpc.senate.gov/_files/Feb07 06DoDIntellMS.pdf, accessed February 21, 2006.

129. Tenet, *At the Center of the Storm*, 302, 309, 341–358.
130. Murray Waas, "Key Bush Intelligence Briefing Kept from Hill Panel," *National Journal*, November 22, 2005.
131. Bonin, *Arrows of the Night*, 201–202.
132. *The 9/11 Commission Report*, 336.
133. Peter Baker reports that Bush admitted to the need to go to Afghanistan first, but "when we have dealt with Afghanistan," he said, "we must come back to Iraq"; Baker, *Days of Fire*, 151–152. Con Coughlin's account suggests that Iraq hung in the background. Blair suggested that they had to deal effectively with AQ and the Taliban first, and Bush agreed: "Iraq," one participant claims Bush told Blair, "we keep for another day." Coughlin reports that, at dinner, Bush specifically said that although he would not go after Iraq at first, he reserved the right to go after Saddam later. Con Coughlin, *American Ally: Tony Blair and the War on Terror* (New York: HarperCollins, 2006), 168, 203.
134. Sir Christopher Meyer, "How Britain Failed to Check Bush in the Run Up to War," *Guardian*, November 7, 2005.
135. Rumsfeld, *Known and Unknown*, 424.
136. Rumsfeld, *Known and Unknown*, 425. Bush confirms the event: "Two months after 9/11," Bush explains—referring to a November or December time frame—"I asked Don Rumsfeld to review the existing battle plans for Iraq"; George W. Bush, *Decision Points* (New York: Crown, 2010), 234. Cheney claims he and Bush had already spoken and he was the one who urged Bush to direct Rumsfeld to get started; Cheney, *In My Time*, 368–369. As noted below, there are other reports of a very similar discussion on November 21, which may be the reference Bush is making.
137. This note is quoted in Mark Danner, "Rumsfeld's War and Its Consequences Now," *The New York Review of Books*, December 19, 2013; also cited in Baker, *Days of Fire*, 160.
138. Donald Rumsfeld, Memorandum for the President, "Strategic Thoughts," September 30, 2001, declassified May 7, 2009, available at DoD FOIA site, Rumsfeld folder.
139. At the beginning of October, OSD produced a "Strategic Guidance" briefing that reflected this same direction. A version has now been declassified in full, and we can see the complete range of targets on the minds of Rumsfeld and his Defense planners. As "Threats," the briefing listed the well-known roster of enemies, including terrorist

organizations and "states that harbor, sponsor, finance, or otherwise support those terrorist organizations." The "objectives" of the campaign were to "disrupt, damage and destroy" terrorist organizations, but also to go well beyond that—to "convince or compel states to sever all ties and terminate terrorist activity within their borders," and to "Disrupt, damage and destroy internal control mechanisms and the military capacity, including WMD, of regimes that continue to support WMD." The core means to achieve these goals was described as "Marshal, coordinate and synchronize all instruments of US national power—diplomatic, financial, intelligence, military and other—in the planning, execution and exploitation of a global campaign against terrorism sustainable for the foreseeable future." The briefing outlined a "Strategic Concept" for the war: It would be a government-wide campaign of many instruments and "extended duration," a "series of continuing, synchronized actions conducted in parallel along multiple lines of operation to: Break the determination of terrorist leaders, states and non-state actors that support terrorism; [and] Deny their ability to react effectively." The next slide got even more specific. Under "War Aims," it included "terrorists and state supporters defeated," and included two critical boxes. One was headed "Plans and Operations Against Terrorist Organizations, Possibly Including," a list that included al Qaeda, Hamas, Hezbollah, Islamic Jihad, and "Others." The adjacent box was headed "Plans and Operations Against State Regimes That Support Terrorists, Possibly Including" the Taliban in Afghanistan, Iraq, Iran, Syria, Libya, Sudan—and, again, "Others." The goal was clear, and ambitious: that "No state has the resolve or ability to continue harboring, sponsoring or otherwise supporting terrorists of global reach"; Department of Defense, "Campaign Against Terrorism: Strategic Guidance for the US Department of Defense," October 2, 2001, declassified January 29, 2008, released with documents made available to Donald Rumsfeld under MDR authority, available at DoD FOIA website.

140. Interviewee 24.
141. Interviewee 12.
142. Interviewees 34, 35, and 58; and Eric Schmitt and Thom Shanker, *Counterstrike: The Untold Story of America's Secret Campaign against al Qaeda* (New York: Times Books, 2011), 23–24.
143. Schmitt and Shanker, *Counterstrike*, 24.
144. Interviewee 58.
145. Interviewees 36, 58; Schmitt and Shanker, *Counterstrike*, 42.
146. Keller, "The World According to Colin Powell," 4–5.
147. Quote from http://abcnews.go.com/2020/Politics/story?id=1105979&page=1, accessed January 24, 2006.
148. Tony Blair, letter to George W. Bush, October 11, 2001, declassified by UK Iraq Inquiry.
149. Baker, *Days of Fire*, 168–169.
150. Presidential public affairs official Scott McClellan recalls that "one event with an enormous impact on President Bush's mind-set," something that "has been almost forgotten by many people," was the anthrax attacks. Bush was "determined not to let another terrorist attack happen on his watch and to challenge regimes believed

to be seeking weapons of mass destruction"; Scott McClellan, *What Happened: Inside the Bush White House and Washington's Culture of Deception* (New York: PublicAffairs, 2008), 108–112.

151. Evan Thomas, "The Shot Heard Round the World." *Newsweek*, February 27, 2006, 26.

152. Hayes, *Cheney*, 358.

153. Interviewee 6.

154. Haass, *War of Necessity*, 203.

155. Feith, *War and Decision,* 75.

156. Woodward, *Bush at War*, 310.

157. Interviewee 9.

158. One senior Blair advisor told Con Coughlin, "Although Blair took a keen interest in the Iraq issue before 9/11, it never crossed his mind that a military invasion could be launched to remove Saddam from power. He realized after Afghanistan that it was possible to make a difference, and that it was possible to rid the world of rotten regimes. The experience in Afghanistan was a real eye-opener for him"; Con Coughlin, *American Ally: Tony Blair and the War on Terror* (New York: HarperCollins, 2006), 209.

159. Woodward, *Bush at War*, 339.

160. Morell, *The Great War of Our Time*, 75–76.

161. Rumsfeld, *Known and Unknown*, 402.

162. Rumsfeld, *Known and Unknown*, 403.

163. Baker, *Days of Fire*, 191.

164. Jonathan Powell, memorandum to Tony Blair, "The War: What Comes Next," November 15, 2001, declassified by UK Iraq Inquiry.

165. Interviewee 12.

166. Interviewee 55.

167. Woodward, *Plan of Attack*, 1–3. There remains some ambiguity between two reported Bush-Rumsfeld conversations: the one on September 26, and this November 21 interaction. Public reports of both suggest that the content was essentially the same: look into the war plan with Iraq, do it quietly. It would seem that if the order was given in September, there would not have been a need for a second discussion in November. Either way, multiple sources have confirmed the essence of the direction at some combination of discussions from late September to late November 2001.

168. General Richard B. Myers (Ret.), *Eyes on the Horizon: Serving on the Front Lines of National Security* (New York: Threshold Editions, 2009), Kindle edition, loc. 3834, 4087.

169. Untitled memorandum, November 27, 2001, stamped "Unclassified," available at the George Washington University National Security Archive, https://nsarchive2.gwu.edu//NSAEBB/NSAEBB326/doc08.pdf.

170. Interviewee 63.

171. "Attachment 2 to Letter of 3 December 2001—IRAQ: Further Thoughts," sent to Sir David Manning from Richard Dearlove's private secretary, December 3, 2001,

declassified by UK Iraq Inquiry. Another attachment to that memo asked, "If the US heads for direct action [in Iraq], have we ideas which could divert them to an alternative course?" "Attachment 1 to Letter of 3 December 2001: IRAQ," sent to Sir David Manning from Richard Dearlove's private secretary, December 3, 2001, declassified by UK Iraq Inquiry. One memo from Blair's chief of staff, noted as having been filed between November 30 and December 3, lists as the lead objective of a new Iraq policy, "Removal of Saddam and replacement by a new, more moderate regime." But the concept was still support for oppositionists: Under "Plan," the memo suggested "Diplomatic campaign followed by military campaign (without large-scale coalition ground forces) . . . Campaign to end only with the replacement of Saddam"; Memorandum, Chief of Staff to PM, "Iraq: Change of Heart or Change of Regime," November 30–December 3, 2001, declassified by UK Iraq Inquiry. This plan is also described in detail in "IRAQ: Further Thoughts," which proposes declaring that the United States and United Kingdom "want regime change in Baghdad and we are ready to provide air support to coup makers."

172. "The War Against Terrorism—the Second Phase," December 4, 2001, declassified by UK Iraq Inquiry.

173. "IRAQ: Further Thoughts" memo.

174. Tommy Franks, *American Soldier* (New York: Regan Books, 2004), 328–335, 344–345; Gordon and Trainor, *Cobra II*, 27–32; Myers, *Eyes on the Horizon*, loc. 3899.

175. DeLong, *A General Speaks Out*, 66, 71.

176. Franks, *American Soldier*, 346–356, 366; Rumsfeld, *Known and Unknown*, 429–431; Myers, *Eyes on the Horizon*, loc. 3969. There is some disagreement in the sources about the exact date of the Crawford briefing, but it appears to have been either on the twenty-eighth or twenty-ninth. More evidence that discussions of Iraq were gaining steam by the end of 2001 comes from a memo from the head of the Intelligence and Research branch at State, Carl Ford, to Undersecretary Marc Grossman, dated December 14, 2001 (and declassified May 18, 2006), titled "Europe—Iraqi WMD Threat and the War on Terrorism." The memo dealt, Ford's cover sheet explained, with how European countries might react "should the US attack Iraq without clear evidence that it was culpable for the events of 9/11."

177. Woodward, *Plan of Attack*, 66.

178. Interviewee 3.

179. Special Inspector General for Iraqi Reconstruction, *Hard Lessons: The Iraq Reconstruction Experience* (Washington, DC: US Government Printing Office, 2009), 3, 7, available at http://www.sigir.mil/files/HardLessons/Hard_Lessons_Report.pdf.

180. Interviewee 4; also Interviewee 58.

181. Kessler, "US Decision on Iraq Has Puzzling Past."

182. Another press report, this one from the fall of 2002, quotes sources in the US government as suggesting that a de facto regime change decision was made in late 2001. "President Bush's determination to oust Iraq's Saddam Hussein by military force if necessary was set last fall without a formal decision-making meeting or the intelligence assessment that customarily precedes such a momentous decision," suggests the *USA Today* article, cowritten by the paper's senior defense and intelligence

reporters. The debate after that time, their sources contended, "has been about the means to accomplish that end." They quoted one "senior administration official" who admitted that the decision "kind of evolved, but it's not clear and neat"; it was, the official said, "policymaking by osmosis." Then–national security adviser Condoleezza Rice admitted on the record, "There wasn't a flash moment. There's no decision meeting. But Iraq had been on the radar screen—that it was a danger and that it was something you were going to have to deal with eventually"; John Diamond, Judy Keen, Dave Moniz, Susan Page and Barbara Slavin, "Iraq Course Set from Tight White House Circle," *USA Today*, September 11, 2002, available at http://www.usatoday.com/news/world/2002-09-10-iraq-war_x.htm.

183. Interviewee 3.
184. Interviewee 39.
185. Haass, *War of Necessity*, 216.
186. Haass, *War of Necessity*, 211.

Chapter 5: Justifying Invasion

1. Interviewee 8.
2. George W. Ball, *The Past Has Another Pattern: Memoirs* (New York: W. W. Norton, 1982), 422.
3. Dominic D. P. Johnson and Dominic Tierney, "The Rubicon Theory of War: How the Path to Conflict Reaches the Point of No Return," *International Security* 36, no. 1 (Summer 2011): 13.
4. Heinz Keckhausen and Peter M. Gollwitzer, "Thought Contents and Cognitive Functioning in Motivational versus Volitional States of Mind," *Motivation and Emotion* 11, no. 2 (June 1987): 103.
5. Peter M. Gollwitzer, "Action Phases and Mindsets," in *Handbook of Motivation and Cognition*, vol. 2., ed. E. T. Higgins and R. M. Sorrentino (New York: Guilford Press, 1990), 57.
6. Robert Kagan and William Kristol, "What to Do About Iraq," *Weekly Standard*, January 21, 2002, 23–25.
7. Interviewee 56. "It became an industrial base issue," another said—they simply needed more time to have all the required equipment and munitions ready; Interviewee 55. Part of the reason for the confusion, as another source put it, was how difficult it was to tell when getting ready for war turned into a decision to wage one. "Sorting out the preparation phases from the decision phases is tricky," he said; Interviewee 27.
8. Interviewee 11. Some officials did not get a sense of an urgent rush to war; Interviewee 57.
9. Karen DeYoung, *Soldier: The Life of Colin Powell* (New York: Alfred A. Knopf, 2006), 376.
10. Michael Isikoff and David Corn, *Hubris: The Inside Story of Spin, Scandal, and the Selling of the Iraq War* (New York: Crown, 2006), 7–8.
11. George Tenet, *At the Center of the Storm* (New York: HarperPerennial, 2007), 306–307.

12. Dick Cheney, *In My Time: A Personal and Political Memoir* (New York: Simon and Schuster, 2011), 370–371. On this meeting see also Bob Woodward, *Plan of Attack* (New York: Simon and Schuster, 2004), 72–73.

13. Interviewee 54.

14. Condoleezza Rice, *No Higher Honor: A Memoir of My Years in Washington* (New York: Crown, 2011), 171–172. A *New Republic* article from December 2003, based on interviews with former government officials, cites what it argues to be a crucial tête-à-tête between George Bush and Dick Cheney. It occurred in "early 2002," the magazine reports (based on later references, this probably refers to January), and Vice President Cheney "spoke to President George W. Bush from the heart." The war in Afghanistan had gone far more easily than anyone had expected, the account reports Cheney as arguing, and now it was time to look to "the next phase of the war on terrorism," which was "toppling Saddam Hussein." Cheney reportedly argued that he had changed his mind since 1991: the first Bush administration's choice not to go all the way to Baghdad had been a mistake, and now President Bush "had a chance to correct it." Cheney's "plea was enormously successful," the account concludes; it quotes a former NSC official who claimed a sense that by February, "the decision was taken"; Spencer Ackerman and Franklin Foer, "The Radical," *New Republic*, December 1, 2003, 17.

15. Cheney, *In My Time*, 387. At the same time, Capitol Hill staffers sympathetic to the cause—Danielle Pletka in the Senate and Steve Rademaker in the House—had drafted legislation providing $25 million in Defense funds to Iraqi exiles, guaranteeing $12 million of it to Chalabi's INC. The legislation's first draft would have put the program entirely under Defense, but this was furiously resisted by Richard Armitage, who managed to add language requiring State concurrence. Eventually a $30 million tranche appeared in the war supplemental budget without specific mention of the INC—but was deleted by the Congress; Dov S. Zakheim, *A Vulcan's Tale: How the Bush Administration Mismanaged the Reconstruction of Afghanistan* (Washington, DC: Brookings Institution Press, 2011), 161–163.

16. Interviewee 54. Deputy Director James Pavitt's instruction to "scare them" is recounted in Isikoff and Corn, *Hubris*, 8.

17. Burrough et al., "Path to War," 240. Frum's own recollection was that his assignment was to make "our best case for going after Iraq"; David Frum, *The Right Man: The Surprise Presidency of George W. Bush* (New York: Random House, 2003), 224.

18. Jeffrey Goldberg, "The Believer," *New Yorker*, February 13 and 20, 2006, 60.

19. Elisabeth Bumiller, *Condoleezza Rice: An American Life* (New York: Random House, 2007), 173–175. Frum gives an account of adding Iran to the speech in *The Right Man*, 237.

20. Charles Krauthammer, "Redefining the War," *The Washington Post*, February 1, 2002.

21. *Comprehensive Report of the Special Advisor to the DCI on Iraq's WMD*, vol. 1 of 3, September 30, 2004, 61; hereafter cited as the Duelfer Report.

22. Tommy Franks describes the briefing in *American Soldier* (New York: Regan Books, 2004), 373. The session is also recounted in Woodward, *Plan of Attack*, 98–103.

23. Warren P. Strobel and John Walcott, "Bush Has Decided to Overthrow Hussein," McClatchy Washington Bureau, February 13, 2002.

24. Rice, *No Higher Honor*, 172.

25. Michael R. Gordon and Bernard E. Trainor, *Cobra II: The Inside Story of the Invasion and Occupation of Iraq* (New York: Pantheon Books, 2006), 51–52. In his memoirs, Franks tries to dance around the obvious falsehood by saying, "It was the truth. In May 2002, we were offering the President options, not a plan"; Franks, *American Soldier*, 425. This is patently ridiculous. They were more than five months into extremely intensively development of a *war plan*, specifically directed by the president, an order relayed to Franks by "his boss," the secretary of defense. How that allows the statement he made is unclear.

26. Zakheim, *A Vulcan's Tale*, 157–159.

27. Tenet, *At the Center of the Storm*, 386–387.

28. Interviewee 53.

29. Tenet, *At the Center of the Storm*, 386.

30. Rowan Scarborough, *Rumsfeld's War: The Untold Story of America's Anti-Terrorist Commander* (Washington, DC: Regnery Publishing, 2004), 45, and Isikoff and Corn, *Hubris,* 9–10.

31. Woodward, *Plan of Attack*, 108.

32. Mike Tucker and Charles S. Faddis, *Operation Hotel California: The Clandestine War in Iraq* (Guilford, CT: The Lyons Press, 2009).

33. Interviewee 54.

34. Evan Thomas, Tamara Lipper, and Roy Gutman, "Chemistry in the War Cabinet," *Newsweek*, January 28, 2002, 26. This report offered a hagiographic portrait of the emerging national security team. "Measured by the usual backstabbing standards of Washington," it argued, "Rumsfeld and Powell—and the rest of George W. Bush's war cabinet—have got along famously." It described Rumsfeld as a "gruff but reassuringly macho presence at the Pentagon's televised midday briefings." Even by January such comments were simply not suitable for national members of the press doing their job of checking governmental power.

35. Cable from British Embassy Washington to Foreign Ministry, "US/Iraq: The Momentum Builds," February 13, 2002, declassified by UK Iraq Inquiry.

36. "By the first few months of 2002," Meyer would later explain, "it was clear that Bush was determined to implement the official American policy of regime change." By that time, Meyer claims, "Tony Blair had already taken the decision to support regime change, though he was discreet about saying so in public"; Christopher Meyer, "How Britain Failed to Check Bush," *Guardian,* November 7, 2005.

37. Jim Hoagland, "Facing the Music on Iraq," *Washington Post,* February 17, 2002, B7.

38. As one summary of postwar interviews with Iraqi senior officials concludes, "Saddam did not realize how dangerous this new round of bargaining and obstructionism was to his regime until it was too late"; Charles A. Duelfer and Stephen Benedict Dyson, "Chronic Misperception and International Conflict," *International Security* 36, no. 1 (Summer 2011): 90.

39. Hans Blix, *Disarming Iraq* (New York: Pantheon Books, 2004), 60.

40. Interviewee 66.

41. Interviewee 9.

42. Scott McClellan, *What Happened: Inside the Bush White House and Washington's Culture of Deception* (New York: PublicAffairs, 2008), 127–129.

43. US Department of Defense News Transcript, "DoD News Briefing—Secretary Rumsfeld and Gen. Myers," February 12, 2002, available at http://www.defenselink.mil/transcripts/transcript.aspx?transcriptid=2636.

44. Douglas J. Feith, *War and Decision: Inside the Pentagon at the Dawn of the War on Terrorism* (New York: Harper, 2008), 237–238.

45. Interviewee 24. Another participant described them as "a very comprehensive review of all the issues that would be necessary to accomplish, *if* the decision were taken for a war"; Interviewee 38. Department of State officials who described the interagency process for Karen DeYoung's biography of Colin Powell spoke in very similar terms. "Since there had been no official policy decision on invading Iraq, the meetings had an air of unreality about them. . . . 'We knew what we were talking *about*, but we didn't know what we were talking *for*,' recalled one State Department participant. 'We didn't know whether secretly a decision had been made.'" By about June, State representatives to the meetings began to get the uneasy feeling that their OSD and OVP counterparts were "too cocky," one State official told DeYoung. "It's like they know something we don't." DeYoung, *Soldier*, 398–399.

46. Interviewee 24; other information from Interviewee 7.

47. Tenet, *At the Center of the Storm*, 307–308.

48. Interviewee 7. Even Doug Feith, anxious as he was to get going with war planning, worried about the lack of rigor. "Looking back on the interagency decision-making process," he writes, "I am struck by its lack of clarity. On issue after issue, where there were disagreements they were not brought to the surface to be presented to the President for decision. Rather, basic disagreements were allowed to remain unresolved—as long as a degree of consensus could be produced on immediate next steps"; Feith, *War and Decision,* 245.

49. Interviewee 7.

50. Interviewee 44.

51. Interviewee 52.

52. Interviewee 24.

53. Interviewee 24.

54. Interviewee 54.

55. On this distinction see Bob Woodward, *State of Denial* (New York: Simon and Schuster, 2006), 117.

56. Special Inspector General for Iraqi Reconstruction, *Hard Lessons: The Iraq Reconstruction Experience* (Washington, D.C.: US Government Printing Office, 2009), 7, available at http://www.sigir.mil/files/HardLessons/Hard_Lessons_Report.pdf.

57. Bumiller, *Condoleezza Rice*, 184.

58. Cheney, *In My Time*, 404–406.

59. Rice, *No Higher Honor*, 17.

60. John Grainger, memorandum, "Iraq: Regime Change," March 21, 2002, declassified as part of the UK Iraq inquiry.

61. Overseas and Defence Secretariat, Cabinet Office, "Iraq: Options Paper," March 8, 2002, available at www.downingstreetmemo.com.

62. Cheney, *In My Time*, 377.

63. David Manning, "Prime Minister: Your Trip to the US," March 14, 2002, available at www.downingstreetmemo.com.

64. Strobel and Walcott, "Bush Has Decided to Overthrow Hussein."

65. Cheney, *In My Time*, 372–374.

66. Interviewee 64.

67. Stephen F. Hayes, *Cheney: The Untold Story of America's Most Powerful and Controversial Vice President* (New York: HarperCollins, 2007), 371–373.

68. Michael Elliott and James Carney, "First Stop Iraq," *Time*, March 31, 2003, 172.

69. British Embassy Washington, Confidential and Personal Memo from Ambassador Christopher Meyer to Sir David Manning, March 18, 2002; available at www.downingstreetmemo.com.

70. Meyer, "How Britain Failed to Check Bush."

71. British Embassy memo, March 18, 2002.

72. British Embassy memo, March 18, 2002.

73. Nicholas Lemann, "The Next World Order," *New Yorker*, April 1, 2002, posted online March 25, available online at http://www.newyorker.com/archive/2002/04/01/020401fa_FACT1.

74. Jack Straw, "Prime Minister: Crawford/Iraq," March 25, 2002, available at www.downingstreetmemo.com.

75. Con Coughlin, *American Ally: Tony Blair and the War on Terror* (New York: HarperCollins, 2006), 221–224.

76. Meyer, "How Britain Failed to Check Bush." Blair's essential message was confirmed in several British government documents that have been revealed. One in particular states quite clearly that Blair "said that the UK would support military action to bring about regime change, provided that certain conditions were met: efforts had been made to construct a coalition/shape public opinion, the Israeli-Palestine Crisis was quiescent, and the options for action to eliminate Iraq's WMD through the UN weapons inspectors had been exhausted." Cabinet Office, "Conditions for Military Action."

77. Robin Cook, *The Point of Departure* (London: Simon and Schuster, 2004), 135.

78. Woodward, *Plan of Attack*, 119–120.

79. According to one declassified State briefing, State "planning on the transition" for a post-Saddam Iraq started as early as October 2001; topics for working groups were vetted beginning in February 2002. US Department of State, "Future of Iraq Project," PowerPoint presentation, November 1, 2002, declassified June 16, 2005. After some debates about using outside contractors to conduct the analysis—among others, Ahmad Chalabi reportedly wanted his INC to do it—State determined that it would have to oversee the program itself. In an interesting sidelight, State was

originally going to contract out to the Middle East Institute, a Washington think-tank, to run the process. They had a $5 million grant all set and awarded—and then someone in the government noticed that the Institute director, former State Near East Bureau head Edward Walker, had referred to the "axis of evil" notion as "ridiculous." OSD and OVP people rushed in to cancel the contract; Deputy Secretary of State Richard Armitage reportedly called Congressman Henry Hyde with an appeal to support the grant, to no avail. It was cancelled. Jim Hoagland, "The Iraq Intrigues," *Washington Post*, May 3, 2002, A27.

The project was run by the Office of Northern Gulf Affairs; a State official named Thomas Warrick directed it. It eventually boasted seventeen working groups, ranging from transitional justice to oil and energy to civil society. Specifically, the working groups were Transitional Justice; Public Finance; Democratic Principles; Public Health and Humanitarian Issues; Public Outreach; Water, Agriculture & the Environment; Economy and Infrastructure; Local Government; Defense Policy; Oil & Energy; Education; Anti-Corruption Issues; Civil Society-Capacity Building; Building a Free Media; Return of Refugees and Internally Displaced Persons; Foreign Policy; and Preserving Iraq's Cultural Heritage. Marc Grossman, under secretary for political affairs, "Testimony before the Senate Foreign Relations Committee," February 11, 2003, available at www.state.gov/p/17616.htm, accessed February 21, 2006.

80. David L. Phillips, *Losing Iraq: Inside the Postwar Reconstruction Fiasco* (Boulder, CO: Westview Books, 2005), 37. This process is also described in George Packer, *The Assassin's Gate: America in Iraq* (New York: Farar, Straus and Giroux, 2005), 66–67. The consultant and expert on postconflict transitions David Phillips participated in these efforts. He wrote that "the goal was not to achieve consensus but to build a sense of solidarity and common purpose between Iraqis who were coming together to plan their country's recovery." Ahmad Chalabi, spurned in his effort to have the INC coordinate the whole project, at first would not participate and suggested that the effort be shuttered. When it was clear that it would proceed, Chalabi reportedly realized he had no choice but to join and try to influence its outcomes; Phillips, *Losing Iraq*, 38.

81. One participant described it as a program "to put together émigré Iraqis with experience and competence that we felt would be needed in a postwar Iraq"; Interviewee 44.

82. DeYoung, *Soldier*, 397–398.

83. This would have been the Contingency Planning and Peacekeeping Office within State's Political-Military Bureau, excluded partly due to turf issues between State regional and functional bureaus; Donald R. Drechsler, "Reconstituting the Interagency Process after Iraq," *Journal of Strategic Studies* 28, no. 1 (2005): 17.

84. Interviewee 29. Ali Allawi concludes that it was a "half-hearted and unreal attempt to tackle the issues that would confront the overseers of a country with a devastated economy and a dictatorial political culture. Most of the groups dealt with issues on which participants had no up-to-date information, or any immediate experience"; Ali A. Allawi, *The Occupation of Iraq: Winning the War, Losing the Peace* (New Haven, CT: Yale University Press, 2007), 83.

85. Interviewee 5.

86. Interviewee 44.

87. Rice, *No Higher Honor*, 175.

88. Kevin M. Woods, with Michael R. Pease, Mark E. Stout, Williamson Murray, and James G. Lacey, *Iraqi Perspectives Project: A View of Operation Iraqi Freedom from Saddam's Senior Leadership* (Norfolk, VA: Joint Center for Operational Analysis, US Joint Forces Command, March 2006), 29.

89. John Nixon, *Debriefing the President: The Interrogation of Saddam Hussein* (New York: Blue Rider Press, 2016), 83,

90. Woodward, *State of Denial*, 91; see also 179.

91. For example, Interviewee 1, Interviewee 24.

92. Interviewee 7.

93. Interviewee 7.

94. Department of Defense, "Scenarios for the 'End Game,'" April 23, 2002, declassified and released in DoD FOIA process, available at DoD FOIA site.

95. Donald Rumsfeld, *Known and Unknown* (New York: Sentinel, 2011), 398.

96. In February 2001, long before 9/11, Rumsfeld had issued a snowflake ordering that democratization initiatives be "de-emphasized"; Zakheim, *A Vulcan's Tale*, 186.

97. Testimony of Donald Rumsfeld on US Policy toward Iraq, Hearing before the House Committee on Armed Services, 177-2, September 18, 2002, available at http://commdocs.house.gov/committees/security/has261000.000/has261000_0.htm.

98. Michael Morell, *The Great War of Our Time* (New York: 12 Books, 2015), 86–87.

99. Blix, *Disarming Iraq*, 62–67.

100. Charles A. Duelfer and Stephen Benedict Dyson, "Chronic Misperception and International Conflict," *International Security* 36, no. 1 (Summer 2011): 86–92.

101. Joyce Battle, ed., "Saddam Hussein Talks to the FBI," National Security Archive Electronic Briefing Book No. 279, Interview Session Number 4, February 13, 2004.

102. Duelfer and Dyson, "Chronic Misperception and International Conflict," 91.

CHAPTER 6: MUDDLING TOWARD WAR

1. David Frum, *The Right Man: The Surprise Presidency of George W. Bush* (New York: Random House, 2003), 190.

2. Quoted in David Rose, "Neo Culpa," *Vanity Fair*, November 3, 2006, available at http://www.vanityfair.com/news/2006/12/neocons200612.

3. Douglas J. Feith, *War and Decision: Inside the Pentagon at the Dawn of the War on Terrorism* (New York: Harper, 2008), 468.

4. Tom Ricks, "Some Top Military Brass Favor Status Quo in Iraq," *Washington Post*, July 28, 2002, A1.

5. Steven Mufson, "Scowcroft Urges Restraint against Iraq," *Washington Post*, August 5, 2002.

6. Bob Woodward, *Plan of Attack* (New York: Simon and Schuster, 2004), 149.

7. These quotes come from Mufson, "Scowcroft Urges Restraint against Iraq."

8. Feith, *War and Decision*, 276; Nora Bensahel et al., *After Saddam: Prewar Planning and the Occupation of Iraq* (Santa Monica, CA: The RAND Corporation, 2008), 22–23.

9. Interviewee 51.

10. Gordon W. Rudd, *Reconstructing Iraq: Regime Change, Jay Garner, and the ORHA Story* (Lawrence: University Press of Kansas, 2011), 53.

11. Interviewee 51.

12. Richard Haass, *War of Necessity, War of Choice: A Memoir of Two Iraq Wars* (New York: Simon and Schuster, 2009), 5–6.

13. Interviewee 7.

14. Interviewee 54.

15. US Department of State and Broadcasting Board of Governors, Office of Inspector General, Review of Awards to Iraqi National Congress Support Foundation, September 2001, report released by Department of State FOIA process, available at State IG FOIA website.

16. Donald Rumsfeld, "Iraqi Exile Support," January 8, 2002, available at www .rumsfeld.com. Outside the government, Chalabi backers retaliated by leaking to the *Wall Street Journal* the minutes of a May 2002 meeting from the State inspector general that purportedly claim that State officials were using the investigation as a pretext to "shut down the INC." The *Journal* took this as evidence that the State Department was trying to "hijack the peace" by eliminating Chalabi from the equation; "Smearing Mr. Chalabi," *Wall Street Journal*, April 10, 2003.

17. Interviewee 44.

18. Jim Hoagland—the Chalabi supporter writing for the *Post*—reported in May 2002 that the State Department inspector general was trying to "strangle" the INC "with red tape"—and thus kill off "the only Iraqi opposition group with a record of fighting against Saddam Hussein and for democracy in Iraq"; Jim Hoagland, "The Iraq Intrigues," *Washington Post*, May 3, 2002, A27.

19. George Packer, *The Assassin's Gate: America in Iraq* (New York: Farrar, Straus and Giroux, 2005), 147; Interviewee 8.

20. Interviewee 11.

21. Doug Feith's memoir confirms that at a July 25, 2002, Deputies lunch, he announced that State and DIA had agreed on the transfer; Feith, *War and Decision*, 277.

22. Jonathan S. Landay, "US Halts Funding to Iraqi Group," *The Philadelphia Inquirer*, May 19, 2004.

23. Richard Bonin, *Arrows of the Night: Ahmad Chalabi's Long Journey to Triumph in Iraq* (New York: Doubleday, 2011), 2, 173.

24. Interviewee 44.

25. Phillips, *Losing Iraq*, 7–8, 67–68.

26. Interviewee 24.

27. Interviewee 8.

28. Interviewee 12. Aram Roston's volume on Chalabi quotes a journalist who followed the exile for years as saying that Wolfowitz was the one neocon "from whom he recalls hearing the smallest doubts about Chalabi"—but that even Wolfowitz *did* express some doubt, saying, "I'm not one of the people who thinks Ahmad Chalabi is the best thing since sliced bread"; Aram Roston, *The Man Who Pushed America to War: The Extraordinary Life, Adventures, and Obsesions of Ahmad Chalabi* (New York:

Nation Books, 2008), 203. Another former senior official agreed that Rumsfeld never fell in love with Chalabi; Interviewee 42.

29. Interviewee 54. Another senior official found no strong push for a government-in-exile with Chalabi at its head; the consensus, he thought, was that 'we would have to wait and see," that Iraqis inside the country would need to have a major voice; Interviewee 38. For his part, Doug Feith claims in his book that "I never advocated that the United States should select Iraq's leader, and I never heard Wolfowitz argue for favoring a particular Iraqi leader, whether Chalabi or anyone else"; Feith, *War and Decision,* 254. In his own memoirs, Rumsfeld writes with a studied distance, saying he found Chalabi talented but had no desire to anoint him: Donald Rumsfeld, *Known and Unknown* (New York: Sentinel, 2011), 489.

30. Interviewee 60. Another senior official with knowledge of the thinking of these cabinet members dismisses the idea that they were snowed by exiles. John Hannah in Cheney's office, he says, was close to Francis Brooke of the INC. He describes the exiles as "one of Cheney's means of information gathering" but says they were not committed to any one person or set of people; Interviewee 64. A former senior Defense official told me, "Some people in DoD respected him, but the press stories about the Pentagon championing Chalabi were much overstated. The real passion regarding Chalabi was more on the negative side than the positive. There were people in the CIA and State Department who were passionately antagonistic to Chalabi"; Interviewee 9. Doug Feith's perspective on this can be found in Douglas J. Feith, *War and Decision: Inside the Pentagon at the Dawn of the War on Terrorism* (New York: Harper, 2008), 190–191.

31. Interviewee 1.

32. Michael Isikoff and David Corn, *Hubris: The Inside Story of Spin, Scandal, and the Selling of the Iraq War* (New York: Crown, 2006), 52.

33. Interviewee 8. At their March 17 lunch, British Ambassador Meyer asked Wolfowitz about the debates within the administration between pro- and anti-Chalabi factions. Wolfowitz initially claimed neutrality—though, "as the conversation developed," Meyer reported to London, "it became clear that Wolfowitz was far more pro-INC than not." Wolfowitz suggested that some people were pushing to exclude the INC, and he strongly opposed this option. "It was true that Chalabi was not the easiest person to work with," Wolfowitz said. "But he had a good record in bringing high-grade defectors out of Iraq" (or so Wolfowitz continued to think at the time). "The CIA stubbornly refused to believe this," Wolfowitz told Meyer. "They unreasonably denigrated the INC because of their fixation with Chalabi." British Embassy memo, March 18, 2002.

34. Interviewee 44.

35. Cited in Dov S. Zakheim, *A Vulcan's Tale: How the Bush Administration Mismanaged the Reconstruction of Afghanistan* (Washington, DC: Brookings Institution Press, 2011), 163.

36. Bonin, *Arrows of the Night,* 229, 235–240.

37. Joseph L. Galloway, Jonathan S. Landay, Warren P. Strobel, and John Walcott, "Postwar Planning for Iraq 'Ignored,'" *Philadelphia Inquirer,* October 17, 2004, 1.

One former senior official insisted that quotes implying that the United States wanted to anoint Chalabi may have come from lower-level people; President Bush clearly refused to pick and choose among exiles; Interviewee 9.

38. Interviewee 5.

39. Interviewee 8.

40. For an internal DoD take on the meeting, see Office of the Assistant Secretary of Defense memo, "Iraqi Opposition Military Conference Meeting," July 16, 2002, declassified through DoD FOIA process, available at DoD FOIA website. A relevant report is a January 2003 "Future of Iraq Project Progress Report," describing the meeting of a working group held in Washington. The group had discussed, among other things, a disturbing fact—Iraq's Nationality Law. "Right now, essentially," the memo explained, "**no external Iraqi oppositionist is eligible to vote or hold office in a future Iraqi government** because almost all have been stripped of their Iraqi citizenship." Not to be deterred by an unfortunate fact of the laws of the country they were about to invade, the authors of the memo concluded simply, "This law will have to be changed before the first Iraqi election can be held"; no author specified, "Future of Iraq Project—Progress Report," n.d. but presumably January 2003 because it is reporting on a meeting of January 9–10, 2003, declassified through DoD FOIA process, available at DoD FOIA website. Emphasis in original.

41. Peter W. Rodman, "Support for Iraqi Opposition," May 9, 2002, declassified October 2010, available at www.rumsfeld.com. The memo is discussed in Feith, *War and Decision*, 252, although Feith's characterization of it does not entirely match the actual language in the memo.

42. Donald Rumsfeld, "Supporting the Iraqi Opposition," July 1, 2002, declassified October 12, 2010, available at www.rumsfeld.com.

43. John Kingdon, *Agendas, Alternatives, and Public Policies* (New York: HarperCollins, 1984), 1.

44. Kingdon, *Agendas, Alternatives, and Public Policies*, 134.

45. Policy entrepreneurs are people willing to "invest their resources—time, energy, reputation, and sometimes money"—into a campaign for changed policy; Kingdon, *Agendas, Alternatives, and Public Policies*, 129; see also Nelson W. Polsby, *Political Innovation in America: The Politics of Policy Initiation* (New Haven, CT: Yale University Press), 55, 173–174.

46. Kingdon, *Agendas, Alternatives, and Public Policies*, 93–94; see also 129.

47. Interviewee 3.

48. Interviewee 4. Some writings on policy communities and entrepreneurs suggest that such a trigger is essential—that the ideas cherished by entrepreneurs will lay dormant for years until aided by what Kingdon calls a "focusing event" that can help them push the idea through a "policy window." Sometimes these events can be passing and secondary but still used as fuel for policy change; at other times, "crises come along that simply bowl over everything standing in the way of prominence on the agenda"; Kingdon, *Agendas, Alternatives, and Public Policies*, 101; on focusing events and policy windows, see also 95–105 and 174–177.

49. Polsby, *Political Innovation in America*, 169.

50. The text of the memo itself, as well as many of the accompanying memos that I will cite, is available at www.downingstreetmemo.com.

51. David Manning, "Your Trip to the US." A March 22, 2002, memo from the political director at the Foreign Office, Peter Ricketts, to Foreign Secretary Jack Straw recognized that "we are left with a problem of bringing public opinion to accept the imminence of a threat from Iraq"; P. F. Ricketts, "Iraq: Advice for the Prime Minister," March 22, 2002, available at www.downingstreetmemo.com.

52. Cabinet Office, "Iraq: Conditions for Military Action."

53. Department of Defense, "Declaratory Policy on WMD," classified by USDP Feith, August 2002, declassified through DoD FOIA process and available on DoD FOIA website.

54. Another declassified Top Secret memo on the same subject began with a summary of its "Fundamental Premise": "Inspections cannot succeed in ridding Iraq of its WMD *unless* Iraq cooperates." The next sentence offered a crucial clue as to the purpose of inspections for people with such beliefs: "Therefore, the *inspectors' purpose is not to uncover WMD but to determine whether Saddam has decided to cooperate.*" The text then laid out a process by which the United States would discredit inspections, ratchet up military pressure, and flow more coalition forces to the region. The final stage would be an ultimatum demanding a "complete an accurate declaration," an end to attacks on coalition aircraft, and "complete cooperation with the inspectors." The "ultimatum's deadline," the memo concluded, "would be determined by military factors—when the US would be in the most advantageous position to begin armed conflict"; Department of Defense, "Post-UNSCR Strategy for Iraq," n.d., declassified through DoD FOIA process and available on DoD FOIA website. Emphasis in original.

Other internal Defense Department memos from this period gave at least lip service to the idea of inspections as an alternative to war—though the clear implication hanging behind them was that the alternative was hardly feasible. One undated memo titled "Dealing with Iraqi WMD: The Inspection Option" said it straight out: "Eliminating this WMD threat may ultimately require military action. However, we may first want to try to put in place an inspection regime" based on existing international legal foundations such as the Gulf War cease-fire and UN Security Council Resolution 687. This regime would have to be incredibly robust, led by US inspectors, with immediate access to any site without delay. Even then, the memo was hardly sanguine: it called attention to Iraq's ability to spoof every inspection system to date and argued that "even the most intrusive inspection system regime can only hinder Iraqi WMD/missile development, not eliminate it." It said inspections are of little value without good intelligence—"and the international community has no effective response to Saddam's defiance. Sanctions are not sufficiently coercive and not sustainable"; Department of Defense, "Dealing with Iraqi WMD: The Inspection Option," n.d., declassified through DoD FOIA process and available on DoD FOIA website.

55. Interviewee 7.

56. Interviewee 44.

57. Interviewee 13.

58. Interviewee 64.

59. Colin Powell, *My American Journey* (New York: Ballantine Books, 1995), 213.

60. Interviewee 27. See also Karen DeYoung, *Soldier: The Life of Colin Powell* (New Yorl: Alfred A. Knopf, 2006), 5, 431.

61. Woodward, *Plan of Attack,* 148–153; the original account was published in *Bush at War*, 331–334.

62. Woodward, *Plan of Attack,* 151. See also DeYoung, *Soldier*, 403.

63. DeYoung, *Soldier*, 401–402.

64. This somewhat different tone—the "here's how to get to your end goal" rather than the "please, Mr. President, consider these risks" tone—is apparent in the account of the discussion in Robert Draper, *Dead Certain: The Presidency of George W. Bush* (New York: The Free Press, 2007), 179–180.

65. Woodward, *Plan of Attack,* 151.

66. Condoleezza Rice, *No Higher Honor: A Memoir of My Years in Washington* (New York: Crown, 2011), 21.

67. Feith, *War and Decision*, 284–286.

68. Feith, *War and Decision*, 286–287. For Rumsfeld's summary of his own views see Bob Woodward, *State of Denial* (New York: Simon and Schuster, 2006), 130–131.

69. Quoted at http://www.hughhewitt.com/blog/g/bcb02904-68f1-4d8e-9758-8561 8344cb0a.

70. Barton Gellman and Walter Pincus, "Depiction of Threat Outgrew Supporting Evidence," *Washington Post*, August 10, 2003, A1; Elisabeth Bumiller, *Condoleezza Rice: An American Life* (New York: Random House, 2007), 191.

71. Scott McClellan, *What Happened: Inside the Bush White House and Washington's Culture of Deception* (New York: PublicAffairs, 2008), 134, 142, 144.

72. Toby Harnden, "Americans Firm on Toppling Saddam," *Telegraph UK*, August 14, 2002, available at http://www.telegraph.co.uk/news/main.jhtml?xml=/news /2002/08/14/wpoll14.xml, accessed February 21, 2006. The poll was performed by the *Washington Post* and ABC News.

73. David W. Moore, "Majority of Americans Favor Attacking Iraq to Oust Saddam Hussein," Gallup.com, https://news.gallup.com/poll/6658/majority-americans-favor -attacking-iraq-oust-saddam-hussein.aspx, accessed November 14, 2018.

74. Phillips, *Losing Iraq*, 42.

75. US Department of State, Press Statement, "Meeting of Iraqi Opposition Leaders," August 8, 2002. Unclassified, released March 29, 2006, available at State Department FOIA site.

76. Ali A. Allawi, *The Occupation of Iraq: Winning the War, Losing the Peace* (New Haven, CT: Yale University Press, 2007), 82.

77. Bumiller, *Condoleezza Rice*, 187; Rice, *No Higher Honor*, 179; Woodward, *Plan of Attack*, 154.

78. Gordon and Trainor, *Cobra II*, 72–73.

79. Bumiller, *Condoleezza Rice*, 187; DeYoung, *Soldier*, 406.

80. Drechsler, "Reconstituting the Interagency Process after Iraq," 9; Interviewee 5.

81. Interviewee 27.

82. Interviewee 71.

83. Interviewee 14.

84. Interviewee 63.

85. Gordon W. Rudd, *Reconstructing Iraq: Regime Change, Jay Garner and the ORHA Story* (Lawrence: University Press of Kansas, 2011), 43.

86. Interviewee 6.

87. Interviewee 71.

88. Interviewee 44. The same source described it as, "We set it up and we fly it in" with the invasion; the thinking was, the day Saddam was gone, there would be a new prime minister, and the power transition would begin. One odd piece of evidence is available on the declassified documents. On Rodman's August 17 memo, Feith has written the following in forwarding it to Rumsfeld: "Worth reading, though I don't think that Peter's recommendations are necessarily inconsistent with creating a US-led transitional civil authority." As it happened, Feith's forecast would prove accurate; at the time, however, Defense claimed to be holding up a rapid-transition model as a strict alternative to an occupation authority, and Feith himself would claim to be aghast when Paul Bremer announced that outcome. So either he changed his mind or he didn't recognize the significance of the distinction at this point. The "concept was," Condoleezza Rice told the *New York Times*, "that we would defeat the army, but the institutions would hold, everything from ministries to police forces. You were going to bring new leadership but that we were going to keep the body in place"; Michael R. Gordon, "The Strategy to Secure Iraq Did Not Foresee a 2nd War," *New York Times*, October 19, 2004.

89. Quoted in Charles H. Ferguson, *No End in Sight: Iraq's Descent Into Chaos* (New York: PublicAffairs, 2008), 88.

90. Interviewee 3.

91. Department of Defense, "The Case Against Iraq," August 23, 2002, classified by USDP Feith, declassified and released in DoD FOIA process; available at DoD FOIA site.

92. Interviewee 43.

93. Interviewee 42.

94. James Fallows, "The Fifty-First State?" *The Atlantic*, November 2002, 54–55.

95. Galloway et al., "Postwar Planning."

96. Interviewee 6.

97. Kevin Whitelaw, "After the Fall," *US News and World Report*, December 2, 2002, available at http://www.usnews.com/usnews/news/articles/021202/archive_038289.htm, accessed February 8, 2006.

98. Transcript of interview with Vice President Cheney on *Meet the Press*, September 8, 2002, available at http://www.mtholyoke.edu/acad/intrel/bush/meet.htm, accessed February 21, 2006.

99. Fallows, "The Fifty-First State?" 56–59.

100. Bill Keller, "The Sunshine Warrior," *New York Times Magazine*, September 22, 2002, 51.

101. Interviewee 29. See also Feith, *War and Decision*, 277–278.

102. Peter W. Rodman, "Who Will Govern Iraq?" August 17, 2002, declassified July 16, 2010, available at www.rumsfeld.com.

103. Feith, *War and Decision*, 252.

104. Jonathan Weisman and Mike Allen, "Officials Argue for Fast US Exit from Iraq," *Washington Post*, April 21, 2003.

105. Interviewee 39.

106. Feith, *War and Decision*, 190.

107. US Department of State, "Future of Iraq Project," PowerPoint presentation, November 1, 2002, declassified June 16, 2005.

108. Interviewee 8.

109. Lt. Gen. John H. Cushman (Ret.), "Planning and Early Execution of the War in Iraq: An Assessment of Military Participation," Harvard University Program on Information Resources, January 2007, 16, available at http://www.west-point.org /publications/cushman/ForArmyWarCollege.pdf.

110. Interviewees 18, 20, 21.

111. Interviewee 37.

112. Interviewee 20.

113. Interviewee 12.

114. Interviewee 21. Colonel Kevin Benson, a planner working these issues, would later write that "This additional workload, coupled with [other issues], kept the pressure on all planners and the staff in general"; Colonel Kevin C. M. Benson, "OIF Phase IV: A Planner's Reply to Brigadier Aylwin-Foster," *Military Review*, March–April 2006, 62.

115. Interviewee 21.

116. Haass, *War of Necessity*, 253.

117. Trent Lott, *Herding Cats: A Life in Politics* (New York: William Morrow, 2005), 235.

118. Lott, *Herding Cats*, 236.

119. Interviewee 54.

120. Dick Cheney, *In My Time: A Personal and Political Memoir* (New York: Simon and Schuster, 2011), 389.

121. DeYoung, *Soldier*, 408.

122. George Tenet, *At the Center of the Storm: My Years at the CIA* (New York: Harper-Collins, 2007), 315–316.

123. Rice, *No Higher Honor*, 180. See also Peter Baker, *Days of Fire: Bush and Cheney in the White House* (New York: Doubleday, 2013), 210–211.

124. Joint Staff, Department of Defense, "Operation Iraqi Freedom (OIF), History Brief," May 14, 2003, declassified through DoD FOIA process, available on DoD FOIA website. Also Rowan Scarborough, *Rumsfeld's War* (Washington, DC: Regnery Publishing, 2004), 175.

125. Condoleezza Rice, "Principals' Committee Review of Iraq Policy Paper," October 29, 2002, available at http://www.waranddecision.com/docLib/20080402_IraqGoals Strategy.pdf.

126. Special Inspector General for Iraqi Reconstruction, *Hard Lessons: The Iraq Reconstruction Experience* (Washington, D.C.: US Government Printing Office,

2009), 9, available at http://www.sigir.mil/files/HardLessons/Hard_Lessons_Report
.pdf.

127. CNN, "W.H.: Bush to Seek Hill's OK on Iraq Strikes," August 29, 2002, available at http://articles.cnn.com/2002-08-29/us/cheney.iraq_1_cheney-and-other
-administration-iraq-strikes-military-action?_s=PM:US.

128. Another memo from the same date rejected the idea that amnesty for Saddam
could be an alternative to military action. "Regime change does not necessarily
equal war—there are other ways to change the regime." As an example, the memo
suggested that "it might be possible to induce Saddam and his inner circle to give
up." But after a review of the idea, the memo concluded that it was unlikely that
"Saddam and his closest cronies would accept such an offer," and indeed there were
severe risks were he to do so—for example, Saddam's acceptance of amnesty could
"demoralize members of the opposition." Therefore, the conclusion was clear: "Pros
and cons, below, assume that offer will not be accepted by Saddam." "Amnesty and
Regime Change," August 23, 2002, Classified by USDP Feith, declassified and
released in DoD FOIA process; available at DoD FOIA site. See also Department
of Defense, OSD/ISA/NESA, August 19, 2002, "Discussion Paper for the 20
August 2002 PC Meeting on Iraq; Iraq: Saddam's Options in a Conflict With the
US," declassified through DoD FOIA process, available at DoD FOIA site.

129. Rice, *No Higher Honor*, 186–187. A background paper prepared for Rice and Stephen Hadley by NSC advisor Philip Zelikow in August clearly reflects the thinking
of people heading toward war. Iraqi disarmament was the objective, Zelikow wrote,
but no inspections regime would work "if Saddam Hussein continues to run the
country." Zelikow was perhaps unintentionally direct about the implications of one
approach: "Framing our international strategy around a 'return of inspectors,'" he
explained, "requires us to obtain UNSC agreement to an absurdly intrusive and
unworkable inspection regime, transparently rigged as a casus belli." This would,
of course, become precisely the adopted policy, the same notion that had been
appearing in British documents for months. Zelikow had an alternative: an international demand for Saddam Hussein to leave Iraq, followed by the imposition of
a UN Transition Administration (headed, he proposed, by Lakhdar Brahimi). As
precedents he listed a number of places where the international community had
determined that a regime had to go—though two of the three "especially analo-
gous" ones were Afghanistan and Haiti, neither of which avoided the requirement
for intervention. He portrayed this option as a "last *peaceful* chanced to settle the
Iraq conflict." Philip Zelikow, "IRAQ: An International Strategy that is an Alternative to 'Inspections,'" August 2002, available in Philip Zelikow document collection,
http://faculty.virginia.edu/zelikow/documents/nationalsecuritypolicy.pdf.

130. Interviewee 64.
131. Interviewee 6.
132. Packer, *Assassin's Gate*, 45.

Chapter 7: A Juggernaut for War

1. Donald Rumsfeld, "Kosovo," attachment to letter to Joshua Bolten, April 28,
1999, available at www.rumsfeld.com.

2. George W. Ball, *The Past Has Another Pattern: Memoirs* (New York: W. W. Norton, 1982), 376.

3. John McCain, foreword to David Halberstam, *The Best and Brightest* (New York: The Modern Library, 2002).

4. Douglas J. Feith, *War and Decision: Inside the Pentagon at the Dawn of the War on Terrorism* (New York: Harper, 2008), 258. CENTCOM deputy chief Michael DeLong has written that the idea came originally from Chalabi, who sold it to Wolfowitz, but as we have seen it had been floating around US Iraq planning since the Clinton administration; Lt. Gen. Michael DeLong, *A General Speaks Out: The Truth About the Wars in Afghanistan and Iraq* (St. Paul, MN: Zenith Publishing, 2007), 80.

5. As early as April 8, 2002, Rumsfeld wrote to the principals, recommending that they make "full use" of the Iraqi Liberation Act, whatever that meant; Donald Rumsfeld, Memo to Rice, "Military Assistance Under the Iraqi Liberation Act (ILA)," August 12, 2002, available at www.rumsfeld.com. Donald Rumsfeld, "Memorandum for the Chairman of the Joint Chiefs of Staff, Subj: Planning Guidance for Iraqi Opposition Training," n.d. but indications are July 16, 2002; available at www.rumsfeld.com.

6. This account comes from George Tenet, *At the Center of the Storm: My Years at the CIA* (New York: HarperCollins, 2007), 397–398; and Interviewee 8.

7. Donald Rumsfeld, "Memorandum for the Chairman of the Joint Chiefs of Staff, Subj: Planning Guidance for Iraqi Opposition Training," n.d. but indications are July 16, 2002; available at www.rumsfeld.com.

8. Feith, *War and Decision*, 259, 279–280, 381–385; Joint Staff, Department of Defense, "Operation Iraqi Freedom (OIF), History Brief," May 14, 2003, declassified through DoD FOIA process, available on DoD FOIA website. Meanwhile Rumsfeld, according to Feith, "never made the training program a personal project." In August 2002 the Principals Committee approved the concept, but it took until December 28 for Rumsfeld to issue a formal order.

9. Michael R. Gordon and Bernard E. Trainor, *Cobra II: The Inside Story of the Invasion and Occupation of Iraq* (New York: Pantheon Books, 2006), 106–107. They claim that, as the numbers stayed small, Wolfowitz reportedly urged Franks to allow three thousand Iraqi exiles to be brought over from Iran, in batches of three hundred, to join the group.

10. Interviewee 32.

11. Interviewee 25.

12. Interviewee 11. The site was widely reported at the time—including in official US Defense Department press releases; see http://archive.defense.gov/news/newsarticle.aspx?id=29394.

13. Interviewee 32.

14. Interviewee 25 and Joint Staff, "OIF History Brief." One US official intimately involved in the issue said, "I never understood" what the Free Iraqi Force "was supposed to do. I heard everything from a praetorian guard to prison guards"; Interviewee 8. At one February 2003 speech to Iraqi exiles in which he invited them to join the force, Wolfowitz limited the description to saying that "the Free Iraqi Force

will be integrated with US forces to serve as guides, translators, and experts on civil affairs"; "Deputy Secretary of Defense Paul Wolfowitz Iraqi Forum for Democracy," Dearborn, Michigan, February 23, 2003; http://www.usembassy.it/file2003_02 /alia/a3022407.htm.

15. Interviewees 25, 32. They were, at the same time, highly secretive, and concerned that their identities not become known—perhaps worried that Saddam's long arm would retaliate against them or their families even at that late date. One result was that they demanded to be paid in cash—they didn't want to have to deposit checks or have other records with their identities. But their morale remained high.

16. Interviewee 25.

17. Interviewee 8.

18. Interviewee 25.

19. *Washington Post* columnist Jim Hoagland was taking the INC bait, hook, line, and sinker. In late October 2002, he wrote that the "tip-off" that war planning was "moving into its final phase . . . comes from a decision to begin military training of Iraqi exile forces and dissidents who can be spirited out of Iraq." He pointed to a six- to eight-week training course—ludicrous, trying to turn civilians into fighters in that time—and a target number of three to five thousand, who would "help keep order once their country is liberated"; Jim Hoagland, "A Matter of Weeks," *Washington Post*, October 25, 2002, A29. Later he would claim that the program stalled because the US military dragged its feet: Jim Hoagland, "Siren Song," *Washington Post*, February 23, 2003, B7.

20. HQ TRADOC, After Action Review, Free Iraqi Force Operations, May 21, 2003; available at DoD FOIA declassification site.

21. Aram Roston, *The Man Who Pushed America to War: The Extraordinary Life, Adventures, and Obsessions of Ahmad Chalabi* (New York: Nation Books, 2008), 235.

22. DeLong, *A General Speaks Out*, 80.

23. Bob Woodward, *Plan of Attack* (New York: Simon and Schuster, 2004), 416. As Richard Clarke has written, "I doubt that anyone ever had the chance to make the case to [President Bush] that attacking Iraq would actually make America less secure. . . . Certainly he did not hear that from the small circle of advisors who alone are the people whose views he respects and trusts." Richard A. Clarke, *Against All Enemies* (New York: Free Press, 2004), 244.

24. Interviewee 3.

25. Interviewee 71.

26. Interviewee 54.

27. One senior official watched Wolfowitz, Feith, and the other OSD officials push their plans for Iraq and the postwar designs along. The "policy guys were in their own world," he said. They never worried about how they were going to actually implement what they imagined. They were "so busy fighting with the State Department that they assumed—well, things will get done," events would take care of themselves; Interviewee 1.

28. Interviewee 66.

29. Richard Haass, *War of Necessity, War of Choice: A Memoir of Two Iraq Wars* (New York: Simon and Schuster, 2009), 223–224, 214.

30. Interviewee 36.

31. Interviewee 5.

32. Condoleezza Rice, *No Higher Honor: A Memoir of My Years in Washington* (New York: Crown, 2011), 189–190.

33. Feith, *War and Decision*, 316–317. See also Bob Woodward, *State of Denial: Bush at War, Part III* (New York: Simon and Schuster, 2006), 92.

34. Donald Rumsfeld, *Known and Unknown* (New York: Sentinel, 2011), 486. Interviewee 39 confirmed that this was a major constraint inside the administration.

35. Interviewee 42.

36. Interviewee 5.

37. Special Inspector General, *Hard Lessons*, 20. As Feith himself realizes—and as was being widely reported in the press—CENTCOM was busily developing a plan *to go to war*. Feith tries to wriggle out of this: "War planning," he says, "is a routine matter in military organizations," whereas postwar planning is not; Feith, *War and Decision*, 347. But that will not wash; it was obvious to everyone that the planning underway by the summer of 2002 was far beyond routine.

38. On July 8, 2002, Colin Powell had sent out a cable to a host of US embassies in Europe, Japan, Chile, Argentina, South Africa, and elsewhere stating that, to "prepare for the transition" to a democratic Iraqi regime, they would be establishing working groups under the Future of Iraq Project; State Department Cable, July 8, 2002, "Future of Iraq Expert Working Groups," declassified June 25, 2005. The State Department was telling US embassies to broadcast an imminent Iraqi regime change and to invite help. Meanwhile, at the Defense Department, no one wanted to plan for the postwar phase of a conflict because it might look like they were actually going to war.

39. Interviewee 44.

40. Elisabeth Bumiller, *Condoleezza Rice: An American Life* (New York: Random House, 2007), 191–192.

41. See the discussion in Scott McClellan, *What Happened: Inside the Bush White House and Washington's Culture of Deception* (New York: PublicAffairs, 2008), 131–132.

42. Phillips, *Losing Iraq*, 45.

43. Phillips, *Losing Iraq*, 46, 54. The effort was riven with factional infighting, largely between State, on the one hand, and Defense and the vice president's office on the other. George Packer quotes an Iraqi exile, Feisal Istrabadi, as viewing two US officials, one from State and one from Cheney's office, "standing on the sidewalk outside a fancy London restaurant, screaming at each other"; George Packer, *The Assassin's Gate: America in Iraq* (New York: Farrar, Straus and Giroux, 2005), 79. See also his discussions of Kanan Makiya's suspicions of Americans who didn't really want democracy, pp. 67 and 83.

44. If the London meeting were "any indication of how the various factions in Iraq would get along," Phillips writes, "Iraq's future was beckoningly bright." Phillips, *Losing Iraq*, 54.

45. Interviewee 44.

46. Tenet, *At the Center of the Storm*, 317–318. This report is mentioned in Select Committee on Intelligence, United States Senate, *Report on Prewar Intelligence Assessments about Postwar Iraq*, 110th Congress, S. Report 110-76, May 2007, 104.

47. Tenet, *At the Center of the Storm*, 318.

48. Gordon and Trainor, *Cobra II*, 74.

49. Robert Draper, *Dead Certain: The Presidency of George W. Bush* (New York: The Free Press, 2007), 178.

50. George W. Bush, "President's Remarks at the United Nations General Assembly," September 12, 2002, available at http://www.whitehouse.gov/news/releases/2002/09/20020912-1.html.

51. Interviewee 38.

52. Cook, *The Point of Departure*, 204–205.

53. Tenet, *At the Center of the Storm*, 319; and Interviewee 19.

54. Republican Policy Committee, United States Senate, "Disaggregating the Pentagon Offices: The Department of Defense, the Office of Special Plans and Iraq Pre-War Intelligence," February 7, 2006, 3, available at http://rpc.senate.gov/_files/Feb07 06DoDIntellMS.pdf, accessed February 21, 2006; Interviewee 9. As Feith would put it in a 2003 press briefing, it was called Special Plans "because at the time, calling it Iraq Planning Office might have undercut . . . our diplomatic efforts with regard to Iraq and the U.N. and elsewhere"; Douglas Feith and William Luti, "DoD Briefing on Policy and Intelligence Matters," Department of Defense News Transcript, June 4, 2003, available at www.defenselink.mil/transcripts/2003/tr20030604-0248.html, accessed February 21, 2006.

55. Republican Policy Committee, "Disaggregating the Pentagon Offices," 3.

56. It was sent to DIA, according to Luti, "to ensure that proper tradecraft was used, accounting procedures." In regard to whether defector testimony was crucial, Luti replied, "No, there's been no basis for that. None whatsoever"; Feith and Luti, "DoD Briefing."

57. The text of the Iraq letter is available at http://www.sfgate.com/cgi-bin/article.cgi?f=/news/archive/2002/09/16/international1954EDT0706.DTL, accessed February 16, 2006.

58. Hans Blix, *Disarming Iraq* (New York: Pantheon Books, 2004), 74–75, 11.

59. Testimony of Donald Rumsfeld on US Policy toward Iraq, Hearing before the House Committee on Armed Services: 177-2, September 18, 2002, available at http://commdocs.house.gov/committees/security/has261000.000/has261000_0.htm.

60. Robin Cook, *The Point of Departure* (London: Simon & Schuster UK, 2003), 212–217.

61. A partial transcript of the resolution can be found at http://www.cooperativeresearch.org/archive/2002/usukgov100102.htm, accessed February 15, 2006.

62. Paul Reynolds, "Analysis: Battle of Iraq Resolutions," BBC News, posted September 30, 2002; available at http://news.bbc.co.uk/2/hi/americas/2288074.stm, accessed February 15, 2006; Michael R. Gordon, "A Draft US Plan on Iraq Inspections Authorizes Force," *New York Times*, September 28, 2002. Hans Blix wrote later that when he first read the draft, it "made my few hairs stand up. It read more like a US Defense Department document than like one drafted by the UN"; Blix, *Disarming Iraq*, 76.

63. Department of Defense, ISA/NESA, "A Political Roadmap to a New Iraqi Government," October 2, 2002, declassified through DoD FOIA process, available at DoD FOIA site.

64. Eight days after that memo, Luti's office of Near East and South Asian Affairs generated another document—the "Pros and Cons of a Provisional Government." Should the United States form one, composed of exiles, "prior to liberation"? Doing so would demonstrate the "seriousness" of war planning, could spark defections from Iraqi forces, increase "pressure on Saddam," and provide a better "legal basis/ political cover for post-liberation governance." Risks included factional disputes and constraining US flexibility. Luti's conclusion was stark: "Tell the Iraqi opposition that the US Government will promptly recognize [a provisional government] comprising most of the major Iraqi opposition groups." OSD/SP/NESA, "Pros and Cons of a Provisional Government," October 10, 2002, declassified through DoD FOIA process, available at DoD FOIA website.

65. Interviewee 12.

66. David Phillips claims that on the US side, the dominant role of Cheney's office continued to be felt. Department of State officials "Ryan Crocker and [David] Pearce were far too timid about confronting Kanan [Makiya] and his [INC] cohorts," Phillips claims. The meeting began to show "deep divisions in the Iraqi opposition," Phillips contends. "The gap between exiles and other Iraqis was more of a chasm than a subtle difference of opinion." Phillips, *Losing Iraq*, 77–87. For good insights into Kanan Makiya, see Packer, *Assassin's Gate*, 78–79. See also Larry Diamond, *Squandered Victory: The American Occupation and the Bungled Effort to Bring Democracy to Iraq* (New York: Times Books, 2005), 27–28.

67. Packer, *Assassin's Gate*, 68.

68. Department of Defense, OSD/ISA/NESA, "SecDef Directive to Military Governor of Iraq" and "Structure, Organization, and Staffing of the US Military administration," October 7, 2002, declassified through DoD FOIA process, available at DoD FOIA website.

69. Meyer, "How Britain Failed to Check Bush."

70. Donald Rumsfeld, memo to Gen. Franks, "The North," September 30, 2002, available at www.rumsfeld.com.

71. Woodward, *Plan of Attack*, 188–189; Bumiller, *Condoleezza Rice*, 191. A week later, an OSD Policy memo was generated, titled "Victory in Iraq." It was just a series of bullet points. The first section was titled, "Definition of Immediate Victory," and this was basically removing Saddam from power, establishing a US-led "military administration" in Iraq (including subgoals like "No significant armed resistance to military administration" and "Elimination of terrorist bases and safe haven"). The "Definition of Ultimate Victory" read as follows: "Replacement by a broad-based, representative government that: Renounces WMD. Doesn't support terrorism. Seeks to live in peace with its neighbors. Respects individual rights of all Iraqis." See Department of Defense, OSD Policy, "Victory in Iraq," October 18, 2002, declassified through DoD FOIA process, available at DoD FOIA website.

72. Trent Lott, *Herding Cats: A Life in Politics* (New York: William Morrow, 2005), 239.

73. Paul R. Pillar, "Intelligence, Policy, and the War in Iraq," *Foreign Affairs* 85, no. 2 (March–April 2006).

74. Quoted in Rumsfeld, *Known and Unknown*, 436–437.

75. Special Inspector General for Iraqi Reconstruction, *Hard Lessons: The Iraq Reconstruction Experience* (Washington, DC: US Government Printing Office, 2009), 10, available at http://www.sigir.mil/files/HardLessons/Hard_Lessons_Report.pdf.

76. Interviewee 5, Interviewee 29, and Interviewee 40. See also Nora Bensahel et al., *After Saddam: Prewar Planning and the Occupation of Iraq* (Santa Monica, CA: The RAND Corporation, 2008), 91. I encountered different views of who initiated this second working group. Some published accounts and high-level interviewees said that Miller did so in a conversation with Abrams. Some sources I spoke with suggested that part of the initiative came from the senior AID official Wendy Chamberlin, just back to Washington from field assignments in August 2002, who got together with Robin Cleveland at OMB—an old friend—and decided that planning for postwar development needed to begin.

77. Interviewees 33, 40.

78. Interviewee 40.

79. Interviewee 62.

80. Interviewee 16.

81. Interviewee 40.

82. Interviewee 16. One report quoted a participant saying that information only went PowerPoint deep; "It was all guesstimates made on top of suppositions." They were making dangerous assumptions about the very infrastructure that was so decayed: confronted with UN reports on a collapsing electricity grid, the group decided that Iraq's oil wealth would pay for the necessary upgrades. The group never received adequate information about plans for postinvasion security, only vague assurances that the Defense Department was handling the issue; Special Inspector General, *Hard Lessons*, 11.

83. Interviewee 61. This incident is also described in Association for Diplomatic Studies and Training, Oral History Interview, Ambassador Frank Almaguer, January 23, 2004, 227–232, available at https://adst.org/wp-content/uploads/2013/12/Almaguer-Frank-1.pdf.

84. Interviewee 64.

85. Interviewee 28.

86. Interviewee 23; Interviewee 28; Special Inspector General, *Hard Lessons*, 18.

87. Interviewee 23.

88. Special Inspector General, *Hard Lessons*, 21, 31.

89. The president's remarks can be found at http://www.whitehouse.gov/news/releases/2002/10/20021016-1.html, accessed February 15, 2006.

90. Special Inspector General, *Hard Lessons*, 12–13.

91. Peter W. Rodman, memo for Donald Rumsfeld, "Replies to questions in William Raspberry column," October 1, 2002, released through DoD FOIA process, available at DoD FOIA site in Rumsfeld documents basket.

92. Interviewee 22.
93. Woodward, *State of Denial*, 79.
94. Bumiller, *Condoleezza Rice*, 195.
95. Interviewee 11.
96. Karen DeYoung, *Soldier: The Life of Colin Powell* (New York: Alfred A. Knopf, 2006), 418–419.
97. Blix, *Disarming Iraq*, 86–89.
98. Interviewee 12.
99. Rumsfeld, *Known and Unknown*, 480.
100. "Iraq: An Illustrative List of Potential Problems to Be Considered and Addressed," October 15, 2002, declassified through OSD, released in "Set of Documents Released to Secretary Rumsfeld Through MDR," document set available at http://www.dod.gov/pubs/foi/SecretaryRumsfeld/DocumentsReleasedToSecretary RumsfeldUnderMDR.pdf.
101. David von Drehle, "Wrestling with History: Sometimes You Have to Fight the War You Have, Not the War You Wish You Had," *Washington Post Magazine*, November 13, 2005, 12.
102. Rice, *No Higher Honor*, 192.
103. Interviewee 51.
104. Rumsfeld, *Known and Unknown*, 481.
105. Quoted in Special Inspector General, *Hard Lessons*, 33.
106. Gordon W. Rudd, *Reconstructing Iraq: Regime Change, Jay Garner, and the ORHA Story* (Lawrence: University Press of Kansas, 2011), 54–55.
107. Tommy Franks, *American Soldier* (New York: Regan Books, 2004), 419–424. Part of the issue may have been Franks's personality. Gruff, powerful, impatient with subordinates, his former deputy Lt. Gen. Michael DeLong (Ret.) has described him as someone who had his own way of wanting things done—and "God help you if you tried to deviate from it"; Lt. Gen. Michael DeLong, *A General Speaks Out: The Truth About the Wars in Afghanistan and Iraq* (St. Paul, MN: Zenith Publishing, 2007), 7.
108. Interviewee 11. The official army history concludes that army planners were "assured that other elements of the US Government would handle the larger issues involved in planning for and executing PH IV operations"; Donald P. Wright and Timothy R. Reese, *On Point II: Transition to the New Campaign—the United States Army in Operation Iraqi Freedom, May 2003–January 2005* (Ft. Leavenworth, KS: Combat Studies Institute, June 2008), 76.
109. Special Inspector General, *Hard Lessons*, 35.
110. The risks of chaos in the aftermath were hardly unknown. State's Future of Iraq Project briefings had spoken of the "need for urgent environmental assessments in hours after regime change," and things like the "importance of getting the electrical grid up and running immediately," which could "go a long way to determining Iraqis' attitudes towards Coalition forces." Without a coherent postwar plan for security, none

of this was likely to materialize; US Department of State, "Future of Iraq Project," PowerPoint presentation, November 1, 2002, declassified June 16, 2005.

111. General Richard B. Myers (Ret.), *Eyes on the Horizon: Serving on the Front Lines of National Security* (New York: Threshold Editions, 2009), Kindle edition, loc. 5657.

112. Interviewee 18. As Major General William Webster, deputy commander of CFLCC, would later tell an official army history, "All along, General Franks said that the Secretary of Defense wanted us to quickly leave and turn over post-hostilities to international organizations (IOs) and nongovernmental organizations (NGOs) led by ORHA. That was the notion"; quoted in Wright and Reese, *On Point II*, 140–141.

113. Colonel Kevin C. M. Benson, "OIF Phase IV: A Planner's Reply to Brigadier Aylwin-Foster," *Military Review*, March–April 2006, 61–62. They kept refining the plan and developed a more detailed Phase IV plan, which they called ECLIPSE II, in homage to the World War II predecessor—not being aware that such a reference would be completely anathema to OSD planners who wanted no part of a formal occupation. A thoughtful comparison of the two ECLIPSE plans is Lt. Col. Kenneth O. McGreedy, "Waging Peace: Operations ECLIPSE I and II—Some Implications for Future Operations," US Army War College, March 2004, available at http://www.smallwarsjournal.com/documents/mcgreedy.pdf.

114. Wright and Reese, *On Point II*, 74.

115. Interviewee 1.

116. Interviewee 33.

117. Interviewee 7.

118. Interviewee 69.

119. Interviewees 22, 24.

120. Interviewee 9.

121. Interviewee 12.

122. Interviewee 10.

123. Interviewee 30.

124. Tenet, *At the Center of the Storm*, 311–315.

125. Later in Iraq, one ORHA staffer would write that visitors from OSD were stopping in and talking about the need to finish up Iraq quickly. "We needed to 're-cock' [and] move onto Iran and possibly Syria," they were saying—talk that the official thought was "mumbled and half serious" until he kept hearing it from more and more people; Don Eberly, *Liberate and Leave: Fatal Flaws in the Early Strategy for Postwar Iraq* (Minneapolis, MN: Zenith Press, 2009), 104.

126. Kevin M. Woods, with Michael R. Pease, Mark E. Stout, Williamson Murray, and James G. Lacey, *Iraqi Perspectives Project: A View of Operation Iraqi Freedom from Saddam's Senior Leadership* (Norfolk, VA: Joint Center for Operational Analysis, US Joint Forces Command, March 2006), 25–29.

127. Woods, *Iraqi Perspectives Project*, 29.

128. See the UN press release at http://www.un.org/News/Press/docs/2002/sc7564.doc .htm, accessed February 15, 2006.

129. Blix, *Disarming Iraq*, 91–96.

130. Donald Rumsfeld, Draft Memorandum for the President [with cover memo to CJCS requesting review], "Next Steps on Iraq," November 13, 2002, declassified July 16, 2002, released to Donald Rumsfeld with documents released under MDR, available at DoD FOIA site.

131. Ali A. Allawi, *The Occupation of Iraq: Winning the War, Losing the Peace* (New Haven, CT: Yale University Press, 2007), 85.

132. Phillips, *Losing Iraq*, 92.

133. Zalmay Khalilzad, *The Envoy: From Kabul to the White House, My Journey through a Turbulent World* (New York: St. Martin's Press, 2016), 152–153. Iraqis were no more anxious for US domination of the postwar: "The Iraqi opposition was united in demanding immediate control of the country when the regime crumbled," State consultant David Phillips explains. "They rejected all US efforts to establish either a military transitional government or a transitional body under the supervision of a US general"; Phillips, *Losing Iraq*, 94–101.

134. Doug Feith admits that Chalabi had made a play, weeks beforehand, to demand that the INC "serve as the conference host." Feith's office had discreetly put him off; Feith, *War and Decision*, 379.

135. Jim Hoagland, "So Long, Saddam," *The Washington Post*, December 13, 2002, A45.

136. Feith, *War and Decision*, 379.

137. Woodward, *State of Denial*, 103–104.

138. Blix, *Disarming Iraq*, 101–102.

139. Blix, *Disarming Iraq*, 107–108.

140. Feith, *War and Decision*, 341–342.

141. George W. Bush, *Decision Points* (New York: Crown, 2010), 224.

142. Dick Cheney, *In My Time: A Personal and Political Memoir* (New York: Simon and Schuster, 2011), 395.

143. Woodward, *Plan of Attack,* 249. See also Peter Baker, *Days of Fire: Bush and Cheney in the White House* (New York: Doubleday, 2013), 239–240. See Tenet, *At the Center of the Storm*, 361–370.

144. Tenet, *At the Center of the Storm*, 369–370.

145. Interviewee 4.

146. Jonathan S. Landay, "Lack of Hard Evidence of Iraqi Weapons Worries Top US Officials," McClatchy Washington Bureau, September 6, 2002.

147. Interviewee 42.

148. Joint Staff, "Iraq: Status of WMD Programs," September 5, 2002, declassified January 6, 2011, released to Donald Rumsfeld with documents released under MDR, available at DoD FOIA site.

149. Interviewee 56.

150. Sergei L. Loiko and Maggie Farley, "Inspectors 'Have Zilch' Thus Far," *Los Angeles Times*, December 31, 2002. See also "Iraqis Cooperate with Inspectors," *Seattle Post-Intelligencer News Services*, December 4, 2002.

151. Interviewee 56.

152. Interviewee 63.

153. CIA, "Iraq's Weapons of Mass Destruction Programs," October 2002, available at http://www.gwu.edu/~nsarchiv/NSAEBB/NSAEBB254/doc01.pdf.

154. *Comprehensive Report of the Special Advisor to the DCI on Iraq's WMD*, vol. 1 of 3, September 30, 2004, 62–63; hereafter cited as the Duelfer Report.

155. US Department of Defense, "Proposed US Approach to Dealing with the Iraq WMD Declaration," December 18, 2002, declassified with documents delivered to Donald Rumsfeld under MDR, available at DoD FOIA site.

156. Rumsfeld, *Known and Unknown*, 442.

157. Bumiller, *Condoleezza Rice*, 197–198.

158. Interviewee 4.

159. Interviewee 33.

160. Interviewee 38.

161. Interviewee 33.

162. Interviewee 45.

163. Interviewee 55.

164. Rumsfeld, *Known and Unknown*, 457.

CHAPTER 8: "ALL IS TBD"—ON THE VERGE OF WAR

1. Quoted in David Rose, "Neo Culpa," *Vanity Fair*, November 3, 2006, available at http://www.vanityfair.com/news/2006/12/neocons200612.

2. P. J. O'Rourke, "How Harold Ramis Invented Baby Boom Comedy with 'Animal House,'" *The Daily Beast*, February 27, 2014, at http://www.thedailybeast.com/articles/2014/02/27/how-harold-ramis-invented-baby-boom-comedy-with-animal-house.html.

3. George W. Ball, *The Past Has Another Pattern: Memoirs* (New York: W. W. Norton, 1982), 375–376.

4. Evan Thomas, Richard Wolffe, and Michael Isikoff, "Where Are Iraq's WMDs?" *Newsweek*, June 1, 2003. See also Neil Macfarquhar, "Iraq Says UN Teams Have Found No Weapons," *New York Times*, January 3, 2003.

5. Hans Blix, *Disarming Iraq* (New York: Pantheon Books, 2004), 123, 134, 137.

6. Elisabeth Bumiller, *Condoleezza Rice: An American Life* (New York: Random House, 2007), 202.

7. Bumiller, *Condoleezza Rice*, 201; Bob Woodward, *Plan of Attack* (New York: Simon and Schuster, 2004), 254.

8. Blix, *Disarming Iraq*, 109–110.

9. Interviewee 56.

10. No author, presumed OSD; January 17, 2003, "Considerations for Post-liberation Iraq," declassified June 29, 2007, through DoD FOIA process, available at DoD FOIA website. Interestingly, the original document was classified SECRET Rel Turkey, meaning the document was intended for potential sharing with Turkey.

11. OSD Policy, "Draft Agreement between USG and 'Iraqi Interim Authority' (IIA)," March 3, 2003, declassified December 1, 2008, released to Donald Rumsfeld with documents released under MDR, available at DoD FOIA site.

12. James Dobbins et al., *Occupying Iraq: A History of the Coalition Provisional Authority* (Santa Monica, CA: The RAND Corporation, 2009), 31. One participant in the ESG process described the interim government plan as "a chart" rather than a true proposal. "A huge amount of OSD staff work" went into the IIA, "but it was never codified" into something specific and real. They "never came to grips with who would be in the government" after liberation; Interviewee 14. These issues were further muddied in a February 2003 briefing titled "A Provisional Government for Iraq?" It argued that initial control of such issues as "providing security, law and order" and "law enforcement" would fall to US entities—a Combined Joint Task Force and then a "Civilian Administrator." Both would report to Rumsfeld "to maintain the unity of leadership," the briefing suggested. "In lieu of a provisional government," the briefing noted, Iraqis would help run their own government through a variety of mechanisms—a "consultative council," a "judicial council," local governments—but it was quite clear that these were, initially at least, advisory bodies to a US control system. As late as February 14, however, this briefing was still making the case for a provisional government (to be dominated by exiles) as a better means to the legitimacy of US actions. OSD Policy, "A Provisional Government for Iraq?" February 14, 2003, declassified April 2, 2009, and available at the DoD FOIA site.

13. The poll's results can be found at http://abcnews.go.com/sections/world/DailyNews/iraqpoll021217.html, accessed February 15, 2006.

14. Ari Berman, "Polls Suggest Media Failure in Pre-War Coverage," *Editor & Publisher*, March 26, 2003, available at http://www.editorandpublisher.com/eandp/news/article_display.jsp?vnu_content_id=1848576, accessed February 15, 2006.

15. Dana Milbank and Claudia Deane, "Hussein Link to 9/11 Lingers in Many Minds," *Washington Post*, September 6, 2003, A1.

16. Woodward, *Plan of Attack*, 260; George Packer, *The Assassin's Gate: America in Iraq* (New York: Farrar, Straus and Giroux, 2005), 96–97; Robert Draper, *Dead Certain: The Presidency of George W. Bush* (New York: The Free Press, 2007), 187–189; Zalmay Khalilzad, *The Envoy: From Kabul to the White House, My Journey through a Turbulent World* (New York: St. Martin's Press, 2016), 157. Bush seemed "unfocused" to some of the participants, but Zalmay Khalilzad would later write that he "peppered the Iraqis with questions"—not the first time the president would seem both deeply engaged and detached to different people in the same meeting.

17. Jim Hoagland, "Making the Case," *The Washington Post*, January 26, 2003, B7.

18. Packer, *Assassin's Gate*, 111.

19. Khalilzad, *The Envoy*, 158.

20. Interviewee 22.

21. Interviewee 30. Another source remembers the directive coming from Rumsfeld, and Feith merely passing it down—"The Secretary wants to know." Interviewee 31.

22. The study was later published: Richard H. Shultz, *In the Aftermath of War: US Support for Reconstruction and Nation-Building in Panama following Just Cause* (Maxwell Air Force Base, AL: Air University Press, August 1993).

23. A summary memo of the public order plan, with Busby listed as author, can be found at http://www.waranddecision.com/docLib/20080420_SummaryPublic OrderPlan.pdf.
24. Interviewee 31.
25. Interviewee 30.
26. Action memo for under secretary of defense for policy, "Maintaining Public Order during Combat Operations in Iraq," February 9, 2003, 1, available at www.warand decision.com.
27. Action memo, "Maintaining Public Order," Background/Planning Considerations, 1.
28. Interviewee 42.
29. Interviewee 42. Doug Feith's book *War and Decision* relates this story in telling ways. Feith describes a situation in which he ran the issue up the flagpole, giving a copy of the memo to Peter Pace, then vice chairman of the Joint Chiefs, and to CENTCOM, but getting little traction. It is odd that he would have left it there: if the memo had persuaded him that the issue was critical, he could, and should, have elevated it to Rumsfeld. You don't just "ship thought pieces to CENTCOM"; Interviewee 30. If you want action, you take the issue to the Secretary of Defense, and you get him to raise it with General Franks, and you say, "Why isn't there a plan for postwar security?" But none of that happened.
30. Interviewee 31.
31. Department of Defense, "Post-War Tasks," January 31, 2003, declassified through DoD FOIA processes, available at DoD FOIA website.
32. Karen DeYoung, *Soldier: The Life of Colin Powell* (New York: Alfred A. Knopf, 2006), 459, argued that Powell requested the assessment. A source (Interviewee 38) told me that Powell did *not* request it—that the Iraq staff in NEA asked to write it, and Ryan Crocker and his team sent it to Powell; another source suggested he found out years later that Powell and Armitage *had* in fact asked for such an assessment. Yet another source (Interviewee 44) described the process as being one in which word came down (as it turns out, presumably from the top) saying, "You State folks who are so skeptical, give us your worst-case assessment. What could go wrong?"
33. Michael Morell, *The Great War of Our Time* (New York: 12 Books, 2015), 98–99.
34. Joseph L. Galloway, Jonathan S. Landay, Warren P. Strobel, and John Walcott, "Postwar Planning for Iraq 'Ignored,'" *Philadelphia Inquirer*, October 17, 2004, 1.
35. Conrad C. Crane and W. Andrew Terrill, "Reconstructing Iraq: Challenges and Missions for Military Forces in a Post-Conflict Scenario," US Army War College, Strategic Studies Institute, February 2003, 2.
36. They represented, therefore, not merely the work of one analyst or agency—in fact they were not "written" in large measure by the analyst often attributed, Paul Pillar, only supervised by him—but the consensus view of Iraq and Middle East analysts across the intelligence community. Richard Haass explains that *he* commissioned the studies, in part because no one else was doing it; Richard Haass, *War of Necessity, War of Choice: A Memoir of Two Iraq Wars* (New York: Simon and Schuster, 2009), 254.

37. Paul R. Pillar, "The Right Stuff," *The National Interest*, September–October 2007, 53, 58. In the end the resulting reports were technically not National Intelligence Estimates; they were "Intelligence Community Assessments," a slightly different sort of product not vetted by the director of the CIA or the National Foreign Intelligence Board; Select Committee on Intelligence, United States Senate, *Report on Prewar Intelligence Assessments about Postwar Iraq*, 110th Congress, S. Report 110-76, May 2007, 3–4.

38. National Intelligence Council, "Principal Challenges in Post-Saddam Iraq," January 2003, included in Senate Select Committee on Intelligence, *Report on Prewar Intelligence Assessments about Postwar Iraq*, 54–83ff. The quotes below are drawn from pages 57, 60–61, 64, and 70; and Pillar, "The Right Stuff," 54–55.

39. Quoted in Senate Select Committee on Intelligence, *Report on Prewar Intelligence Assessments about Postwar Iraq*, 103–104.

40. Interviewee 22.

41. Interviewee 5.

42. Interviewee 12.

43. Interviewee 12.

44. DeYoung, *Soldier*, 429; and Interviewee 64.

45. Interviewee 11.

46. Bob Woodward, *State of Denial: Bush at War, Part III* (New York: Simon and Schuster, 2006), 107.

47. Peter Baker, *Days of Fire: Bush and Cheney in the White House* (New York: Doubleday, 2013), 243.

48. Donald Rumsfeld, *Known and Unknown* (New York: Sentinel, 2011), 453–454.

49. A declassified version is available at https://fas.org/irp/offdocs/nspd/nspd-24.pdf.

50. Interviewee 5.

51. Some of those to whom I spoke recall a deputies' meeting at which Doug Feith discussed the document. Another source recalled a Principals Committee meeting where Donald Rumsfeld passed out a paper, "the back page of which held a big signature of George Bush." Donald Rumsfeld's website released a "draft" NSPD, prepared on January 7, 2003, in Doug Feith's office, and sent over to NSC staff as the basis for NSPD-24; OSD Policy, "Draft NSPD on Post-war Planning Office," January 7, 2003, attachment to Douglas Feith, "Establishing the DoD Postwar Planning Office," memo to Secretary of Defense, January 8, 2003, available at www.rumsfeld.com. One senior defense official remembers part of Rumsfeld's motivation being to take control from those who might have desired a long-term perspective to US operations. Rumsfeld wanted the effort centralized with those who had the resources—but also with the "guys who wanted to get it done right, [and] quickly get home. And the people who were motivated to be in a hurry were DoD"; Interviewees 23, 33, 40, and 42.

52. Interviewees 40, 23, and 33.

53. Interviewee 10.

54. Interviewee 23.

55. Interview with Jay Garner, *Frontline* documentary, "Truth, War and Consequences," available at http://www.pbs.org/wgbh/pages/frontline/shows/truth/interviews /garner.html; Woodward, *State of Denial*, 103–106.
56. Interviewee 33.
57. Woodward, *State of Denial*, 149–150.
58. Interviewee 3.
59. Interviewee 14. Another told me that Defense officials often didn't attend, and when they did, very often they did not actively participate—it was, he said, "One more symptom of a larger phenomenon: The national security team was not playing nicely at any level." Interviewee 38. One senior official told me, "Rumsfeld hated Frank [Miller], and was sure he was doing this [the ESG] on his own hook" in order to meddle in Defense business; Interviewee 64. Interviewee 71 commented simply, "Miller wasn't Rumsfeld's favorite."
60. Interviewee 5.
61. Interviewee 16 and Special Inspector General for Iraqi Reconstruction, *Hard Lessons: The Iraq Reconstruction Experience* (Washington, DC: US Government Printing Office, 2009), 34, available at http://www.sigir.mil/files/HardLessons/Hard_Lessons _Report.pdf.
62. Interviewee 42.
63. Interviewee 27.
64. Some examples can be found in Woodward, *State of Denial*, 108–110, 176–177; Interviews 5, 7, and 11.
65. Interviewee 71.
66. Bumiller, *Condoleezza Rice*, 204.
67. Interviewee 71.
68. Interviewee 12; also Interviewees 28 and 10.
69. Interviewee 5.
70. Condoleezza Rice, *No Higher Honor: A Memoir of My Years in Washington* (New York: Crown, 2011), 192.
71. Interviewee 64.
72. Julia Preston, "An Attack on Iraq Not Yet Justified, France Warns US," *New York Times*, January 21, 2003.
73. I have spoken to some former senior officials who shared his frustration: one suggested that de Villepin had given some indications that the French had long understood the language of "grave consequences" to mean military force, and Powell thought they were on the same page; Interviewee 27.
74. One official observing Powell's diplomacy closely would later tell me that "Even in August 2002, I think there were still possibilities we could avoid war—if you acted like you were going to do this, it was possible that you could force the collapse of Saddam Hussein, spark a revolt. At some point he might just give it up. We could have played out more of this." But then you get the de Villepin change of stance on the second resolution—and a "bizarre alliance on the 20th of January [2003] between France and the Pentagon," because both wanted the diplomatic track to

end. The president was by that time "clearly leaning" toward war, and "the failure of
the second resolution, and especially the French" action, "takes any argument Powell has about further delay and wipes it out"; Interviewee 4. A senior White House
official agreed: the president was trying to set up a process to coerce Saddam into
backing down short of war, he insisted. The strategy was to avoid war if possible, but
to do that we had to "be seen as preparing for war, because that's what put maximum
pressure on Saddam. If you could convince him that his regime survival was at stake,
that was the one thing that might cause him to change his mind" about his course.
A second resolution, the official said, had become key to getting Saddam to believe
this position. But France, Germany, and Russia undercut this position; Interviewee
39. A former State official would later tell journalists that, by destroying Powell's
carefully calibrated UN route alternative strategy, the French foreign minister had
ruined whatever hope there was of sidetracking the rush to invasion. "On that day,"
he would later reflect, "we were going to war"; Michael Isikoff and David Corn,
Hubris: The Inside Story of Spin, Scandal, and the Selling of the Iraq War (New York:
Crown, 2006), 176. This is of course misleading; the United States was going to war
long before the French foreign minister tried to stand in the way.

75. One official told me that, before the second resolution fiasco, at least some French
officials were essentially begging the administration: "Just go to war. Don't put us on
the spot. If you're going to go to war, go. But don't ask us for a second resolution."
Tony Blair, however, needed the second resolution for domestic political purposes,
and so the die was cast—until the process collapsed, as everyone knew it would;
Interviewee 22.

   On January 26, William Luti in the policy shop at Defense prepared a memo for
Donald Rumsfeld. It was a "Read Ahead" for a principals meeting on "Diplomacy re
Iraq." The memo implies that no one knew the exact agenda of the coming meeting;
Luti scribbled at the top of the memo, "SECDEF: Not knowing the topic (other
than 'diplomacy') I divined this paper from thin air." What is interesting about the
memo is Luti's description of "The plan (as we know it)" for diplomacy. On the next
day (January 27), it explained, Hans Blix would make his next report on Iraqi compliance. American UN ambassador Negroponte would respond that Iraq was failing
to comply (the "USG position," the memo said, would be "Iraq has failed both tests
of 1441: full declaration and active cooperation"). On February 3, "Secretary Powell
in open session in the Security Council . . . Makes 'The Case.'" And then, for the
month of February: "Inspections continue. Build coalition—continue making the
case. . . . Continue positioning forces." William Luti, "Read Ahead for Principles
[sic] Meeting on 'Diplomacy re Iraq,'" January 26, 2003, declassified July 8, 2010,
declassified with papers delivered to Donald Rumsfeld under MDR, available at
DoD FOIA site.

76. Michael R. Gordon, and James Risen, "Findings of UN Group Undercut US Assertion," *New York Times*, January 28, 2003, A9.

77. Blix, *Disarming Iraq*, 139–141.

78. Blix, *Disarming Iraq*, 141–142.

79. Judith Miller and Julia Preston, "Blix Says He Saw Nothing to Prompt a War," *New York Times*, January 31, 2003, A10.

80. Meyer, "How Britain Failed to Check Bush."

81. No author (likely Office of Reconstruction and Humanitarian Assistance), "Civil Administration Team," January 29, 2003, declassified through DoD FOIA process, available at DoD FOIA website. A second memo drafted that day begins with a section on "Guiding Principles/Assumptions." Rather in tension with Donald Rumsfeld's earlier promises about the minimal costs of an Iraq war, the very first guiding principle made clear that "we are engaged in resource unconstrained planning." The last one outlined a critical assumption being made for postwar planning. "Sufficient Iraqi infrastructure and acceptable levels of technocratic talent will exist," it said, "to provide a suitable basis for all Phase IV activities." No author, "Memo to Deputy Director," January 29, 2003, declassified through DoD FOIA process, available at DoD FOIA site.

82. For her remarks, see http://transcripts.cnn.com/TRANSCRIPTS/0302/05/lkl.00 .html, accessed February 15, 2006.

83. For the transcript of Bush's remarks, see http://www.whitehouse.gov/news /releases/2003/02/20030206-17.html, accessed February 15, 2006.

84. UK Joint Intelligence Committee, "Iraq After 9/11—The Terrorist Threat," November 28, 2001, declassified by UK Iraq Inquiry.

85. Morell, *The Great War of Our Time*, 88.

86. Interviewee 11.

87. Interviewee 11.

88. Morell, *The Great War of Our Time*, 93–98.

89. Morell, *The Great War of Our Time*, 95–96.

90. Blix, *Disarming Iraq*, 153–155.

91. Jim Hoagland, "An Old Trooper's Smoking Gun," *Washington Post*, February 6, 2003, A37.

92. Isikoff and Corn, *Hubris*, 190.

93. See, for example, Amanda Terkel, "*Washington Post* Editorial Board Attempts to Erase Its Pre-War Rush to Invasion," ThinkProgress, May 1, 2008, at https://thinkprogress .org/washington-post-editorial-board-attempts-to-erase-its-pre-war-rush-to-invasion -8d93a991b3da/; and the *Bill Moyers Journal* episode of April 25, 2007, "Buying the War," at http://www.pbs.org/moyers/journal/btw/transcript1.html. One 2007 study found a somewhat mixed picture; see Alexander G. Nikolaev and Douglas V. Porpora. "Talking War: How Elite US Newspaper Editorials and Opinion Pieces Debated the Attack on Iraq," *Sociological Focus* 40, no. 1 (2007). But many of the more public discussions and information were biased in the direction of support for war.

94. "Irrefutable," *Washington Post*, February 6, 2003. On the *Post*'s role see James Fallows, "Why We Won't Learn from Iraq," *The Atlantic*, March 19, 2013, at https://www .theatlantic.com/politics/archive/2013/03/why-we-wont-learn-from-iraq/274140/.

95. Eric Alterman, "Never Apologize, Never Explain," Center for American Progress, March 4, 2004, at https://www.americanprogress.org/issues/general/news/2004/03 /04/597/think-again-never-apologize-never-explain/.

96. David Remnick, "Making a Case," *New Yorker*, February 3, 2003.

97. George F. Will, "After Powell, Before War," *Newsweek*, February 17, 2003.

98. George F. Will, "Enough Said About Inspections," *Washington Post*, January 30, 2003.

99. George F. Will, "Disregarding the Deniers," *Washington Post*, February 6, 2003.

100. Marc Grossman, under secretary for political affairs, "Testimony before the Senate Foreign Relations Committee," February 11, 2003, available at www.state .gov/p/17616.htm, accessed February 21, 2006.

101. Douglas Feith, under secretary of defense for policy, "Testimony before the Senate Committee on Foreign Relations," February 11, 2003, available at http://www .usembassy.it/file2003_02/alia/a3021102.htm, accessed February 21, 2006.

102. No author specified (possibly Justice or Defense Department), "Justice Sector Major Decision Issues," February 6, 2003, declassified through Defense Department FOIA process, available at DoD FOIA site. Emphasis/underlining in original.

103. US Department of State Information Memorandum, "Iraq Contingency Planning," to Under Secretary Dobriansky, February 7, 2003, released in part June 15, 2005.

104. Interviewee 50.

105. The official with whom I spoke believes Dobriansky raised the issue with more senior State officials, to little avail. Another official in a position to know believes Dobrianski tried to support the message of the memo but does not recall details of what occurred; Interviewee 52.

106. Blix, *Disarming Iraq*, 176–193.

107. Con Coughlin, *American Ally: Tony Blair and the War on Terror* (New York: Harper-Collins, 2006), 278.

108. Coughlin, *American Ally*, 281–289.

109. "Statement by France to Security Council," *New York Times*, February 14, 2003.

110. The speech is available, and these quotes are drawn from the version, at http:// www.au.af.mil/au/awc/awcgate/dod/sp20030214-secdef0024.htm.

111. He did not see "resolving other countries' internal political disputes, paving roads, erecting power lines, policing streets, building stock markets, and organizing democratic governmental bodies were missions for our men and women in uniform," he would confess in his memoir; Rumsfeld, *Known and Unknown*, 482.

112. Office of Reconstruction and Humanitarian Assistance, "Inter-Agency Rehearsal and Planning Conference," February 21–22, 2003. Downloaded from Department of Defense FOIA Site.

113. A later slide continued the wishful thinking. On a list of "facilities and infrastructure we hope will be intact following hostilities to facilitate our work," the civil administration group of ORHA listed the "entire oil infrastructure," "facilities associated with local, civilian police," "court and prison facilities," banks, the electrical grid, radio and television stations, and "all key buildings/facilities of the ministries and agencies for which CIVAD is responsible."

114. These same, bracing assumptions can be found on an undated memo without an author but surely assembled by the same team; Department of Defense, "Police,

Justice and Prisons in Iraq: Concept of Post-Conflict Operations," declassified through DoD FOIA process, available at DoD FOIA website.

115. ORHA, Post-Conflict Planning Group, Civil Administration Section, Justice Sector, Briefing, n.d., declassified through DoD FOIA process, available at DoD FOIA website.

116. Interviewee 16.

117. Special Inspector General, *Hard Lessons*, 43.

118. Interviewee 16.

119. Interviewee 62.

120. Interviewee 41. One ORHA planner said it was "apparent to everybody that we were doing this on a wing and a prayer. But it was a fait accompli at that point, and we were going to have to make it work somehow"; Interviewee 10.

121. Interviewee 7.

122. Interviewee 11.

123. Interviewee 45.

124. Interviewee 45, and the same comment and recollection was relayed to me by another participant in the meeting. Garner has publicly portrayed the sessions in more optimistic terms. The rock drill and other similar events were "really useful," he told the PBS show *Frontline*, "because then we began to find out where all the dots were and what we had to do to connect each one of those dots. . . . It was a good drill, and we were able to put everything together and to begin to horizontally coordinate all the plans"; *Frontline* interview with Jay Garner, "Truth, War and Consequences."

125. Special Inspector General, *Hard Lessons*, 43.

126. Woodward, *State of Denial*, 125.

127. George W. Bush, "President Discusses the Future of Iraq," Washington Hilton Hotel, February 26, 2003.

128. "Deputy Secretary of Defense Paul Wolfowitz Iraqi Forum for Democracy," Dearborn, Michigan, February 23, 2003, available at http://www.usembassy.it /file2003_02/alia/a3022407.htm.

129. Interviewee 41.

130. Interviewee 17.

131. Quoted in *The World According to Dick Cheney*, Showtime documentary.

132. George W. Bush, *Decision Points* (New York: Crown, 2010), 251.

133. From Bill Sizemore, "The Christian With Four Aces," *The Virginia Quarterly Review* (Spring 2008): 79, available at http://www.vqronline.org/articles/2008/spring /sizemore-christian-aces/. See also "Robertson: I Warned Bush on Iraq Casualties," October 20, 2004, Cable News Network, reprinted at www.commondreams.org /headlines04/1020-05.htm.

134. Interviewee 69.

135. Interviewee 59.

136. Interviewee 69.

137. As one participant put it, there was little enthusiasm for ORHA's mission at State, partly because of Rumsfeld's clear bias against State's role. "It was, 'if you don't want us, we're not going to play the game.'" Special Inspector General, *Hard Lessons*, 37.

138. Interviewee 10.

139. United States Institute of Peace, Iraq Experience Project, Oral History Interview, Larry Crandall, September 20, 2004, 4–5.

140. Strange contradictions appear in various documents that have emerged. One early, undated ORHA briefing includes as its objective to "conduct the detailed planning . . . with respect to the administration of Iraq *throughout the transition to an Iraqi-led authority.*" On the next slide, under its "Charter," the slide lists the massive range of jobs already referred to: humanitarian relief, "protect natural resources and infrastructure," aid reconstruction, rebuild "key civilian services," "stabilize the justice sector and provide law enforcement services," dismantle WMD, and then: "Transition to Iraqi-led authority representing the free will of the Iraqi people." Department of Defense, Office of Reconstruction and Humanitarian Assistance, briefing, n.d., declassified and released in DoD FOIA process, available at DoD FOIA site. This would seem to rule out the Coalition Provisional Authority as an interim phase. Meanwhile, before the war began, in March 2003, there were already documents circulating within DoD that were draft orders from an entity called the CPA; Department of Defense, "Instructions to Iraqi Armed Forces" and "Instructions to the Citizens of Iraq," Coalition Provisional Authority Directives, March 18, 2003, Office of the Under Secretary of Defense for Policy, declassified June 2007, available at DoD FOIA site. The directives are signed by Tommy Franks.

141. Interviewee 65.

142. Interviewee 60.

143. Don Eberly, *Liberate and Leave: Fatal Flaws in the Early Strategy for Postwar Iraq* (Minneapolis, MN: Zenith Press, 2009), 28.

144. Interviewee 10, Interviewee 16; James Dobbins et al., *Occupying Iraq: A History of the Coalition Provisional Authority* (Santa Monica, CA: RAND Corporation, 2009), 5, 8; Nora Bensahel et al., *After Saddam: Prewar Planning and the Occupation of Iraq* (Santa Monica, CA: RAND Corporation, 2008), 54, 56, 58.

145. Special Inspector General, *Hard Lessons*, 42.

146. Interviewee 62.

147. Interviewee 40.

148. Interviewee 9.

149. Interviewee 12.

150. Interviewee 9.

151. Tommy Franks, *American Soldier* (New York: Regan Books, 2004), 424, 442.

152. Interviewee 10.

153. Eberly, *Liberate and Leave*, 34, 36.

154. Special Inspector General, *Hard Lessons*, 40.

155. Interviewee 43.

156. Interviewee 43.

157. Rumsfeld, *Known and Unknown*, 452–453.

158. House Budget Committee, "Department of Defense Budget Priorities for Fiscal Year 2004," February 27, 2003, 8–10, available at http://frwebgate.access.gpo.gov/cgi-bin/getdoc.cgi?dbname=108_house_hearings&docid=f:85421.pdf, accessed March 13, 2006.

159. Paul Wolfowitz, "Remembering the Future," *National Interest*, Spring 2000, 39–40.
160. The transcript of the press conference can be found at http://www.whitehouse.gov /news/releases/2003/03/20030306-8.html, accessed February 17, 2006.
161. CNN, "Transcript of Blix's U.N. Presentation," March 7, 2003, available at http://www.cnn.com/2003/US/03/07/sprj.irq.un.transcript.blix/, accessed February 28, 2006.
162. Blix, *Disarming Iraq*, 210.
163. Douglas J. Feith, *War and Decision: Inside the Pentagon at the Dawn of the War on Terrorism* (New York: Harper, 2008), 403–409.
164. In the March 7 meeting, Armitage argued against forcing an IIA with a US flavor; Cheney, interestingly, argued in favor of control. The problem with Armitage's idea was that it appeared to commit the United States to several months of unalloyed occupation while it "consulted" with Iraqis to find a "legitimate local" IIA group. Rumsfeld claims that the meeting ended without a clear decision; Rumsfeld, *Known and Unknown*, 491.
165. Interviewee 69.
166. Gordon and Trainor, *Cobra II*, 160. Which precise meeting or meetings these were is unclear, but the claims were offered some time between mid-February and early March. Woodward, *State of Denial*, 122, for example, suggests that Franks offered his infamous assertion about "lord mayors" in a February 14 briefing.
167. George Tenet, *At the Center of the Storm* (New York: HarperPerennial, 2007), 420. Confirming evidence comes from Interviewee 5 and Rice, *No Higher Honor*, 189–190.
168. The text of Bush's radio address is available at http://www.whitehouse.gov/news /releases/2003/03/20030308-1.html, accessed February 17, 2006.
169. BBC News, "Iraq, Tony, and the Truth: Timeline," available at http://news.bbc.co .uk/1/hi/programmes/panorama/4336727.stm, accessed February 21, 2006.
170. These two briefings were declassified in 2003. They are "Post-War Planning Issues" (the March 10 briefing, though undated), declassified September 26, 2003, and now marked "Unclassified"; and a second set beginning with a slide titled "Dealing with the 'Foreign Ministry,'" the March 12 set, also marked "Unclassified" and declassified on the same day.
171. Interviewee 33; Interviewee 13.
172. Rumsfeld claims in his memoirs that "CENTCOM plans hinged on a key intelligence assumption that proved to be inaccurate: The existing Iraqi police could be helpful in keeping order." He quotes, not from the CIA brief itself, but from Defense Department notes at one meeting that claim to summarize its conclusions: Iraqi "police and justice personnel appear to have extensive professional training." That is actually from the March 10 briefing slides, which have now been declassified. Rumsfeld, *Known and Unknown*, 476.
173. The one CIA report dealing with the Iraqi police mentioned in a 2007 Senate survey of postwar Iraq estimates makes no clear finding about their reliability, and in fact emphasizes only how little the agency knew about the Iraqi police at the local level; Select Committee on Intelligence, United States Senate, *Report on Prewar Intelligence Assessments about Postwar Iraq*, 110th Congress, S. Report 110-76, May

2007, 94–95. One senior State official working postwar stability issues recalled reading a "two page memo" from the CIA on the Iraqi police, but what it mostly made clear, he recalled, was that "they had no information and no sources"; Interviewee 50.

174. Woodward, *State of Denial*, 119.

175. Later, when Paul Bremer had taken much more extreme actions, Defense official Peter Rodman did a memo for Rumsfeld laying out the multiple briefings in which the decision had clearly been taken to keep it together. Peter Rodman, "Disbanding the Iraqi Army," May 24, 2006, declassified December 1, 2008, posted to the Rumsfeld archive of documents, http://papers.rumsfeld.com/.

176. On these issues see also Feith, *War and Decision*, 367.

177. Interviewee 42. For his part, Rumsfeld in his memoirs claims he was so concerned about the state of postwar governance that, the day after the March 10 NSC meeting, he saw Bush and volunteered *himself* as the initial civilian administrator on the ground in Baghdad. He asked to go to Iraq for the first two weeks of the postwar to get all the ducks in a row. Bush did not like the idea of his defense secretary stuck in Baghdad with a world of national security issues to deal with, and turned the offer down; Rumsfeld, *Known and Unknown*, 491–492.

178. NBC News, *Meet the Press*, transcript of interview with Vice President Dick Cheney, March 16, 2003, available at http://www.mtholyoke.edu/acad/intrel/bush/cheneymeetthepress.htm, accessed February 28, 2006.

179. CBS News, "Interrogator Shares Saddam's Confessions." See also CIA, "Misreading Intentions: Iraq's Reaction to Inspections Created Picture of Deception," January 5, 2006, 11. Approved for release June 5, 2012.

180. Interviewee 27.

181. Donald Rumsfeld, "Kosovo," attachment to letter to Joshua Bolten, April 28, 1999, available at www.rumsfeld.com.

CHAPTER 9: THE AFTERMATH

1. Interviewee 54.

2. Interview with Ahmad Chalabi, *Frontline* documentary, "Truth, War and Consequences," available at http://www.pbs.org/wgbh/pages/frontline/shows/truth/interviews/chalabi.html.

3. C. M. Bowra, "The Tragic Vision," in Marsh H. McCall Jr., ed., *Aeschylus: A Collection of Critical Essays* (Englewood Cliffs, NJ: Prentice Hall, 1972), 28.

4. Douglas J. Feith, *War and Decision: Inside the Pentagon at the Dawn of the War on Terrorism* (New York: Harper, 2008), 449.

5. An updated survey of evidence on this point is Glenn Kessler, "The Cheneys' Claim of a 'Deep, Longstanding, Far-Reaching Relationship Between al-Qaeda and Saddam," *Washington Post*, July 17, 2014. For a contemporaneous intelligence judgment, see the British Joint Intelligence Committee Assessment, "Iraq After September 11—the Terrorist Threat," November 28, 2001, declassified by the UK Iraq Inquiry.

6. United States Institute of Peace, Iraq Experience Project, Oral History Interview, Lt. Col. Chris Hughes, October 29, 2004, 3.

7. Oral History Interview, Lt. Col. Chris Hughes, October 29, 2004, 7–8.

8. Oral History Interview, Lt. Col. Chris Hughes, 37.

9. Dick Cheney, *In My Time: A Personal and Political Memoir* (New York: Simon and Schuster, 2011), 400.

10. Max Hastings, *Winston's War, 1940–1945* (New York: Knopf, 2010), 423.

11. Hastings, *Winston's War*, 424, 425. The occupation is also described in Keith Lowe, *Savage Continent: Europe in the Aftermath of World War II* (New York: St. Martin's Press, 2012), 296–314.

12. Quoted in Amikam Nachmani, "Civil War and Foreign Intervention in Greece: 1946–1949," *Journal of Contemporary History* 25, no. 4 (October 1990): 493, 497–498.

13. Nachmani, "Civil War and Foreign Intervention in Greece," 489.

14. Quoted in Lowe, *Savage Continent*, 71.

15. Lowe, *Savage Continent*, xiii.

16. Lowe, *Savage Continent*, xv, 76, 179–184, 262, 359; the Acheson quote is from p. 1. See also Hastings, *Winston's War*, 422.

17. Interviewee 64.

18. Interviewee 43.

19. Interview with US Army officer, Washington, D.C., February 2010.

20. Reflections from Interviewee 37.

21. Interviewee 48.

22. Interviewee 63.

23. United States Institute of Peace, Iraq Experience Project, Oral History Interview, Mr. Jay Bachar, July 19, 2004, 5–6.

24. Interviewee 16.

25. Interviewee 42.

26. Interviewee 16.

27. Interviewee 53.

28. On this process see Bob Woodward, *State of Denial* (New York: Simon and Schuster, 2006), 93, 102–103.

29. Hans Blix, *Disarming Iraq* (New York: Pantheon, 2004), 257.

30. Interviewee 42.

31. Interviewee 46.

32. Interviewee 47.

33. Interviewee 46.

34. Interviewee 47.

35. Interviewee 49.

36. The Adelman quote comes from Peter Baker, *Days of Fire: Bush and Cheney in the White House* (New York: Doubleday, 2013), 266; and the Rice example from Condoleezza Rice, *No Higher Honor: A Memoir of My Years in Washington* (New York: Crown, 2011), 208.

37. Interviewee 53.

38. Interviewee 54.
39. Tommy Franks, cable to Rumsfeld, April 16, 2003, declassified April 17, 2003, released in released in "Set of Documents Released to Secretary Rumsfeld Through MDR," available at DoD FOIA site.
40. Interviewee 69.
41. The following account is derived from a number of sources, including Interviewee 8.
42. Interviewee 59.
43. Interviewee 16.
44. Don Eberly, *Liberate and Leave: Fatal Flaws in the Early Strategy for Postwar Iraq* (Minneapolis, MN: Zenith Press, 2009), 33. A senior British official who was dealing with the administration at high levels has agreed, saying that "there wasn't a settled view within the US administration on what the day after plan would like right up until—indeed, until after the conflict." Debates between Defense, State, and NSC were clearly apparent just days before the war. "It was pretty chaotic." Dominick Chilcott, testimony to UK Iraq Inquiry, December 8, 2009, 12–13, available at http://www.iraqinquiry.org.uk/media/40483/20091208chilcott-final.pdf.
45. Zalmay Khalilzad, *The Envoy: From Kabul to the White House, My Journey through a Turbulent World* (New York: St. Martin's Press, 2016), 169.
46. Interviewee 38.
47. Slide from CENTCOM planning PowerPoint, August 2002, declassified June 16, 2005.
48. Karen DeYoung, *Soldier: The Life of Colin Powell* (New York: Alfred A. Knopf, 2006), 463.
49. Interviewee 10. One US Army foreign affairs officer dispatched to help with the governance process concluded that, given all the challenges and constraints, "by the time we hit Iraq we had to make it up as we went. . . . It was completely ad hoc, piecemeal, for the entire country. . . . It was a mess. . . . We had no idea where it was going to go and how we were going to do this." United States Institute of Peace, Iraq Experience Project, Oral History Interview, Col. P. J. Dermer, August 22, 2004, 2, 4, available at http://www.usip.org/library/oh/sops/iraq/gov/dermer.pdf.
50. Interviewee 12.
51. Interviewee 63.
52. OSD Policy, "Iraqi Interim Authority Implementation Concept—Summary," "Iraqi Interim Authority Action Plan," and memo from Donald Rumsfeld to Principals, subject, "Iraqi Interim Authority (IIA) Action Plan," March 30, 2003, declassified March 30, 2008, released with documents released to Donald Rumsfeld under MDR, available on DoD FOIA site.
53. OSD Policy, "Talking Points on the Iraqi Interim Authority," March 31, 2003, declassified July 18, 2010, released with documents released to Donald Rumsfeld under MDR, available at DoD FOIA site.
54. Donald Rumsfeld, "Iraqi Interim Authority," memo to President Bush, April 1, 2003, available at www.rumsfeld.com.
55. Special Inspector General for Iraqi Reconstruction, *Hard Lessons: The Iraq Reconstruction Experience* (Washington, D.C.: US Government Printing Office, 2009), 71, available at http://www.sigir.mil/files/HardLessons/Hard_Lessons_Report.pdf.

56. Phillips, *Losing Iraq*, 136.
57. Department of Defense News Transcript, "Deputy Secretary Wolfowitz and Gen Pace—NBC 'Meet the Press,'" April 6, 2003, available at http://www.defense link.mil/transcripts/2003/t04062003_tdod0406mtp.html, accessed March 9, 2006.
58. Interviewee 10.
59. Nora Bensahel et al., *After Saddam: Prewar Planning and the Occupation of Iraq* (Santa Monica, CA: RAND Corporation, 2008), 59.
60. United States Institute of Peace, Iraq Experience Project, Oral History Interview, Denise Dauphinais, July 27, 2004, 18–19.
61. Interviewee 10. See also Don Eberly, *Liberate and Leave: Fatal Flaws in the Early Strategy for Postwar Iraq* (Minneapolis, MN: Zenith Press, 2009), 33–34.
62. Special Inspector General for Iraqi Reconstruction, *Hard Lessons: The Iraq Reconstruction Experience* (Washington, DC: US Government Printing Office, 2009), 48, available at http://www.sigir.mil/files/HardLessons/Hard_Lessons_Report .pdf.
63. Interviewee 16.
64. Interviewee 59.
65. Interviewee 65.
66. Interviewee 42.
67. Interviewee 5.
68. Interviewee 60.
69. Interviewee 65.
70. Special Inspector General, *Hard Lessons*, 55.
71. Ali A. Allawi, *The Occupation of Iraq: Winning the War, Losing the Peace* (New Haven, CT: Yale University Press, 2007), 102.
72. Interviewee 62.
73. Interviewee 62.
74. Special Inspector General, *Hard Lessons*, 54.
75. Eberly, *Liberate and Leave*, 66.
76. Eberly, *Liberate and Leave*, 128–130.
77. Bensahel et al., *After Saddam*, 162.
78. Interviewee 8. Khalilzad's memoirs do not specify a time frame but agree with the broad thrust of the account; see *The Envoy*, 170–171.
79. At the Nasiriyah meeting, on April 15, about seventy-five Iraqis attended a fairly disorganized session. Exile leaders had been delayed in Qatar, so the meeting began with only the internals. When the exiles arrived, they "sat at separate tables," according to Jay Garner. "They didn't mingle" interview with Jay Garner, *Frontline* documentary, "Truth, War and Consequences," available at http://www.pbs.org /wgbh/pages/frontline/shows/truth/interviews/garner.html. Ali Allawi writes that this session generated little momentum toward an IIA; Allawi, *The Occupation of Iraq*, 101.
80. Feith, *War and Decision*, 418, 420. For a British view of the limitations and risks of the IIA, see the declassified memo "Iraq Red Team: The Future of Governance in Iraq," April 11, 2003, released as part of the UK Iraq Inquiry.

81. Timothy P. Wright and Timothy Reese, *On Point II: Transition to the New Campaign—the United States Army in Operation Iraqi Freedom* (Ft. Leavenworth, KS: Combat Studies Institute Press, US Army Combined Arms Center, 2008), 142.

82. Michael R. Gordon, "The Strategy to Secure Iraq Did Not Foresee a 2nd War," *New York Times*, October 19, 2004, 1.

83. Peter Ford, "Disorder Deepens in Liberated Baghdad," *Christian Science Monitor*, May 12, 2003.

84. Allawi, *The Occupation of Iraq*, 103–104.

85. Interview with Kanan Makiya, *Frontline* documentary, "Truth, War and Consequences," available at http://www.pbs.org/wgbh/pages/frontline/shows/truth/interviews/makiya.html. Zalmay Khalilzad admits that the conference quickly turned into a "noisy meeting with passionate outbursts and diatribes against the United States. The United States was failing to deliver security and services to the Iraqi people, delegates complained. 'Why did you overthrow the system that existed if you didn't have a plan to replace it with something better'?" The meeting "was teetering on the edge of total disorder"; Khalilzad, *The Envoy*, 172.

86. Jonathan Weisman and Mike Allen, "Officials Argue for Fast US Exit from Iraq," *Washington Post*, April 21, 2003.

87. Khalilzad, *The Envoy*, 172.

88. Allawi, *The Occupation of Iraq*, 104.

89. Interview with Ahmad Chalabi, *Frontline* documentary, "Truth, War and Consequences," available at http://www.pbs.org/wgbh/pages/frontline/shows/truth/interviews/chalabi.html.

90. J. Paul Bremer, *My Year in Iraq: The Struggle to Build a Future of Hope* (New York: Simon and Schuster, 2006), 12.

91. Quoted in Patrick E. Tyler and Edmund L. Andrews, "US Overhauls Administration to Govern Iraq," *New York Times*, May 12, 2003.

92. Michael Hirsh, "Our New Civil War," *Newsweek*, May 12, 2003.

93. Condoleezza Rice, "Promoting the National Interest," *Foreign Affairs* 79, no. 1 (January–February 2000).

94. Bradley Graham, *By His Own Rules: The Ambitions, Successes, and Ultimate Failures of Donald Rumsfeld* (New York: PublicAffairs, 2009), 404–405; and Feith, *War and Decision*, 437–438.

95. Interviewee 39.

96. Susan Sachs, "Opposition Groups Work to Complete Assembly Plan," *New York Times*, May 7, 2003; Interviewee 38.

97. DeYoung, *Soldier*, 465.

98. The episode is described in James Dobbins et al., *Occupying Iraq: A History of the Coalition Provisional Authority* (Santa Monica, CA: The RAND Corporation, 2009), 1. It does not appear as such in Bremer's memoirs; Bremer does mention that he was contacted by Libby and Wolfowitz but does not offer details of the conversation; L. Paul Bremer, *My Year in Iraq: The Struggle to Build a Future of Hope* (New York: Simon and Schuster, 2006), 6–7.

99. David Rennie, "US Diplomat to Be Iraq's Next Governor," *The Guardian*, May 2, 2003; Mike Allen, "Expert on Terrorism to Direct Rebuilding," *New York Times*, May 2, 2003; Douglas Jehl, "Aftereffects: Postwar Plans; Iraq's US Overseer Is Praised by Rumsfeld," *New York Times*, May 3, 2003.

100. Bremer, *My Year in Iraq*, 9–10.

101. Bremer, *My Year in Iraq*, 12.

102. Bremer, *My Year in Iraq*, 11–12.

103. George W. Bush, *Decision Points* (New York: Crown, 2010), 258–259.

104. He says as much in his memoirs; Khalilzad, *The Envoy*, 173. The NSC spokesman was still making the same assumption, telling the press on May 6 that Khalilzad would stay on—and also that Garner would remain in place as a sort of operational deputy to Bremer; James Dao and Eric Schmitt, "Aftereffects: Postwar Planning— President Picks a Special Envoy to Rebuild Iraq," *New York Times*, May 7, 2003; on Rumsfeld's offer to Garner, see Dobbins et al., *Occupying Iraq*, 9.

105. Reports differ as to the exact way in which the hammer fell. Karen DeYoung writes that Condoleezza Rice told Khalilzad directly he had to stand down. I spoke to a source who said Khalilzad left the Rice meeting still thinking he had a continuing mandate, only to hear later that Feith's office had vetoed the plan; Interviewee 8.

106. Roger Cohen, "The MacArthur Lunch," *New York Times*, August 27, 2007; and Khalilzad, *The Envoy*, 174–175. According to one account, Powell called Rice and appealed for Khalilzad. She replied that Bremer would only take the job on the condition of his removal. They would have to live with it; Graham, *By His Own Rules*, 401.

107. Cohen, "The MacArthur Lunch."

108. Interviewee 64.

109. Interviewee 9.

110. Bremer later told Bradley Graham he was "flabbergasted" that anyone in the Washington interagency could have pronounced themselves confused: "There is simply no case to be made that they didn't know what I was doing." Graham, *By His Own Rules*, 406.

111. Allawi, *The Occupation of Iraq*, 105, 110.

112. Khalilzad, *The Envoy*, 174–175.

113. OSD Policy, "Read Ahead for [ ] Meeting on IIA," May 8, 2003, declassified through DoD FOIA process, available at DoD FOIA website.

114. Michael R. Gordon, "Fear of Baghdad Unrest Prompts a Halt in Sending Troops Home," *New York Times*, May 15, 2003.

115. See, for example, Peter Slevin, "US Bans More Iraqis from Jobs," *Washington Post*, May 17, 2003.

116. An extensive treatment of this decision and its implications can be found in Charles Ferguson, *No End in Sight* (New York: PublicAffairs, 2008), 163–233.

117. Edmund L. Andrews, "Envoy's Letter Counters Bush on Dismantling of Iraq Army," *New York Times*, September 4, 2007.

118. Michael R. Gordon, "Fateful Choice on Iraq Army Bypassed Debate," *New York Times*, March 17, 2008.

119. Bush, *Decision Points*, 259.

120. Andrews, "Envoy's Letter."

121. Khalilzad, *The Envoy*, 175.

122. Dobbins et al., *Occupying Iraq*, 49, 51.

123. Michael R. Gordon and Eric Schmitt, "US Plans to Reduce Forces in Iraq, With Help of Allies," *New York Times*, May 3, 2003, 1.

124. Rajiv Chandrasekaran, *Imperial Life in the Emerald City: Inside Iraq's Green Zone* (New York: Alfred A. Knopf, 2006), 91–92.

125. Interviewee 16.

126. Interviewee 50.

127. Interviewee 59.

128. Oral History Interview, Denise Dauphinais, 21–22.

129. Donald Rumsfeld, "Memorandum for the President," September 9, 2003, declassified September 18, 2008, released with documents released to Donald Rumsfeld under MDR, available at DoD FOIA website.

130. Interviewee 64.

131. Ferguson, *No End in Sight*, 143–144.

132. "A whole bunch of kids out there . . . hovered around him," in the perception of an experienced national security official; Interviewee 62.

133. Interviewee 64.

134. Interviewee 65.

135. Jim Hoagland, "Getting to Know the Iraqis," *The Washington Post*, July 20, 2003, B7.

136. "Deputy Secretary of Defense Paul Wolfowitz Iraqi Forum for Democracy," Dearborn, Michigan, February 23, 2003, available at http://www.usembassy.it /file2003_02/alia/a3022407.htm.

137. Liz Sly, "Baghdad Gets Its Groove Back," *Washington Post*, August 26, 2018.

138. Ali Soufan, "Al-Qaeda is Thriving, Despite Our Endless War. Can We Ever Defeat It?" *BuzzFeed News*, October 29, 2018.

139. Idrees Ali, "US General Says Conditions for Islamist Extremism Still Linger," Reuters, October 16, 2018.

140. The quotes in this section are from John Nixon, *Debriefing the President: The Interrogation of Saddam Hussein* (New York: Blue Rider Press, 2016), 71, 24, 4, 128, 158.

141. Oral History Interview, Lt. Col. Chris Hughes, 37–38.

CHAPTER 10: LESSONS

1. Carl von Clausewitz, *On War*, ed. and trans. Michael Howard and Peter Paret (Princeton, NJ: Princeton University Press, 1976), 88–89.

2. Aeschylus, *Persians*, in *Aeschylus: Complete Plays*, vol. 2, trans. Carl H. Mueller (Hanover, NH: Smith and Kraus, 2002), 130–131.

3. Interviewee 42.

4. Aeschylus, *Persians*, 153, 157, 159, 160. See also Albin Lesky, *Greek Tragedy*, trans. H. A. Frankfort (London: Ernest Benn, 1967), 62.

5. Clark, *The Sleepwalkers*, 561.

6. Robert Buzzanco, "Don Draper Does Vietnam (a.k.a., Ken Burns Teaches the War in 10 Easy Lessons)," *Diplomatic History* 42, no. 3 (2018): 380–383.

7. Just how decisive specific *individuals* have to be in order to be negligent is the subject of some debate. Some standards, such as those developed for war crimes, have suggested that culpability can only apply in cases where people are directly responsible for actions—simply demonstrating that they knew, or should have known, about violations is not enough; see Dakota S. Rudesill, "Precision War and Responsibility: Transformational Military Technology and the Duty of Care Under the Laws of War," *Yale Journal of International Law* 32, no. 2 (2007): 525.

8. These criteria, and the quote, can be found at https://injury.findlaw.com/accident -injury-law/proving-fault-what-is-negligence.html.

9. Interviewee 39.

10. Quoted in Jim Rasenberger, *The Brilliant Disaster: JFK, Castro, and America's Doomed Invasion of Cuba's Bay of Pigs* (New York: Scribner, 2011), 394.

11. Richard Myers, chairman at the time, relates at least one episode in which President Bush met with the Chiefs and asked whether "they had any reservations about our preparedness. Each service chief and combatant commander spoke in turn. The consensus was that the US military was ready, and everyone agreed there were no show stoppers if the President were to commit to war." General Richard B. Myers (Ret.), *Eyes on the Horizon: Serving on the Front Lines of National Security* (New York: Threshold Editions, 2009), Kindle edition, loc. 4146.

12. Newbold's story is eloquently told in David Margolick, "The Night of the Generals," *Vanity Fair*, March 5, 2007.

13. Quoted in Bob Woodward, *Plan of Attack* (New York: Simon and Schuster, 2004), 118.

14. Patrick Porter, *Blunder: Britain's War in Iraq* (Oxford: Oxford University Press, 2018), 9–10.

15. Douglas J. Feith, "Inside the Inside Story," *Wall Street Journal*, May 6, 2007.

16. Interviewee 5.

17. An especially poignant example of this effect is the story of General Newbold, who fully acknowledges sitting in meetings with Donald Rumsfeld and failing to speak his mind, in part because he knew he would "risk Rumsfeld's famously withering wrath." See Margolick, "The Night of the Generals."

18. In James C. Thomson's brilliant short "autopsy" of the causes of Vietnam, published in 1968, the framing power of concepts, ideas, and worldviews figures prominently; see Thompson, "How Could Vietnam Happen?" 47–49. My argument here has much in common with Patrick Porter's superb catalogue, in *Blunder*, of the role of "bad ideas" in fostering the British decision for war.

19. Robert A. Burton, *On Being Certain: Believing You Are Right Even When You're Not* (New York: St. Martin's Griffin, 2008), xiii.

20. Jonathan Haidt, "The Emotional Dog and Its Rational Tail: A Social Intuitionist Approach to Moral Judgment," *Psychological Review* 108, no. 4 (2011): 814–815, 817–818, 829.

21. John Agresto, *Mugged by Reality: The Liberation of Iraq and the Failure of Good Intentions* (New York: Encounter Books, 2007), 5, 184.

22. Burton, *On Being Certain*, 177–178, 220.

INDEX

Michael J. Mazarr is a senior political scientist at the RAND Corporation. He has been a faculty member and associate dean at the US National War College and senior fellow and project leader at the Center for Strategic and International Studies. He served in the US Navy Reserve and has worked as an aide to the chairman of the Joint Chiefs of Staff and as a defense staffer on Capitol Hill. He holds degrees from Georgetown University and the University of Maryland School of Public Affairs.

PublicAffairs is a publishing house founded in 1997. It is a tribute to the standards, values, and flair of three persons who have served as mentors to countless reporters, writers, editors, and book people of all kinds, including me.

I. F. STONE, proprietor of *I. F. Stone's Weekly*, combined a commitment to the First Amendment with entrepreneurial zeal and reporting skill and became one of the great independent journalists in American history. At the age of eighty, Izzy published *The Trial of Socrates*, which was a national bestseller. He wrote the book after he taught himself ancient Greek.

BENJAMIN C. BRADLEE was for nearly thirty years the charismatic editorial leader of *The Washington Post*. It was Ben who gave the *Post* the range and courage to pursue such historic issues as Watergate. He supported his reporters with a tenacity that made them fearless and it is no accident that so many became authors of influential, best-selling books.

ROBERT L. BERNSTEIN, the chief executive of Random House for more than a quarter century, guided one of the nation's premier publishing houses. Bob was personally responsible for many books of political dissent and argument that challenged tyranny around the globe. He is also the founder and longtime chair of Human Rights Watch, one of the most respected human rights organizations in the world.

·   ·   ·

For fifty years, the banner of Public Affairs Press was carried by its owner Morris B. Schnapper, who published Gandhi, Nasser, Toynbee, Truman, and about 1,500 other authors. In 1983, Schnapper was described by *The Washington Post* as "a redoubtable gadfly." His legacy will endure in the books to come.

Peter Osnos, *Founder*